THE COMPLETE AIR FRYER COOKBOOK FOR BEGINNERS

The Guide with Healthy & Budget-Friendly Recipes to Live a Better Life. Discover Tips & Tricks To Fry, Grill, Roast, and Bake Your Daily Meals

Michelle Blanch

© Copyright 2022 - All rights reserved.
Michelle Blanch

The content contained within this book may not be reproduced, duplicated, or transmitted without direct written permission from the author or the publisher.

Under no circumstances will any blame or legal responsibility be held against the publisher, or author, for any damages, reparation, or monetary loss due to the information contained within this book. Either directly or indirectly.

Legal Notice:

This book is copyright protected. This book is only for personal use. You cannot amend, distribute, sell, use, quote, or paraphrase any part, or the content within this book, without the consent of the author or publisher.

Disclaimer Notice:

Please note the information contained within this document is for educational and entertainment purposes only. All effort has been executed to present accurate, up-to-date, and reliable, complete information. No warranties of any kind are declared or implied. Readers acknowledge that the author is not engaging in the rendering of legal, financial, medical, or professional advice. The content within this book has been derived from various sources. Please consult a licensed professional before attempting any techniques outlined in this book.

By reading this document, the reader agrees that under no circumstances is the author responsible for any losses, direct or indirect, which are incurred as a result of the use of the information contained within this document, including, but not limited to, errors, omissions, or inaccuracies.

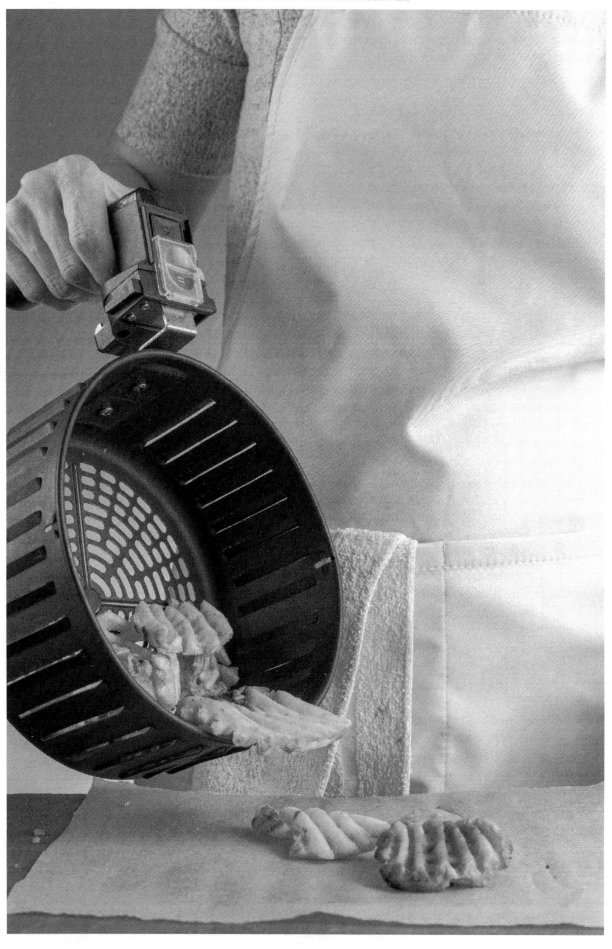

Table of Contents

INTRODUCTION **14**
    AIR FRYER BENEFITS 14
    USE AND MAINTENANCE 15
    CLEANING AND STORAGE 15
    TIPS FOR USING AIR FRYER 16

CHAPTER 1 : BREAKFAST RECIPES **17**
1. COCONUT-BLUEBERRY CEREAL 17
2. AIR TOASTED CHEESE SANDWICH 17
3. CITRUS BLUEBERRY BREAKFAST MUFFINS 18
4. PEANUT BUTTER AND JELLY BREAKFAST DONUTS .. 18
5. RASPBERRY OATMEAL 18
6. BACON, EGG AND CHEESE BREAKFAST HASH 19
7. AIR TOASTED FRENCH TOAST 19
8. BREAKFAST RADISH HASH BROWNS 19
9. BREAKFAST EGG AND TOMATOES 19
10. MAPLE GLAZED SAUSAGES AND FIGS 19
11. BREAKFAST STRATA 20
12. SCRAMBLED EGGS WONTON CUPS 20
13. SHEET PAN SHAKSHUKA 20
14. BREAKFAST CASSEROLE 20
15. AIR-FRIED OMELET 21
16. SUNNY SIDE UP EGG TARTS 21
17. CRUNCHY ZUCCHINI HASH BROWNS 21
18. FRENCH TOAST 21
19. SAUSAGE OMELET 21
20. ZUCCHINI FRITTERS 22
21. SCRAMBLED EGG 22
22. SAUSAGE WRAPS 22
23. BACON BRUSSELS SPROUTS 22
24. SAUSAGE SWISS CHEESE EGG BITE 23
25. SPICY CHICKEN WINGS 23
26. FAJITA CHICKEN 23
27. LEMON CHICKEN BREASTS 23
28. SALMON DILL PATTIES 23
29. CHICKEN FRITTERS 24
30. DELICIOUS CHICKEN BURGER PATTIES 24
31. TUNA PATTIES 24
32. SAUSAGE CHEESE BREAKFAST FRITTATA 24
33. HAM EGG BITES 25
34. PEPPERONI OMELET 25
35. PANCETTA AND HOTDOG OMELET 25
36. CHEESE GARLIC QUICHE 25
37. EASY CHEESY BREAKFAST EGGS 25
38. CHEESY CHICKEN FRITTERS 26
39. CHEDDAR CHEESE OMELET 26
40. GRUYERE CHEESE EGG BITE 26
41. CHEDDAR CHEESE BROCCOLI EGG BITE 26
42. CHEESE SAUSAGE PEPPER FRITTATA 26
43. COTTAGE CHEESE EGG CUPS 27
44. CHEESE MUSHROOM FRITTATA 27
45. CHEESE OMELET 27
46. CHEESE MUSHROOM EGG BAKE 27
47. CHEESE EGG FRITTATA 27
48. CHEESE HAM EGG CUPS 28
49. CHEESE VEGETABLE FRITTATA 28
50. CHEESY BROCCOLI BITES 28
51. EGG IN A HOLE 28
52. SIMPLE EGG SOUFFLÉ 29
53. BREAKFAST SCRAMBLE CASSEROLE 29
54. COWBOY QUICHE 29
55. SCRAMBLED EGGS 29
56. EGG SAUSAGE SPINACH CUPS 29
57. BREAKFAST EGGS AVOCADO 30
58. EGG BACON CHEESE BITES 30
59. EGG HAM BITES 30
60. EGG CHEESE MUSTARD BAKE 30
61. BREAKFAST EGG BITES 30
62. EGG STUFFED PEPPERS 31
63. EGGS IN BREAD CUPS 31
64. SPINACH BAKED EGGS 31
65. EASY BREAKFAST FRITTATA 31
66. GREEN CHILIS EGG BITE 31
67. ROASTED PEPPER EGG BITE 32
68. BROCCOLI BELL PEPPER FRITTATA 32
69. SPINACH TOMATO FRITTATA 32
70. BASIL FETA EGG BITE 32

CHAPTER 2: BEEF, PORK, AND LAMB RECIPES **33**
71. CRISP PORK CHOPS 33
72. PARMESAN PORK CHOPS 33
73. MEATLOAF SLIDERS 33
74. QUICK & EASY STEAK 33
75. PERFECT CHEESEBURGER 34
76. STEAK BITES WITH MUSHROOMS 34
77. SIMPLE & TASTY PORK CHOPS 34
78. SIMPLE AIR FRYER STEAK 34
79. QUICK & TENDER PORK CHOPS 34
80. PORK WITH MUSHROOMS 35
81. QUICK & SIMPLE BRATWURST WITH VEGETABLES . 35
82. DELICIOUS CHEESEBURGERS 35
83. ASIAN SIRLOIN STEAKS 35
84. SOFT & JUICY BEEF KABOBS 35
85. ASIAN FLAVORS BEEF BROCCOLI 36
86. JUICY RIB EYE STEAK 36
87. CHEESY & JUICY PORK CHOPS 36
88. STUFFED PEPPERS 36
89. LAMB PATTIES 36
90. LEMON MUSTARD LAMB CHOPS 37
91. ITALIAN SAUSAGE MEATBALLS 37
92. YUMMY MEATBALLS 37
93. TASTY PORK BITES 37
94. FLAVORFUL PORK TENDERLOIN 38
95. SPICY LAMB CHOPS 38

96. Quick & Easy Meatballs 38
97. Easy Pesto Pork Chops 38
98. Moist Lamb Roast 38
99. Dried Herbs Lamb Chops 39
100. Crispy Pork Chops 39
101. Garlic Thyme Pork Chops 39
102. Pork Strips 39
103. Mushrooms Meatballs 39
104. Flavorful Kabab 40
105. Grilled Pork Shoulder 40
106. Beef Satay 40
107. Beefy Steak Topped with Chimichurri Sauce 40
108. Cheesy Ground Beef and Mac Taco Casserole 40
109. Garlic and Bell Pepper Beef 41
110. Beef and Green Onion Marinade 41
111. Short Ribs and Beer Sauce 41
112. Beef and Cabbage Mix 42
113. Short Ribs and Special Sauce 42
114. Beef Patty in Mushroom Sauce 42
115. Greek Beef Meatballs Salad 42
116. Beef Stuffed Squash 43
117. Beef Casserole 43
118. Burgundy Beef Mix 43
119. Sirloin Steaks and Pico de Gallo 43
120. Mexican Beef Mix 44
121. Coffee Flavored Steak 44
122. Seasoned Beef Roast 44
123. Simple Beef Sirloin Roast 44
124. Simple Beef Patties 45
125. Easy Beef Roast 45
126. Beef Sirloin Roast 45
127. Air Fried Grilled Steak 45
128. Air Fryer Beef Casserole 45
129. Charred Onions & Steak Cube BBQ 46
130. Beef Ribeye Steak 46
131. Air Fryer Roast Beef 46
132. Salt-and-Pepper Beef Roast 46
133. Prime Rib Roast 46
134. Beef Tenderloin 47
135. Perfect Rump Roast 47
136. Slow Roasted Beef Short Ribs 47
137. Sirloin Roast Beef 47
138. Roasted Hamburgers 47
139. Pan-Seared Roasted Strip Steak 47
140. London Broil Steak 48
141. Summer Sausage 48
142. Meatball Venison 48
143. Smoked Ham Sausage 48
144. Venison Loaf 49
145. Bologna 49
146. Squirrel Dish 49
147. Swedish Meatballs 49
148. Spaghetti and Meatballs 50
149. Cheese Garlicky Pork Chops 50
150. Garlic Lemon Pork Chops 50
151. Herb Cheese Pork Chops 51
152. Tender Pork Chops 51
153. Asian Pork Chops 51
154. Easy & Delicious Pork Chops 51
155. Dash Seasoned Pork Chops 51
156. Easy Pork Butt 52
157. Sweet and Sour Pork 52
158. Pork Ratatouille 52
159. Cheddar Pork Meatballs 52
160. Almond Pork Bite 53
161. Stuffed Pork Chops 53
162. Crispy Breaded Pork 53
163. Lemongrass Pork Chops 54
164. BBQ Pork Ribs 54
165. Spicy Pork Chops 54
166. Easy Pork Patties 54
167. Lemon Pepper Seasoned Pork Chops 55
168. Flavorful Pork Chops 55
169. Pesto Pork Chops 55
170. Coconut Butter Pork Chops 55
171. Crispy Pork Chops 55
172. BBQ Lamb 56
173. Lamb Meatballs 56
174. Glazed Lamb Chops 56
175. Garlic Lamb Shank 56
176. Indian Meatball with Lamb 57
177. Roasted Lamb 57
178. Lamb Gyro 57
179. Lemon Lamb Rack 57
180. Juicy & Savory Lamb Chops 58
181. Lamb Patties 58
182. Dijon Garlic Lamb Chops 58
183. Flavorful Cumin Lamb 58
184. Juicy & Tender Lemon Mustard Lamb Chops 59
185. Lamb Balls 59
186. Spicy Lamb Steak 59
187. Easy Greek Lamb Chops 59
188. Delicious Za'atar Lamb Chops 60
189. Quick & Easy Lamb Chops 60
190. Dried Herb Lamb Chops 60
191. Moist Lamb Roast 60
192. Thyme Lamb Chops 60
193. Baked Lamb Chops 61
194. Meatballs 61
195. Rosemary Roasted Leg of Lamb 61

CHAPTER 3: POULTRY RECIPES 62

196. Air Fried Whole Chicken 62
197. Air Roasted Turkey 62
198. Spanish Chicken Bake 62
199. Barbeque Air Fried Chicken 63
200. Saucy Chicken with Leeks 63
201. Chili Chicken Slider 63
202. Spicy Chicken Ginger Soup 64
203. Chicken with Artichoke Hearts 64
204. Chicken Shawarma 64

#	Recipe	Page
205.	Tender & Juicy Chicken	64
206.	Greek Chicken	65
207.	Roasted Pepper Chicken	65
208.	Chicken Paillard	65
209.	Greek Tomato Olive Chicken	65
210.	Crispy Crusted Chicken	66
211.	Apple Chicken	66
212.	Easy Slow Cook Chicken	66
213.	Broccoli Chicken Casserole	66
214.	Chicken Meatballs	67
215.	Tasty Caribbean Chicken	67
216.	Asian Chicken Wings	67
217.	Chili Garlic Chicken Wings	67
218.	Delicious Tandoori Chicken	68
219.	Mexican Chicken Lasagna	68
220.	Chicken Fajita Casserole	68
221.	Baked Chicken Mushrooms	68
222.	Chicken Cacciatore	69
223.	Ranch Chicken	69
224.	Caesar Chicken	69
225.	Simple & Easy Slow Cook Chicken	69
226.	Mustard Chicken	70
227.	Chicken Thighs with Rosemary	70
228.	Baked Chicken Tenders	70
229.	Chicken Curry Salad	70
230.	Herb Roasted Turkey Breast	70
231.	Shredded Chicken Sandwich	71
232.	Dijon Stuffed Chicken	71
233.	Air Fried Turkey Breast with Basil	71
234.	Buttermilk Brined Turkey Breast	71
235.	Turkey Meatloaf	71
236.	Simple Turkey Breast	72
237.	Turkey Chili	72
238.	Turkey Divan Casserole	72
239.	Turkey Broccoli Casserole	73
240.	Homemade Turkey Breakfast Sausage	73
241.	Sweet Potato, Onion, and Turkey Sausage Hash	73
242.	Easy Turkey Breakfast Patties	73
243.	Turkey Spinach Patties	73
244.	Tasty Turkey Fajitas	74
245.	Turkey Broccoli Fritters	74
246.	Spicy Turkey Wings	74
247.	Nutritious Turkey & Veggies	74
248.	Turkey Spinach Meatballs	74
249.	Tender Turkey Legs	75
250.	Grilled Quail	75
251.	Turkey Breasts	75
252.	BBQ Chicken Breasts	75
253.	Rotisserie Chicken	75
254.	Honey-Mustard Chicken Breasts	76
255.	Chicken Parmesan Wings	76
256.	Air Fryer Chicken	76
257.	Whole Chicken	76
258.	Honey Duck Breasts	76
259.	Creamy Coconut Chicken	76
260.	Buffalo Chicken Tenders	77
261.	Teriyaki Wings	77
262.	Lemony Drumsticks	77
263.	Parmesan Chicken Tenders	77
264.	Easy Lemon Chicken Thighs	77
265.	Air Fryer Grilled Chicken Breasts	78
266.	Perfect Chicken Parmesan	78
267.	Honey and Wine Chicken Breasts	78
268.	Crispy Honey Garlic Chicken Wings	78
269.	Chicken-Fried Steak Supreme	79
270.	Lemon-Pepper Chicken Wings	79
271.	Air Fried Chili Chicken	79
272.	Air-Fried Lemon Chicken	80
273.	Baked Chicken Thighs	80
274.	Turkey Wraps with Sauce	80
275.	Air Roasted Chicken Drumsticks	81
276.	Scrumptious Turkey Wraps	81
277.	Air Roasted Whole Chicken	81

CHAPTER 4: FISH AND SEAFOOD RECIPES 82

#	Recipe	Page
278.	Lobster Tails with Lemon Butter	82
279.	Tuna Patties	82
280.	Crispy Fish Sticks	82
281.	Delicious White Fish	82
282.	Salmon Patties	83
283.	Perfect Salmon Fillets	83
284.	Flavorful Parmesan Shrimp	83
285.	Simple Air Fryer Salmon	83
286.	Shrimp with Veggie	83
287.	Nutritious Salmon	84
288.	Shrimp Scampi	84
289.	Lemon Chili Salmon	84
290.	Pesto Salmon	84
291.	Walnut Salmon	84
292.	Lemon Shrimp	85
293.	Grilled Catfish Fillets	85
294.	Grilled Cod Fillets Mixed with Grapes Salad and Fennel	85
295.	Crispy Paprika Fish Fillets	85
296.	Lemony Tuna	86
297.	Grilled Soy Salmon Fillets	86
298.	Tender & Juicy Salmon	86
299.	Lemon Garlic White Fish	86
300.	Parmesan White Fish Fillets	87
301.	Ginger Garlic Salmon	87
302.	Quick & Easy Salmon	87
303.	Healthy Salmon Patties	87
304.	Garlic Yogurt Salmon Fillets	87
305.	Parmesan Basil Salmon	88
306.	Flavorful Curry Cod Fillets	88
307.	Dukkah Crusted Salmon	88
308.	Herbed Salmon	88
309.	Cod Steaks and Plum Sauce	88
310.	Flavored Grilled Salmon	89
311.	Grilled Lemony Saba Fish	89
312.	Orange Sauce with Trout Fillet	89
313.	Grilled Parsley and Thyme Salmon	89
314.	Grilled Mustard Salmon	90

315. Tabasco Shrimps 90
316. Onion Pepper Shrimp 90
317. Old Bay Shrimp 90
318. Shrimp with Vegetables 90
319. Delicious Buttery Shrimp 91
320. Mexican Shrimp Fajitas 91
321. Crisp & Juicy Cajun Shrimp 91
322. Lime Garlic Shrimp Kababs 91
323. Tasty Chipotle Shrimp 91
324. Tasty Shrimp Fajitas 91
325. Easy Coconut Shrimp 92
326. Shrimp & Vegetable Dinner 92
327. Lemon Garlic Shrimp 92
328. Easy Cajun Shrimp 92
329. Sweet and Savory Breaded Shrimp 92
330. Bacon-Wrapped Shrimp 93
331. Spicy Scallops 93
332. Pesto Scallops 93
333. Old Bay Seasoned Crab Cakes 93
334. Lemon Garlic Scallops 94
335. Lemon Caper Scallops 94
336. Cajun Scallops 94
337. Flavorful Crab Cakes 94
338. Healthy Crab Cakes 94
339. Crisp Bacon Wrapped Scallops 95
340. Soy and Ginger Shrimp 95
341. Quick Paella 95
342. Steamed Salmon and Sauce 95
343. Indian Fish Fingers 96
344. Flying Fish 96
345. Pistachio-Crusted Lemon-Garlic Salmon .. 96
346. Salmon Noodles 96
347. Fried Calamari 97
348. Mustard-Crusted Fish Fillets 97
349. Fish and Vegetable Tacos 97
350. Lighter Fish and Chips 97
351. Snapper with Fruit 98
352. Tuna Wraps 98
353. Tuna and Fruit Kebabs 98
354. Asian Swordfish 98
355. Salmon Spring Rolls 99
356. Salmon on Bed of Fennel and Carrot 99
357. Scallops with Green Vegetables 99
358. Butter Up Salmon 99
359. Lemon Salmon 100
360. Hearty Spiced Salmon 100
361. Cajun Shrimp 100
362. Air Fried Dragon Shrimp 100
363. Fish Tacos 100
364. Asian Coconut Shrimp 101
365. Mahi Fahrenheit with Herby Buttery Drizzle 101
366. Classic Lemon Pepper Haddock 101
367. Fried Scallops with Saffron Cream Sauce ... 102
368. Easy Crab Cakes 102
369. Sweet Asian Style Salmon 102
370. Zesty Ranch Fish Fillets 102
371. Dill Fish Chops 103
372. Easy Fish Sticks with Chili Ketchup Sauce ... 103
373. Packet Lobster Tail 103
374. Shrimp and Green Beans 103
375. Crab Dip 104
376. Sesame Shrimp 104
377. Salmon and Cauliflower Rice 104
378. Trout and Mint 104
379. Salmon and Coconut Sauce 104
380. Simple Salmon 105
381. Salmon and Sauce 105
382. Parmesan Cod 105
383. Cod and Endives 105
384. Cod and Tomatoes 106
385. Salmon Burgers 106
386. Air Fried Haddock Fillets 106
387. Crispy Coated Scallops 106
388. Tasty Tuna Loaf 106
389. Maryland Crab Cakes 107
390. Mediterranean Sole 107
391. Spicy Grilled Halibut 107
392. Tropical Shrimp Skewers 108
393. Seafood Mac n Cheese 108
394. Crispy Air Fried Sushi Roll 108
395. Honey Glazed Salmon 109
396. Parmesan Shrimp 109
397. Bacon-Wrapped Scallops 109
398. Air Fryer Fish Tacos 109
399. Salmon Croquettes 109
400. Friedamari 110
401. Air Fryer Salmon Patties 110
402. Bang Frieda Mari Panko Breaded Fried Shrimp 110
403. 3-Ingredient Air Fryer Catfish 110
404. Fish in Parchment Paper 111
405. Buttery Scallops 111
406. Crusted Scallops 111
407. Lobster Tails with White Wine Sauce 111
408. Broiled Lobster Tails 112
409. Paprika Lobster Tail 112
410. Lobster Tails with Lemon Butter 112
411. Sheet Pan Seafood Bake 112

CHAPTER 5: SIDE DISHES 113

412. Tasty Potato Fries 113
413. Roasted Broccoli Cauliflower 113
414. Arugula Artichoke Dip 113
415. Roasted Vegetables Salad 113
416. Delicious Potato Patties 114
417. Garlicky Cauliflower Florets 114
418. Zucchini Patties 114
419. Parmesan Hassel back Potatoes 114
420. Flavorful Herb Potatoes 115
421. Baked Egg Tomato 115
422. Baked Zucchini Eggplant 115
423. Veggie Tots 115
424. Spinach Bake 116

425. NOT YOUR AVERAGE ZUCCHINI PARMESAN CHIPS 116
426. SKY-HIGH ROASTED CORN 116
427. RAVISHING AIR-FRIED CARROTS WITH HONEY GLAZE 116
428. FLAMING BUFFALO CAULIFLOWER BITES 116
429. PLEASANT AIR-FRIED EGGPLANT 117
430. CAULIFLOWER HASH 117
431. ASPARAGUS WITH ALMONDS 117
432. ZUCCHINI CUBES 117
433. SWEET POTATO & ONION MIX 117
434. SPICY EGGPLANT CUBES 118
435. ROASTED GARLIC HEAD 118
436. WRAPPED ASPARAGUS 118
437. BAKED YAMS WITH DILL 118
438. HONEY ONIONS 118
439. DELIGHTFUL ROASTED GARLIC SLICES 119
440. COCONUT OIL ARTICHOKES 119
441. ROASTED MUSHROOMS 119
442. MASHED YAMS 119
443. CAULIFLOWER RICE 119
444. SHREDDED CABBAGE 120
445. FRIED LEEKS RECIPE 120
446. BRUSSELS SPROUTS AND TOMATOES MIX RECIPE 120
447. RADISH HASH RECIPE 120
448. BROCCOLI SALAD RECIPE 120
449. CHILI BROCCOLI 120
450. PARMESAN BROCCOLI AND ASPARAGUS 120
451. BUTTER BROCCOLI MIX 121
452. BALSAMIC KALE 121
453. KALE AND OLIVES 121
454. KALE AND MUSHROOMS MIX 121
455. ROASTED ZUCCHINI 121
456. CRISPY & SPICY EGGPLANT 122
457. CURRIED EGGPLANT SLICES 122
458. SPICED GREEN BEANS 122
459. AIR FRYER BASIL TOMATOES 122
460. AIR FRYER RATATOUILLE 123
461. GARLICKY CAULIFLOWER FLORETS 123
462. PARMESAN BRUSSELS SPROUTS 123
463. FLAVORFUL TOMATOES 123
464. HEALTHY ROASTED CARROTS 123
465. CURRIED CAULIFLOWER WITH PINE NUTS ... 124
466. THYME SAGE BUTTERNUT SQUASH 124
467. GRILLED CAULIFLOWER 124
468. STUFFED ZUCCHINI 124
469. VINEGAR VEGGIES 125
470. GARLICKY MIXED VEGGIES 125
471. MEDITERRANEAN VEGGIES 126
472. MARINATED VEGGIE SKEWERS 126
473. PINEAPPLE & VEGGIE SKEWERS 126
474. BUTTERED CORN 127
475. GUACAMOLE 127

CHAPTER 6: VEGAN AND VEGETARIAN RECIPES 128

476. BEANS AND VEGGIES MIX 128
477. SALSA BEANS 128
478. SUPREME AIR-FRIED TOFU 128
479. SWEET & TANGY MUSHROOMS 128
480. CHEESY BROCCOLI RICE 129
481. MAC & CHEESE 129
482. TOFU WITH CAULIFLOWER 129
483. POTATO CASSEROLE 129
484. ASPARAGUS STRATA 130
485. ZUCCHINI EGG BAKE 130
486. CURRIED CAULIFLOWER 130
487. BABY POTATOES 130
488. BAKED VEGETABLES 131
489. DILL MASHED POTATO 131
490. CREAM POTATO 131
491. CHARD WITH CHEDDAR 131
492. CHILI SQUASH WEDGES 131
493. HONEY CARROTS WITH GREENS 132
494. SOUTH ASIAN CAULIFLOWER FRITTERS 132
495. AIR FRIED CAULIFLOWER RICE 132
496. ROASTED APPLE SWEET POTATOES 132
497. GREEN BEANS WITH CARROTS 133
498. WINTER VEGETARIAN FRITTATA 133
499. CHEESY BROCCOLI CASSEROLE 133
500. BUFFALO CAULIFLOWER 133
501. CAULIFLOWER BITES 134
502. ONION RINGS 134
503. ZUCCHINI PARMESAN CHIPS 134
504. JALAPEÑO CHEESE BALLS 134
505. GLAZED CARROTS 135
506. FLATBREAD 135
507. CREAMY CABBAGE 135
508. CREAMY POTATOES 135
509. GREEN BEANS AND CHERRY TOMATOES 135
510. CRISPY BRUSSELS SPROUTS AND POTATOES . 136
511. AIR FRIED LEEKS 136
512. CRISPY BROCCOLI 136
513. GARLIC-ROASTED BELL PEPPERS 136
514. ASPARAGUS WITH GARLIC 136
515. CHEESY ROASTED SWEET POTATOES 136
516. SALTY LEMON ARTICHOKES 137
517. ASPARAGUS & PARMESAN 137
518. CORN ON COBS 137
519. ONION GREEN BEANS 137
520. SPICY ASIAN BRUSSELS SPROUTS 137
521. HEALTHY MUSHROOMS 138
522. CHEESE STUFF PEPPERS 138
523. CHEESY BRUSSELS SPROUTS 138
524. SPICY BRUSSELS SPROUTS 138
525. AIR FRIED TASTY EGGPLANT 138
526. AIR FRYER BROCCOLI & BRUSSELS SPROUTS 139
527. SPICY ASPARAGUS SPEARS 139
528. STUFFED MUSHROOMS 139
529. CHEESY BROCCOLI CAULIFLOWER 139
530. BROCCOLI WITH HERBS AND CHEESE 139
531. ALMOND FLOUR BATTERED 'N CRISPED ONION RINGS 140

532. Spanish-Style Eggs with Manchego Cheese 140
533. Tamarind Glazed Sweet Potatoes 140
534. Mediterranean style Eggs with Spinach .. 140
535. Thai Roasted Veggies 141
536. Spicy Zesty Broccoli with Tomato Sauce .. 141
537. Fried Squash Croquettes 141
538. Cheese Stuffed Mushrooms with Horseradish Sauce 141
539. Creamy Spinach and Mushroom Lasagna .. 142
540. Roasted Cauliflower with Pepper Jack Cheese 142
541. Family Favorite Stuffed Mushrooms 142
542. Famous Fried Pickles 143
543. Asian Stir Fry 143
544. Cauliflower Crust Pizza 143
545. Roasted Squash Puree 144
546. Kale Slaw and Strawberry Salad + Poppy seed Dressing 144
547. Tomato Bites with Creamy Parmesan Sauce 144
548. Simple Green Beans with Butter 144
549. Creamy Cauliflower and Broccoli 145
550. Balsamic Artichokes 145
551. Cheesy Artichokes 145
552. Beet Salad with Parsley Dressing 145
553. Blue Cheese Salad and Beets 146
554. Broccoli Salad 146
555. Brussels Sprout with Tomatoes Mix 146
556. Cheesy Brussels Sprout 146
557. Spicy Cabbage 147
558. Sweet Baby Carrots 147
559. Zucchini Mix and Herbed Eggplant 147
560. Sweet Potato Toast 147
561. Stuffed Portabella Mushroom 147
562. Pumpkin Quesadillas 148
563. Toasted-Baked Tofu cubes 148
564. Stuffed Squash 148
565. Sriracha Roasted Potatoes 148
566. Brussel Sprouts, Mango, Avocado Salsa Tacos 148
567. Spaghetti Squash Burrito Bowls 149
568. Baked Oatmeal 149
569. Healthy Mixed Vegetables 149
570. Easy Roasted Vegetables 149
571. Easy & Crispy Brussels Sprouts 150
572. Garlic Green Beans 150
573. Simple Vegan Broccoli 150
574. Sesame Carrots 150
575. Asparagus with Almonds 150
576. Easy Roasted Carrots 150
577. Asian Broccoli 151
578. Healthy Squash & Zucchini 151
579. Crunchy Fried Cabbage 151
580. Quick Vegetable Kebabs 151
581. Easy Soy Garlic Mushrooms 151
582. Spicy Edamame 152
583. Balsamic Mushrooms 152
584. Mediterranean Vegetables 152
585. Simple Roasted Okra 152
586. Air Fried Vegetables 152
587. Air Broiled Mushrooms 153
588. Hydrated Potato Wedges 153
589. Crispy Baked Tofu 153
590. Spiced Tempeh 153
591. Steamed Broccoli 154
592. Air Fried Brussel Sprouts 154

CHAPTER 7 : RICE AND GRAINS RECIPES .. 155

593. Rice and Calamari Mix 155
594. Curry Rice 155
595. Pesto Rice 155
596. Mango and Berries Rice 155
597. Nutty Rice 155
598. Pine Nuts Quinoa 155
599. Beans and Corn 156
600. Corn and Pine Nuts Mix 156
601. Carrots Rice 156
602. Ginger Rice 156
603. Rice and Radishes 156
604. Quinoa and Shrimp 156
605. Oregano Salsa Rice 157
606. Chestnut Rice 157
607. Beef Quinoa Mix 157
608. Shallots Wild Rice 157
609. Squash Quinoa 157
610. Garlic Black Beans and Potatoes 157
611. Parsley Beans 158
612. Chili Beans and Quinoa 158
613. Thyme Beans 158
614. Millet Pudding 158
615. Bulgur and Peas 158
616. Fennel and Peas Quinoa 158
617. Beans and Kale 159
618. Garlic Barley Mix 159
619. Quinoa and Broccoli Salad 159
620. Spring Onions and Tomatoes Beans 159
621. Cracked What Mix 159
622. Creamy Beans Mix 160
623. Walnuts Bulgur Mix 160
624. Minty Bulgur 160
625. Couscous and Veggies 160
626. Coriander Couscous 160
627. Hydrated Kale Chips 160

CHAPTER 8 : APPETIZERS AND SNACKS 161

628. Feta Tater Tots 161
629. Cauliflower Poppers 161
630. Fish Nuggets 161
631. Buffalo Chicken Wings 161
632. Bacon-Wrapped Shrimp 162
633. Crispy Coconut Prawns 162
634. Pancetta Wrapped Shrimp 162
635. Haddock Nuggets 162

#	Recipe	Page
636.	Taco Seasoned Kale Chips	163
637.	Chili Beef Nachos	163
638.	Sausage Potato & Zucchini Skewers	163
639.	Salted Maple Pecan Granola	163
640.	Bacon-Wrapped Hot Dogs	164
641.	Double-Baked Stuffed Potato	164
642.	Garlic Bread	164
643.	Butter Baked Mussels	164
644.	Air Fried Zucchini Fries	165
645.	Blue Cheese Caesar Chicken Wings	165
646.	Sweet & Spicy Korean Chicken Wings	165
647.	Honey Mustard Chicken Legs	166
648.	Margherita Pizza	166
649.	Pepperoni Pizza	166
650.	Avocado Baked Egg	167
651.	Rotisserie Chicken	167
652.	Rustic Grilled Cheese	167
653.	Chicken Wraps	167
654.	Chicken Mushroom Bites	168
655.	Potato Tater Tots	168
656.	Plantain Chips	168
657.	Crispy Asparagus	168
658.	Breaded Ravioli	169
659.	Beef Enchilada Dip	169
660.	Cheesy Stuffed Sliders	169
661.	Philly Egg Rolls	169
662.	Mozzarella Cheese Sticks	170
663.	Buffalo Quesadillas	170
664.	Crispy Sausage Bites	170
665.	Puffed Asparagus Spears	171
666.	Wonton Poppers	171
667.	Party Pull Apart	171
668.	Easy Cheesy Stuffed Mushrooms	171
669.	Roasted Peanuts	172
670.	Roasted Cashews	172
671.	French Fries	172
672.	Spicy Carrot Fries	172
673.	Maple Carrot Fries	173
674.	Squash Fries	173
675.	Dill Pickle Fries	173
676.	Mozzarella Sticks	173
677.	Apple Chips	174
678.	Beet Chips	174
679.	Potato Chips	174
680.	Buttered Corn	174
681.	Bread Sticks	175
682.	Polenta Sticks	175
683.	Crispy Eggplant Slices	175
684.	Simple Cauliflower Poppers	176
685.	Crispy Cauliflower Poppers	176
686.	Broccoli Poppers	176
687.	Cheesy Broccoli Bites	176
688.	Mixed Veggie Bites	177
689.	Risotto Bites	177
690.	Rice Flour Bites	177
691.	Potato Croquettes	177
692.	Bacon Croquettes	178
693.	Chicken & Veggie Nuggets	178
694.	Cod Nuggets	179
695.	Crispy Prawns	179
696.	Breaded Shrimp	179
697.	Bacon Wrapped Shrimp	179
698.	Mixed Berries Crisp	180
699.	Duck, Fat: Roasted Red Potatoes	180
700.	Chicken Wings with Alfredo Sauce	180
701.	Crispy Squash	180
702.	Classic French Fries	181
703.	BBQ Chicken	181
704.	Turkey Meatballs with Spaghetti Squash	181
705.	Turkey & Mushroom Casserole	181
706.	Prosciutto-Wrapped Asparagus	182
707.	Coconut Shrimp	182
708.	Rice Bites	182
709.	Grilled Tomato Salsa	182
710.	Parmesan French Fries	183
711.	Fish Sticks	183
712.	Homemade Fries	183
713.	Fried Garlic Pickles	183
714.	Zucchini Strips with Marinara Dip	184
715.	Greek Potatoes	184
716.	Ranch Chicken Fingers	184
717.	Crunchy Parmesan Asparagus	184
718.	Bacon Bell Peppers	185
719.	Corn & Carrot Fritters	185
720.	Butter Baked Nuts	185
721.	Eggs Spinach Side	186
722.	Squash and Cumin Chili	186
723.	Fried Up Avocados	186
724.	Hearty Green Beans	186
725.	Parmesan Cabbage Wedges	186
726.	Extreme Zucchini Fries	187
727.	Easy Fried Tomatoes	187
728.	Roasted Up Brussels	187
729.	Roasted Brussels and Pine Nuts	187
730.	Low-Calorie Beets Dish	187
731.	Broccoli and Parmesan Dish	188
732.	Bacon and Asparagus Spears	188
733.	Healthy Low Carb Fish Nugget	188
734.	Fried Up Pumpkin Seeds	188
735.	Decisive Tiger Shrimp Platter	188
736.	Air Fried Olives	189
737.	Bacon-Wrapped Dates	189
738.	Bacon-Wrapped Shrimp and Jalapeño	189
739.	Breaded Artichoke Hearts	189
740.	Bruschetta with Basil Pesto	190
741.	Cajun Zucchini Chips	190
742.	Cheesy Apple Roll-Ups	190
743.	Cheesy Jalapeño Poppers	190
744.	Cheesy Steak Fries	190
745.	Crispy Breaded Beef Cubes	191
746.	Coriander Artichokes	191
747.	Spinach and Artichokes Sauté	191

748. Green Beans ... 191
749. Bok Choy and Butter Sauce ... 191
750. Turmeric Mushroom ... 191
751. Creamy Fennel ... 192
752. Air Fried Green Tomatoes ... 192
753. Seasoned Potato Wedges ... 192
754. Honey Roasted Carrots ... 192
755. Onion Rings ... 192
756. Chicken Kebab ... 193
757. Mac and Cheese Balls ... 193
758. Cauliflower Fritters ... 193
759. Loaded Tater Tot Bites ... 193
760. Italian-Style Tomato-Parmesan Crisps ... 194
761. Baked Cheese Crisps ... 194
762. Puerto Rican Tostones ... 194
763. Cajun Cheese Sticks ... 194
764. Classic Deviled Eggs ... 194
765. Barbecue Little Smokies ... 194
766. Paprika Potato Chips ... 195
767. Cheddar Dip ... 195
768. Coated Avocado Tacos ... 195
769. Roasted Corn with Butter and Lime ... 195
770. Batter-Fried Scallions ... 195
771. Heirloom Tomato with Baked Feta ... 196
772. Crispy Potato Skins ... 196
773. Beets and Carrots ... 196
774. Broccoli Crisps ... 196
775. Maple Syrup Bacon ... 196
776. Low-Carb Pizza Crust ... 197
777. Colby Potato Patties ... 197
778. Turkey Garlic Potatoes ... 197
779. Creamy Scrambled Eggs ... 197
780. Bacon-Wrapped Onion Rings ... 197
781. Grilled Cheese ... 198
782. Peppered Puff Pastry ... 198
783. Horseradish Mayo & Gorgonzola Mushrooms ... 198
784. Crumbed Beans ... 198
785. Croutons ... 199
786. Cheese Lings ... 199
787. Sweet Potato Wedges ... 199
788. Spiced Almonds ... 199
789. Crispy Cauliflower Bites ... 199
790. Roasted Coconut Carrots ... 200
791. Spicy Grilled Turkey Breast ... 200
792. Teriyaki Turkey Bowls ... 200
793. Thai Turkey Stir Fry ... 200
794. Turkey Enchiladas ... 201
795. Baked Potatoes with Bacon ... 201
796. Walnut & Cheese Filled Mushrooms ... 201
797. Air-Fried Chicken Thighs ... 201
798. Simple Buttered Potatoes ... 202
799. Homemade Peanut Corn Nuts ... 202
800. Corn-Crusted Chicken Tenders ... 202
801. Choco Hazelnut Croissant ... 202
802. Blueberry Muffin Surprise ... 202
803. Blueberry Crumble ... 202
804. Golden Caramelized Pear Tart ... 203
805. Middle East Baklava ... 203
806. Chocolate Donuts ... 203
807. Coconut Pancake ... 204
808. Cinnamon Rolls ... 204

CHAPTER 9: SWEETS AND DESSERTS ... 205

809. Easy Baked Chocolate Mug Cake ... 205
810. Angel Food Cake ... 205
811. Fried Peaches ... 205
812. Apple Dumplings ... 205
813. Apple Pie in Air Fryer ... 206
814. Raspberry Cream Roll-Ups ... 206
815. Air Fryer Chocolate Cake ... 206
816. Banana-Choco Brownies ... 206
817. Chocolate Donuts ... 207
818. Air Fryer Cinnamon Rolls ... 207
819. Easy Air Fryer Donuts ... 207
820. Chocolate Soufflé for Two ... 207
821. Fried Bananas with Chocolate Sauce ... 208
822. Apple Hand Pies ... 208
823. Chocolaty Banana Muffins ... 208
824. Bread Pudding with Cranberry ... 208
825. Black and White Brownies ... 209
826. Sweet Cream Cheese Wontons ... 209
827. Baked Apple ... 209
828. Coffee and Blueberry Cake ... 209
829. Cinnamon Sugar Roasted Chickpeas ... 210
830. Cherry-Choco Bars ... 210
831. Cinnamon Fried Bananas ... 210
832. Coconutty Lemon Bars ... 210
833. Awesome Chinese Doughnuts ... 210
834. Banana and Walnuts Muffins ... 211
835. Vanilla Spiced Soufflé ... 211
836. Apricot Blackberry Crumble ... 211
837. Roasted Pineapples with Vanilla Zest ... 211
838. Chocolate Cup cakes ... 212
839. Crispy Bananas ... 212
840. Stuffed Baked Apples ... 212
841. Cinnamon Apple Chips ... 212
842. Apple Chips with Dip ... 213
843. Delicious Spiced Apples ... 213
844. Tasty Cheese Bites ... 213
845. Apple Chips ... 213
846. Gooey Cinnamon Smores ... 214
847. Sweetened Plantains ... 214
848. Pear Crisp ... 214
849. Easy Pears Dessert ... 214
850. Vanilla Strawberry Mix ... 214
851. Sweet Bananas and Sauce ... 214
852. Cinnamon Apples and Mandarin Sauce ... 215
853. Cocoa Berries Cream ... 215
854. Sweet Vanilla Rhubarb ... 215
855. Cherries and Rhubarb Bowls ... 215
856. Pumpkin Bowls ... 215
857. Buttery Fennel and Garlic ... 215
858. Lemon Mousse ... 216

#	Entry	Page
859.	Glazed Banana	216
860.	Raspberry Danish	216
861.	Blueberry Muffins	216
862.	Cranberry Cupcakes	217
863.	Zucchini Mug Cake	217
864.	Chocolate Brownies	217
865.	Apple Crisp	218
866.	Banana and Walnut Cake	218
867.	Perfect Cinnamon Toast	218
868.	Apple Pie in Air Fryer	218
869.	Banana Brownies	219
870.	Chocolate Soufflé for Two	219
871.	Blueberry Lemon Muffins	219
872.	Raspberry Cream Roll-Ups	219
873.	Black and White Brownies	220
874.	Baked Apple	220
875.	Cinnamon Fried Bananas	220
876.	Awesome Chinese Doughnuts	221
877.	Crispy Bananas	221
878.	Air Fried Banana and Walnuts Muffins	221
879.	Nutty Mix	221
880.	Vanilla Spiced Soufflé	221
881.	Chocolate Cup Cakes	222
882.	Air Baked Cheesecake	222
883.	Air Roasted Nuts	222
884.	Air Fried White Corn	223
885.	Fruit Cake	223
886.	Hydrated Apples	223
887.	Nutty Slice	223
888.	Energy Brownies	223
889.	Air Fry Toaster Oven Bars	224
890.	Self-Saucing Banana Pudding	224
891.	Chocolate Lava Cake	224
892.	Banana and Walnut Bread	224
893.	Choco-Peanut Mug Cake	225
894.	Raspberry-Coco Desert	225
895.	Almond Cherry Bars	225
896.	Coffee Flavored Doughnuts	225
897.	Simple Strawberry Cobbler	226
898.	Easy Pumpkin Pie	226
899.	Simple Cheesecake	226
900.	Strawberry Donuts	226
901.	Apricot Blackberry Crumble	227
902.	Ginger Cheesecake	227
903.	Coconut Donuts	227
904.	Blueberry Cream	227
905.	Blackberry Chia Jam	227
906.	Mixed Berries Cream	227
907.	Cinnamon-Spiced Acorn Squash	228
908.	Pear Sauce	228
909.	Brownie Muffins	228
910.	Chocolate Mug Cake	228
911.	Chocolate Soufflé	228
912.	Chocolate Cake	229
913.	Chocolate Chip Air Fryer Cookies	229
914.	Doughnuts	229
915.	Cherry-Choco Bars	230
916.	Crusty Apple Hand Pies	230
917.	Pancakes Nutella-Stuffed	230
918.	Spiced Pear Sauce	230
919.	Saucy Fried Bananas	230
920.	Macaroons	231
921.	Orange Cake	231
922.	Carrot Cake	231
923.	Easy Baked Chocolate Mug Cake	231
924.	Fried Peaches	232
925.	Apple Dumplings	232
926.	Air Fryer Chocolate Cake	232
927.	Banana-Choco Brownies	232
928.	Easy Air Fryer Donuts	233
929.	Fried Bananas with Chocolate Sauce	233
930.	Chocolaty Banana Muffins	233
931.	Sweet Cream Cheese Wontons	233
932.	Air Fryer Cinnamon Rolls	234
933.	Bread Pudding with Cranberry	234

CHAPTER 10: BREAD RECIPES 235

#	Entry	Page
934.	Mini Pizza	235
935.	Artichoke with Red Pepper Pizza	235
936.	Flatbread	235
937.	Artichoke Turkey Pizza	236
938.	Bacon Cheeseburger Pizza	236
939.	Bacon Lettuce Tomato Pizza	236
940.	Breakfast Pizza	236
941.	French Bread Pizza	237
942.	Vegetable Pizza Pan Supreme	237
943.	Garlic Bread Pizza	237
944.	Cheesy Pepperoni Pizza Bites	237
945.	Cheesy BBQ Chicken Pizza	238
946.	Eggplant Pizza	238
947.	Veggie Pizza	238
948.	Grill Pizza Sandwiches	238
949.	Basil Pizza	238
950.	PowerXL Air Fryer Grill-baked Grilled Cheese	239
951.	Cheese Chili Toast	239
952.	Cheese Pizza	239
953.	Garlic Bread	239
954.	Pepperoni Pizza	239
955.	Egg Sandwich	240
956.	Grilled Cheese Sandwich	240
957.	Beef and Seeds Burgers	240
958.	Thai Pork Burgers	240
959.	Cheesy Philly Steaks	241
960.	Cheese & Egg Breakfast Sandwich	241
961.	Peanut Butter & Banana Sandwich	241
962.	Super Cheesy Sandwiches	241
963.	Simple Cuban Sandwiches	242
964.	Hot Ham and Cheese Sandwich	242
965.	Philly Cheesesteak Sandwiches	242
966.	Chicken Focaccia Bread Sandwiches	242
967.	Guacamole Turkey Burgers	242
968.	Bread Pudding	243

- 969. Cheesy Bread Pudding 243
- 970. Chocolate Bread Pudding 243
- 971. Fast Pumpkin Pudding 243
- 972. Coconut Berry Pudding 244
- 973. Pineapple Pudding 244
- 974. Cocoa Pudding 244
- 975. Cauliflower Pudding 244
- 976. Tuna and Lettuce Wraps 244
- 977. Crunchy Chicken Egg Rolls 244
- 978. Golden Cabbage and Mushroom Spring Rolls 245
- 979. Korean Beef and Onion Tacos 245
- 980. Cheesy Sweet Potato and Bean Burritos . 246
- 981. Golden Chicken and Yogurt Taquitos 246
- 982. Cod Tacos with Salsa 246
- 983. Golden Spring Rolls 247
- 984. Fast Cheesy Bacon and Egg Wraps 247
- 985. Chicken-Lettuce Wraps 247
- 986. Chicken Pita Sandwich 248
- 987. Veggie Salsa Wraps 248
- 988. Cheesy Shrimp Sandwich 248
- 989. Smoky Chicken Sandwich 248
- 990. Nugget and Veggie Taco Wraps 249
- 991. Cheesy Greens Sandwich 249
- 992. Cheesy Chicken Sandwich 249
- 993. Lettuce Fajita Meatball Wraps 249
- 994. Easy Homemade Hamburgers 250
- 995. Easy Beef Burritos 250
- 996. Beef Parmigiana Sliders 250
- 997. Chicago-Style Beef Sandwich 250
- 998. Mediterranean Burgers with Onion Jam 251
- 999. Italian Piadina Sandwich 251
- 1000. Taco Stuffed Avocados 251
- 1001. Beef Taco Roll-Ups with Cotija Cheese.. 251
- 1002. Quick Sausage and Veggie Sandwiches ... 252
- 1003. Cheesy Beef Burrito 252
- 1004. Burgers with Caramelized Onions 252

30 DAY MEAL PLAN 253

AIR FRYER COOKING CHART 254

MEASUREMENT CONVERSION 255

BONUS 1—HOW TO REHEAT FOOD 256

   Recipe for Reheating Food 256

BONUS 2—COOKING FROZEN FOODS 257

CONCLUSION 258

Introduction

An Air Fryer is an electric kitchen appliance that cooks food by rapidly circulating warm air around it instead of using a heat source such as a stove, oven, or toaster.

This differs from other types of "fryers" in that it usually uses much less oil or shortening.

The primary purpose of an Air Fryer is to provide a healthier option than deep frying in oil because the heating and cooking process happens rapidly in the confined environment where food is cooked, much like boiling water can kill germs in the water.

An additional benefit is the loss of fat, which saves time and money spent on cooking oils and fats.

An Air Fryer also facilitates the faster preparation of food.

In addition to making foods healthier than they would be in the oven or on the stovetop, an Air Fryer is also more energy-efficient than other types of frying as it requires less heat to cook. Many models of Air Fryers are equipped with an indicator light that signals when the oil or shortening is getting too hot so that users do not burn their food. Air Fryers can cost anywhere from $50 to several hundred dollars.

The most expensive ones typically include digital settings that can be programmed, such as timers and temperature controls.

Apart from frying, an Air Fryer can be utilized as a food dehydrator drying vegetables, fruits, and meat jerky for further uses. However, any leftover pellets need to be discarded when cleaning the interior compartment of an Air Fryer.

The performance of an Air Fryer is entirely dependent on its quality, and the cleanliness of the food being cooked.

If the food has any foreign matter or debris stuck to it, this will determine how well that item can be fried in an Air Fryer.

Foods with sticky substances such as bread crumbs or cornmeal may not work as well if they are stuck on them.

Foods that are too fatty will also cause problems with performance because they take longer to dry after cooking.

This can result in oily residues inside the Air Fryer when it is used again at a later date.

If an Air Fryer is used with ingredients that have a lot of oil or grease, it can leave foul odors that may remain after using it later on.

Air Fryer Benefits

It is a device that quickly and easily cooks your favorite foods. Whether you are looking to eat healthier or just want to cut calories, the Air Fryer has many benefits over traditional methods.

1. **Bakes How You Want:** To cook golden-brown fries, whip up your crispy wings in half the time without using a deep fryer. To make shrimp kebabs with minimal mess, or cook perfectly juicy burgers in less time than a burger grill! The possibilities are endless! Use what exactly suits your taste buds and needs best.
2. **Crust-Free:** The heat from the appliance is contained inside, eliminating the crusts from your favorite slices of bread, rolls, and crustless biscuits.
3. **Precise Control:** There are many options when it comes to cooking with an Air Fryer. This makes it easy for you to cook exactly what you want each day. No more burnt food or spend time trying to figure out the most efficient way to get dishes cooked for a family dinner.
4. **Diverse Options:** Air Fryers can be used as toasters, cake makers, and for grilling vegetables.
5. **Use it for Anything:** Many people that own an Air Fryer use it for far more than just fried foods. They can be used as toasters, cake makers, and for grilling vegetables.
6. As the name suggests, an Air Fryer works through air rather than oil. The device is constructed with a heating element below the food being cooked and keeps the outside dry so that it does not absorb extra fats or grease. This means healthier meals with less clean-up!
7. Air frying uses less oil than normal frying, but it still gives you some of that deep-fried flavor without all the hassle or extra calories. The Air Fryer keeps the inside temperature below 400°F, ensuring that your food is not overcooked.
8. The Air Fryer uses far less oil than traditional methods of frying, which can make a big difference when it comes to your health. You can enjoy fried foods without the added fat and calories that come with regular deep fryers. Air frying uses 80% less oil than normal frying and cooks your foods in half the time as well!
9. A lot of fried food is delicious, but there is no denying it's unhealthy. The Air Fryer helps to cut down on all the fat involved in cooking, making dinner healthier without sacrificing flavor. Since the temperature of the machine is around 300°F, you don't need to worry about burning your food. No matter how sensitive your recipe is, the Air Fryer will keep it tasting great!
10. The appliance has a lot of benefits over traditional methods of frying. It cooks more quickly than other devices and uses 80% less oil in the process too! Food cooks up crisp on the outside and tender on the inside, just like it would if you were frying it — only without all that extra fat.
11. Using an Air Fryer is a healthy alternative to other types of cooking.

How it Works

An Air Fryer works by circulating hot air around the cooking chamber. This heat and circulation system provides cooking power and a quick, relatively even heating effect that allows for a wide variety of frying options, from French fries to corn on the cob to Brussels sprouts. Despite popular belief, using an Air Fryer as opposed to deep frying is quite easy if you follow our simple steps below. The main difference between deep-frying and air frying is that one uses a lot of oil, while the other uses almost none at all.

Step 1: Prepare Your Air Fryer

First off, if your Air Fryer has any removable accessories or parts (such as baskets), make sure you remove them and clean them thoroughly before you start cooking. This will help to make your cooking experience a little less messy. You can use an Air Fryer without any of its accessories, but some people find that using baskets or skewers can be helpful for flipping foods or putting foods on top of the basket.

Step 2: Prep Your Ingredients

Next, you'll want to go through the ingredients and prepare them for cooking. For example, if you were going to be cooking chicken nuggets, you would start by removing the skin and cutting it into bite-sized pieces. You may also wish to slice up any vegetables that go along with your meal. After a little bit of preparation, everything is ready for cooking!

Step 3: Use the Appropriate Setting

You'll need to consult your user's manual if you're using a different brand of Air Fryer than we did, but for the most part, you can find instructions on the product's packaging for how to use the Air Fryer. Most Air Fryers come with one or two settings, and typically that will be listed right on the product packaging. Here are some of those settings: A high setting will cook food at a higher temperature than lower settings. This makes it better for cooking foods that require more intense heat such as fried eggs or chicken breasts. A low setting is best used for foods like veggies and even baking items (such as fan-shaped cookies).

Step 4: Put the Air Fryer to Work!

After you've successfully set up your Air Fryer, it's time to start cooking with it! If you have any cooking accessories, such as baskets or skewers, please make sure to put them back in place. That will help you to flip items.

Now that your Air Fryer is ready to cook, simply take some of your favorite foods and put them in the middle slot on your Air Fryer. Make sure that all of the items are at least 3 inches apart. You can also add food to the top and bottom slots. Every Air Fryer is different, so make sure you check to see what setting your Air Fryer uses and adjust accordingly. Most Air Fryers will have a little button that you can use to adjust the temperature; some may even have knobs on the side of the product.

When it's time to cook, don't forget that turning on your Air Fryer should be done with caution! Excessively high temperatures or prolonged cooking times can damage your appliance; so, make sure to keep an eye out for any faint odors or smoke (if your Air Fryer emits any) and make sure to reduce the heat if either happens.

Step 5: Enjoy Your Delicious Air Fried Food!

Once you've cooked your food, it's time to enjoy it!

Use and Maintenance

Air Fryers are great for cooking vegetables, chicken and steak, fish fillets, and breaded meat. They are also fun to play with because you can cook foods in other shapes and textures that typical cooking methods will not allow.

Air Fryers are designed to make you healthier because they use less oil and fewer calories than preparing the food in a conventional oven.

The procedure for using an Air Fryer is very simple. You just need to fill water and oil into the basket of an Air Fryer. Then, you cook up your dinner as usual in your conventional oven and after taking it out, set it into the basket of your Air Fryer. Maintenance is very simple. You just need to remove the basket from the base of the Air Fryer and wash it with warm water. You should not soak it in water as this may damage the inner parts of your Air Fryer. If you cannot spend time and money on buying a separate appliance for each dish you want to cook, then one of the best options that you have is an Air Fryer. If you know how to use and maintain it properly, it can prove to be one of the most efficient cooking appliances for your home as well.

Most Air Fryers come with a user manual and you should read it before using your device.

Cleaning and Storage

1. Always clean and wipe the Air Fryer grill after every usage.
2. Clean the outside of the appliance with a warm, damp cloth and a mild detergent.
3. To clean the door, mildly brush both flanks with warm soapy water and a moist cloth. Do not immerse the appliance in water or wash it in the dishwasher.
4. Clean the gadget's interior using hot water, a mild detergent, and a non-scratch sponge. Do not rub the heating coils because they are brittle and can break. Then rinse the appliance well with a clean, damp cloth. Do not leave standing water inside the machine.
5. If necessary, remove unwanted food residue with a non-abrasive cleaning brush.
6. Food adhering to accessories should be soaked in warm soapy water for easy removal. Hand washing is recommended.
7. Unplug the appliance and allow it to cool totally.
8. Ensure all parts and accessories are clean and dry.
9. Place the appliance in a clean and dry place.

Tips for Using Air Fryer

1. Smaller foods generally require a slightly shorter cooking time than larger ones.
2. Large sizes or quantities of food may require longer cooking time than smaller sizes or quantities.
3. Turning or flipping food midway through the cooking process ensures that food cooks evenly.
4. Sandwiches that are typically cooked in an oven can also be cooked in the Air Fryer.
5. Use the pre-made dough to make filled sandwiches quickly and easily. It requires less cooking time than homemade dough.
6. Using a can or plate is also recommended when cooking fragile or whole foods.
7. It's easy to make mistakes when using an Air Fryer. Avoid these common pitfalls:
   - Not monitoring the temperature of the Air Fryer, which can lead to uneven cooking and food burning.
   - Putting in too much food, which can cause it to be overcooked and dry out — or not get crisp enough on the outside because it takes too long.
   - Using ingredients that are too cold or thick by not allowing them time for boiling, which can lead to uneven cooking.
   - Not allowing enough time for the Air Fryer to preheat, which can lead to uneven cooking.
   - Not monitoring temperatures at different heights in the Air Fryer basket during cooking to ensure a variety of textures.
   - Stirring food too much, which can cause it to stick together.
   - Overcrowding the basket with too much food so that it doesn't cook evenly or crisply.
   - Overfilling the Air Fryer basket with too much food, which can cause it to overheat and shut off due to lack of circulation.
   - Using food that isn't fresh by not allowing it time for cooking.
   - Using oil and butter in one cooking process instead of separately, which can lead to sticking.
   - Pushing down on the lid to create a vacuum seal.
   - Not making sure that the Air Fryer and foods are cleaned thoroughly after each use.
   - Using salty ingredients that shouldn't be boiled together by not allowing them time for boiling can lead to uneven cooking.
   - Using frozen foods that aren't thawed properly, which can lead to sticking.
   - Not monitoring Air Fryer temperatures between batches or between different heights in the cooking basket can lead to uneven cooking.
   - Storing foods in a container other than an air-tight one such as foil or plastic bags.
   - Storing foods too long without consuming them.
   - Adding more than one tablespoon of olive oil at one time when cooking in an Air Fryer. Air frying too much olive oil leads to poor results and a foul taste.
   - Not paying attention to where the appliance gets stuck when air frying. Air Fryers tend to get stuck at the top, so it's important to shake and rotate foods once they have cooked halfway so that they turn out crispy on all sides.
   - Using cheese or tomato sauce that is too cold by not allowing it time for boiling, which can lead to uneven cooking.
   - Not using a timer for the Air Fryer, which can cause uneven cooking.
   - Cooking frozen foods and then reheating leftovers in an Air Fryer, which can lead to uneven cooking and food burning.
   - Using too much oil or butter in one cooking process, which can lead to sticking.
   - Only using frozen vegetables and fruits without thawing them beforehand leads to uneven cooking. Whereas, fresh vegetables don't need to be thawed before being cooked with an Air Fryer.
   - Using a slow cooker instead of an Air Fryer: Slow cookers don't circulate heat well and can lead to sticking.
   - Not using a slow cooker for foods that require long cooking times.

CHAPTER 1:
Breakfast Recipes

1. Coconut-Blueberry Cereal

Preparation Time: 20 minutes
Cooking Time: 20 minutes
Servings: 4
Ingredients:

- 1/2 cup dried blueberries
- 1/2 cup unsweetened coconut flakes
- 1 cup pumpkin seeds
- 2 cups chopped pecans
- 6 medium dates, pitted
- 1/3 cup coconut oil
- 2 tsp. cinnamon
- 1/2 tsp. sea salt

Directions:

1. Add coconut oil, dates, and half the pecans to a food processor; pulse until finely ground.
2. Add pumpkin seeds and the remaining pecans and continue pulsing until roughly chopped.
3. Transfer the mixture to a large bowl and add cinnamon, vanilla, and salt; spread on a baking sheet/pan that can fit in your air fry toaster oven and set on bake at 325°F for about 20 minutes or until browned.
4. Remove from oven and let cool slightly before stirring in blueberries and coconut.
5. Enjoy!

Nutrition:
Calories: 372; Carbs: 12 g; Fat: 25.2 g; Protein: 20.1 g.

2. Air Toasted Cheese Sandwich

Preparation Time: 15 minutes
Cooking Time: 20 minutes
Servings: 2
Ingredients:

- 2 eggs
- 4 slices of bread of choice
- 4 slices turkey
- 4 slices ham
- 6 tbsp. half and half cream
- 2 tsp. melted butter
- 4 slices Swiss cheese
- 1/4 tsp. pure vanilla extract
- Powdered sugar and raspberry jam for serving

Directions:

1. Mix the eggs, vanilla, and cream in a bowl and set it aside.
2. Make a sandwich with the bread layered with cheese slice, turkey, ham, cheese slice, and the top slice of bread to make two sandwiches. Gently press on the sandwiches to somewhat flatten them.
3. Spread out kitchen aluminum foil and cut it about the same size as the sandwich and spread the melted butter on the surface of the foil.
4. Dip the sandwich in the egg mixture and let it soak for about 20 seconds on each side. Repeat this for the other sandwich. Place the soaked sandwiches on the prepared foil sheets then place them on the basket in your fryer.
5. Set on toast and cook for 12 minutes; then flip the sandwiches and brush with the remaining butter and cook for another 5 minutes or until well browned.
6. Place the cooked sandwiched on a plate and top with the powdered sugar and serve with a small bowl of raspberry jam.
7. Enjoy!

Nutrition:
Calories: 735; Carbs: 13.4 g; Fat: 47.9 g; Protein: 40.8 g.

3. Citrus Blueberry Breakfast Muffins

Preparation Time: 15 minutes
Cooking Time: 15 minutes
Servings: 3-4
Ingredients:

- 2-1/2 cups cake flour
- 1/2 cup sugar
- 1/4 cup light cooking oil such as avocado oil - 1/2 cup heavy cream
- 1 cup fresh blueberries
- 2 eggs
- Zest and juice from 1 orange
- 1 tsp. pure vanilla extract
- 1 tsp. brown sugar for topping

Directions:

1. Start by combining the oil, heavy cream, eggs, orange juice, and vanilla extract in a large bowl then set it aside.
2. Separately, combine the flour and sugar until evenly mixed; then pour little by little into the wet ingredients.
3. Combine well unlit well blended but careful not to over mix.
4. Preheat your Air Fryer toast oven at 320°F.
5. Gently fold the blueberries into the batter and divide them into cupcake holders, preferably silicone cupcake holders as you won't have to grease them. Alternatively, you can use cupcake paper liners on any cupcake holders/ tray you could be having.
6. Sprinkle the tops with brown sugar and pop the muffins in the fryer.
7. Bake for about 12 minutes. Use a toothpick to check for readiness. When the muffins have evenly browned and an inserted toothpick comes out clean, they are ready.
8. Take out the muffins and let them cool.
9. Enjoy!

Nutrition:
Calories: 289; Carbs: 12.8 g; Fat: 32 g; Protein: 21.1 g.

4. Peanut Butter and Jelly Breakfast Donuts

Preparation Time: 15 minutes
Cooking Time: 12 minutes
Servings: 4
Ingredients:
For the Donuts:

- 1-1/4 cups all-purpose flour
- 1/2 tsp. baking soda
- 1/2 tsp. baking powder
- 1/3 cup sugar
- 1/2 cup buttermilk
- 1 large egg
- 1 tsp. pure vanilla extract
- 3 tbsp. unsalted, melted, and divided into 2+1
- 3/4 tsp. salt

For the Glaze:

- 2 tbsp. milk
- 1/2 cup powdered sugar
- 2 tbsp. smooth peanut butter
- Sea salt to taste

For the Filling:

- 1/2 cup strawberry or blueberry jelly

Directions:

1. Whisk together all the dry ingredients for the donut in a large bowl.
2. Separately combine the egg, buttermilk, melted butter, and vanilla extract.
3. Create a small well at the center of the dry ingredients and pour in the egg mixture. Use a fork to combine the ingredients then finish off with a spatula.
4. Place the dough on a floured surface and knead. It will start sticky but as you knead, it's going to come together.
5. Roll out the dough to make a 3/4-inch-thick circle. Use a cookie cutter, or the top part of a cup to cut the dough into rounds.
6. Place the donuts on parchment paper and then into your Air Fryer toast oven. You may have to cook in batches depending on the size of your oven.
7. Set on a bagel for 12 minutes at 350°F.
8. Use a pastry bag or squeeze bottle to fill the donuts with jelly.
9. Combine the glaze ingredients and drizzle on top of the donuts. Enjoy!

Nutrition:
Calories: 430; Carbs: 66.8 g; Fat: 14.6 g; Protein: 9.1 g.

5. Raspberry Oatmeal

Preparation Time: 10 minutes
Cooking Time: 40 minutes
Servings: 4
Ingredients:

- 1 cup shredded coconut
- 2 tsp. stevia - 1 tsp. cinnamon powder
- 2 cups. almond milk
- 1/2 cup raspberries

Directions:

1. Mix all the ingredients in a bowl.
2. Pour into the Air Fryer baking pan.
3. Transfer to the PowerXL Air Fryer Grill
4. Using the knob, select bake/pizza mode.
5. Adjust the temperature to 360°F.
6. Bake for 15 minutes.
7. Serve and enjoy.

Serving Suggestions: Garnish with coconut.
Nutrition:
Calories: 172; Fat: 5 g; Carb: 5 g; Protein: 6g.

6. Bacon, Egg and Cheese Breakfast Hash
Preparation Time: 15 minutes
Cooking Time: 35 minutes
Servings: 4
Ingredients:
- 2 slices bacon - 4 tiny potatoes
- 1/4 tomato - 1 egg
- 1/4 cup shredded cheese

Directions:
1. Preheat the PowerXL Air Fryer Grill to 200°C/ 400°F on bake mode. Set bits of bacon on a double-layer tin foil.
2. Cut the vegetables to place over the bacon. Crack an egg over it.
3. Shape the tin foil into a bowl and cook it in the PowerXL Air Fryer Grill at 177°C/ 350°F for 15–20 minutes. Put some shredded cheese on top.

Nutrition:
Calories: 150.5; Carbs: 18 g; Protein: 6 g; Fat: 6g.

7. Air Toasted French Toast
Preparation Time: 5 minutes
Cooking Time: 20 minutes
Servings: 3
Ingredients:
- 6 slices preferred bread
- 3/4 cup milk
- 3 eggs
- 1 tsp. pure vanilla extract
- 1 tbsp. ground cinnamon

Directions:
1. Combine all the ingredients except the bread in a medium bowl until well mixed.
2. Dip each slice of bread into the egg mix. Gently shake the excess off and place it in a greased pan.
3. Air toast in the fryer, for 6 minutes.
4. To serve, drizzle with maple syrup.

Nutrition:
Calories: 245; Carbs: 28.5 g; Fat: 7.5 g; Protein: 14.9 g.

8. Breakfast Radish Hash Browns
Preparation Time: 10 minutes
Cooking Time: 13 minutes
Servings: 2
Ingredients:
- 1 lb. radishes, clean and sliced
- 1 onion, sliced
- 1 tbsp. olive oil
- 1 tsp. onion powder
- 1 tsp. garlic powder
- 1/2 tsp. paprika
- 1/4 tsp. pepper
- 1/2 tsp. salt

Directions:
1. Toss sliced radishes and onion with olive oil.
2. Coat the Air Fryer basket with cooking spray.
3. Put the radish and onion mixture into the Air Fryer basket and cook at 360°F for 8 minutes.
4. Transfer the radish and onion mixture into the mixing bowl. Add onion powder, garlic powder, paprika, pepper, and salt and toss well.
5. Return the radish and onion mixture into the Air Fryer basket and cook for 5 minutes more.
6. Serve and enjoy.

Nutrition:
Calories: 125; Fat: 7.4 g; Carbohydrates: 13.6 g; Sugar: 3.2 g; Protein: 3.6 g; Cholesterol: 0 mg.

9. Breakfast Egg and Tomatoes
Preparation Time: 15 minutes
Cooking Time: 30 minutes
Servings: 2
Ingredients:
- Salt and pepper to taste
- 2 eggs
- 2 large tomatoes

Directions:
1. Preheat the Air Fryer by selecting the bake/pizza mode.
2. Adjust the temperature to 375°F.
3. Cut off the top of the tomatoes, scoop out the seed and flesh.
4. Break the egg into each tomato and transfer it to the PowerXL Air Fryer baking tray.
5. Bake for 24 minutes.
6. Serve and enjoy.

Serving Suggestions: Garnish with chopped parsley
Nutrition:
Calories: 95; Fat: 5 g; Carbs: 5.5 g; Protein: 7g.

10. Maple Glazed Sausages and Figs
Preparation Time: 10 minutes
Cooking Time: 40 minutes
Servings: 2
Ingredients:
- 2 tbsp. maple syrup
- 2 tbsp. balsamic vinegar
- 2 packages (12 ounces each) fully cooked chicken, cooked garlic sausages
- 8 fully ripe fresh figs, cut lengthwise
- 1/2 large sweet onion, minced
- 1-1/2 lb. Swiss chard, with sliced stems, minced leaves
- 2 tsp. olive oil
- Salt and pepper

Directions:
1. Preheat the PowerXL Air Fryer Grill to 232°C/ 450°F, mix syrup with 1 tablespoon of vinegar in a tiny bowl. Put sausages with figs on a one-layer foil-lined oven tray.
2. Roast for 8–10 minutes by grazing the syrup mix throughout the cooking.
3. Cook the onions in the PowerXL Air Fryer Grill in a bowl with wrapping for 9 minutes.
4. Mix oil and seasoning with 1 tsp. of vinegar. Serve the chards with figs and sausages.

Nutrition:

Calories: 450; Carbs: 42 g; Protein: 34 g; Fat: 17 g.

11. Breakfast Strata

Preparation Time: 6 hours
Cooking Time: 2 hours
Servings: 8
Ingredients:
- 18 eggs
- 2 packs croutons
- 1 pack cheddar
- Salt & pepper
- 1 pack chopped spinach
- 3 cups milk
- 3 cups chopped ham
- 1 jar Red Peppers

Directions:
1. Preheat the PowerXL Air Fryer Grill to 135°C/ 275°F.
2. Grease the pan with a non-stick spray.
3. Spread layers of ham, spinach, cheese, croutons, and red peppers.
4. Pour eggs mixed with milk and seasoning in the pan and refrigerate.
5. Bake for 2 hours and leave to rest for 15 minutes.

Nutrition:
Calories: 140; Carbs: 6 g; Protein: 16 g; Fat: 5 g.

12. Scrambled Eggs Wonton Cups

Preparation Time: 15 minutes
Cooking Time: 10 minutes
Servings: 3
Ingredients:
- 6 wonton wrappers
- 6 eggs
- 3 Breakfast sausages
- 2 large peppers
- 4 mushrooms
- 3 onions
- Butter
- Salt and pepper to taste

Directions:
1. Preheat the PowerXL Air Fryer Grill to 177°C/ 350°F.
2. Make the scrambled eggs.
3. Fold the wrappers brushed with butter into the muffin pan.
4. Mix the ingredients in a bowl and put them in the wrappers. Bake for 10 minutes.

Nutrition:
Calories: 130; Carbs: 7 g; Protein: 9 g; Fat: 7 g.

13. Sheet Pan Shakshuka

Preparation Time: 15 minutes
Cooking Time: 10 minutes
Servings: 4
Ingredients:
- 4 large eggs
- 1 large Anaheim chili, chopped
- 2 tbsp. vegetable oil
- 1/2 cup onion, chopped
- 1 tsp. cumin, ground
- 2 minced garlic cloves
- 1/2 cup feta cheese
- 1/2 tsp. paprika
- 1 can tomatoes
- Salt & pepper

Directions:
1. Sauté the chili and onions in vegetable oil until tender.
2. Pour in the remaining ingredients except for eggs and cook until thick.
3. Make 4 pockets to pour in the eggs.
4. Bake for 10 minutes at 191°C/ 375°F in the PowerXL Air Fryer Grill.
5. Top it off with feta.

Nutrition:
Calories: 219; Carbs: 20 g; Protein: 10 g; Fat: 11 g.

14. Breakfast Casserole

Preparation Time:
Cooking Time: 40 minutes
Servings: 4
Ingredients:
- 3 tbsp. brown sugar
- 1/2 cup of flour
- 1/2 tsp. cinnamon powder
- 4 tbsp. margarine
- 2 tbsp. white sugar

For the Casserole
- 2 eggs
- 2-1/2 tbsp. white flour
- 1 tsp. baking powder
- 1 tsp. baking soda
- 2 tbsp. sugar
- 4 tbsp. margarine
- 1/2 cup of milk
- 1-1/3 cup of blueberries
- 1 tbsp. lemon zest

Directions:
1. Preheat the PowerXL Air Fryer Grill by selecting the pizza/bake mode.
2. Adjust the temperature to 300°F.
3. In a bowl, mix the casserole ingredients; then pour them into the PowerXL Air Fryer Grill baking pan.
4. In a separate bowl, mix white sugar with flour, margarine, white sugar, and cinnamon.
5. Mix until a crumbly mixture is achieved; spread over the blueberries mixture.
6. Transfer to the PowerXL Air Fryer Grill and bake for 30 minutes.

Serving Suggestions: Serve with a glass of juice.
Nutrition:
Calories: 101; Fat: 9.4 g; Carbs: 0.3 g; Protein: 7 g.

15. Air-Fried Omelet

Preparation Time: 10 minutes
Cooking Time: 10 minutes
Servings: 2
Ingredients:

- 3 large eggs
- 100g ham, cut into small pieces
- 1/4 cup milk
- 3/4 cup mixed vegetables (mushrooms, scallions, bell pepper)
- 1/4 cup mixed cheddar and mozzarella cheese
- 1 tsp. mixed herbs
- Salt and freshly ground pepper to taste

Directions:

1. Combine the eggs and milk in a medium bowl; then add in the remaining ingredients apart from the cheese and mixed herbs. Beat well using a fork.
2. Pour the egg mixture into an evenly greased pan then; place it in the basket of your air fry toaster oven.
3. Set on bake to 350°F for 10 minutes.
4. Sprinkle the cheese and mixed herbs on the omelet halfway through cooking time.
5. Gently loosen the omelet from the sides of the pan using a spatula. Serve hot!

Nutrition:
Calories: 278; Carbs: 1.3 g; Fat: 4.6 g; Protein: 24.1 g.

16. Sunny Side up Egg Tarts

Preparation Time: 15 minutes
Cooking Time: 20 minutes
Servings: 2
Ingredients:

- 4 eggs
- 3/4 cup shredded Gruyere cheese (or preferred cheese)
- 1 sheet puff pastry
- Minced chives for topping

Directions:

1. Start by flouring a clean surface; then gently roll out your sheet of puff pastry and divide it into four equal squares.
2. If you have a small Air Fryer toast oven, start with two squares but if it's big enough, go ahead and place the squares on the basket and cook for about 8–10 minutes or until they turn golden brown.
3. Whilst still in the basket, gently make an indentation at the center of each square and sprinkle 2–4 tablespoons of shredded cheese in the well then crack an egg on top.
4. Cook for 5–10 minutes or to desired doneness. Remove from Air Fryer toast oven, sprinkle with chives and you are ready to eat!

Nutrition:
Calories: 403; Carbs: 10.8 g; Fat: 29.4 g; Protein: 24.6 g.

17. Crunchy Zucchini Hash Browns

Preparation Time: 30 minutes
Cooking Time: 15 minutes
Servings: 3
Ingredients:

- 4 medium zucchinis, peeled and grated
- 1 tsp. onion powder
- 1 tsp. garlic powder - 2 tbsp. almond flour
- 1-1/2 tsp. chili flakes
- Salt and freshly ground pepper to taste
- 2 tsp. olive oil

Directions:

1. Put the grated zucchini in between layers of kitchen towel and squeeze to drain excess water. Pour a teaspoon of oil in a pan, preferably non-stick, over medium heat and sauté the potatoes for about 3 minutes.
2. Transfer the zucchini to a shallow bowl and let cool. Sprinkle the zucchini with the remaining ingredients and mix until well combined.
3. Transfer the zucchini mixture to a flat plate and pat it down to make 1 compact layer. Put it in the fridge and let it sit for 20 minutes.
4. Set your Air Fryer toast oven to 360°F.
5. Meanwhile, take out the flattened zucchini and divide it into equal portions using a knife or cookie cutter.
6. Lightly brush your Air Fryer toast oven's basket with the remaining teaspoon of olive oil.
7. Gently place the zucchini pieces into the greased basket and fry for 12–15 minutes, flipping the hash browns halfway through. Enjoy hot!

Nutrition:
Calories: 195; Carbs: 10.4 g; Fat: 13.1 g; Protein: 9.6 g.

18. French Toast

Preparation Time: 5 minutes
Cooking Time: 10 minutes
Servings: 4
Ingredients:

- 2 slices bread
- 1 tsp. liquid vanilla
- 3 eggs
- 1 tbsp. margarine

Directions:

1. Preheat the PowerXL Air Fryer Grill by setting it to toast/pizza mode.
2. Adjust the temperature to 375°F; insert the pizza tray.
3. In a bowl, whisk the eggs and vanilla.
4. Spread the margarine on the bread, transfer it into the egg and allow it to soak.
5. Place on the PowerXL Air Fryer pizza rack and time to 6 minutes, flip after 3 minutes.

Serving Suggestions: Serve topped with yogurt and honey.
Nutrition:
Calories: 99; Fat: 0.2 g; Carbs: 7 g; Protein: 5 g.

19. Sausage Omelet

Preparation Time: 12 minutes
Cooking Time: 23 minutes
Servings: 2
Ingredients:

- 2 sausages, chopped

- 1 yellow onion
- 1 bacon slice
- 4 eggs

Directions:
1. Preheat the PowerXL Air Fryer Grill by selecting air fry mode.
2. Adjust temperature to 320°F and time to 5 minutes.
3. In a bowl, mix all the ingredients.
4. Pour into the Air Fryer baking tray.
5. Transfer into the PowerXL Air Fryer Grill.
6. Air fry for 10 minutes.
7. Serve and enjoy!

Serving Suggestions: Serve with toast bread.
Directions & Cooking Tips: Add a handful of cheese to the egg mixture.
Nutrition:
Calories: 156; Fat: 21 g; Carbs: 27 g; Protein: 17 g.

20. Zucchini Fritters

Preparation Time: 8 minutes
Cooking Time: 20 minutes
Servings: 4
Ingredients:
- 10 oz. zucchini
- 7 oz. halloumi cheese
- 2 eggs
- 1/4 cup all-purpose flour
- 1 tsp. dried dill
- Salt and black pepper to taste

Directions:
1. Preheat the PowerXL Air Fryer Grill by selecting bake/pizza mode.
2. Adjust temperature to 360°F and time to 5 minutes.
3. In a bowl, mix all the ingredients.
4. Make small fritters from the mixture.
5. Place them on the Air Fryer baking tray.
6. Transfer into the PowerXL Air Fryer Grill.
7. Bake for 7 minutes.
8. Serve and enjoy!

Serving Suggestions: Serve with Vegetable salad.
Nutrition:
Calories: 170; Fat: 15 g; Carbs: 7 g; Protein: 12 g.

21. Scrambled Egg

Preparation Time: 10 minutes
Cooking Time: 20 minutes
Servings: 1
Ingredients:
- 2 eggs
- 2 tbsp. Butter
- 1/4 cup cheese
- 1 tomato

Directions:
1. Preheat the PowerXL Air Fryer Grill by selecting air fry mode.
2. Adjust temperature to 290°F and time to 5 minutes.
3. Grease the baking tray with butter.
4. In a bowl, mix all the ingredients.
5. Pour into the Air Fryer baking tray.
6. Transfer into the PowerXL Air Fryer Grill.
7. Air fry for 7 minutes.

Serving Suggestions: Serve with toast bread.
Nutrition:
Calories: 206; Fat: 11.3 g; Carbs: 3 g; Protein: 12 g.

22. Sausage Wraps

Preparation Time: 10 minutes
Cooking Time: 20 minutes
Servings: 2
Ingredients:
- 1 cup Mozzarella cheese
- 8 sausages
- 8 crescent rolled dough

Directions:
1. Preheat the PowerXL Air Fryer Grill by selecting bake/pizza mode.
2. Adjust temperature to 380°F and Timer to 5 minutes.
3. Open the dough, arrange cheese at one end.
4. Add the sausage and roll, secure with a toothpick.
5. Arrange the sausage wrap in the Air Fryer baking tray.
6. Transfer into the PowerXL Air Fryer Grill.
7. Bake for 7 minutes.
8. Serve and enjoy.

Serving Suggestions: Serve with ketchup or BBQ sauce.
Nutrition:
Calories: 230; Fat: 7 g; Carbs: 5 g; Protein: 10 g.

23. Bacon Brussels Sprouts

Preparation Time: 10 minutes
Cooking Time: 30 minutes
Servings: 4
Ingredients:
- 1 lb. Brussels sprouts, cut into half
- 1/2 avocado, diced
- 1/4 cup onion, sliced
- 4 bacon slices, cut into pieces
- 1 tsp. garlic powder
- 3 tbsp. lemon juice
- 2 tbsp. balsamic vinegar
- 3 tbsp. olive oil
- Pepper
- Salt

Directions:
1. In a small bowl, whisk together oil, garlic powder, 2 tablespoons of lemon juice, and salt.
2. In a mixing bowl, toss Brussels sprouts with 3 tablespoons of oil mixture.
3. Add Brussels sprouts into the Air Fryer basket and cook at 370°F for 20 minutes. Toss halfway through.
4. Now top with bacon and onion and cook for 10 minutes more.
5. Transfer the Brussels sprout mixture into the large bowl. Add basil, avocado, remaining oil mixture, and lemon juice. Toss well.
6. Serve and enjoy.

Nutrition:
Calories: 248; Fat: 16.5 g; Carbohydrates: 15.5 g; Sugar: 4.5 g; Protein: 11.7 g; Cholesterol: 21 mg.

24. Sausage Swiss Cheese Egg Bite

Preparation Time: 10 minutes
Cooking Time: 5 minutes
Servings: 7
Ingredients:
- 4 eggs
- 1 tbsp. green onion, chopped
- 1/4 cup mushrooms, chopped
- 1/4 cup sausage, cooked and crumbled
- 1/2 cup cottage cheese, crumbled
- 1/2 cup Swiss cheese, shredded
- Pepper
- Salt

Directions:
1. Grease egg mold with cooking spray and set it aside.
2. In a bowl, beat eggs until frothy. Add remaining ingredients into the eggs and stir to mix.
3. Pour egg mixture into the prepared egg mold.
4. Place egg mold into the Air Fryer basket and cook at 330°F for 5 minutes.
5. Serve and enjoy.

Nutrition:
Calories: 82; Fat: 5.1 g; Carbohydrates: 1.3 g; Sugar: 0.4 g; Protein: 7.7 g; Cholesterol: 10 mg.

25. Spicy Chicken Wings

Preparation Time: 10 minutes
Cooking Time: 25 minutes
Servings: 4
Ingredients:
- 2 lb. chicken wings
- 1/2 tsp. Worcestershire sauce
- 1/2 tsp. Tabasco
- 6 tbsp. butter, melted
- 12 oz. hot sauce

Directions:
1. Coat the Air Fryer basket with cooking spray.
2. Add chicken wings into the Air Fryer basket and cook at 380°F for 25 minutes. Shake basket after every 5 minutes.
3. Meanwhile, in a mixing bowl, combine hot sauce, Worcestershire sauce, and melted butter. Set aside. Add chicken wings and toss well.
4. Serve and enjoy.

Nutrition:
Calories: 594; Fat: 34.4 g; Carbohydrates: 1.6 g; Sugar: 1.2 g; Protein: 66.2 g; Cholesterol: 248 mg.

26. Fajita Chicken

Preparation Time: 10 minutes
Cooking Time: 17 minutes
Servings: 4
Ingredients:
- 4 chicken breasts, make horizontal cuts on each piece
- 1/2 red bell pepper, sliced
- 2 tbsp. fajita seasoning
- 1/2 green bell pepper, sliced
- 2 tbsp. olive oil
- 1/2 cup cheddar cheese, shredded
- 1 onion, sliced
- Pepper
- Salt

Directions:
1. Line Air Fryer basket with aluminum foil.
2. Preheat the Air Fryer to 380°F.
3. Rub oil and seasoning all over the chicken breast.
4. Place chicken into the Air Fryer basket and top with peppers and onion.
5. Cook for 15 minutes. Top with cheese and cook for 1–2 minutes more.
6. Serve and enjoy.

Nutrition:
Calories: 431; Fat: 22.6 g; Carbohydrates: 8.2 g; Sugar: 2.7 g; Protein: 46.4 g; Cholesterol: 145 mg.

27. Lemon Chicken Breasts

Preparation Time: 10 minutes
Cooking Time: 20 minutes
Servings: 4
Ingredients:
- 4 chicken breasts, skinless and boneless
- 1 preserved lemon
- 1 tbsp. olive oil

Directions:
1. Add all ingredients into the bowl and mix well. Set aside for 10 minutes.
2. Coat the Air Fryer basket with cooking spray.
3. Place chicken into the Air Fryer basket and cook at 400°F for 20 minutes.
4. Serve and enjoy.

Nutrition:
Calories: 312; Fat: 14.4 g; Carbohydrates: 1.4 g; Sugar: 0.4 g; Protein: 42.4 g; Cholesterol: 130 mg.

28. Salmon Dill Patties

Preparation Time: 10 minutes
Cooking Time: 10 minutes
Servings: 2
Ingredients:
- 1 egg
- 14 oz. salmon
- 1 tsp. dill weed
- 1/2 cup almond flour
- 1/4 cup onion, diced
- Pepper
- Salt

Directions:
1. Line Air Fryer basket with parchment paper.
2. Add all ingredients into the mixing bowl and combine well.
3. Make patties from the mixture and place them into the Air Fryer basket.

4. Cook at 370°F for 10 minutes. Turn patties halfway through.
5. Serve and enjoy.

Nutrition:
Calories: 341; Fat: 18 g; Carbohydrates: 3.3 g; Sugar: 1 g; Protein: 43 g; Cholesterol: 169 mg.

29. Chicken Fritters

Preparation Time: 10 minutes
Cooking Time: 10 minutes
Servings: 4
Ingredients:
- 1 lb. ground chicken
- 1/2 tsp. onion powder
- 1/2 tsp. garlic powder
- 1/2 cup parmesan cheese, shredded
- 1/2 tbsp. dill, chopped
- 1/2 cup almond flour
- 2 tbsp. green onions, chopped
- Pepper
- Salt

Directions:
1. Line Air Fryer basket with parchment paper.
2. Add all ingredients into a large bowl and mix until well combined.
3. Make patties from the mixture and place them into the Air Fryer basket.
4. Cook at 350°F for 10 minutes. Turn patties halfway through.
5. Serve and enjoy.

Nutrition:
Calories: 280; Fat: 12.9 g; Carbohydrates: 2.2 g; Sugar: 0.4 g; Protein: 37.8 g; Cholesterol: 110 mg.

30. Delicious Chicken Burger Patties

Preparation Time: 10 minutes
Cooking Time: 25 minutes
Servings: 5
Ingredients:
- 1 lb. ground chicken
- 1 egg, lightly beaten
- 1 cup Monterey jack cheese, grated
- 1 cup carrot, grated
- 1 cup cauliflower, grated
- 1/8 tsp. red pepper flakes
- 2 garlic cloves, minced
- 1/2 cup onion, minced
- 3/4 cup almond flour
- Pepper
- Salt

Directions:
1. Line Air Fryer basket with parchment paper.
2. Add all ingredients into the mixing bowl and combine well.
3. Make patties from the mixture and place them into the Air Fryer basket.
4. Cook at 400°F for 25 minutes. Turn patties halfway through.
5. Serve and enjoy.

Nutrition:
Calories: 314; Fat: 16.6 g; Carbohydrates: 5.9 g; Sugar: 2.4 g; Protein: 34.6 g; Cholesterol: 134 mg.

31. Tuna Patties

Preparation Time: 10 minutes
Cooking Time: 10 minutes
Servings: 10
Ingredients:
- 15 oz. can tuna, drained and flaked
- 1 celery stalk, chopped
- 3 tbsp. parmesan cheese, grated
- 1/2 cup almond flour
- 1 tbsp. lemon juice
- 2 eggs, lightly beaten
- 1/2 tsp. dried herbs
- 1/2 tsp. garlic powder
- 2 tbsp. onion, minced
- Pepper
- Salt

Directions:
1. Line Air Fryer basket with parchment paper.
2. Add all ingredients into the large bowl and mix until well combined.
3. Make patties from the mixture and place them into the Air Fryer basket in batches.
4. Cook at 360°F for 10 minutes. Turn patties halfway through.
5. Serve and enjoy.

Nutrition:
Calories: 86; Fat: 2.9 g; Carbohydrates: 0.9 g; Sugar: 0.3 g; Protein: 13.7 g; Cholesterol: 49 mg.

32. Sausage Cheese Breakfast Frittata

Preparation Time: 10 minutes
Cooking Time: 10 minutes
Servings: 2
Ingredients:
- 2 eggs
- 1 tbsp. spring onions, chopped
- 1 breakfast sausage patty, chopped
- 1 tbsp. butter, melted
- 2 tbsp. cheddar cheese
- 1 tbsp. bell peppers, chopped
- Pepper
- Salt

Directions:
1. Grease the Air Fryer safe pan with cooking spray and set it aside.
2. Add chopped sausage patty in the prepared pan and air fry at 350°F for 5 minutes.
3. Meanwhile, in a bowl whisk together eggs, pepper, and salt. Add bell peppers, spring onions, and mix well.
4. Once sausages are cooked, pour the egg mixture into the pan and mix well.
5. Sprinkle with cheese and air fry at 350°F for 5 minutes.

6. Serve and enjoy.

Nutrition:
Calories: 202; Fat: 14.1 g; Carbohydrates: 6.7 g; Sugar: 3.5 g; Protein: 13 g; Cholesterol: 186 mg.

33. Ham Egg Bites
Preparation Time: 10 minutes
Cooking Time: 12 minutes
Servings: 8
Ingredients:
- 6 eggs
- 1/2 cup cheddar cheese, shredded
- 1 cup ham, diced
- 2 tbsp. cream
- 1/4 tsp. garlic powder
- 1/4 tsp. onion powder
- Pepper
- Salt

Directions:
1. In a bowl, whisk eggs with the remaining ingredients.
2. Pour egg mixture into the silicone muffin molds.
3. Place molds into the Air Fryer basket and cook at 300°F for 12–14 minutes.
4. Serve and enjoy.

Nutrition:
Calories: 106; Fat: 7.2 g; Carbohydrates: 1.2 g; Sugar: 0.4 g; Protein: 8.8 g; Cholesterol: 140 mg.

34. Pepperoni Omelet
Preparation Time: and **Cooking Time:** 25 minutes
Servings: 2
Ingredients:
- 2 tbsp. milk
- 4 eggs
- 10 pepperoni slices
- Salt and ground black pepper to taste

Directions:
1. Preheat the PowerXL Air Fryer Grill by selecting air fry mode.
2. Adjust temperature to 350°F and time to five minutes.
3. In a bowl, mix all the ingredients.
4. Pour into the Air Fryer baking tray.
5. Transfer into the PowerXL Air Fryer Grill.
6. Air fry for 12 minutes.
7. Serve and enjoy!

Nutrition:
Calories: 456; Fat: 32.9 g; Carbs: 6.2 g; Protein: 22 g.

35. Pancetta and Hotdog Omelet
Preparation Time: and **Cooking Time:** 20 minutes
Servings: 2
Ingredients:
- 1 pancetta, chopped
- 1/4 tsp. dried rosemary
- 2 hot dogs, chopped
- 1/2 tsp. dried parsley
- 2 small onions, chopped

Directions:
1. In a bowl, crack the egg.
2. Add the remaining ingredients and mix; pour into the Air Fryer baking tray.
3. Adjust temperature to 320°F.
4. Set time to 5 minutes.
5. Open the door and arrange your baking pan.
6. Air fry for 10 minutes.
7. Serve and enjoy.

Nutrition:
Calories: 185; Fat: 10.5 g; Carbs: 6 g; Protein: 15 g.

36. Cheese Garlic Quiche
Preparation Time: 10 minutes
Cooking Time: 30 minutes
Servings: 4
Ingredients:
- 6 eggs
- 1/2 cup onion, chopped
- 1/8 tsp. cayenne
- 1/8 tsp. nutmeg
- 8 oz. cheddar cheese, grated
- 4 bacon slices, cooked and chopped
- 3/4 cup coconut milk
- 1/2 tsp. garlic, minced
- 1 tbsp. olive oil
- Pepper
- Salt

Directions:
1. Grease the Air Fryer safe pan with cooking spray and set it aside.
2. Heat oil in a pan over medium fire. Add onion and sauté for 5 minutes.
3. Add garlic and sauté for 30 seconds. Remove pan from heat and set it aside to cool.
4. In a mixing bowl, whisk eggs with milk, pepper, and salt. Stir in sautéed onion garlic, cayenne, nutmeg, bacon, and cheese.
5. Pour egg mixture into the prepared pan.
6. Place pan in the Air Fryer basket and cook at 350°F for 25 minutes.
7. Serve and enjoy.

Nutrition:
Calories: 566; Fat: 47.6 g; Carbohydrates: 5.5 g; Sugar: 2.9 g; Protein: 30.7 g; Cholesterol: 326 mg.

37. Easy Cheesy Breakfast Eggs
Preparation Time: 10 minutes
Cooking Time: 5 minutes
Servings: 1
Ingredients:
- 2 eggs
- 1 tsp. parmesan cheese, grated
- 2 tbsp. cheddar cheese, shredded
- 2 tbsp. heavy cream
- Pepper
- Salt

Directions:
1. Grease ramekin dish with cooking spray and set it aside.
2. In a small bowl, whisk eggs with parmesan cheese, cheddar cheese, heavy cream, pepper, and salt.
3. Pour egg mixture into the prepared ramekin dish.
4. Place ramekin dish into the Air Fryer basket and cook at 330°F for 5 minutes.
5. Serve and enjoy.

Nutrition:
Calories: 332; Fat: 27.5 g; Carbohydrates: 2.3 g; Sugar: 0.8 g; Protein: 19.7 g; Cholesterol: 393 mg.

38. Cheesy Chicken Fritters

Preparation Time: 10 minutes
Cooking Time: 25 minutes
Servings: 4
Ingredients:
- 1 lb. ground chicken
- 3/4 cup almond flour
- 1 egg, lightly beaten
- 1 garlic clove, minced
- 1 1/2 cup mozzarella cheese, shredded
- 1/2 cup shallots, chopped
- 2 cups broccoli, chopped
- Pepper
- Salt

Directions:
1. Line the Air Fryer basket with parchment paper.
2. Add all ingredients into a bowl and mix until well combined.
3. Make patties from the mixture and place them into the Air Fryer basket.
4. Cook at 390°F for 15 minutes. Turn patties and cook for 10 minutes more.
5. Serve and enjoy.

Nutrition:
Calories: 322; Fat: 14.2 g; Carbohydrates: 8.2 g; Sugar: 1.1 g; Protein: 40.1 g. Cholesterol: 147 mg.

39. Cheddar Cheese Omelet

Preparation Time: 10 minutes
Cooking Time: 7 minutes
Servings: 1
Ingredients:
- 3 eggs - 1/2 tsp. soy sauce
- 2 tbsp. cheddar cheese, grated
- 1 onion, chopped - 1/4 tsp. garlic powder
- 1/4 tsp. onion powder

Directions:
1. Grease the Air Fryer pan with cooking spray and set it aside.
2. In a bowl, whisk eggs with the remaining ingredients. Pour egg mixture into the prepared pan.
3. Place the pan in the Air Fryer basket and cook at 350°F for 6–7 minutes.

Nutrition:
Calories: 127; Fat: 4.9 g; Carbohydrates: 12.4 g; Sugar: 4.5 g; Protein: 9 g; Cholesterol: 15 mg.

40. Gruyere Cheese Egg Bite

Preparation Time: 10 minutes
Cooking Time: 5 minutes
Servings: 7
Ingredients:
- 4 eggs
- 1/4 cup bacon, cooked and crumbled
- 1/2 cup cottage cheese, crumbled
- 1/2 cup gruyere cheese, shredded

Directions:
1. Coat the egg mold with cooking spray and set it aside.
2. In a bowl, beat eggs until frothy. Add the remaining ingredients and stir to mix.
3. Pour the egg mixture into the prepared egg mold.
4. Place the egg mold into the Air Fryer basket and cook at 330°F for 5 minutes.

Nutrition:
Calories: 86; Fat: 5.6 g; Carbohydrates: 0.8 g; Sugar: 0.3 g; Protein: 7.9 g; Cholesterol: 104 mg.

41. Cheddar Cheese Broccoli Egg Bite

Preparation Time: 10 minutes
Cooking Time: 5 minutes
Servings: 7
Ingredients:
- 4 eggs
- 1/4 cup broccoli, cooked and chopped
- 1/2 cup cottage cheese, crumbled
- 1/2 cup cheddar cheese, shredded

Directions:
1. Coat the egg mold with cooking spray and set it aside.
2. In a bowl, beat eggs until frothy. Add the remaining ingredients and stir to mix.
3. Pour the egg mixture into the prepared egg mold. Place the egg mold into the Air Fryer basket and cook at 330°F for 5 minutes.

Nutrition:
Calories: 84; Fat: 5.5 g; Carbohydrates: 1.1 g; Sugar: 0.3 g; Protein: 7.5 g; Cholesterol: 103 mg.

42. Cheese Sausage Pepper Frittata

Preparation Time: 10 minutes
Cooking Time: 20 minutes
Servings: 2
Ingredients:
- 4 eggs, lightly beaten
- 1 green onion, chopped
- 3 tbsp. bell pepper, diced
- 1/2 cup Monterey jack cheese
- 1/4 lb. breakfast sausage, cooked and crumbled
- Pepper
- Salt

Directions:
1. Preheat the Air Fryer to 360°F.

2. Grease the Air Fryer pan with cooking spray and set it aside.
3. In a bowl, whisk eggs with the remaining ingredients. Pour the egg mixture into the prepared pan.
4. Place the pan in the Air Fryer basket and cook for 18–20 minutes. Serve and enjoy.

Nutrition:
Calories: 411; Fat: 29.6 g; Carbohydrates: 10.7 g; Sugar: 7.2 g; Protein: 26.8 g; Cholesterol: 390 mg.

43. Cottage Cheese Egg Cups

Preparation Time: 10 minutes
Cooking Time: 15 minutes
Servings: 6
Ingredients:
- 3 eggs, lightly beaten
- 2 tbsp. green chilies, diced
- 2 tbsp. cottage cheese
- 1 tbsp. coconut milk
- 2 tbsp. cheddar cheese, shredded
- Pepper
- Salt

Directions:
1. Coat the egg mold with cooking spray and set it aside.
2. In a bowl, whisk eggs with milk, pepper, and salt. Add cheddar cheese, green chilies, and cottage cheese. Stir well.
3. Pour the egg mixture into a prepared egg mold.
4. Place the egg mold into the Air Fryer basket and cook at 350°F for 15 minutes.
5. Serve and enjoy.

Nutrition:
Calories: 53; Fat: 3.7 g; Carbohydrates: 1.1 g; Sugar: 0.6 g; Protein: 4.2 g; Cholesterol: 85 mg.

44. Cheese Mushroom Frittata

Preparation Time: 10 minutes
Cooking Time: 6 minutes
Servings: 2
Ingredients:
- 3 eggs
- 2 mushrooms, chopped
- 2 tbsp. onion, chopped
- 1/4 bell pepper, diced
- 2 tbsp. cheddar cheese, shredded
- 2 tbsp. coconut milk
- Pepper
- Salt

Directions:
1. Grease the Air Fryer safe pan with cooking spray and set it aside.
2. In a bowl, whisk eggs with milk, pepper, and salt. Add remaining ingredients and stir well.
3. Pour the egg mixture into the prepared pan
4. Place the pan in the Air Fryer basket and cook at 400°F for 6 minutes.
5. Serve and enjoy.

Nutrition:
Calories: 170; Fat: 12.6 g; Carbohydrates: 4.1 g; Sugar: 2.5 g; Protein: 11.2 g; Cholesterol: 253 mg.

45. Cheese Omelet

Preparation Time: 10 minutes
Cooking Time: 8 minutes
Servings: 2
Ingredients:
- 2 eggs
- 1/4 cup cheddar cheese, shredded
- 1/4 cup heavy cream

Directions:
1. Grease the Air Fryer safe pan with cooking spray and set it aside.
2. In a bowl, whisk eggs with cream, pepper, and salt.
3. Pour the egg mixture into the prepared pan. Place the pan in the Air Fryer basket and cook at 350°F for 4 minutes.
4. Sprinkle cheese on top and cook for 4 minutes more.

Nutrition:
Calories: 172; Fat: 14.6 g; Carbohydrates: 1 g; Sugar: 0.4 g; Protein: 9.4 g; Cholesterol: 199 mg.

46. Cheese Mushroom Egg Bake

Preparation Time: 10 minutes
Cooking Time: 8 minutes
Servings: 1
Ingredients:
- 2 eggs
- 1/2 cup ham, diced
- 1/4 cup cheddar cheese, shredded
- 1/4 cup coconut milk
- 2 mushrooms, sliced
- 1 tbsp. green onion, chopped

Directions:
1. Grease the Air Fryer safe pan with cooking spray and set it aside.
2. In a bowl, whisk eggs with cheese, milk, pepper, and salt. Add ham, mushrooms, and green onion. Stir well.
3. Pour egg mixture into the prepared pan.
4. Place pan into the Air Fryer basket and cook at 330°F for 8 minutes.
5. Serve and enjoy.

Nutrition:
Calories: 498; Fat: 38.3 g; Carbohydrates: 8.6 g; Sugar: 3.6 g; Protein: 31.9 g; Cholesterol: 396 mg.

47. Cheese Egg Frittata

Preparation Time: 10 minutes
Cooking Time: 6 minutes
Servings: 2
Ingredients:
- 4 eggs
- 1/3 cup cheddar cheese, shredded
- 1/2 cup half and half
- Pepper
- Salt

Directions:

1. Grease the Air Fryer-safe pan with cooking spray and set it aside.
2. In a small bowl, whisk eggs with cheese, half and half, pepper, and salt. Pour the egg mixture into the prepared pan. Place the pan in the Air Fryer basket and cook at 320°F for 6 minutes. Serve and enjoy.

Nutrition:
Calories: 281; Fat: 22 g; Carbohydrates: 3.6 g; Sugar: 0.9 g; Protein: 17.6 g; Cholesterol: 370 mg.

48. Cheese Ham Egg Cups

Preparation Time: 10 minutes
Cooking Time: 5 minutes
Servings: 4
Ingredients:
- 4 eggs
- 1/2 cup cheddar cheese, shredded
- 4 tbsp. heavy cream
- 1/2 cup ham, diced
- Pepper - Salt

Directions:
1. Grease four ramekins with cooking spray and set them aside. In a small bowl, whisk eggs with cheese, heavy cream, ham, pepper, and salt.
2. Pour the egg mixture into the prepared ramekins. Place ramekins into the Air Fryer basket and cook at 300°F for 5 minutes. Serve and enjoy.

Nutrition:
Calories: 199; Fat: 16.1 g; Carbohydrates: 1.6 g, Sugar: 0.4 g; Protein: 12.2 g; Cholesterol: 209 mg.

49. Cheese Vegetable Frittata

Preparation Time: 10 minutes
Cooking Time: 10 minutes
Servings: 6
Ingredients:
- 4 eggs
- 3 tbsp. heavy cream
- 1/2 cup cheddar cheese, shredded
- 1/4 cup leek, diced
- 1 cup spinach, diced
- 1 cup mushrooms, diced
- Pepper
- Salt

Directions:
1. Grease the Air Fryer safe pan with cooking spray and set it aside.
2. In a bowl, whisk together eggs, heavy cream, pepper, and salt.
3. Add cheese, leek, spinach, and mushrooms, and stir well.
4. Pour egg mixture into the prepared pan.
5. Place the pan in the Air Fryer basket and cook at 300°F for 10 minutes.
6. Serve and enjoy.

Nutrition:
Calories: 112; Fat: 8.9 g; Carbohydrates: 1.7 g; Sugar: 0.7 g; Protein: 6.8 g; Cholesterol: 129 mg.

50. Cheesy Broccoli Bites

Preparation Time: 15 minutes
Cooking Time: 12 minutes
Servings: 4
Ingredients:
- 2 cups broccoli florets
- 2 eggs, beaten
- 1 ¼ cups Cheddar cheese, grated
- ¼ cup Parmesan cheese, grated
- 1 ¼ cups breadcrumbs
- Salt and freshly ground black pepper, to taste

Directions:
1. In a kitchen appliance, add the broccoli and pulse until finely chopped.
2. In a big bowl, add the chopped broccoli and remaining ingredients.
3. Make small equal-sized balls from the mixture.
4. Arrange the balls onto a baking sheet and refrigerate for at least a half-hour.
5. Turn the "Temperature Knob" of the PowerXL Air Fryer Grill to line the temperature to 360°F.
6. Turn the "Function Knob" to settle on "Air Fry." Turn the "Timer Knob" to line the time for 12 minutes. After preheating, arrange the balls in the Air Fryer basket in a single layer.
7. Insert the Air Fryer basket at position 2 of the Air Fryer Grill. When the cooking time is over, transfer the balls onto a platter. Serve warm.

Nutrition:
Calories: 383; Fat: 19.8 g; Carbs: 28 g; Protein: 23 g.

51. Egg in a Hole

Preparation Time: 5 minutes
Cooking Time: 5 minutes
Servings: 1
Ingredients:
- 1 slice bread
- 1 tsp. butter softened
- 1 egg
- 1 tbsp. shredded Cheddar cheese
- 2 tsp. diced ham

Directions:
1. Preheat the Air Fryer to 330°F (166°C). Place a baking dish in the Air Fryer basket.
2. On a flat surface, cut a hole in the center of the bread slice with a 2 1/2-inch-diameter biscuit cutter.
3. Spread the butter lightly on each side of the bread slice and transfer it to the baking dish.
4. Crack the egg into the hole, then season as desired with salt and pepper. Scatter the shredded cheese and diced ham on top.
5. Bake in the preheated Air Fryer for 5 minutes until the bread is lightly browned and the egg is cooked to your preference.
6. Remove from the basket and serve hot.

Nutrition:
Calories: 243; Fat: 14.5 g; Carbs: 15.4 g; Protein: 12.6 g.

52. Simple Egg Soufflé

Preparation Time: 5 minutes
Cooking Time: 8 minutes
Servings: 2
Ingredients:
- 2 eggs
- 1/4 tsp. chili pepper
- 2 tbsp. heavy cream
- 1/4 tsp. pepper
- 1 tbsp. parsley, chopped

Directions:
1. In a bowl, whisk eggs with remaining gradients.
2. Grease two ramekins with cooking spray.
3. Pour egg mixture into the prepared ramekins and place them into the Air Fryer basket.
4. Cook soufflé at 390°F for 8 minutes

Nutrition:
Calories: 116; Fat: 10 g; Carbs: 1.1 g; Protein: 6 g.

53. Breakfast Scramble Casserole

Preparation Time: 20 minutes
Cooking Time: 10 minutes
Servings: 4
Ingredients:
- 6 slices bacon
- 6 eggs
- Cooking oil
- ½ cup chopped red bell pepper
- ½ cup chopped green bell pepper
- ½ cup chopped onion
- ¾ cup shredded Cheddar cheese

Directions:
1. In a pan, over medium-high heat, cook the bacon for 5 to 7 minutes, flipping to evenly crisp.
2. Dry out on paper towels, crumble, and set it aside. In a medium bowl, whisk the eggs. Add salt and pepper to taste.
3. Spray a barrel pan with cooking oil. Make sure to cover the bottom and sides of the pan.
4. Add the beaten eggs, crumbled bacon, red bell pepper, green bell pepper, and onion to the pan.
5. Place the pan in the Air Fryer and cook for 6 minutes. Open the Air Fryer and sprinkle the cheese over the casserole. Cook for an additional 2 minutes.

Nutrition:
Calories: 116; Fat: 10 g; Carbs: 1.1 g; Protein: 6 g.

54. Cowboy Quiche

Preparation Time: 30 minutes
Cooking Time: 1 hour
Servings: 8
Ingredients:
- 1 red potato with sliced skin (keep it short)
- 1 onion, minced
- 1/2 jalapeno with minced seeds
- 1 stick butter, melted
- 10 white mushrooms, minced
- 5–7 bacon strips
- 1/2 cup of sliced ham
- 1/2 red pepper, minced
- 1/2 green pepper, minced
- 1/4 cup of grated Cheddar
- 1/4 cup of grated Gruyere
- 6 eggs
- 12 ounces milk
- pint heavy cream
- 1 tsp. ground nutmeg
- 2 unbaked (9-inch) pie doughs

Directions:
1. Preheat the PowerXL Air Fryer Grill to 177°C/ 350°F. Put the veggies on a parchment paper-filled tray.
2. Put some melted butter with salt and pepper over vegetables and bake for a quarter-hour.
3. Put mushrooms separately in a parchment paper-filled tray with melted butter on top. Cook for five minutes.
4. Cook bacon strips on a special tray until crisp.
5. Put minced ham inside the PowerXL Air Fryer Grill and cook everything properly.
6. Mix all the ingredients to blend properly.
7. Stir eggs, milk, and cream separately. Add some salt, black pepper, and nutmeg. Blend properly.
8. Add the ingredients in a pan containing raw crust with the egg mixture. Bake for 35 minutes.

Nutrition:
Calories: 257.9; Carbs: 24 g; Protein: 11.6 g; Fat: 9 g.

55. Scrambled Eggs

Preparation Time: 2 minutes
Cooking Time: 5 minutes
Servings: 2
Ingredients:
- 1/2 tbsp. unsalted butter
- 2 large eggs
- 1 tbsp. water kosher salt
- Fresh ground pepper

Directions:
1. Turn the fan on for air circulation.
2. Put seasoned eggs on the lightly greased pan and canopy with foil.
3. Cook for 5–10 minutes or until the eggs are set.
4. Use a spatula to stir the eggs and scrape the edges.

Nutrition:
Calories: 149; Carbs: 1 g; Protein: 12 g; Fat: 6.7 g.

56. Egg Sausage Spinach Cups

Preparation Time: 10 minutes
Cooking Time: 10 minutes
Servings: 2
Ingredients:
- 1/4 cup egg beaters
- 4 tbsp. sausage, cooked and crumbled
- 4 tsp. jack cheese, shredded

- 4 tbsp. spinach, chopped

Directions:
1. Grease two ramekins with cooking spray and set them aside.
2. In a mixing bowl, whisk together all ingredients until well combined.
3. Pour mixture into the prepared ramekins.
4. Place ramekins into the Air Fryer basket and cook at 330°F for 10 minutes.

Nutrition:
Calories: 306; Fat: 23.4 g; Carbohydrates: 2.4 g; Sugar: 0.2 g; Protein: 20.9 g; Cholesterol: 72 mg.

57. Breakfast Eggs Avocado

Preparation Time: 10 minutes
Cooking Time: 9 minutes
Servings: 2
Ingredients:
- 2 eggs
- 1 avocado, cut in half and remove the seed
- Pinch red pepper flakes

Directions:
1. Break one egg into each avocado half. Season with red pepper flakes, pepper, and salt.
2. Place avocado halves into the Air Fryer basket and heat at 400°F for 5 minutes or until eggs are cooked.

Nutrition:
Calories: 268; Fat: 24 g; Carbohydrates: 9.1 g; Sugar: 0.9 g; Protein: 7.5 g; Cholesterol: 164 mg.

58. Egg Bacon Cheese Bites

Preparation Time: 10 minutes
Cooking Time: 13 minutes
Servings: 4
Ingredients:
- 4 eggs
- 1/4 cup cheddar cheese, shredded
- 4 bacon slices, cooked and crumbled
- 1/2 small bell pepper, diced
- 1/2 onion, diced
- 4 tsp. coconut milk

Directions:
1. Grease four ramekins with cooking spray.
2. Crack 1 egg into each ramekin; then add 1 teaspoon of coconut milk into each one.
3. Top each one off with bacon, bell pepper, onion, and cheese. Season with pepper and salt. Place ramekins into the Air Fryer basket and cook at 300°F for 10–13 minutes.

Nutrition:
Calories. 216; Fat: 15.9 g; Carbohydrates: 3.4 g; Sugar: 1.9 g; Protein: 14.8 g; Cholesterol: 192 mg.

59. Egg Ham Bites

Preparation Time: 10 minutes
Cooking Time: 12 minutes
Servings: 8
Ingredients:
- 6 eggs
- 1/2 cup cheddar cheese, shredded
- 1 cup ham, diced
- 2 tbsp. cream
- 1/4 tsp. garlic powder
- 1/4 tsp. onion powder

Directions:
1. In a bowl, whisk eggs with the remaining ingredients.
2. Pour egg mixture into the silicone muffin molds. Place the molds into the Air Fryer basket and cook at 300°F for 12–14 minutes or until eggs are cooked.

Nutrition:
Calories: 106; Fat: 7.2 g; Carbohydrates: 1.2 g; Sugar: 0.4 g; Protein: 8.8 g; Cholesterol: 140 mg.

60. Egg Cheese Mustard Bake

Preparation Time: 10 minutes
Cooking Time: 25 minutes
Servings: 3
Ingredients:
- 6 eggs
- 1/4 tsp. dry mustard
- 2 tbsp. butter, melted
- 1/4 lb. cheddar cheese, grated
- 1/2 cup coconut milk

Directions:
1. Grease the Air Fryer safe pan with cooking spray and set it aside.
2. In a bowl, whisk eggs with milk, mustard, pepper, and salt. Stir in cheese.
3. Pour the egg mixture into the prepared pan.
4. Place the pan in the Air Fryer basket and cook at 350°F for 25 minutes.

Nutrition:
Calories: 439; Fat: 38.6 g; Carbohydrates: 3.5 g; Sugar: 2.3 g; Protein: 21.6 g; Cholesterol: 387 mg.

61. Breakfast Egg Bites

Preparation Time: 10 minutes
Cooking Time: 5 minutes
Servings: 6
Ingredients:
- 4 eggs
- 1/4 cup cheddar cheese, shredded
- 4 tsp. almond milk

Directions:
1. Grease egg bite molds with cooking spray and set them aside. In a bowl, whisk eggs with cheese, milk, pepper, and salt.
2. Pour egg mixture into the prepared mold.
3. Place the mold into the Air Fryer basket and cook at 330°F for 5 minutes. Make sure eggs are lightly browned in color on top.
4. Serve and enjoy.

Nutrition:
Calories: 69; Fat: 5.3 g; Carbohydrates: 0.5 g; Sugar: 0.4 g; Protein: 4.9 g; Cholesterol: 114 mg.

62. Egg Stuffed Peppers

Preparation Time: 10 minutes
Cooking Time: 13 minutes
Servings: 2
Ingredients:

- 4 eggs
- 1 bell pepper, halved, and seeds removed
- A pinch red pepper flakes
- Pepper
- Salt

Directions:

1. Crack two eggs into each bell pepper half.
2. Season with red pepper flakes, pepper, and salt.
3. Place bell pepper halves into the Air Fryer basket and cook at 390°F for 13 minutes.
4. Serve and enjoy.

Nutrition:
Calories: 145; Fat: 8.9 g; Carbohydrates: 5.3 g; Sugar: 3.7 g; Protein: 11.7 g; Cholesterol: 327 mg.

63. Eggs in Bread Cups

Preparation Time: 10 minutes
Cooking Time: 23 minutes
Servings: 4
Ingredients:

- 4 bacon slices
- 2 bread slices, crust removed
- 4 eggs
- Salt and freshly ground black pepper, to taste

Directions:

1. Grease 4 cups of the muffin pan and put it aside.
2. Heat a frypan over a medium-high fire and cook the bacon slices for about 2–3 minutes.
3. With a slotted spoon, transfer the bacon slice onto a paper towel-lined plate to chill.
4. Break each bread slice in half.
5. Arrange one bread slice half in each of the prepared muffin cups and press slightly.
6. Now, arrange one bacon slice over each bread slice in a circular shape.
7. Crack one egg into each muffin cup and sprinkle with salt and black pepper.

Nutrition:
Calories: 235; Fat: 16.7 g; Carbs: 3.4 g; Protein: 16 g.

64. Spinach Baked Eggs

Preparation Time: 10 minutes
Cooking Time: 8 minutes
Servings: 2
Ingredients:

- 2 eggs
- 1/4 tsp. parsley, chopped
- 1/4 tsp. thyme
- 1/4 cup spinach, chopped

Directions:

1. Preheat the Air Fryer to 350°F.
2. Grease two ramekins with cooking spray and set them aside.
3. In a bowl, whisk eggs with the remaining ingredients.
4. Pour the egg mixture into the prepared ramekins.
5. Place the ramekins into the Air Fryer basket and cook for 5–8 minutes.
6. Serve and enjoy.

Nutrition:
Calories: 70; Fat: 4.4 g; Carbohydrates: 2 g; Sugar: 0.9 g; Protein: 5.8 g; Cholesterol: 164 mg.

65. Easy Breakfast Frittata

Preparation Time: 10 minutes
Cooking Time: 15 minutes
Servings: 2
Ingredients:

- 1 cup egg whites- 1/4 cup mushrooms, sliced
- 1/4 cup tomato, sliced
- 2 tbsp. coconut milk
- 2 tbsp. chives, chopped

Directions:

1. Grease the Air Fryer safe pan with cooking spray and set it aside.
2. Preheat the Air Fryer to 320°F.
3. In a bowl, whisk eggs with pepper and salt. Add remaining ingredients and mix well.
4. Pour the egg mixture into the prepared pan.
5. Place the pan in the Air Fryer basket and cook for 15 minutes.

Nutrition:
Calories: 105; Fat: 3.9 g; Carbohydrates: 3.1 g; Sugar: 2.2 g; Protein: 14.2 g; Cholesterol: 0 mg.

66. Green Chilis Egg Bite

Preparation Time: 10 minutes
Cooking Time: 5 minutes
Servings: 7
Ingredients:

- 4 eggs - 1/4 cup green chilis, diced
- 1/2 cup cottage cheese, crumbled
- 1/2 cup pepper jack cheese, shredded

Directions:
1. Coat the egg mold with cooking spray and set it aside.
2. In a bowl, beat eggs until frothy. Add remaining ingredients into the eggs and stir to mix.
3. Pour the egg mixture into the prepared egg mold. Place the egg mold into the Air Fryer basket and cook at 330°F for 5 minutes.

Nutrition:
Calories: 57; Fat: 3.1 g; Carbohydrates: 1.4 g; Sugar: 0.5 g; Protein: 5.5 g; Cholesterol: 96 mg.

67. Roasted Pepper Egg Bite
Preparation Time: 10 minutes
Cooking Time: 5 minutes
Servings: 7
Ingredients:
- 4 eggs - 1/4 cup spinach, chopped
- 1/2 roasted red pepper, chopped
- 1 tbsp. green onion, chopped
- 1/2 cup cottage cheese, crumbled

Directions:
1. Grease egg mold with cooking spray and set it aside.
2. In a bowl, beat eggs until frothy. Add remaining ingredients into the eggs and stir to mix.
3. Pour the egg mixture into the prepared egg mold. Place the egg mold into the Air Fryer basket and cook at 330°F for 5 minutes.

Nutrition:
Calories: 82; Fat: 5.3 g; Carbohydrates: 1.3 g; Sugar: 0.5 g; Protein: 7.5 g; Cholesterol: 102 mg.

68. Broccoli Bell Pepper Frittata

Preparation Time: 10 minutes
Cooking Time: 17 minutes
Servings: 2
Ingredients:
- 3 eggs
- 2 tbsp. cheddar cheese, shredded - 2 tbsp. cream
- 1/2 cup bell pepper, chopped
- 1/2 cup broccoli florets, chopped
- 1/4 tsp. garlic powder
- 1/4 tsp. onion powder

Directions:
1. Grease the Air Fryer pan with cooking spray. Add bell peppers and broccoli into the pan.
2. Place the pan in the Air Fryer basket and cook at 350°F for 7 minutes. In a bowl, whisk eggs with cheese, cream, garlic powder, onion powder, pepper, and salt.
3. Pour the egg mixture over broccoli and bell pepper and cook for 10 minutes more.

Nutrition:
Calories: 150; Fat: 9.7 g; Carbohydrates: 5.3 g; Sugar: 2.9 g; Protein: 11.2 g; Cholesterol: 255 mg.

69. Spinach Tomato Frittata

Preparation Time: 10 minutes
Cooking Time: 7 minutes
Servings: 2
Ingredients:
- 2 eggs
- 1/4 cup fresh spinach, chopped
- 1/4 cup tomatoes, chopped
- 2 tbsp. cream

Directions:
1. Grease the Air Fryer pan with cooking spray and set it aside.
2. In a bowl, whisk eggs with the remaining ingredients.
3. Pour the egg mixture into the prepared pan. Place the pan in the Air Fryer basket and cook at 330°F for 7 minutes.

Nutrition:
Calories: 90; Fat: 6.3 g; Carbohydrates: 1.8 g; Sugar: 1.2 g; Protein: 16.8 g; Cholesterol: 170 mg.

70. Basil Feta Egg Bite
Preparation Time: 10 minutes
Cooking Time: 5 minutes
Servings: 7
Ingredients:
- 4 eggs
- 1 tbsp. fresh basil, chopped
- 1/4 cup sun-dried tomatoes, diced
- 1/4 cup feta cheese, crumbled
- 1/2 cup cottage cheese, crumbled

Directions:
1. Coat the egg mold with cooking spray and set it aside.
2. In a bowl, beat the eggs until frothy. Add the remaining ingredients and stir to mix.
3. Pour the egg mixture into the prepared egg mold.

Nutrition:
Calories: 66; Fat: 4 g; Carbohydrates: 1.3 g; Sugar: 0.6 g, Protein: 6.2 g; Cholesterol: 100 mg.

CHAPTER 2:
Beef, Pork, and Lamb Recipes

71. Crisp Pork Chops

Preparation Time: 10 minutes
Cooking Time: 12 minutes
Serve: 6
Ingredients:
- 1 1/2 lbs. pork chops, boneless
- 1 tsp paprika
- 1 tsp creole seasoning
- 1 tsp garlic powder
- 1/4 cup parmesan cheese, grated
- 1/3 cup almond flour

Directions:
1. Preheat the air fryer to 360 F.
2. Add all ingredients except pork chops in a zip-lock bag.
3. Add pork chops in the bag. Seal bag and shake well to coat pork chops.
4. Remove pork chops from zip-lock bag and place in the air fryer basket.
5. Cook pork chops for 10-12 minutes.
6. Serve and enjoy.

Nutrition: Calories 230 Fat 11 g Carbohydrates 2 g Sugar 0.2 g Protein 27 g Cholesterol 79 mg

72. Parmesan Pork Chops

Preparation Time: 10 minutes
Cooking Time: 15 minutes
Serve: 4
Ingredients:
- 4 pork chops, boneless
- 4 tbsp parmesan cheese, grated
- 1 cup pork rind
- 3 eggs, lightly beaten
- 1/2 tsp chili powder
- 1/2 tsp onion powder
- 1 tsp paprika - 1/4 tsp pepper
- 1/2 tsp salt

Directions:
1. Preheat the air fryer to 400 F.
2. Season pork chops with pepper and salt.
3. Add pork rind in food processor and process until crumbs form.
4. Mix together pork rind crumbs and seasoning in a large bowl.
5. Place egg in a separate bowl.
6. Dip pork chops in egg mixture then coat with pork crumb mixture and place in the air fryer basket.
7. Cook pork chops for 12-15 minutes.
8. Serve and enjoy.

Nutrition: Calories 329 Fat 24 g Carbohydrates 1 g Sugar 0.4 g Protein 23 g Cholesterol 158 mg

73. Meatloaf Sliders

Preparation Time: 10 minutes
Cooking Time: 10 minutes
Serve: 8
Ingredients:
- 1 lb. ground beef
- 1/2 tsp dried tarragon
- 1 tsp Italian seasoning
- 1 tbsp Worcestershire sauce
- 1/4 cup ketchup
- 1/4 cup coconut flour
- 1/2 cup almond flour
- 1 garlic clove, minced
- 1/4 cup onion, chopped
- 2 eggs, lightly beaten
- 1/4 tsp pepper
- 1/2 tsp sea salt

Directions:
1. Add all ingredients into the mixing bowl and mix until well combined.
2. Make the equal shape of patties from mixture and place on a plate. Place in refrigerator for 10 minutes.
3. Spray air fryer basket with cooking spray.
4. Preheat the air fryer to 360 F.
5. Place prepared patties in air fryer basket and cook for 10 minutes.
6. Serve and enjoy.

Nutrition: Calories 228 Fat 16 g Carbohydrates 6 g Sugar 2 g Protein 13 g Cholesterol 80 mg

74. Quick & Easy Steak

Preparation Time: 10 minutes
Cooking Time: 7 minutes
Serve: 2
Ingredients:
- 12 oz steaks
- 1/2 tbsp unsweetened cocoa powder
- 1 tbsp Montreal steak seasoning
- 1 tsp liquid smoke
- 1 tbsp soy sauce

- Pepper
- Salt

Directions:
1. Add steak, liquid smoke, and soy sauce in a zip-lock bag and shake well.
2. Season steak with seasonings and place in the refrigerator for overnight.
3. Place marinated steak in air fryer basket and cook at 375 F for 5 minutes.
4. Turn steak to another side and cook for 2 minutes more.
5. Serve and enjoy.

Nutrition: Calories 356 Fat 8.7 g Carbohydrates 1.4 g Sugar 0.2 g Protein 62.2 g Cholesterol 153 mg

75. Perfect Cheeseburger
Preparation Time: 5 minutes
Cooking Time: 12 minutes
Serve: 2

Ingredients:
- 1/2 lb. ground beef
- 1/4 tsp onion powder
- 2 cheese slices
- 1/4 tsp pepper
- 1/8 tsp salt

Directions:
1. In a bowl, mix together ground beef, onion powder, pepper, and salt.
2. Make two equal shapes of patties from meat mixture and place in the air fryer basket.
3. Cook patties at 370 F for 12 minutes. Turn patties halfway through.
4. Once air fryer timer goes off then place cheese slices on top of each patty and close the air fryer basket for 1 minute.
5. Serve and enjoy.

Nutrition: Calories 325 Fat 16.4 g Carbohydrates 0.8 g Sugar 0.3 g Protein 41.4 g Cholesterol 131 mg

76. Steak Bites with Mushrooms
Preparation Time: 10 minutes
Cooking Time: 18 minutes
Serve: 3

Ingredients:
- 1 lb. steaks, cut into 1/2-inch cubes
- 1/2 tsp garlic powder
- 1 tsp Worcestershire sauce
- tbsp butter, melted
- 8 oz mushrooms, sliced
- Pepper
- Salt

Directions:
1. Add all ingredients into the large mixing bowl and toss well.
2. Spray air fryer basket with cooking spray.
3. Preheat the air fryer to 400 F.
4. Add steak mushroom mixture into the air fryer basket and cook at 400 F for 15-18 minutes. Shake basket twice.
5. Serve and enjoy.

Nutrition: Calories 388 Fat 15.5 g Carbohydrates 3.2 g Sugar 1.8 g Protein 57.1 g Cholesterol 156 mg

77. Simple & Tasty Pork Chops
Preparation Time: 10 minutes
Cooking Time: 9 minutes
Serve: 4

Ingredients:
- 4 pork chops, boneless
- 2 tsp onion powder
- 1 tsp smoked paprika
- 1/2 cup parmesan cheese, grated
- 2 tbsp olive oil
- 1/2 tsp pepper
- 1 tsp kosher salt

Directions:
1. Brush pork chops with olive oil.
2. In a bowl, mix together parmesan cheese and spices.
3. Spray air fryer basket with cooking spray.
4. Coat pork chops with parmesan cheese mixture and place in the air fryer basket.
5. Cook pork chops at 375 F for 9 minutes. Turn halfway through.
6. Serve and enjoy.

Nutrition: Calories 332 Carbohydrates 1.1 g Sugar 0.3 g Protein 19.3 g Cholesterol 71 mg

78. Simple Air Fryer Steak
Preparation Time: 10 minutes
Cooking Time: 18 minutes
Serve: 2

Ingredients:
- 12 oz steaks, 3/4-inch thick
- 1 tsp garlic powder
- 1 tsp olive oil
- ½ teaspoon Pepper
- ½ tsp Salt

Directions:
1. Coat steaks with oil and season with garlic powder, pepper, and salt.
2. Preheat the air fryer to 400 F.
3. Place steaks in air fryer basket and cook for 15-18 minutes. Turn halfway through.
4. Serve and enjoy.

Nutrition: Calories 363 Carbohydrates 1.1 g Sugar 0.3 g Protein 61.7 g Cholesterol 153 mg

79. Quick & Tender Pork Chops
Preparation Time: 5 minutes
Cooking Time: 14 minutes
Serve: 3

Ingredients:
- 3 pork chops, rinsed and pat dry
- 1/4 tsp smoked paprika
- 1/2 tsp garlic powder
- 2 tsp olive oil
- ½ tsp Pepper

- ½ teaspoon Salt

Directions:
1. Coat pork chops with olive oil and season with paprika, garlic powder, pepper, and salt.
2. Place pork chops in air fryer basket and cook at 380 F for 10-14 minutes. Turn halfway through.
3. Serve and enjoy.

Nutrition: Calories 285 Carbohydrates 0.5 g Sugar 0.1 g Protein 18.1 g Cholesterol 69 mg

80. Pork with Mushrooms
Preparation Time: 10 minutes
Cooking Time: 18 minutes
Serve: 4

Ingredients:
- 1 lb. pork chops, rinsed and pat dry
- 1/2 tsp garlic powder
- 1 tsp soy sauce
- 1 tbsp butter, melted
- 8 oz mushrooms, halved
- Pepper
- Salt

Directions:
1. Preheat the air fryer to 400 F.
2. Cut pork chops into the 3/4-inch cubes and place in a large mixing bowl.
3. Add remaining ingredients into the bowl and toss well.
4. Transfer pork and mushroom mixture into the air fryer basket and cook for 15-18 minutes. Shake basket halfway through.
5. Serve and enjoy.

Nutrition: Calories 428 Carbohydrates 2.2 g Sugar 1.1 g Protein 27.5 g Cholesterol 113 mg

81. Quick & Simple Bratwurst with Vegetables
Preparation Time: 10 minutes
Cooking Time: 20 minutes
Serve: 6

Ingredients:
- package bratwurst, sliced 1/2-inch rounds
- 1/2 tbsp Cajun seasoning
- 1/4 cup onion, diced - 1 bell pepper, sliced

Directions:
1. Add all ingredients into the large mixing bowl and toss well.
2. Line air fryer basket with foil.
3. Add vegetable and bratwurst mixture into the air fryer basket and cook at 390 F for 10 minutes.
4. Toss well and cook for 10 minutes more.
5. Serve and enjoy.

Nutrition: Calories 63 Fat 4 g Carbohydrates 4 g Sugar 2 g Protein 2 g Cholesterol 10 mg

82. Delicious Cheeseburgers
Preparation Time: 10 minutes
Cooking Time: 12 minutes
Serve: 4

Ingredients:
- 1 lb. ground beef
- 4 cheddar cheese slices
- 1/2 tsp Italian seasoning
- Pepper - Salt

Directions:
1. Spray air fryer basket with cooking spray.
2. In a bowl, mix together ground beef, Italian seasoning, pepper, and salt.
3. Make four equal shapes of patties from meat mixture and place into the air fryer basket.
4. Cook at 375 F for 5 minutes. Turn patties to another side and cook for 5 minutes more.
5. Place cheese slices on top of each patty and cook for 2 minutes more. Serve and enjoy.

Nutrition: Calories 325 Fat 16.5 g Carbohydrates 0.4 g Sugar 0.2 g Protein 41.4 g Cholesterol 131 mg

83. Asian Sirloin Steaks
Preparation Time: 10 minutes
Cooking Time: 20 minutes
Serve: 2

Ingredients:
- 12 oz sirloin steaks
- 1 tbsp garlic, minced
- 1 tbsp ginger, grated
- 1/2 tbsp Worcestershire sauce
- 1 1/2 tbsp soy sauce
- 1 tbsp erythritol
- Pepper
- Salt

Directions:
1. Add steaks in a large zip-lock bag along with remaining ingredients. Shake well and place in the refrigerator for overnight.
2. Spray air fryer basket with cooking spray.
3. Place marinated steaks in air fryer basket and cook at 400 F for 10 minutes.
4. Turn steaks to another side and cook for 10-15 minutes more.
5. Serve and enjoy.

Nutrition: Calories 342 Fat 10 g Carbohydrates 5 g Sugar 1 g Protein 52 g Cholesterol 152 mg

84. Soft & Juicy Beef Kabobs
Preparation Time: 10 minutes
Cooking Time: 10 minutes
Serve: 4

Ingredients:
- 1 lb. beef, cut into chunks
- 1 bell pepper, cut into 1-inch pieces
- 2 tbsp soy sauce
- 1/3 cup sour cream
- 1/2 onion, cut into 1-inch pieces

Directions:
1. In a medium bowl, mix together soy sauce and sour cream.

2. Add beef into the bowl and coat well and place in the refrigerator for overnight.
3. Thread marinated beef, bell peppers, and onions onto the soaked wooden skewers.
4. Place in air fryer basket and cook at 400 F for 10 minutes. Turn halfway through.
5. Serve and enjoy.

Nutrition: Calories 251 Fat 15 g Carbohydrates 4 g Sugar 2 g Protein 23 g Cholesterol 85 mg

85. Asian Flavors Beef Broccoli

Preparation Time: 10 minutes
Cooking Time: 15 minutes
Serve: 3

Ingredients:
- 1/2 lb. steak, cut into strips
- 2 tsp garlic, minced
- 1 tsp ginger, minced
- 2 tbsp sesame oil
- 1 1/2 tbsp soy sauce
- 1 tbsp oyster sauce
- 1 lb. broccoli florets
- 1 tbsp sesame seeds, toasted

Directions:
1. Add all ingredients except sesame seeds into the large mixing bowl and toss well. Place bowl in the refrigerator for 1 hour.
2. Add marinated steak and broccoli into the air fryer basket and cook at 350 F for 15 minutes.
3. Shake basket 2-3 times while cooking.
4. Garnish with sesame seeds and serve.

Nutrition: Calories 265 Fat 14 g Carbohydrates 12.5 g Sugar 2 g Protein 21 g Cholesterol 45 mg

86. Juicy Rib Eye Steak

Preparation Time: 10 minutes
Cooking Time: 14 minutes
Serve: 2

Ingredients:
- 2 medium rib-eye steaks
- 1/4 tsp garlic powder
- 1/4 tsp onion powder
- 1 tsp olive oil
- Pepper
- Salt

Directions:
1. Coat steaks with oil and season with garlic powder, onion powder, pepper, and salt.
2. Preheat the air fryer to 400 F.
3. Place steaks into the air fryer basket and cook for 14 minutes. Turn halfway through.
4. Serve and enjoy.

Nutrition: Calories 469 Fat 31 g Carbohydrates 3 g Sugar 0.5 g Protein 44 g Cholesterol 135 mg

87. Cheesy & Juicy Pork Chops

Preparation Time: 10 minutes
Cooking Time: 8 minutes
Serve: 2

Ingredients:
- 4 pork chops
- 1/4 cup cheddar cheese, shredded
- 1/2 tsp garlic powder
- 1/2 tsp salt

Directions:
1. Preheat the air fryer to 350 F.
2. Rub pork chops with garlic powder and salt and place in the air fryer basket.
3. Cook pork chops for 4 minutes.
4. Turn pork chops to another side and cook for 2 minutes. Add cheese on top of pork chops and cook for 2 minutes more.
5. Serve and enjoy.

Nutrition: Calories 465 Fat 22 g Carbohydrates 2 g Sugar 0.6 g Protein 61 g Cholesterol 190 mg

88. Stuffed Peppers

Preparation Time: 10 minutes
Cooking Time: 8 minutes
Serve: 2

Ingredients:
- 2 bell peppers, remove stems and seeds
- 4 oz cheddar cheese, shredded
- 1 1/2 tsp Worcestershire sauce
- 1/2 cup tomato sauce
- 8 oz ground beef
- 1 tsp olive oil
- 1 garlic clove, minced
- 1/2 onion, chopped
- 1/2 tsp pepper
- 1/2 tsp salt

Directions:
1. Preheat the air fryer to 390 F.
2. Sauté garlic and onion in the olive oil in a small pan until softened.
3. Add meat, 1/4 cup tomato sauce, Worcestershire sauce, half cheese, pepper, and salt and stir well to combine.
4. Stuff meat mixture into each pepper and top with remaining cheese and tomato sauce.
5. Spray air fryer basket with cooking spray.
6. Place stuffed peppers into the air fryer basket and cook for 15-20 minutes.
7. Serve and enjoy.

Nutrition: Calories 530 Fat 28.7 g Carbohydrates 14 g Sugar 10.8 g Protein 51 g Cholesterol 161 mg

89. Lamb Patties

Preparation Time: 10 minutes
Cooking Time: 20 minutes
Serve: 4

Ingredients:
- 1 1/2 lbs. ground lamb

- 1/3 cup feta cheese, crumbled
- 1 tsp oregano
- 1/4 tsp pepper
- 1/2 tsp salt

Directions:
1. Preheat the air fryer to 375 F.
2. Add all ingredients into the bowl and mix until well combined.
3. Spray air fryer basket with cooking spray.
4. Make the equal shape of patties from meat mixture and place into the air fryer basket.
5. Cook lamb patties for 10 minutes then turn to another side and cook for 10 minutes more.
6. Serve and enjoy.

Nutrition: Calories 351 Fat 15.2 g Carbohydrates 0.8 g Sugar 0.5 g Protein 49.6 g Cholesterol 164 mg

90. Lemon Mustard Lamb Chops

Preparation Time: 10 minutes
Cooking Time: 15 minutes
Serve: 4

Ingredients:
- 8 lamb chops
- tbsp lemon juice
- 1 tsp tarragon
- 1/2 tsp olive oil
- ½ tbsp Dijon mustard
- Pepper
- Salt

Directions:
1. Preheat the air fryer to 390 F.
2. In a small bowl, mix together mustard, lemon juice, tarragon, and olive oil.
3. Brush mustard mixture over lamb chops.
4. Place lamb chops in air fryer basket and cook for 15 minutes. Turn halfway through.
5. Serve and enjoy.

Nutrition: Calories 328 Fat 13.4 g Carbohydrates 0.6 g Sugar 0.2 g Protein 48.1 g Cholesterol 153 mg

91. Italian Sausage Meatballs

Preparation Time: 10 minutes
Cooking Time: 15 minutes
Serve: 8

Ingredients:
- 1 lb. Italian sausage
- 1 lb. ground beef
- 1/2 tsp Italian seasoning
- 1/2 tsp red pepper flakes
- 1 1/2 cups parmesan cheese, grated
- 2 egg, lightly beaten
- 2 tbsp parsley, chopped
- 2 garlic cloves, minced
- 1/4 cup onion, minced
- Pepper
- Salt

Directions:
1. Add all ingredients into the large mixing bowl and mix until well combined.
2. Spray air fryer basket with cooking spray.
3. Make meatballs from bowl mixture and place into the air fryer basket.
4. Cook at 350 F for 15 minutes.
5. Serve and enjoy.

Nutrition: Calories 334 Fat 21.9 g Carbohydrates 1 g Sugar 0.3 g Protein 31.4 g Cholesterol 143 mg

92. Yummy Meatballs

Preparation Time: 10 minutes
Cooking Time: 20 minutes
Serve: 8

Ingredients:
- 2 lbs. ground beef
- 3 eggs, lightly
- 1/2 cup fresh parsley, minced
- 2 tsp cinnamon
- 1 tsp dried oregano
- 1 tsp cumin
- 1 cup almond flour
- 1 garlic cloves, minced
- 1 onion, grated
- 1 tsp pepper - 2 tsp salt

Directions:
1. Preheat the air fryer to 370 F.
2. Spray air fryer basket with cooking spray.
3. Add all ingredients into the large bowl and mix until well combined.
4. Make small balls from mixture and place into the air fryer basket and cook for 20 minutes.
5. Serve and enjoy.

Nutrition: Calories 325 Fat 16 g Carbohydrates 6 g Sugar 1 g Protein 40 g Cholesterol 125 mg

93. Tasty Pork Bites

Preparation Time: 10 minutes
Cooking Time: 21 minutes
Serve: 6

Ingredients:
- 2 eggs, lightly beaten
- 1 lb. pork tenderloin, cut into cubes
- ¼ cup almond flour
- ½ tsp ground coriander
- ½ tsp paprika
- ½ tsp lemon zest
- ½ tsp kosher salt

Directions:
1. In a shallow bowl, whisk eggs.
2. In a shallow dish, mix together almond flour, coriander, paprika, lemon zest, and salt.
3. Dip each pork cube in egg then coat with almond flour mixture.
4. Preheat the air fryer to 365 F.
5. Spray air fryer basket with cooking spray.
6. Add coated pork cubes into the air fryer basket and cook for 14 minutes.

7. Turn pork cubes to another side and cook for 7 minutes more.
8. Serve and enjoy.

Nutrition: Calories 135 Fat 4 g Carbohydrates 0.2 g Sugar 0.1 g Protein 21 g Cholesterol 111 mg

94. Flavorful Pork Tenderloin

Preparation Time: 10 minutes
Cooking Time: 15 minutes
Serve: 3

Ingredients:
- lb. pork tenderloin
- 1 tbsp vinegar
- 2 garlic cloves, minced
- 1 tbsp butter
- ½ tsp onion powder
- ½ tsp garlic powder
- ½ tsp cinnamon
- 1 tsp sage
- ½ tsp saffron

Directions:
1. In a small bowl, mix together saffron, onion powder, garlic powder, cinnamon, and sage.
2. Rub pork tenderloin with the saffron mixture.
3. Now rub pork tenderloin with garlic and vinegar and let sit for 10 minutes.
4. Preheat the air fryer to 320 F.
5. Place pork tenderloin into the air fryer and top with butter.
6. Cook for 15 minutes.
7. Slice and serve.

Nutrition: Calories 327 Fat 16 g Carbohydrates 2 g Sugar 0.3 g Protein 40 g Cholesterol 140 mg

95. Spicy Lamb Chops

Preparation Time: 10 minutes
Cooking Time: 10 minutes
Serve: 6

Ingredients:
- 1½ lbs. lamb chops
- 1 tbsp butter, melted
- 1 tbsp olive oil
- 1 ½ tsp cayenne pepper
- 1 tsp garlic powder
- 1 tsp onion powder
- ½ tsp red chili flakes
- 1 tsp chili pepper
- ½ tsp lime zest

Directions:
1. In a large bowl, mix together oil, butter, lime zest, chili pepper, chili flakes, onion powder, garlic powder, and cayenne pepper.
2. Add lamb chops to the bowl and coat well with marinade and place in the refrigerator for 30 minutes.
3. Spray air fryer basket with cooking spray.
4. Place marinated pork chops into the air fryer basket and cook for 10 minutes. Turn pork chops halfway through.
5. Serve and enjoy.

Nutrition: Calories 253 Fat 12 g Carbohydrates 1 g Sugar 0.4 g Protein 32 g Cholesterol 105 mg

96. Quick & Easy Meatballs

Preparation Time: 10 minutes
Cooking Time: 12 minutes
Serve: 4

Ingredients:
- 4 oz lamb meat, minced
- 1 tbsp oregano, chopped
- ½ tbsp lemon zest
- 1 egg, lightly beaten
- Pepper - Salt

Directions:
1. Add all ingredients into the bowl and mix until well combined.
2. Spray air fryer basket with cooking spray.
3. Make balls from bowl mixture and place into the air fryer basket and cook at 400 F for 12 minutes.
4. Serve and enjoy.

Nutrition: Calories 72 Fat 3 g Carbohydrates 1 g Sugar 0.2 g Protein 10 g Cholesterol 66 mg

97. Easy Pesto Pork Chops

Preparation Time: 10 minutes
Cooking Time: 18 minutes
Serve: 5

Ingredients:
- 5 pork chops
- 3 tbsp basil pesto
- 2 tbsp almond flour
- 1 tbsp olive oil

Directions:
1. Spray pork chops with cooking spray.
2. Coat pork chops with pesto and sprinkles with almond flour.
3. Place pork chops into the air fryer basket and cook at 350 F for 18 minutes.
4. Serve and enjoy.

Nutrition: Calories 321 Fat 26 g Carbohydrates 3 g Sugar 0.5 g Protein 21 g Cholesterol 241 mg

98. Moist Lamb Roast

Preparation Time: 5 minutes
Cooking Time: 1 hour 30 minutes
Serve: 4

Ingredients:
- 2 1/2 lbs. lamb leg roast
- 1 tbsp dried rosemary
- 3 garlic cloves, sliced
- 1 tbsp olive oil
- Pepper
- Salt

Directions:
1. Make small cuts on meat using a sharp knife.
2. Poke garlic slices into the cuts. Season meat with pepper and salt.
3. Mix together oil and rosemary and rub over the meat.

4. Place meat into the air fryer and cook at 400 F for 15 minutes.
5. Turn temperature to 320 F for 1 hour 15 minutes.
6. Serve and enjoy.

Nutrition: Calories 595 Fat 25 g Carbohydrates 2 g Sugar 0 g Protein 85 g Cholesterol 423 mg

99. Dried Herbs Lamb Chops

Preparation Time: 10 minutes
Cooking Time: 20 minutes
Serve: 4

Ingredients:
- 1 lb. lamb chops
- 1 tsp oregano
- 1 tsp thyme
- 1 tsp rosemary
- 1 tbsp fresh lemon juice
- 2 tbsp olive oil
- 1 tsp coriander
- 1/4 tsp pepper
- 1 tsp salt

Directions:
1. Add all ingredients except lamb chops into the zip-lock bag.
2. Add lamb chops to the bag. Seal bag and shake well and place in the fridge for overnight.
3. Place marinated lamb chops into the air fryer.
4. Cook at 390 F for 3 minutes. Turn lamb chops to another side and cook for 4 minutes more.
5. Serve and enjoy.

Nutrition: Calories 275 Fat 16 g Carbohydrates 1 g Sugar 0.5 g Protein 30 g Cholesterol 124 mg

100. Crispy Pork Chops

Preparation Time: 10 minutes
Cooking Time: 20 minutes
Serve: 4

Ingredients:
- 4 pork chops, boneless
- 2 eggs, lightly beaten
- 1 cup almond flour
- 1/4 cup parmesan cheese, grated
- 1 tbsp onion powder
- 1/2 tbsp garlic powder
- 1/2 tbsp pepper
- 1/2 tsp sea salt

Directions:
1. Preheat the air fryer to 350 F.
2. Spray air fryer basket with cooking spray.
3. In a bowl, mix together almond flour, parmesan cheese, onion powder, garlic powder, pepper, and salt.
4. Whisk eggs in a shallow bowl.
5. Dip pork chops into the egg then coat with almond mixture and place into the air fryer basket.
6. Cook pork chops for 10 minutes. Turn pork chops to another side and cook for 10 minutes more.
7. Serve and enjoy.

Nutrition: Calories 450 Fat 35 g Carbohydrates 9 g Sugar 3 g Protein 28 g Cholesterol 231 mg

101. Garlic Thyme Pork Chops

Preparation Time: 10 minutes
Cooking Time: 15 minutes
Serve: 8

Ingredients:
- 8 pork chops, boneless
- 5 garlic cloves, minced
- 1 cup parmesan cheese
- 1 tbsp butter, melted
- 1 tsp thyme
- 1 tbsp parsley
- 1 tbsp coconut oil
- 1/4 tsp pepper
- 1/2 tsp sea salt

Directions:
1. Preheat the air fryer to 400 F.
2. Spray air fryer basket with cooking spray.
3. In a bowl, mix together butter, spices, cheese, and coconut oil.
4. Rub butter mixture on top of pork chops and place into the air fryer basket.
5. Cook for 10 minutes. Turn to another side and cook for 10 minutes more.
6. Serve and enjoy.

Nutrition: Calories 355 Fat 29 g Carbohydrates 2 g Sugar 0 g Protein 23 g Cholesterol 125 mg

102. Pork Strips

Preparation Time: 10 minutes
Cooking Time: 10 minutes
Serve: 2

Ingredients:
- 4 pork loin chops
- 1 tbsp swerve
- 1 tbsp soy sauce
- 1/8 tsp ground ginger
- 1 garlic clove, chopped
- 1/2 tsp balsamic vinegar

Directions:
1. Tenderize meat and season with pepper and salt.
2. In a bowl, mix together sweetener, soy sauce, and vinegar. Add ginger and garlic and set aside.
3. Add pork chops into the marinade mixture and marinate for 2 hours.
4. Preheat the air fryer to 350 F.
5. Add marinated meat into the air fryer and cook for 5 minutes on each side.
6. Cut into strips and serve.

Nutrition: Calories 551 Fat 39.8 g Carbohydrates 9.9 g Sugar 8.8 g Protein 36.6 g Cholesterol 138 mg

103. Mushrooms Meatballs

Preparation Time: 10 minutes
Cooking Time: 20 minutes
Serve: 2

Ingredients:
- 1/2 lb. ground beef
- 2 tbsp onion, chopped
- 2 mushrooms, diced
- 1/4 tsp pepper
- 2 tbsp parsley, chopped
- 1/4 cup almond flour
- 1/2 tsp salt

Directions:
1. In a mixing bowl, combine together all ingredients until well combined.
2. Make small balls from meat mixture and place into the air fryer basket.
3. Cook at 350 F for 20 minutes.
4. Serve and enjoy.

Nutrition: Calories 269 Fat 8 g Carbohydrates 10 g Sugar 2 g Protein 34 g Cholesterol 105 mg

104. Flavorful Kabab

Preparation Time: 10 minutes
Cooking Time: 10 minutes
Serve: 2

Ingredients:
- 1/2 lb. ground beef
- 2 tbsp parsley, chopped
- 1/2 tbsp olive oil
- 1 1/2 tbsp kabab spice mix
- 1/2 tbsp garlic, minced
- 1/2 tsp salt

Directions:
1. Add all ingredients into the bowl and mix well combined.
2. Divide mixture into the two equal portions and give it to kabab shape.
3. Place kababs into the air fryer basket and cook at 370 F for 10 minutes.
4. Serve and enjoy.

Nutrition: Calories 245 Fat 11 g Carbohydrates 1 g Sugar 0 g Protein 35 g Cholesterol 103 mg

105. Grilled Pork Shoulder

Preparation Time: 10 minutes
Cooking Time: 15 minutes
Serve: 2

Ingredients:
- 1/2 lb. pork shoulder, cut into 1/2-inch slices
- 1/2 tsp Swerve
- 1/2 tbsp sesame oil
- 1/2 tbsp rice wine
- 1/2 tbsp soy sauce
- 1 tbsp green onion, sliced
- 1/2 tbsp sesame seeds
- 1/4 tsp cayenne pepper
- 1/2 tbsp garlic, minced
- 1/2 tbsp ginger, minced
- 1 tbsp gochujang
- 1/2 onion, sliced

Directions:
1. In a large bowl, mix together all ingredients and place in the refrigerator for 60 minutes.
2. Place air fryer grill pan into the air fryer.
3. Add pork mixture into the air fryer and cook at 400 F for 15 minutes. Turn halfway through.
4. Serve and enjoy.

Nutrition: Calories 405 Fat 30 g Carbohydrates 7 g Sugar 3 g Protein 28 g Cholesterol 105 mg

106. Beef Satay

Preparation Time: 10 minutes
Cooking Time: 8 minutes
Serve: 2

Ingredients:
- 1 lb. beef flank steak, sliced into long strips
- 1 tsp hot sauce
- 1 tbsp Swerve
- 1 tbsp garlic, minced
- 1 tbsp ginger, minced
- 1 tbsp soy sauce
- 1/2 cup cilantro, chopped
- 1 tsp ground coriander
- 1 tbsp fish sauce
- 1 tbsp olive oil

Directions:
1. Add all ingredients into the zip-lock bag and shake well. Place into the fridge for 1 hour.
2. Add marinated meat into the air fryer basket and cook at 400 F for 8 minutes. Turn halfway through.
3. Serve and enjoy.

Nutrition: Calories 690 Fat 36 g Carbohydrates 10 g Sugar 6 g Protein 74 g Cholesterol 205 mg

107. Beefy Steak Topped with Chimichurri Sauce

Preparation Time: 5 Minutes
Cooking Time: 60 Minutes
Servings: 6

Ingredients:
- 1 cup commercial chimichurri
- 3 pounds' steak
- Salt and pepper to taste

Directions:
1. Place all ingredients in a Ziploc bag and marinate in the fridge for 2 hours.
2. Preheat the air fryer to 390°F.
3. Place the grill pan accessory in the air fryer.
4. Grill the skirt steak for 20 minutes per batch.
5. Flip the steak every 10 minutes for even grilling.

Nutrition: Calories: 507 Fat: 27g Protein: 63 G

108. Cheesy Ground Beef and Mac Taco Casserole

Preparation Time: 10 Minutes
Cooking Time: 25 Minutes

Servings: 5
Ingredients:
- 1-ounce shredded Cheddar cheese
- 1-ounce shredded Monterey Jack cheese
- 2 tablespoons chopped green onions
- 1/2 (10.75 ounce) can condensed tomato soup
- 1/2-pound lean ground beef
- 1/2 cup crushed tortilla chips
- 1/4-pound macaroni, cooked according to manufacturer's Directions:
- 1/4 cup chopped onion
- 1/4 cup sour cream (optional)
- 1/2 (1.25 ounce) package taco seasoning mix
- 1/2 (14.5 ounce) can diced tomatoes

Directions:
1. Lightly grease baking pan of air fryer with cooking spray. Add onion and ground beef. For 10 minutes, cook on 360°F. Halfway through cooking time, stir and crumble ground beef.
2. Add taco seasoning, diced tomatoes, and tomato soup. Mix well. Mix in pasta.
3. Sprinkle crushed tortilla chips. Sprinkle cheese.
4. Cook for 15 minutes at 390°F until tops are lightly browned and cheese is melted.
5. Serve and enjoy.

Nutrition: Calories: 329 Fat: 17g Protein: 15.6g

109. Garlic and Bell Pepper Beef

Preparation Time: 30 minutes
Cooking Time: 21 minutes
Servings: 4
Ingredients:
- 11 oz. steak fillets (sliced)
- 1/2 cup beef stock
- 2 tbsp. olive oil
- 2 tbsp. fish sauce
- 4 cloves garlic (pressed)
- 1 red pepper (cut into thin strips)
- 4 green onions (sliced)
- 1 tbsp. sugar - 2 tsp. cornflour
- Black pepper to taste

Directions:
1. In a pan, add beef, oil, garlic, black pepper, and bell pepper. Stir, cover, and keep in the refrigerator for 30 minutes.
2. Preheat the Air Fryer to 360°F.
3. Put the pan to the Air Fryer and cook for 14 minutes. In a bowl, mix sugar and fish sauce. Pour over the beef and cook for an additional 7 minutes. Serve and enjoy.

Nutrition:
Calories: 243; Fat: 3 g; Carbs: 24 g; Protein: 38 g.

110. Beef and Green Onion Marinade

Preparation Time: 10 minutes
Cooking Time: 20 minutes
Servings: 4
Ingredients:
- 1 lb. lean beef
- 1 cup soy sauce
- 5 garlic cloves (minced)
- 1/4 cup sesame seeds
- 1/2 cup of water
- 1 tsp. black pepper
- 1/4 cup brown sugar
- 1 cup green onion

Directions:
1. In a bowl, add soy sauce, onions, sugar, water, garlic, sesame seed, and pepper; whisk. Add the beef and toss to coat, leave for 10 minutes.
2. Preheat the Air Fryer to 390°F; drain the beef and transfer it to the Air Fryer. Cook for 20 minutes.
3. Serve with salad and enjoy.

Nutrition:
Calories: 329; Fat: 8 g; Carbs: 24 g; Protein: 22 g.

111. Short Ribs and Beer Sauce

Preparation Time: 15 minutes
Cooking Time: 43 minutes
Servings: 6
Ingredients:
- 4 lb. short ribs (cut into small pieces)
- 1 dried Portobello mushroom
- 1 yellow onion (chopped)
- 1 cup chicken stock

- 6 thyme sprigs (chopped)
- 1/4 cup tomato paste
- 1 bay leaf
- 1 cup dark beer
- Salt and pepper to taste

Directions:
1. Preheat the Air Fryer to 350°F.
2. In a pan that fits into your Air Fryer, heat oil over medium fire. Add onion, stock, tomato paste, beer, mushroom, bay leaf, and thyme. Simmer for 3–5minutes.
3. Add the rib and transfer it to the Air Fryer. Cook for 40 minutes.
4. Bon appetite!

Nutrition:
Calories: 300; Fat: 7 g; Carbs: 18 g; Protein: 23 g.

112. Beef and Cabbage Mix
Preparation Time: 10 minutes
Cooking Time: 40 minutes
Servings: 6
Ingredients:
- 2-1/2 lb. beef brisket
- 3 garlic cloves, preferably pressed
- 1 cup beef stock
- 1 cabbage cut into wedges
- 2 bay leaves
- 4 carrots, chopped
- 2 turnips (cut into smaller pieces)
- Salt and black pepper to taste

Directions:
1. Preheat the Air Fryer to 360°F.
2. Put the beef in a pan. Add the stock, salt, pepper, carrots, cabbage, bay leaves, garlic, and turnip. Stir, transfer to the Air Fryer, and cover. Cook for 40 minutes.
3. Serve and enjoy.

Nutrition:
Calories: 355; Fat: 16 g; Carbs: 18 g; Protein: 24 g.

113. Short Ribs and Special Sauce
Preparation Time: 10 minutes
Cooking Time: 46 minutes
Servings: 4
Ingredients:
- 4 lb. short ribs
- 1/2 cup soy sauce
- 3 cloves garlic (pressed)
- 1/2 cup water
- 2 tbsp. sesame oil
- 1/4 cup rice wine
- 3 ginger slices
- 1/4 cup pear juice
- 1 tsp. vegetable oil
- 2 green onions chopped

Directions:
1. Preheat the Air Fryer to 350°F.
2. Heat oil in a pan; then put green onions, garlic, and ginger. Stir and cook for 1 minute.
3. Add the rib and the remaining ingredients, transfer to the Air Fryer and cook for 35 minutes.
4. Serve and enjoy.

Nutrition:
Calories: 321; Fat: 12 g; Carbs: 20 g; Protein: 14 g.

114. Beef Patty in Mushroom Sauce
Preparation Time: 15 minutes
Cooking Time: 22 minutes
Servings: 6
Ingredients:
- 2 lb. ground beef
- 3/4 cup flour
- 1 tbsp. onion flakes
- 1/2 tsp. garlic powder
- 1/4 cup beef stock
- 1 tbsp. chopped parsley
- 1 tbsp. soy sauce
- Salt and pepper to taste
- 2 tbsp. bacon fat
- 1/4 cup sour cream
- Salt and black pepper to taste

Directions:
1. Preheat the Air Fryer to 350°F.
2. In a bowl, mix beef, pepper, salt, garlic powder, 1 tablespoon of soy sauce, ¼ cup beef stock, parsley, onions flakes, and flour. Stir and shape six patties. Move it into the Air Fryer and cook for 14 minutes.
3. While the patties are still cooking, heat butter in a pan on medium fire. Add the mushroom and cook for 4 minutes with constant stirring. Add onions and cook for another 4 minutes. incorporate the soy sauce and sour cream and simmer. Remove from heat.
4. Serve patties with mushroom sauce.

Nutrition:
Calories: 235; Fat: 23 g; Carbs: 6 g; Protein: 32 g.

115. Greek Beef Meatballs Salad
Preparation Time: 10 minutes
Cooking Time: 10 minutes
Servings: 6
Ingredients:
- 17 oz. ground beef
- 1 cup baby spinach
- 5 bread slices, cubed
- 1/4 cup parsley
- 1/4 cup milk
- 1/4 cup chopped mint
- 1 yellow onion (minced)
- 2 garlic cloves (minced)
- 2-1/2 tsp. dried oregano
- Cooking spray
- Salt and pepper to taste

Directions:

1. Preheat the Air Fryer to 370°F.
2. Add the bread and milk and allow to soak for 3 minutes. Squeeze and transfer to another bowl.
3. To the bread in the bowl, add egg, salt, pepper, mint, parsley, garlic, and onion. Stir and shape into balls using an ice-cream scooper.
4. Grease the meatballs with cooking spray. Place them in your Air Fryer and cook for 10 minutes.
5. In a bowl, mix spinach, cucumber, and tomatoes. Add the meatball, oil, pepper, salt, lemon juice, and yogurt. Toss and serve.

Nutrition:
Calories: 200; Fat: 4 g; Carbs: 13 g; Protein: 27g.

116. Beef Stuffed Squash
Preparation Time: 10 minutes
Cooking Time: 40 minutes
Servings: 2
Ingredients:
- 1 lb. ground beef
- 1 tsp. dried oregano
- 1 spaghetti squash (pricked)
- 3 garlic cloves (minced)
- 28 oz. canned tomatoes (chopped)
- 1 Portobello mushroom (sliced)
- 1/2 tsp. dried thyme
- 1 green bell pepper (chopped)
- 1/4 tsp. cayenne pepper
- 1 yellow onion (diced)
- Salt and pepper to taste

Directions:
1. Preheat the Air Fryer to 350°F. Transfer the spaghetti squash into the Air Fryer and cook for 20 minutes. Remove and transfer to the cutting board and cut into halves. Remove and discard the seeds.
2. Heat a pan over medium fire. Add the beef, garlic, onions, mushroom. Stir and cook until the meat is golden brown. Add the remaining ingredients except for the squash and allow them to cook for 10 minutes.
3. Stuff the squash with the beef mix and transfer it into the Air Fryer; cook for 10 minutes at 360°F.
4. Serve and enjoy.

Nutrition:
Calories: 260; Fat: 7 g; Carbs: 14 g; Protein: 10 g.

117. Beef Casserole
Preparation Time: 15 minutes
Cooking Time: 35 minutes
Servings: 12
Ingredients:
- 2 lb. beef
- 2 tsp. mustard
- 2 cups grated mozzarella
- 1 tbsp. olive oil
- 2 cups chopped eggplant
- 28 oz. canned tomatoes (chopped)
- 1 tsp. dried oregano
- 2 tsp. Worcestershire sauce
- 2 tbsp. chopped parsley
- 16 oz. tomato sauce
- Salt and pepper to taste

Directions:
1. Preheat the Air Fryer to 360°F.
2. In a bowl, add eggplant, salt, pepper, and oil. Mix to coat.
3. In a separate bowl, add beef, mustard, salt, pepper, and Worcestershire sauce; stir well. Pour the mixture into a pan that fits into your Air Fryer and spread evenly; add the eggplant mix and tomato sauce. Sprinkle with parsley and oregano.
4. Transfer to the Air Fryer and cook for 35 minutes.
5. Serve and enjoy.

Nutrition:
Calories: 200; Fat: 12 g; Carbs: 16 g; Protein: 15 g.

118. Burgundy Beef Mix
Preparation Time: 10 minutes
Cooking Time: 1 hour 5 minutes
Servings: 7
Ingredients:
- 2 lb. beef chuck roast, cut into smaller cubes
- 4 carrots (chopped)
- 1 cup water
- 1 cup. beef stock
- 3 tbsp. almond flour
- 2 yellow onions (chopped)
- 1 tbsp. chopped thyme
- 2 celery ribs (chopped)
- 1/2 lb. mushroom (sliced)
- 15 oz. canned tomatoes (chopped)
- 1/2 tsp. mustard powder
- Salt and black pepper to taste

Directions:
1. Preheat the Air Fryer to 300°F.
2. Place a pot over high heat; then place the meat and brown on all sides for 3–5 minutes. Add the tomato, carrot, onions, celery, mushroom, salt, pepper, mustard, stock, and thyme; stir.
3. In a bowl, add water and flour; stir. Add to the pot and transfer into the Air Fryer and cook for 1 hour.
4. Serve and enjoy.

Nutrition:
Calories: 275; Fat: 13 g; Carbs: 17 g; Protein: 28 g.

119. Sirloin Steaks and Pico de Gallo
Preparation Time: 10 minutes
Cooking Time: 10 minutes
Servings: 4
Ingredients:
- 4 medium sirloin steak
- 1 tsp. onion powder
- 1/2 tbsp. sweet paprika
- 1 tsp. garlic powder

- 2 tbsp. chili powder
- 1 tsp. ground cumin
- Salt and pepper to taste

For the Pico de Gallo:
- 2 tomatoes (chopped)
- 2 tbsp. lime juice
- 1 jalapeño (chopped)
- 1 small red onion (chopped)
- 1/4 cup chopped cilantro
- 1 small red onion (diced)
- 1/4 tsp. cumin
- 1 red onion (chopped)

Directions:
1. Preheat the Air Fryer to 360°F.
2. In a bowl, mix chili powder, onion powder, salt, pepper, garlic powder, paprika, and 1 tablespoon of cumin. Rub the combination on both sides of the steak; then transfer to your Air Fryer. Cook for 10 minutes.
3. Mix all the Pico de Gallo ingredients in a bowl and add pepper to taste.
4. Serve the steak with the Pico de Gallo at the side. Enjoy.

Nutrition:
Calories: 200; Fat: 12 g; Carbs: 15 g; Protein: 18 g.

120. Mexican Beef Mix

Preparation Time: 10 minutes
Cooking Time: 1 hour 10 minutes
Servings: 8
Ingredients:
- 2 lb. beef roast, cubes
- 2 green bell peppers (chopped)
- 6 garlic cloves (minced)
- 2 tbsp. olive oil
- 4 jalapenos (chopped)
- 2 yellow onions (diced)
- 1/2 cup of water
- 14 oz. canned tomatoes (chopped)
- 1/2 cup black olive (pitted and chopped)
- 1 and 1/2 tsp. ground cumin
- Salt and pepper to taste

Directions:
1. Preheat the Air Fryer to 300°F.
2. In a pan, add all the ingredients and stir; transfer to the Air Fryer and cook for 1 hour 10 minutes.
3. Serve garnished with olives.

Nutrition:
Calories: 305; Fat: 14 g; Carbs: 1825 g.

121. Coffee Flavored Steak

Preparation Time: 10 minutes
Cooking Time: 15 minutes
Servings: 4
Ingredients:
- 4 rib-eye steak
- 2 tbsp. garlic powder
- 2 tbsp. chili powder
- 1-1/2 tbsp. ground coffee
- 2 tbsp. onion powder
- 1/2 tbsp. sweet paprika
- A pinch cayenne pepper
- 1/4 tsp. ground ginger
- Black pepper to taste
- 1/4 tsp. ground coriander

Directions:
1. Preheat the Air Fryer to 360°F.
2. In a bowl, mix all the ingredients, excluding the steak, and stir. Rub the steak thoroughly with the mixture.
3. Transfer to the Air Fryer and cook for 15 minutes.
4. Serve and enjoy.

Nutrition:
Calories: 160; Fat: 10 g; Carbs: 14 g; Protein: 12 g.

122. Seasoned Beef Roast

Preparation Time: 10 minutes
Cooking Time: 45 minutes
Servings: 10
Ingredients:
- 3 pounds beef top roast
- 1 tbsp. olive oil
- 2 tbsp. Montreal steak seasoning

Directions:
1. Coat the roast with oil and then rub with the seasoning generously.
2. With kitchen twines, tie the roast to keep it compact. Arrange the roast onto the cooking tray.
3. Select "Air Fry" and then alter the temperature to 360°F. Set the timer for 45 minutes and press "Start."
4. If the display shows "Add Food," insert the cooking tray in the center position.
5. When the display shows "Turn Food," do nothing.
6. When cooking time is complete, take away the tray from Vortex.
7. Place the roast onto a platter for about 10 minutes before slicing.
8. With a sharp knife, cut the roast into desired sized slices and serve.

Nutrition:
Calories: 269; Fat: 9.9 g; Carbs: 0 g; Fiber: 0 g.

123. Simple Beef Sirloin Roast

Preparation Time: 10 minutes
Cooking Time: 50 minutes
Servings: 8
Ingredients:
- 2½ pounds sirloin roast
- Salt and ground black pepper, as required

Directions:
1. Rub the roast with salt and black pepper generously.
2. Insert the rotisserie rod through the roast.
3. Insert the rotisserie forks, one on each rod's side, to secure the rod to the chicken.
4. Select "Roast" and then adjust the temperature to 350°F.
5. Set the timer for 50 minutes and press "Start."

6. When the display shows "Add Food," press the red lever down.
7. Weight the left side of the rod into the Vortex.
8. Now, turn the rod's left side into the groove along the metal bar so it will not move.
9. Then, close the door and touch "Rotate." Press the red lever to release the rod when the cooking time is complete.
10. Remove the roast from the Vortex.
11. Place the roast onto a platter for about 10 minutes before slicing.
12. With a sharp knife, cut the roast into desired-sized slices and serve.

Nutrition:
Calories: 201; Fat: 8.8 g; Carbs: 0 g; Protein: 28.9 g.

124. Simple Beef Patties
Preparation Time: 10 minutes
Cooking Time: 13 minutes
Servings: 4
Ingredients:
- 1 lb. ground beef
- ½ tsp. garlic powder
- ¼ tsp. onion powder
- Pepper
- Salt

Directions:
1. Preheat the Instant Vortex Air Fryer oven to 400°F.
2. Add ground meat, garlic powder, onion powder, pepper, and salt into a bowl and mix until well combined.
3. Make even shape patties from the meat mixture and arrange them into the Air Fryer pan.
4. Place a pan in Instant Vortex Air Fryer oven.
5. Cook patties for 10 minutes. Turn them after 5 minutes.
6. Serve and enjoy.

Nutrition:
Calories: 212; Fat: 7.1 g; Carbs: 0.4 g; Protein: 34.5 g.

125. Easy Beef Roast
Preparation Time: 10 minutes
Cooking Time: 45 minutes
Servings: 6
Ingredients:
- 2 ½ lb. beef roast
- 2 tbsp. Italian seasoning

Directions:
1. Arrange roast on the rotisserie spite.
2. Rub roast with Italian seasoning, then insert into the Instant Vortex Air Fryer oven.
3. Air fry at 350°F for 45 minutes or until the roast internal temperature reaches 145°F.
4. Slice and serve.

Nutrition:
Calories: 365; Fat: 13.2 g; Carbs: 0.5 g; Protein: 57.4 g.

126. Beef Sirloin Roast
Preparation Time: 10 minutes
Cooking Time: 50 minutes
Servings: 8
Ingredients:
- 1 tbsp. smoked paprika
- 1 tsp. ground cumin
- 1 tsp. garlic powder
- Salt and freshly ground black pepper, to taste
- 2½ pounds sirloin roast

Directions:
1. In a bowl, mix the spices, salt, and black pepper.
2. Rub the roast with spice mixture generously.
3. Place the sirloin roast into the greased baking pan.
4. Press the "Power Button" of the PowerXL Digital Air Fryer and turn the dial to select "Air Roast" mode.
5. Press the "Time Button" and again turn the dial to set the cooking time to 50 minutes.
6. Now push "Temp Button" and rotate the dial to set the temperature at 350°F.
7. Press the "Start/Pause" button to start.
8. When the unit beeps to show that it is preheated, open the lid and insert the baking pan in the oven.
9. When cooking time is complete, open the lid and place the roast onto a platter for about 10 minutes before slicing.
10. With a sharp knife, cut the beef roast into desired sized slices and serve.

Nutrition:
Calories: 260; Fat: 11.9 g; Sat Fat: 4.4 g; Carbohydrates: 0.4 g; Fiber: 0.1 g; Sugar: 0.1 g; Protein: 38 g.

127. Air Fried Grilled Steak
Preparation Time: 6 minutes
Cooking Time: 40 minutes
Servings: 2
Ingredients:
- 2 sirloin steaks
- 3 tbsp. butter, melted
- 3 tbsp. olive oil
- Salt and pepper, to taste

Directions:
1. Preheat the Smart Air Fryer Oven for 5 minutes at 350°F.
2. Season the sirloin steaks with olive oil, salt, and pepper.
3. Place the beef in the Air Fryer basket and put the basket into the oven.
4. Select GRILL. Grill for 40 minutes at 350°F.
5. Once cooked, serve with butter.

Nutrition:
Calories: 1536; Fat: 123.7 g; Protein: 103.4 g.

128. Air Fryer Beef Casserole
Preparation Time: 7 minutes
Cooking Time: 30 minutes
Servings: 4
Ingredients:
- 1 green bell pepper, seeded and chopped
- 1 onion, chopped
- 1-lb. ground beef
- 3 cloves of garlic, minced
- 6 cups eggs, beaten

Directions:
1. Preheat the Smart Air Fryer Oven for 5 minutes at 325°F.

2. In a baking dish, mix the ground beef, onion, garlic, olive oil, and bell pepper.
3. Add beaten eggs to a large bowl.
4. Season the ground beef mixture with salt and pepper and pour in the beaten eggs and give a good stir.
5. Place the dish with the beef and egg mixture in the Air Fryer.
6. Place the rack on the middle shelf of the Smart Air Fryer Oven.
7. Select BAKE. Set temperature to 325°F, and time to 30 minutes.
8. When done, remove from the oven and rest for 5 minutes. Serve warm.

Nutrition:
Calories: 1520; Fat: 125.1 g; Protein: 87.9 g.

129. Charred Onions & Steak Cube BBQ

Preparation Time: 8 minutes
Cooking Time: 40 minutes
Servings: 3
Ingredients:
- 1 cup red onions, cut into wedges
- 1 tbsp. dry mustard
- 1-lb. boneless beef sirloin, cut into cubes
- Salt and pepper, to taste

Directions:
1. Preheat the Air Fryer to 390°F.
2. Place the grill rack in the Air Fryer. Toss all the listed ingredients in a bowl and mix until everything is coated with the seasonings.
3. Place on the grill rack and put the rack in the oven.
4. Select GRILL. Grill for 40 minutes.
5. Halfway through the cooking time, give a stir to cook evenly.
6. When done, transfer to a plate and enjoy.

Nutrition:
Calories: 260; Fat: 10.7 g; Protein: 35.5 g.

130. Beef Ribeye Steak

Preparation Time: 6 minutes
Cooking Time: 10 minutes
Servings: 4
Ingredients:
- 4 (8-oz.) rib-eye steaks
- 1 tbsp. McCormick Grill Mates Montreal Steak Seasoning
- Salt and pepper, to taste

Directions:
1. Season the steaks with salt, pepper, and seasoning.
2. Place two steaks in the Smart Air Fryer Oven grill rack.
3. Select GRILL and grill for 5 minutes at 400°F.
4. Open the Air Fryer and flip the steaks. Then cook for an additional 5 minutes.
5. Remove the cooked steaks from the Smart Air Fryer Oven to a plate.
6. Repeat for the remaining two steaks.
7. Serve warm.

Nutrition:
Calories: 293; Fat: 22 g; Fiber: 0 g; Protein: 23 g.

131. Air Fryer Roast Beef

Preparation Time: 7 minutes
Cooking Time: 20 minutes
Servings: 6
Ingredients:
- Roast beef
- 1 tbsp. olive oil
- Seasonings of choice

Directions:
1. Preheat your Smart Air Fryer Oven to 160°F.
2. Place the beef roast in a bowl and toss with olive oil and desired seasonings.
3. Put seasoned roast into the Air Fryer.
4. Select ROAST and set the temperature to 160°F and time to 20 minutes.
5. Turn the roast when the timer sounds and cook another 10 minutes.
6. Serve hot.

Nutrition:
Calories: 267; Fat: 8 g; Carbs: 1 g; Protein: 21 g.

132. Salt-and-Pepper Beef Roast

Preparation Time: 4 hours
Cooking Time: 30 minutes
Servings: 12–14
Ingredients:
- 4–6lb. boned beef cross rib roast
- 1/4 cup coarse salt
- 1/4 cup sugar
- 2 tbsp. coarse-ground pepper
- 1/2 cup prepared horseradish

Directions:
1. Mix salt with sugar in a bowl. Pat the mixture on the beef, and marinate for 3–4 hours.
2. Mix 1.5 teaspoon of salt, pepper, and horseradish.
3. Put the beef on a rack in a 9"x13" pan and rub the horseradish mixture.
4. Roast in 176°C/ 350°F in the PowerXL Air Fryer Grill. Check if the internal temperature is 120–125°C.
5. Let it rest for 20 minutes and then slice the meat thinly across the grain.

Nutrition:
Calories: 267; Carbs: 1.3 g; Protein: 20 g; Fat: 19 g.

133. Prime Rib Roast

Preparation Time: 60 minutes
Cooking Time: 45 minutes
Servings: 4–6
Ingredients:
- Prime Rib Roast
- Butter
- Salt and pepper

Directions:
1. Cut the fat parts from each side of the meat, and put it inside the PowerXL Air Fryer Grill.

2. Cook at 230°C/ 450°F for 15 minutes. Lower it to 165°C/ 325°F afterward.
3. Check if the internal temperature has reached 110°C/ 225°F and serve.

Nutrition:
Calories: 290; Protein: 19.2 g; Fat: 23.1 g.

134. Beef Tenderloin
Preparation Time: 60 minutes
Cooking Time: 10 minutes
Servings: 6
Ingredients:
- 5 lb. beef tenderloin
- Vegetable oil
- Spices, salt, and pepper

Directions:
1. Preheat the PowerXL Air Fryer Grill to 180°C/ 350°F. Cut extra fat from it.
2. Gently rub tenderloin with vegetable oil and seasoning.
3. Cook it in the PowerXL Air Fryer Grill for 20–30 minutes.

Nutrition:
Calories: 179; Protein: 26 g; Fat: 7.6 g.

135. Perfect Rump Roast
Preparation Time: 2 hours
Cooking Time: 20 minutes
Servings: 5
Ingredients:
- 4 lb. rump roast
- 3 garlic cloves
- 1 tbsp. each salt, pepper
- 1 onion
- 1 cup water

Directions:
1. Preheat the PowerXL Air Fryer Grill to 260°C/ 500°F
2. Make 4-5 cuts on the roast, and fill with salt, pepper, and garlic.
3. Season some more before searing for 20 minutes. Add water and minced onion.
4. Cook in the PowerXL Air Fryer Grill at 180°C/ 350°F for 1.5 hours.

Nutrition:
Calories: 916.8; Carbs: 4.4 g; Protein: 94.6 g; Fat: 55.2 g.

136. Slow Roasted Beef Short Ribs
Preparation Time: 10 minutes
Cooking Time: 3 hours
Servings: 6
Ingredients:
- 5 lb. beef short ribs
- 1/3 cup brown sugar
- 1 tsp. garlic powder
- 1 tsp. onion powder
- 1/4 tsp. marjoram
- 1/2 tsp. kosher salt
- 1/4 tsp. thyme
- 1 pinch cayenne pepper

Directions:
1. Pat the ribs dry.
2. Rub the ingredients on each rib, put them in a sealed plastic bag, and freeze overnight.
3. Preheat the PowerXL Air Fryer Grill to 150°C/ 300°F, and put ribs on a rack in a roasting pan.
4. Roast for around 3 hours.

Nutrition:
Calories: 791; Carbs: 19 g; Protein: 79 g; Fat: 42 g.

137. Sirloin Roast Beef
Preparation Time: 90 minutes
Cooking Time: 15 minutes
Servings: 6
Ingredients:
- 3.3 lb. sirloin Beef
- 2 tbsp. vegetable oil
- 6 ounces red wine
- 14 ounces beef consommé

Directions:
1. Preheat the PowerXL Air Fryer Grill to 200°C/ 400°F.
2. Season the sirloin and cook it at medium heat in oil for 5 minutes, turning regularly.
3. Roast it in the PowerXL Air Fryer Grill for 15 minutes to make it medium-rare. Flip it halfway. Remove it when the internal temperature is 145°F and cover with foil.
4. Make a gravy with the fat residue on the pan and some wine. Add beef consommé to the sauce and simmer for 5 minutes. Strain when completed and pour on the roast.

Nutrition:
Calories: 179; Protein: 22 g; Fat: 9.4 g.

138. Roasted Hamburgers
These juicy hamburgers can be made at any time of the year!
Preparation Time: 15 minutes
Cooking Time: 10 minutes
Servings: 6
Ingredients:
- 1–1/2 tsp. kosher salt - 2 lb. ground beef
- 1 tbsp. Worcestershire sauce
- 1/2 tsp. freshly ground black pepper
- 6 toasted hamburger buns
- Hamburger toppings

Directions:
1. Preheat the PowerXL Air Fryer Grill to 230°C/ 450°F and line a rimmed baking sheet with aluminum foil with some salt to absorb drippings.
2. Season meat by hand and split it up into 6 parts to shape into 3"x1" disks. Place burgers an inch apart on a wire rack and roast for 10–16 minutes at 135°C/ 250°F for medium-rare meat.

Nutrition:
Calories: 131.6; Carbs: 8.7 g; Protein: 13.1 g; Fat: 4.1 g.

139. Pan-Seared Roasted Strip Steak
Preparation Time: 20 minutes
Cooking Time: 10 minutes
Servings: 2

Ingredients:
- 1 3-inch strip steak
- 1 tbsp. butter
- Meat tenderizer
- Coarsely Ground Black Pepper

Directions:
1. Cut and season the room-temperature meat.
2. Preheat the PowerXL Air Fryer Grill to 200°C/ 400°F.
3. Sear the steak in butter over medium-high heat evenly for 2–3 minutes after an hour of resting.
4. Cook in the PowerXL Air Fryer Grill for 7 minutes to achieve medium-rare.

Nutrition:
Calories: 253.6; Carbs: 0.2 g; Protein: 21.1 g; Fat: 18.1 g,

140. London Broil Steak

Preparation Time: 50 minutes
Cooking Time: 20 minutes
Servings: 6
Ingredients:
- 2 lb. London broil top-round steak
- Kosher salt
- Freshly ground black pepper
- 1/4 cup extra-virgin olive oil
- 1/2 lemon juice
- 2 tbsp. brown sugar
- 1 tbsp. Worcestershire sauce
- 4 cloves garlic, diced
- 1/4 cup balsamic vinegar

Directions:
1. Marinate the steak in the refrigerator for at least 20 minutes.
2. Preheat the PowerXL Air Fryer Grill to 190°C/ 375°F and cook the steak for 6–8 minutes on each side.

Nutrition:
Calories: 173; Protein: 26.1 g; Fat: 7.7 g.

141. Summer Sausage

Preparation Time: 40 minutes
Cooking Time: 4 hours
Servings: 6
Ingredients:
- 2-1/2 tsp. cracked black pepper
- 5 lb. ground venison
- 3 tsp. tender quick salt
- 2-1/2 tsp. mustard seeds
- 1 tsp. liquid smoke
- 2-1/2 tsp. garlic salt
- 1 tsp. hickory salt

Directions:
1. In a bowl, mix ground venison, mustard seed, black pepper, and liquid smoke.
2. Add tender quick salt, garlic salt, and hickory salt.
3. Cut into 6 long rolls.
4. Place it on the PowerXL Air Fryer Grill.
5. Set the PowerXL Air Fryer Grill to the broil function.
6. Cook for 4 hours at 150°F.

Serving Suggestions: Serve with ketchup.
Directions & Cooking Tips: Rinse venison well.
Nutrition:
Calories: 140; Fat: 10 g; Carbs: 3 g; Protein: 13 g.

142. Meatball Venison

Preparation Time: 10 minutes
Cooking Time: 30 minutes
Servings: 4
Ingredients:
- 1 tsp. salt
- 1 lb. ground venison
- 1/2 tsp. nutmeg
- 1-1/2 can of water
- 1 egg
- 1 cup bread crumbs
- 1 can mushroom soup
- 1/2 tsp. thyme
- 1 packet dried onion soup

Directions:
1. Mix salt, egg, meat, nutmeg, bread crumbs, and thyme in a bowl.
2. Shape into small balls.
3. Place the meatball on the PowerXL Air Fryer Grill pan.
4. Set the PowerXL Air Fryer Grill to the Air Fry function. Cook for 30 minutes at 350°F.
5. Serve with mushroom soup.

Serving Suggestions: Serve with dried onion soup.
Directions & Cooking Tips: Rinse the meat well.
Nutrition:
Calories: 57; Fat: 2 g; Carbs: 2 g; Protein: 10 g.

143. Smoked Ham Sausage

Preparation Time: 5 minutes
Cooking Time: 15 minutes
Servings: 4
Ingredients:
- 1-1/2 tsp. sage
- Cayenne
- 1 tsp. thyme
- 3 lb. venison- 1 tsp. salt
- 1 lb. smoked ham
- 1 tsp. ground pepper
- 1/2 lb. bacon

Directions:
1. In a bowl, mix venison, thyme, sage, ground pepper, salt, and cayenne.
2. Cut the meats into pieces.
3. Mix all ingredients.
4. Shape platter out of it.
5. Place the platter on the PowerXL Air Fryer Grill pan.
6. Set the PowerXL Air Fryer Grill to the broil function.
7. Cook for 15 minutes at 400°F.

Serving Suggestions: Serve with fries.
Directions & Cooking Tips: Rinse meats well.

Nutrition:
Calories: 112; Fat: 8 g; Carbs: 4 g; Protein: 10 g.

144. Venison Loaf
Preparation Time: 10 minutes
Cooking Time: 1 hour
Servings: 4
Ingredients:
- Chopped onion
- 1 lb. sausage
- 1 cup milk
- 2 eggs
- 8 ounces barbecue sauce
- 2 cups cracker crumbs
- Tomato sauce
- 1 lb. ground venison

Directions:
1. Mix cracker crumbs, milk, ground venison, and barbecue sauce in a bowl.
2. Add sausage, eggs, and onion.
3. Place the mixture on the PowerXL Air Fryer Grill pan.
4. Set the PowerXL Air Fryer Grill to the Air Fry function. Bake for 1 hour at 350°F.
5. Serve immediately or allow cooling before serving.

Serving Suggestions: Serve with tomato sauce.
Directions & Cooking Tips: Mix the ingredients homogeneously.
Nutrition:
Calories: 116; Fat: 10 g; Carbs: 1.1 g; Protein: 6 g.

145. Bologna
Preparation Time: 10 minutes
Cooking Time: 45 minutes
Servings: 5
Ingredients:
- 1-1/2 tsp. liquid smoke
- 2 lb. ground venison
- 1 cup water
- 2 tbsp. tender-quick salt
- 1/2 tsp. garlic powder
- 4 tsp. onion powder

Directions:
1. Mix liquid smoke, garlic powder, water, and onion powder in a bowl. Add tender-quick salt and ground venison.
2. Make rolls from the mixture.
3. Place the rolls on the PowerXL Air Fryer Grill pan.
4. Set the PowerXL Air Fryer Grill at the broil function. Cook for 45 minutes at 300°F.

Serving Suggestions: Serve with tomato sauce.
Directions & Cooking Tips: Make the roll smooth.
Nutrition:
Calories: 249; Fat: 21 g; Carbs: 1 g; Protein: 16g

146. Squirrel Dish
Preparation Time: 40 minutes
Cooking Time: 1 hour 30 minutes
Servings: 4
Ingredients:
- 1/2 cup onion powder
- 1 can tomatoes
- 1/2 dozen potatoes
- 1 squirrel
- Vegetable oil
- Salt
- 1 cup flour
- Pepper

Directions:
1. Cut the meats into cubes.
2. Add flour, salt, and pepper.
3. Add potatoes and onions.
4. Place the mixture on the PowerXL Air Fryer Grill pan.
5. Set the PowerXL Air Fryer Grill to Air Fry function.
6. Cook for 1 hour 30 minutes at 350°F.
7. Serve immediately.

Serving Suggestions: Serve with tomato sauce.
Directions & Cooking Tips: Rinse the squirrel meat well.
Nutrition:
Calories: 103; Fat: 3 g; Carbs: 4 g; Protein: 19 g.

147. Swedish Meatballs
Preparation Time: 10 minutes
Cooking Time: 40 minutes
Servings: 10
Ingredients:
- 1-pound ground beef
- 1-pound ground pork
- 1/5 cup panko breadcrumbs
- 1/5 onion, chopped
- 1 tsp. salt
- 1/5 tsp. ground black pepper
- 1/4 tsp. nutmeg
- 1 tsp. garlic powder
- 2 tbsp. plus 2 tsp. Worcestershire sauce, divided
- 1/4 cup butter
- 1/4 cup flour
- 3 cups beef broth
- 1 sprig fresh thyme

Directions:
1. Combine beef, pork, panko breadcrumbs, onion, salt, black pepper, nutmeg, garlic powder, onion powder, egg, parsley, ¼ cup heavy cream, and pour 2 teaspoons of Worcestershire sauce into a bowl. Use the mixture to form 30 meatballs.
2. Place the inner pot in the PowerXL Fast Cooker.
3. Press the sauté button and then the program dial to select the beef set. Press the program selection again to confirm the default setting and start the cooking cycle (170°C for 20 minutes).
4. Put the butter in the inner pot and cook until the butter has melted.
5. Add flour and cook for 3 minutes.
6. Turn in the broth and simmer for not less than 10 to 11 minutes.

7. Click the Cancel button. Add the thyme, meatballs, and the rest of the Worcestershire cream and sauce.
8. Place the lid on the PowerXL Quick Cooker and turn the lid counterclockwise. The lid is locked and the pressure relief valve is closed.
9. Press the start button, scroll to the meat setting, and press the program wheel. Press the timer button, scroll to set the cooking time to 4 minutes, and press the program wheel to start the cooking cycle.
10. When the timer reaches 0, the PowerXL Quick Pot will automatically switch to keep warm. Press the Cancel button. Let the PowerXL Fast Cooker sit to naturally relieve the pressure. Turn the steam switch to open. Once the steam is released, the lid should be removed.

Nutrition:
Calories: 42; Fat: 0.5 g; Carbs: 10 g; Protein: 1 g.

148. Spaghetti and Meatballs

Preparation Time: 10 minutes
Cooking Time: 40 minutes
Servings: 8
Ingredients:
- 2 tbsp. olive oil
- 1 small onion, chopped
- 6 cloves garlic, chopped, divided
- 2 (28 ounces) cans of tomato paste
- 10 basil leaves
- 1 tsp. sea salt
- 1 tsp. sugar
- 1 tsp. ground black pepper, divided
- 1/5 cup chopped parsley, divided
- 2 pounds ground beef
- 4 eggs
- 3/4 cup breadcrumbs
- 1/5 cup milk
- 1/5 onion, chopped
- 1 tsp. salt
- 1/5 cup grated parmesan cheese
- 1 pound cooked spaghetti

Directions:
1. Place the inner pot on the PowerXL Fast Cooker.
2. Press the Sauté button, scroll to the Vegetable setting, and press the program selection. Press the timer button, scroll to set the cooking time to 20 minutes, and press the program wheel to start the cooking cycle.
3. Put olive oil, chopped onions, and 4 chopped garlic cloves in the inner pot and cook until translucent.
4. Add tomato puree, basil, sea salt, sugar, ½ teaspoon of black pepper, and ¼ cup of parsley; cook for 10 minutes. Make the sauce. Press the Cancel button.
5. Mix the beef, eggs, breadcrumbs, milk, chopped onions, salt, parmesan, the remaining garlic, black pepper, and parsley in a bowl. Form meatballs from the mixture.
6. Place the meatballs in the hot sauce.
7. Place the lid on the PowerXL Quick Cooker and turn the lid counter-clockwise. The lid is locked and the pressure relief valve is closed.
8. Press the start button, scroll to the meat setting, and press the program wheel. Press the timer button, set the cooking time to 20 minutes, and press the program wheel to start the cooking cycle.
9. When the timer reaches 0, the PowerXL Quick Pot will automatically switch to keeping warm. Press the Cancel button. Turn the steam release switch to open. Remove the lid once steam is released.
10. Remove the meatballs from the inner pot and serve over the cooked spaghetti.

Nutrition:
Calories: 57; Fat: 2 g; Carbs: 2 g; Protein: 10 g.

149. Cheese Garlicky Pork Chops

Preparation Time: 10 minutes
Cooking Time: 20 minutes
Servings: 8
Ingredients:
- 8 pork chops, boneless
- 3/4 cup parmesan cheese
- 2 tbsp. butter, melted
- 2 tbsp. coconut oil
- 1 tsp. thyme
- 1 tbsp. parsley
- 5 garlic cloves, minced
- 1/4 tsp. pepper
- 1/2 tsp. sea salt

Directions:
1. Coat the Air Fryer basket with cooking spray.
2. Preheat the Air Fryer to 400°F.
3. In a bowl, mix butter, spices, parmesan cheese, and coconut oil.
4. Brush butter mixture on top of pork chops, place it into the Air Fryer basket and cook for 20 minutes. Turn pork chops halfway through.
5. Serve and enjoy.

Nutrition:
Calories: 344; Fat: 28.2: g; Carbohydrates: 1.1 g; Sugar: 0 g; Protein: 21.2 g; Cholesterol: 83 mg.

150. Garlic Lemon Pork Chops

Preparation Time: 10 minutes
Cooking Time: 20 minutes
Servings: 5
Ingredients:
- 2 lb. pork chops
- 2 tbsp. fresh lemon juice
- 2 tbsp. garlic, minced
- 1 tbsp. fresh parsley
- 1 1/2 tbsp. olive oil
- Pepper
- Salt

Directions:
1. In a small bowl, mix garlic, parsley, olive oil, and lemon juice. Season pork chops with pepper and salt.

2. Pour garlic mixture over the pork chops; coat well and allow to marinate for 30 minutes.
3. Add marinated pork chops into the Air Fryer basket and cook at 400°F for 20 minutes. Turn pork chops halfway through.
4. Serve and enjoy.

Nutrition:
Calories: 623; Fat: 49.4 g; Carbohydrates: 1.3 g; Sugar: 0.2 g; Protein: 41.1 g; Cholesterol: 156 mg.

151. Herb Cheese Pork Chops

Preparation Time: 10 minutes
Cooking Time: 9 minutes
Servings: 2
Ingredients:
- 2 pork chops, boneless - 1 tsp. paprika
- 3 tbsp. parmesan cheese, grated
- 1/3 cup almond flour
- 1/2 tsp. Cajun seasoning
- 1 tsp. herb de Provence

Directions:
1. Preheat the Air Fryer to 350°F.
2. Mix almond flour, Cajun seasoning, herb de Provence, paprika, and parmesan cheese. Coat pork chops with cooking spray.
3. Coat pork chops with almond flour mixture and place them into the Air Fryer basket; cook for 9 minutes.
4. Serve and enjoy.

Nutrition:
Calories: 360; Fat: 27.3 g; Carbohydrates: 2.4 g; Sugar: 0.3 g; Protein: 26.7 g; Cholesterol: 85 mg.

152. Tender Pork Chops

Preparation Time: 10 minutes
Cooking Time: 13 minutes
Servings: 4
Ingredients:
- 4 pork chops, boneless
- 1/2 tsp. granulated garlic
- 1/2 tsp. celery seeds
- 1/2 tsp. parsley
- 1/2 tsp. granulated onion
- 2 tsp. olive oil
- 1/2 tsp. salt

Directions:
1. Coat the Air Fryer basket with cooking spray.
2. In a small bowl, mix the seasonings and sprinkle over the pork chops.
3. Place pork chops into the Air Fryer basket and cook at 350°F for 5 minutes. Turn the pork chops and cook for 8 minutes more.
4. Serve and enjoy.

Nutrition:
Calories: 278; Fat: 22.3 g; Carbohydrates: 0.4 g; Sugar: 0.1 g; Protein: 18.1 g; Cholesterol: 69 mg.

153. Asian Pork Chops

Preparation Time: 10 minutes
Cooking Time: 12 minutes
Servings: 2
Ingredients:
- 2 pork chops
- 1 tsp. black pepper
- 3 tbsp. lemongrass, chopped
- 1 tbsp. shallot, chopped
- 1 tbsp. garlic, chopped
- 1 tsp. liquid stevia
- 1 tbsp. sesame oil
- 1 tbsp. fish sauce
- 1 tsp. soy sauce

Directions:
1. In a mixing bowl, pour the ingredients over the pork chops and mix well. Place in refrigerator for 2 hours.
2. Preheat the Air Fryer to 400°F.
3. Place marinated pork chops into the Air Fryer basket and cook for 12 minutes. Turn pork chops after 7 minutes.
4. Serve and enjoy.

Nutrition:
Calories: 340; Fat: 26.8 g; Carbohydrates: 5.3 g; Sugar: 0.4 g; Protein: 19.3 g; Cholesterol: 69 mg.

154. Easy & Delicious Pork Chops

Preparation Time: 10 minutes
Cooking Time: 15 minutes
Servings: 4
Ingredients:
- 4 pork chops
- 2 tsp. parsley
- 2 tsp. garlic, grated
- 1/4 tsp. garlic powder
- 1/4 tsp. onion powder
- 1 tbsp. olive oil
- 1 tbsp. butter
- Pepper - Salt

Directions:
1. Preheat the Air Fryer to 350°F.
2. In a large bowl, mix seasonings, garlic, butter, and oil.
3. Add pork chops to the bowl and mix well. Place in refrigerator overnight.
4. Place the marinated pork chops into the Air Fryer basket and cook for 15 minutes. Turn them after 7 minutes.
5. Serve and enjoy.

Nutrition:
Calories: 315; Fat: 26.3 g; Carbohydrates: 0.8 g; Sugar: 0.1 g; Protein: 18.2 g; Cholesterol: 76 mg.

155. Dash Seasoned Pork Chops

Preparation Time: 10 minutes
Cooking Time: 20 minutes
Servings: 2
Ingredients:
- 2 pork chops, boneless
- 1 tbsp. dash seasoning
- Pepper

- Salt

Directions:
1. Coat the Air Fryer basket with cooking spray.
2. Rub seasoning all over the pork chops.
3. Place seasoned pork chops into the Air Fryer basket and cook at 360°F for 20 minutes. Turn halfway through.
4. Serve and enjoy.

Nutrition:
Calories: 256; Fat: 19.9 g; Carbohydrates: 0 g; Sugar: 0 g; Protein: 18 g; Cholesterol: 69 mg.

156. Easy Pork Butt

Preparation Time: 10 minutes
Cooking Time: 20 minutes
Servings: 4
Ingredients:
- 1 1/2 lb. pork butt, chopped into pieces
- 1/4 cup jerk paste

Directions:
1. Coat the Air Fryer basket with cooking spray.
2. Add meat and jerk paste into the bowl and coat well. Place in the refrigerator overnight.
3. Preheat the Air Fryer to 390°F.
4. Place the marinated meat into the Air Fryer basket and cook for 20 minutes. Turn halfway through.
5. Serve and enjoy.

Nutrition:
Calories: 339; Fat: 12.1 g; Carbohydrates: 0.8 g; Sugar: 0.6 g; Protein: 53 g; Cholesterol: 156 mg.

157. Sweet and Sour Pork

Preparation Time: 25 minutes
Cooking Time: 12 minutes
Servings: 4
Ingredients:
- 2 pounds pork cut into chunks
- 2 large eggs - 1 tsp. olive oil
- 1 cup cornstarch
- Salt and freshly ground black pepper to taste
- 1/4 tsp. Chinese spice
- Oil Mister

Directions:
1. Preheat the PowerXL Air Fryer Grill by selecting grill mode.
2. Adjust temperature to 350°F and time to 5 minutes.
3. Whisk egg and olive oil in a bowl.
4. Add breadcrumbs to another bowl.
5. Dip the pork in the egg mixture.
6. Then coat with the breadcrumb mixture.
7. Transfer it into the PowerXL Air Fryer Grill.
8. Grill for 12 minutes, flipping halfway.
9. Serve and enjoy!

Serving Suggestions: Serve with ketchup or tomato sauce.
Directions & Cooking Tips: Add spice to taste.
Nutrition:
Calories: 256; Fat: 7 g; Carbs: 10 g; Protein: 21 g.

158. Pork Ratatouille

Preparation Time: 20 minutes
Cooking Time: 55 minutes
Servings: 4
Ingredients:
- 4 pork sausages

For Ratatouille
- pepper, chopped
- 15 oz. tomatoes, chopped
- 2 zucchinis, chopped
- 1 red chili, chopped
- 1 eggplant, chopped
- 2 sprigs fresh thyme
- 1 medium red onion, chopped
- 1 tbsp. balsamic vinegar
- 2 garlic cloves, minced

Directions:
1. Preheat the PowerXL Air Fryer Grill by selecting pizza/bake mode.
2. Adjust temperature to 392°F and time to 10 minutes.
3. Combine zucchini, eggplant, onions, and oil in the cooking tray.
4. Transfer to the PowerXL Air Fryer Grill and bake for 20 minutes.
5. Remove and add the remaining Ratatouille Ingredients.
6. Transfer to the PowerXL Air Fryer Grill and cook for an additional 20 minutes.
7. Remove and season with salt and pepper.
8. Add the sausage to the Pizza tray.
9. Cook for 15 minutes flipping halfway.
10. Serve and enjoy.

Serving Suggestions: Serve the sausage with the Ratatouille.
Directions & Cooking Tips: The vegetable must be well cooked.
Nutrition:
Calories: 233; Fat: 11 g; Carbs: 4 g; Protein: 23 g.

159. Cheddar Pork Meatballs

The cheddar pork meatball is super delicious, succulent, and juicy. It is a creative way of putting your pork to good use.

Preparation Time: 25 minutes
Cooking Time: 15 minutes
Servings: 6
Ingredients:
- 1 lb. ground pork
- 1/2 tsp. maple syrup
- 1 large onion, chopped
- 2 tsp. mustard
- Salt and black pepper to taste
- 1/2 cup chopped basil leaves
- 2 tbsp. grated cheddar cheese

Directions:
1. Preheat the PowerXL Air Fryer Grill by selecting air fry mode.
2. Adjust temperature to 390°F and time to 5 minutes.
3. Combine all the ingredients in a bowl.

4. Form small balls.
5. Arrange them on the Air Fryer baking tray.
6. Transfer it into the PowerXL Air Fryer Grill.
7. Air fry for 10 minutes; flip, and cook for another 5 minutes.
8. Serve and enjoy!

Serving Suggestions: Serve with noodles and marinara sauce.
Directions & Cooking Tips: Use an ice-cream scooper to form the balls.
Nutrition:
Calories: 300; Fat: 24 g; Carbs: 3 g; Protein: 16 g.

160. Almond Pork Bite

Preparation Time: 25 minutes
Cooking Time: 20 minutes
Servings: 10
Ingredients:

- 16 oz. sausage meat
- 1 whole egg, beaten
- 1/3 cup chopped onion
- 2 tbsp. almonds, chopped
- 1/2 tsp. pepper
- 2 tbsp. dried sage
- 1/3 cup sliced apples, sliced
- 1/2 tsp. salt

Directions:
1. Preheat the PowerXL Air Fryer Grill by selecting grill mode.
2. Adjust temperature to 350°F and time to 5 minutes.
3. Combine all the ingredients in a bowl.
4. Pour into a Ziploc bag and marinate for 15 minutes.
5. Form cutlets.
6. Arrange them on the PowerXL Air Fryer Grill grilling plate.
7. Transfer them into the PowerXL Air Fryer Grill.
8. Grill for 20 minutes.
9. Serve and enjoy!

Serving Suggestions: Serve with heavy cream.
Directions & Cooking Tips: Drain the marinade.
Nutrition:
Calories: 391; Fat: 16 g; Carbs: 32 g; Protein: 19 g.

161. Stuffed Pork Chops

Stuffed pork chops are the perfect recipe for a house party, can be ready in less than an hour, and the taste is just wow!
Preparation Time: 30 minutes
Cooking Time: 20 minutes
Servings: 4
Ingredients:

- 8 pork chops
- 2 tbsp. olive
- 1/4 tsp. pepper
- 4 cups stuffing mix
- 1/2 tsp. salt
- 4 garlic cloves, minced
- 2 tbsp. sage leaves

Directions:
1. Preheat the PowerXL Air Fryer Grill by selecting Air Fryer mode.
2. Adjust temperature to 350°F and time to 5 minutes.
3. Cut a hole in the pork chops and fill it with stuffing mix.
4. In a bowl, combine the remaining ingredients.
5. Add the pork chops and leave them to marinate for 10 minutes.
6. Arrange the pork chops on the PowerXL Air Fryer Grill grilling plate.
7. Transfer them into the PowerXL Air Fryer Grill.
8. Air fry for 20 minutes.
9. Serve and enjoy!

Serving Suggestions: Serve with salad.
Directions & Cooking Tips: Drain the marinade.
Nutrition:
Calories: 300; Fat: 13 g; Carbs: 19 g; Protein: 21 g.

162. Crispy Breaded Pork

Crispy breaded pork is tender meat that's has a crispy outside and a juicy inside.
Preparation Time: 10 minutes
Cooking Time: 15 minutes
Servings: 6
Ingredients:

- 6 (3/4- inch thick) center-cut boneless pork chops
- olive oil spray
- 1-1/4 tsp. sweet paprika
- kosher salt
- 1/2 tsp. onion powder
- 1 large egg, beaten
- 1/2 cup panko crumbs
- 1/3 cup crushed cornflakes crumbs
- 1/4 tsp. chili powder
- 2 tbsp. grated parmesan cheese
- 1/2 tsp. garlic powder
- 1/8 tsp. black pepper

Directions:
1. Preheat the PowerXL Air Fryer Grill by selecting Air Fryer mode.
2. Adjust temperature to 390°F and time to 5 minutes.
3. Season the pork chops on both sides with salt.
4. In a bowl, combine the remaining ingredients except for the egg.
5. Beat the egg in another bowl.
6. Dip pork chops in eggs then in breadcrumb mixture.
7. Arrange the pork chops on the Air Fryer baking tray, sprinkle with oil.
8. Transfer them into the PowerXL Air Fryer Grill.
9. Air fry for 6 minutes per side.
10. Serve and enjoy!

Serving Suggestions: Serve with tomato sauce or ketchup.
Directions & Cooking Tips: You can dip the pork chops twice in the eggs and breadcrumb mixture.
Nutrition:
Calories: 281; Fat: 12 g; Carbs: 7 g; Protein: 31 g.

163. Lemongrass Pork Chops

This lemongrass is known for the aroma and flavor they add to foods. This is not different as it gives the meal a nice fragrance.

Preparation Time: 2 hours
Cooking Time: 20 minutes
Servings: 4
Ingredients:
- 3 pork chops
- 4 stalks lemongrass, trimmed and chopped
- 1-1/4 tsp. soy sauce
- 2 garlic cloves, minced
- 1-1/2 tbsp. sugar
- 2 shallots, chopped
- 2 tbsp. olive oil
- 1-1/4 tsp. fish sauce
- 1-1/2 tsp. black pepper

Directions:
1. Combine all the ingredients in a bowl.
2. Add the pork chops and allow to marinate for 2 hours.
3. Preheat the PowerXL Air Fryer Grill by selecting Grill/air fry mode.
4. Adjust temperature to 390°F and time to 5 minutes.
5. Remove the pork chops and arrange them on the grilling plate.
6. Transfer them into the PowerXL Air Fryer Grill
7. Air fry for 6 minutes, flip and air fry for additional 7 minutes.
8. Serve and enjoy!

Serving Suggestions: Serve with sautéed asparagus.
Directions & Cooking Tips: Marinate for at least 2 hours to get a nice savory taste.
Nutrition:
Calories: 342; Fat: 10 g; Carbs: 4 g; Protein: 30 g.

164. BBQ Pork Ribs

Preparing the BBQ pork Rib with the PowerXL Air Fryer Grill produces a tender and juicy pork meat. The recipe can be prepared for a small outdoor gathering.

Preparation Time: 5 hours
Cooking Time: 25 minutes
Servings: 3
Ingredients:
- 1 lb. pork ribs, cut into smaller pieces
- 1 tsp. soy sauce
- 1 tsp. sesame oil
- 1 tsp. oregano
- 1 tbsp. Plus 1 tbsp. maple syrup
- 3 tbsp. barbecue sauce
- Salt and black pepper to taste
- 2 cloves garlic, minced
- 1 tbsp. cayenne pepper

Directions:
1. Combine all the ingredients in a bowl.
2. Add the pork chops allow to marinate for 5 hours.
3. Preheat the PowerXL Air Fryer Grill by selecting Grill/air fry mode.
4. Adjust temperature to 390°F and time to 5 minutes.
5. Remove the pork chops and arrange them on the grilling plate.
6. Transfer them into the PowerXL Air Fryer Grill.
7. Air fry for 15 minutes, flip, and brush with the remaining tablespoon of maple syrup.
8. Air fry for another 10 minutes.
9. Serve and enjoy!

Serving Suggestions: Serve with maple syrup.
Directions & Cooking Tips: Drain the marinade.
Nutrition:
Calories: 346; Fat: 11 g; Carbs: 5 g; Protein: 22 g.

165. Spicy Pork Chops

Preparation Time: 10 minutes
Cooking Time: 10 minutes
Servings: 4
Ingredients:
- 4 pork chops
- 1 1/2 tsp. olive oil
- 1/2 tsp. dried sage
- 1/4 tsp. chili powder
- 1/2 tsp. cayenne pepper
- 1/2 tsp. black pepper
- 1/2 tsp. ground cumin
- 1 tsp. paprika
- 1/2 tsp. garlic salt

Directions:
1. Preheat the Air Fryer to 400°F.
2. In a small bowl, mix paprika, garlic salt, sage, pepper, chili powder, cayenne pepper, and cumin.
3. Rub pork chops with spice mixture and place them into the Air Fryer basket. Coat pork chops from the top with cooking spray.
4. Cook for 10 minutes. Turn halfway through.

Nutrition:
Calories: 277; Fat: 21.9 g; Carbohydrates: 1.1 g; Sugar: 0.2 g; Protein: 18.3 g; Cholesterol: 69 mg.

166. Easy Pork Patties

Preparation Time: 10 minutes
Cooking Time: 35 minutes
Servings: 6
Ingredients:
- 2 lb. ground pork
- 1/2 cup almond flour
- 1 egg, lightly beaten
- 1 onion, minced
- 1 carrot, minced
- 1 tsp. garlic powder
- 1 tsp. paprika

Directions:
1. Add all ingredients into the large bowl and mix until well combined.
2. Make small patties from the meat mixture and place them into the Air Fryer basket and cook at 375°F for 20 minutes.

3. Turn pork patties and cook for 15 minutes more.

Nutrition:
Calories: 254; Fat: 7.3 g; Carbohydrates: 3.8 g; Sugar: 1.6 g; Protein: 41.4 g; Cholesterol: 138 mg.

167. Lemon Pepper Seasoned Pork Chops

Preparation Time: 10 minutes
Cooking Time: 15 minutes
Servings: 4
Ingredients:
- 4 pork chops, boneless
- 1 tsp. lemon-pepper seasoning
- Salt

Directions:
1. Season pork chops with lemon pepper seasoning, and salt.
2. Place pork chops into the Air Fryer basket and cook at 400°F for 15 minutes.

Nutrition:
Calories: 257; Fat: 19.9 g; Carbohydrates: 0.3 g; Sugar: 0 g; Protein: 18 g; Cholesterol: 69 mg.

168. Flavorful Pork Chops

Preparation Time: 10 minutes
Cooking Time: 16 minutes
Servings: 4
Ingredients:
- 4 pork chops, boneless
- 2 tsp. olive oil
- 1/2 tsp. celery seed
- 1/2 tsp. parsley
- 1/2 tsp. onion powder
- 1/2 tsp. garlic powder
- 1/2 tsp. salt

Directions:
1. Brush pork chops with olive oil.
2. Mix celery seed, parsley, onion powder, garlic powder, and salt and sprinkle over pork chops.
3. Place pork chops into the Air Fryer basket and cook at 350°F for 16 minutes. Turn pork chops halfway through.

Nutrition:
Calories: 279; Fat: 22.3 g; Carbohydrates: 0.6 g; Sugar: 0.2 g; Protein: 18.1 g; Cholesterol: 69 mg.

169. Pesto Pork Chops

Preparation Time: 10 minutes
Cooking Time: 18 minutes
Servings: 5
Ingredients:
- 5 pork chops
- 1 tbsp. basil pesto
- 2 tbsp. almond flour
- Pepper
- Salt

Directions:
1. Coat pork chops with cooking spray.
2. Rub basil pesto on top of pork chops and coat with almond flour.
3. Place pork chops into the Air Fryer basket and cook at 350°F for 18 minutes.
4. Serve and enjoy.

Nutrition:
Calories: 320; Fat: 25.5 g; Carbohydrates: 2.4 g; Sugar: 0.4 g; Protein: 20.4 g; Cholesterol: 69 mg.

170. Coconut Butter Pork Chops

Preparation Time: 10 minutes
Cooking Time: 15 minutes
Servings: 2
Ingredients:
- 4 pork chops
- 1 tbsp. coconut oil
- 1 tbsp. coconut butter
- 2 tsp. parsley
- 2 tsp. garlic, grated
- Pepper
- Salt

Directions:
1. Preheat the Air Fryer to 350°F.
2. In a large bowl, mix garlic, butter, coconut oil, parsley, pepper, and salt.
3. Rub garlic mixture over the pork chops. Wrap marinated pork chops into the foil and place them in the refrigerator for 1 hour.
4. Remove pork chops from foil and place them into the Air Fryer basket and cook for 15 minutes. Turn pork chops after 7 minutes.
5. Serve and enjoy.

Nutrition:
Calories: 686; Fat: 57.1 g; Carbohydrates: 5 g; Sugar: 1 g; Protein: 37.2 g; Cholesterol: 138 mg.

171. Crispy Pork Chops

Preparation Time: 10 minutes
Cooking Time: 20 minutes
Servings: 4
Ingredients:
- 4 pork chops, boneless
- 2 eggs, lightly beaten
- 1 cup almond flour
- 1/4 cup parmesan cheese, grated
- 1 tbsp. onion powder
- 1 tbsp. garlic powder
- 1/2 tbsp. black pepper
- 1/2 tsp. sea salt

Directions:
1. Coat the Air Fryer basket with cooking spray. Preheat the Air Fryer to 350°F.
2. In a shallow bowl, mix almond flour, parmesan cheese, onion powder, garlic powder, pepper, and salt.
3. Whisk eggs in a shallow dish.
4. Dip pork chops into the egg; then coat with almond flour mixture.

5. Place coated pork chops into the Air Fryer basket and cook for 20 minutes. Turn pork chops halfway through.
6. Serve and enjoy.

Nutrition:
Calories: 363; Fat: 27 g; Carbohydrates: 5.3 g; Sugar: 1.6 g; Protein: 24.9 g; Cholesterol: 155 mg.

172. BBQ Lamb

Preparation Time: 90 minutes
Cooking Time: 15 minutes
Servings: 8
Ingredients:
- 4 lb. boneless leg of lamb, cut into 2-inch chunks
- 2-1/2 tbsp. herb salt
- 2 tbsp. olive oil

Directions:
1. Preheat the PowerXL Air Fryer Grill by selecting Air Fryer mode.
2. Adjust the temperature to 390°F; set time to 5 minutes.
3. Season the meat with salt and olive oil.
4. Arrange it on the Air Fryer baking tray.
5. Transfer it to the PowerXL Air Fryer Grill.
6. Air fry for 15 minutes, flipping halfway through.
7. Serve and enjoy.

Serving Suggestions: Serve with marinara sauce.
Directions & Cooking Tips: Work in batches.
Nutrition:
Calories: 341; Fat: 16 g; Carbs: 1 g; Protein: 26 g.

173. Lamb Meatballs

Preparation Time: 15 minutes
Cooking Time: 15 minutes
Servings: 12
Ingredients:
- 1 lb. ground lamb
- 1/2 cup breadcrumbs
- 1 lemon, juiced and zested
- 1/4 cup milk
- 2 egg yolks
- 1 tsp. ground cumin
- 1 tsp. dried oregano
- 1/2 tsp. salt
- 1 tsp. ground coriander
- 1/2 tsp. black pepper
- 3 garlic cloves, minced
- 1/4 cup fresh parsley, chopped
- 1/2 cup crumbled feta cheese

Directions:
1. Preheat the PowerXL Air Fryer Grill by selecting Broil mode.
2. Adjust the temperature to 390°F, set time to 5 minutes.
3. Combine all the ingredients in a bowl.
4. Form 12 balls.
5. Arrange them on the Air Fryer baking tray.
6. Transfer them to the PowerXL Air Fryer Grill.
7. Cook for 12 minutes.
8. Serve and enjoy.

Serving Suggestions: Serve with tzatziki sauce.
Directions & Cooking Tips: Rub olive oil on your hand when forming the meatballs.
Nutrition:
Calories: 129; Fat: 6.4 g; Carbs: 4.9 g; Protein: 25 g.

174. Glazed Lamb Chops

Preparation Time: 30 minutes
Cooking Time: 15 minutes
Servings: 4
Ingredients:
- 4 (4-ounce) lamb loin chops
- 1 tbsp. Dijon mustard
- 1 tsp. honey
- 1/2 tbsp. fresh lime juice
- 1/2 tsp. olive oil
- Salt and ground black pepper, as required

Directions:
1. Preheat the PowerXL Air Fryer Grill by selecting Air Fryer mode.
2. Adjust the temperature to 390°F, set time to 5 minutes.
3. Combine all the ingredients in a bowl.
4. Add the chops and toss to coat.
5. Arrange them on the Air Fryer baking tray.
6. Transfer them to the PowerXL Air Fryer Grill.
7. Air fry for 15 minutes, flipping halfway through.
8. Serve and enjoy.

Serving Suggestions: Serve while still hot.
Directions & Cooking Tips: Leave to marinate for a few minutes.
Nutrition:
Calories: 224; Fat: 4 g; Carbs: 2 g; Protein: 19 g.

175. Garlic Lamb Shank

Preparation Time: 15 minutes
Cooking Time: 24 minutes
Servings: 4
Ingredients:
- 17 oz. lamb shanks
- 2 tbsp. garlic, peeled and coarsely chopped
- 1 tsp. kosher salt
- 1/2 cup chicken stock
- 1 tbsp. dried parsley
- 1 tsp. dried rosemary
- 4 oz. chive stems, chopped
- 1 tsp. butter
- 1 tsp. nutmeg
- 1/2 tsp. ground black pepper

Directions:
1. Make the cuts in the lamb shank and fill the cuts with the chopped garlic.
2. Sprinkle the lamb shank with kosher salt, dried parsley, dried rosemary, nutmeg, and ground black pepper.
3. Stir the spices on the lamb shank gently.
4. Preheat the PowerXL Air Fryer Grill by selecting air fry mode.
5. Adjust the temperature to 380°F; set time to 5 minutes.

6. Put the butter, chives, and chicken stock in the Air Fryer baking tray.
7. Add the lamb shank and air fry the meat for 24 minutes.
8. Serve and enjoy.

Serving Suggestions: Serve with the cooking liquid.
Directions & Cooking Tips: Add spices to taste.
Nutrition:
Calories: 205; Fat: 8.2 g; Carbs: 3 g; Protein: 28 g.

176. Indian Meatball with Lamb
Preparation Time: 10 minutes
Cooking Time: 14 minutes
Servings: 8
Ingredients:
- 1 lb. ground lamb
- 1 garlic clove, minced
- 1 egg
- 1 tbsp. butter
- 4 oz. chive stems, grated
- 1/4 tbsp. turmeric
- 1/3 tsp. cayenne pepper
- 1/4 tsp. bay leaf
- 1 tsp. ground coriander
- 1 tsp. salt
- 1 tsp. ground black pepper

Directions:
1. Combine all the ingredients in a bowl.
2. Preheat the PowerXL Air Fryer by selecting the air fry mode.
3. Adjust the temperature to 390°F and time to 5 minutes.
4. Put the butter in the Air Fryer baking tray and melt it.
5. Form the meatballs.
6. Place them in the Air Fryer baking tray.
7. Transfer them to the PowerXL Air Fryer Grill.
8. Cook the dish for 14 minutes.
9. Stir the meatballs twice during the cooking.

Serving Suggestions: Serve with salad and sauce.
Directions & Cooking Tips: Use an ice-cream scooper to form the balls.
Nutrition:
Calories: 300; Fat: 13 g; Carbs: 19 g; Protein: 21 g.

177. Roasted Lamb
Preparation Time: 60 minutes
Cooking Time: 1 hour 30 minutes
Servings: 4
Ingredients:
- 2-1/2 pounds lamb leg roast, slits carved
- 1 tbsp. olive oil
- 2 garlic cloves, sliced into smaller slithers
- 1 tbsp. dried rosemary
- Cracked Himalayan rock salt and cracked peppercorns, to taste

Directions:
1. Make the cuts in the lamb roast and insert them with garlic.
2. Sprinkle the lamb roast with kosher salt, rosemary, and ground black pepper.
3. Brush with oil.
4. Preheat the PowerXL Air Fryer Grill by selecting air fry mode.
5. Adjust the temperature to 380°F; set the timer to 5 minutes.
6. Place the lamb roast on the baking pan.
7. Transfer it to the PowerXL Air Fryer Grill.
8. Air fry for 1 hour 15 minutes.
9. Serve and enjoy.

Serving Suggestions: Serve with mushroom sauce.
Directions & Cooking Tips: Leave to marinate for some minutes.
Nutrition:
Calories: 246; Fat: 7 g; Carbs: 9 g; Protein: 33 g.

178. Lamb Gyro
Preparation Time: 20 minutes
Cooking Time: 20 minutes
Servings: 4
Ingredients:
- 1-pound ground lamb
- 1/2 onion sliced
- 1/4 cup mint, minced
- 1/4 red onion, minced
- 1/8 tsp. rosemary
- 1/2 tsp. salt
- 1/2 tsp. black pepper
- 3/4 cup hummus
- 4 slices pita bread
- 1/2 cucumber, peeled and sliced into thin rounds
- 1 cup romaine lettuce, shredded
- 1 Roma tomato, diced
- 1/4 cup parsley, minced
- 2 cloves garlic, minced
- 12 mint leaves, minced

Directions:
1. Preheat the PowerXL Air Fryer Grill by selecting broil mode.
2. Adjust the temperature to 370°F; set time to 5 minutes.
3. Mix lamb with onions, mint, parsley, garlic, salt, rosemary, and pepper.
4. Form into patties.
5. Arrange them in a lined Air Fryer baking tray.
6. Transfer them to the PowerXL Air Fryer Grill.
7. Air fry for 20 minutes, flipping halfway through.
8. Assemble the gyro with the remaining ingredients.
9. Serve and enjoy.

Serving Suggestions: Serve drizzled with tzatziki sauce.
Directions & Cooking Tips: Mix until well incorporated.
Nutrition:
Calories: 309; Fat: 14.6 g; Carbs: 29 g; Protein: 19 g.

179. Lemon Lamb Rack
Preparation Time: 30 minutes
Cooking Time: 30 minutes
Servings: 4
Ingredients:
- 1/4 cup olive oil

- 3 tbsp. garlic, minced
- 1/3 cup dry white wine
- 1 tbsp. lemon zest, grated
- 2 tbsp. lemon juice
- 1-1/2 tsp. dried oregano, crushed
- 1 tsp. thyme leaves, minced
- Salt and black pepper
- 4 lamb rack
- 1 lemon, sliced

Directions:
1. Preheat the PowerXL Air Fryer Grill by selecting Air Fryer mode.
2. Adjust the temperature to 370°F; set time to 5 minutes.
3. Whisk all the ingredients together in a bowl.
4. Pour into the Air Fryer baking tray.
5. Add the lamb rack.
6. Top with lemon.
7. Transfer it to the PowerXL Air Fryer Grill.
8. Air fry for 30 minutes, flipping halfway through.
9. Serve and enjoy.

Serving Suggestions: Serve with the juice.
Directions & Cooking Tips: Leave to marinate for a few minutes.
Nutrition:
Calories: 288; Fat: 7 g; Carbs: 5 g; Protein: 16 g.

180. Juicy & Savory Lamb Chops

Preparation Time: 10 minutes
Cooking Time: 10 minutes
Servings: 1
Ingredients:
- 1/3 lb. lamb chop
- 1 tbsp. mixed fresh herbs, chopped
- 1/2 tbsp. olive oil
- 1/2 tbsp. Dijon mustard
- Pepper
- Salt

Directions:
1. Season lamb chop with pepper and salt.
2. In a small bowl, mix oil, mustard, and mixed herbs.
3. Brush the lamb chop from both sides with the oil mixture.
4. Place the lamb chop into the Air Fryer basket and cook at 375°F for 10 minutes. Turn halfway through.

Nutrition:
Calories: 350; Fat: 18.5 g; Carbohydrates: 1.2 g; Sugar: 0.1 g; Protein: 43 g; Cholesterol: 136 mg.

181. Lamb Patties

Preparation Time: 10 minutes
Cooking Time: 30 minutes
Servings: 4
Ingredients:
- 1 lb. ground lamb meat
- 1 egg, lightly beaten
- 1/2 tbsp. garlic, minced
- 1 spring onion, chopped
- 1/4 cup almond flour
- 1 tbsp. basil, chopped
- 1 tbsp. cilantro, chopped
- Pepper
- Salt

Directions:
1. Coat the Air Fryer basket with cooking spray.
2. Add all ingredients into the bowl and mix until well combined.
3. Make small patties from the meat mixture and place them into the Air Fryer basket. Cook at 390°F for 30 minutes. Turn patties halfway through.
4. Serve and enjoy.

Nutrition:
Calories: 260; Fat: 17 g; Carbohydrates: 1.1 g; Sugar: 0.2 g; Protein: 23 g; Cholesterol: 121 mg.

182. Dijon Garlic Lamb Chops

Preparation Time: 10 minutes
Cooking Time: 17 minutes
Servings: 4
Ingredients:
- 8 lamb chops
- 1 tsp. cayenne pepper
- 1 tsp. cumin powder
- 1 tsp. garlic, minced
- 1 tsp. soy sauce - 2 tsp. olive oil
- 2 tsp. Dijon mustard
- 1/4 tsp. salt

Directions:
1. Add lamb chops and remaining ingredients into the zip-lock bag. Seal the bag, shake well, and place it in the refrigerator for 30 minutes.
2. Place the marinated lamb chops into the Air Fryer basket and cook at 350°F for 17 minutes. Turn lamb chops halfway through.
3. Serve and enjoy.

Nutrition:
Calories: 445; Fat: 19.1 g; Carbohydrates: 0.9 g; Sugar: 0.1 g; Protein: 63.6 g; Cholesterol: 203 mg.

183. Flavorful Cumin Lamb

Preparation Time: 10 minutes
Cooking Time: 10 minutes
Servings: 4
Ingredients:
- 1 lb. lamb, cut into 1/2-inch pieces
- 1/4 tsp. Swerve
- 12 red chili peppers, chopped
- 1 tbsp. garlic, minced
- 1 tbsp. soy sauce
- 2 tbsp. olive oil
- 1/2 tsp. cayenne
- 1 1/2 tbsp. ground cumin
- 1 tsp. kosher salt

Directions:
1. Add lamb pieces and remaining ingredients into the zip-lock bag. Seal the bag, shake well, and place it in the refrigerator for 30 minutes.
2. Place the marinated lamb pieces into the Air Fryer basket and cook at 360°F for 10 minutes. Shake basket halfway through.
3. Serve and enjoy.

Nutrition:
Calories: 291; Fat: 16 g; Carbohydrates: 3.3 g; Sugar: 0.8 g; Protein: 32.8 g; Cholesterol: 102 mg.

184. Juicy & Tender Lemon Mustard Lamb Chops

Preparation Time: 10 minutes
Cooking Time: 15 minutes
Servings: 4
Ingredients:
- 8 lamb chops
- 1 tbsp. fresh lemon juice
- 1 tsp. tarragon
- 1/2 tsp. olive oil
- 2 tbsp. mustard
- Pepper
- Salt

Directions:
1. Preheat the Air Fryer to 390°F.
2. In a small bowl, mix lemon juice, tarragon, oil, mustard, pepper, and salt.
3. Brush the lamb chops from both sides with the lemon juice mixture.
4. Place the lamb chops into the Air Fryer basket and cook for 15 minutes. Turn halfway through. Serve and enjoy.

Nutrition:
Calories: 451; Fat: 18.7 g; Carbohydrates: 2.1 g; Sugar: 0.5 g; Protein: 64.6 g, Cholesterol: 203 mg.

185. Lamb Balls

Preparation Time: 10 minutes
Cooking Time: 12 minutes
Servings: 6
Ingredients:
- 1 lb. ground lamb
- 1 lemon juice
- 1 tbsp. dried dill
- 1 tbsp. dried rosemary
- 1 egg, lightly beaten
- 1 lb. ground beef
- Pepper
- Salt

Directions:
1. Coat the Air Fryer basket with cooking spray.
2. Add all ingredients into a bowl and mix until well combined.
3. Make 1-inch balls from the mixture and place them into the Air Fryer basket. Cook at 350°F for 7 minutes.
4. Shake the basket and cook for 5 minutes more.
5. Serve and enjoy.

Nutrition:
Calories: 297; Fat: 11.1 g; Carbohydrates: 0.9 g; Sugar: 0.2 g; Protein: 45.3 g; Cholesterol: 163 mg.

186. Spicy Lamb Steak

Preparation Time: 10 minutes
Cooking Time: 15 minutes
Servings: 4
Ingredients:
- 1 lb. lamb sirloin steaks, boneless
- 1 tsp. cayenne pepper
- 1/2 tsp. ground cardamom
- 1 tsp. ground cinnamon
- 1 tsp. ground fennel
- 1 tsp. garam masala
- 4 garlic cloves
- 1 tbsp. ginger
- 1/2 onion
- 1 tsp. kosher salt

Directions:
1. Add all ingredients except lamb steaks into the blender and blend until a smooth paste is formed.
2. Add lamb steaks and blended paste into a bowl and mix well. Place it in the refrigerator for 30 minutes.
3. Coat the Air Fryer basket with cooking spray.
4. Place the marinated lamb steaks into the Air Fryer basket and cook at 330°F for 15 minutes. Turn halfway through.
5. Serve and enjoy.

Nutrition:
Calories: 76; Fat: 2.3 g; Carbohydrates: 4.6 g; Sugar: 0.7 g; Protein: 9.7 g; Cholesterol: 0 mg.

187. Easy Greek Lamb Chops

Preparation Time: 10 minutes
Cooking Time: 10 minutes
Servings: 4
Ingredients:
- 2 lb. lamb chops
- 2 tsp. garlic, minced
- 2 tsp. dried oregano
- 1/4 cup fresh lemon juice
- 1/4 cup olive oil
- Pepper
- Salt

Directions:
1. In a bowl, mix lemon juice, oil, oregano, garlic, pepper, and salt. Add lamb chops to the bowl and coat well.
2. Add lamb chops into the Air Fryer basket and cook at 400°F for 10 minutes. Turn halfway through.
3. Serve and enjoy.

Nutrition:
Calories: 538; Fat: 29.4 g; Carbohydrates: 1.3 g; Sugar: 0.4 g; Protein: 64 g; Cholesterol: 204 mg.

188. Delicious Za'atar Lamb Chops

Preparation Time: 10 minutes
Cooking Time: 10 minutes
Servings: 4
Ingredients:
- 8 lamb chops, trimmed
- 1 tbsp. za'atar
- 1/2 lemon
- 1 tsp. olive oil
- 2 garlic cloves, crushed
- Pepper
- Salt

Directions:
1. Preheat the Air Fryer to 400°F.
2. Rub lamb chops with garlic and oil.
3. Squeeze lemon juice over lamb chops and season with za'atar, pepper, and salt.
4. Place the lamb chops into the Air Fryer basket and cook for 10 minutes. Turn halfway through.
5. Serve and enjoy.

Nutrition:
Calories: 435; Fat: 17.9 g; Carbohydrates: 1.2 g; Sugar: 0.2 g; Protein: 63.4 g; Cholesterol: 203 mg.

189. Quick & Easy Lamb Chops

Preparation Time: 10 minutes
Cooking Time: 5 minutes
Servings: 2
Ingredients:
- 4 lamb chops
- 1/2 tbsp. fresh oregano, chopped
- 1 1/2 tbsp. olive oil
- 1 garlic clove, minced
- Pepper
- Salt

Directions:
1. Preheat the Air Fryer to 400°F.
2. Mix garlic, olive oil, oregano, pepper, and salt; rub all over lamb chops.
3. Place the lamb chops into the Air Fryer basket and cook for 5 minutes.
4. Serve and enjoy.

Nutrition:
Calories: 514; Fat: 27.1 g; Carbohydrates: 1.3 g; Sugar: 0.1 g; Protein: 63.4 g; Cholesterol: 203 mg.

190. Dried Herb Lamb Chops

Preparation Time: 10 minutes
Cooking Time: 8 minutes
Servings: 4
Ingredients:
- 1 lb. lamb chops
- 1 tsp. oregano
- 1 tsp. thyme
- 1 tsp. rosemary
- 2 tbsp. fresh lemon juice
- 2 tbsp. olive oil
- 1 tsp. coriander
- 1 tsp. salt

Directions:
1. Add all ingredients into the zip-lock bag. Then, add the lamb chops.
2. Seal the bag, shake well and place it in the fridge overnight.
3. Place the marinated lamb chops into the Air Fryer basket and cook at 390°F for 8 minutes. Turn lamb chops halfway through.
4. Serve and enjoy.

Nutrition:
Calories: 276; Fat: 15.5 g; Carbohydrates: 0.8 g; Sugar: 0.2 g; Protein: 32 g; Cholesterol: 102 mg.

191. Moist Lamb Roast

Preparation Time: 10 minutes
Cooking Time: 1 hour 30 minutes
Servings: 4
Ingredients:
- 2.75 lb. lamb leg roast, make slits on top of the meat
- 2 garlic cloves, sliced
- 1 tbsp. olive oil
- 1 tbsp. dried rosemary
- Pepper
- Salt

Directions:
1. Stuff sliced garlic into the slits of lamb. Season with pepper and salt.
2. Mix oil and rosemary; rub all over the meat.
3. Place the meat into the Air Fryer basket and cook at 400°F for 15 minutes.
4. Turn temperature to 320°F for 1 hour 15 minutes.
5. Serve and enjoy.

Nutrition:
Calories: 670; Fat: 45 g; Carbohydrates: 1.1 g; Sugar: 0 g; Protein: 58.1 g; Cholesterol: 221 mg.

192. Thyme Lamb Chops

Preparation Time: 10 minutes
Cooking Time: 12 minutes
Servings: 4
Ingredients:
- 4 lamb chops - 3 tbsp. olive oil
- 1 tbsp. dried thyme
- 3 garlic cloves, minced
- Pepper _ Salt

Directions:
1. Preheat the Air Fryer to 390°F.
2. In a small bowl, mix thyme, oil, and garlic.
3. Season the lamb chops with pepper and salt and rub with thyme oil mixture.
4. Place the chops into the Air Fryer basket and cook for 12 minutes. Turn halfway through.
5. Serve and enjoy.

Nutrition:
Calories: 305; Fat: 18.8 g; Carbohydrates: 1.2 g; Sugar: 0 g; Protein: 31.8 g; Cholesterol: 101 mg.

193. Baked Lamb Chops

Preparation Time: 10 minutes
Cooking Time: 30 minutes
Servings: 4
Ingredients:

- 4 lamb chops
- 1 1/2 tsp. tarragon
- 1 1/2 tsp. ginger
- 1 tsp. garlic powder
- 1 tsp. ground cinnamon
- Pepper
- Salt

Directions:

1. Add garlic powder, cinnamon, tarragon, ginger, pepper, and salt into the zip-lock bag and mix well. Then add lamb chops to the bag.
2. Seal the bag, shake well, and place it in the fridge for 2 hours.
3. Place the marinated lamb chops into the Air Fryer basket and cook at 375°F for 20 minutes.
4. Turn the lamb chops and cook for 10 minutes more.
5. Serve and enjoy.

Nutrition:
Calories: 216; Fat: 8.3 g; Carbohydrates: 1.6 g; Sugar: 0.2 g; Protein: 31.8 g; Cholesterol: 101 mg.

194. Meatballs

Preparation Time: 10 minutes
Cooking Time: 15 minutes
Servings: 4
Ingredients:

- 1 lb. ground lamb
- 1 tsp. onion powder
- 1 tbsp. garlic, minced
- 1 tsp. ground coriander
- 1 tsp. ground cumin
- Pepper
- Salt

Directions:

1. Add all ingredients into the large bowl and mix until well combined.
2. Make meatballs from the mixture, place them into the Air Fryer basket, and cook at 400°F for 15 minutes.
3. Serve and enjoy.

Nutrition:
Calories: 218; Fat: 8.5 g; Carbohydrates: 1.4 g; Sugar: 0.2 g; Protein: 32.1 g; Cholesterol: 102 mg.

195. Rosemary Roasted Leg of Lamb

Preparation Time: 30 minutes
Cooking Time: 90 minutes
Servings: 6–8
Ingredients:

- 5–6 lb. boneless leg of lamb
- 2 tbsp. olive oil
- 5–6 cloves garlic, peeled and minced
- 2 tbsp. minced rosemary leaves
- 1 tbsp. kosher salt
- Freshly ground black pepper

Directions:

1. Preheat the PowerXL Air Fryer Grill to 190°C/ 375°F. Graze the lamb with olive oil.
2. Pat all the ingredients on the lamb and put it in the baking pan.
3. Cook for 90 minutes and check if the internal temperature has reached 125°C/ 250°F for rare and 135°C/ 275°F for medium-rare.
4. Remove it from the PowerXL Air Fryer Grill, and wrap it with aluminum foil.

Nutrition:
Calories: 136; Carbs: 0.3 g; Protein: 23 g; Fat: 1.4 g.

CHAPTER 3:
Poultry Recipes

196. Air Fried Whole Chicken

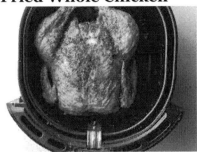

Preparation Time: 10 minutes
Cooking Time: 25 minutes
Servings: 10
Ingredients:
- 1 Whole chicken
- 1 tbsp. oil
- 1 tsp. garlic powder
- 1 tsp. onion powder
- 1 tsp. paprika
- 1 tsp. Italian seasoning
- Salt or pepper to taste
- 1-1/2 cup chicken broth

Directions:
1. Truss and wash up the chicken.
2. Preheat the PowerXL Air Fryer Grill by selecting Air fry/grill mode.
3. Adjust the temperature to 390°F; set time to 5 minutes.
4. Mix the season and rub the chicken with half of it.
5. Place the chicken in the baking tray and add the broth.
6. Transfer to the PowerXL Air Fryer Grill.
7. Air fry for 25 minutes.
8. Flip the chicken and rub it with the remaining seasoning.
9. Air fry for another 10 minutes. Enjoy.

Serving Suggestions: Enjoy with salad.
Directions & Cooking Tips: The juice can be used to prepare the sauce.
Nutrition:
Calories: 431; Fat: 26 g; Carbs: 3 g; Protein: 42 g.

197. Air Roasted Turkey

Preparation Time: 10 minutes
Cooking Time: 40 minutes
Servings: 6
Ingredients:
- 2-3/4 pounds turkey breast
- 2 tbsp. unsalted butter
- 1 tbsp. chopped fresh rosemary
- 1 tsp. chopped fresh chives
- 1 tsp. minced fresh garlic
- 1/4 tsp. black pepper
- 1/2 tsp. salt

Directions:
1. Preheat your Air Fryer toast oven to 350°F.
2. In a bowl, mix chives, rosemary, garlic, salt, and pepper until well combined. Add in butter and mash until well blended.
3. Rub the turkey breast with the herbed butter and then add to the Air Fryer toast oven basket; air roast for 20 minutes.
4. Turn the turkey breast and air roast for another 20 minutes.
5. Transfer the cooked turkey onto an aluminum foil and wrap; let rest for at least 10 minutes and then slice it up. Serve warm.

Nutrition:
Calories: 263; Carbs: 0.3 g; Fat: 10.1 g; Protein: 40.2 g.

198. Spanish Chicken Bake

Preparation Time: 10 minutes
Cooking Time: 25 minutes
Servings: 4
Ingredients:

- 4 chicken thighs, boneless
- 1/2 onion, quartered
- 1/8 cup chorizo
- 1/2 red onion, quartered
- 1/2 lb. potatoes, quartered
- 4 garlic cloves
- 1/4 tsp. dried oregano
- 4 tomatoes, quartered
- 1/4 tsp. paprika powder
- 1/2 green bell pepper, julienned
- Salt and black pepper

Directions:
1. Preheat the PowerXL Air Fryer Grill by selecting Pizza/Bake mode.
2. Adjust the temperature to 390°F; set time to 5 minutes.
3. Combine all the ingredients.
4. Pour into the Air Fryer baking tray.
5. Transfer to the PowerXL Air Fryer Grill.
6. Bake for 25 minutes.
7. Enjoy

Serving Suggestions: Serve with rice and salad.
Directions & Cooking Tips: Season the chicken.
Nutrition:
Calories: 290; Fat: 7 g; Carbs: 19 g; Protein: 12 g.

199. Barbeque Air Fried Chicken

Preparation Time: 10 minutes
Cooking Time: 20 minutes
Servings: 10
Ingredients:

- 2 lb. chicken
- 1 tsp. liquid smoke
- 2 cloves Fresh garlic smashed
- 1/2 cup apple cider vinegar
- 1 Tbsp. Kosher salt
- 1 Tbsp. freshly ground black pepper
- 2 tsp. garlic powder
- 1.5 cups barbecue sauce
- 1/4 cup light brown sugar + more for sprinkling

Directions:
1. Combine all the ingredients.
2. Add the meat and leave to marinate for some minutes.
3. Preheat the PowerXL Air Fryer Grill by selecting Air fry mode.
4. Adjust the temperature to 390°F; set time to 5 minutes.
5. Pour into the Air Fryer baking tray.
6. Transfer to the PowerXL Air Fryer Grill.
7. Air fry for 20 minutes, flip halfway done.
8. Enjoy.

Serving Suggestions: Serve with the juice.
Directions & Cooking Tips: Leave to marinate for some minutes.
Nutrition:
Calories: 360; Fat: 16 g; Carbs: 17 g; Protein: 27 g.

200. Saucy Chicken with Leeks

Preparation Time: 10 minutes
Cooking Time: 18 minutes
Servings: 10
Ingredients:

- 6 chicken legs, boneless and skinless
- 2 leeks sliced
- 1/2 tsp. smoked cayenne pepper
- 2 tbsp. olive oil
- 2 large-sized tomatoes, chopped
- 1/2 tsp. dried oregano
- 3 cloves garlic, minced
- A dash ground nutmeg

Directions:
1. Combine all the ingredients.
2. Add the meat and leave to marinate for some minutes.
3. Preheat the PowerXL Air Fryer Grill by selecting Air fry mode.
4. Adjust the temperature to 390F; set time to 5 minutes.
5. Arrange the leeks on the PowerXL grill baking tray.
6. Add the chicken on top.
7. Transfer it to the PowerXL Air Fryer Grill.
8. Air fry for 18 minutes, flip halfway done.
9. Enjoy.

Serving Suggestions: Serve with hoisin sauce.
Directions & Cooking Tips: For tastier meat, leave to marinate overnight.
Nutrition:
Calories: 280; Fat: 16 g; Carbs: 2 g; Protein: 19 g.

201. Chili Chicken Slider

Preparation Time: 10 minutes
Cooking Time: 18 minutes
Servings: 4
Ingredients:

- 1-1/2 cups chicken, minced
- 1/3 tsp. paprika
- 1/2 tbsp. chili sauce
- 3 cloves garlic, peeled and minced
- 1 tsp. ground black pepper, or to taste
- 1/2 tsp. fresh basil, minced
- 1-1/2 tbsp. coconut aminos
- 1/3 cup scallions, peeled and chopped
- 1/2 tsp. grated fresh ginger
- 1 tsp. salt

Directions:
1. Preheat the PowerXL Air Fryer Grill by selecting grill mode.
2. Adjust the temperature to 355°F, set time to 5 minutes.
3. Combine all the ingredients in a bowl
4. Form into patties.
5. Arrange them on the PowerXL grill grilling plate.
6. Transfer them to the PowerXL Air Fryer Grill.
7. Air fry for 18 minutes, flip halfway done.
8. Enjoy.

Serving Suggestions: Serve with bread.

Directions & Cooking Tips: Make sure the ingredients are well incorporated.
Nutrition:
Calories: 366; Fat: 6 g; Carbs: 4 g; Protein: 56 g.

202. Spicy Chicken Ginger Soup
Preparation Time: 10 minutes
Cooking Time: 3 hours
Servings: 4
Ingredients:
- 1 lb. chicken, cooked and diced
- 14 oz. can coconut milk
- 1 tbsp. garlic powder
- 1 cup rice, uncooked
- 2 tbsp. fresh basil, chopped
- 1 tbsp. ground ginger
- 1 tbsp. green curry paste
- 2 tsp. thyme
- 4 cups chicken stock

Directions:
1. Place the inner pot in the PowerXL grill Air Fryer combo base.
2. Add all ingredients into the inner pot and mix well.
3. Cover the inner pot with a glass lid.
4. Select slow cook mode; then press the temperature button and set the timer for 3 hours. Press Start.
5. When the timer reaches 0, press the cancel button.
6. Serve and enjoy.

Nutrition:
Calories: 599; Fat: 28.8 g; Carbohydrates: 46.4 g; Sugar: 4.6 g; Protein: 39.6 g; Cholesterol: 87 mg.

203. Chicken with Artichoke Hearts
Preparation Time: 10 minutes
Cooking Time: 8 hours
Servings: 6
Ingredients:
- 6 chicken thighs, skinless and boneless
- 3 tbsp. fresh lemon juice
- 10 oz. frozen artichoke hearts
- 14 oz. can tomatoes, diced
- 1/2 tsp. garlic powder
- 1 tsp. dried basil
- 1 tsp. dried oregano
- 15 olives, pitted
- Pepper
- Salt

Directions:
1. Place the inner pot in the PowerXL grill Air Fryer combo base.
2. Add all ingredients into the inner pot and mix well.
3. Cover the inner pot with a glass lid.
4. Select slow cook mode; then press the temperature button and set the timer for 8 hours. Press Start.
5. When the timer reaches 0, press the cancel button.
6. Serve and enjoy.

Nutrition:
Calories: 330; Fat: 12.2 g; Carbohydrates: 9.5 g; Sugar: 3 g; Protein: 44.6 g; Cholesterol: 130 mg.

204. Chicken Shawarma
Preparation Time: 10 minutes
Cooking Time: 3 hours
Servings: 5
Ingredients:
- 1 1/4 lb. chicken thigh, skinless and boneless
- 1 tsp. garlic powder
- 1 tsp. cumin
- 2 tbsp. garlic, minced
- 1/2 cup Greek yogurt
- 1/4 cup chicken stock
- 1/4 tsp. ground coriander
- 1/4 tsp. cinnamon
- 1/2 tsp. curry powder
- 1/2 tsp. dried parsley
- 1 tsp. paprika
- 1/4 cup fresh lemon juice
- 1 1/2 tbsp. tahini
- 1 tbsp. olive oil
- Pepper
- Salt

Directions:
1. Place the inner pot in the PowerXL grill Air Fryer combo base.
2. Add all ingredients into the inner pot and mix well.
3. Cover the inner pot with a glass lid.
4. Select slow cook mode; then press the temperature button and set the timer for 3 hours. Press Start.
5. When the timer reaches 0, press the cancel button. Serve and enjoy.

Nutrition:
Calories: 295; Fat: 14.3 g; Carbohydrates: 4.2 g; Sugar: 1.4 g; Protein: 36.2 g; Cholesterol: 102 mg.

205. Tender & Juicy Chicken
Preparation Time: 10 minutes
Cooking Time: 40 minutes
Servings: 6
Ingredients:
- 2 lb. chicken thighs, skinless and boneless
- 8 garlic cloves, sliced
- 2 tbsp. olive oil
- 2 tbsp. fresh parsley, chopped
- 1 fresh lemon juice
- Pepper
- Salt

Directions:
1. Place chicken on a baking dish and season with pepper and salt.
2. Sprinkle parsley and garlic over the chicken and drizzle oil and lemon juice on top.

3. Place the inner pot in the PowerXL grill Air Fryer combo base.
4. Place the baking dish in the inner pot.
5. Cover the inner pot with an air frying lid.
6. Select Bake mode; then set the temperature to 450°F and time for 40 minutes. Press Start.
7. When the timer reaches 0, press the cancel button.
8. Serve and enjoy.

Nutrition:
Calories: 336; Fat: 16 g, Carbohydrates: 1.6 g; Sugar: 0.2 g; Protein: 44.1 g; Cholesterol: 135 mg.

206. Greek Chicken

Preparation Time: 10 minutes
Cooking Time: 6 hours
Servings: 4
Ingredients:
- 4 chicken breasts, skinless and boneless
- 1/4 cup fresh lemon juice
- 2 tsp. dried oregano
- 1 tbsp. garlic, minced
- 1 cup chicken stock
- 3/4 tbsp. lemon zest
- 1 tsp. kosher salt

Directions:
1. Place the inner pot in the PowerXL grill Air Fryer combo base.
2. Add all ingredients into the inner pot and mix well.
3. Cover the inner pot with a glass lid.
4. Select slow cook mode; then press the temperature button and set the timer for 6 hours. Press Start.
5. When the timer reaches 0, press the cancel button.
6. Serve and enjoy.

Nutrition:
Calories: 290; Fat: 11.2 g; Carbohydrates: 1.9 g; Sugar: 0.6 g; Protein: 42.8 g; Cholesterol: 130 mg.

207. Roasted Pepper Chicken

Preparation Time: 10 minutes
Cooking Time: 4 hours
Servings: 4
Ingredients:
- 2 lb. chicken breasts, skinless and boneless
- 3 tbsp. red wine vinegar
- 1 onion, diced
- 1/2 cup olives
- 10 oz. roasted red peppers, drained and chopped
- 1/2 cup feta cheese, crumbled
- 1 tsp. dried thyme
- 1 tsp. dried oregano
- 1 tbsp. garlic, minced
- 1 tbsp. olive oil
- 1/4 tsp. pepper
- 1/2 tsp. kosher salt

Directions:
1. Place the inner pot in the PowerXL grill Air Fryer combo base.
2. Add all ingredients into the inner pot and mix well.
3. Cover the inner pot with a glass lid.
4. Select slow cook mode; then press the temperature button and set the timer for 4 hours. Press Start.
5. When the timer reaches 0, press the cancel button. Serve and enjoy.

Nutrition:
Calories: 567; Fat: 26.3 g; Carbohydrates: 10 g; Sugar: 5.1 g; Protein: 69.6 g; Cholesterol: 219 mg.

208. Chicken Paillard

Preparation Time: 10 minutes
Cooking Time: 25 minutes
Servings: 8
Ingredients:
- 4 chicken breasts, skinless and boneless
- 1/2 cup olives, diced
- 1 small onion, sliced
- 1 fennel bulb, sliced
- 28 oz. can tomatoes, diced
- 1/4 cup fresh basil, chopped
- 1/4 cup fresh parsley, chopped
- 1/4 cup pine nuts
- 2 tbsp. olive oil
- Pepper
- Salt

Directions:
1. Arrange the chicken in a baking dish and season with pepper and salt and drizzle with oil.
2. In a bowl, mix olives, tomatoes, pine nuts, onion, fennel, pepper, and salt.
3. Pour olive mixture over chicken.
4. Place the inner pot in the PowerXL grill Air Fryer combo base.
5. Place the baking dish into the inner pot.
6. Cover the inner pot with an air frying lid.
7. Select Bake mode; then set the temperature to 450°F and time for 25 minutes. Press Start.
8. When the timer reaches 0, press the cancel button. Serve and enjoy.

Nutrition:
Calories: 242; Fat: 12.8 g; Carbohydrates: 9.3 g; Sugar: 3.9 g; Protein: 23.2 g; Cholesterol: 65 mg.

209. Greek Tomato Olive Chicken

Preparation Time: 10 minutes
Cooking Time: 18 minutes
Servings: 4
Ingredients:
- 4 chicken breasts, boneless and halves
- 15 olives, pitted and halved
- 2 cups cherry tomatoes
- 3 tbsp. olive oil
- 3 tbsp. capers, rinsed and drained
- Pepper
- Salt

Directions:

1. In a bowl, toss tomatoes, capers, olives, and olive oil. Set it aside.
2. Season chicken with pepper and salt.
3. Place chicken in the baking dish and top with tomato mixture. Place the inner pot in the PowerXL grill Air Fryer combo base. Place the baking dish into the inner pot.
4. Cover the inner pot with an air frying lid.
5. Select Bake mode; then set the temperature to 475°F and time for 18 minutes. Press Start.
6. When the timer reaches 0, press the cancel button.
7. Serve and enjoy.

Nutrition:
Calories: 241; Fat: 15 g; Carbohydrates: 4.9 g; Sugar: 2.4 g; Protein: 22.3 g; Cholesterol: 64 mg.

210. Crispy Crusted Chicken
Preparation Time: 10 minutes
Cooking Time: 30 minutes
Servings: 4
Ingredients:
- 1 egg, lightly beaten
- 2 tbsp. butter, melted
- 4 chicken breasts, skinless and boneless
- 1 tsp. water
- 3 cups corn flakes, crushed
- 1 tsp. poultry seasoning
- Pepper
- Salt

Directions:
1. Season chicken with poultry seasoning, pepper, and salt.
2. In a shallow bowl, whisk together egg and water.
3. In a separate shallow bowl, mix crushed cornflakes and melted butter.
4. Dip chicken into the egg mixture; then coat with crushed cornflakes.
5. Place the inner pot in the PowerXL grill Air Fryer combo base.
6. Place the coated chicken into the inner pot.
7. Cover the inner pot with an air frying lid.
8. Select Bake mode; then set the temperature to 400°F and time for 30 minutes. Press Start.
9. When the timer reaches 0, press the cancel button.
10. Serve and enjoy.

Nutrition:
Calories: 421; Fat: 17.7 g; Carbohydrates: 18.6 g; Sugar: 1.5 g; Protein: 45.1 g; Cholesterol: 186 mg.

211. Apple Chicken
Preparation Time: 10 minutes
Cooking Time: 45 minutes
Servings: 2
Ingredients:
- 2 chicken breasts, skinless and boneless
- 12 Ritz cracker, crushed
- 10 oz. can condensed cheddar cheese soup
- 1 apple, sliced
- Pepper
- Salt

Directions:
1. Season chicken with pepper and salt and place it into the baking dish. Arrange sliced apple on top of the chicken. Sprinkle crushed crackers on top.
2. Place the inner pot in the PowerXL grill Air Fryer combo base. Place the baking dish into the inner pot.
3. Cover the inner pot with an air frying lid.
4. Select Bake mode; then set the temperature to 350°F and time for 45 minutes. Press Start.
5. When the timer reaches 0, press the cancel button.
6. Serve and enjoy.

Nutrition:
Calories: 924; Fat: 38.2 g; Carbohydrates: 87 g; Sugar: 21.4 g; Protein: 51.8 g; Cholesterol: 136 mg.

212. Easy Slow Cook Chicken
Preparation Time: 10 minutes
Cooking Time: 6 hours
Servings: 4
Ingredients:
- 4 chicken breasts, skinless and boneless
- 1 tsp. ground black pepper
- 1 tbsp. dried onion, minced
- 10.5 oz. can cream mushroom soup

Directions:
1. Place the inner pot in the PowerXL grill Air Fryer combo base.
2. Place the chicken breasts into the inner pot.
3. Mix the cream of mushroom soup, onion, and black pepper and pour over the chicken.
4. Cover the inner pot with a glass lid.
5. Select slow cook mode; then press the temperature button and set the timer for 6 hours. Press Start.
6. When the timer reaches 0, press the cancel button.
7. Serve and enjoy.

Nutrition:
Calories: 318; Fat: 12.1 g; Carbohydrates: 6.6 g; Sugar: 1.7 g; Protein: 43.2 g; Cholesterol: 132 mg.

213. Broccoli Chicken Casserole
Preparation Time: 10 minutes
Cooking Time: 45 minutes
Servings: 4
Ingredients:
- 4 chicken breasts, skinless and boneless
- 1 cup Ritz crackers, crushed
- 1/2 tsp. paprika
- 10.5 oz. can cheddar cheese soup
- 10 oz. frozen broccoli florets
- 1 cup sharp cheddar cheese, shredded
- 1 cup milk
- Black pepper
- Kosher salt

Directions:
1. Place the inner pot in the PowerXL grill Air Fryer combo base.
2. Season the chicken with pepper and salt and place it into the inner pot.

3. In a large bowl, mix milk, cheddar cheese, paprika, cheddar cheese soup, half crackers, and broccoli; pour over the chicken.
4. Top with remaining crackers.
5. Cover the inner pot with an air frying lid.
6. Select Bake mode; then set the temperature to 350°F and time for 45 minutes. Press Start.
7. When the timer reaches 0, press the cancel button.
8. Serve and enjoy.

Nutrition:
Calories: 533; Fat: 25.4 g; Carbohydrates: 16.5 g, Sugar: 6.1 g; Protein: 53.6 g; Cholesterol: 168 mg.

214. Chicken Meatballs
Preparation Time: 10 minutes
Cooking Time: 10 minutes
Servings: 4
Ingredients:
- 1 lb. ground chicken
- 1 tbsp. soy sauce
- 1/4 cup shredded coconut
- 1 tsp. sesame oil
- 1 tsp. sriracha
- 1 tbsp. hoisin sauce
- 1/2 cup fresh cilantro, chopped
- 2 green onions, chopped
- Pepper
- Salt

Directions:
1. Add all ingredients into a large bowl and mix until well combined.
2. Make small balls from the meat mixture.
3. Place the inner pot in the PowerXL grill Air Fryer combo base.
4. Place the grill plate in the inner pot. Cover.
5. Select Air Fry mode; then set the temperature to 350°F and time for 10 minutes. Press Start.
6. Let the appliance preheat for 3 minutes.
7. Open the lid then place meatballs on the grill plate.
8. Serve and enjoy.

Nutrition:
Calories: 258; Fat: 11.4 g; Carbohydrates: 3.7 g; Sugar: 1.7 g; Protein: 33.5 g; Cholesterol: 101 mg.

215. Tasty Caribbean Chicken
Preparation Time: 10 minutes
Cooking Time: 10 minutes
Servings: 8
Ingredients:
- 3 lb. chicken thigh, skinless and boneless
- 3 tbsp. coconut oil, melted
- 1/2 tsp. ground nutmeg
- 1/2 tsp. ground ginger
- 1 tbsp. cayenne
- 1 tbsp. cinnamon
- 1 tbsp. coriander powder
- Pepper - Salt

Directions:
1. In a small bowl, mix all the ingredients, except chicken.
2. Rub bowl mixture all over the chicken.
3. Place the inner pot in the PowerXL grill Air Fryer combo base.
4. Place the grill plate in the inner pot. Cover.
5. Select Air Fry mode; then set the temperature to 390°F and time for 10 minutes. Press Start.
6. Let the appliance preheat for 3 minutes.
7. Open the lid, then place the chicken on the grill plate.
8. Serve and enjoy.

Nutrition:
Calories: 373; Fat: 17.9 g; Carbohydrates: 1.2 g; Sugar: 0.1 g; Protein: 49.3 g; Cholesterol: 151 mg.

216. Asian Chicken Wings
Preparation Time: 10 minutes
Cooking Time: 30 minutes
Servings: 2
Ingredients:
- 4 chicken wings
- 1 tbsp. Chinese spice
- 1 tsp. mixed spice
- 1 tbsp. soy sauce
- Pepper
- Salt

Directions:
1. Add chicken wings into the bowl. Add remaining ingredients and toss well.
2. Place the inner pot in the PowerXL grill Air Fryer combo base.
3. Place the grill plate in the inner pot. Cover.
4. Select Air Fry mode; then set the temperature to 350°F and time for 30 minutes. Press Start.
5. Let the appliance preheat for 3 minutes.
6. Open the lid; then place chicken wings on the grill plate.
7. Serve and enjoy.

Nutrition:
Calories: 429; Fat: 17.3 g; Carbohydrates: 2.1 g; Sugar: 0.6 g; Protein: 62.4 g; Cholesterol: 178 mg.

217. Chili Garlic Chicken Wings
Preparation Time: 10 minutes
Cooking Time: 20 minutes
Servings: 4
Ingredients:
- 12 chicken wings
- 1 tsp. granulated garlic
- 1 tbsp. chili powder
- 1/2 tbsp. baking powder
- 1/2 tsp. sea salt

Directions:
1. Add chicken wings into a large bowl and toss with remaining ingredients.
2. Place the inner pot in the PowerXL grill Air Fryer combo base.
3. Place the grill plate in the inner pot. Cover.

4. Select Air Fry mode; then set the temperature to 410°F and time for 20 minutes. Press Start.
5. Let the appliance preheat for 3 minutes.
6. Open the lid; then place chicken wings on the grill plate.
7. Serve and enjoy.

Nutrition:
Calories: 580; Fat: 22.6 g; Carbohydrates: 2.4 g; Sugar: 0.3 g; Protein: 87.1 g; Cholesterol: 267 mg.

218. Delicious Tandoori Chicken

Preparation Time: 10 minutes
Cooking Time: 15 minutes
Servings: 4
Ingredients:
- 1 lb. chicken tenders, cut in half
- 1/4 cup yogurt
- 1 tsp. paprika
- 1 tsp. garam masala
- 1 tsp. turmeric
- 1 tsp. cayenne pepper
- 1/4 cup parsley, chopped
- 1 tbsp. garlic, minced
- 1 tbsp. ginger, minced
- 1 tsp. salt

Directions:
1. Add all ingredients into the large bowl and mix well. Place in refrigerator for 30 minutes.
2. Place the inner pot in the PowerXL grill Air Fryer combo base.
3. Place the grill plate in the inner pot. Cover.
4. Select Air Fry mode; then set the temperature to 350°F and time for 15 minutes. Press Start.
5. Let the appliance preheat for 3 minutes.
6. Open the lid; then place marinated chicken on the grill plate.
7. Serve and enjoy.

Nutrition:
Calories: 240; Fat: 8.9 g; Carbohydrates: 3.9 g; Sugar: 1.3 g; Protein: 34.2 g; Cholesterol: 102 mg.

219. Mexican Chicken Lasagna

Preparation Time: 10 minutes
Cooking Time: 15 minutes
Servings: 15
Ingredients:
- 1 1/2 lb. chicken breast, cooked and shredded
- 3/4 cup sour cream
- 2 cup cheese, shredded
- 4 tortillas
- 1 tsp. dry onion, minced
- 2 tsp. ground cumin
- 2 tbsp. chili powder
- 1 cup salsa

Directions:
1. Mix chicken, dried onion, cumin, chili powder, salsa, and sour cream.
2. Spread half chicken mixture in a baking dish; then place 2 tortillas on top.
3. Sprinkle 1/2 cheese over the tortillas; then repeat the layers.
4. Place the inner pot in the PowerXL grill Air Fryer combo base.
5. Place the baking dish into the inner pot.
6. Cover the inner pot with an air frying lid.
7. Select Bake mode; then set the temperature to 390°F and time for 15 minutes. Press Start.
8. When the timer reaches 0, press the cancel button.
9. Serve and enjoy.

Nutrition:
Calories: 160; Fat: 9 g; Carbohydrates: 5.3 g; Sugar: 0.8 g; Protein: 14.5 g; Cholesterol: 50 mg.

220. Chicken Fajita Casserole

Preparation Time: 10 minutes
Cooking Time: 15 minutes
Servings: 4
Ingredients:
- 1 lb. cooked chicken, shredded
- 7 oz. cheddar cheese, shredded
- 2 tbsp. tex-mix seasoning
- 1 onion, sliced
- Pepper
- Salt

Directions:
1. Mix all ingredients except 2 ounces of shredded cheese in a baking dish.
2. Spread remaining cheese on top.
3. Place the inner pot in the PowerXL grill Air Fryer combo base.
4. Place the baking dish into the inner pot.
5. Cover the inner pot with an air frying lid.
6. Select Bake mode; then set the temperature to 390°F and time for 15 minutes. Press Start.
7. When the timer reaches 0, press the cancel button.
8. Serve and enjoy.

Nutrition:
Calories: 641; Fat: 44.1 g; Carbohydrates: 13.3 g; Sugar: 4.3 g; Protein: 50.2 g; Cholesterol: 199 mg.

221. Baked Chicken Mushrooms

Preparation Time: 10 minutes
Cooking Time: 30 minutes
Servings: 4
Ingredients:
- 2 lb. chicken breasts, halved
- 1/3 cup sun-dried tomatoes
- 8 oz. mushrooms, sliced
- 1/2 cup mayonnaise
- 1 tsp. salt

Directions:
1. Grease the baking dish with butter and set it aside.
2. Place the chicken into the baking dish and top with sun-dried tomatoes, mushrooms, mayonnaise, and salt. Mix well.

3. Place the inner pot in the PowerXL grill Air Fryer combo base.
4. Place the baking dish into the inner pot.
5. Cover the inner pot with an air frying lid.
6. Select Bake mode; then set the temperature to 390°F and time for 30 minutes. Press Start.
7. When the timer reaches 0, press the cancel button.
8. Serve and enjoy.

Nutrition:
Calories: 560; Fat: 26.8 g; Carbohydrates: 9.5 g; Sugar: 3.2 g; Protein: 67.8 g; Cholesterol: 209 mg.

222. Chicken Cacciatore

Preparation Time: 10 minutes
Cooking Time: 5 hours
Servings: 2
Ingredients:
- 1 3/4 lb. chicken thighs
- 1 cherry pepper
- 1 small onion, chopped
- 6 oz. cremini mushrooms
- 1 medium red pepper
- 14 oz. tomato paste
- 1 tbsp. capers
- 1 fresh rosemary sprig
- 1 garlic clove
- 1 cup chicken broth
- Pepper
- Salt

Directions:
1. Place the inner pot in the PowerXL grill Air Fryer combo base.
2. Whisk together tomato paste and broth in a bowl.
3. Season the chicken with pepper and salt.
4. Place the seasoned chicken into the inner pot.
5. Add the remaining ingredients; then pour tomato paste mixture over chicken.
6. Cover the inner pot with a glass lid.
7. Select slow cook mode; then press the temperature button and set the timer for 5 hours. Press Start.
8. When the timer reaches 0, press the cancel button.
9. Serve and enjoy.

Nutrition:
Calories: 1002; Fat: 31.4 g; Carbohydrates: 51.4 g; Sugar: 30.5 g; Protein: 129.2 g; Cholesterol: 353 mg.

223. Ranch Chicken

Preparation Time: 10 minutes
Cooking Time: 4 hours
Servings: 2
Ingredients:
- 3 chicken breasts, skinless and boneless
- 1 1/2 tbsp. dry ranch seasoning
- 1 1/2 tbsp. taco seasoning
- 1/4 cup water
- 2 garlic cloves, minced

Directions:
1. Place the inner pot in the PowerXL grill Air Fryer combo base.
2. Add chicken to the inner pot.
3. In a small bowl, whisk together the remaining ingredients and pour over the chicken.
4. Cover the inner pot with a glass lid.
5. Select slow cook mode; then press the temperature button and set the timer for 4 hours. Press Start.
6. When the timer reaches 0, press the cancel button.
7. Shred the chicken using a fork and serve.

Nutrition:
Calories: 465; Fat: 17.5 g; Carbohydrates: 2.6 g; Sugar: 0 g; Protein: 64.8 g; Cholesterol: 198 mg.

224. Caesar Chicken

Preparation Time: 10 minutes
Cooking Time: 6 hours
Servings: 2
Ingredients:
- 2 chicken breasts, skinless and boneless
- 1/4 cup creamy Caesar dressing
- 1/4 tsp. dried parsley
- 2 tbsp. fresh basil, chopped
- 1/8 tsp. black pepper
- 1/8 tsp. salt

Directions:
1. Place the inner pot in the PowerXL grill Air Fryer combo base.
2. Add all ingredients into the inner pot and stir well.
3. Cover the inner pot with a glass lid.
4. Select slow cook mode; then press the temperature button and set the timer for 6 hours. Press Start.
5. When the timer reaches 0, press the cancel button.
6. Shred the chicken using a fork and serve.

Nutrition:
Calories: 378; Fat: 19.8 g; Carbohydrates: 3.2 g; Sugar: 2 g; Protein: 42.3 g; Cholesterol: 135 mg.

225. Simple & Easy Slow Cook Chicken

Preparation Time: 10 minutes
Cooking Time: 4 hours
Servings: 2
Ingredients:
- 1/4 lb. chicken, boneless
- 8 oz. salsa
- 7 oz. condensed cheddar soup

Directions:
1. Place the inner pot in the PowerXL grill Air Fryer combo base.
2. Add all ingredients into the inner pot and mix well.
3. Cover the inner pot with a glass lid.
4. Select slow cook mode; then press the temperature button and set the timer for 4 hours. Press Start.
5. When the timer reaches 0, press the cancel button.
6. Shred the chicken using a fork and serve.

Nutrition:
Calories: 550; Fat: 12.9 g; Carbohydrates: 17 g; Sugar: 5.1 g; Protein: 85.6 g; Cholesterol: 222 mg.

226. Mustard Chicken

Preparation Time: 10 minutes
Cooking Time: 4 hours
Servings: 2
Ingredients:
- 1 lb. chicken breast, skinless, boneless and cut into pieces
- 2 tbsp. soy sauce
- 1/4 cup orange juice
- 1/2 cup ground mustard
- 1/4 cup honey
- 2 tbsp. water
- 2 tbsp. cornstarch

Directions:
1. Place the inner pot in the PowerXL grill Air Fryer combo base.
2. Add chicken into the inner pot.
3. In a small bowl, combine soy sauce, orange juice, ground mustard, and honey.
4. Pour the bowl mixture over the chicken.
5. Cover the inner pot with a glass lid.
6. Select slow cook mode; then press the temperature button and set the timer for 4 hours. Press Start.
7. When the timer reaches 0, press the cancel button.
8. Mix water and cornstarch and pour over the chicken mixture and stir well.
9. Serve and enjoy.

Nutrition:
Calories: 626; Fat: 17.1 g; Carbohydrates: 60.5 g; Sugar: 40.4 g; Protein: 59.3 g; Cholesterol: 145 mg.

227. Chicken Thighs with Rosemary

Preparation Time: 5 minutes
Cooking Time: 1 hour 20 minutes
Servings: 4
Ingredients:
- 4 chicken thighs, with the bone and skin
- Rosemary sprigs
- A large potato, cut into cubes
- 1 onion
- 2 tbsp. olive oil
- 2 garlic cloves
- Salt and pepper
- 1/2 tsp. chicken seasoning powder

Directions:
1. Preheat the PowerXL Air Fryer Grill at 218°C/ 425°F.
2. Put the rosemary sprigs on the baking pan with cooking spray.
3. Bake the remaining ingredients for half an hour.
4. Season the chicken thighs and bake for 35 minutes.

Nutrition:
Calories: 670; Carbs: 14 g; Protein: 47 g; Fat: 46 g.

228. Baked Chicken Tenders

Preparation Time: 30 minutes
Cooking Time: 15–18 minutes
Servings: 6–8
Ingredients:
- 1-1/2 lb. boneless chicken tenders
- 2 eggs
- 2 tsp. butter, melted
- 2/3 cup graham crackers
- 2/3 cup breadcrumbs
- Barbecue sauce
- Salt and pepper for seasoning

Directions:
1. Preheat the PowerXL Air Fryer Grill to 232°C/ 450°F and spray some oil on the baking pan.
2. Combine the crackers, breadcrumbs, and butter until smooth.
3. Beat the eggs in another bowl with salt and pepper.
4. Dip the chicken pieces in the eggs first and then the breadcrumbs.
5. Bake for 15–18 minutes.

Nutrition:
Calories: 362; Carbs: 16.5 g; Protein: 58 g; Fat: 5.8 g,

229. Chicken Curry Salad

Preparation Time: 30 minutes
Cooking Time: 30 minutes
Servings: 4
Ingredients:
- 3 chicken breasts cut into cubes
- 1 tbsp. Dijon mustard
- 1/2 cup mayo
- Chopped celery
- A cup red grapes, cut into halves
- 1 tbsp. sour cream
- Salt and pepper for seasoning
- 2 tbsp. cilantro, chopped
- 1-1/2 tbsp. spice mix

Directions:
1. Cook boneless chicken for half an hour at 149°C/ 300°F in the PowerXL Air Fryer Grill.
2. Combine the remaining ingredients.
3. Add the cooked chicken and grapes to the mixture. Mix them well.
4. Put a plastic wrap on the bowl and refrigerate overnight before serving.

Nutrition:
Calories: 325; Carbs: 13 g; Protein: 37 g; Fat: 14 g.

230. Herb Roasted Turkey Breast

Moving away from the chicken recipes to another delicacy.
Preparation Time: 10 minutes
Cooking Time: 2 hours and 30 minutes
Servings: 6
Ingredients:
- 1/2 tsp. minced garlic
- 1 turkey breast, thawed
- 1 tsp. thyme, ground
- 1/2 cup softened butter
- Crushed rosemary leaves

- Salt and pepper for seasoning

Directions:
1. Preheat the PowerXL Air Fryer Grill at 204°C/ 400°F.
2. Place the turkey breast on the pan after applying cooking spray.
3. Mix the remaining ingredients and use a brush to rub them onto the breast evenly.
4. Roast for 2-1/2 hours and let it rest for 15.

Nutrition:
Calories: 360; Carbs: 1 g; Protein: 72 g; Fat: 5 g.

231. Shredded Chicken Sandwich

Preparation Time: 10 minutes
Cooking Time: 15 minutes
Servings: 2
Ingredients:
- Shredded chicken
- Mayo
- Lettuce
- Salt and pepper
- 2 slices whole-grain bread

Directions:
1. Toast bread with butter in the PowerXL Air Fryer Grill.
2. Mix all the other ingredients until smooth. Cut the slices into halves and fill them up with the mixture.

Nutrition:
Calories: 368; Carbs: 51 g; Protein: 25 g; Fat: 7.2 g.

232. Dijon Stuffed Chicken

Preparation Time: 30 minutes
Cooking Time: 40 minutes
Servings: 4
Ingredients:
- 2 chicken breasts
- 1 potato, cubed
- 1 tsp Dijon mustard
- Salt and pepper
- 2 slices provolone cheese
- 2 tsp. olive oil
- 1/2 apple
- Spinach

Directions:
1. Preheat the PowerXL Air Fryer Grill to 218°C/ 425°F.
2. Bake the potatoes for 10 minutes.
3. Make 2 slits on the breasts and rub in some Dijon mustard.
4. Put the apple slices and cheese slices in the slits and rub with salt, pepper, and olive oil.
5. Bake for 30 minutes.

Nutrition:
Calories: 340; Carbs: 6 g; Protein: 35 g; Fat: 19 g.

233. Air Fried Turkey Breast with Basil

Preparation Time: 15 minutes
Cooking Time: 1 hour
Servings: 4
Ingredients:
- 2 pounds turkey breasts, bone-in skin-on
- 2 tbsp. olive oil
- Coarse sea salt and ground black pepper, to taste
- 1 tsp. fresh basil leaves, chopped
- 2 tbsp. lemon zest, grated

Directions:
1. Preheat the PowerXL Air Fryer Grill by selecting air fry mode. Adjust the temperature to 330°F; set time to 5 minutes. Rub olive on all sides of the turkey breast.
2. Sprinkle with salt, pepper, lemon zest, and basil.
3. Arrange the turkey on the PowerXL grill Pizza rack.
4. Transfer it to the PowerXL Air Fryer Grill.
5. Air fry for 30 minutes. Flip and air fry for another 28 minutes. Enjoy!

Serving Suggestions: Serve with a lemon wedge.
Directions & Cooking Tips: Leave to marinate for a few minutes.
Nutrition:
Calories: 390; Fat: 24 g; Carbs: 2 g; Protein: 41 g.

234. Buttermilk Brined Turkey Breast

Preparation Time: 12 hours
Cooking Time: 35 minutes
Servings: 8
Ingredients:
- 3-1/2 pounds boneless, skinless turkey breast
- 3/4 cup brine from a can of olives
- 1 fresh rosemary sprig
- 2 fresh thyme sprigs
- 1/2 cup buttermilk

Directions:
1. Combine all the ingredients.
2. Add the turkey and pour into a sealable bag.
3. Leave to marinate for 12 hours in the refrigerator.
4. Preheat the PowerXL Air Fryer Grill by selecting Air Fry mode.
5. Adjust the temperature to 350°F; set time to 5 minutes.
6. Arrange the chicken on the PowerXL grill baking tray.
7. Transfer it to the PowerXL Air Fryer Grill.
8. Air fry for 20 minutes, flip halfway done
9. Enjoy

Serving Suggestions: Serve with Rice or pasta.
Directions & Cooking Tips: Drain the marinade.
Nutrition:
Calories: 215; Fat: 3 g; Carbs: 8 g; Protein: 32 g.

235. Turkey Meatloaf

Preparation Time: 20 minutes
Cooking Time: 20 minutes
Servings: 4
Ingredients:
- 1-pound ground turkey
- 1/4 cup salsa verde
- 1/2 cup fresh breadcrumbs
- 1 cup grated Monterey Jack cheese
- 2 garlic cloves, minced
- 1/2 tsp. dried oregano, crushed
- 1 cup onion, chopped

- 1 cup kale leaves, trimmed and finely chopped
- 1 tsp. red chili powder
- 1/2 tsp. ground cumin
- Salt and ground black pepper to taste

Directions:
1. Preheat the PowerXL Air Fryer Grill by selecting Pizza/Bake mode.
2. Adjust the temperature to 350°F; set time to 5 minutes.
3. Mix all the ingredients.
4. Place the turkey on the PowerXL grill baking tray.
5. Transfer it to the PowerXL Air Fryer Grill.
6. Bake for 20 minutes. Enjoy.

Serving Suggestions: Serve with any sauce or toppings of choice.
Directions & Cooking Tips: Thoroughly combine the ingredients.
Nutrition:
Calories: 430; Fat: 20 g; Carbs: 15 g; Protein: 41 g.

236. Simple Turkey Breast

Preparation Time: 20 minutes
Cooking Time: 40 minutes
Servings: 5
Ingredients:
- 3 lb. bone-in turkey breast
- Salt and black pepper, as required
- 1 tbsp. olive oil

Directions:
1. Preheat the PowerXL Air Fryer Grill by selecting Air Fry mode.
2. Adjust the temperature to 360°F; set time to 5 minutes.
3. Season the turkey with salt and pepper.
4. Rub with olive oil.
5. Arrange the seasoned turkey on the PowerXL grill Pizza rack.
6. Transfer it to the PowerXL Air Fryer Grill.
7. Air fry for 20 minutes.
8. Flip and air fry for an additional 20 minutes.
9. Enjoy.

Serving Suggestions: Serve with salad.
Directions & Cooking Tips: Additional spices can be used.
Nutrition:
Calories: 213; Fat: 22 g; Carbs: 1 g; Protein: 13 g.

237. Turkey Chili

Preparation Time: 15 minutes
Cooking Time: 30 minutes
Servings: 6
Ingredients:
- 1 tbsp. extra-virgin olive oil
- 1 pound (454 g) lean ground turkey
- 1 large onion, diced
- 3 garlic cloves, minced
- 1 red bell pepper, seeded and diced
- 1 cup chopped celery
- 2 tbsp. chili powder
- 1 tbsp. ground cumin
- 1 (28-ounce / 794-g) can reduced-salt diced tomatoes
- 1 (15-ounce / 425-g) can low-sodium kidney beans, drained and rinsed
- 2 cups low-sodium chicken broth

Directions:
1. In a large pot, heat the oil over medium fire. Add the turkey, onion, and garlic. Stir regularly, until the turkey is cooked through.
2. Add the bell pepper, celery, chili powder, and cumin. Stir well and continue to cook for 1 minute.
3. Add the tomatoes with their liquid, kidney beans, and chicken broth. Bring to a boil, reduce the heat to low, and simmer for 20 minutes.

Nutrition:
Calories: 276; Fat: 10 g; Protein: 23 g; Carbs: 27 g; Sugars: 7 g; Fiber: 8 g; Sodium: 556 mg.

238. Turkey Divan Casserole

Preparation Time: 10 minutes
Cooking Time: 50 minutes
Servings: 6
Ingredients:
- Nonstick cooking spray
- 3 tsp. extra-virgin olive oil, divided
- 1 pound (454 g) turkey cutlets
- ¼ tsp. freshly ground black pepper, divided
- ¼ cup chopped onion
- 2 garlic cloves, minced
- 2 tbsp. whole-wheat flour
- ½ cup shredded Swiss cheese, divided
- ½ tsp. dried thyme
- 4 cups chopped broccoli
- ¼ cup coarsely ground almonds

Directions:
1. In a skillet, heat 1 teaspoon of oil over medium fire. Season the turkey with salt and ⅛ teaspoon of pepper. Sauté the turkey cutlets for 5 to 7 minutes on each side until cooked through. Transfer to a cutting board, cool briefly, and cut into bite-size pieces.
2. In the same pan, heat the remaining 2 teaspoons of oil over medium-high fire. Sauté the onion for 3 minutes until it begins to soften. Add the garlic and continue cooking for another minute.
3. Stir in the flour and mix well. Whisk in the almond milk, broth, and remaining 1/8 teaspoon of pepper; continue whisking until smooth. Add ¼ cup of cheese and the thyme, and continue stirring until the cheese is melted.
4. In a baking dish, arrange the broccoli on the bottom. Cover with half the sauce. Place the turkey pieces on top of the broccoli, and cover with the remaining sauce. Sprinkle with the remaining ¼ cup of cheese and the ground almonds.
5. Bake for 35 minutes until the sauce is bubbly and the top is browned.

Nutrition: Calories: 207; Fat: 8 g; Protein: 25 g; Carbs: 9 g; Sugars: 2 g; Fiber: 3 g; Sodium: 128 mg.

239. Turkey Broccoli Casserole

Preparation Time: 10 minutes
Cooking Time: 30 minutes
Servings: 6
Ingredients:

- 2-1/2 cups turkey breast, cubed and cooked
- 16 oz. broccoli, chopped and drained
- 1-1/2 cups milk; fat-free
- 1 cup cheddar cheese, low-fat, shredded
- 10 oz. cream chicken soup. low sodium and low fat

What you will need from the store cupboard:

- 8 oz. egg substitute
- ¼ tsp. poultry seasoning
- ¼ cup sour cream, low fat
- 2 cups seasoned stuffing cubes

Directions:

1. Bring together the egg substitute, soup, milk, pepper, sour cream, salt, and poultry seasoning in a big bowl.
2. Now stir in the broccoli, turkey, ¾ cup of cheese, and stuffing cubes.
3. Transfer to a baking dish. Apply cooking spray. Bake for 10 minutes. Sprinkle the remaining cheese. Bake for another 5 minutes. Keep it aside for 5 minutes. Serve.

Nutrition: Calories: 303; Carbohydrates: 26g, Fiber 3g, Sugar 0.8 g; Cholesterol: 72mg, Total Fat 7 g; Protein: 33 g.

240. Homemade Turkey Breakfast Sausage

Preparation Time: 10 minutes
Cooking Time: 10 minutes
Servings: 8
Ingredients:

- 1-pound lean ground turkey
- ½ tsp. dried sage
- ½ tsp. dried thyme
- ½ tsp. freshly ground black pepper
- ¼ tsp. ground fennel seeds
- 1 tsp. extra-virgin olive oil

Directions:

1. In a large mixing bowl, combine the ground turkey, salt, sage, thyme, pepper, and fennel. Mix well.
2. Shape the meat into 8 small, round patties.
3. Heat the olive oil in a skillet over medium-high fire. Cook the patties in the skillet for 3 to 4 minutes on each side until browned.
4. Serve warm, or store in an airtight container in the refrigerator for up to 3 days or in the freezer for up to 1 month.

Nutrition: Calories: 92; Total Fat: 5 g; Protein: 11 g; Carbohydrates: 0 g; Sugars: 0 g; Fiber: 0 g; Sodium: 156 mg.

241. Sweet Potato, Onion, and Turkey Sausage Hash

Preparation Time: 10 minutes
Cooking Time: 25 minutes
Servings: 4
Ingredients:

- 1 tbsp. extra-virgin oil
- 2 medium sweet potatoes, cut into ½-inch dice
- ½ recipe Homemade Turkey Breakfast Sausage (here)
- 1 small onion, chopped
- ½ red bell pepper, seeded and chopped
- 2 garlic cloves, minced

Directions:

1. In a large skillet, heat the oil over medium-high flame. Add the sweet potatoes and cook, stirring occasionally, for 12 to 15 minutes until they brown and begin to soften.
2. Add the turkey sausage in bulk, onion, bell pepper, and garlic. Heat for 5 to 6 minutes until the turkey sausage is cooked through and the vegetables soften.
3. Garnish with parsley and serve warm.

Nutrition:
Calories: 190; Total Fat: 9 g; Protein: 12 g; Carbohydrates: 16 g; Sugars: 7 g; Fiber: 3 g; Sodium: 197 mg.

242. Easy Turkey Breakfast Patties

Preparation Time: 10 minutes
Cooking Time: 10 minutes
Servings: 8
Ingredients:

- 1 pound (454 g) lean ground turkey
- ½ tsp. dried thyme
- ½ tsp. dried sage
- ½ tsp. salt
- ½ tsp. freshly ground black pepper
- ¼ tsp. ground fennel seeds
- 1 tsp. extra-virgin olive oil

Directions:

1. Mix the ground turkey, thyme, sage, salt, pepper, and fennel in a large bowl; stir until well combined.
2. Form the turkey mixture into 8 equal-sized patties with your hands.
3. In a skillet, heat the olive oil over a medium-high fire. Cook the patties for 3 to 4 minutes per side.

Nutrition:
Calories: 91; Fat: 4.8 g; Protein: 11.2 g; Carbs: 0.1 g; Fiber: 0.1 g; Sugar: 0 g; Sodium: 155 mg.

243. Turkey Spinach Patties

Preparation Time: 10 minutes
Cooking Time: 20 minutes
Servings: 4
Ingredients:

- 1 lb. ground turkey
- 1 1/2 cups fresh spinach, chopped
- 1 tsp. Italian seasoning
- 1 tbsp. olive oil
- 1 tbsp. garlic, minced
- 4 oz. feta cheese, crumbled

Directions:

1. Add ground turkey and remaining ingredients into the mixing bowl and mix until well combined.
2. Make four equal shapes of patties from the turkey mixture and place them into the Air Fryer basket.
3. Cook for 20 minutes.

Nutrition:
Calories: 336; Fat: 22.4 g; Carbohydrates: 2.4 g; Sugar: 1.3 g; Protein: 35.5 g; Cholesterol: 142 mg.

244. Tasty Turkey Fajitas

Preparation Time: 10 minutes
Cooking Time: 20 minutes
Servings: 4
Ingredients:
- 1 lb. turkey breast, boneless, skinless, and cut into 1/2-inch slices
- 1/4 cup fresh cilantro, chopped
- 1 jalapeno pepper, chopped
- 1 onion, sliced
- 2 bell pepper, sliced into strips
- 1 1/2 tbsp. olive oil
- 2 limes juiced
- 1/2 tsp. onion powder
- 1 tsp. garlic powder
- 1/2 tbsp. oregano
- 1/2 tsp. paprika
- 1 tbsp. chili powder

Directions:
1. In a small bowl, mix onion powder, garlic powder, oregano, paprika, cumin, chili powder, and pepper.
2. Squeeze one lime juice over turkey breast; then sprinkle the spice mixture.
3. Brush turkey breast with 1 tablespoon of olive oil and set it aside.
4. Add onion and bell peppers into a medium bowl and toss with remaining oil. Preheat the Air Fryer to 375°F.
5. Add onion and bell peppers into the Air Fryer basket and cook for 8 minutes. Shake basket and cook for 5 minutes more. Add jalapenos and cook for 5 minutes. Shake basket and add sliced turkey over vegetables and cook for 8 minutes.

Nutrition:
Calories: 211; Fat: 7.8 g; Carbohydrates: 16.2 g; Sugar: 9.1 g; Protein: 20.9 g; Cholesterol: 49 mg.

245. Turkey Broccoli Fritters

Preparation Time: 10 minutes
Cooking Time: 10 minutes
Servings: 8
Ingredients:
- 1 lb. turkey thighs, boneless, skinless cut into small pieces
- 2 cups broccoli florets, steamed and chopped
- 1 cup cheddar cheese, shredded
- 1/2 cup almond flour
- 1/2 tsp. garlic powder - 2 eggs, lightly beaten

Directions:

1. Coat the Air Fryer basket with cooking spray.
2. Add turkey and remaining ingredients into the mixing bowl; mix until well combined.
3. Make small fritters from the chicken mixture and place them into the Air Fryer basket.
4. Cook the turkey fritters at 400°F for 8 minutes. Turn them and cook for 2 minutes more.

Nutrition:
Calories: 199; Fat: 10.9 g; Carbohydrates: 2.3 g; Sugar: 0.6 g; Protein: 22.4 g; Cholesterol: 106 mg.

246. Spicy Turkey Wings

Preparation Time: 10 minutes
Cooking Time: 30 minutes
Servings: 4
Ingredients:
- 2 lb. turkey wings
- 2 tsp. garlic powder
- 4 tsp. chili powder
- 3 tbsp. olive oil

Directions:
1. Add turkey wings and remaining ingredients into the ziplock bag and shake well to coat.
2. Place turkey wings into the Air Fryer basket and cook at 380°F for 30 minutes. Toss every 5 minutes.

Nutrition:
Calories: 534; Fat: 27.8 g; Carbohydrates: 2.5 g; Sugar: 0.5 g; Protein: 66.2 g; Cholesterol: 202 mg.

247. Nutritious Turkey & Veggies

Preparation Time: 10 minutes
Cooking Time: 10 minutes
Servings: 4
Ingredients:
- 1 lb. turkey breast, boneless and cut into bite-size pieces
- 1 tbsp. Italian seasoning
- 1/2 tsp. garlic powder
- 1/2 tsp. chili powder
- 2 tbsp. olive oil
- 2 garlic cloves, minced
- 1/2 onion, chopped
- 1 cup bell pepper, chopped
- 1 zucchini, chopped
- 1 cup broccoli florets

Directions:
1. Preheat the Air Fryer to 400°F.
2. Add turkey and remaining ingredients into a large mixing bowl and toss well.
3. Put them into the Air Fryer basket and heat for 10 minutes or until turkey is cooked. Shake Air Fryer basket halfway through.

Nutrition:
Calories: 235; Fat: 11.2 g; Carbohydrates: 8 g; Sugar: 3.8 g; Protein: 25.9 g; Cholesterol: 75 mg.

248. Turkey Spinach Meatballs

Preparation Time: 10 minutes
Cooking Time: 10 minutes

Servings: 4
Ingredients:
- 1 lb. ground turkey
- 3/4 cup almond flour
- 1/4 cup feta cheese, crumbled
- 2 tbsp. parmesan cheese, grated
- 1/4 cup sun-dried tomatoes, drained
- 2 tsp. garlic
- 3 cups baby spinach

Directions:
1. Add spinach, sun-dried tomatoes, and 1 teaspoon of garlic into the food processor and process until a paste is formed.
2. Add the mixture into a large mixing bowl. Add the remaining ingredients and mix until well combined.
3. Make small meatballs from the mixture and place them into the Air Fryer basket.
4. Cook meatballs at 400°F for 10 minutes.

Nutrition:
Calories: 303; Fat: 14.7 g; Carbohydrates: 3.5 g; Sugar: 1 g; Protein: 38.4 g; Cholesterol: 114 mg.

249. Tender Turkey Legs

Preparation Time: 10 minutes
Cooking Time: 27 minutes
Servings: 4
Ingredients:
- 4 turkey legs
- 1/4 tsp. thyme
- 1/4 tsp. oregano
- 1/4 tsp. rosemary
- 1 tbsp. butter

Directions:
1. Season the turkey legs with pepper and salt.
2. In a small bowl, mix butter, thyme, oregano, and rosemary.
3. Rub the butter mixture all over the turkey legs.
4. Place the turkey legs into the Air Fryer basket and cook for 27 minutes.

Nutrition:
Calories: 182; Fat: 9.9 g; Carbohydrates: 1.9 g; Sugar: 0.1 g; Protein: 20.2 g; Cholesterol: 68 mg.

250. Grilled Quail

Preparation Time: 10 minutes
Cooking Time: 1 hour 55 minutes
Servings: 6
Ingredients:
- 6 ounces quail
- 1 cup bouillon
- 6 bacon strips
- 2 cups Stuffing
- 1 tbsp Worcestershire sauce
- Pepper and salt to taste

Directions:
1. Split the quail.
2. Sprinkle pepper and salt on the quail.
3. Add stuffing and bouillon
4. Wrap quail and bacon strips together.
5. Sprinkle with Worcestershire sauce.
6. Place it in the PowerXL Air Fryer Grill basket.
7. Set the PowerXL Air Fryer Grill to grill function.
8. Cook for 1 hour 45 minutes.
9. Serve immediately or allow cooling before serving.

Nutrition:
Calories: 134; Fat: 5 g; Carbs: 3 g; Protein: 21 g.

251. Turkey Breasts

Preparation Time: 5 minutes
Cooking Time: 1 hour
Servings: 4
Ingredients:
- 3 lb. boneless turkey breast
- ¼ cup mayonnaise
- 2 tsp. poultry seasoning
- salt and pepper to taste
- 1/2 tsp. garlic powder

Directions:
1. Preheat the Air Fryer to 360°F. Season the turkey with mayonnaise, seasoning, salt, garlic powder, and black pepper. Cook in the Air Fryer for 1 hour at 360°F.
2. Turn after every 15 minutes. The turkey is done when its internal temperature reaches 165°F.

Nutrition:
Calories: 558; Carbs: 1 g; Fat: 18 g; Protein: 98 g.

252. BBQ Chicken Breasts

Preparation Time: 5 minutes
Cooking Time: 15 minutes
Servings: 4
Ingredients:
- 4 (about 6 oz. each) boneless, skinless chicken breast
- 2 tbsp. BBQ seasoning
- Cooking spray

Directions:
1. Rub the chicken with BBQ seasoning and marinate in the refrigerator for 45 minutes. Preheat the Air Fryer at 400°F. Grease the basket with oil and place the chicken.
2. Then spray oil on top. Cook for 13 to 14 minutes. Flipping at the halfway mark. Serve.

Nutrition:
Calories: 131; Carbs: 2 g; Fat: 3 g; Protein: 24 g.

253. Rotisserie Chicken

Preparation Time: 5 minutes
Cooking Time: 1 hour
Servings: 4
Ingredients:
- 1 whole chicken, cleaned and patted dry
- 2 tbsp. olive oil
- 1 tbsp. seasoned salt

Directions:
1. Remove the giblet packet from the cavity. Rub the chicken with oil and salt. Place it in the Air Fryer basket, breast-side down. Cook at 350°F for 30 minutes.

2. Then flip and cook another 30 minutes. Chicken is done when it reaches 165°F.

Nutrition:
Calories: 534; Carbs 0 g; Fat: 36 g; Protein: 35 g.

254. Honey-Mustard Chicken Breasts

Preparation Time: 5 minutes
Cooking Time: 25 minutes
Servings: 6
Ingredients:
- 6 (6-oz, each) Boneless, skinless chicken breasts
- 2 tbsp. minced fresh rosemary
- 3 tbsp. honey
- 1 tbsp. Dijon mustard
- Salt and pepper to taste

Directions:
1. Combine the mustard, honey, pepper, rosemary, and salt in a bowl. Rub the chicken with this mixture.
2. Grease the Air Fryer basket with oil. Air fry the chicken at 350°F for 20 to 24 minutes or until the chicken reaches 165°F.
3. Serve.

Nutrition:
Calories: 236; Carbs: 9.8 g; Fat: 5 g; Protein: 38 g.

255. Chicken Parmesan Wings

Preparation Time: 5 minutes
Cooking Time: 15 minutes
Servings: 4
Ingredients:
- 2 lb. chicken wings cut into drumettes, pat dried
- 1/2 cup Parmesan, plus 6 tbsp. grated
- 1 tsp. Herbs de Provence
- 1 tsp. paprika
- Salt to taste

Directions:
1. Combine the parmesan, herbs, paprika, and salt in a bowl and rub the chicken with this mixture. Preheat the Air Fryer at 350°F.
2. Grease the basket with cooking spray. Cook for 15 minutes. Flip once at the halfway mark. Garnish with parmesan and serve.

Nutrition:
Calories: 490; Carbs: 1 g; Fat: 22 g; Protein: 72 g.

256. Air Fryer Chicken

Preparation Time: 5 minutes
Cooking Time: 30 minutes
Servings: 4
Ingredients:
- 2 lb. chicken wings
- Salt and pepper to taste
- Cooking spray

Directions:
1. Flavor the chicken wings with salt and pepper.
2. Grease the Air Fryer basket with cooking spray. Add chicken wings and cook at 400F for 35 minutes.
3. Flip 3 Times during cooking for even cooking. Serve.

Nutrition:
Calories: 277; Carbs: 1 g; Fat: 8 g; Protein: 50 g.

257. Whole Chicken

Preparation Time: 5 minutes
Cooking Time: 40 minutes
Servings: 6
Ingredients:
- 1 (2 1/2 pounds) whole chicken washed and pat dried
- 2 tbsp. dry rub
- 1 tsp. salt
- Cooking spray

Directions:
1. Preheat the Air Fryer at 350°F. Rub the dry rub on the chicken. Then rub with salt. Cook it at 350°F for 45 minutes. After 30 minutes, flip the chicken and finish cooking.
2. Chicken is done when it reaches 165°F.

Nutrition:
Calories: 412; Carbs: 1 g; Fat: 28 g; Protein: 35 g.

258. Honey Duck Breasts

Preparation Time: 5 minutes
Cooking Time: 25 minutes
Servings: 2
Ingredients:
- 1 smoked duck breast, halved
- 1 tsp. honey
- 1 tsp. tomato paste
- 1 tbsp. mustard
- 1/2 tsp. apple vinegar

Directions:
1. Mix tomato paste, honey, mustard, and vinegar in a bowl. Whisk well. Add duck breast pieces and coat well. Cook in the Air Fryer at 370°F for 15 minutes.
2. Remove the duck breast from the Air Fryer and add more honey mixture. Coat again. Cook again at 370°F for 6 minutes. Serve.

Nutrition:
Calories: 274 Carbs 22g Fat 11 g; Protein: 13 g.

259. Creamy Coconut Chicken

Preparation Time: 5 minutes
Cooking Time: 25 minutes
Servings: 4
Ingredients:
- 4 big chicken legs
- 5 tsp. turmeric powder
- 2 tbsp. grated Ginger
- Salt and black pepper to taste
- 4 tbsp. coconut cream

Directions:
1. In a bowl, mix salt, pepper, ginger, turmeric, and cream. Whisk. Add chicken pieces, coat, and marinate for 2 hours.
2. Transfer chicken to the preheated Air Fryer and cook at 370°F for 25 minutes.

3. Serve.
Nutrition:
Calories: 300; Carbs: 22 g; Fat: 4 g; Protein: 20 g.

260. Buffalo Chicken Tenders
Preparation Time: 5 minutes
Cooking Time: 20 minutes
Servings: 4
Ingredients:
- 1 pound boneless, skinless chicken tenders
- ¼ cup hot sauce
- 1 1/2 ounces, finely ground pork rinds
- 1 tsp. chili powder
- 1 tsp. garlic powder

Directions:
1. Put the chicken breasts in a bowl and pour hot sauce over them. Toss to coat. Mix ground pork rinds, chili powder, and garlic powder in another bowl.
2. Place each tender in the ground pork rinds and coat well. With wet hands, press down the pork rinds into the chicken. Place the tender in a single layer into the Air Fryer basket. Cook at 375°F for 20 minutes. Flip once. Serve.

Nutrition:
Calories: 160; Carbs: 0.6 g; Fat: 4.4 g; Protein: 27.3 g.

261. Teriyaki Wings
Preparation Time: 5 minutes
Cooking Time: 25 minutes
Servings: 4
Ingredients:
- 2 pounds chicken wings
- 1/2 cup teriyaki sauce
- 2 tsp. minced garlic
- ¼ tsp. ground ginger
- 2 tsp. baking powder

Directions:
1. Except for the baking powder, place all ingredients in a bowl and marinate for 1 hour in the refrigerator. Place wings into the Air Fryer basket and sprinkle with baking powder.
2. Gently rub into wings. Cook at 400°F for 25 minutes. Shake the basket two or three times during cooking. Serve.

Nutrition:
Calories: 446; Carbs 3.1 g; Fat: 29.8 g; Protein: 41.8 g.

262. Lemony Drumsticks
Preparation Time: 5 minutes
Cooking Time: 25 minutes
Servings: 2
Ingredients:
- 2 tsp. baking powder
- 1/2 tsp. garlic powder
- 8 Chicken drumsticks
- 4 tbsp. melted salted butter
- 1 tbsp. lemon pepper seasoning

Directions:
1. Sprinkle garlic powder and baking powder over drumsticks and rub them into chicken skin. Place drumsticks into the Air Fryer basket. Cook at 375F for 25 minutes. Flip the drumsticks once halfway through the Cooking Time.
2. Remove from oven. Mix seasoning and butter in a bowl. Add drumsticks to the bowl and toss to coat. Serve.

Nutrition:
Calories: 532; Carbs: 1.2 g; Fat: 32.3 g; Protein: 48.3 g.

263. Parmesan Chicken Tenders
Preparation Time: 5 minutes
Cooking Time: 10 minutes
Servings: 4
Ingredients:
- 1-pound chicken tenderloins
- 3 large egg whites
- 1/2 cup Italian-style bread crumbs
- ¼ cup grated Parmesan cheese

Directions:
1. **Preparing the Ingredients.** Spray the Cuisinart Air Fryer basket with olive oil. Trim off any white fat from the chicken tenders. In a bowl, whisk the egg whites until frothy. In a separate small mixing bowl, combine the bread crumbs and Parmesan cheese. Mix well.
2. Dip the chicken tenders into the egg mixture, then into the Parmesan and bread crumbs. Shake off any excess bread. Place the chicken tenders in the greased Cuisinart Air Fryer basket in a single layer. Generously spray the chicken with olive oil to avoid powdery, uncooked breading.
3. **Air Frying.** Set the temperature of your Cuisinart AF to 370°F. Set the timer and bake for 4 minutes. Using tongs, flip the chicken tenders and bake for 4 minutes more. Check that the chicken has reached an internal temperature of 165°F. Add cooking time if needed. Once the chicken is fully cooked, serve and enjoy.

Nutrition:
Calories: 210 Fat: 4 g; Saturated fat: 1 g; Carbohydrate: 10 g; Fiber: 1 g; Sugar: 1 g; Protein: 33 g.

264. Easy Lemon Chicken Thighs
Preparation Time: 5 minutes
Cooking Time: 10 minutes
Servings: 4
Ingredients:
- Salt and black pepper to taste
- 2 tbsp. olive oil
- 2 tbsp. Italian seasoning
- 2 tbsp. freshly squeezed lemon juice
- 1 lemon, sliced

Directions:
1. Place the chicken thighs in a medium mixing bowl and season them with salt and pepper. Add the olive oil, Italian seasoning, and lemon juice and toss until the chicken thighs are thoroughly coated with oil. Add the sliced lemons. Place the chicken thighs into the Air Fryer basket in a single layer.
2. Set the temperature of your AF to 350°F. Set the timer and cook for 10 minutes. Using tongs, flip the chicken. Reset

the timer and cook for 10 minutes more. Check that the chicken has reached an internal temperature of 165°F. Add cooking time if needed. Once the chicken is fully cooked, serve, and enjoy.

Nutrition:
Calories: 325; Carbs: 1 g; Fat: 26 g; Protein: 20 g.

265. Air Fryer Grilled Chicken Breasts

Preparation Time: 5 minutes
Cooking Time: 14 minutes
Servings: 4
Ingredients:
- 1/2 tsp. garlic powder
- salt and black pepper to taste
- 1 tsp. dried parsley
- 2 tbsp. olive oil, divided
- 3 boneless, skinless chicken breasts

Directions:
3. **Preparing the Ingredients.** In a small bowl, combine the garlic powder, salt, pepper, and parsley. Using 1 tablespoon of olive oil and half of the seasoning mix, rub each chicken breast with oil and seasonings. Place the chicken breast in the Air Fryer basket.
4. **Air Frying.** Set the temperature of your Cuisinart AF to 370°F. Set the timer and grill for 7 minutes.
5. Using tongs, flip the chicken and brush the remaining olive oil and spices onto the chicken. Reset the timer and grill for 7 minutes more. Check that the chicken has reached an internal temperature of 165°F. Add cooking time if needed.
6. When the chicken is cooked, transfer it to a platter and serve.

Nutrition:
Calories: 182; Carbs: 0 g; Fat: 9 g; Protein: 26 g.

266. Perfect Chicken Parmesan

Preparation Time: 5 minutes
Cooking Time: 25 minutes
Servings: 2
Ingredients:
- 2 large white meat chicken breasts, approximately 5–6 ounces
- 1 cup breadcrumbs (Panko brand works well)
- 2 medium-sized eggs
- Pinch salt and pepper
- 1 tbsp. dried oregano
- 1 cup marinara sauce
- 2 slices provolone cheese
- 1 tbsp. parmesan cheese

Directions:
1. **Preparing the Ingredients.** Cover the basket of the Power Air Fryer XL with a lining of tin foil, leaving the edges uncovered to allow air to circulate through the basket.
2. Preheat the Air Fryer to 350F.
3. In a mixing bowl, whisk the eggs until fluffy, and the yolks and whites are fully combined; set it aside.
4. In a separate mixing bowl, combine the breadcrumbs, oregano, salt, and pepper, and set it aside.
5. One by one, dip the raw chicken breasts into the bowl with dry ingredients, coating both sides; submerge into the bowl with wet ingredients, then dip again into the dry ingredients. This double coating will ensure an extra crisp and delicious air-fry!
6. Lay the coated chicken breasts on the foil covering the Power Air Fryer Basket in a single flat layer.
7. **Air Frying.** Set the Power Air Fryer XL timer for 10 minutes.
8. After 10 minutes, the Air Fryer will turn off. The chicken should be mid-way cooked and the breaded coating starting to brown.
9. Use tongs, turn each piece of chicken over to ensure a full all-over fry.
10. Reset the Air Fryer to 320F for another 10 minutes.
11. While the chicken is cooking, pour half the marinara sauce into a 7-inch heat-safe pan.
12. After 10 minutes, when the Air Fryer shuts off, remove the fried chicken breasts using tongs and set them in the marinara-covered pan. Drizzle the remaining marinara sauce over the fried chicken; then place the slices of provolone cheese atop both of them and sprinkle the parmesan cheese over the entire pan.
13. Reset the Air Fryer to 350 for 5 minutes.
14. After 5 minutes, when the Air Fryer shuts off, remove the dish from the Air Fryer using tongs or oven mitts. The chicken will be perfectly crisped and the cheese melted and lightly toasted. Serve while hot!

Nutrition:
Calories: 210; Fat: 20 g; Protein: 18 g; Sugar: 0 g.

267. Honey and Wine Chicken Breasts

Preparation Time: 5 minutes
Cooking Time: 15 minutes
Servings: 4
Ingredients:
- 2 chicken breasts, rinsed and halved
- 1 tbsp. melted butter
- 1/2 tsp. freshly ground pepper
- 3/4 tsp. sea salt, or to taste
- 1 tsp. paprika
- 1 tsp. dried rosemary
- 2 tbsp. dry white wine
- 1 tbsp. honey

Directions:
1. **Preparing the Ingredients.** Firstly, pat the chicken breasts dry. Lightly coat them with the melted butter.
2. Then, add the remaining ingredients.
3. **Air Frying.** Transfer them to the Air Fryer basket; bake for about 15 minutes at 330°F. Serve warm and enjoy

Nutrition:
Calories: 189; Fat: 14 g; Protein: 11 g; Sugar: 1 g.

268. Crispy Honey Garlic Chicken Wings

Preparation Time: 10 minutes
Cooking Time: 20 minutes

Servings: 8
Ingredients:
- 1/8 cup water
- 1/2 tsp. salt
- 4 tbsp. minced garlic
- ¼ cup vegan butter
- ¼ cup raw honey
- ¾ cup almond flour
- 16 chicken wings

Directions:
1. **Preparing the Ingredients.** Rinse off and dry chicken wings well.
2. Spray the Air Fryer basket with olive oil.
3. Coat chicken wings with almond flour and add coated wings to the Power Air Fryer XL.
4. **Air Frying.** Set temperature to 380°F, and time to 25 minutes. Cook shaking every 5 minutes.
5. When the timer goes off, cook 5–10 minutes at 400°F till the skin becomes crispy and dry.
6. As chicken cooks, melt butter in a saucepan and add garlic. Sauté garlic 5 minutes. Add salt and honey, simmer for 20 minutes. Make sure to stir every so often, so the sauce does not burn. Add a bit of water after 15 minutes to ensure the sauce does not harden.
7. Remove chicken wings from the Air Fryer and coat in sauce. Enjoy!

Nutrition:
Calories: 435; Fat: 19 g; Protein: 31 g; Sugar: 6 g.

269. Chicken-Fried Steak Supreme

Preparation Time: 10 minutes
Cooking Time: 30 minutes
Servings: 8
Ingredients:
- 1/2-pound chicken breast
- 1 cup breadcrumbs (Panko brand works well)
- 2 medium-sized eggs
- A pinch salt and pepper
- 1/2 tbsp. ground thyme

Directions:
1. **Preparing the Ingredients.** Cover the basket of the Power Air Fryer XL with a lining of tin foil, leaving the edges uncovered to allow air to circulate through the basket. Preheat the Air Fryer to 350F. In a mixing bowl, beat the eggs until fluffy and until the yolks and whites are fully combined; set it aside. In a separate mixing bowl, combine the breadcrumbs, thyme, salt, and pepper; and set it aside. One by one, dip each piece of raw steak into the bowl with dry ingredients, coating all sides; then submerge into the bowl with wet ingredients, then dip again into the dry ingredients. This double coating will ensure an extra-crisp air fry. Lay the coated steak pieces on the foil covering the air-fryer basket in a single flat layer.
2. **Air Frying.** Set the Power Air Fryer XL Timer for 15 minutes. After 15 minutes, the Air Fryer will turn off. The steak should be mid-way cooked and the breaded coating starting to brown. Using tongs, turn each piece of steak over to ensure a full all-over fry. Reset the Air Fryer to 320 for 15 minutes. After 15 minutes, when the Air Fryer shuts off, remove the fried steak strips using tongs and set them on a serving plate. Eat as soon as cool enough to handle and enjoy!

Nutrition:
Calories: 180; Fat: 10 g; Protein: 15 g; Sugar: 0 g.

270. Lemon-Pepper Chicken Wings

Preparation Time: 10 minutes
Cooking Time: 20 minutes
Servings: 4
Ingredients:
- 8 whole chicken wings
- Juice of 1/2 lemon
- 1/2 tsp. garlic powder
- 1 tsp. onion powder
- Salt
- Pepper
- ¼ cup low-fat buttermilk
- 1/2 cup all-purpose flour
- Cooking oil

Directions:
1. **Preparing the Ingredients.** Put the wings in a sealable plastic bag. Drizzle the wings with lemon juice. Season with garlic powder, onion powder, salt, and pepper to taste.
2. Seal the bag. Shake thoroughly to combine the seasonings and coat the wings.
3. Pour the buttermilk and the flour into separate bowls large enough to dip the wings.
4. Spray the PowerXL Air Fryer basket with cooking oil.
5. One at a time, dip the wings in the buttermilk and then the flour.
6. **Air Frying.** Place the wings in the Power Air Fryer XL basket. It is okay to stack them on top of each other. Spray the wings with cooking oil, being sure to spray the bottom layer. Cook for 5 minutes.
7. Remove the basket and shake it to ensure all of the pieces will cook fully.
8. Return the basket to the Power Air Fryer XL and continue cooking the chicken. Repeat shaking every 5 minutes until a total of 20 minutes has passed. Cool before serving.

Nutrition:
Calories: 347; Fat: 12 g; Protein: 46 g; Fiber: 1 g.

271. Air Fried Chili Chicken

Preparation Time: 25 minutes
Cooking Time: 10 minutes
Servings: 4
Ingredients:
- 1/2 tbsp. sesame oil
- 1 tbsp. low-sodium soy sauce
- 1 tbsp. cornstarch
- 450g chicken thighs, skinless, boneless, diced
- 1/2 tbsp. peanut oil
- 1 red onion, chopped

- 1 tbsp. minced fresh ginger
- 2 cups snow peas
- 1 tbsp. chili garlic sauce
- 1 mango, peeled, chopped
- 1/8 tsp. sea salt
- 1/8 tsp. black pepper

Directions:
1. In a large mixing bowl, combine sesame oil, soy sauce, cornstarch, and chicken; let sit for at least 20 minutes.
2. In the pan from your Air Fryer toast oven, heat peanut oil and then sauté ginger and onion for about 2 minutes; add snow peas and stir fry for about 1 minute.
3. Add chicken with the marinade and transfer to your Air Fryer toast oven. Air fry for 5 minutes at 350°F or until chicken is browned.
4. Add chili sauce, mango, and pepper; continue stir-frying for 1 minute or until chicken is cooked through and mango is tender. Serve the stir fry over cooked brown rice.

Nutrition: Calories: 330; Carbs: 11.8 g; Fat: 24.1 g; Protein: 26 g.

272. Air-Fried Lemon Chicken

Preparation Time: 10 minutes
Cooking Time: 15 minutes
Servings: 4
Ingredients:
- 4 boneless skinless chicken breasts
- ½ tsp. organic cumin
- 1 tsp. sea salt (real salt)
- 1/4 tsp. black pepper
- 1/2 cup butter, melted
- 1 lemon 1/2 juiced, 1/2 thinly sliced
- 1 cup chicken bone broth
- 1 can pitted green olives
- 1/2 cup red onions, sliced

Directions:
1. Liberally season the chicken breasts with sea salt, cumin, and black pepper.
2. Preheat your Air Fryer toast oven to 370 and brush the chicken breasts with the melted butter.
3. Air fry in the pan of your air fry toaster oven for about 5 minutes until evenly browned.
4. Add all remaining Ingredients and air broil for 10 minutes. Serve hot!

Nutrition: Calories: 310; Carbs: 10.2 g; Fat: 9.4 g; Protein: 21.8 g.

273. Baked Chicken Thighs

Preparation Time: 15 minutes
Cooking Time: 35 minutes
Servings: 4
Ingredients:
- 500g (1 lb.) chicken thighs
- 1 tsp. red pepper flakes
- 1 tsp. sweet paprika
- 1 tsp. freshly ground black pepper
- 1 tsp. dried oregano
- 1 tsp. curry powder
- 1 tbsp. garlic powder
- 1–2 tbsp. coconut oil

Directions:
1. Start by preheating your Air Fryer toast oven to 370°F and preparing the basket of the fryer by lining it with parchment paper.
2. Combine all the spices in a small bowl then set it aside. Now arrange the thighs on your prepared basket with the skin side down (remember to first pat the skin dry with kitchen towels).
3. Sprinkle the upper side of the chicken thighs with half the seasoning mix, flip them over and sprinkle the lower side with the remaining seasoning mix.
4. Bake for about 30 minutes until the chicken thighs are cooked through and the skin is crisp. Turn once halfway through cooking time. To make the skin crispier, increase the heat to 400°F and bake for 5 more minutes.
5. Enjoy!

Nutrition:
Calories: 281; Carbs: 3 g; Fat: 13 g; Protein: 36.8 g.

274. Turkey Wraps with Sauce

Preparation Time: 10 minutes
Cooking Time: 16 minutes
Servings: 6
Ingredients:
Wraps
- 4 large collard leaves, stems removed
- 1 medium avocado, sliced
- 1/2 cucumber, thinly sliced
- 1 cup diced mango
- 6 large strawberries, thinly sliced
- 6 (200g) grilled turkey breasts, diced
- 24 mint leaves

Dipping Sauce
- 2 tbsp. almond butter
- 2 tbsp. coconut cream
- 1 bird eye chili, finely chopped
- 2 tbsp. unsweetened applesauce
- 1/4 cup fresh lime juice
- 1 tsp. sesame oil
- 1 tbsp. apple cider vinegar
- 1 tbsp. tahini
- 1 clove garlic, crushed
- 1 tbsp. grated fresh ginger
- 1/8 tsp. sea salt

Directions:
For the chicken breasts:
1. Start by setting your Air Fryer toast oven to 350°F.
2. Lightly coat the basket of the Air Fryer toast oven with oil.
3. Season the turkey with salt and pepper. Arrange it on the prepared basket and air fry for 8 minutes on each side.
4. Once done, remove from Air Fryer toast oven and set on a platter to cool slightly then dice them up.

For the wraps:

5. Divide the veggies and diced turkey breasts equally among the four large collard leaves; fold bottom edges over the filling, and then both sides.
6. Roll very tightly up to the end of the leaves; secure with toothpicks and cut each in half.

Make the sauce:

7. Combine all the sauce ingredients in a blender and blend until very smooth. Divide between bowls and serve with the wraps.

Nutrition:
Calories: 389; Carbs: 11.7 g; Fat: 38.2 g; Protein: 26 g.

275. Air Roasted Chicken Drumsticks

Preparation Time: 10 minutes
Cooking Time: 20 minutes
Servings: 4
Ingredients:

- 1 tbsp. olive oil
- 1-1/2 red onions, diced
- 1-1/2 tsp. salt
- 8 chicken drumsticks
- Zest of 1/4 lemon
- 8 cloves garlic
- 2/3 cup diced tinned tomatoes
- 2 tbsp. sweet balsamic vinegar

Directions:

1. Set your Air Fryer toast oven to 370°F and add the oil, onions, and 1/2 teaspoon of salt to the pan of your Air Fryer toast oven. Cook for 2 minutes until golden.
2. Add the chicken drumsticks and sprinkle with the rest of the salt, pepper, and chili; then add the thyme, garlic cloves, and lemon zest. Add in balsamic vinegar and tomatoes and spread the mixture between the drumsticks.
3. Air roast for about 20 minutes or until done to desire.
4. Serve the creamy chicken over rice, pasta, or potatoes or with a side of vegetables.
5. Enjoy!

Nutrition:
Calories: 329; Carbs: 13.3 g; Fat: 0.4 g; Protein: 20.8 g.

276. Scrumptious Turkey Wraps

Preparation Time: 15 minutes
Cooking Time: 10 minutes
Servings: 4
Ingredients:

- 250g ground turkey
- 1/2 small onion, finely chopped
- 1 garlic clove, minced
- 2 tbsp. extra virgin olive oil
- 1 head lettuce
- 1 tsp. cumin
- 1/2 tbsp. fresh ginger, sliced
- 2 tbsp. apple cider vinegar
- 2 tbsp. freshly chopped cilantro
- 1 tsp. freshly ground black pepper
- 1 tsp. sea salt

Directions:

1. Sauté garlic and onion in extra virgin olive oil until fragrant and translucent in your Air Fryer toast oven pan at 350°F.
2. Add turkey and cook well for 5-8 minutes or until done to desire.
3. Add in the remaining ingredients and continue cooking for 5 minutes more.
4. To serve, ladle a spoonful of turkey mixture onto a lettuce leaf and wrap. Enjoy!

Nutrition:
Calories: 197; Carbs: 8.4 g; Fat: 17.9 g; Protein: 13.4 g.

277. Air Roasted Whole Chicken

Preparation Time: 15 minutes
Cooking Time: 50 minutes
Servings: 12
Ingredients:

- 1 full chicken, dissected
- 2 tbsp. extra virgin olive oil
- 2 tbsp. chopped garlic
- 2 tsp. sea salt
- 1 tbsp. chopped fresh thyme
- 1 tbsp. chopped fresh rosemary

Fruit Compote

- 1 apple, diced
- 1/2 cup red grapes, halved, seeds removed
- 12 dried apricots, sliced
- 16 dried figs, coarsely chopped
- 1/2 cup chopped red onion
- 2 tsp. liquid stevia
- 1/2 tsp. salt
- 1/2 tsp. pepper

Directions:

1. In a small bowl, stir together thyme, rosemary, garlic, salt, and pepper and rub the mixture over the pork.
2. Light your Air Fryer toast oven and set it to 320°F. Place the chicken on the basket and air roast for 10 minutes.
3. Increase the temperature and cook for another 10 minutes, turning the chicken pieces once. Increase the temperature one more time to 400°F and cook for 5 minutes to get a crispy finish.
4. **Make Fruit** Compote: In a saucepan, combine all ingredients and cook over medium heat, stirring, for about 25 minutes or until liquid is reduced to a quarter.
5. Once the chicken is cooked, serve hot with a ladle of fruit compote.
6. Enjoy!

Nutrition:
Calories: 511; Carbs: 15 g; Fat: 36.8 g; Protein: 31.5 g

CHAPTER 4:
Fish and Seafood Recipes

278. Lobster Tails with Lemon Butter
Preparation Time: 10 minutes
Cooking Time: 8 minutes
Servings: 4
Ingredients
- 4 lobster tails, shell cut from the top
- 1 tablespoon fresh parsley, chopped
- 2 garlic cloves, pressed
- 1 teaspoon Dijon mustard
- 1/4 teaspoon salt
- 1/8 teaspoon black pepper
- 1 1/2 tablespoon olive oil
- 1 1/2 tablespoon fresh lemon juice
- 4 tablespoon butter, divided

Directions:
1. Place the lobster tails in the oven's baking tray.
2. Whisk rest of the ingredients in a bowl and pour over the lobster tails.
3. Press "Power Button" of Air Fry Oven and turn the dial to select the "Broil" mode.
4. Press the Time button and again turn the dial to set the cooking time to 8 minutes.
5. Now push the Temp button and rotate the dial to set the temperature at 350 degrees F.
6. Once preheated, place the lobster's baking tray in the oven and close its lid.
7. Serve warm.

Nutrition: Calories 281 Total Fat 11g Saturated Fat 4g Cholesterol 242mg Sodium 950mg Total Carbohydrate 8g Dietary Fiber 1g Total Sugars 2g Protein 29g

279. Tuna Patties
Preparation Time: 10 minutes
Cooking Time: 10 minutes
Servings: 2
Ingredients:
- 2 cans tuna
- 1/2 lemon juice
- 1/2 tsp onion powder
- 1 tsp garlic powder
- 1/2 tsp dried dill
- 1 1/2 tbsp. mayonnaise
- 1 1/2 tbsp. almond flour
- 1/4 tsp pepper
- 1/4 tsp salt

Directions:
1. Preheat the air fryer to 400 F.
2. Add all ingredients in a mixing bowl and mix until well combined.
3. Spray air fryer basket with cooking spray.
4. Make four patties from mixture and place in the air fryer basket.
5. Cook patties for 10 minutes at 400 F if you want crispier patties then cook for 3 minutes more.
6. Serve and enjoy.

Nutrition: Calories 414 Fat 20.6 g Carbohydrates 5.6 g Sugar 1.3 g Protein 48.8 g Cholesterol 58 mg

280. Crispy Fish Sticks
Preparation Time: 10 minutes
Cooking Time: 10 minutes
Servings: 4
Ingredients:
- 1 lb. white fish, cut into pieces
- 3/4 tsp Cajun seasoning
- 1 1/2 cups pork rind, crushed
- 2 tbsp. water
- 2 tbsp. Dijon mustard
- 1/4 cup mayonnaise
- Pepper
- Salt

Directions:
1. Spray air fryer basket with cooking spray.
2. In a small bowl, whisk together mayonnaise, water, and mustard.
3. In a shallow bowl, mix together pork rind, pepper, Cajun seasoning, and salt.
4. Dip fish pieces in mayo mixture and coat with pork rind mixture and place in the air fryer basket.
5. Cook at 400 F for 5 minutes. Turn fish sticks to another side and cook for 5 minutes more.
6. Serve and enjoy.

Nutrition: Calories 397 Fat 36.4 g Carbohydrates 4 g Sugar 1 g Protein 14.7 g Cholesterol 4 mg

281. Delicious White Fish
Preparation Time: 10 minutes
Cooking Time: 10 minutes
Servings: 2
Ingredients:
- 12 oz. white fish fillets
- 1/2 tsp onion powder
- 1/2 tsp lemon pepper seasoning
- 1/2 tsp garlic powder
- 1 tbsp. olive oil
- Pepper
- Salt

Directions:
1. Spray air fryer basket with cooking spray.

2. Preheat the air fryer to 360 F.
   3. Coat fish fillets with olive oil and season with onion powder, lemon pepper seasoning, garlic powder, pepper, and salt.
   4. Place fish fillets in air fryer basket and cook for 10-12 minutes.
   5. Serve and enjoy.

Nutrition: Calories 358 Fat 19.8 g Carbohydrates 1.3 g Sugar 0.4 g Protein 41.9 g Cholesterol 131 mg

282. Salmon Patties

Preparation Time: 10 minutes
Cooking Time: 7 minutes
Servings: 2
Ingredients:
- 8 oz. salmon fillet, minced
- 1 lemon, sliced
- 1/2 tsp garlic powder
- 1 egg, lightly beaten
- 1/8 tsp salt

Directions:
1. Add all ingredients except lemon slices into the bowl and mix until well combined.
2. Spray air fryer basket with cooking spray.
3. Place lemon slice into the air fryer basket.
4. Make the equal shape of patties from salmon mixture and place on top of lemon slices into the air fryer basket.
5. Cook at 390 F for 7 minutes.
6. Serve and enjoy.

Nutrition: Calories 184 Fat 9.2 g Carbohydrates 1 g Sugar 0.4 g Protein 24.9 g Cholesterol 132 mg

283. Perfect Salmon Fillets

Preparation Time: 10 minutes
Cooking Time: 15 minutes
Servings: 2
Ingredients:
- 2 salmon fillets
- 1/2 tsp garlic powder
- 1/4 cup plain yogurt
- 1 tsp fresh lemon juice
- 1 tbsp. fresh dill, chopped
- 1 lemon, sliced
- Pepper
- Salt

Directions:
1. Place lemon slices into the air fryer basket.
2. Season salmon with pepper and salt and place on top of lemon slices into the air fryer basket.
3. Cook salmon at 330 F for 15 minutes.
4. Meanwhile, in a bowl, mix together yogurt, garlic powder, lemon juice, dill, pepper, and salt.
5. Place salmon on serving plate and top with yogurt mixture.
6. Serve and enjoy.

Nutrition: Calories 195 Fat 7 g Carbohydrates 6 g Sugar 2 g Protein 24 g Cholesterol 65 mg

284. Flavorful Parmesan Shrimp

Preparation Time: 10 minutes
Cooking Time: 10 minutes
Servings: 6
Ingredients:
- 2 lbs. cooked shrimp, peeled and deveined
- 2 tbsp. olive oil
- 1/2 tsp onion powder
- 1 tsp basil
- 1/2 tsp oregano
- 2/3 cup parmesan cheese, grated
- 3 garlic cloves, minced
- 1/4 tsp pepper

Directions:
1. In a large mixing bowl, combine together garlic, oil, onion powder, oregano, pepper, and cheese.
2. Add shrimp in a bowl and toss until well coated.
3. Spray air fryer basket with cooking spray.
4. Add shrimp into the air fryer basket and cook at 350 F for 8-10 minutes.
5. Serve and enjoy.

Nutrition: Calories 233 Fat 7.9 g Carbohydrates 3.2 g Sugar 0.1 g Protein 35.6 g Cholesterol 32 m

285. Simple Air Fryer Salmon

Preparation Time: 5 minutes
Cooking Time: 10 minutes
Servings: 2
Ingredients:
- 2 salmon fillets, skinless and boneless
- 1 tsp olive oil
- Pepper
- Salt

Directions:
1. Coat salmon fillets with olive oil and season with pepper and salt.
2. Place salmon fillets in air fryer basket and cook at 360 F for 8-10 minutes.
3. Serve and enjoy.

Nutrition: Calories 256 Fat 13.3 g Carbohydrates 0 g Sugar 0 g Protein 34.5 g Cholesterol 78 mg

286. Shrimp with Veggie

Preparation Time: 10 minutes
Cooking Time: 20 minutes
Servings: 4
Ingredients:
- 50 small shrimp
- 1 tbsp. Cajun seasoning
- 1 bag of frozen mix vegetables
- 1 tbsp. olive oil

Directions:
1. Line air fryer basket with aluminum foil.
2. Add all ingredients into the large mixing bowl and toss well.
3. Transfer shrimp and vegetable mixture into the air fryer basket and cook at 350 F for 10 minutes.
4. Toss well and cook for 10 minutes more.

5. Serve and enjoy.

Nutrition: Calories 101 Fat 4 g Carbohydrates 14 g Sugar 1 g Protein 2 g Cholesterol 3 mg

287. Nutritious Salmon

Preparation Time: 10 minutes
Cooking Time: 10 minutes
Servings: 2

Ingredients:
- 2 salmon fillets
- 1 tbsp. olive oil
- 1/4 tsp ground cardamom
- 1/2 tsp paprika
- Salt

Directions:
1. Preheat the air fryer to 350 F.
2. Coat salmon fillets with olive oil and season with paprika, cardamom, and salt and place into the air fryer basket.
3. Cook salmon for 10-12 minutes. Turn halfway through.
4. Serve and enjoy.

Nutrition: Calories 160 Fat 1 g Carbohydrates 1 g Sugar 0.5 g Protein 22 g Cholesterol 60 mg

288. Shrimp Scampi

Preparation Time: 10 minutes
Cooking Time: 10 minutes
Servings: 4

Ingredients:
- 1 lb. shrimp, peeled and deveined
- 10 garlic cloves, peeled
- 2 tbsp. olive oil
- 1 fresh lemon, cut into wedges
- 1/4 cup parmesan cheese, grated
- 2 tbsp. butter, melted

Directions:
1. Preheat the air fryer to 370 F.
2. Mix together shrimp, lemon wedges, olive oil, and garlic cloves in a bowl.
3. Pour shrimp mixture into the air fryer pan and place into the air fryer and cook for 10 minutes.
4. Drizzle with melted butter and sprinkle with parmesan cheese.
5. Serve and enjoy.

Nutrition: Calories 295 Fat 17 g Carbohydrates 4 g Sugar 0.1 g Protein 29 g Cholesterol 260 mg

289. Lemon Chili Salmon

Preparation Time: 10 minutes
Cooking Time: 17 minutes
Servings: 4

Ingredients:
- 2 lbs. salmon fillet, skinless and boneless
- 2 lemon juice - 1 orange juice
- 1 tbsp. olive oil
- 1 bunch fresh dill - 1 chili, sliced
- Pepper - Salt

Directions:
1. Preheat the air fryer to 325 F.
2. Place salmon fillets in air fryer baking pan and drizzle with olive oil, lemon juice, and orange juice.
3. Sprinkle chili slices over salmon and season with pepper and salt.
4. Place pan in the air fryer and cook for 15-17 minutes.
5. Garnish with dill and serve.

Nutrition: Calories 339 Fat 17.5 g Carbohydrates 2 g Sugar 2 g Protein 44 g Cholesterol 100 mg

290. Pesto Salmon

Preparation Time: 10 minutes
Cooking Time: 16 minutes
Servings: 4

Ingredients:
- 25 oz. salmon fillet
- 1 tbsp. green pesto
- 1 cup mayonnaise
- 1/2 oz. olive oil
- 1 lb. fresh spinach
- 2 oz. parmesan cheese, grated
- Pepper
- Salt

Directions:
1. Preheat the air fryer to 370 F.
2. Spray air fryer basket with cooking spray.
3. Season salmon fillet with pepper and salt and place into the air fryer basket.
4. In a bowl, mix together mayonnaise, parmesan cheese, and pesto and spread over the salmon fillet.
5. Cook salmon for 14-16 minutes.
6. Meanwhile, in a pan sauté spinach with olive oil until spinach is wilted, about 2-3 minutes. Season with pepper and salt.
7. Transfer spinach in serving plate and top with cooked salmon.
8. Serve and enjoy.

Nutrition: Calories 545 Fat 39.6 g Carbohydrates 9.5 g Sugar 3.1 g Protein 43 g Cholesterol 110 mg Parmesan

291. Walnut Salmon

Preparation Time: 10 minutes
Cooking Time: 12 minutes
Servings: 4

Ingredients:
- 4 salmon fillets
- 1/4 cup parmesan cheese, grated
- 1/2 cup walnuts
- 1 tsp olive oil
- 1 tbsp. lemon rind

Directions:
1. Preheat the air fryer to 370 F.
2. Spray an air fryer baking dish with cooking spray.
3. Place salmon on a baking dish.
4. Add walnuts into the food processor and process until finely ground. Mix ground walnuts with parmesan cheese, oil, and lemon rind. Stir well.

5. Spoon walnut mixture over the salmon and press gently. Place in the air fryer and cook for 12 minutes.
6. Serve and enjoy.

Nutrition: Calories 420 Fat 27.4 g Carbohydrates 2 g Sugar 0.3 g Protein 46.3 g Cholesterol 98 mg

292. Lemon Shrimp

Preparation Time: 10 minutes
Cooking Time: 8 minutes
Servings: 2
Ingredients:
- 12 oz. shrimp, peeled and deveined
- 1 lemon sliced - 1/4 tsp garlic powder
- 1/4 tsp paprika - 1 tsp lemon pepper
- 1 lemon juice - 1 tbsp. olive oil

Directions:
1. In a bowl, mix together oil, lemon juice, garlic powder, paprika, and lemon pepper.
2. Add shrimp to the bowl and toss well to coat.
3. Spray air fryer basket with cooking spray.
4. Transfer shrimp into the air fryer basket and cook at 400 F for 8 minutes.
5. Garnish with lemon slices and serve.

Nutrition: Calories 381 Fat 17.1 g Carbohydrates 4.1 g Sugar 0.6 g Protein 50.6 g Cholesterol 358 mg

293. Grilled Catfish Fillets

Preparation Time: 10 minutes
Cooking Time: 20 minutes
Servings: 5
Ingredients:
- 1 tbsp. parsley - 5 fillets catfish
- Sweet paprika - 1 tbsp. olive oil
- Black pepper - Salt - 1 tbsp. lemon juice

Directions:
1. Drizzle catfish fillets with oil, pepper, salt, and paprika.
2. Place it in the PowerXL Air Fryer Grill basket.
3. Set the basket to position 6 in the PowerXL Air Fryer Grill.
4. Set the PowerXL Air Fryer Grill to Air Fryer/Grill at 1450F. Grill for about 20 minutes.
5. Serve immediately.

Serving Suggestions: Serve with lemon juice.
Directions & Cooking Tips: Rinse catfish fillet well
Nutrition:
Calories: 320; Fat: 10 g; Carbs: 0 g; Protein: 56 g.

294. Grilled Cod Fillets Mixed with Grapes Salad and Fennel

Preparation Time: 10 minutes
Cooking Time: 30 minutes
Servings: 3
Ingredients:
- 1 tbsp. olive oil
- 1/2 cup pecans
- 1 sliced fennel bulb.
- 3 black cod fillets
- Black pepper and salt
- 1 cup grapes

Directions:
1. Rub oil all over the fish fillets.
2. Sprinkle with pepper and salt.
3. Place the fish on the PowerXL Air Fryer Grill basket.
4. Place the basket at position 6 in the PowerXL Air Fryer Grill.
5. Set the PowerXL Air Fryer Grill to Air Fryer/Grill function at 1450F.
6. Grill for about 10 minutes.
7. Mix grapes, pecans, oil, and fennel in another bowl; sprinkle with pepper and salt.
8. Place the mixture in the PowerXL Air Fryer Grill basket.
9. Set the PowerXL Air Fryer Grill to the Air Fry function.
10. Cook for about 5 minutes at 400°F.
11. Serve cod with grape and fennel mix.

Serving Suggestions: Serve with maple syrup.
Directions & Cooking Tips: Divide the cod while serving.
Nutrition:
Calories: 154; Fat: 3 g; Carbs: 0 g; Protein: 34 g.

295. Crispy Paprika Fish Fillets

Preparation Time: 5 minutes
Cooking Time: 15 minutes
Servings: 4
Ingredients:
- 1/2 cup seasoned breadcrumbs
- 1 tbsp. balsamic vinegar

- 1/2 tsp. seasoned salt
- 1 tsp. paprika
- 1/2 tsp. ground black pepper
- 1 tsp. celery seed
- 2 fish fillets, halved
- 1 egg, beaten

Directions:
1. **Preparing the Ingredients.** Pour the vinegar, salt, breadcrumbs, paprika, celery seeds, and ground black pepper into your food processor. Leave it for 30 seconds.
2. Then cover the fish fillets using the beaten egg; then put them into the breadcrumb's mixture.
3. **Air Frying.** Cook it at 350°F for around 15 minutes.

Nutrition:
Calories: 185; Fat: 11 g; Protein: 21 g; Sugar: 0 g.

296. Lemony Tuna

Preparation Time: 10 minutes
Cooking Time: 10 minutes
Servings: 4
Ingredients:
- 2 (6-ounce) cans water-packed plain tuna
- 2 tsp. Dijon mustard
- 1/2 cup breadcrumbs
- 1 tbsp. fresh lime juice
- 2 tbsp. fresh parsley, chopped
- 1 egg
- Hot sauce
- 3 tbsp. canola oil
- Salt and freshly ground black pepper

Directions:
1. **Preparing the Ingredients.** Get the majority of the liquid from the canned tuna.
2. In a bowl, add the fish, mustard, crumbs, citrus juice, parsley, and hot sauce; mix till well combined. Add a little canola oil if it seems too dry. Add egg, salt, and stir to combine. Make the patties from the tuna mixture. Refrigerate the tuna patties for about 2 hours.
3. **Air Frying.** Preheat the Air Fryer oven to 355°F. Cook for about 10–12 minutes.

Nutrition:
Calories: 345; Fat: 1 g; Protein: 18 g; Fiber: 4 g.

297. Grilled Soy Salmon Fillets

Preparation Time: 5 minutes
Cooking Time: 8 minutes
Servings: 4
Ingredients:
- 4 salmon fillets
- 1/4 tsp. ground black pepper
- 1/2 tsp. cayenne pepper
- 1/2 tsp. salt
- 1 tsp. onion powder
- 1 tbsp. fresh lemon juice
- 1/2 cup soy sauce
- 1/2 cup water
- 1 tbsp. honey
- 2 tbsp. extra-virgin olive oil

Directions:
1. **Preparing the Ingredients.** Firstly, pat the salmon fillets dry using kitchen towels. Season the salmon with black pepper, cayenne pepper, salt, and onion powder.
2. To make the marinade, combine lemon juice, soy sauce, water, honey, and olive oil. Marinate the salmon for at least 2 hours in your refrigerator.
3. Arrange the fish fillets on a grill basket in your PowerXL Air Fryer oven.
4. **Air Frying.** Bake at 330°F for 8 to 9 minutes, or until salmon fillets are easily flaked with a fork.
5. Work with batches and serve warm.

Nutrition:
Calories: 254; Fat: 4 g; Protein: 29 g; Fiber: 1 g.

298. Tender & Juicy Salmon

Preparation Time: 10 minutes
Cooking Time: 7 minutes
Servings: 2
Ingredients:
- 2 salmon fillets
- 2 tsp. paprika
- 2 tsp. olive oil
- Pepper
- Salt

Directions:
1. Rub salmon fillets with oil, paprika, pepper, and salt.
2. Place fillets into the Air Fryer basket and cook at 390°F for 7 minutes.
3. Serve and enjoy.

Nutrition:
Calories: 282; Fat: 15.9 g; Carbohydrates: 1.2 g; Sugar: 0.2 g; Protein: 34.9 g; Cholesterol: 78 mg.

299. Lemon Garlic White Fish

Preparation Time: 10 minutes
Cooking Time: 10 minutes
Servings: 2
Ingredients:
- 12 oz. white fish fillets
- 1/2 tsp. onion powder
- 1/2 tsp. lemon-pepper seasoning
- 1/2 tsp. garlic powder
- Pepper
- Salt

Directions:
1. Preheat the Air Fryer to 360°F.
2. Coat the fish fillets with cooking spray and season with onion powder, lemon pepper seasoning, garlic powder, pepper, and salt.
3. Place parchment paper in the bottom of the Air Fryer basket. Place the fish fillets into the Air Fryer basket and cook for 6–10 minutes. Serve and enjoy.

Nutrition:
Calories: 298; Fat: 12.8 g; Carbohydrates: 1.4 g; Sugar: 0.4 g; Protein: 41.9 g; Cholesterol: 131 mg.

300. Parmesan White Fish Fillets

Preparation Time: 10 minutes
Cooking Time: 10 minutes
Servings: 4
Ingredients:
- 1 lb. white fish fillets
- 1/2 tsp. lemon-pepper seasoning
- 1/4 cup parmesan cheese
- 1/4 cup coconut flour

Directions:
1. In a shallow dish, mix coconut flour, parmesan cheese, and lemon pepper seasoning.
2. Coat white fish fillets from both sides with cooking spray.
3. Coat fish fillets with coconut flour mixture.
4. Place coated fish fillets into the Air Fryer basket and cook at 400°F for 10 minutes. Turn fish fillets halfway through.
5. Serve and enjoy.

Nutrition:
Calories: 220; Fat: 10 g; Carbohydrates: 0.9 g; Sugar: 0.1 g; Protein: 29.9 g; Cholesterol: 92 mg.

301. Ginger Garlic Salmon

Preparation Time: 10 minutes
Cooking Time: 10 minutes
Servings: 2
Ingredients:
- 2 salmon fillets, boneless and skinless
- 2 tbsp. mirin
- 2 tbsp. soy sauce
- 1 tbsp. olive oil
- 2 tbsp. scallions, minced
- 1 tbsp. ginger, grated
- 2 garlic cloves, minced

Directions:
1. Add salmon fillets into the zip-lock bag.
2. In a small bowl, mix mirin, soy sauce, olive oil, scallions, ginger, and garlic and pour over salmon. Seal the bag, shake well, and place it in the refrigerator for 30 minutes.
3. Place marinated salmon fillets into the Air Fryer basket and cook at 360°F for 10 minutes. Serve and enjoy.

Nutrition:
Calories: 345; Fat: 18.2 g; Carbohydrates: 11.6 g; Sugar: 4.5 g; Protein: 36.1 g; Cholesterol: 78 mg.

302. Quick & Easy Salmon

Preparation Time: 10 minutes
Cooking Time: 12 minutes
Servings: 2
Ingredients:
- 2 salmon fillets
- 1/2 tsp. hot sauce
- 3 tbsp. coconut aminos
- 1 garlic clove, minced
- 1 tsp. ginger, grated
- 1 tsp. sesame seeds, toasted

Directions:
1. Add salmon fillets into the zip-lock bag.
2. Mix hot sauce, coconut aminos, garlic, and ginger and pour over salmon. Seal the bag and place it in the refrigerator for 30 minutes.
3. Place marinated salmon fillets into the Air Fryer basket and cook at 400°F for 6 minutes. Turn salmon and brush with marinade and cook for 6 minutes more or until ready. Serve and enjoy.

Nutrition:
Calories: 272; Fat: 11.8 g; Carbohydrates: 6 g; Sugar: 0.1 g; Protein: 35 g; Cholesterol: 78 mg.

303. Healthy Salmon Patties

Preparation Time: 10 minutes
Cooking Time: 7 minutes
Servings: 2
Ingredients:
- 8 oz. salmon fillet, minced
- 1/4 tsp. garlic powder
- 1 egg, lightly beaten
- 1 lemon, sliced
- 1/8 tsp. salt

Directions:
1. In a bowl, mix minced salmon, garlic powder, egg, and salt until well combined.
2. Make two patties from the salmon mixture.
3. Preheat the Air Fryer to 390°F.
4. Place the sliced lemon on the bottom of the Air Fryer basket; then place the salmon patties on top. Cook for 7 minutes. Serve and enjoy.

Nutrition:
Calories: 191; Fat: 9.3 g; Carbohydrates: 3.1 g; Sugar: 1 g; Protein: 25.2 g; Cholesterol: 132 mg.

304. Garlic Yogurt Salmon Fillets

Preparation Time: 10 minutes
Cooking Time: 15 minutes
Servings: 2
Ingredients:
- 2 salmon fillets
- 1/2 tsp. garlic powder
- 1/4 cup Greek yogurt
- 1 tsp. fresh lemon juice
- 1 tbsp. fresh dill, chopped
- 1 lemon, sliced
- Pepper
- Salt

Directions:
1. Place lemon slices in the bottom of the Air Fryer basket.
2. Season salmon fillets with pepper and salt and place on the lemon slices in the Air Fryer basket.
3. Cook salmon fillets at 330°F for 15 minutes.
4. Place the cooked salmon fillets on a serving plate.
5. Mix yogurt, dill, lemon juice, and garlic powder.
6. Pour the yogurt mixture over the cooked salmon and serve.

Nutrition:

Calories: 277; Fat: 11.9 g; Carbohydrates: 5.6 g; Sugar: 2.4 g; Protein: 38.8 g; Cholesterol: 80 mg.

305. Parmesan Basil Salmon
Preparation Time: 10 minutes
Cooking Time: 7 minutes
Servings: 4
Ingredients:
- 4 salmon fillets
- 3 tbsp. parmesan cheese, grated
- 5 fresh basil leaves, minced
- 3 tbsp. mayonnaise
- 1/2 lemon juice
- Pepper
- Salt

Directions:
1. Preheat the Air Fryer to 400°F.
2. Coat the Air Fryer basket with cooking spray.
3. Season salmon with pepper, lemon juice, and salt.
4. In a small bowl, mix cheese, basil, and mayonnaise.
5. Spread the cheese mixture on top of the salmon fillets. Place them into the Air Fryer basket and cook for 7 minutes.
6. Serve and enjoy.

Nutrition:
Calories: 316, Fat 17.1 g; Carbohydrates: 3.2 g; Sugar: 0.8 g; Protein: 38.3 g; Cholesterol: 89 mg.

306. Flavorful Curry Cod Fillets
Preparation Time: 10 minutes
Cooking Time: 10 minutes
Servings: 2
Ingredients:
- 2 cod fillets, defrost, and pat dry with a paper towel
- 1 tbsp. Thai basil, sliced
- 1/8 tsp. garlic powder
- 1/8 tsp. paprika
- 1/4 tsp. curry powder
- 1 tbsp. butter, melted
- 1/8 tsp. sea salt

Directions:
1. In a small bowl, mix curry powder, garlic powder, paprika, and salt; set it aside.
2. Line Air Fryer basket with aluminum foil.
3. Place the cod fillets into the Air Fryer basket. Brush the fillets with butter and sprinkle with a dry spice mixture.
4. Cook at 360°F for 8 minutes. Drizzle with remaining butter and cook for 2 minutes more. Garnish with basil and serve.

Nutrition:
Calories: 143; Fat: 6.8 g; Carbohydrates: 0.4 g; Sugar: 0.1 g; Protein: 20.2 g; Cholesterol: 70 mg.

307. Dukkah Crusted Salmon
Preparation Time: 10 minutes
Cooking Time: 10 minutes
Servings: 2
Ingredients:
- 1 tbsp. dukkah
- 12 oz. salmon fillets - A pinch salt

Directions:
1. Preheat the Air Fryer to 390°F.
2. Season the salmon with salt and sprinkle dukkah on top of salmon fillets.
3. Place the salmon fillets into the Air Fryer basket and cook for 10 minutes. Serve and enjoy.

Nutrition:
Calories: 248; Fat: 12.3 g; Carbohydrates: 0.8 g; Sugar: 0 g; Protein: 33.8 g; Cholesterol: 75 mg.

308. Herbed Salmon
Preparation Time: 10 minutes
Cooking Time: 5 minutes
Servings: 2
Ingredients:
- 8 oz. salmon fillets
- 2 tbsp. olive oil
- 1 tbsp. lemon herb butter
- 1/4 tsp. paprika
- 1 tsp. Herb de Provence
- Pepper
- Salt

Directions:
1. In a small bowl, mix paprika, Herb de Provence, pepper, and salt.
2. Rub salmon fillets with oil and spice mixture.
3. Place salmon fillets into the Air Fryer basket and cook at 390°F for 5-8 minutes.
4. Melt lemon herb butter and pour over salmon just before serving.

Nutrition:
Calories: 305; Fat: 24.2 g; Carbohydrates: 1.2 g; Sugar: 0 g; Protein: 22.5 g; Cholesterol: 58 mg.

309. Cod Steaks and Plum Sauce
Preparation Time: 10 minutes
Cooking Time: 30 minutes
Servings: 3
Ingredients:
- 1 tbsp. plum sauce
- 1/2 tsp. garlic powder
- 3 large cod steaks - Cooking spray
- 1/2 tsp. ginger powder
- Black pepper and salt
- 1/4 tsp. turmeric powder

Directions:
1. Drizzle the cod steaks with cooking spray.
2. Add pepper, ginger powder, salt, turmeric powder, and garlic powder.
3. Place the coated cod steaks in the PowerXL Air Fryer Grill.
4. Set the function to Air Fryer/Grill.
5. Grill for about 20 minutes at 360°F.
6. Flip while cooking for uniformity.
7. Heat plum sauce over medium heat for 2 minutes at reheat function. Divide the cod steaks and serve immediately

Serving Suggestions: Serve with plum sauce.
Directions & Cooking Tips: Allow the steaks to rest for some minutes before grilling.
Nutrition:
Calories: 330; Fat: 3 g; Carbs: 25 g; Protein: 30 g.

310. Flavored Grilled Salmon
Preparation Time: 60 minutes
Cooking Time: 8 minutes
Servings: 3
Ingredients:
- 3 chopped scallions
- 2 tbsp. lemon juice
- 1/3 cup water
- 3 salmon fillets
- 1/2 tsp. garlic powder
- 2 tbsp. olive oil
- Black pepper and salt
- 1/3 cup soy sauce
- 1/3 cup brown sugar

Directions:
1. Mix soy sauce, sugar, lemon juice, and salmon fillets in a bowl.
2. Add oil, garlic powder, pepper, water, and salt.
3. Refrigerate for 1 hour
4. Place the salmon fillet in the PowerXL Air Fryer Grill basket.
5. Set the PowerXL Air Fryer Grill to Air Fryer/Grill.
6. Allow to grill for about 8 minutes at 360°F.

Nutrition:
Calories: 269; Fat: 29 g; Carbs: 0 g; Protein: 51 g.

311. Grilled Lemony Saba Fish
Preparation Time: 10 minutes
Cooking Time: 8 minutes
Servings: 1
Ingredients:
- 2 tbsp. lemon juice
- 2 tbsp. minced garlic
- Black pepper and salt
- 2 tbsp. olive oil
- 4 saba fish fillet
- 3 chopped red chili pepper

Directions:
1. Drizzle the fish with oil and sprinkle salt and pepper. Add chili, lemon juice, and garlic.
2. Toss well.
3. Place the fish on the PowerXL Air Fryer Grill basket at position 6.
4. Set the PowerXL Air Fryer Grill to Air Fryer/Grill.
5. Grill for about 8 minutes at 360F.
6. Flip while cooking.
7. Serve immediately.

Serving Suggestions: Serve with fries and ketchup.
Nutrition:
Calories: 231; Fat: 17 g; Carbs: 0.2 g; Protein: 22 g.

312. Orange Sauce with Trout Fillet
Preparation Time: 10 minutes
Cooking Time: 10 minutes
Servings: 5
Ingredients:
- 1 tbsp. minced ginger
- 5 chopped spring onion
- Black pepper and salt
- 1 orange juice and zest
- 1 tbsp. olive oil
- 5 trout fillets

Directions:
1. Sprinkle pepper and salt over the trout fillet.
2. Brush the fillets with olive oil.
3. Transfer the fillets to the PowerXL Air Fryer Grill pan.
4. Add spring onion, orange juice and zest, and ginger to the grill pan.
5. Set the PowerXL Air Fryer Grill to Air Fryer/Grill.
6. Grill for about 10 minutes at 360°F.
7. Serve immediately.

Serving Suggestions: Serve with the orange sauce.
Directions & Cooking Tips: Remove the skin and bone of the trout fillets.
Nutrition:
Calories: 348; Fat: 14 g; Carbs: 15 g; Protein: 42 g.

313. Grilled Parsley and Thyme Salmon
Preparation Time: 10 minutes
Cooking Time: 12 minutes
Servings: 5
Ingredients:
- 5 parsley sprigs
- 5 salmon fillets
- 1 chopped yellow onion
- 3 tbsp. olive oil
- 3 sliced tomatoes
- 5 thyme sprigs
- Black pepper and salt
- 1 lemon juice

Directions:
1. Pour 1 tablespoon of oil on the PowerXL Air Fryer Grill pan.
2. Add the sliced tomatoes to the grill pan.
3. Sprinkle pepper and salt on the tomatoes.
4. Pour another tablespoon of oil into the grill pan.
5. Place onion, fish, parsley spring, lemon juice, and thyme sprig on the tomatoes.
6. Transfer the pan to the PowerXL Air Fryer Grill basket.
7. Set the PowerXL Air Fryer Grill to Air Fryer/Grill.
8. Set the timer to 12 minutes and the temperature at 360°F.
9. Serve immediately.

Serving Suggestions: Serve with your favorite sauce.
Directions & Cooking Tips: Debone the fillets.
Nutrition:
Calories: 290; Fat: 10 g; Carbs: 15 g; Protein: 32 g.

314. Grilled Mustard Salmon

Preparation Time: 15 minutes
Cooking Time: 10 minutes
Servings: 2
Ingredients:

- 1 tbsp. coconut oil
- 2 large salmon fillets
- 2 tbsp. mustard - 1 tbsp. maple extract
- Black pepper and salt

Directions:

1. Mix mustard, salmon, maple extract, pepper, and salt in a bowl.
2. Drizzle the fish with cooking oil.
3. Place the fish on the PowerXL Air Fryer Grill basket at position 6.
4. Set the PowerXL Air Fryer Grill to Air Fryer/Grill.
5. Set the timer to 10 minutes at 370°F.
6. Serve immediately.

Serving Suggestions: Remove the salmon bone before cooking.
Directions & Cooking Tips: Serve with maple syrup.
Nutrition:
Calories: 300; Fat: 22 g; Carbs: 2.5 g; Protein: 25 g.

315. Tabasco Shrimps

Preparation Time: 15 minutes
Cooking Time: 10 minutes
Servings: 5
Ingredients:

- 1 tsp. oregano
- Black pepper and pepper
- 1-pound shrimp
- 1/2 tsp. smoked paprika
- 1 tsp. Tabasco sauce
- 1 tsp. red pepper flakes
- 1/2 tsp. parsley
- 2 tbsp. olive oil
- 2 tbsp. water

Directions:

1. Mix shrimps, pepper, salt, and water in a bowl.
2. Add pepper flakes, parsley, paprika, tabasco sauce, and oregano.
3. Mix well.
4. Preheat the PowerXL Air Fryer Grill.
5. Place the mixture on the PowerXL Air Fryer Grill basket.
6. Set the PowerXL Air Fryer Grill to Air Fryer/Grill.
7. Grill for 10 minutes at 370°F.

Serving Suggestions: Serve with salad.
Directions & Cooking Tips: Rinse shrimp well before coating.
Nutrition:
Calories: 210; Fat: 13 g; Carbs: 2 g; Protein: 22 g.

316. Onion Pepper Shrimp

Preparation Time: 10 minutes
Cooking Time: 12 minutes
Servings: 4
Ingredients:

- 1 lb. shrimp, peeled, deveined, & tails removed
- 1/8 tsp. cayenne pepper
- 1/2 tsp. garlic powder
- 1 tsp. chili powder
- 1 tbsp. olive oil
- 1/2 onion, cut into 1-inch chunks
- 1 red bell pepper, cut into 1-inch chunks

Directions:

1. Add shrimp and remaining ingredients into the mixing bowl and toss well.
2. Add shrimp mixture into the Air Fryer basket and cook at 330°F for 10-12 minutes. Shake Air Fryer basket halfway through.

Nutrition:
Calories: 183; Fat: 5.6 g; Carbohydrates: 5.9 g; Sugar: 2.2 g; Protein: 26.4 g; Cholesterol: 239 mg.

317. Old Bay Shrimp

Preparation Time: 10 minutes
Cooking Time: 10 minutes
Servings: 4
Ingredients:

- 12 oz. shrimp, peeled
- 3.25 oz. pork rind, crushed
- 1 1/2 tsp. old bay seasoning
- 1/4 cup mayonnaise

Directions:

1. In a shallow bowl, mix crushed pork rind and old bay seasoning.
2. Add shrimp and mayonnaise and toss well.
3. Coat shrimp with pork rind mixture and place it into the Air Fryer basket.
4. Cook shrimp at 380°F for 10 minutes.

Nutrition:
Calories: 290; Fat: 14.6 g; Carbohydrates: 4.8 g; Sugar: 0.9 g; Protein: 34.3 g; Cholesterol: 216 mg.

318. Shrimp with Vegetables

Preparation Time: 10 minutes
Cooking Time: 10 minutes
Servings: 4
Ingredients:

- 1 lb. shrimp, peeled and deveined
- 1 tsp. ginger, minced
- 1 tsp. garlic, minced
- 2 tsp. sesame oil - 2 tbsp. olive oil
- 4 tbsp. soy sauce
- 1 lb. mushrooms, quartered
- 1 green bell pepper, sliced
- 1 lb. zucchini, cut into quarter-inch pieces

Directions:

1. Add shrimp and remaining ingredients into the mixing bowl and toss well.
2. Add shrimp mixture into the Air Fryer basket and cook for 10 minutes. Shake basket halfway through.

Nutrition:
Calories: 278; Fat: 11.8 g; Carbohydrates: 13.3 g; Sugar: 5.7 g; Protein: 32.1 g, Cholesterol: 239 mg.

319. Delicious Buttery Shrimp
Preparation Time: 10 minutes
Cooking Time: 6 minutes
Servings: 4
Ingredients:
- 12 large shrimp, peeled and deveined
- 3 garlic cloves, minced
- 3 tbsp. butter, melted

Directions:
1. In a bowl, add shrimp, garlic, butter, pepper, and salt. Marinate for 15 minutes.
2. Remove shrimp from marinade, place it into the Air Fryer basket, and cook for 6 minutes. Pour reserved marinade over shrimp and serve.

Nutrition:
Calories: 99; Fat: 8.9 g, Carbohydrates: 1 g; Sugar: 0 g; Protein: 4 g; Cholesterol: 58 mg.

320. Mexican Shrimp Fajitas
Preparation Time: 10 minutes
Cooking Time: 8 minutes
Servings: 4
Ingredients:
- 1 lb. jumbo shrimp, peeled and deveined
- 1 tsp. chili powder
- 1 tsp. paprika
- 1 oz. fajita seasoning
- 2 garlic cloves, minced
- 1 tbsp. olive oil - 1 onion, sliced
- 1 yellow bell pepper, sliced
- 1 red bell pepper, sliced

Directions:
1. Add shrimp and remaining ingredients into the large mixing bowl and toss well.
2. Add shrimp mixture into the Air Fryer basket and cook at 400°F for 8 minutes. Shake basket halfway through.

Nutrition:
Calories: 173; Fat: 3.9 g; Carbohydrates: 13.6 g; Sugar: 6.3 g; Protein: 21.4 g; Cholesterol: 233 mg.

321. Crisp & Juicy Cajun Shrimp
Preparation Time: 10 minutes
Cooking Time: 10 minutes
Servings: 4
Ingredients:
- 1 lb. shrimp, peeled and deveined
- 1 tbsp. olive oil
- 1/2 tsp. Cajun seasoning
- 1 garlic clove, minced

Directions:
1. Add shrimp, oil, Cajun seasoning, garlic, pepper, and salt into the mixing bowl. Toss well and refrigerate for 1 hour.
2. Add shrimp mixture into the Air Fryer basket and cook at 350°F for 8-10 minutes. Turn halfway through.

Nutrition:
Calories: 166; Fat: 5.4 g; Carbohydrates: 2 g; Sugar: 0 g; Protein: 25.9 g; Cholesterol: 239 mg.

322. Lime Garlic Shrimp Kababs
Preparation Time: 10 minutes
Cooking Time: 8 minutes
Servings: 2
Ingredients:
- 1 cup raw shrimp - 1 lime juice
- 1 garlic clove, minced

Directions:
1. Preheat the Air Fryer to 350°F.
2. In a bowl, mix shrimp, lime juice, garlic, pepper, and salt.
3. Thread shrimp onto the skewers and place them into the Air Fryer basket; cook for 8 minutes. Turn halfway through.

Nutrition:
Calories: 201; Fat: 2.8 g; Carbohydrates: 4.9 g; Sugar: 0.4 g; Protein: 37.2 g; Cholesterol: 342 mg.

323. Tasty Chipotle Shrimp
Preparation Time: 10 minutes
Cooking Time: 8 minutes
Servings: 4
Ingredients:
- 1 1/2 lb. shrimp, peeled and deveined
- 2 tbsp. olive oil
- 4 tbsp. lime juice
- 1/4 tsp. ground cumin
- 2 tsp. chipotle in adobo

Directions:
1. Add shrimp, oil, lime juice, cumin, and chipotle in a ziplock bag. Seal the bag, shake well, and place it in the refrigerator for 30 minutes.
2. Thread marinated shrimp onto skewers and place them into the Air Fryer basket.
3. Cook at 350°F for 8 minutes.

Nutrition:
Calories: 274; Fat: 10 g; Carbohydrates: 6.4 g; Sugar: 0.7 g; Protein: 39 g; Cholesterol: 359 mg.

324. Tasty Shrimp Fajitas
Preparation Time: 10 minutes
Cooking Time: 22 minutes
Servings: 12
Ingredients:
- 1 lb. shrimp, tail-off
- 2 tbsp. taco seasoning
- 1/2 cup onion, diced
- 1 green bell pepper, diced
- 1 red bell pepper, diced

Directions:
1. Coat the Air Fryer basket with cooking spray.
2. Add shrimp, taco seasoning, onion, and bell peppers into the mixing bowl; toss well.

3. Place the shrimp mixture into the Air Fryer basket and cook at 390°F for 12 minutes.
4. Stir shrimp mixture and cook for 10 minutes more.

Nutrition:
Calories: 55; Fat: 0.8 g; Carbohydrates: 2.7 g; Sugar: 1.2 g; Protein: 9 g; Cholesterol: 80 mg.

325. Easy Coconut Shrimp
Preparation Time: 10 minutes
Cooking Time: 8 minutes
Servings: 8
Ingredients:
- 2 eggs, lightly beaten
- 1 lb. large shrimp, peeled and deveined
- 1 cup unsweetened flaked coconut
- 1/4 cup coconut flour

Directions:
1. In a small bowl, add coconut flour.
2. In a shallow bowl, add eggs. In a separate shallow bowl, add flakes coconut.
3. Coat shrimp with coconut flour; then dip in eggs and finally coat with flaked coconut.
4. Coat the Air Fryer basket with cooking spray.
5. Place the coated shrimp into the Air Fryer basket and cook at 400°F for 6–8 minutes. Turn shrimp halfway through.

Nutrition:
Calories: 112; Fat: 4.8 g; Carbohydrates: 5.1 g; Sugar: 0.7 g; Protein: 12.9 g; Cholesterol: 122 mg.

326. Shrimp & Vegetable Dinner
Preparation Time: 10 minutes
Cooking Time: 10 minutes
Servings: 4
Ingredients:
- 1 lb. jumbo shrimp, cleaned and peeled
- 2 tbsp. olive oil
- 1 bell pepper, cut into 1-inch pieces
- 8 oz. yellow squash, sliced into 1/4-inch half moons
- 1 medium zucchini, sliced into 1/4-inch half moons
- 6 oz. sausage, cooked and sliced
- 1 tbsp. Cajun seasoning
- 1/4 tsp. kosher salt

Directions:
1. Add shrimp and remaining ingredients into the large mixing bowl; toss well to coat.
2. Preheat the Air Fryer to 400°F.
3. Add shrimp mixture into the Air Fryer basket and cook for 10 minutes. Shake Air Fryer basket 3 times during the process.

Nutrition:
Calories: 312; Fat: 19.3 g; Carbohydrates: 5.8 g; Sugar: 5.4 g; Protein: 30.1 g; Cholesterol: 269 mg.

327. Lemon Garlic Shrimp
Preparation Time: 10 minutes
Cooking Time: 15 minutes
Servings: 3
Ingredients:
- 1 lb. shrimp, peeled and deveined
- 1/4 tsp. garlic powder
- 1 tbsp. olive oil
- 1/2 fresh lemon
- 2 tbsp. fresh parsley, chopped

Directions:
1. Toss shrimp with garlic powder, olive oil, pepper, and salt.
2. Add shrimp into the Air Fryer basket and cook at 400°F for 12–15 minutes. Shake basket halfway through.
3. Transfer shrimp to the serving bowl.
4. Squeeze lemon juice over shrimp.
5. Garnish with parsley and serve.

Nutrition:
Calories: 224; Fat: 7.3 g; Carbohydrates: 3.6 g; Sugar: 0.3 g; Protein: 34.7 g; Cholesterol: 318 mg.

328. Easy Cajun Shrimp
Preparation Time: 10 minutes
Cooking Time: 6 minutes
Servings: 2
Ingredients:
- 1/2 lb. shrimp, peeled and deveined
- 1 tbsp. olive oil
- 1/4 tsp. paprika
- 1/2 tsp. old bay seasoning
- 1/2 tsp. cayenne pepper
- A pinch salt

Directions:
1. Preheat the Air Fryer to 390°F.
2. Add shrimp and remaining ingredients into the mixing bowl; toss well to coat.
3. Add shrimp into the Air Fryer basket and cook for 6 minutes.

Nutrition:
Calories: 197; Fat: 9 g; Carbohydrates: 2.1 g; Sugar: 0.1 g; Protein: 25.9 g; Cholesterol: 239 mg.

329. Sweet and Savory Breaded Shrimp
Preparation Time: 5 minutes
Cooking Time: 20 minutes
Servings: 2
Ingredients:
- 1/2-pound fresh shrimp, peeled from their shells and rinsed
- 2 raw eggs
- 1/2 cup breadcrumbs (we like Panko, but any brand or home recipe will do)
- 1/2 white onion, peeled and rinsed, and finely chopped
- 1 tsp. ginger-garlic paste
- 1/2 tsp. turmeric powder
- 1/2 tsp. red chili powder
- 1/2 tsp. cumin powder
- 1/2 tsp. black pepper powder
- 1/2 tsp. dry mango powder
- A pinch salt

Directions:

1. **Preparing the Ingredients.** Cover the basket of the XL Air Fryer Oven with a lining of tin foil, leaving the edges uncovered to allow air to circulate through the basket.
2. Preheat the XL Air Fryer oven to 350°F.
3. In a mixing bowl, whisk the eggs until fluffy and the yolks and whites are fully combined.
4. Dunk all the shrimp in the egg mixture, fully submerging.
5. In a separate mixing bowl, combine the bread crumbs with all the dry ingredients until evenly blended.
6. One by one, coat the egg-covered shrimp in the mixed dry ingredients so that they get fully covered, and place them on the foil-lined air-fryer basket.
7. **Air Frying.** Set the air-fryer timer to 20 minutes.
8. Halfway through the cooking time, shake the handle of the air-fryer so that the breaded shrimp jostles inside and fry coverage is even.
9. After 20 minutes, when the fryer shuts off, the shrimp will be perfectly cooked and their breaded crust golden-brown and delicious! Using tongs, remove from the Air Fryer oven and set on a serving dish to cool.

Nutrition:
Calories: 195; Fat: 11 g; Protein: 25 g; Sugar: 0 g.

330. Bacon-Wrapped Shrimp
Preparation Time: 5 minutes
Cooking Time: 5 minutes
Servings: 4
Ingredients:
- 1¼ pound tiger shrimp, peeled and deveined
- 1-pound bacon

Directions:
1. **Preparing the Ingredients.** With a slice of bacon, wrap each shrimp.
2. Refrigerate for about 20 minutes.
3. **Air Frying.** Arrange the shrimp in the oven rack/basket. Place the rack on the middle shelf of the XL Air Fryer oven. Cook for about 5–7 minutes.

Nutrition:
Calories: 190; Fat: 11 g; Protein: 21 g; Sugar: 0 g.

331. Spicy Scallops
Preparation Time: 10 minutes
Cooking Time: 8 minutes
Servings: 4
Ingredients:
- 1 lb. scallops, thawed, washed, and pat dry with a paper towel
- 1 tsp. garlic powder
- 1 tbsp. chili powder
- 1 tbsp. paprika
- 2 tbsp. onion flakes
- Pepper
- Salt

Directions:
1. Coat the Air Fryer basket with cooking spray.
2. In a mixing bowl, add scallops and remaining Ingredients; toss well.
3. Add scallops into the Air Fryer basket and cook at 340°F for 8 minutes. Shake basket halfway through. Serve and enjoy.

Nutrition:
Calories: 122; Fat: 1.4 g; Carbohydrates: 7.3 g; Sugar: 1.4 g; Protein: 19.9 g; Cholesterol: 37 mg.

332. Pesto Scallops
Preparation Time: 10 minutes
Cooking Time: 8 minutes
Servings: 4
Ingredients:
- 1 lb. sea scallops
- 2 tsp. garlic, minced
- 3 tbsp. heavy cream
- 1/4 cup basil pesto
- 1 tbsp. olive oil
- Pepper
- Salt

Directions:
1. In a small pan, mix oil, heavy cream, garlic, basil pesto, pepper, and salt. Simmer for 2–3 minutes.
2. Add scallops into the Air Fryer basket and cook at 320°F for 5 minutes.
3. Turn scallops and cook for 3 minutes more.
4. Transfer scallops into the mixing bowl. Pour sauce over the scallops and toss to coat.
5. Serve and enjoy.

Nutrition:
Calories: 171; Fat: 8.5 g; Carbohydrates: 3.5 g; Sugar: 0 g; Protein: 19.4 g; Cholesterol: 53 mg.

333. Old Bay Seasoned Crab Cakes
Preparation Time: 10 minutes
Cooking Time: 10 minutes
Servings: 5
Ingredients:
- 2 eggs
- 1/4 cup almond flour
- 2 tsp. dried parsley
- 1 tbsp. dried celery
- 1 tsp. old bay seasoning
- 1 1/2 tbsp. Dijon mustard
- 2 1/2 tbsp. mayonnaise
- 18 oz. can lump crab meat, drained
- 1/2 tsp. salt

Directions:
1. Line Air Fryer basket with aluminum foil.
2. Add all ingredients into the mixing bowl and mix until well combined. Place mixture in the refrigerator for 10 minutes.
3. Make five equal shapes of patties from the mixture and place them onto the aluminum foil in the Air Fryer basket.
4. Cook at 320°F for 10 minutes. Turn patties halfway through. Serve and enjoy.

Nutrition:

Calories: 139; Fat: 13.3 g; Carbohydrates: 4.2 g; Sugar: 0.7 g; Protein: 17.6 g; Cholesterol: 125 mg.

334. Lemon Garlic Scallops

Preparation Time: 10 minutes
Cooking Time: 8 minutes
Servings: 4
Ingredients:
- 1 lb. sea scallops, pat dry with paper towels
- 1 tsp. fresh thyme
- 1 garlic clove, minced
- 2 tbsp. fresh lemon juice
- 1/4 cup olive oil
- Pepper
- Salt

Directions:
1. Season scallops with pepper and salt.
2. Coat the Air Fryer basket with cooking spray.
3. Add scallops into the Air Fryer basket and cook at 400°F for 5–8 minutes or until the internal temperature of the scallops reaches 120°F. Transfer the scallops to the serving bowl. Heat olive oil in a pan on medium fire. Add garlic and sauté until garlic softens. Add lemon juice and whisk until sauce is heated through. Pour olive oil mixture over the cooked scallops. Garnish with thyme and serve.

Nutrition:
Calories: 212; Fat: 13.5 g; Carbohydrates: 3.3 g; Sugar: 0.2 g; Protein: 19.2 g; Cholesterol: 37 mg.

335. Lemon Caper Scallops

Preparation Time: 10 minutes
Cooking Time: 6 minutes
Servings: 2
Ingredients:
- 8 large sea scallops, clean and pat dry with a paper towel
- 1/2 tsp. garlic, chopped
- 1 tsp. lemon zest, grated
- 2 tsp. capers, chopped
- 2 tbsp. fresh parsley, chopped
- 1/4 cup olive oil
- Pepper
- Salt

Directions:
1. Season scallops with pepper and salt.
2. Coat the Air Fryer basket with cooking spray.
3. Place scallops into the Air Fryer basket and cook at 400°F for 6 minutes or until the internal temperature of scallops reaches 120°F.
4. In a small bowl, mix oil, garlic, lemon zest, capers, and parsley; drizzle over the scallops and serve.

Nutrition:
Calories: 325; Fat: 26.2 g; Carbohydrates: 3.7 g; Sugar: 0.1 g; Protein: 20.4 g; Cholesterol: 40 mg.

336. Cajun Scallops

Preparation Time: 10 minutes
Cooking Time: 6 minutes
Servings: 1
Ingredients:
- 6 scallops, clean and pat dry with a paper towel
- 1/2 tsp. Cajun seasoning - Salt

Directions:
1. Preheat the Air Fryer to 400°F.
2. Line the Air Fryer basket with aluminum foil and grease with cooking spray.
3. Place the scallops into the Air Fryer basket.
4. Season the scallops with Cajun seasoning and salt and cook for 6 minutes. Turn scallops halfway through.
5. Serve and enjoy.

Nutrition:
Calories: 158; Fat: 1.4 g; Carbohydrates: 4.3 g; Sugar: 0 g; Protein: 30.2 g; Cholesterol: 59 mg.

337. Flavorful Crab Cakes

Preparation Time: 10 minutes
Cooking Time: 10 minutes
Servings: 4
Ingredients:
- 8 oz. lump crab
- 1 tsp. old bay seasoning
- 1 tbsp. Dijon mustard
- 2 tbsp. almond flour
- 2 tbsp. mayonnaise
- 2 tbsp. green onion, chopped
- 1/4 cup bell pepper, chopped
- Pepper
- Salt

Directions:
1. Add lump crab and remaining ingredients into a bowl and mix until well combined.
2. Make four equal shapes of patties from the mixture and place them into the Air Fryer basket.
3. Coat the top of the patties with cooking spray.
4. Cook at 370°F for 10 minutes.
5. Serve and enjoy.

Nutrition:
Calories: 156; Fat: 14.2 g; Carbohydrates: 6.7 g; Sugar: 1.5 g; Protein: 11.6 g; Cholesterol: 34 mg.

338. Healthy Crab Cakes

Preparation Time: 10 minutes
Cooking Time: 10 minutes
Servings: 4
Ingredients:
- 8 oz. lump crab meat
- 2 tbsp. butter, melted
- 2 tsp. Dijon mustard
- 1 tbsp. mayonnaise
- 1 egg, lightly beaten
- 1/2 tsp. old bay seasoning
- 1 green onion, sliced
- 2 tbsp. parsley, chopped
- 1/4 cup almond flour
- Pepper

- Salt

Directions:
1. Add crab meat, mustard, mayonnaise, egg, old bay seasoning, green onion, parsley, almond flour, pepper, and salt into a bowl; mix until well combined.
2. Make four equal shapes of patties from the mixture, place them on a waxed paper-lined dish, and refrigerate for 30 minutes. Brush melted butter over both sides of the patties and place them into the Air Fryer basket.
3. Cook patties at 350°F for 10 minutes. Turn halfway through. Serve and enjoy.

Nutrition:
Calories: 136; Fat: 13.7 g; Carbohydrates: 2.8 g; Sugar: 0.5 g; Protein: 10.3 g; Cholesterol: 89 mg.

339. Crisp Bacon Wrapped Scallops

Preparation Time: 10 minutes
Cooking Time: 8 minutes
Servings: 4
Ingredients:
- 16 scallops, clean and pat dry with paper towels
- 8 bacon slices, cut each slice in half
- Pepper
- Salt

Directions:
1. Preheat the Air Fryer to 400°F.
2. Place bacon slices into the Air Fryer basket and cook for 3 minutes. Turn halfway through.
3. Wrap each scallop in a bacon slice and secure it with a toothpick. Season with pepper and salt.
4. Coat-wrapped scallops with cooking spray and place them into the Air Fryer basket.
5. Cook scallops for 8 minutes. Turn halfway through.
6. Serve and enjoy.

Nutrition:
Calories: 311; Fat: 16.8 g; Carbohydrates: 3.4 g; Sugar: 0 g; Protein: 34.2 g; Cholesterol: 81 mg.

340. Soy and Ginger Shrimp

Preparation Time: 8 minutes
Cooking Time: 10 minutes
Servings: 4
Ingredients:
- 2 tbsp. olive oil
- 2 tbsp. scallions, finely chopped
- 2 cloves garlic, chopped
- 1 tsp. fresh ginger, grated
- 1 tbsp. dry white wine
- 1 tbsp. balsamic vinegar
- 1/4 cup soy sauce
- 1 tbsp. sugar
- 1-pound shrimp
- Salt and ground black pepper, to taste

Directions:
1. **Preparing the Ingredients.** To make the marinade, warm the oil in a saucepan; cook all ingredients, except the shrimp, salt, and black pepper. Now, let it cool.
2. Marinate the shrimp, covered, at least an hour, in the refrigerator.
3. **Air Frying.** After that, bake the shrimp at 350°F for 8 to 10 minutes (depending on the size), turning once or twice. Season the prepared shrimp with salt and black pepper and serve right away.

Nutrition:
Calories: 165; Carbs: 5.8; Fat: 4.5 g; Protein: 24 g; Fiber: 0 g.

341. Quick Paella

Preparation Time: 7 minutes
Cooking Time: 15 minutes
Servings: 4
Ingredients:
- 1 (10-ounce) package frozen cooked rice, thawed
- 1 (6-ounce) jar artichoke hearts, drained and chopped
- 1/4 cup vegetable broth
- 1/2 tsp. turmeric
- 1/2 tsp. dried thyme
- 1 cup frozen cooked small shrimp
- 1/2 cup frozen baby peas
- 1 tomato, diced

Directions:
1. **Preparing the Ingredients.** In a 6-by-6-by-2-inch pan, combine the rice, artichoke hearts, vegetable broth, turmeric, and thyme; stir gently.
2. **Air Frying.** Place in the XL Air Fryer oven and bake for 8 to 9 minutes or until the rice is hot. Remove from the Air Fryer oven and gently stir in the shrimp, peas, and tomato. Cook for 5 to 8 minutes or until the shrimp and peas are hot and the paella is bubbling.

Nutrition:
Calories: 345; Fat: 1 g; Protein: 18 g; Fiber: 4 g.

342. Steamed Salmon and Sauce

Preparation Time: 5 minutes
Cooking Time: 10 minutes
Servings: 2
Ingredients:
- 1 cup water
- 2 x 6 oz. fresh salmon
- 1 tsp. vegetable oil
- ½ cup plain Greek yogurt
- ½ cup sour cream
- 1 tbsp. finely chopped dill (keep a bit for garnishing)
- A pinch salt to taste

Directions:
1. Pour the water into the tray of the Air Fryer oven and start heating to 285 Fahrenheit.
2. Drizzle oil over the fish and spread it. Salt the fish to taste.
3. Now pop it into the Air Fryer oven for 10 minutes.
4. In the meantime, mix the yogurt, cream, dill, and a bit of salt to make the sauce. When the fish is done, serve with the sauce and garnish with sprigs of dill.

Nutrition:
Calories: 185; Fat: 11 g; Protein: 21 g; Sugar: 0 g.

343. Indian Fish Fingers

Preparation Time: 35 minutes
Cooking Time: 15 minutes
Servings: 4
Ingredients:
- 1/2-pound fish fillet
- 1 tbsp. finely chopped fresh mint leaves or any fresh herbs
- 1/3 cup bread crumbs
- 1 tsp. ginger garlic paste or ginger and garlic powders
- 1 hot green chili finely chopped
- 1/2 tsp. paprika
- A generous pinch black pepper
- Salt to taste
- 3/4 tbsp. lemon juice
- 3/4 tsp. garam masala powder
- 1/3 tsp. rosemary
- 1 egg

Directions:
1. Start by removing any skin on the fish, washing, and patting dry. Cut the fish into fingers.
2. In a medium bowl mix all ingredients except for fish, mint, and bread crumbs. Bury the fingers in the mixture and refrigerate for 30 minutes.
3. Remove them from the fridge and mix in mint leaves.
4. In a separate bowl beat the egg; pour bread crumbs into a third bowl. Dip the fingers in the egg bowl; then toss them in the bread crumbs bowl.
5. Put the fingers into the oven rack/basket. Place the rack on the middle shelf of the Air Fryer oven. Set temperature to 360°F, and time to 15 minutes, toss the fingers halfway through.

Nutrition:
Calories: 187; Fat: 7 g; Protein: 11 g; Fiber: 1 g.

344. Flying Fish

Preparation Time: 5 minutes
Cooking Time: 12 minutes
Servings: 6
Ingredients:
- 1 tbsp. oil
- 3–4 oz. breadcrumbs
- 1 whisked whole egg in a saucer/soup plate
- 6 fresh fish fillets
- Fresh lemon (For serving)

Directions:
1. Preheat the Air Fryer to 350°F. Mix the crumbs and oil until it looks nice and loose.
2. Dip the fish in the egg and coat lightly, then move on to the crumbs. Make sure the fillet is covered evenly.
3. Cook in the Air Fryer oven basket for roughly 12 minutes—depending on the size of the fillets you are using.
4. Serve with fresh lemon and chips to complete the duo.

Nutrition:
Calories: 480; Fat: 37 g; Carbohydrates: 9 g; Protein: 49 g.

345. Pistachio-Crusted Lemon-Garlic Salmon

Preparation Time: 5 minutes
Cooking Time: 20 minutes
Servings: 6
Ingredients:
- medium-sized salmon filets
- raw eggs
- ounces melted butter
- 1 clove garlic, peeled and finely minced
- 1 large-sized lemon
- 1 tsp. salt
- 1 tbsp. parsley, rinsed, patted dry, and chopped
- 1 tsp. dill, rinsed, patted dry, and chopped
- ½ cup pistachio nuts, shelled and coarsely crushed

Directions:
1. Cover the basket of the Air Fryer with a lining of tin foil, leaving the edges uncovered to allow air to circulate through the basket.
2. Preheat the Air Fryer oven to 350°F.
3. In a mixing bowl, beat the eggs until fluffy and the yolks and whites are fully combined.
4. Add the melted butter, lemon juice, minced garlic, parsley, and dill; stir thoroughly.
5. One by one, dunk the salmon filets into the wet mixture, then roll them in the crushed pistachios, coating completely.
6. Place the coated salmon fillets in the Air Fryer oven basket.
7. Set the Air Fryer oven timer for 10 minutes.
8. When the Air Fryer shuts off, after 10 minutes, the salmon will be partially cooked and the crust begins to crisp. Using tongs, turn each of the fish filets over.
9. Reset the Air Fryer oven to 350°F for another 10 minutes.
10. After 10 minutes, when the Air Fryer shuts off, the salmon will be perfectly cooked and the pistachio crust will be toasted and crispy. Using tongs, remove from the Air Fryer and serve.

Nutrition:
Calories: 185; Fat: 11 g; Protein: 21 g; Sugar: 0 g.

346. Salmon Noodles

Preparation Time: 5 minutes
Cooking Time: 16 minutes
Servings: 4
Ingredients:
- 1 salmon fillet
- 1 tbsp. teriyaki marinade
- ½ oz, soba noodles, cooked and drained
- 1 oz. firm tofu
- 1 oz. mixed salad
- 1 cup broccoli
- 1 tbsp olive oil
- Salt and pepper to taste

Directions:
1. Season the salmon with salt and pepper to taste, then coat with the teriyaki marinade. Set aside for 15 minutes.

2. Preheat the Air Fryer oven at 350°F, then cook the salmon for 8 minutes. Whilst the Air Fryer is cooking the salmon, start slicing the tofu into small cubes. Next, slice the broccoli into smaller chunks. Drizzle with olive oil. Once the salmon is cooked, put the broccoli and tofu into the Air Fryer oven tray for another 8 minutes.
3. Plate the salmon and broccoli tofu mixture over the soba noodles. Add the mixed salad to the side and serve.

Nutrition:
Calories: 185 Fat 11 g; Protein: 21 g; Sugar 0 g.

347. Fried Calamari

Preparation Time: 8 minutes
Cooking Time: 15 minutes
Servings: 6–8
Ingredients:

- ½ tsp. salt
- ½ tsp. Old Bay seasoning
- 1/3 cup plain cornmeal
- ½ cup semolina flour
- ½ cup almond flour
- 5–6 cup olive oil
- 1 ½ pounds baby squid

Directions:

1. Rinse squid in cold water and slice tentacles, keeping just ¼-inch of the hood in one piece.
2. Combine 1–2 pinches of pepper, salt, Old Bay seasoning, cornmeal, and both flours. Dredge squid pieces into the flour mixture and place them into the Air Fryer basket.
3. Spray liberally with olive oil.
4. Cook for 15 minutes at 345°F till coating turns golden brown.

Nutrition:
Calories: 211; Carbohydrates: 55 g; Fat: 6 g; Protein: 21 g.

348. Mustard-Crusted Fish Fillets

Preparation Time: 5 minutes
Cooking Time: 8 to 11 minutes
Servings: 4
Ingredients:

- 1 tsp. low-sodium yellow mustard
- 1 tbsp. freshly squeezed lemon juice
- (3.5-ounce) sole fillets
- ½ tsp. dried thyme
- ½ tsp. dried marjoram
- ⅛ tsp. freshly ground black pepper
- 1 slice low-sodium whole-wheat bread, crumbled
- 1 tsp. olive oil

Directions:

1. In a small bowl, mix the mustard and lemon juice. Spread this evenly over the fillets. Place them in the Air Fryer basket.
2. In another small bowl, mix the thyme, marjoram, pepper, bread crumbs, and olive oil. Mix until combined.
3. Gently but firmly press the spice mixture onto the top of each fish fillet.
4. Bake for 8 to 11 minutes at 320°F, or until the fish reaches an internal temperature of at least 145°F on a meat thermometer and the topping is browned and crisp. Serve immediately.

Nutrition:
Calories: 142; Fat: 4 g; Saturated Fat: 1 g; Protein: 20 g; Carbohydrates: 5 g; Sodium: 140 g; Fiber: 1 g; Sugar: 1 g.

349. Fish and Vegetable Tacos

Preparation Time: 15 minutes
Cooking Time: 9 to 12 minutes
Servings: 4
Ingredients:

- 1lb. white fish fillets, such as sole
- tsp. olive oil
- tbsp. freshly squeezed lemon juice, divided
- 1 1/2 cups chopped red cabbage
- 1 large carrot, grated
- 1/2 cup low-sodium salsa
- 1/3 cup low-fat Greek yogurt
- Soft low-sodium whole-wheat tortillas

Directions:

1. Brush the fish with olive oil and sprinkle with 1 tablespoon of lemon juice. Air-fry in the Air Fryer basket for 9 to 12 minutes at 390°F, or until the fish just flakes when tested with a fork.
2. Meanwhile, in a medium bowl, stir together the remaining 2 tablespoons of lemon juice, red cabbage, carrot, salsa, and yogurt.
3. When the fish is cooked, remove it from the Air Fryer basket and break it up into large pieces.
4. Offer the fish, tortillas, and the cabbage mixture, and let each person assemble a taco.

Nutrition:
Calories: 209; Fat: 3 g; Saturated Fat: 0 g; Protein: 18 g; Carbohydrates: 30 g; Sodium: 116 g; Fiber: 1 g; Sugar: 4 g.

350. Lighter Fish and Chips

Preparation Time: 10 minutes
Cooking Time: 11 to 15 minutes (chips); 10 to 14 minutes (cod fillets)
Servings: 4
Ingredients:

- russet potatoes, peeled, thinly sliced, rinsed, and patted dry
- 1 egg white
- 1 tbsp. freshly squeezed lemon juice
- 1/3 cup ground almonds
- slices low-sodium whole-wheat bread, finely crumbled
- 1/2 tsp. dried basil - (4-ounce) cod fillets

Directions:

1. Preheat the oven to warm.
2. Put the potato slices in the Air Fryer basket and air-fry for 11 to 15 minutes at 390°F, or until crisp and brown. With tongs, turn the fries twice during cooking.
3. Meanwhile, in a shallow bowl, beat the egg white and lemon juice until frothy.
4. On a plate, mix the almonds, bread crumbs, and basil.

5. One at a time, dip the fillets into the egg white mixture and then into the almond–bread crumb mixture to coat. Place the coated fillets on a wire rack to dry while the fries cook.
6. When the potatoes are done, transfer them to a baking sheet and keep warm in the oven on low heat.
7. Air-fry the fish in the Air Fryer basket for 10 to 14 minutes, or until the fish reaches an internal temperature of at least 140°F on a meat thermometer and the coating is browned and crisp. Serve immediately with the potatoes.

Nutrition:
Calories: 247; Fat: 5 g; Saturated Fat: 0 g; Protein: 27 g; Carbohydrates: 25 g; Sodium: 131 g; Fiber: 3 g; Sugar: 3 g.

351. Snapper with Fruit
Preparation Time: 15 minutes
Cooking Time: 9 to 13 minutes
Servings: 4
Ingredients:
- (4-ounce) red snapper fillets
- tsp. olive oil
- nectarines, halved and pitted
- plums, halved and pitted
- 1 cup red grapes
- 1 tbsp. freshly squeezed lemon juice
- 1 tbsp. honey
- ½ tsp. dried thyme

Directions:
1. Put the red snapper in the Air Fryer basket and drizzle with the olive oil. Air-fry for 4 minutes at 390°F.
2. Remove the basket and add the nectarines and plums. Scatter the grapes overall.
3. Drizzle with the lemon juice and honey and sprinkle with thyme.
4. Return the basket to the Air Fryer and air-fry for 5 to 9 minutes more, or until the fish flakes when tested with a fork and the fruit is tender. Serve immediately.

Nutrition:
Calories: 245; Fat: 4 g; Saturated Fat: 1 g; Protein: 25 g; Carbohydrates: 28 g; Sodium: 73 g; Fiber: 3 g; Sugar: 24 g.

352. Tuna Wraps
Preparation Time: 10 minutes
Cooking Time: 4 to 7 minutes
Servings: 4
Ingredients:
- 1-pound fresh tuna steak, cut into 1-inch cubes
- 1 tbsp. grated fresh ginger
- garlic cloves, minced
- ½ tsp. toasted sesame oil
- low-sodium whole-wheat tortillas
- ¼ cup low-fat mayonnaise
- cups shredded romaine lettuce
- 1 red bell pepper, thinly sliced

Directions:
1. In a medium bowl, mix the tuna, ginger, garlic, and sesame oil. Let it stand for 10 minutes.
2. Grill the tuna in the Air Fryer for 4 to 7 minutes at 390°F, or until done to your liking and lightly browned.
3. Make wraps with tuna, tortillas, mayonnaise, lettuce, and bell pepper. Serve immediately.

Nutrition:
Calories: 288; Fat: 7 g; Saturated Fat: 2 g; Protein: 31 g; Carbohydrates: 26 g; Sodium: 135 g; Fiber: 1 g; Sugar: 1 g.

353. Tuna and Fruit Kebabs
Preparation Time: 15 minutes
Cooking Time: 8 to 12 minutes
Servings: 4
Ingredients:
- 1-pound tuna steaks, cut into 1-inch cubes
- ½ cup canned pineapple chunks, drained, juice reserved
- ½ cup large red grapes
- 1 tbsp. honey
- tsp. grated fresh ginger
- 1 tsp. olive oil
- Pinch cayenne pepper

Directions:
1. Thread the tuna, pineapple, and grapes on 8 bamboo or 4 metal skewers that fit in the Air Fryer.
2. In a small bowl, whisk the honey, 1 tablespoon of reserved pineapple juice, ginger, olive oil, and cayenne. Brush this mixture over the kebabs. Let them stand for 10 minutes.
3. Grill the kebabs for 8 to 12 minutes at 370°F, or until the tuna reaches an internal temperature of at least 145°F on a meat thermometer, and the fruit is tender and glazed, brushing once with the remaining sauce. Discard any remaining marinade. Serve immediately.

Nutrition:
Calories: 181; Fat: 2 g; Saturated Fat: 0 g; Protein: 18 g; Carbohydrates: 13 g; Sodium: 43 g; Fiber: 1 g; Sugar: 12 g.

354. Asian Swordfish
Preparation Time: 10 minutes
Cooking Time: 6 to 11 minutes
Servings: 4
Ingredients:
- (4-ounce) swordfish steaks
- ½ tsp. toasted sesame oil
- 1 jalapeño pepper, finely minced
- garlic cloves, grated
- 1 tbsp. grated fresh ginger
- ½ tsp. Chinese five-spice powder
- ⅛ tsp. freshly ground black pepper
- tbsp. freshly squeezed lemon juice

Directions:
1. Place the swordfish steaks on a work surface and drizzle with the sesame oil.
2. In a small bowl, mix the jalapeño, garlic, ginger, five-spice powder, pepper, and lemon juice. Rub this mixture into the fish and let it stand for 10 minutes.
3. Roast the swordfish in the Air Fryer for 6 to 11 minutes at 380°F, or until the swordfish reaches an internal

temperature of at least 140°F on a meat thermometer. Serve immediately.

Nutrition:
Calories: 187; Fat: 6 g; Saturated Fat: 1 g; Protein: 29g Carbohydrates: 2 g; Sodium: 132 g; Fiber: 0 g; Sugar: 1 g.

355. Salmon Spring Rolls

Preparation Time: 20 minutes
Cooking Time: 8 to 10 minutes
Servings: 4
Ingredients:

- ½ pound salmon fillet
- 1 tsp. toasted sesame oil
- 1 onion, sliced
- rice paper wrappers
- 1 yellow bell pepper, thinly sliced
- 1 carrot, shredded
- ⅓ cup chopped fresh flat-leaf parsley
- ¼ cup chopped fresh basil

Directions:

1. Put the salmon in the Air Fryer basket and drizzle with the sesame oil. Add the onion. Air-fry for 8 to 10 minutes, or until the salmon just flakes when tested with a fork and the onion is tender.
2. Meanwhile, fill a small shallow bowl with warm water. One at a time, dip the rice paper wrappers into the water and place them on a work surface.
3. Top each wrapper with one-eighth each of the salmon and onion mixture, yellow bell pepper, carrot, parsley, and basil. Roll up the wrapper, folding in the sides, to enclose the ingredients.
4. If you like, bake in the Air Fryer at 380°F for 7 to 9 minutes, until the rolls are crunchy. Cut the rolls in half to serve.

Nutrition: Calories: 95; Fat: 2 g; Saturated Fat: 0 g; Protein: 13g Carbohydrates: 8 g; Sodium: 98 g; Fiber: 2 g; Sugar: 2 g.

356. Salmon on Bed of Fennel and Carrot

Preparation Time: 15 minutes
Cooking Time: 13 to 14 minutes
Servings: 4
Ingredients:

- 1 fennel bulb, thinly sliced
- 1 large carrot, peeled and sliced
- 1 small onion, thinly sliced
- ¼ cup low-fat sour cream
- ¼ tsp. coarsely ground pepper
- (5 ounces) salmon fillets

Directions:

1. Combine the fennel, carrot, and onion in a bowl and toss.
2. Put the vegetable mixture into a 6-inch metal pan. Roast in the Air Fryer for 4 minutes at 400°F or until the vegetables are crisp-tender.
3. Remove the pan from the Air Fryer. Stir in the sour cream and sprinkle the vegetables with the pepper.
4. Top with the salmon fillets.
5. Return the pan to the Air Fryer. Roast for another 9 to 10 minutes or until the salmon just barely flakes when tested with a fork.

Nutrition: Calories: 253; Fat: 9 g; Saturated Fat: 1 g; Protein: 31 g; Carbohydrates: 12 g; Sodium: 115 g; Fiber: 3 g; Sugar: 5 g.

357. Scallops with Green Vegetables

Preparation Time: 15 minutes
Cooking Time: 8 to 11 minutes
Servings: 4
Ingredients:

- 1 cup green beans
- 1 cup frozen peas
- 1 cup frozen chopped broccoli
- tsp. olive oil
- ½ tsp. dried basil
- ½ tsp. dried oregano
- ounces sea scallops

Directions:

1. In a large bowl, toss the green beans, peas, and broccoli with olive oil. Place them in the Air Fryer basket. Air-fry for 4 to 6 minutes, or until the vegetables are crisp-tender.
2. Remove the vegetables from the Air Fryer basket and sprinkle them with the herbs. Set aside. In the Air Fryer basket, put the scallops and air-fry for 4 to 5 minutes at 400°F, or until the scallops are firm and reach an internal temperature of just 145°F on a meat thermometer. Toss scallops with the vegetables and serve immediately.

Nutrition:
Calories: 124; Fat: 3 g; Saturated Fat: 0 g; Protein: 14 g; Carbohydrates: 11 g; Sodium: 56 g; Fiber: 3 g; Sugar: 5 g.

358. Butter Up Salmon

Preparation Time: 10 minutes
Cooking Time: 20 minutes
Servings: 2
Ingredients:

- 2 pieces (6 ounces) salmon fillets
- Salt and pepper to taste
- 1 tbsp. butter, melted

Directions:

1. Season salmon fillet well with salt and pepper, coat them with butter.
2. Press "Power Button" on your Air Fryer and select "Air Fry" mode.
3. Press the Time Button and time to 20 minutes.
4. Push Temp Button and set temp to 320°F.
5. Press the "Start/Pause" button and start the device.
6. Once the appliance beeps to indicated that it is pre-heated, transfer fillets to a greased Air Fryer basket and push them into the oven.
7. Serve and enjoy!

Nutrition:
Calories: 270; Fat: 16 g; Saturated Fat: 5.2 g; Carbohydrates: 0 g; Fiber: 0 g; Sodium: 193 mg; Protein: 33 g.

359. Lemon Salmon

Preparation Time: 10 minutes
Cooking Time: 8 minutes
Servings: 3
Ingredients:

- 1 ½ pounds salmon
- ½ tsp. red chili powder
- Salt and pepper to taste
- 1 lemon, cut into slices
- 1 tbsp. fresh dill, chopped

Directions:

1. Season salmon with chili powder, salt, and pepper generously.
2. Press "Power Button" on your Air Fryer and select "Air Fry" mode.
3. Press the Time Button and time to 8 minutes.
4. Push Temp Button and set temp to 375°F.
5. Press the "Start/Pause" button and start the device.
6. Once the appliance beeps to indicate that it is pre-heated, arrange salmon fillets in the Air Fryer cooking basket.
7. Push into Air Fryer Oven and cook until the timer runs out.
8. Garnish with fresh dill and serve hot!

Nutrition:
Calories: 305; Fat: 14 g; Saturated Fat: 2 g; Carbohydrates: 1.3 g; Fiber: 0.4 g; Sodium: 156 mg; Protein: 44 g.

360. Hearty Spiced Salmon

Preparation Time: 10 minutes
Cooking Time: 11 minutes
Servings: 2
Ingredients:

- 1 tsp. smoked paprika
- 1 tsp. cayenne pepper
- 1 tsp. onion powder
- 1 tsp. garlic powder
- Salt and pepper to taste
- 2 pieces (6 ounces) salmon fillets
- 1 tsp. olive oil

Directions:

1. Take a small bowl and add spices; mix them well.
2. Drizzle salmon fillets with oil, rub the fillets with spice mixture.
3. Press "Power Button" on your Air Fryer and select "Air Fry" mode.
4. Press the Time Button and time to 11 minutes.
5. Push Temp Button and set temp to 390°F.
6. Press the "Start/Pause" button and start the device.
7. Once the appliance beeps to indicate that it is pre-heated, arrange salmon fillets in the Air Fryer cooking basket.
8. Push into Air Fryer Oven and cook until the timer runs out.
9. Serve and enjoy!

Nutrition:
Calories: 280; Fat: 15 g; Saturated Fat: 2 g; Carbohydrates: 3 g; Fiber: 1 g; Sodium: 0.8 mg; Protein: 33 g.

361. Cajun Shrimp

Preparation Time: 10 minutes
Cooking Time: 7 minutes
Servings: 4
Ingredients:

- 1 ¼ pound tiger shrimp, about 16-20 pieces
- ¼ tsp. cayenne pepper
- ½ tsp. old bay seasoning
- ¼ tsp. smoked paprika
- A pinch salt
- 1 tbsp. olive oil

Directions:

1. Preheat your Air Fryer to 390°F in "AIR FRY" mode.
2. Take a mixing bowl and add ingredients (except shrimp), mix well.
3. Dip the shrimp into the spice mixture and oil.
4. Transfer the shrimp to your cooking basket and cook for 5 minutes. Serve and enjoy!

Nutrition:
Calories: 180; Fat: 2 g; Saturated Fat: 1 g; Carbohydrates: 5 g; Fiber: 0 g; Sodium: 970 mg; Protein: 23 g.

362. Air Fried Dragon Shrimp

Preparation Time: 10 minutes
Cooking Time: 10 minutes
Servings: 4
Ingredients:

- 1 pound raw shrimp, peeled and deveined
- 1 ½ cup soy sauce
- 2 eggs
- 1 tbsp. olive oil
- 1 cup yellow onion, diced
- ¼ cup flour
- ½ tsp. red pepper, ground
- ½ tsp. ginger, grounded

Directions:

1. Preheat your Air Fryer to 350°F in "AIR FRY" mode.
2. Add all the ingredients to make the batter, except for the shrimp.
3. Set it aside for 10 minutes.
4. Dip each shrimp into the batter to coat all sides. Place them on the Air Fryer basket.
5. Cook for 10 minutes.
6. Serve and enjoy!

Nutrition:
Calories: 600; Fat: 6 g; Saturated Fat: 2 g; Carbohydrates: 59 g; Fiber: 8 g; Sodium: 690 mg; Protein: 31 g.

363. Fish Tacos

Preparation Time: 10 minutes
Cooking Time: 9 minutes
Servings: 4
Ingredients:

- 4 cod fillets, cut into 1-inch cubes
- Salt and black pepper to taste
- ½ lime, juiced

- ½ cup all-purpose flour
- 1 large egg, lightly beaten
- 1 cup panko breadcrumbs
- Olive oil for brushing
- 4 medium corn tortillas
- ½ cup shredded red cabbage
- 1 medium avocado, pitted, peeled, and chopped
- 1 tbsp. chopped fresh cilantro
- 1 cup sour cream
- Lime wedges for serving

Directions:
1. Insert the dripping pan in the bottom part of the Air Fryer and preheat the oven at Air Fry mode at 400°F for 2 to 3 minutes. Lightly brush the rotisserie basket with some olive oil and set it aside.
2. Season the fish with salt, black pepper, and lime juice.
3. Pour the flour onto a plate and the breadcrumbs onto another. Dredge the fish pieces lightly on the flour, then in the eggs, and the breadcrumbs. Put the coated fish in the rotisserie basket and fit into the oven using the rotisserie lift.
4. Cook for 9 minutes or until the fish pieces are golden brown.
5. To serve, lay the tortillas individually on a clean, flat surface and add the fish pieces. Top with cabbage, avocado, cilantro, sour cream, and lime wedges. Serve immediately.

Nutrition:
Calories: 275; Total Fat: 11.34 g; Total Carbs: 19.39 g; Fiber: 25 g; Protein: 23.37 g; Sugar: 1.5 g; Sodium: 422mg.

364. Asian Coconut Shrimp

Preparation Time: 10 minutes
Cooking Time: 8 minutes
Servings: 4
Ingredients:
- ½ cup all-purpose flour
- 2 large eggs
- 2/3 cup unsweetened coconut flakes
- 1/3 cup panko breadcrumbs
- 24 medium shrimps
- Salt and black pepper to taste
- Olive oil

Directions:
1. Insert the dripping pan in the bottom part of the Air Fryer and preheat the oven at Air Fry mode at 400°F for 2 to 3 minutes. Lightly brush the rotisserie basket with some olive oil and set it aside.
2. Pour the flour into a shallow plate, whisk the eggs in a bowl, and mix the coconut flakes with breadcrumbs on another plate.
3. Season the shrimps with salt, black pepper, and dredge lightly in the flour. Proceed to coat in the eggs and then, generously, in the breadcrumbs mixture.
4. Spray the coated shrimps with some olive oil and arrange them in the rotisserie basket. Fit the basket in the oven using the rotisserie lift and set the timer for 8 minutes or until the shrimps are golden brown.
5. When ready, transfer the shrimps to serving plates and serve warm with sweet coconut dipping sauce.

Nutrition:
Calories: 190; Total Fat: 7.16 g; Total Carbs: 20.88 g; Fiber: 2 g; Protein: 10.32 g; Sugar: 5.95 g; Sodium: 281 mg.

365. Mahi Fahrenheit with Herby Buttery Drizzle

Preparation Time: 10 minutes
Cooking Time: 12 minutes
Servings: 4
Ingredients:
- 4 (6 oz.) Mahi Fahrenheit fillets
- Salt and black pepper to taste
- Olive oil for spraying
- 2/3 cup butter, melted
- 1 tbsp. chopped fresh parsley
- ½ tbsp. chopped fresh dill

Directions:
1. Insert the dripping pan in the bottom part of the Air Fryer and preheat the oven at Bake mode at 400°F for 2 to 3 minutes.
2. Season the Mahi Fahrenheit fillets with salt, black pepper, and grease lightly with some olive oil. Lay the fish on the cooking tray and fit onto the middle rack of the oven.
3. Close the lid and set the timer for 12 minutes.
4. Once the fish cooks, transfer to a serving platter. Whisk the butter with the parsley and dill. Drizzle the mixture on the fish before serving.
5. Enjoy immediately.

Nutrition:
Calories: 529; Total Fat: 46.54 g; Total Carbs: 9.25 g; Fiber: 5.6 g; Protein: 20.26 g; Sugar: 1.28 g; Sodium: 422 mg.

366. Classic Lemon Pepper Haddock

Preparation Time: 10 minutes
Cooking Time: 12 minutes
Servings: 4
Ingredients:
- ¼ cup all-purpose flour
- 2 egg whites
- 1/3 cup panko breadcrumbs
- 1 tsp. lemon pepper
- 4 (8 oz.) haddock fillets
- Salt to taste
- Lemon slices
- Chopped parsley to garnish

Directions:
1. Insert the dripping pan in the bottom part of the Air Fryer and preheat the oven at Air Fry mode at 400°F for 2 to 3 minutes.
2. Pour the flour into a shallow plate, mix the breadcrumbs and lemon peppers in another shallow dish, whisk the egg whites lightly in a medium bowl, and season the fish lightly with salt.
3. Dredge the fish lightly in the flour, coat in the egg whites, and then generously in the breadcrumbs mixture.

4. Lay the fish on the cooking tray, grease lightly with cooking spray, and fit onto the middle rack of the oven. Close the Air Fryer and set the timer for 12 minutes.
5. Once the fish cooks, transfer it to a serving platter. Serve immediately with the lemon and parsley garnish.

Nutrition:
Calories: 208; Total Fat: 1.22 g; Total Carbs: 10.95 g; Fiber: 1.1 g; Protein: 36.88 g; Sugar: 2.14 g; Sodium: 476 mg.

367. Fried Scallops with Saffron Cream Sauce

Preparation Time: 5 minutes
Cooking Time: 2 minutes
Servings: 4
Ingredients:
- Olive oil for greasing
- 24 scallops, cleaned
- 2/3 cup heavy cream
- tbsp. freshly squeezed lemon juice
- ¼ tsp. dried crushed saffron threads

Directions:
1. Insert the dripping pan in the bottom part of the Air Fryer and preheat the oven at Air Fry mode 400°F for 2 to 3 minutes.
2. Lightly brush the rotisserie basket with some olive oil and fill it with the scallops.
3. Close and fit the basket in the oven using the rotisserie lift and cook for 2 minutes or until the scallops are golden brown on the outside.
4. Meanwhile, in a medium bowl, quickly whisk the heavy cream lemon juice and saffron threads.
5. When the scallops are ready, transfer them to a serving plate and drizzle the sauce on top.
6. Enjoy immediately.

Nutrition:
Calories: 77; Total Fat: 7.73 g; Total Carbs: 1.05 g; Fiber: 0 g; Protein: 1.15 g; Sugar: 0.66 g; Sodium: 31 mg.

368. Easy Crab Cakes

Preparation Time: 10 minutes
Cooking Time: 10 minutes
Servings: 4
Ingredients:
- 4 oz. lump crab
- 1 medium red bell pepper, deseeded and diced
- 2 scallions, finely chopped
- 1 tbsp. mayonnaise
- 1 tbsp. panko bread crumbs
- 1 tbsp. Dijon mustard
- 1 tsp. old bay seasoning
- Olive oil for spraying
- Lemon wedges for serving

Directions:
1. Insert the dripping pan in the bottom part of the Air Fryer and preheat the oven at Bake mode at 370°F for 2 to 3 minutes.
2. Meanwhile, in a medium bowl, mix all the ingredients except for the olive oil and lemon wedges until evenly distributed. Form 4 to 6 firm patties from the mixture, arrange on the cooking tray, and grease lightly with some olive oil. You may do this in two batches.
3. Fit the cooking tray on the middle rack and close the oven. Set the timer to 10 minutes. Cook until the timer reads to the end and the crab cakes are golden brown and well compacted.
4. Remove the crab cakes from the oven and serve with lemon wedges.

Nutrition:
Calories: 246; Total Fat: 6.19 g; Total Carbs: 13.65 g; Fiber: 1.5 g; Protein: 33.16 g; Sugar: 3.65 g; Sodium: 338 mg.

369. Sweet Asian Style Salmon

Preparation Time: 10 minutes
Cooking Time: 12 minutes
Servings: 4
Ingredients:
- 2 garlic cloves, minced
- tbsp. fresh ginger paste
- 1 tsp. fresh orange zest
- ½ cup fresh orange juice
- ¼ cup of soy sauce
- 1 tbsp. plain vinegar
- 1 tbsp. olive oil
- Salt to taste
- 4 (5 oz.) salmon fillets

Directions:
1. In a large bowl, mix all the ingredients except for the fish. Place the fish in the sauce. Spoon the sauce well on top and cover the bowl with plastic wrap. Allow marinating at room temperature for 30 minutes.
2. After 30 minutes, insert the dripping pan in the bottom part of the Air Fryer and preheat the oven at Bake mode at 400°F for 2 to 3 minutes. Using tongs, remove the fish from the sauce, making sure to shake off some marinade of the fish and place it in the cooking tray. You can work in two batches.
3. Slide the tray onto the top rack of the oven, close the oven, and cook for 12 minutes, flipping the fish after 6 minutes.
4. Once ready, transfer the fish to serving plates and serve warm with steamed greens.

Nutrition:
Calories: 132, Total Fat: 7.39 g; Total Carbs: 8.72 g; Fiber: 0.5 g; Protein: 7.2 g; Sugar: 5.96 g; Sodium: 257 mg.

370. Zesty Ranch Fish Fillets

Preparation Time: 10 minutes
Cooking Time: 13 minutes
Servings: 4
Ingredients:
- ¾ cup finely crushed cornflakes or panko breadcrumbs
- tbsp. dry ranch-style dressing mix
- tsp. fresh lemon zest
- ½ tbsp. olive oil

- eggs, beaten
- white fish fillets
- Lemon wedges to garnish

Directions:
1. Insert the dripping pan in the bottom part of the Air Fryer and preheat the oven at Air Fry mode at 400°F for 2 to 3 minutes.
2. Mix the cornflakes, dressing mix, lemon zest, and oil on a shallow plate, and then pour the eggs on another.
3. Working in two batches, dip the fish into the egg
4. Drip off excess egg, and coat well in the cornflakes mixture on both sides.
5. Place the fish on the cooking tray and fix the tray on the middle rack of the oven. Close the oven and set the timer for 13 minutes. Cook until the fish is golden brown.
6. Transfer to a serving plate and serve with the lemon wedges.

Nutrition:
Calories: 409; Total Fat: 23.84 g; Total Carbs: 3.79 g; Fiber: 0.5 g; Protein: 42.55 g; Sugar: 1.41 g; Sodium: 322 mg.

371. Dill Fish Chops
Preparation Time: 10 minutes
Cooking Time: 11 minutes
Servings: 4
Ingredients:
- 4 (5 oz.) cod fillets, cut into 2-inch cubes
- ½ cup tapioca starch
- 2 eggs
- 1 cup almond flour
- 1 ½ dried fish seasoning
- 1 ½ dried dill
- Salt and black pepper to taste
- ½ tsp. mustard powder
- Olive oil for greasing

Directions:
1. Insert the dripping pan in the bottom part of the Air Fryer and preheat the oven at Air Fry mode at 390°F for 2 to 3 minutes.
2. Pour the tapioca starch on a shallow plate. Beat the eggs in a medium bowl. Mix the almond flour, fish seasoning dill, salt, black pepper, and mustard powder on another plate.
3. Lightly coat the fish cubes in the starch, then dip in the eggs, and coat generously in the mustard mixture until well coated on all sides.
4. Spray the coated fish with a little olive oil and put it in the rotisserie basket. Fit the basket in the oven using the rotisserie ling and close the oven. Set the timer for 11 minutes and cook until the fish is golden brown on the outside.
5. Transfer the crusted fish onto serving plates and serve warm with your favorite sauce.

Nutrition:
Calories: 206; Total Fat: 4.02 g; Total Carbs: 18.18 g; Fiber: 0.4 g; Protein: 22.79 g; Sugar: 1.31 g; Sodium: 398mg.

372. Easy Fish Sticks with Chili Ketchup Sauce
Preparation Time: 10 minutes
Cooking Time: 12 minutes
Servings: 4
Ingredients:
- 4 fish sticks, store-bought
- ½ cup tomato ketchup
- 1 tbsp. Sriracha sauce
- 1 tbsp. chopped fresh parsley to garnish
- Sliced pickles for serving

Directions:
1. Insert the dripping pan in the bottom part of the Air Fryer and preheat the oven at Air Fry mode at 390°F for 2 to 3 minutes.
2. Arrange the fish sticks on the cooking tray and fit them onto the middle rack of the oven. Close and set the timer for 12 minutes and cook until the fish sticks are golden brown and crispy.
3. Meanwhile, in a small bowl, mix the tomato ketchup, Sriracha sauce, and parsley until well combined and set it aside for serving.
4. When the fish is ready, transfer onto serving plates and serve warm with the sauce and pickles.

Nutrition:
Calories: 341; Total Fat: 2.53 g; Total Carbs: 1.13 g; Fiber: 0.4 g; Protein: 73.57 g; Sugar: 0.69 g; Sodium: 568 mg.

373. Packet Lobster Tail
Preparation Time: 10 minutes
Cooking Time: 27 minutes
Servings: 2
Ingredients:
- 6 oz. lobster tails, halved
- 1 tbsp. salted butter; melted.
- 1 tsp. dried parsley.
- ½ tsp. Old Bay seasoning
- Juice of ½ medium lemons

Directions:
1. Place the two halved tails on an aluminum foil. Drizzle with butter, Old Bay seasoning, and lemon juice.
2. Seal the foil packets, completely covering tails. Place them into the Air Fryer basket
3. Adjust the temperature to 375°F and set the timer for 12 minutes. Once done, sprinkle with dried parsley and serve immediately.

Nutrition:
Calories: 234; Total Fat: 19 g; Saturated Fat: 0 g; Cholesterol: 0 mg; Sodium: 0 mg; Total Carbs: 7 g; Fiber: 1 g; Sugar: 0 g; Protein: 23 g.

374. Shrimp and Green Beans
Preparation Time: 10 minutes
Cooking Time: 20 minutes
Servings: 4
Ingredients:
- ½ lb. green beans; trimmed and halved

- 1 lb. shrimp; peeled and deveined
- ¼ cup ghee; melted
- 1 tbsp. cilantro; chopped.
- Juice of 1 lime
- A pinch salt and black pepper

Directions:
1. In a pan that fits your Air Fryer, mix all the ingredients, toss, introduce in the fryer and cook at 360°F for 15 minutes shaking the fryer halfway. Divide into bowls and serve

Nutrition:
Calories: 222; Total Fat: 8 g; Saturated Fat: 0 g; Cholesterol: 0 mg; Sodium: 0 mg; Total Carbs: 5 g; Fiber: 3 g; Sugar: 0 g; Protein: 10 g.

375. Crab Dip
Preparation Time: 8 minutes
Cooking Time: 10 minutes
Servings: 4
Ingredients:
- 1 oz. full-fat cream cheese; softened.
- 1 (6-oz.) can lump crabmeat
- ¼ cup chopped pickled jalapeños.
- ¼ cup full-fat sour cream.
- ¼ cup sliced green onion
- ½ cup shredded Cheddar cheese
- ¼ cup full-fat mayonnaise
- 1 tbsp. lemon juice
- ½ tsp. hot sauce

Directions:
1. Place all ingredients into a 4-cup round baking dish and stir until fully combined. Place dish into the Air Fryer basket. Adjust the temperature to 400°F and set the timer for 8 minutes. Dip will be bubbling and hot when done. Serve warm.

Nutrition:
Calories: 441; Total Fat: 38 g; Saturated Fat: 0 g; Cholesterol: 0 mg; Sodium: 0 mg; Total Carbs: 2 g; Fiber: 6 g; Sugar: 0 g; Protein: 18 g.

376. Sesame Shrimp
Preparation Time: 8 minutes
Cooking Time: 15 minutes
Servings: 4
Ingredients:
- 1 lb. shrimp; peeled and deveined
- 1 tbsp. olive oil
- 1 tbsp. sesame seeds, toasted
- ½ tsp. Italian seasoning
- A pinch salt and black pepper

Directions:
1. Take a bowl, mix the shrimp with the rest of the ingredients, and toss well. Put the shrimp in the Air Fryer's basket, cook at 370°F for 12 minutes, divide into bowls and serve,

Nutrition:
Calories: 199; Total Fat: 11 g; Saturated Fat: 0 g; Cholesterol: 0 mg; Sodium: 0 mg; Total Carbs: 4 g; Fiber: 2 g; Sugar: 0 g; Protein: 11 g.

377. Salmon and Cauliflower Rice
Preparation Time: 10 minutes
Cooking Time: 30 minutes
Servings: 4
Ingredients:
- 4 salmon fillets; boneless
- ½ cup chicken stock - 1 cup cauliflower, riced
- 1 tbsp. butter; melted - 1 tsp. turmeric powder
- Salt and black pepper to taste

Directions:
1. In a pan that fits your Air Fryer, mix the cauliflower rice with the other ingredients except for the salmon and toss.
2. Arrange the salmon fillets over the cauliflower rice, put the pan in the fryer, and cook at 360°F for 25 minutes, flipping the fish after 15 minutes.
3. Divide everything between plates and serve

Nutrition:
Calories: 241; Total Fat: 12 g; Saturated Fat: 0 g; Cholesterol: 0 mg; Sodium: 0 mg; Total Carbs: 6 g; Fiber: 2 g; Sugar: 0 g; Protein: 12 g.

378. Trout and Mint
Preparation Time: 10 minutes
Cooking Time: 21 minutes
Servings: 4
Ingredients:
- 1 avocado, peeled, pitted, and roughly chopped.
- 4 rainbow trout
- 1/3 pine nuts
- 1 cup olive oil + 3 tbsp.
- 1 cup parsley; chopped.
- 2 garlic cloves; minced
- ½ cup mint; chopped.
- Zest of 1 lemon
- Juice of 1 lemon
- A pinch salt and black pepper

Directions:
1. Pat dry the trout, season with salt and pepper, and rub with 3 tablespoons of oil.
2. Put the fish in your Air Fryer's basket and cook for 8 minutes on each side. Divide the fish between plates and drizzle half of the lemon juice all over.
3. In a blender, combine the rest of the oil with the remaining lemon juice, parsley, garlic, mint, lemon zest, pine nuts, and the avocado and pulse well. Spread this over the trout and serve.

Nutrition:
Calories: 240; Total Fat: 12 g; Saturated Fat: 0 g; Cholesterol: 0 mg; Sodium: 0 mg; Total Carbs: 6 g; Fiber: 4 g; Sugar: 0 g; Protein: 9 g.

379. Salmon and Coconut Sauce
Preparation Time: 25 minutes
Cooking Time: 20 minutes

Servings: 4
Ingredients:
- 4 salmon fillets; boneless
- 1/3 cup heavy cream
- ¼ cup lime juice
- ½ cup coconut; shredded
- ¼ cup coconut cream
- 1 tsp. lime zest; grated
- A pinch salt and black pepper

Directions:
1. Take a bowl, mix all the ingredients except the salmon, and whisk.
2. Arrange the fish in a pan that fits your Air Fryer. Drizzle the coconut sauce all over, put the pan in the machine, and cook at 360°F for 20 minutes.
3. Divide between plates and serve

Nutrition:
Calories: 227; Total Fat: 12 g; Saturated Fat: 0 g; Cholesterol: 0 mg; Sodium: 0 mg; Total Carbs: 4 g; Fiber: 2 g; Sugar: 0 g; Protein: 9 g.

380. Simple Salmon
Preparation Time: 10 minutes
Cooking Time: 15 minutes
Servings: 2
Ingredients:
- 2 (4-oz.) salmon fillets, skin removed
- 1 medium lemon
- tbsp. unsalted butter; melted
- ½ tsp. dried dill
- ½ tsp. garlic powder

Directions:
1. Place each fillet on a 5" × 5" square of aluminum foil. Drizzle with butter and sprinkle with garlic powder.
2. Zest half of the lemon and sprinkle zest over salmon. Slice the other half of the lemon and lay two slices on each piece of salmon.
3. Sprinkle dill over salmon. Gather and fold foil at the top and sides to fully close packets.
4. Place foil packets into the Air Fryer basket. Adjust the temperature to 400°F and set the timer for 12 minutes. The salmon will be easily flaked and have an internal temperature of at least 145°F when fully cooked.

Nutrition:
Calories: 252; Total Fat: 15 g; Saturated Fat: 0 g; Cholesterol: 0 mg; Sodium: 0 mg; Total Carbs: 2 g; Fiber: 4 g; Sugar: 0 g; Protein: 29 g.

381. Salmon and Sauce
Preparation Time: 10 minutes
Cooking Time: 25 minutes
Servings: 4
Ingredients:
- 4 salmon fillets; boneless
- 2 garlic cloves; minced
- ¼ cup ghee; melted
- ½ cup heavy cream
- 1 tbsp. chives; chopped.
- 1 tsp. lemon juice - 1 tsp. dill; chopped.
- A pinch salt and black pepper

Directions:
1. Take a bowl and mix all the ingredients except the salmon and whisk well.
2. Arrange the salmon in a pan that fits the Air Fryer. Drizzle the sauce all over, introduce the pan in the machine, and cook at 360°F for 20 minutes. Divide everything between plates and serve

Nutrition:
Calories: 220; Total Fat: 14 g; Saturated Fat: 0 g; Cholesterol: 0 mg; Sodium: 0 mg; Total Carbs: 5 g; Fiber: 2 g; Sugar: 0 g; Protein: 12 g.

382. Parmesan Cod
Preparation Time: 10 minutes
Cooking Time: 20 minutes
Servings: 4
Ingredients:
- 4 cod fillets; boneless
- A drizzle olive oil
- 2 spring onions; chopped.
- 1 cup parmesan
- 1 tbsp. balsamic vinegar
- Salt and black pepper to taste

Directions:
1. Season fish with salt, pepper, grease with the oil, and coat it in parmesan.
2. Put the fillets in your Air Fryer's basket and cook at 370°F for 14 minutes.
3. Meanwhile, in a bowl, mix the spring onions with salt, pepper, and vinegar; whisk.
4. Divide the cod between plates, drizzle the spring onions mix all over, and serve with a side salad

Nutrition:
Calories: 220; Total Fat: 12 g; Saturated Fat: 0 g; Cholesterol: 0 mg; Sodium: 0 mg; Total Carbs: 5 g; Fiber: 2 g; Sugar: 0 g; Protein: 13 g.

383. Cod and Endives
Preparation Time: 10 minutes
Cooking Time: 25 minutes
Servings: 4
Ingredients:
- 4 salmon fillets; boneless
- endives; shredded
- tbsp. olive oil - ½ tsp. sweet paprika
- Salt and black pepper to the taste

Directions:
1. In a pan that fits the Air Fryer, combine the fish with the rest of the ingredients. Toss, introduce in the fryer and cook at 350°F for 20 minutes, flipping the fish halfway
2. Divide between plates and serve right away

Nutrition:

Calories: 243; Total Fat: 13 g; Saturated Fat: 0 g; Cholesterol: 0 mg; Sodium: 0 mg; Total Carbs: 6 g; Fiber: 3 g; Sugar: 0 g; Protein: 14 g.

384. Cod and Tomatoes

Preparation Time: 10 minutes
Cooking Time: 20 minutes
Servings: 4
Ingredients:
- 1 cup cherry tomatoes; halved
- 4 cod fillets, skinless and boneless
- 1 tbsp. olive oil - 1 tbsp. cilantro; chopped.
- Salt and black pepper to taste

Directions:
1. In a baking dish that fits your Air Fryer, mix all the ingredients; toss gently.
2. Introduce it in your Air Fryer and cook at 370°F for 15 minutes.
3. Divide everything between plates and serve right away.

Nutrition:
Calories: 248; Total Fat: 11 g; Saturated Fat: 0 g; Cholesterol: 0 mg; Sodium: 0 mg; Total Carbs: 5 g; Fiber: 2 g; Sugar: 0 g; Protein: 11 g.

385. Salmon Burgers

Preparation Time: 10 minutes
Cooking Time: 10 minutes
Servings: 4
Ingredients:
- 1 (14.75 oz.) can salmon, drain & flake
- ¼ cup onion, chopped fine - 1 egg
- ¼ cup multi-grain crackers, crushed
- 1 tsp. fresh dill, chopped - ¼ tsp. pepper
- Nonstick cooking spray

Directions:
1. In a medium bowl, combine all ingredients. Form into 4 patties.
2. Lightly grease fryer basket with cooking spray. Place the baking pan in position 2 of the oven.
3. Set oven to Air Fryer on 350°F.
4. Place the patties in the basket and set them on the baking pan. Set timer for 8 minutes. Cook until burgers are golden brown, turning over halfway through cooking time. Serve on toasted buns with a choice of toppings.

Nutrition:
Calories: 330; Total Fat: 10 g; Saturated Fat: 2 g; Cholesterol: 0 mg; Sodium: 643 mg; Total Carbs: 11 g; Fiber: 0 g; Sugar: 0 g; Protein: 24 g.

386. Air Fried Haddock Fillets

Preparation Time: 10 minutes
Cooking Time: 20 minutes
Servings: 8
Ingredients:
- Nonstick cooking spray - 2 egg whites
- ½ tsp. dill - ½ tsp. pepper
- 1 cup cornflakes, crushed
- 1 lb. haddock fillets, cut in 8 pieces

Directions:
1. Place baking pan in position 2 of the oven. Lightly grease fryer basket with cooking spray.
2. In a shallow bowl, whisk together egg whites, dill, and pepper.
3. Place crushed cornflakes in a separate shallow dish.
4. Dip fish in egg mixture, then cornflakes, coating completely. Place it in the fryer basket.
5. Place the basket and set the Air Fryer to 400°F. Cook 18-20 minutes, turning over halfway through, until fish flakes easily with a fork. Serve.

Nutrition:
Calories: 193; Total Fat: 1 g; Saturated Fat: 0 g; Cholesterol: 0 mg; Sodium: 568 mg; Total Carbs: 7 g; Fiber: 0 g; Sugar: 1 g; Protein: 39 g.

387. Crispy Coated Scallops

Preparation Time: 10 minutes
Cooking Time: 10 minutes
Servings: 4
Ingredients:
- Nonstick cooking spray
- 1 lb. sea scallops, patted dry
- 1 tsp. onion powder - ½ tsp. pepper
- 1 egg - 1 tbsp. water
- ¼ cup Italian breadcrumbs
- Paprika
- 1 tbsp. fresh lemon juice

Directions:
1. Lightly grease fryer basket with cooking spray. Place baking pan in position 2 of the oven.
2. Sprinkle the scallops with onion powder and pepper.
3. In a shallow dish, whisk together egg and water.
4. Place bread crumbs in a separate shallow dish.
5. Dip scallops in egg then bread crumbs coating them lightly. Place them in the fryer basket and lightly coat with cooking spray. Sprinkle with paprika.
6. Place the basket in the Air Fryer and set it to 400°F. Bake for 10–12 minutes until scallops are firm on the inside and golden brown on the outside. Drizzle with lemon juice and serve.

Nutrition:
Calories: 122; Total Fat: 2 g; Saturated Fat: 1 g; Cholesterol: 0 mg; Sodium: 563 mg; Total Carbs: 10 g; Fiber: 1 g; Sugar: 1 g; Protein: 0 g.

388. Tasty Tuna Loaf

Preparation Time: 10 minutes
Cooking Time: 45 minutes
Servings: 6
Ingredients:
- Nonstick cooking spray
- 1 oz. can chunk white tuna in water, drain & flake
- ¾ cup bread crumbs
- 1 onion, chopped fine
- 2 eggs, beaten
- ¼ cup milk
- ½ tsp. fresh lemon juice

- ½ tsp. dill
- 1 tbsp. fresh parsley, chopped
- ½ tsp. salt - ½ tsp. pepper

Directions:
1. Place rack in position 1 of the oven. Grease a 9-inch loaf pan with cooking spray.
2. In a large bowl, combine all ingredients until thoroughly mixed. Spread evenly in prepared pan. Set oven to bake on 350°F for 45 minutes. After 5 minutes, place the pan in the oven and cook for 40 minutes, or until the top is golden brown. Slice and serve.

Nutrition:
Calories: 169; Total Fat: 5 g; Saturated Fat: 1 g; Cholesterol: 0 mg; Sodium: 540 mg; Total Carbs: 13 g; Fiber: 1 g; Sugar: 3 g; Protein: 18 g.

389. Maryland Crab Cakes

Preparation Time: 10 minutes
Cooking Time: 10 minutes
Servings: 6
Ingredients:
- Nonstick cooking spray
- 3 eggs
- 1 cup Panko breadcrumbs
- 1 stalk celery, chopped
- tbsp. mayonnaise
- 1 tsp. Worcestershire sauce
- ¼ cup mozzarella cheese, grated
- 1 tsp. Italian seasoning
- 1 tbsp. fresh parsley, chopped
- 1 tsp. pepper
- ¾ lb. lump crabmeat, drained

Directions:
1. Place baking pan in position 2 of the oven. Lightly grease the fryer basket with cooking spray.
2. In a large bowl, combine all ingredients except crab meat; mix well.
3. Fold in crab carefully so it retains some chunks. Form mixture into 12 patties.
4. Place patties in a single layer in the fryer basket. Place the basket on the baking pan.
5. Set oven to Air Fryer on 350°F for 10 minutes. Cook until golden brown, turning over halfway through cooking time. Serve immediately.

Nutrition:
Calories: 172; Total Fat: 8 g; Saturated Fat: 2 g; Cholesterol: 0 mg; Sodium: 527 mg; Total Carbs: 14 g; Fiber: 1 g; Sugar: 1 g; Protein: 16 g.

390. Mediterranean Sole

Preparation Time: 15 minutes
Cooking Time: 20 minutes
Servings: 6
Ingredients:
- Nonstick cooking spray
- tbsp. olive oil
- scallions, sliced thin
- cloves garlic, diced fine
- tomatoes, chopped
- ½ cup dry white wine
- tbsp. fresh parsley, chopped fine
- 1 tsp. oregano
- 1 tsp. pepper
- lb. sole, cut in 6 pieces
- oz. feta cheese, crumbled

Directions:
1. Place the rack in position 1 of the oven. Grease an 8x11-inch baking dish with cooking spray.
2. Heat the oil in a medium skillet over medium fire. Add scallions and garlic and cook until tender, stirring frequently.
3. Add the tomatoes, wine, parsley, oregano, and pepper. Stir to mix. Simmer for 5 minutes, or until sauce thickens. Remove from heat.
4. Pour half the sauce on the bottom of the prepared dish. Lay fish on top; then pour the remaining sauce. Sprinkle with feta.
5. Set the oven to bake at 400°F for 25 minutes. After 5 minutes, place the baking dish on the rack and cook 15–18 minutes or until fish flakes easily with a fork. Serve immediately.

Nutrition:
Calories: 220; Total Fat: 12 g; Saturated Fat: 4 g; Cholesterol: 0 mg; Sodium: 631 mg; Total Carbs: 6 g; Fiber: 2 g; Sugar: 4 g; Protein: 22 g.

391. Spicy Grilled Halibut

Preparation Time: 30 minutes
Cooking Time: 15 minutes
Servings: 4
Ingredients:
- ½ cup fresh lemon juice
- 2 jalapeno peppers, seeded and chopped fine
- 6 oz. halibut fillets
- Nonstick cooking spray
- ¼ cup cilantro, chopped

Directions:
1. In a small bowl, combine lemon juice and chilies; mix well.
2. Place fish in a large Ziploc bag and add marinade. Toss to coat. Refrigerate for 30 minutes.
3. Lightly spray the baking pan with cooking spray. Set oven to broil on 400°F for 15 minutes.
4. After 5 minutes, lay fish on the pan and place in position 2 of the oven. Cook for 10 minutes, or until fish flakes easily with a fork. Turn fish over and brush with marinade halfway through cooking time.
5. Sprinkle with cilantro before serving.

Nutrition:
Calories: 328; Total Fat: 24 g; Saturated Fat: 4 g; Cholesterol: 0 mg; Sodium: 137 mg; Total Carbs: 3 g; Fiber: 0 g; Sugar: 1 g; Protein: 25 g.

392. Tropical Shrimp Skewers

Preparation Time: 15 minutes
Cooking Time: 5 minutes
Servings: 4
Ingredients:

- 1 tbsp. lime juice
- 1 tbsp. honey
- ¼ tsp. red pepper flakes
- ¼ tsp. pepper
- ¼ tsp. ginger
- Nonstick cooking spray
- 1 lb. medium shrimp, peel, devein and leave tails on
- 2 cups peaches drained and chopped
- ½ green bell pepper, chopped fine
- ¼ cup scallions, chopped

Directions:

1. Soak 8 small wooden skewers in water for 15 minutes.
2. In a small bowl, whisk together lime juice, honey, and spices Transfer 2 tablespoons of the mixture to a medium bowl.
3. Place the baking pan in position 2 of the oven. Lightly grease the fryer basket with cooking spray. Set oven to broil on 400°F for 10 minutes.
4. Thread 5 shrimp on each skewer and brush both sides with marinade. Place them in the basket and after 5 minutes, place them on the baking pan. Cook 4-5 minutes or until shrimp turn pink.

Nutrition:
Calories: 181; Total Fat: 1 g; Saturated Fat: 0 g; Cholesterol: 0 mg; Sodium: 650 mg; Total Carbs: 27 g; Fiber: 2 g; Sugar: 21 g; Protein: 16 g.

393. Seafood Mac n Cheese

Preparation Time: 20 minutes
Cooking Time: 30 minutes
Servings: 8
Ingredients:

- Nonstick cooking spray
- 16 oz. macaroni
- 3 tbsp. butter, divided
- ¾ lb. medium shrimp, peeled, deveined, and cut into ½-inch pieces
- ½ cup Italian panko bread crumbs
- 1 cup onion, chopped fine
- 1 ½ tsp. garlic, diced fine
- 1/3 cup flour
- 1 1/3 cup sharp cheddar cheese, grated
- ½ lb. lump crab meat, cooked

Directions:

1. Place a wire rack in position 1 of the oven. Coat a 7x11-inch baking dish with cooking spray.
2. Cook macaroni according to package directions, shortening cooking time by 2 minutes. Drain and rinse with cold water.
3. Melt 1 tablespoon of butter in a large skillet over med-high heat. Add shrimp and cook, stirring until they turn pink. Remove from heat.
4. Melt the remaining butter in a large saucepan over medium heat. Once melted, mix with bread crumbs in a small bowl.
5. Add onions and garlic to the saucepan and cook, stirring until they soften.
6. Whisk in flour and cook 1 minute, until smooth.
7. Whisk in milk until there are no lumps. Bring to a boil, reduce heat and simmer until thickened, whisking constantly.
8. Whisk in seasonings. Stir in cheese until melted and smooth. Fold in macaroni and seafood. Transfer to prepared dish. Sprinkle bread crumb mixture evenly over top.

Nutrition:
Calories: 672; Total Fat: 26 g; Saturated Fat: 15 g; Cholesterol: 0 mg; Sodium: 0 mg; Total Carbs: 68 g; Fiber: 7 g; Sugar: 7 g; Protein: 39 g.

394. Crispy Air Fried Sushi Roll

Preparation Time: 5 minutes
Cooking Time: 15 minutes
Servings: 12
Ingredients:
Kale Salad:

- 1 tbsp. sesame seeds
- ¾ tsp. soy sauce
- ¼ tsp. ginger
- 1/8 tsp. garlic powder
- ¾ tsp. toasted sesame oil
- ½ tsp. rice vinegar
- 1 ½ cup chopped kale

Sushi Rolls:

- ½ a sliced avocado
- sheets sushi nori
- 1 batch cauliflower rice

Sriracha Mayo:

- Sriracha sauce
- ¼ cup vegan mayo

Coating:

- ½ cup panko breadcrumbs

Directions:

1. Combine all of the kale salad Ingredients, tossing well. Set to the side.
2. Lay out a sheet of nori and spread a handful of rice on it. Then place 2–3 tablespoons of kale salad over rice, followed by avocado. Roll up sushi.
3. To make mayo, whisk mayo Ingredients together until smooth.
4. Add breadcrumbs to a bowl. Coat sushi rolls in crumbs till coated and add to the Air Fryer.
5. Cook rolls for 10 minutes to 390°F, shaking gently at 5 minutes. Slice each roll into 6–8 pieces and enjoy!

Nutrition:
Calories: 267; Total Fat: 13 g; Saturated Fat: 0 g; Cholesterol: 0 mg; Sodium: 0 mg; Total Carbs: 0 g; Fiber: 0 g; Sugar: 3 g; Protein: 6 g.

395. Honey Glazed Salmon

Preparation Time: 5 minutes
Cooking Time: 20 minutes
Servings: 2
Ingredients:
- 1 tsp. water
- 1 tsp. rice wine vinegar
- 1 tbsp. raw honey
- 2 salmon fillets

Directions:
1. Combine water, vinegar, honey, and soy sauce. Pour half of this mixture into a bowl.
2. Place salmon in one bowl of marinade and let chill for 2 hours.
3. Ensure your Air Fryer is preheated to 356F and add salmon.
4. Cook for 8 minutes, flipping halfway through. Baste salmon with some of the remaining marinade mixture and cook another 5 minutes.
5. To make a sauce to serve salmon, pour the remaining marinade mixture into a saucepan, heating till simmering. Let simmer for 2 minutes. Serve drizzled over salmon!

Nutrition:
Calories: 390; Total Fat: 8 g; Saturated Fat: 0 g; Cholesterol: 0 mg; Sodium: 0 mg; Total Carbs: 0 g; Fiber: 0 g; Sugar: 5 g; Protein: 16 g

396. Parmesan Shrimp

Preparation Time: 5 minutes
Cooking Time: 10 minutes
Servings: 4 - 6
Ingredients:
- 1 tbsp. olive oil
- 1 tsp. onion powder
- 1 tsp. basil
- ½ tsp. oregano
- 1 tsp. pepper
- 2/3 cup grated parmesan cheese
- minced garlic cloves
- pounds jumbo cooked shrimp (peeled/deveined)

Directions:
1. Mix all seasonings and gently toss shrimp with the mixture.
2. Spray olive oil into the Air Fryer basket and add seasoned shrimp.
3. Cook 8–10 minutes to 350°F.
4. Squeeze lemon juice over shrimp right before eating!

Nutrition:
Calories: 351; Total Fat: 11 g; Saturated Fat: 0 g; Cholesterol: 0 mg; Sodium: 0 mg; Total Carbs: 0 g; Fiber: 0 g; Sugar: 1 g; Protein: 19 g

397. Bacon-Wrapped Scallops

Preparation Time: 5 minutes
Cooking Time: 10 minutes
Servings: 4
Ingredients:
- 1 tsp. paprika
- 1 tsp. lemon pepper
- 4 slices center-cut bacon
- 20 raw sea scallops

Directions:
1. Rinse and drain scallops, placing on paper towels to soak up excess moisture.
2. Cut slices of bacon into 4 pieces.
3. Wrap each scallop with a piece of bacon, using toothpicks to secure. Sprinkle wrapped scallops with paprika and lemon pepper.
4. Spray the Air Fryer basket with olive oil and add scallops.
5. Cook 5–6 minutes at 400°F, making sure to flip halfway through.

Nutrition:
Calories: 389; Total Fat: 17 g; Saturated Fat: 0 g; Cholesterol: 0 mg; Sodium: 0 mg; Total Carbs: 0 g; Fiber: 0 g; Sugar: 1 g; Protein: 210 g.

398. Air Fryer Fish Tacos

Preparation Time: 5 minutes
Cooking Time: 15 minutes
Servings: 4
Ingredients:
- 1-pound cod
- 1 tbsp. cumin
- ½ tbsp. chili powder
- 1 ½ cups almond flour
- 1 ½ cups coconut flour
- 2 eggs

Directions:
1. Whisk beer and eggs together.
2. Whisk flours, pepper, salt, cumin, and chili powder together.
3. Slice cod into large pieces and coat in egg mixture, then flour mixture.
4. Spray the bottom of your Air Fryer basket with olive oil and add coated codpieces.
5. Cook for 15 minutes at 375°F.
6. Serve on lettuce leaves topped with homemade salsa!

Nutrition:
Calories: 178; Total Fat: 10 g; Saturated Fat: 0 g; Cholesterol: 0 mg; Sodium: 0 mg; Total Carbs: 0 g; Fiber: 0 g; Sugar: 1 g; Protein: 19 g.

399. Salmon Croquettes

Preparation Time: 5 minutes
Cooking Time: 15 minutes
Servings: 6–8
Ingredients:
- 1 cup Panko breadcrumbs
- 1 cup Almond flour
- 2 egg whites
- 1 tbsp. chopped chives
- 1 tbsp. minced garlic cloves
- ½ cup chopped onion

- 2/3 cup grated carrots
- 1 pound chopped salmon fillet

Directions:
1. Mix all ingredients, except for breadcrumbs, flour, and egg whites.
2. Shape mixture into balls. Then coat them in flour, then egg, and then breadcrumbs. Drizzle with olive oil.
3. Add coated salmon balls to the Air Fryer and cook for 6 minutes at 350F. Shake and cook an additional 4 minutes until golden in color.

Nutrition:
Calories: 503; Total Fat: 9 g; Saturated Fat: 0 g; Cholesterol: 0 mg; Sodium: 0 mg; Total Carbs: 61 g; Fiber: 0 g; Sugar: 4 g; Protein: 5 g.

400. Friedamari

Preparation Time: 5 minutes
Cooking Time: 15 minutes
Servings: 6 - 8
Ingredients:
- ½ tsp. salt
- ½ tsp. Old Bay seasoning
- 1/3 cup plain cornmeal
- ½ cup semolina flour
- ½ cup almond flour
- 5–6 cups olive oil
- 1 ½ pounds baby squid

Directions:
1. Rinse the squid in cold water and slice tentacles, keeping just ¼-inch of the hood in one piece.
2. Combine 1–2 pinches of pepper, salt, Old Bay seasoning, cornmeal, and both flours. Dredge squid pieces into flour mixture and place into the Air Fryer. Spray liberally with olive oil.
3. Cook for 15 minutes at 345°F till coating turns a golden brown.

Nutrition:
Calories: 211; Total Fat: 6 g; Saturated Fat: 0 g; Cholesterol: 0 mg; Sodium: 0 mg; Total Carbs: 0 g; Fiber: 0 g; Sugar: 1 g; Protein: 21 g.

401. Air Fryer Salmon Patties

Preparation Time: 5 minutes
Cooking Time: 15 minutes
Servings: 4
Ingredients:
- 1 tbsp. olive oil
- 1 tbsp. ghee
- ¼ tsp. salt
- 1/8 tsp. pepper
- 1 can wild Alaskan pink salmon

Directions:
1. Drain a can of salmon into a bowl and keep liquid. Discard skin and bones.
2. Add salt, pepper, and egg to salmon, mixing well with hands. Make patties.
3. Dredge in flour and the remaining egg. If it seems dry, spoon reserved salmon liquid from the can onto patties.
4. Add patties to the Air Fryer. Cook for 7 minutes at 378°F till golden, making sure to flip once during the cooking process.

Nutrition:
Calories: 437; Total Fat: 12 g; Saturated Fat: 0 g; Cholesterol: 0 mg; Sodium: 0 mg; Total Carbs: 55 g; Fiber: 0 g; Sugar: 2 g; Protein: 24 g.

402. Bang Frieda Mari Panko Breaded Fried Shrimp

Preparation Time: 5 minutes
Cooking Time: 15 minutes
Servings: 4
Ingredients:
- 1 tsp. paprika
- 1 tbsp Montreal chicken seasoning
- ¾ cup panko bread crumbs
- ½ cup almond flour - 1 egg white
- 1-pound raw shrimp (peeled and deveined)

Bang Frieda Mari Sauce:
- ¼ cup sweet chili sauce - 1 tbsp. sriracha sauce
- 1/3 cup plain Greek yogurt

Directions:
1. Ensure your Air Fryer is preheated to 400°F.
2. Season all shrimp with seasonings.
3. Add flour to one bowl, egg white in another, and breadcrumbs to a third.
4. Dip seasoned shrimp in flour, then egg whites, and then breadcrumbs.
5. Spray coated shrimp with olive oil and add to Air Fryer basket.
6. Cook for 4 minutes, flip, and cook an additional 4 minutes.
7. To make the sauce, mix all sauce ingredients until smooth.

Nutrition:
Calories: 212; Total Fat: 1 g; Saturated Fat: 0 g; Cholesterol: 0 mg; Sodium: 0 mg; Total Carbs: 12 g; Fiber: 0 g; Sugar: 0.5 g; Protein: 37 g.

403. 3-Ingredient Air Fryer Catfish

Preparation Time: 5 minutes
Cooking Time: 15 minutes
Servings: 4
Ingredients:
- 1 tbsp. chopped parsley - 1 tbsp. olive oil
- ¼ cup seasoned fish fry
- 4 catfish fillets

Directions:
1. Ensure your Air Fryer is preheated to 400°F.
2. Rinse off catfish fillets and pat dry.
3. Add fish fry seasoning to Ziploc baggie, then catfish. Shake the bag and ensure the fish gets well coated.
4. Spray each fillet with olive oil.
5. Add fillets to the Air Fryer basket. Cook 10 minutes. Then flip and cook another 2–3 minutes.

Nutrition:

Calories: 208; Total Fat: 5 g; Saturated Fat: 0 g; Cholesterol: 0 mg; Sodium: 0 mg; Total Carbs: 8 g; Fiber: 0 g; Sugar: 0.5 g; Protein: 17 g.

404. Fish in Parchment Paper
Preparation Time: 10 minutes
Cooking Time: 25 minutes
Servings: 2
Ingredients:
- 1 oz. cod fillets thawed
- 1 tbsp. oil
- 1/2 cup julienned carrots
- 2 sprigs tarragon
- 1/2 cup red peppers
- 1/2 tsp. black pepper
- 2 pats melted butter

Directions:
1. Take a bowl and add melted butter, tarragon, 1/2 teaspoon of salt, and lemon juice. Combine well until you get a creamy sauce.
2. Add the julienned vegetable and stir well. Set it aside. Slice two squares of parchment big enough to hold the fish and vegetables.
3. Coat the fish fillets with cooking oil spray and apply salt and pepper to the sides. Lay one filet down on each parchment square.
4. Top each fillet with half of the vegetables. Pour any leftover sauce over the vegetables. Fold over the parchment paper and crimp the sides to hold the fish, veggies, and sauce carefully inside the packet.

Nutrition:
Calories: 251; Total Fat: 12 g; Saturated Fat: 0 g; Cholesterol: 0 mg; Sodium: 0 mg; Total Carbs: 8 g; Fiber: 2 g; Sugar: 0 g; Protein: 26 g.

405. Buttery Scallops
Preparation Time: 10 minutes
Cooking Time: 25 minutes
Servings: 8
Ingredients:
- 2 lb. scallops
- 6 tbsp. butter, melted
- 2 tbsp. dry white wine
- 1 tbsp. lemon juice
- 1/2 cup parmesan cheese, grated
- 1 tsp. salt
- 1/2 tsp. black pepper
- 1 tsp. garlic powder

Directions:
1. Mix everything in a bowl except scallops.
2. Toss in scallops and mix well to coat them.
3. Spread the scallops with the sauce on a baking tray.
4. Press the "Power" button of the Air Fryer and turn the dial to select the "bake" mode.
5. Press the Time button and again turn the dial to set the cooking time to 25 minutes.
6. Now push the temp button and rotate the dial to set the temperature at 350°F.
7. Once preheated, place the scallop's baking tray in the oven and close its lid.
8. Serve warm.

Nutrition:
Calories: 227 Fat: 10.1 g; Carbohydrate: 5.6 g; Protein: 27.8 g.

406. Crusted Scallops
Preparation Time: 10 minutes
Cooking Time: 20 minutes
Servings: 4
Ingredients:
- 1-1/2 lb. bay scallops, rinsed
- 3 garlic cloves, minced
- 1/2 cup panko crumbs
- 1 tsp. onion powder
- 4 tbsp. butter, melted
- 1/2 tsp. cayenne pepper
- 1 tsp. garlic powder
- 1/4 cup parmesan cheese, shredded

Directions:
1. Mix everything in a bowl except scallops.
2. Toss in scallops and mix well to coat them.
3. Spread the scallops with the sauce on a baking tray.
4. Press the "Power" button of the Air Fryer and turn the dial to select the "Bake" mode.
5. Press the Time button and again turn the dial to set the cooking time to 20 minutes.
6. Now push the temp button and rotate the dial to set the temperature at 400°F.
7. Once preheated, place the scallop baking tray in the oven and close its lid.

Nutrition:
Calories: 242 Fat: 11.1 g; Carbohydrate: 11.1 g; Protein: 23.8 g.

407. Lobster Tails with White Wine Sauce
Preparation Time: 10 minutes
Cooking Time: 14 minutes
Servings: 4
Ingredients:
- 4 lobster tails, shell cut from the top
- 1/2 onion, quartered
- 1/2 cup butter
- 1/3 cup wine
- 1/4 cup honey
- 6 garlic cloves crushed
- 1 tbsp. lemon juice
- 2 tbsp. fresh chopped parsley

Directions:
1. Place the lobster tails in the oven's baking tray.
2. Whisk the rest of the ingredients in a bowl and pour over the lobster tails.
3. Press the "Power" button of the Air Fryer and turn the dial to select the "Broil" mode.

4. Press the Time button and again turn the dial to set the cooking time to 14 minutes.
5. Now push the temp button and rotate the dial to set the temperature at 350°F.
6. Once preheated, place the lobster baking tray in the oven and close its lid.
7. Serve warm.

Nutrition:
Calories: 340 Fat: 23.1 g; Carbohydrate: 20.4 g; Protein: 0.7 g.

408. Broiled Lobster Tails

Preparation Time: 10 minutes
Cooking Time: 6 minutes
Servings: 4
Ingredients:
- 2 lobster tails, shell cut from the top
- 1/2 cup butter, melted
- 1/2 tsp. ground paprika
- Salt to taste
- White pepper, to taste
- 1 lemon, juiced

Directions:
1. Place the lobster tails in the oven's baking tray.
2. Whisk the rest of the ingredients in a bowl and pour over the lobster tails.
3. Press the "Power" button of the Air Fryer and turn the dial to select the "Broil" mode.
4. Press the Time button and again turn the dial to set the cooking time to 6 minutes.
5. Now push the temp button and rotate the dial to set the temperature at 350°F.

Nutrition:
Calories: 227, Fat: 23.1 g; Carbohydrate: 0.2 g; Protein: 20.3 g.

409. Paprika Lobster Tail

Preparation Time: 10 minutes
Cooking Time: 10 minutes
Servings: 4
Ingredients:
- 2 (4 to 6 oz.) lobster tails, shell cut from the top
- 1/8 tsp. salt
- 1/8 tsp. black pepper
- 1/8 tsp. paprika
- 1/2 lemon, cut into wedges

Directions:
1. Place the lobster tails in the oven's baking tray.
2. Whisk the rest of the ingredients in a bowl and pour over the lobster tails.
3. Press the "Power" button of the Air Fryer and turn the dial to select the "Broil" mode.
4. Press the Time button and again turn the dial to set the cooking time to 10 minutes.
5. Now push the temp button and rotate the dial to set the temperature at 350°F.
6. Once preheated, place the lobster baking tray in the oven and close its lid.

Nutrition:
Calories: 204 Fat: 12.5 g; carbohydrate: 0.2 g; Protein: 21.7 g.

410. Lobster Tails with Lemon Butter

Preparation Time: 10 minutes
Cooking Time: 8 minutes
Servings: 4
Ingredients:
- 4 lobster tails, shell cut from the top
- 1 tbsp. fresh parsley, chopped
- 2 garlic cloves, pressed
- 1 tsp. Dijon mustard
- 1/4 tsp. salt
- 1/8 tsp. black pepper
- 1-1/2 tbsp. olive oil
- 1-1/2 tbsp. fresh lemon juice
- 4 tbsp. butter, divided

Directions:
1. Place the lobster tails in the oven's baking tray.
2. Whisk the rest of the ingredients in a bowl and pour over the lobster tails.
3. Press the "Power" button of the Air Fryer and turn the dial to select the "Broil" mode.
4. Press the Time button and again turn the dial to set the cooking time to 8 minutes.
5. Now push the temp button and rotate the dial to set the temperature at 350°F.

Nutrition:
Calories: 281; Fat: 18.1 g; Carbohydrate: 0.8 g; Protein: 27.9 g.

411. Sheet Pan Seafood Bake

Preparation Time: 10 minutes
Cooking Time: 14 minutes
Servings: 4
Ingredients:
- 2 corn ears, husked and diced
- 1 lb. red potatoes, boiled, diced
- 2 lb. clams, scrubbed
- 1 lb. shrimp, peeled and de-veined
- 12 oz. sausage, sliced
- 1/2 red onion, sliced
- Fresh parsley for garnish

Directions:
1. Toss all the veggies, corn, seafood, oil, and seasoning in a baking tray.
2. Press the "Power" button of the Air Fryer and turn the dial to select the "Broil" mode.
3. Press the Time button and again turn the dial to set the cooking time to 14 minutes.
4. Now push the temp button and rotate the dial to set the temperature at 425°F. Once preheated, place the seafood baking tray in the oven and close its lid. Serve warm.

Nutrition:
Calories: 532; Fat: 35.6 g; carbohydrate: 26.3 g; Protein: 28.7 g.

CHAPTER 5: Side Dishes

412. Tasty Potato Fries
Preparation Time: 10 minutes
Cooking Time: 20 minutes
Servings: 2
Ingredients:
- 1 lb potatoes, wash, peel and cut into fry's shape
- 1/4 tsp chili powder
- 1/2 tbsp olive oil
- 1/4 tsp smoked paprika
- Salt

Directions:
1. Spray air fryer basket with cooking spray.
2. Add potato fries in a large bowl and drizzle with olive oil. Season with paprika, chili powder, and salt.
3. Add potato fries into the air fryer basket.
4. Place air fryer basket into the oven and select air fry mode set Omni to the 370 F for 20 minutes. Stir twice.
5. Serve and enjoy.

Nutrition: Calories 188 Fat 8 g Carbohydrates 36 g Sugar 7 g Protein 9 g Cholesterol 0 mg
1. Remove when done and serve.

Nutrition: Calories 105, Total Fat 9g, Carbs 3g, Protein 3g

413. Roasted Broccoli Cauliflower
Preparation Time: 5 minutes
Cooking Time: 15 minutes
Servings: 12
Ingredients:
- 4 cups broccoli florets
- 1/3 cup parmesan cheese, grated and divided
- 4 cups cauliflower florets
- 6 garlic cloves, minced
- 1/3 cup olive oil
- Pepper
- Salt

Directions:
1. Preheat the oven to 400 F.
2. Add cauliflower, broccoli, half cheese, garlic, and olive oil in a bowl and toss well. Season with pepper and salt.
3. Arrange broccoli and cauliflower mixture on a prepared baking dish.
4. Select bake mode and set the Omni to 400 F for 15 minutes once the oven beeps, place the baking dish into the oven. Just before serving add remaining cheese and toss well.
5. Serve and enjoy.

Nutrition: Calories 86 Fat 9 g Carbohydrates 5 g Sugar 3 g Protein 4 g Cholesterol 4 mg

414. Arugula Artichoke Dip
Preparation Time: 5 minutes
Cooking Time: 30 minutes
Servings: 4
Ingredients:
- 15 oz artichoke hearts, drained
- 1 tsp Worcestershire sauce
- 3 cups arugula, chopped
- 1 cup cheddar cheese, shredded
- 1 tbsp onion, minced
- 1/2 cup mayonnaise

Directions:
1. Blend all ingredients until smooth.
2. Pour artichoke mixture into baking dish.
3. Select bake mode and set the Omni to 350 F for 30 minutes once the oven beeps, place the baking dish into the oven.
4. Serve with crackers and enjoy.

Nutrition: Calories 284 Fat 14 g Carbohydrates 16 g Sugar 8 g Protein 12 g Cholesterol 37 mg

415. Roasted Vegetables Salad
Preparation Time: 5 Minutes
Cooking Time: 85 Minutes
Servings: 5
Ingredients
- 3 eggplants
- 1 tbsp of olive oil
- 3 medium zucchini
- 1 tbsp of olive oil
- 4 large tomatoes, cut them in eighths
- 4 cups of one shaped pasta
- 2 peppers of any color
- 1 cup of sliced tomatoes cut into small cubes
- 2 teaspoon of salt substitute
- 8 tbsp of grated parmesan cheese
- ½ cup of Italian dressing
- Leaves of fresh basil

Directions:
1. Preparing the Ingredients. Wash your eggplant and slice it off then discard the green end. Make sure not to peel.
2. Slice your eggplant into1/2 inch of thick rounds. 1/2 inch)
3. Pour 1tbsp of olive oil on the eggplant round.

4. Air Frying. Put the eggplants in the basket of the Cuisinart air fryer oven and then toss it in the air fryer oven. Cook the eggplants for 40 minutes. Set the heat to 360 °F
5. Meanwhile, wash your zucchini and slice it then discard the green end. But do not peel it.
6. Slice the Zucchini into thick rounds of ½ inch each. Toss your ingredients
7. Add 1 tbsp of olive oil.
8. Air Frying. Cook the zucchini for 25 minutes on a heat of 360° F and when the time is off set it aside.
9. Wash and cut the tomatoes.
10. Air Frying. Arrange your tomatoes in the basket of the Cuisinart air fryer oven. Set the timer to 30 minutes. Set the heat to 350° F
11. When the time is off, cook your pasta according to the pasta guiding directions, empty it into a colander. Run the cold water on it and wash it and drain the pasta and put it aside.
12. Meanwhile, wash and chop your peppers and place it in a bow
13. Wash and thinly slice your cherry tomatoes and add it to the bowl. Add your roasted veggies.
14. Add the pasta, a pinch of salt, the topping dressing, add the basil and the pram and toss everything together. (It is better to mix with your hands). Set the ingredients together in the refrigerator, and let it chill
15. Serve your salad and enjoy it!

Nutrition: CALORIES: 209; FAT: 17G; PROTEIN: 6G; SUGAR: 5

416. Delicious Potato Patties

Preparation Time: 10 minutes
Cooking Time: 8 minutes
Servings: 2
Ingredients:
- 1 egg, beaten
- 1/4 tsp onion powder
- 1/4 tsp garlic powder
- 1 cup mashed potatoes
- 2 tbsp green onion, chopped
- 1 cup breadcrumbs
- 1/2 cup flour
- 1/2 cup cheddar cheese, shredded
- Pepper
- Salt

Directions:
1. In a bowl, mix together mashed potatoes, green onion, cheese, onion powder, and garlic powder.
2. Add flour, egg, and breadcrumbs in three separate bowls.
3. Make patties from potato mixture then roll in flour, dip in eggs, and coat with breadcrumbs.
4. Place patties on a cooking pan.
5. Place cooking pan into the oven and select air fry mode set Omni to the 370 F for 8 minutes.
6. Serve and enjoy.

Nutrition: Calories 577 Fat 12 g Carbohydrates 88 g Sugar 1 g Protein 23 g Cholesterol 114 mg

417. Garlicky Cauliflower Florets

Preparation Time: 5 minutes
Cooking Time: 20 minutes
Servings: 4
Ingredients:
- 5 cups cauliflower florets
- 1/2 tsp cumin powder
- 1/2 tsp coriander powder
- 6 garlic cloves, chopped
- 4 tablespoons olive oil
- 1/2 tsp salt

Directions:
1. Combine all ingredients into the large bowl and toss well.
2. Add cauliflower florets into the air fryer basket.
3. Place air fryer basket into the oven and select air fry mode set Omni to the 400 F for 20 minutes. Stir twice.
4. Serve and enjoy.

Nutrition: Calories 159 Fat 12 g Carbohydrates 2 g Sugar 1 g Protein 8 g Cholesterol 0 mg

418. Zucchini Patties

Preparation Time: 5 minutes
Cooking Time: 15 minutes
Servings: 6
Ingredients:
- 1 egg, beaten
- 1/4 tsp garlic powder
- 1/4 tsp basil, dried
- 1 1/2 cups zucchini, shredded
- 1/4 cup breadcrumbs
- 1/4 cup cheddar cheese, shredded
- 1/8 tsp pepper
- 1/4 tsp salt

Directions:
1. Place shredded zucchini on a paper towel and pat dry.
2. Add zucchini and remaining ingredients into the bowl and mix well.
3. Drop a tablespoon of mixture on a prepared cooking pan and lightly flatten with a spoon.
4. Select bake mode and set the Omni to 425 F for 15 minutes once the oven beeps, place the cooking pan into the oven.
5. Serve and enjoy.

Nutrition: Calories 52 Fat 6 g Carbohydrates 4 g Sugar 9 g Protein 1 g Cholesterol 32 mg

419. Parmesan Hassel back Potatoes

Preparation Time: 10 minutes
Cooking Time: 40 minutes
Servings: 2
Ingredients:
- 2 potatoes, make the thin slices
- 2 tbsp butter, melted

- 3 tbsp mushrooms, sliced
- 4 tbsp parmesan cheese, grated
- Pepper
- Salt

Directions:
1. Spray the cooking pan with cooking spray and set aside.
2. Slide mushroom slices into each slit.
3. Place potatoes on cooking pan and brush with half-melted butter.
4. Place cooking pan into the oven and select air fry mode set Omni to the 350 F for 20 minutes.
5. Turn potatoes to the other side and brush with remaining butter and air fry for 20 minutes more.
6. Sprinkle with parmesan cheese and serve.

Nutrition: Calories 345 Fat 18 g Carbohydrates 38 g Sugar 6 g Protein 14 g Cholesterol 51 mg

420. Flavorful Herb Potatoes

Preparation Time: 10 minutes
Cooking Time: 25 minutes
Servings: 2

Ingredients:
- 3/4 lb potatoes, diced into 1-inch pieces
- 1/4 tsp dried oregano
- 1/4 tsp garlic powder
- 1/4 tsp dried basil
- 1/4 tsp pepper
- 1/4 tsp salt

Directions:
1. Spray the cooking pan with cooking spray and set aside.
2. Add potatoes, basil, oregano, garlic powder, pepper, and salt in a bowl and toss well.
3. Transfer potatoes on a cooking pan.
4. Place cooking pan into the oven and select air fry mode set Omni to the 400 F for 25 minutes. Stir twice.
5. Serve and enjoy.

Nutrition: Calories 120 Fat 2 g Carbohydrates 23 g Sugar 1 g Protein 3 g Cholesterol 0 mg

421. Baked Egg Tomato

Preparation Time: 5 minutes
Cooking Time: 30 minutes
Servings: 2

Ingredients:
- 2 eggs
- 1 tsp fresh parsley
- 2 large fresh tomatoes
- Pepper
- Salt

Directions:
1. Cut the top of the tomato and spoon out the tomato innards.
2. Break the egg in each tomato. Place tomatoes on the cooking pan.
3. Select bake mode and set the Omni to 350 F for 30 minutes once the oven beeps, place the cooking pan into the oven.
4. Season with pepper, and salt.
5. Garnish with parsley and serve.

Nutrition: Calories 96 Fat 7 g Carbohydrates 5 g Sugar 1 g Protein 2 g Cholesterol 164 mg

422. Baked Zucchini Eggplant

Preparation Time: 5 minutes
Cooking Time: 35 minutes
Servings: 6

Ingredients:
- 3 medium zucchini, sliced
- 1 medium eggplant, sliced
- 1 tbsp olive oil
- 4 garlic cloves, minced
- 1/4 tsp pepper
- 3 oz parmesan cheese, grated
- 1/4 cup parsley, chopped
- 1/4 cup basil, chopped
- 1 cup cherry tomatoes, halved
- 1/4 tsp salt

Directions:
1. Spray baking dish with cooking spray.
2. In a bowl, add cherry tomatoes, eggplant, zucchini, olive oil, garlic, cheese, basil, pepper, and salt toss well until combined.
3. Transfer eggplant mixture into the baking dish.
4. Select bake mode and set the Omni to 350 F for 35 minutes once the oven beeps, place the baking dish into the oven.
5. Garnish with parsley and serve.

Nutrition: Calories 110 Fat 8 g Carbohydrates 14 g Sugar 8 g Protein 7 g Cholesterol 10 mg

423. Veggie Tots

Preparation Time: 10 minutes
Cooking Time: 10 minutes
Servings: 2

Ingredients:
- 1 egg
- 1 carrot, grated & squeeze out the liquid
- 1/4 cup breadcrumbs
- 1 zucchini, grated & squeeze out the liquid
- 1/4 cup parmesan cheese, grated
- Pepper
- Salt

Directions:
1. Spray air fryer basket with cooking spray.
2. Mix all ingredients into the bowl
3. Make tots from mixture and place into the air fryer basket.
4. Place air fryer basket into the oven and select air fry mode set Omni to the 400 F for 15 minutes.
5. Serve and enjoy.

Nutrition: Calories 153 Fat 8 g Carbohydrates 17 g Sugar 2 g Protein 10 g Cholesterol 91 mg

424. Spinach Bake

Preparation Time: 10 minutes
Cooking Time: 10 minutes
Servings: 6
Ingredients:
- 10 oz baby spinach
- 1 cup cheddar cheese, shredded
- 1/2 cup mayonnaise
- 2/3 cup yogurt
- 1/4 cup parmesan cheese, shredded
- 1/2 onion, chopped
- 2 tsp garlic powder

Directions:
1. Add all ingredients into the mixing bowl and stir to combine and pour into the baking dish.
2. Select bake mode and set the Omni to 400 F for 10 minutes once the oven beeps, place the baking dish into the oven. Serve and enjoy.

Nutrition: Calories 203 Fat 12 g Carbohydrates 13 g Sugar 1 g Protein 4 g Cholesterol 29 mg

425. Not Your Average Zucchini Parmesan Chips

Preparation Time: 5 minutes
Cooking Time: 10 minutes
Servings: 4
Ingredients:
- 2 thinly sliced zucchinis - 1 beaten egg
- ½ cup of panko breadcrumbs
- ½ cup of grated Parmesan cheese
- salt and black pepper

Directions:
1. Prepare your zucchini by using a mandolin or a knife to slice the zucchinis thinly.
2. Use a cloth to pat dry the zucchini chips.
3. Then using a bowl, add the eggs and beat it properly. After that, pick another bowl, and add the breadcrumbs, Parmesan cheese, salt, and black pepper.
4. Dredge the zucchini chips into the egg mixture and then cover it with the Parmesan-breadcrumb mixture.
5. Grease the battered zucchini chips with a nonstick cooking spray and place it inside your air fryer.
6. Cook it for 8 minutes at a 350 degrees Fahrenheit.
7. Once done, carefully remove it from your air fryer and sprinkle another teaspoon of salt to give it some taste. Serve and enjoy!

Nutrition: Calories: 100, Fat: 6g, Protein: 4g, Carbohydrates 9g, Dietary Fiber: 1.8g

426. Sky-High Roasted Corn

Preparation Time: 5 minutes
Cooking Time: 10 minutes
Servings: 4
Ingredients:
- 4 ears of husk-less corn
- 1 tablespoon of olive oil - 1 teaspoon of salt
- 1 teaspoon of black pepper

Directions:
1. Heat up your air fryer to 400 Fahrenheit.
2. Sprinkle the ears of corn with the olive oil, salt and black pepper.
3. Place it inside your air fryer and cook it for 10 minutes at 400 degrees Fahrenheit.
4. Serve and enjoy!

Nutrition: Calories: 100, Fat: 1g, Protein: 3g, Dietary Fiber: 3g, Carbohydrates: 22g

427. Ravishing Air-Fried Carrots with Honey Glaze

Preparation Time: 5 minutes
Cooking Time: 10 minutes
Servings: 1
Ingredients:
- 3 cups of chopped into ½-inch pieces carrots
- 1 tablespoon of olive oil
- 2 tablespoons of honey
- 1 tablespoon of brown sugar
- salt and black pepper

Directions:
1. Heat up your air fryer to 390 Fahrenheit.
2. Using a bowl, add and toss the carrot pieces, olive oil, honey, brown sugar, salt, and the black pepper until it is properly covered.
3. Place it inside your air fryer and add the seasoned glazed carrots.
4. Cook it for 12 minutes at a 390 degrees Fahrenheit, and then shake after 6 minutes. Serve and enjoy!

Nutrition: Calories: 90, Fat: 3.5g, Dietary Fiber: 2g, Carbohydrates: 13g, Protein: 1g

428. Flaming Buffalo Cauliflower Bites

Preparation Time: 5 minutes
Cooking Time: 20 minutes
Servings: 4
Ingredients:
- 1 large chopped into florets cauliflower head
- 3 beaten eggs
- 2/3 cup of cornstarch
- 2 tablespoons of melted butter
- ¼ cup of hot sauce

Directions:
1. Heat up your air fryer to 360 Fahrenheit.
2. Using a large mixing bowl, add and mix the eggs and the cornstarch a properly.
3. Add the cauliflower, gently toss it until it is properly covered with the batter, shake it off in case of any excess batter and set it aside.
4. Grease your air fryer basket with a nonstick cooking spray and add the cauliflower bites which will require you to work in batches.
5. Cook the cauliflower bites for 15 to 20 minutes or until it has a golden-brown color and a crispy texture, while still shaking occasionally.

6. Then, using a small mixing bowl, add and mix the melted butter and hot sauce properly.
7. Once the cauliflower bites are done, remove it from your air fryer and place it into a large bowl. Pour the buffalo sauce over the cauliflower bites and toss it until it is properly covered.
8. Serve and enjoy!

Nutrition: Calories: 240, Fat: 5.5g, Dietary Fiber: 6.3g, Protein: 8.8g, Carbohydrates: 37g

429. Pleasant Air-Fried Eggplant

Preparation Time: 5 minutes
Cooking Time: 20 minutes
Servings: 4
Ingredients:
- 2 thinly sliced or chopped into chunks eggplants
- 1 teaspoon of salt
- 1 teaspoon of black pepper
- 1 cup of rice flour
- 1 cup of white wine

Directions:
1. Using a bowl, add the rice flour, white wine and mix properly until it gets smooth.
2. Add the salt, black pepper and stir again.
3. Dredge the eggplant slices or chunks into the batter and remove any excess batter.
4. Heat up your air fryer to 390 Fahrenheit.
5. Grease your air fryer basket with a nonstick cooking spray.
6. Add the eggplant slices or chunks into your air fryer and cook it for 15 to 20 minutes or until it has a golden brown and crispy texture, while still shaking it occasionally.
7. Carefully remove it from your air fryer and allow it to cool off. Serve and enjoy!

Nutrition: Calories: 380, Fat: 15g, Protein: 13g, Dietary Fiber: 6.1g, Carbohydrates: 51g

430. Cauliflower Hash

Preparation Time: 10 minutes
Cooking Time: 15 minutes
Servings: 6
Ingredients:
- 1-pound cauliflower
- 2 eggs
- 1 teaspoon salt
- ½ teaspoon ground paprika
- 4-ounce turkey fillet, chopped

Directions:
1. Wash the cauliflower, chop, and set aside.
2. In a different bowl, crack the eggs and whisk well.
3. Add the salt and ground paprika; stir.
4. Place the chopped turkey in the air fryer basket and cook it for 4 minutes at 365° F, stirring halfway through.
5. After this, add the chopped cauliflower and stir the mixture.
6. Cook the turkey/cauliflower mixture for 6 minutes more at 370° F, stirring it halfway through.
7. Then pour in the whisked egg mixture and stir it carefully.
8. Cook the cauliflower hash for 5 minutes more at 365° F.
9. When the cauliflower hash is done, let it cool and transfer to serving bowls. Serve; enjoy.

Nutrition: Calories 143, Fat 9.5, Fiber 2, Carbs 4.5, Protein 10.4

431. Asparagus with Almonds

Preparation Time: 10 minutes
Cooking Time: 5 minutes
Servings: 2
Ingredients:
- 9 ounces asparagus
- 1 teaspoon almond flour
- 1 tablespoon almond flakes
- ¼ teaspoon salt - 1 teaspoon olive oil

Directions:
1. Combine the almond flour and almond flakes; stir the mixture well.
2. Sprinkle the asparagus with the olive oil and salt.
3. Shake it gently and coat in the almond flour mixture.
4. Place the asparagus in the air fryer basket and cook at 400° F for 5 minutes, stirring halfway through.
5. Then cool a little and serve.

Nutrition: Calories 143, Fat 11, Fiber 4.6, Carbs 8.6, Protein 6.4

432. Zucchini Cubes

Preparation Time: 7 minutes
Cooking Time: 8 minutes
Servings: 2
Ingredients:
- 1 zucchini
- ½ teaspoon ground black pepper
- 1 teaspoon oregano
- 2 tablespoons chicken stock
- ½ teaspoon coconut oil

Directions:
1. Chop the zucchini into cubes.
2. Combine the ground black pepper, and oregano; stir the mixture.
3. Sprinkle the zucchini cubes with the spice mixture and stir well.
4. After this, sprinkle the vegetables with the chicken stock.
5. Place the coconut oil in the air fryer basket and preheat it to 360° F for 20 seconds.
6. Then add the zucchini cubes and cook the vegetables for 8 minutes at 390° F, stirring halfway through.
7. Transfer to serving plates and enjoy!

Nutrition: Calories 30, Fat 1.5, Fiber 1.6, Carbs 4.3, Protein 1.4

433. Sweet Potato & Onion Mix

Preparation Time: 10 minutes
Cooking Time: 15 minutes
Servings: 4
Ingredients:
- 2 sweet potatoes, peeled

- 1 red onion, peeled
- 1 white onion, peeled
- 1 teaspoon olive oil - ¼ cup almond milk

Directions:
1. Chop the sweet potatoes and the onions into cubes.
2. Sprinkle the sweet potatoes with olive oil.
3. Place the sweet potatoes in the air fryer basket and cook for 5 minutes at 400° F.
4. Then stir the sweet potatoes and add the chopped onions.
5. Pour in the almond milk and stir gently.
6. Cook the mix for 10 minutes more at 400° F.
7. When the mix is cooked, let it cool a little and serve.

Nutrition: Calories 56, Fat 4.8, Fiber 0.9, Carbs 3.5, Protein 0.6

434. Spicy Eggplant Cubes

Preparation Time: 10 minutes
Cooking Time: 20 minutes
Servings: 2
Ingredients:
- 12 ounces eggplants
- ½ teaspoon cayenne pepper
- ½ teaspoon ground black pepper
- ½ teaspoon cilantro
- ½ teaspoon ground paprika

Directions:
1. Rinse the eggplants and slice them into cubes.
2. Sprinkle the eggplant cubes with the cayenne pepper and ground black pepper.
3. Add the cilantro and ground paprika.
4. Stir the mixture well and let it rest for 10 minutes.
5. After this, sprinkle the eggplants with olive oil and place in the air fryer basket.
6. Cook the eggplants for 20 minutes at 380° F, stirring halfway through.
7. When the eggplant cubes are done, serve them right away!

Nutrition: Calories 67, Fat 2.8, Fiber 6.5, Carbs 10.9, Protein 1.9

435. Roasted Garlic Head

Preparation Time: 5 minutes
Cooking Time: 10 minutes
Servings: 4
Ingredients:
- 1-pound garlic head
- 1 tablespoon olive oil
- 1 teaspoon thyme

Directions:
1. Cut the ends of the garlic head and place it in the air fryer basket.
2. Then sprinkle the garlic head with the olive oil and thyme.
3. Cook the garlic head for 10 minutes at 400° F.
4. When the garlic head is cooked, it should be soft and aromatic.
5. Serve immediately.

Nutrition: Calories 200, Fat 4.1, Fiber 2.5, Carbs 37.7, Protein 7.2

436. Wrapped Asparagus

Preparation Time: 10 minutes
Cooking Time: 5 minutes
Servings: 4
Ingredients:
- 12 ounces asparagus
- ½ teaspoon ground black pepper
- 3-ounce turkey fillet, sliced
- ¼ teaspoon chili flakes

Directions:
1. Sprinkle the asparagus with the ground black pepper and chili flakes.
2. Stir carefully.
3. Wrap the asparagus in the sliced turkey fillet and place in the air fryer basket.
4. Cook the asparagus at 400° F for 5 minutes, turning halfway through cooking.
5. Let the wrapped asparagus cool for 2 minutes before serving.

Nutrition: Calories 133, Fat 9, Fiber 1.9, Carbs 3.8, Protein 9.8

437. Baked Yams with Dill

Preparation Time: 10 minutes
Cooking Time: 8 minutes
Servings: 2
Ingredients:
- 2 yams
- 1 tablespoon fresh dill
- 1 teaspoon coconut oil
- ½ teaspoon minced garlic

Directions:
1. Wash the yams carefully and cut them into halves.
2. Sprinkle the yam halves with the coconut oil and then rub with the minced garlic.
3. Place the yams in the air fryer basket and cook for 8 minutes at 400° F.
4. After this, mash the yams gently with a fork and then sprinkle with the fresh dill.
5. Serve the yams immediately.

Nutrition: Calories 25, Fat 2.3, Fiber 0.2, Carbs 1.2, Protein 0.4

438. Honey Onions

Preparation Time: 10 minutes
Cooking Time: 20 minutes
Servings: 2
Ingredients:
- 2 large white onions
- 1 tablespoon raw honey
- 1 teaspoon water
- 1 tablespoon paprika

Directions:
1. Peel the onions and using a knife, make cuts in the shape of a cross.
2. Then combine the raw honey and water; stir.
3. Add the paprika and stir the mixture until smooth.
4. Place the onions in the air fryer basket and sprinkle them with the honey mixture.
5. Cook the onions for 16 minutes at 380° F.
6. When the onions are cooked, they should be soft.

7. Transfer the cooked onions to serving plates and serve.

Nutrition: Calories 102, Fat 0.6, Fiber 4.5, Carbs 24.6, Protein 2.2

439. Delightful Roasted Garlic Slices

Preparation Time: 10 minutes
Cooking Time: 8 minutes
Servings: 4
Ingredients:
- 1 teaspoon coconut oil
- ½ teaspoon dried cilantro
- ¼ teaspoon cayenne pepper
- 12 ounces garlic cloves, peeled

Directions:
1. Sprinkle the garlic cloves with the cayenne pepper and dried cilantro.
2. Mix the garlic up with the spices, and then transfer to the air fryer basket.
3. Add the coconut oil and cook the garlic for 8 minutes at 400° F, stirring halfway through.
4. When the garlic cloves are done, transfer them to serving plates and serve.

Nutrition: Calories 137, Fat 1.6, Fiber 1.8, Carbs 28.2, Protein 5.4

440. Coconut Oil Artichokes

Preparation Time: 10 minutes
Cooking Time: 13 minutes
Servings: 4
Ingredients:
- 1-pound artichokes
- 1 tablespoon coconut oil
- 1 tablespoon water
- ½ teaspoon minced garlic
- ¼ teaspoon cayenne pepper

Directions:
1. Trim the ends of the artichokes, sprinkle them with the water, and rub them with the minced garlic.
2. Sprinkle with the cayenne pepper and the coconut oil.
3. After this, wrap the artichokes in foil and place in the air fryer basket.
4. Cook for 10 minutes at 370° F.
5. Then remove the artichokes from the foil and cook them for 3 minutes more at 400° F.
6. Transfer the cooked artichokes to serving plates and allow to cool a little.
7. Serve!

Nutrition: Calories 83, Fat 3.6, Fiber 6.2, Carbs 12.1, Protein 3.7

441. Roasted Mushrooms

Preparation Time: 10 minutes
Cooking Time: 5 minutes
Servings: 2
Ingredients:
- 12 ounces mushroom hats
- ¼ cup fresh dill, chopped
- ¼ teaspoon onion, chopped
- 1 teaspoon olive oil
- ¼ teaspoon turmeric

Directions:
1. Combine the chopped dill and onion.
2. Add the turmeric and stir the mixture.
3. After this, add the olive oil and mix until homogenous.
4. Then fill the mushroom hats with the dill mixture and place them in the air fryer basket.
5. Cook the mushrooms for 5 minutes at 400° F.
6. When the vegetables are cooked, let them cool to room temperature before serving.

Nutrition: Calories 73, Fat 3.1, Fiber 2.6, Carbs 9.2, Protein 6.6

442. Mashed Yams

Preparation Time: 10 minutes
Cooking Time: 10 minutes
Servings: 5
Ingredients:
- 1 pound yams
- 1 teaspoon olive oil
- 1 tablespoon almond milk
- ¾ teaspoon salt
- 1 teaspoon dried parsley

Directions:
1. Peel the yams and chop.
2. Place the chopped yams in the air fryer basket and sprinkle with the salt and dried parsley.
3. Add the olive oil and stir the mixture.
4. Cook the yams at 400° F for 10 minutes, stirring twice during cooking.
5. When the yams are done, blend them well with a hand blender until smooth.

Nutrition: Calories 120, Fat 1.8, Fiber 3.6, Carbs 25.1, Protein 1.4

443. Cauliflower Rice

Preparation Time: 10 minutes
Cooking Time: 12 minutes
Servings: 4
Ingredients:
- 14 ounces cauliflower heads
- 1 tablespoon coconut oil
- 2 tablespoons fresh parsley, chopped

Directions:
1. Wash the cauliflower heads carefully and chop them into small pieces of rice.
2. Place the cauliflower in the air fryer and add coconut oil.
3. Stir carefully and cook for 10 minutes at 370° F.
4. Then add the fresh parsley and stir well.
5. Cook the cauliflower rice for 2 minutes more at 400° F.
6. After this, gently toss the cauliflower rice and serve immediately.

Nutrition: Calories 55, Fat 3.5, Fiber 2.5, Carbs 5.4, Protein 2

444. Shredded Cabbage

Preparation Time: 15 minutes
Cooking Time: 15 minutes
Servings: 4
Ingredients:
- 15 ounces cabbage
- ¼ teaspoon salt
- ¼ cup chicken stock
- ½ teaspoon paprika

Directions:
1. Shred the cabbage and sprinkle it with the salt and paprika.
2. Stir the cabbage and let it sit for 10 minutes.
3. Then transfer the cabbage to the air fryer basket and add the chicken stock.
4. Cook the cabbage for 15 minutes at 250° F, stirring halfway through.
5. When the cabbage is soft, it is done.
6. Serve immediately, while still hot

Nutrition: Calories: 132 Fat:2.1 Carbs: 32.1 Protein: 1.78

445. Fried Leeks Recipe

Preparation Time: 5 minutes
Cooking Time: 10 minutes
Servings: 4
Ingredients:
- 4 leeks; ends cut off and halved
- 1 tbsp. butter; melted - 1 tbsp. lemon juice
- Salt and black pepper to the taste

Directions:
1. Coat leeks with melted butter, flavor with salt and pepper, put in your air fryer and cook at 350 °F, for 7 minutes.
2. Arrange on a platter, drizzle lemon juice all over and serve

Nutrition: Calories: 100; Fat: 4; Fiber: 2; Carbs: 6; Protein: 2

446. Brussels Sprouts and Tomatoes Mix Recipe

Preparation Time: 5 minutes
Cooking Time: 10 minutes
Servings: 4
Ingredients:
- 1 lb. Brussels sprouts; trimmed
- 6 cherry tomatoes; halved
- 1/4 cup green onions; chopped. - 1 tbsp. olive oil
- Salt and black pepper to the taste

Directions:
1. Season Brussels sprouts with salt and pepper, put them in your air fryer and cook at 350 °F, for 10 minutes.
2. Transfer them to a bowl, add salt, pepper, cherry tomatoes, green onions and olive oil, toss well and serve.

Nutrition: Calories: 121; Fat: 4; Fiber: 4; Carbs: 11; Protein: 4

447. Radish Hash Recipe

Preparation Time: 5 minutes
Cooking Time: 15 minutes
Servings: 4
Ingredients:
- 1/2 tsp. onion powder
- 1/3 cup parmesan; grated
- 4 eggs - 1 lb. radishes; sliced
- Salt and black pepper to the taste

Directions:
1. In a bowl; mix radishes with salt, pepper, onion, eggs and parmesan and stir well
2. Transfer radishes to a pan that fits your air fryer and cook at 350 °F, for 7 minutes
3. Divide hash on plates and serve.

Nutrition: Calories: 80; Fat: 5; Fiber: 2; Carbs: 5; Protein: 7

448. Broccoli Salad Recipe

Preparation Time: 5 minutes
Cooking Time: 20 minutes
Servings: 4
Ingredients:
- 1 broccoli head; florets separated
- 1 tbsp. Chinese rice wine vinegar
- 1 tbsp. peanut oil
- 6 garlic cloves; minced
- Salt and black pepper to the taste

Directions:
1. In a bowl; mix broccoli with salt, pepper and half of the oil, toss, transfer to your air fryer and cook at 350 °F, for 8 minutes; shaking the fryer halfway
2. Transfer broccoli to a salad bowl, add the rest of the peanut oil, garlic and rice vinegar, toss really well and serve.

Nutrition: Calories: 121; Fat: 3; Fiber: 4; Carbs: 4; Protein: 4

449. Chili Broccoli

Preparation Time: 5 minutes
Cooking Time: 15 minutes
Servings: 4
Ingredients:
- 1-pound broccoli florets
- 2 tablespoons olive oil
- 2 tablespoons chili sauce
- Juice of 1 lime
- A pinch of salt and black pepper

Directions:
1. Combine all of the ingredients in a bowl, and toss well.
2. Put the broccoli in your air fryer's basket and cook at 400 degrees F for 15 minutes.
3. Divide between plates and serve.

Nutrition: Calories 173, Fat 6, Fiber 2, Carbs 6, Protein 8

450. Parmesan Broccoli and Asparagus

Preparation Time: 5 minutes
Cooking Time: 15 minutes
Servings: 4
Ingredients:
- 1 broccoli head, florets separated
- ½ pound asparagus, trimmed

- Juice of 1 lime
- Salt and black pepper to the taste
- 2 tablespoons olive oil
- 3 tablespoons parmesan, grated

Directions:
1. In a small bowl, combine the asparagus with the broccoli and all the other ingredients except the parmesan, toss, transfer to your air fryer's basket and cook at 400 degrees F for 15 minutes.
2. Divide between plates, sprinkle the parmesan on top and serve.

Nutrition: Calories 172, Fat 5, Fiber 2, Carbs 4, Protein 9

451. Butter Broccoli Mix

Preparation Time: 5 minutes
Cooking Time: 15 minutes
Servings: 4
Ingredients:
- 1-pound broccoli florets
- A pinch of salt and black pepper
- 1 teaspoon sweet paprika
- ½ tablespoon butter, melted

Directions:
1. In a small bowl, combine the broccoli with the rest of the ingredients, and toss.
2. Put the broccoli in your air fryer's basket, cook at 350 degrees F for 15 minutes, divide between plates and serve.

Nutrition: Calories 130, Fat 3, Fiber 3, Carbs 4, Protein 8

452. Balsamic Kale

Preparation Time: 2 minutes
Cooking Time: 12 minutes
Servings: 6
Ingredients:
- 2 tablespoons olive oil
- 3 garlic cloves, minced
- 2 and ½ pounds kale leaves
- Salt and black pepper to the taste
- 2 tablespoons balsamic vinegar

Directions:
1. In a pan that fits the air fryer, combine all the ingredients and toss.
2. Put the pan in your air fryer and cook at 300 degrees F for 12 minutes.
3. Divide between plates and serve.

Nutrition: Calories 122, Fat 4, Fiber 3, Carbs 4, Protein 5

453. Kale and Olives

Preparation Time: 5 minutes
Cooking Time: 15 minutes
Servings: 4
Ingredients:
- 1 an ½ pounds kale, torn
- 2 tablespoons olive oil
- Salt and black pepper to the taste
- 1 tablespoon hot paprika
- 2 tablespoons black olives, pitted and sliced

Directions:
1. In a pan that fits the air fryer, combine all the ingredients and toss.
2. Put the pan in your air fryer, cook at 370 degrees F for 15 minutes, divide between plates and serve.

Nutrition: Calories 154, Fat 3, Fiber 2, Carbs 4, Protein 6

454. Kale and Mushrooms Mix

Preparation Time: 5 minutes
Cooking Time: 15 minutes
Servings: 4
Ingredients:
- 1 pound brown mushrooms, sliced
- 1-pound kale, torn
- Salt and black pepper to the taste
- 2 tablespoons olive oil
- 14 ounces coconut milk

Directions:
1. In a pot that fits your air fryer, mix the kale with the rest of the ingredients and toss.
2. Put the pan in the fryer, cook at 380 degrees F for 15 minutes, divide between plates and serve.

Nutrition: Calories 162, Fat 4, Fiber 1, Carbs 3, Protein 5

455. Roasted Zucchini

Preparation Time: 10 minutes
Cooking Time: 10 minutes
Servings: 4
Ingredients:
- 2 medium zucchinis, cut into 1-inch slices
- 1 tsp. lemon zest
- 1 tbsp. olive oil
- Pepper
- Salt

Directions:
1. Toss zucchini with lemon zest, oil, pepper, and salt.
2. Arrange zucchini slices into the Air Fryer basket and cook at 350°F for 10 minutes. Turn halfway through.
3. Serve and enjoy.

Nutrition:

Calories: 46; Fat: 3.7 g; Carbohydrates: 3.4 g; Sugar: 1.7 g; Protein: 1.2 g; Cholesterol: 0 mg.

456. Crispy & Spicy Eggplant

Preparation Time: 10 minutes
Cooking Time: 20 minutes
Servings: 4
Ingredients:
- 1 eggplant, cut into 1-inch pieces
- 1/2 tsp. Italian seasoning
- 1 tsp. paprika
- 1/2 tsp. red pepper
- 1 tsp. garlic powder
- 2 tbsp. olive oil

Directions:
1. Add eggplant and remaining ingredients into the bowl and toss well.
2. Coat the Air Fryer basket with cooking spray.
3. Add eggplant into the Air Fryer basket and cook at 375°F for 20 minutes. Shake basket halfway through. Serve and enjoy.

Nutrition:
Calories: 99; Fat: 7.5 g; Carbohydrates: 8.7 g; Sugar: 4.5 g; Protein: 1.5 g; Cholesterol: 0 mg.

457. Curried Eggplant Slices

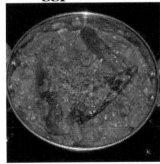

Preparation Time: 10 minutes
Cooking Time: 10 minutes
Servings: 4
Ingredients:
- 1 large eggplant, cut into 1/2-inch slices
- 1 garlic clove, minced
- 1 tbsp. olive oil
- 1/2 tsp. curry powder
- 1/8 tsp. turmeric
- Salt

Directions:
1. Preheat the Air Fryer to 300°F.
2. In a small bowl, mix oil, garlic, curry powder, turmeric, and salt and rub all over eggplant slices.
3. Add eggplant slices into the Air Fryer basket and cook for 10 minutes or until lightly browned.
4. Serve and enjoy.

Nutrition:
Calories: 61; Fat: 3.8 g; Carbohydrates: 7.2 g; Sugar: 3.5 g; Protein: 1.2 g; Cholesterol: 0 mg.

458. Spiced Green Beans

Preparation Time: 10 minutes
Cooking Time: 10 minutes
Servings: 2
Ingredients:
- 2 cups green beans
- 1/8 tsp. ground allspice
- 1/4 tsp. ground cinnamon
- 1/2 tsp. dried oregano
- 2 tbsp. olive oil
- 1/4 tsp. ground coriander
- 1/4 tsp. ground cumin
- 1/8 tsp. cayenne pepper
- 1/2 tsp. salt

Directions:
1. Add all ingredients into a medium bowl and toss well.
2. Coat the Air Fryer basket with cooking spray.
3. Add green beans into the Air Fryer basket and cook at 370°F for 10 minutes. Shake basket halfway through.
4. Serve and enjoy.

Nutrition:
Calories: 158; Fat: 14.3 g; Carbohydrates: 8.6 g; Sugar: 1.6 g; Protein: 2.1 g; Cholesterol: 0 mg.

459. Air Fryer Basil Tomatoes

Preparation Time: 10 minutes
Cooking Time: 25 minutes
Servings: 4
Ingredients:
- 4 large tomatoes, halved
- 1 garlic clove, minced
- 1 tbsp. vinegar
- 1 tbsp. olive oil
- 2 tbsp. parmesan cheese, grated
- 1/2 tsp. fresh parsley, chopped
- 1 tsp. fresh basil, minced
- Pepper
- Salt

Directions:
1. Preheat the Air Fryer to 320°F.
2. In a bowl, mix oil, basil, garlic, vinegar, pepper, and salt. Add tomatoes and stir to coat.
3. Place tomato halves into the Air Fryer basket and cook for 20 minutes.
4. Sprinkle parmesan cheese over tomatoes and cook for 5 minutes more.
5. Serve and enjoy.

Nutrition:

Calories: 87; Fat: 5.4 g; Carbohydrates: 7.7 g; Sugar: 4.8 g; Protein: 3.9 g; Cholesterol: 5 mg.

460. Air Fryer Ratatouille

Preparation Time: 10 minutes
Cooking Time: 15 minutes
Servings: 6
Ingredients:
- 1 eggplant, diced
- 1 onion, diced
- 3 tomatoes, diced
- 1 red bell pepper, diced
- 1 green bell pepper, diced
- 1 tbsp. vinegar
- 2 tbsp. olive oil
- 2 tbsp. herb de Provence
- 2 garlic cloves, chopped
- Pepper
- Salt

Directions:
1. Preheat the Air Fryer to 400°F.
2. Add all ingredients into the bowl, toss well and transfer into the Air Fryer safe dish.
3. Place dish into the Air Fryer basket and cook for 15 minutes. Stir halfway through.
4. Serve and enjoy.

Nutrition:
Calories: 91; Fat: 5 g; Carbohydrates: 11.6 g; Sugar: 6.4 g; Protein: 1.9 g; Cholesterol: 0 mg.

461. Garlicky Cauliflower Florets

Preparation Time: 10 minutes
Cooking Time: 20 minutes
Servings: 4
Ingredients:
- 5 cups cauliflower florets
- 1/2 tsp. cumin powder
- 1/2 tsp. ground coriander
- 6 garlic cloves, chopped
- 4 tbsp. olive oil
- 1/2 tsp. salt

Directions:
1. Add cauliflower florets and remaining Ingredients into the large mixing bowl; toss well.
2. Add cauliflower florets into the Air Fryer basket and cook at 400°F for 20 minutes. Shake basket halfway through.
3. Serve and enjoy.

Nutrition:
Calories: 159; Fat: 14.2 g; Carbohydrates: 8.2 g; Sugar: 3.1 g; Protein: 2.8 g; Cholesterol: 0 mg.

462. Parmesan Brussels Sprouts

Preparation Time: 10 minutes
Cooking Time: 12 minutes
Servings: 4
Ingredients:
- 1 lb. Brussels sprouts, stems removed, halved
- 1/4 cup parmesan cheese, grated
- 2 tbsp. olive oil
- Pepper
- Salt

Directions:
1. Preheat the Air Fryer to 350°F.
2. In a mixing bowl, toss Brussels sprouts with oil, pepper, and salt.
3. Transfer Brussels sprouts into the Air Fryer basket and cook for 12 minutes. Shake basket halfway through.
4. Sprinkle with parmesan cheese and serve.

Nutrition:
Calories: 129; Fat: 8.7 g; Carbohydrates: 10.6 g; Sugar: 2.5 g; Protein: 5.9 g; Cholesterol: 4 mg.

463. Flavorful Tomatoes

Preparation Time: 10 minutes
Cooking Time: 15 minutes
Servings: 4
Ingredients:
- 4 Roma tomatoes, sliced, seeds removed pithy portion
- 1 tbsp. olive oil
- 1/2 tsp. dried thyme
- 2 garlic cloves, minced
- Pepper
- Salt

Directions:
1. Preheat the Air Fryer to 390°F.
2. Toss sliced tomatoes with oil, thyme, garlic, pepper, and salt.
3. Arrange sliced tomatoes into the Air Fryer basket and cook for 15 minutes.
4. Serve and enjoy.

Nutrition:
Calories: 55; Fat: 3.8 g; Carbohydrates: 5.4 g; Sugar: 3.3 g; Protein: 1.2 g; Cholesterol: 0 mg.

464. Healthy Roasted Carrots

Preparation Time: 10 minutes
Cooking Time: 12 minutes
Servings: 4
Ingredients:
- 2 cups carrots, peeled and chopped
- 1 tsp. cumin
- 1 tbsp. olive oil
- 1/4 fresh coriander, chopped

Directions:
1. Toss carrots with cumin and oil and place them into the Air Fryer basket.
2. Cook at 390°F for 12 minutes.
3. Garnish with fresh coriander and serve.

Nutrition:
Calories: 55; Fat: 3.6 g; Carbohydrates: 5.7 g; Sugar: 2.7 g; Protein: 0.6 g; Cholesterol: 0 mg.

465. Curried Cauliflower with Pine Nuts

Preparation Time: 10 minutes
Cooking Time: 10 minutes
Servings: 4
Ingredients:

- 1 small cauliflower head, cut into florets
- 2 tbsp. olive oil
- ¼ cup pine nuts, toasted
- 1 tbsp. curry powder
- ¼ tsp. salt

Directions:

1. Preheat the Air Fryer to 350°F.
2. In a mixing bowl, toss cauliflower florets with oil, curry powder, and salt.
3. Add cauliflower florets into the Air Fryer basket and cook for 10 minutes. Shake basket halfway through.
4. Transfer cauliflower into the serving bowl. Add pine nuts and toss well.
5. Serve and enjoy.

Nutrition:
Calories: 139, Fat: 13.1g, Carbohydrates: 5.5g, Sugar: 1.9g, Protein: 2.7g, Cholesterol: 0 mg.

466. Thyme Sage Butternut Squash

Preparation Time: 10 minutes
Cooking Time: 12 minutes
Servings: 4
Ingredients:

- 2 lb. butternut squash, cut into chunks
- 1 tsp. fresh thyme, chopped
- 1 tbsp. fresh sage, chopped
- 1 tbsp. olive oil
- Pepper
- Salt

Directions:

1. Preheat the Air Fryer to 390°F.
2. In a mixing bowl, toss butternut squash with thyme, sage, oil, pepper, and salt.
3. Add butternut squash into the Air Fryer basket and cook for 10 minutes. Shake basket well and cook for 2 minutes more.
4. Serve and enjoy.

Nutrition:
Calories: 50, Fat: 3.8g, Carbohydrates: 4.2g, Sugar: 2.5g, Protein: 1.4g, Cholesterol: 0 mg.

467. Grilled Cauliflower

Preparation Time: 15 minutes
Cooking Time: 40 minutes
Servings: 4
Ingredients:

- 1 large head of cauliflower, leaves removed and stem trimmed
- Salt, as required
- 4 tbsp. unsalted butter
- ¼ cup hot sauce
- 1 tbsp. ketchup
- 1 tbsp. soy sauce
- ½ cup mayonnaise
- 2 tbsp. white miso
- 1 tbsp. fresh lemon juice
- ½ tsp. ground black pepper
- 2 scallions, thinly sliced

Directions:

1. Sprinkle the cauliflower with salt evenly.
2. Arrange the cauliflower head in a large microwave-safe bowl.
3. With plastic wrap, cover the bowl.
4. With a knife, pierce the plastic a few times to vent.
5. Microwave on high for about 5 minutes.
6. Remove from the microwave and set it aside to cool slightly.
7. In a small saucepan, add butter, hot sauce, ketchup, and soy sauce over medium heat and cook for about 2–3 minutes, stirring occasionally.
8. Brush the cauliflower head with warm sauce evenly.
9. Place the water tray in the bottom of the PowerXL Smokeless Electric Grill.
10. Place about 2 cups of lukewarm water into the water tray.
11. Place the drip pan over the water tray and then arrange the heating element.
12. Now, place the grilling pan over the heating element.
13. Set the temperature settings according to the manufacturer's directions.
14. Cover the grill with a lid and let it preheat.
15. After preheating, remove the lid and grease the grilling pan.
16. Place the cauliflower head over the grilling pan.
17. Cover with the lid and cook for about 10 minutes.
18. Turn the cauliflower over and brush with warm sauce.
19. Cover with the lid and cook for about 25 minutes, flipping and brushing with warm sauce after every 10 minutes.
20. In a bowl, place the mayonnaise, miso, lemon juice, and pepper and beat until smooth.
21. Spread the mayonnaise mixture onto a plate and arrange the cauliflower on top.

Nutrition:
Calories: 261, Total Fat: 22g, Saturated Fat: 8.9g, Cholesterol: 38mg, Sodium: 1300mg, Total Carbs: 15.1g, Fiber: 2.5g, Sugar: 5.4g, Protein: 3.3 g.

468. Stuffed Zucchini

Preparation Time: 20 minutes
Cooking Time: 24 minutes
Servings: 6
Ingredients:

- 3 medium zucchinis, sliced in half lengthwise
- 1 tsp. vegetable oil
- 3 cup corn, cut off the cob
- 1 cup Parmesan cheese, shredded
- 2/3 cup sour cream

- ¼ tsp. hot sauce
- Olive oil cooking spray

Directions:
1. Cut the ends off the zucchini and slice in half lengthwise.
2. Scoop out the pulp from each half of zucchini, leaving the shell.
3. For the filling: in a large pan of boiling water, add the corn over medium heat and cook for about 5–7 minutes.
4. Drain the corn and set it aside to cool.
5. In a large bowl, add corn, half of the parmesan cheese, sour cream, and hot sauce and mix well.
6. Coat the zucchini shells with cooking spray evenly.
7. Place the water tray in the bottom of the PowerXL Smokeless Electric Grill.
8. Place about 2 cups of lukewarm water into the water tray.
9. Place the drip pan over the water tray and then arrange the heating element.
10. Now, place the grilling pan over the heating element.
11. Set the temperature settings according to the manufacturer's directions.
12. Cover the grill with a lid and let it preheat.
13. After preheating, remove the lid and grease the grilling pan.
14. Place the zucchini halves over the grilling pan, flesh side down.
15. Cover with the lid and cook for about 8–10 minutes.
16. Remove the zucchini halves from the grill.
17. Spoon filling into each zucchini half evenly and sprinkle with remaining parmesan cheese.
18. Place the zucchini halves over the grilling pan.
19. Cover with the lid and cook for about 8 minutes.
20. Serve hot.

Nutrition:
Calories: 198, Total Fat: 10.8g, Saturated Fat: 6g, Cholesterol: 21mg, Sodium: 293mg, Total Carbs: 19.3g, Fiber: 3.2g, Sugar: 4.2g, Protein: 9.6 g.

469. Vinegar Veggies

Preparation Time: 15 minutes
Cooking Time: 10 minutes
Servings: 4
Ingredients:
- 3 golden beets, trimmed, peeled, and sliced thinly
- 3 carrots, peeled and sliced lengthwise
- 1 cup zucchini, sliced
- 1 onion, sliced
- ½ cup yam, sliced thinly
- 2 tbsp. fresh rosemary
- 1 garlic clove, minced
- Salt and ground black pepper, as required
- 3 tbsp. vegetable oil
- 2 tsp. balsamic vinegar

Directions:
1. Place all ingredients in a bowl and toss to coat well.
2. Refrigerate to marinate for at least 30 minutes.
3. Place the water tray in the bottom of the PowerXL Smokeless Electric Grill.
4. Place about 2 cups of lukewarm water into the water tray.
5. Place the drip pan over the water tray and then arrange the heating element.
6. Now, place the grilling pan over the heating element.
7. Plugin the PowerXL Smokeless Electric Grill and press the "Power" button to turn it on.
8. Then press the "Fan" button.
9. Set the temperature settings according to the manufacturer's directions.
10. Cover the grill with a lid and let it preheat.
11. After preheating, remove the lid and grease the grilling pan.
12. Place the vegetables over the grilling pan.
13. Cover with the lid and cook for about 5 minutes per side.
14. Serve hot.

Nutrition:
Calories: 184, Total Fat: 10.7g, Saturated Fat: 2.2g, Cholesterol: 0mg, Sodium: 134mg, Total Carbs: 21.5g, Fiber: 4.9g, Sugar: 10g, Protein: 2.7 g.

470. Garlicky Mixed Veggies

Preparation Time: 15 minutes
Cooking Time: 8 minutes
Servings: 4
Ingredients:
- 1 bunch fresh asparagus, trimmed
- 6 ounces fresh mushrooms, halved
- 6 Campari tomatoes, halved
- 1 red onion, cut into 1-inch chunks
- 3 garlic cloves, minced
- 2 tbsp. olive oil
- Salt and ground black pepper, as required

Directions:
1. In a large bowl, add all ingredients and toss to coat well. Place the water tray in the bottom of the PowerXL Smokeless Electric Grill. Place about 2 cups of lukewarm water into the water tray.
2. Place the drip pan over the water tray and then arrange the heating element.
3. Now, place the grilling pan over the heating element. Plugin the PowerXL Smokeless Electric Grill and press the "Power" button to turn it on. Then press the "Fan" button.
4. Set the temperature settings according to the manufacturer's directions.
5. Cover the grill with a lid and let it preheat.
6. After preheating, remove the lid and grease the grilling pan. Place the vegetables over the grilling pan. Cover with the lid and cook for about 8 minutes, flipping occasionally.

Nutrition:
Calories: 137, Total Fat: 7.7g, Saturated Fat: 1.1g, Cholesterol: 0mg, Sodium: 54mg, Total Carbs: 15.6g, Fiber: 5.6g, Sugar: 8.9g, Protein: 5.8 g.

471. Mediterranean Veggies

Preparation Time: 5 minutes
Cooking Time: 10 minutes
Servings: 4
Ingredients:
- 1 cup mixed bell peppers, chopped
- 1 cup eggplant, chopped
- 1 cup zucchini, chopped
- 1 cup mushrooms, chopped
- ½ cup onion, chopped
- ½ cup sun-dried tomato vinaigrette dressing

Directions:
1. In a large bowl, add all ingredients and toss to coat well. Refrigerate to marinate for about 1 hour. Place the water tray in the bottom of the PowerXL Smokeless Electric Grill. Place about 2 cups of lukewarm water into the water tray.
2. Place the drip pan over the water tray and then arrange the heating element.
3. Now, place the grilling pan over the heating element. Plugin the PowerXL Smokeless Electric Grill and press the "Power" button to turn it on. Then press the "Fan" button.
4. Set the temperature settings according to the manufacturer's directions.
5. Cover the grill with a lid and let it preheat.
6. After preheating, remove the lid and grease the grilling pan. Place the vegetables over the grilling pan. Cover with the lid and cook for about 8–10 minutes, flipping occasionally.

Nutrition:
Calories: 159, Total Fat: 11.2g, Saturated Fat: 2g, Cholesterol: 0mg, Sodium: 336mg, Total Carbs: 12.3g, Fiber: 1.9g, Sugar: 9.5g, Protein: 1.6 g

472. Marinated Veggie Skewers

Preparation Time: 20 minutes
Cooking Time: 10 minutes
Servings: 4
Ingredients:
For Marinade:
- 2 garlic cloves, minced
- 2 tsp. fresh basil, minced
- 2 tsp. fresh oregano, minced
- ½ tsp. cayenne pepper
- Sea Salt and ground black pepper, as required
- 2 tbsp. fresh lemon juice
- 2 tbsp. olive oil

For Veggies:
- 2 large zucchinis, cut into thick slices
- 8 large button mushrooms, quartered
- 1 yellow bell pepper, seeded and cubed
- 1 red bell pepper, seeded and cubed

Directions:
1. For the marinade: in a large bowl, add all the ingredients and mix until well combined.
2. Add the vegetables and toss to coat well.
3. Cover and refrigerate to marinate for at least 6–8 hours.
4. Remove the vegetables from the bowl and thread onto pre-soaked wooden skewers.
5. Place the water tray in the bottom of the PowerXL Smokeless Electric Grill.
6. Place about 2 cups of lukewarm water into the water tray.
7. Place the drip pan over the water tray and then arrange the heating element.
8. Now, place the grilling pan over the heating element.
9. Plugin the PowerXL Smokeless Electric Grill and press the "Power" button to turn it on. Then press the "Fan" button.
10. Set the temperature settings according to the manufacturer's directions. Cover the grill with a lid and let it preheat.
11. After preheating, remove the lid and grease the grilling pan.
12. Place the skewers over the grilling pan. Cover with the lid and cook for about 8–10 minutes, flipping occasionally. Serve hot.

Nutrition:
Calories: 122, Total Fat: 7.8g, Saturated Fat: 1.2g, Cholesterol: 0mg, Sodium: 81mg, Total Carbs: 12.7g, Fiber: 3.5g, Sugar: 6.8g, Protein: 4.3 g

473. Pineapple & Veggie Skewers

Preparation Time: 20 minutes
Cooking Time: 15 minutes
Servings: 6
Ingredients:
- 1/3 cup olive oil
- 1½ tsp. dried basil
- ¾ tsp. dried oregano
- Salt and ground black pepper, as required
- 2 zucchinis, cut into 1-inch slices
- 2 yellow squashes, cut into 1-inch slices
- ½ pound whole fresh mushrooms
- 1 red bell pepper, cut into chunks
- 1 red onion, cut into chunks
- 12 cherry tomatoes
- 1 fresh pineapple, cut into chunks

Directions:
1. In a bowl, add oil, herbs, salt, and black pepper; mix well.
2. Thread the veggies and pineapple onto pre-soaked wooden skewers.
3. Brush the veggies and pineapple with the oil mixture evenly.
4. Place the water tray in the bottom of the PowerXL Smokeless Electric Grill.
5. Place about 2 cups of lukewarm water into the water tray.
6. Place the drip pan over the water tray and then arrange the heating element.
7. Now, place the grilling pan over the heating element.
8. Plugin the PowerXL Smokeless Electric Grill and press the "Power" button to turn it on.
9. Then press the "Fan" button.
10. Set the temperature settings according to the manufacturer's directions.

11. Cover the grill with a lid and let it preheat.
12. After preheating, remove the lid and grease the grilling pan.
13. Place the skewers over the grilling pan.
14. Cover with the lid and cook for about 10–15 minutes, flipping occasionally.
15. Serve hot.

Nutrition:
Calories: 220, Total Fat: 11.9g, Saturated Fat: 1.7g, Cholesterol: 0mg, Sodium: 47mg, Total Carbs: 30g, Fiber: 5g, Sugar: 20.4g, Protein: 4.3 g.

474. Buttered Corn
Preparation Time: 10 minutes
Cooking Time: 20 minutes
Servings: 6
Ingredients:
- 6 fresh whole corn on the cob
- ½ cup butter, melted
- Salt, as required

Directions:
1. Husk the corn and remove all the silk.
2. Brush each corn with melted butter and sprinkle with salt.
3. Place the water tray in the bottom of the PowerXL Smokeless Electric Grill.
4. Place about 2 cups of lukewarm water into the water tray.
5. Place the drip pan over the water tray and then arrange the heating element.
6. Now, place the grilling pan over the heating element.
7. Plugin the PowerXL Smokeless Electric Grill and press the "Power" button to turn it on.
8. Then press the "Fan" button.
9. Set the temperature settings according to the manufacturer's directions.
10. Cover the grill with a lid and let it preheat.
11. After preheating, remove the lid and grease the grilling pan.
12. Place the corn over the grilling pan.
13. Cover with the lid and cook for about 20 minutes, rotating after every 5 minutes and brushing with butter once halfway through.
14. Serve warm.

Nutrition:
Calories: 268, Total Fat: 17.2g, Saturated Fat: 10g, Cholesterol: 41mg, Sodium: 159mg, Total Carbs: 29g, Fiber: 4.2g, Sugar: 5g, Protein: 5.2 g.

475. Guacamole
Preparation Time: 15 minutes
Cooking Time: 4 minutes
Servings: 4
Ingredients:
- 2 ripe avocados, halved and pitted
- 2 tsp. vegetable oil
- 3 tbsp. fresh lime juice
- 1 garlic clove, crushed
- ¼ tsp. ground chipotle chile
- Salt, as required
- ¼ cup red onion, chopped finely
- ¼ cup fresh cilantro, chopped finely

Directions:
1. Brush the cut sides of each avocado half with oil.
2. Place the water tray in the bottom of the PowerXL Smokeless Electric Grill.
3. Place about 2 cups of lukewarm water into the water tray.
4. Place the drip pan over the water tray and then arrange the heating element.
5. Now, place the grilling pan over the heating element.
6. Plugin the PowerXL Smokeless Electric Grill and press the "Power" button to turn it on.
7. Then press the "Fan" button.
8. Set the temperature settings according to the manufacturer's directions.
9. Cover the grill with a lid and let it preheat.
10. After preheating, remove the lid and grease the grilling pan.
11. Place the avocado halves over the grilling pan, cut side down.
12. Cook, uncovered, for about 2–4 minutes.
13. Transfer the avocados onto the cutting board and let them cool slightly.
14. Remove the peel and transfer the flesh into a bowl.
15. Add the lime juice, garlic, chipotle, and salt, and with a fork, mash until almost smooth.
16. Stir in onion and cilantro and refrigerate, covered for about 1 hour before serving.

Nutrition:
Calories: 230, Total Fat: 21.9g, Saturated Fat: 4.6g, Cholesterol: 0mg, Sodium: 46mg, Total Carbs: 9.7g, Fiber: 6.9g, Sugar: 0.8g, Protein: 2.1 g.

CHAPTER 6:
Vegan and Vegetarian Recipes

476. Beans and Veggies Mix
Preparation time: 5 minutes
Cooking time: 25 minutes
Servings: 4
Ingredients:
- 2 teaspoons olive oil
- 2 spring onions, chopped
- 1 cup canned red kidney beans, drained
- 1 cup canned white beans, drained
- 2 tablespoons lime juice
- 1 cup mushrooms, halved
- 1 cup zucchinis, cubed
- 1 cup cherry tomatoes, cubed
- 1 red bell pepper, chopped
- 1 tablespoon tomato paste

Directions:
1. Preheat the air fryer at 370 degrees F, add the oil, heat up, add the beans, lime juice and the other ingredients, toss, cook for 25 minutes, and divide everything into bowls.

Nutrition: calories 309, fat 17, fiber 6, carbs 8, protein 4

477. Salsa Beans
Preparation time: 10 minutes
Cooking time: 25 minutes
Servings: 4
Ingredients:
- 2 cups canned black beans, drained
- 1 cup green peas
- 1 cup mild salsa
- ½ teaspoon cumin, ground
- ½ teaspoon chili powder
- ½ teaspoon green chili, minced
- ½ teaspoon ginger, grated
- A pinch of salt and black pepper

Directions:
1. In the air fryer's pan, mix the beans with the peas, salsa and the other ingredients, put the pan in the machine and cook at 370 degrees F for 25 minutes.
2. Divide between plates and serve.

Nutrition: calories 283, fat 4, fiber 8, carbs 34, protein 14

478. Supreme Air-Fried Tofu
Preparation Time: 5 minutes
Cooking Time: 50 minutes
Servings: 4
Ingredients:
- 1 block of pressed and sliced into 1-inch cubes of extra-firm tofu
- 2 tablespoons of soy sauce
- 1 teaspoon of seasoned rice vinegar
- 2 teaspoons of toasted sesame oil
- 1 tablespoon of cornstarch

Directions:
1. Using a bowl, add and toss the tofu, soy sauce, seasoned rice vinegar, sesame oil until it is properly covered.
2. Place it inside your refrigerator and allow to marinate for 30 minutes.
3. Preheat your air fryer to 370 degrees Fahrenheit.
4. Add the cornstarch to the tofu mixture and toss it until it is properly covered.
5. Grease your air fryer basket with a nonstick cooking spray and add the tofu inside your basket.
6. Cook it for 20 minutes at a 370 degrees Fahrenheit, and shake it after 10 minutes.
7. Serve and enjoy!

Nutrition: Calories: 80, Fat: 5.8g, Protein: 5g, Carbohydrates: 3g, Dietary Fiber: 1.2g

479. Sweet & Tangy Mushrooms
Preparation Time: 10 minutes
Cooking Time: 15 minutes
Servings: 4
Ingredients:
- ¼ cup soy sauce
- ¼ cup maple syrup
- ¼ cup balsamic vinegar
- 2 garlic cloves, chopped finely
- ½ teaspoon red pepper flakes, crushed
- 18 ounces cremini mushrooms, halved

Directions:
1. In a bowl, place the soy sauce, honey, vinegar, garlic and red pepper flakes and mix well. Set aside.
2. Place the mushroom into the greased baking pan in a single layer.
3. Select "Bake" of Air Fryer Toaster Oven and then adjust the temperature to 350 degrees F.
4. Set timer for 15 minutes and click "Start" to preheat.
5. After preheating, insert the baking pan in oven.
6. After 8 minutes of cooking, place the honey mixture in baking pan and toss to coat well.
7. Serve hot.

Nutrition: Calories 113 Total Fat 2 g Saturated Fat 0 g Cholesterol 0 mg Sodium 8 mg Total Carbs 27 g Fiber 1 g Sugar 20 g Protein 4 g

480. Cheesy Broccoli Rice
Preparation Time: 5 minutes
Cooking Time: 20 minutes
Servings: 8
Ingredients:
- 1 1/2 cups cooked brown rice
- 1 garlic clove, chopped
- 16 oz frozen broccoli florets
- 1 large onion, chopped
- 1 tbsp butter
- 3 tbsp parmesan cheese, grated
- 15 oz condensed cheddar cheese soup
- 1/3 cup unsweetened almond milk

Directions:
Melt butter Add onion and cook until tender.
1. Add garlic and broccoli and cook until broccoli is tender.
2. Stir in rice, soup, and milk and cook until hot.
3. Stir in cheese and pour broccoli mixture into the 11*8*2-inch baking dish.
4. Select bake mode and set the Omni to 350 F for 20 minutes once the oven beeps, place the baking dish into the oven.
5. Serve and enjoy.

Nutrition: Calories 234 Fat 7 g Carbohydrates 35 g Sugar 4 g Protein 9 g Cholesterol 16 mg

481. Mac & Cheese
Preparation Time: 5 minutes
Cooking Time: 20 minutes
Servings: 10
Ingredients:
- 1 lb cooked macaroni
- 1/2 cup flour
- 1/2 cup butter
- 1/2 cup breadcrumbs
- 12 oz cheddar cheese, shredded
- 4 1/2 cups unsweetened almond milk
- Pepper
- Salt

Directions:
1. Melt butter in a pan over medium heat.
2. Remove pan from heat and slowly add flour, salt, and pepper in melted butter.
3. Add ½ cup milk and stir until well blended.
4. Return to heat and slowly add remaining milk.
5. Add cheese and stir until cheese is melted.
6. Pour over cooked macaroni and stir well.
7. Transfer macaroni in a casserole dish and sprinkle with breadcrumbs.
8. Place casserole dish in Omni toaster oven Bakes at 350 F for 15-20 minutes.
9. Serve and enjoy.

Nutrition: Calories 449 Fat 21 g Carbohydrates 49 g Sugar 8 g Protein 13 g Cholesterol 60 mg

482. Tofu with Cauliflower
Preparation Time: 15 minutes
Cooking Time: 1 minutes
Servings: 2
Ingredients:
- ½ (14-ounce) block firm tofu, pressed and cubed
- ½ small head cauliflower, cut into florets
- 1 tablespoon canola oil
- 1 tablespoon nutritional yeast
- ¼ teaspoon dried parsley
- 1 teaspoon ground turmeric
- ¼ teaspoon paprika
- Salt and ground black pepper, as required

Directions:
1. In a bowl, mix together the tofu, cauliflower and the remaining ingredients.
2. Arrange the tofu mixture in greased basket.
3. Select "Air Fry" of Air Fryer Toaster Oven and then adjust the temperature to 390 degrees F.
4. Set timer for 15 minutes and click "Start" to preheat.
5. After preheating, insert the basket in oven.
6. Flip the tofu mixture once halfway through.
7. When cooking time is complete, remove the basket from oven and serve hot.

Nutrition: Calories 170 Total Fat 16 g Saturated Fat 5 g Cholesterol 0 mg Sodium 113 mg Total Carbs 3 g Fiber 2 g Sugar 3 g Protein 19 g

483. Potato Casserole
Preparation Time: 5 minutes
Cooking Time: 35 minutes
Servings: 6
Ingredients:
- 5 eggs
- 1/2 cup cheddar cheese, shredded
- 2 medium potatoes, diced into 1/2-inch cubes
- 1 green bell pepper, diced
- 1 onion, chopped
- 1 tbsp olive oil
- 3/4 tsp pepper
- 3/4 tsp salt

Directions:
1. Spray 9*9-inch casserole dish with cooking spray and set aside.
2. Heat olive oil in a large pan over medium heat.
3. Add onion and sauté for 1 minute. Add potatoes, bell peppers, ½ tsp black pepper, and 2 tsp salt and sauté for 4 minutes more or until onions are softened.
4. Transfer sautéed vegetables to the prepared casserole dish and spread evenly.
5. In a bowl, whisk eggs, and remaining pepper and salt.

6. Pour egg mixture into the casserole dish and sprinkle cheddar cheese on top.
7. Select bake mode and set the Omni to 350 F for 35 minutes once the oven beeps, place casserole dish into the oven.
8. Serve and enjoy.

Nutrition: Calories 174 Fat 2 g Carbohydrates 19 g Sugar 9 g Protein 6 g Cholesterol 146 mg

484. Asparagus Strata

Preparation Time: 11 minutes;
Cooking Time: 19 minutes;
Servings: 4
Ingredients:
- 6 asparagus spears, cut into 2-inch pieces
- 2 slices whole-wheat bread, cut into ½-inch cubes
- 4 eggs
- 3 tbsp. whole milk
- ½ cup grated Havarti
- 2 tbsp. chopped flat-leaf parsley
- Salt and ground black pepper, to taste
- 1 tbsp. water
- Non-stick cooking spray

Directions:
1. Place the asparagus spears and 1 tbsp. water in a baking pan and place in the basket.
2. Select BAKE. Bake for 5 minutes at 325°F until crisp and tender.
3. Drain the asparagus.
4. Spray the pan with non-stick cooking spray.
5. Place the bread cubes and asparagus into the pan and set aside.
6. Beat the eggs in a bowl, then add the milk until combined.
7. Add the cheese, parsley, salt, and pepper. Pour into the baking pan.
8. Select BAKE. Set temperature to 360°F, and set time to 14 minutes or until the eggs are set, and the top starts to brown.
9. When the cooking time is complete, transfer to a platter and serve hot.

Nutrition: Calories 166, Fat 49 g, Fiber 2 g, Protein 12 g.

485. Zucchini Egg Bake

Preparation Time: 5 minutes
Cooking Time: 30 minutes
Servings: 4
Ingredients:
- 6 eggs - 1/2 tsp dill
- 1/2 tsp oregano
- 1/2 tsp basil
- 1/2 tsp baking powder
- 1/2 cup almond flour
- 1 cup cheddar cheese, shredded
- 1 cup kale, chopped
- 1 onion, chopped
- 1 cup zucchini, shredded and squeezed out all liquid
- 1/2 cup milk- 1/4 tsp salt

Directions:
1. Grease 9*9-inch baking dish and set aside.
2. In a large bowl, whisk eggs with milk.
3. Add remaining ingredients
4. Pour egg mixture into the prepared baking dish.
5. Select bake mode and set the Omni to 375 F for 30 minutes once the oven beeps, place the baking dish into the oven. Serve and enjoy.

Nutrition: Calories 269 Fat 14 g Carbohydrates 9 g Sugar 8 g Protein 13 g Cholesterol 278 mg

486. Curried Cauliflower

Preparation Time: 10 minutes
Cooking Time: 15 minutes
Servings: 4
Ingredients:
- 2 lbs. cauliflower, cut into florets
- 1 1/2 tsp curry powder
- 1 tbsp olive oil
- 1 tbsp cilantro, chopped
- 2 tsp fresh lemon juice
- 1 tsp kosher salt

Directions:
1. Combine cauliflower florets with olive oil in a large bowl.
2. Sprinkle cauliflower florets with curry powder and salt.
3. Spread cauliflower florets onto a cooking pan.
4. Select bake mode and set the Omni to 425 F for 15 minutes once the oven beeps, place the cooking pan into the oven.
5. Return roasted cauliflower florets into the bowl and toss with cilantro and lemon juice.
6. Serve and enjoy.

Nutrition: Calories 90 Fat 9 g Carbohydrates 15 g Sugar 5 g Protein 6 g Cholesterol 0 mg

487. Baby Potatoes

Preparation Time: 10 minutes
Cooking Time: 20 minutes
Servings: 2
Ingredients:
- 12 oz baby potatoes
- 1/4 tsp cumin
- 1/4 tsp paprika
- 1/4 tsp chili powder
- 1/2 tbsp olive oil
- 1/4 tsp garlic salt
- 1/4 tsp pepper
- 1/2 tsp kosher salt

Directions:
1. Add all ingredients into a zip-lock bag and shake well.
2. Transfer potatoes into the air fryer basket.

3. Place air fryer basket into the oven and select air fry mode set Omni to the 370 F for 20 minutes. Stir twice.
4. Serve and enjoy.

Nutrition: Calories 133 Fat 8 g Carbohydrates 22 g Sugar 2 g Protein 6 g Cholesterol 0 mg

488. Baked Vegetables

Preparation Time: 5 minutes
Cooking Time: 20 minutes
Servings: 4
Ingredients:
- 4 bell peppers
- 2 cups mushrooms
- 1/4 tsp black pepper
- 2 tbsp olive oil
- 2 eggplants
- 1 tsp salt

Directions:
1. Cut all vegetables into the small bite-sized pieces and place in a baking dish.
2. Drizzle vegetables with olive oil and season with pepper and salt.
3. Select bake mode and set the Omni to 390 F for 20 minutes once the oven beeps, place the baking dish into the oven.
4. Serve and enjoy.

Nutrition: Calories 174 Fat 9 g Carbohydrates 23 g Sugar 18 g Protein 5 g Cholesterol 0 mg

489. Dill Mashed Potato

Preparation Time: 10 minutes
Cooking Time: 15 minutes
Servings: 2
Ingredients:
- 2 potatoes
- 2 tablespoon fresh dill, chopped
- 1 teaspoon butter
- ½ teaspoon salt - ¼ cup half and half

Directions:
1. Preheat the air fryer to 390 F.
2. Rinse the potatoes thoroughly and place them in the air fryer.
3. Cook the potatoes for 15 minutes.
4. After this, remove the potatoes from the air fryer.
5. Peel the potatoes.
6. Mash the potatoes with the help of the fork well.
7. Then add chopped fresh dill and salt.
8. Stir it gently and add butter and half and half.
9. Take the hand blender and blend the mixture well.
10. When the mashed potato is cooked – serve it immediately. Enjoy!

Nutrition: Calories 211, Fat 5.7, Fiber 5.5, Carbs 36.5, Protein 5.1

490. Cream Potato

Preparation Time: 15 minutes
Cooking Time: 20 minutes
Servings: 2
Ingredients:
- 3 medium potatoes, scrubbed
- ½ teaspoon kosher salt
- 1 tablespoon Italian seasoning
- 1/3 cup cream
- ½ teaspoon ground black pepper

Directions:
1. Slice the potatoes.
2. Preheat the air fryer to 365 F.
3. Make the layer from the sliced potato in the air fryer basket.
4. Sprinkle the potato layer with the kosher salt and ground black pepper.
5. After this, make the second layer of the potato and sprinkle it with Italian seasoning.
6. Make the last layer of the sliced potato and pour the cream.
7. Cook the scallop potato for 20 minutes.
8. When the scalloped potato is cooked – let it chill till the room temperature. Enjoy!

Nutrition: Calories 269, Fat 4.7, Fiber 7.8, Carbs 52.6, Protein 5.8

491. Chard with Cheddar

Preparation Time: 10 minutes
Cooking Time: 11 minutes
Servings: 2
Ingredients:
- 3 oz Cheddar cheese, grated
- 10 oz Swiss chard
- 3 tablespoon cream
- 1 tablespoon sesame oil
- salt and pepper to taste

Directions:
1. Wash Swiss chard carefully and chop it roughly.
2. After this, sprinkle chopped Swiss chard with the salt and ground white pepper.
3. Stir it carefully.
4. Sprinkle Swiss chard with the sesame oil and stir it carefully with the help of 2 spatulas.
5. Preheat the air fryer to 260 F.
6. Put chopped Swiss chard in the air fryer basket and cook for 6 minutes.
7. Shake it after 3 minutes of cooking.
8. Then pour the cream into the air fryer basket and mix it up.
9. Cook the meal for 3 minutes more.
10. Then increase the temperature to 400 F.
11. Sprinkle the meal with the grated cheese and cook for 2 minutes more.
12. After this, transfer the meal in the serving plates. Enjoy!

Nutrition: Calories 272, Fat 22.3, Fiber 2.5, Carbs 6.7, Protein 13.3

492. Chili Squash Wedges

Preparation Time: 10 minutes
Cooking Time: 18 minutes
Servings: 2
Ingredients:
- 11 oz Acorn squash

- ½ teaspoon salt - tablespoon olive oil
- ½ teaspoon chili pepper
- ½ teaspoon paprika

Directions:
1. Cut Acorn squash into the serving wedges.
2. Sprinkle the wedges with the salt, olive oil, chili pepper, and paprika. Massage the wedges gently.
3. Preheat the air fryer to 400 F.
4. Put Acorn squash wedges in the air fryer basket and cook for 18 minutes.
5. Flip the wedges into another side after 9 minutes of cooking. Serve the cooked meal hot. Enjoy!

Nutrition: Calories 125, Fat 7.2, Fiber 2.6, Carbs 16.7, Protein 1.4

493. Honey Carrots with Greens

Preparation Time: 7 minutes
Cooking Time: 12 minutes
Servings: 2
Ingredients:
- 1 cup baby carrot
- ½ teaspoon salt
- ½ teaspoon white pepper
- 1 tablespoon honey
- 1 teaspoon sesame oil

Directions:
1. Preheat the air fryer to 385 F.
2. Combine the baby carrot with the salt, white pepper, and sesame oil.
3. Shake the baby carrot and transfer in the air fryer basket.
4. Cook the vegetables for 10 minutes.
5. After this, add honey and shake the vegetables.
6. Cook the meal for 2 minutes.
7. After this, shake the vegetables and serve immediately.
8. Enjoy!

Nutrition: Calories 83, Fat 2.4, Fiber 2.6, Carbs 16, Protein 0.6

494. South Asian Cauliflower Fritters

Preparation Time: 5 minutes
Cooking Time: 20 minutes
Servings: 4
Ingredients:
- 1 large chopped into florets cauliflower
- 3 tablespoons of Greek yogurt
- 3 tablespoons of flour
- ½ teaspoon of ground turmeric
- ½ teaspoon of ground cumin
- ½ teaspoon of ground paprika
- 12 teaspoon of ground coriander
- ½ teaspoon of salt
- ½ teaspoon of black pepper

Directions:
1. Using a large bowl, add and mix the Greek yogurt, flour, and seasonings properly.
2. Add the cauliflower florets and toss it until it is well covered
3. Heat up your air fryer to 390 degrees Fahrenheit.
4. Grease your air fryer basket with a nonstick cooking spray and add half of the cauliflower florets to it.
5. Cook it for 10 minutes or until it turns golden brown and crispy, then shake it after 5 minutes. (Repeat this with the other half).
6. Serve and enjoy!

Nutrition: Calories: 120, Fat: 4g, Protein: 7.5g, Carbohydrates: 14g, Dietary Fiber: 3.4g

495. Air Fried Cauliflower Rice

Preparation Time: 7 minutes;
Cooking Time: 20 minutes;
Servings: 4
Ingredients:
Round 1:
- 1 tsp. turmeric
- 1 cup diced carrot
- ½ cup diced onion
- 2 tbsp. low-sodium soy sauce
- ½ block of extra firm tofu

Round 2:
- ½ cup frozen peas
- 2 minced garlic cloves
- ½ cup chopped broccoli
- 1 tbsp. minced ginger
- 1 tbsp. rice vinegar
- 1½ tsp. sesame oil
- 2 tbsp. reduced-sodium soy sauce
- 3 cups riced cauliflower

Directions:
1. Preheat the Smart Air Fryer Oven to 370°F.
2. Crumble tofu in a large bowl and toss with all the listed ingredients in Round
3. Transfer the tofu mixture to a baking dish. Place the baking dish in the Smart Air Fryer Oven cooking basket.
4. Select AIR FRY. Set the temperature to 370°F, and set time to 10 minutes and cook 10 minutes, making sure to shake once.
5. In another bowl, toss ingredients from Round 2 together.
6. Add Round 2 mixture to the cooked tofu mixture and cook for another 10 minutes, ensuring to shake every 5 minutes.
7. Enjoy!

Nutrition: Calories 67, Fat 8 g, Protein 3 g.

496. Roasted Apple Sweet Potatoes

Preparation Time: 5 minutes
Cooking Time: 30 minutes
Servings: 2
Ingredients:
- 2 large sweet potatoes, diced
- 2 tsp cinnamon
- 2 large green apples, diced
- 2 tbsp maple syrup

- 1 tbsp olive oil

Directions:
1. In a large bowl, add sweet potatoes, oil, cinnamon, and apples and toss well.
2. Spread sweet potatoes mixture onto the cooking pan.
3. Select bake mode and set the Omni to 400 F for 30 minutes once the oven beeps, place the cooking pan into the oven.
4. Drizzle with maple syrup and serve.

Nutrition: Calories 352 Fat 6 g Carbohydrates 74 g Sugar 37 g Protein 2 g Cholesterol 0 mg

497. Green Beans with Carrots

Preparation Time: 7 minutes;
Cooking Time: 10 minutes;
Servings: 3

Ingredients:
- ½ lb. green beans, trimmed
- ½ lb. carrots, peeled and cut into sticks
- 1 tbsp. olive oil
- Salt and ground black pepper, to taste

Directions:
1. Add all the listed ingredients and toss to coat thoroughly.
2. Place the vegetables in the air fryer basket.
3. AIR FRY at a temperature of 400°F for 10 minutes.
4. When ready, transfer to a plate and serve hot.

Nutrition: Calories 94, Fat 8 g, Carbs 17 g, Protein 2 g.

498. Winter Vegetarian Frittata

Preparation Time: 5 Minutes
Cooking Time: 30 Minutes
Servings: 4

Ingredients
- 1 leek, peeled and thinly sliced into rings
- 2 cloves garlic, finely minced
- 3 medium-sized carrots, finely chopped
- 2 tablespoons olive oil
- 6 large-sized eggs
- Sea salt and ground black pepper, to taste
- 1/2 teaspoon dried marjoram, finely minced
- 1/2 cup yellow cheese of choice

Directions:
1. Preparing the Ingredients. Sauté the leek, garlic, and carrot in hot olive oil until they are tender and fragrant; reserve.
2. In the meantime, preheat your Cuisinart air fryer oven to 330 degrees F.
3. Whisk the eggs along with the salt, ground black pepper, and marjoram.
4. Then, grease the inside of your baking dish with a nonstick cooking spray. Pour the whisked eggs into the baking dish. Stir in the sautéed carrot mixture. Top with the cheese shreds.
5. Air Frying. Place the baking dish in the Cuisinart air fryer oven cooking basket. Cook about 30 minutes and serve warm

Nutrition: Calories: 209; Fat: 17g; Protein: 6g; Sugar: 5

499. Cheesy Broccoli Casserole

Preparation Time: 5 minutes
Cooking Time: 30 minutes
Servings: 6

Ingredients:
- 16 oz frozen broccoli florets, defrosted and drained
- 1/2 tsp onion powder
- 15 oz can cream of mushroom soup
- 1 cup cheddar cheese, shredded
- 1/3 cup unsweetened almond milk

For topping:
- 1 tbsp butter, melted
- 1/2 cup cracker crumbs

Directions:
1. Add all ingredients except topping ingredients into the casserole dish.
2. In a small bowl, mix together cracker crumbs and melted butter and sprinkle over the casserole dish mixture.
3. Select bake mode and set the Omni to 350 F for 30 minutes once the oven beeps, place casserole dish into the oven.
4. Serve and enjoy.

Nutrition: Calories 193 Fat 19 g Carbohydrates 15 g Sugar 4 g Protein 9 g Cholesterol 27 mg

500. Buffalo Cauliflower

Preparation Time: 5 Minutes
Cooking Time: 15 Minutes
Servings: 2

Ingredients
Cauliflower:
- 1 C. panko breadcrumbs
- 1 tsp. salt
- 4 C. cauliflower florets

Buffalo Coating:
- ¼ C. Vegan Buffalo sauce
- ¼ C. melted vegan butter

Directions:
1. Preparing the Ingredients. Melt butter in microwave and whisk in buffalo sauce.
2. Dip each cauliflower floret into buffalo mixture, ensuring it gets coated well. Hold over a bowl till floret is done dripping.
3. Mix breadcrumbs with salt.
4. Air Frying. Dredge dipped florets into breadcrumbs and place into the air fryer oven. Set the temperature to 350°F, and set time to 15 minutes. When slightly browned, they are ready to eat!
5. Serve with your favorite keto dipping sauce!

Nutrition: CALORIES: 194; FAT: 17G; PROTEIN: 10G; SUGAR:

501. Cauliflower Bites

Preparation Time: 10 Minutes
Cooking Time: 18 Minutes
Servings: 4

Ingredients
- 1 Head Cauliflower, cut into small florets
- 1 Tsps. Garlic Powder
- Pinch of Salt and Pepper
- 1 Tbsp Butter, melted
- 1/2 Cup Chili Sauce
- Olive Oil

Directions:
1. Preparing the Ingredients. Place cauliflower into a bowl and pour oil over florets to lightly cover.
2. Season florets with salt, pepper, and the garlic powder and toss well.
3. Air Frying. Place florets into the Cuisinart air fryer oven at 350 degrees for 14 minutes.
4. Remove cauliflower from the Air fryer oven.
5. Combine the melted butter with the chili sauce
6. Pour over the florets so that they are well coated.
7. Return to the Cuisinart air fryer oven and cook for additional 3 to 4 minutes
8. Serve as a side or with ranch or cheese dip as a snack.

Nutrition: CALORIES: 209; FAT: 17G; PROTEIN: 6G; SUGAR: 5

502. Onion Rings

Preparation Time: 10 Minutes
Cooking Time: 10 Minutes
Servings: 4

Ingredients
- 1 large Spanish onion
- 1/2 cup buttermilk
- 2 eggs, lightly beaten
- 3/4 cups unbleached all-purpose flour
- 3/4 cups panko bread crumbs
- 1/2 teaspoon baking powder
- 1/2 teaspoon Cayenne pepper, to taste
- Salt

Directions:
1. Preparing the Ingredients. Start by cutting your onion into 1/2 thick rings and separate. Smaller pieces can be discarded or saved for other recipes.
2. Beat the eggs in a large bowl and mix in the buttermilk, then set it aside.
3. In another bowl combine flour, pepper, bread crumbs, and baking powder.
4. Use a large spoon to dip a whole ring in the buttermilk, then pull it through the flour mix on both sides to completely coat the ring.
5. Air Frying. Cook about 8 rings at a time in your Cuisinart air fryer oven for 8-10 minutes at 360 degrees shaking half way through.

Nutrition: CALORIES: 225; FAT: 8G; PROTEIN: 19G; FIBER: 4G

503. Zucchini Parmesan Chips

Preparation Time: 10 Minutes
Cooking Time: 8 Minutes
Servings: 10

Ingredients
- ½ tsp. paprika
- ½ C. grated parmesan cheese
- ½ C. Italian breadcrumbs
- 1 lightly beaten egg
- 2 thinly sliced zucchinis

Directions:
1. Preparing the Ingredients. Use a very sharp knife or mandolin slicer to slice zucchini as thinly as you can. Pat off extra moisture.
2. Beat egg with a pinch of pepper and salt and a bit of water.
3. Combine paprika, cheese, and breadcrumbs in a bowl.
4. Dip slices of zucchini into the egg mixture and then into breadcrumb mixture. Press gently to coat.
5. Air Frying. With olive oil cooking spray, mist coated zucchini slices. Place into your Cuisinart air fryer oven in a single layer. Set temperature to 350°F, and set time to 8 minutes.
6. Sprinkle with salt and serve with salsa.

Nutrition: CALORIES: 211; FAT: 16G; PROTEIN: 8G; SUGAR: 0G

504. Jalapeño Cheese Balls

Preparation Time: 10 Minutes
Cooking Time: 8 Minutes
Servings: 12

Ingredients
- 4 ounces' cream cheese
- ⅓ cup shredded mozzarella cheese
- ⅓ cup shredded Cheddar cheese
- 2 jalapeños, finely chopped
- ½ cup bread crumbs
- 2 eggs
- ½ cup all-purpose flour
- Salt
- Pepper
- Cooking oil

Directions:
1. Preparing the Ingredients. Combine cream cheese, mozzarella, Cheddar, and jalapeños in bowl. Mix well.
2. Form the cheese mixture into balls about an inch thick. Using a small ice cream scoop works well.
3. Arrange the cheese balls on a sheet pan and place in the freezer for 15 minutes. This will help the cheese balls maintain their shape while frying.
4. Spray the Oven rack/basket with cooking oil. In another small bowl, beat the eggs. In a third small bowl, combine the flour with salt and pepper to taste, and mix well. Remove the cheese balls from the

freezer. Dip the cheese balls in the flour, then the eggs, and then the bread crumbs.
5. Air Frying. Place the cheese balls in the Oven rack/basket. Spray with cooking oil. Place the Rack on the middle-shelf of the Cuisinart air fryer oven. Cook for 8 minutes.
6. Open the air fryer oven and flip the cheese balls. I recommend flipping them instead of shaking, so the balls maintain their form. Cook an additional 4 minutes. Cool before serving.

Nutrition: CALORIES: 96; FAT: 6G; PROTEIN: 4G; SUGAR:

505. Glazed Carrots

Preparation Time: 15 minutes
Cooking Time: 12 minutes
Servings: 4
Ingredients:
- 3 cups carrots, peeled and cut into large chunks
- 1 tablespoon olive oil
- 1 tablespoon maple syrup
- 1 tablespoon fresh parsley, minced
- Salt and ground black pepper, as required

Directions:
1. In a bowl, add the carrot, oil, maple syrup, thyme, salt, and black pepper.
2. Arrange the carrot chunks into the greased basket in a single layer.
3. Select "Air Fry" of Air Fryer Toaster Oven and then adjust the temperature to 390 degrees F.
4. Set timer for 12 minutes and press "Start" to preheat.
5. After preheating, insert the basket in the center position of oven.
6. Flip the carrot chunks once halfway through.
7. When cooking time is complete, remove the basket from oven and serve hot.

Nutrition: Calories 77 Total Fat 5 g Saturated Fat 5 g Cholesterol 0 mg Sodium 97 mg Total Carbs 15 g Fiber 1 g Sugar 1 g Protein 7 g

506. Flatbread

Preparation Time: 5 minutes
Cooking Time: 7 minutes
Servings: 2
Ingredients:
- 1 cup shredded mozzarella cheese
- ¼ cup almond flour
- 1-ounce full-fat cream cheese softened

Directions:
1. Melt mozzarella in the microwave for 30 seconds. Stir in almond flour until smooth.
2. Add cream cheese. Continue mixing until dough forms. Knead with wet hands if necessary.
3. Divide the dough into two pieces and roll out to ¼-inch thickness between two pieces of parchment.
4. Cover the air fryer basket with parchment and place the flatbreads into the air fryer basket. Work in batches if necessary.
5. Cook at 320F for 7 minutes. Flip once at the halfway mark.
6. Serve.

Nutrition: Calories: 296 Fat: 22.6g Carb: 3.3g Protein: 16.3g

507. Creamy Cabbage

Preparation Time: 10 minutes
Cooking Time: 20 minutes
Servings: 2
Ingredients:
- ½ green cabbage head, chopped
- ½ yellow onion, chopped
- Salt and black pepper, to taste
- ½ cup whipped cream
- 1 tablespoon cornstarch

Directions:
1. Put cabbage and onion in the air fryer.
2. In a bowl, mix cornstarch with cream, salt, and pepper. Stir and pour over cabbage.
3. Toss and cook at 400F for 20 minutes.
4. Serve.

Nutrition: Calories: 208 Fat: 10g Carb: 16g Protein: 5g

508. Creamy Potatoes

Preparation Time: 10 minutes
Cooking Time: 20 minutes
Servings: 2
Ingredients:
- ¾ pound potatoes, peeled and cubed
- 1 tablespoon olive oil
- Salt and black pepper, to taste
- ½ tablespoon hot paprika
- ½ cup Greek yogurt

Directions:
1. Place potatoes in a bowl, pour water to cover, and leave aside for 10 minutes. Drain, pat dry, then transfer to another bowl.
2. Add salt, pepper, paprika, and half of the oil to the potatoes and mix.
3. Put potatoes in the air fryer basket and cook at 360F for 20 minutes.
4. In a bowl, mix yogurt with salt, pepper, and the rest of the oil and whisk.
5. Divide potatoes onto plates, drizzle with yogurt dressing, mix, and serve.

Nutrition: Calories: 170 Fat: 3g Carb: 20g Protein: 5g

509. Green Beans and Cherry Tomatoes

Preparation Time: 10 minutes
Cooking Time: 15 minutes
Servings: 2
Ingredients:
- 8 ounces cherry tomatoes
- 8 ounces green beans
- 1 tablespoon olive oil
- Salt and black pepper, to taste

Directions:

1. In a bowl, mix cherry tomatoes with green beans, olive oil, salt, and pepper. Mix.
2. Cook in the air fryer at 400 degrees F for 15 minutes. Shake once.
3. Serve.

Nutrition: Calories: 162 Fat: 6g Carb: 8g Protein: 9g

510. Crispy Brussels Sprouts and Potatoes

Preparation Time: 10 minutes
Cooking Time: 8 minutes
Servings: 2
Ingredients:

- ¾ pound brussels sprouts, washed and trimmed
- ½ cup new potatoes, chopped
- 2 teaspoons bread crumbs
- Salt and black pepper, to taste
- 2 teaspoons butter

Directions:

1. In a bowl, add Brussels sprouts, potatoes, bread crumbs, salt, pepper, and butter. Mix well.
2. Place in the air fryer and cook at 400F for 8 minutes.
3. Serve.

Nutrition: Calories: 152 Fat: 3g Carb: 17g Protein: 4g

511. Air Fried Leeks

Preparation Time: 10 minutes
Cooking Time: 7 minutes
Servings: 2
Ingredients:

- 2 leeks, washed, ends cut, and halved
- Salt and black pepper, to taste
- ½ tablespoon butter, melted
- ½ tablespoon lemon juice

Directions:

1. Rub leeks with melted butter and season with salt and pepper.
2. Lay it inside the air fryer and cook at 350F for 7 minutes.
3. Arrange on a platter. Drizzle with lemon juice and serve.

Nutrition: Calories: 100 Fat: 4g Carb: 6g Protein: 2g

512. Crispy Broccoli

Preparation Time: 10 minutes
Cooking Time: 10 minutes
Servings: 4
Ingredients:

- 1 large head fresh broccoli
- 2 teaspoons olive oil
- tablespoon lemon juice

Directions:

1. Rinse the broccoli and pat dry. Cut off the florets and separate them. You can also use the broccoli stems too; cut them into 1" chunks and peel them.
2. Toss the broccoli, olive oil, and lemon juice in a large bowl until coated.
3. Roast the broccoli in the air fryer, in batches, for 10 to 14 minutes or until the broccoli is crisp-tender and slightly brown around the edges. Repeat with the remaining broccoli. Serve immediately.

Nutrition: Calories: 63; Fat: 2g Protein: 4g; Carbohydrates: 10g; Sodium: 50mg; Fiber: 4g;

513. Garlic-Roasted Bell Peppers

Preparation Time: 5 minutes
Cooking Time: 20 minutes
Servings: 4
Ingredients:

- 4 bell peppers, any colors, stemmed, seeded, membranes removed, and cut into fourths
- 1 teaspoon olive oil
- 4 garlic cloves, minced
- ½ teaspoon dried thyme

Directions:

1. Put the peppers in the basket of the air fryer and drizzle with olive oil. Toss gently. Roast for 15 minutes.
2. Sprinkle with the garlic and thyme. Roast for 3 to 5 minutes more, or until tender. Serve immediately.

Nutrition: Calories: 36; Fat: 1g Protein: 1g; Carbohydrates: 5g; Sodium: 21mg; Fiber: 2g;

514. Asparagus with Garlic

Preparation Time: 5 minutes
Cooking Time: 10 minutes
Servings: 4
Ingredients:

- 1-pound asparagus, rinsed, ends snapped off where they naturally break (see Tip)
- 2 teaspoons olive oil
- 3 garlic cloves, minced
- 2 tablespoons balsamic vinegar
- ½ teaspoon dried thyme

Directions:

1. In a huge bowl, mix the asparagus with olive oil. Transfer to the air fryer basket.
2. Sprinkle with garlic. Roast for 4 to 5 minutes for crisp-tender or for 8 to 11 minutes for asparagus that is crisp on the outside and tender on the inside.
3. Drizzle with the balsamic vinegar and sprinkle with the thyme leaves. Serve immediately.

Nutrition: Calories: 41; Fat: 1g Protein: 3g; Carbohydrates: 6g; Sodium: 3mg;

515. Cheesy Roasted Sweet Potatoes

Preparation Time: 5 minutes
Cooking Time: 20 minutes
Servings: 4
Ingredients:

- 2 large sweet potatoes, peeled and sliced
- 1 teaspoon olive oil
- 1 tablespoon white balsamic vinegar
- 1 teaspoon dried thyme
- ¼ cup grated Parmesan cheese

Directions:

1. In a big bowl, shower the sweet potato slices with the olive oil and toss.
2. Sprinkle with the balsamic vinegar and thyme and toss again.
3. Sprinkle the potatoes with the Parmesan cheese and toss to coat.
4. Roast the slices, in batches, in the air fryer basket for 18 to 23 minutes, tossing the sweet potato slices in the basket once during cooking, until tender.
5. Repeat with the remaining sweet potato slices. Serve immediately.

Nutrition: Calories: 100; Fat: 3g Protein: 4g; Carbohydrates: 15g; Sodium: 132mg;

516. Salty Lemon Artichokes

Preparation Time: 15 minutes
Cooking Time: 45 minutes
Servings: 2
Ingredients:
- 1 lemon
- 2 artichokes
- 1 teaspoon kosher salt
- 1 garlic head
- 2 teaspoon olive oil

Directions:
1. Cut off the edges of the artichokes.
2. Cut the lemon into the halves.
3. Peel the garlic head and chop the garlic cloves roughly.
4. Then place the chopped garlic in the artichokes.
5. Sprinkle the artichokes with the olive oil and kosher salt.
6. Then squeeze the lemon juice into the artichokes.
7. Wrap the artichokes in the foil.
8. Preheat the air fryer to 330 F.
9. Place the wrapped artichokes in the air fryer and cook for 45 minutes.
10. When the artichokes are cooked – discard the foil and serve.
11. Enjoy!

Nutrition: Calories 133, Fat 5, Fiber 9.7, Carbs 21.7, Protein 6

517. Asparagus & Parmesan

Preparation Time: 10 minutes
Cooking Time: 6 minutes
Servings: 2
Ingredients:
- 1 teaspoon sesame oil
- 11 oz asparagus
- 1 teaspoon chicken stock
- ½ teaspoon ground white pepper
- 3 oz Parmesan

Directions:
1. Wash the asparagus and chop it roughly.
2. Sprinkle the chopped asparagus with the chicken stock and ground white pepper.
3. Then sprinkle the vegetables with the sesame oil and shake them.
4. Place the asparagus in the air fryer basket.
5. Cook the vegetables for 4 minutes at 400 F.
6. Meanwhile, shred Parmesan cheese.
7. When the time is over – shake the asparagus gently and sprinkle with the shredded cheese.
8. Cook the asparagus for 2 minutes more at 400 F.
9. After this, transfer the cooked asparagus in the serving plates.
10. Serve and taste it!

Nutrition: Calories 189, Fat 11.6, Fiber 3.4, Carbs 7.9 Protein 17.2

518. Corn on Cobs

Preparation Time: 10 minutes
Cooking Time: 10 minutes
Servings: 2
Ingredients:
- 2 fresh corn on cobs
- 2 teaspoon butter
- 1 teaspoon salt
- 1 teaspoon paprika
- ¼ teaspoon olive oil

Directions:
1. Preheat the air fryer to 400 F.
2. Rub the corn on cobs with the salt and paprika.
3. Then sprinkle the corn on cobs with the olive oil.
4. Place the corn on cobs in the air fryer basket.
5. Cook the corn on cobs for 10 minutes.
6. When the time is over – transfer the corn on cobs in the serving plates and rub with the butter gently.
7. Serve the meal immediately.
8. Enjoy!

Nutrition: Calories 122, Fat 5.5, Fiber 2.4, Carbs 17.6, Protein 3.2

519. Onion Green Beans

Preparation Time: 10 minutes
Cooking Time: 12 minutes
Servings: 2
Ingredients:
- 11 oz green beans
- 1 tablespoon onion powder
- 1 tablespoon olive oil
- ½ teaspoon salt
- ¼ teaspoon chili flakes

Directions:
1. Wash the green beans carefully and place them in the bowl.
2. Sprinkle the green beans with the onion powder, salt, chili flakes, and olive oil.
3. Shake the green beans carefully.
4. Preheat the air fryer to 400 F.
5. Put the green beans in the air fryer and cook for 8 minutes.
6. After this, shake the green beans and cook them for 4 minutes more at 400 F.
7. When the time is over – shake the green beans.
8. Serve the side dish and enjoy!

Nutrition: Calories 1205, Fat 7.2, Fiber 5.5, Carbs 13.9, Protein 3.2

520. Spicy Asian Brussels sprouts

Preparation Time: 10 minutes
Cooking Time: 15 minutes
Servings: 4
Ingredients:
- 1 lb. Brussels sprouts, cut in half (1 green)
- 1 tbsp gochujang (1/2 condiment)
- 1 1/2 tbsp olive oil (1/4 condiment)
- 1/2 tsp salt (1/4 condiment)

Directions:
1. In a bowl, mix olive oil, gochujang, and salt.
2. Add Brussels sprouts into the bowl and toss until well coated.
3. Add Brussels sprouts into the air fryer basket and cook at 360 F for 15 minutes.
4. Serve and enjoy.

Nutrition 94 Calories 5g Fat 4g Protein

521. Healthy Mushrooms

Preparation Time: 10 minutes
Cooking Time: 12 minutes
Servings: 2
Ingredients:
- 8 oz mushrooms, clean and cut into quarters (2 healthy fats)
- 1 tbsp fresh parsley, chopped (1/2 green)
- 1 tsp soy sauce (1/4 condiment)
- 1/2 tsp garlic powder (1/4 condiment)
- 1 tbsp olive oil (1/4 condiment)
- Pepper (1/8 condiment)
- Salt (1/8 condiment)

Directions:
1. Add mushrooms and remaining ingredients into the bowl and toss well.
2. Add mushrooms into the air fryer basket and cook at 380 F for 12 minutes. Stir halfway through.
3. Serve and enjoy.

Nutrition 90 Calories 7g Fat 4g Protein

522. Cheese Stuff Peppers

Preparation Time: 10 minutes
Cooking Time: 8 minutes
Servings: 4
Ingredients:
- 10 jalapeno peppers, halved, remove seeds and stem (4 lean)
- 1/2 cup cheddar cheese (1/4 healthy fat)
- 1/2 cup Monterey jack cheese, shredded (1/4 healthy fat) - 8 oz cream cheese, softened (1/2 healthy fat)

Directions:
1. In a bowl, mix together Monterey jack cheese and cream cheese.
2. Stuff cheese mixture into jalapeno halved.
3. Place jalapeno pepper into the air fryer basket and cook at 370 F for 8 minutes.
4. Serve and enjoy.

Nutrition 365 Calories 33g Fat 13.2g Protein

523. Cheesy Brussels sprouts

Preparation Time: 10 minutes
Cooking Time: 12 minutes
Servings: 4
Ingredients:
- 1 lb. Brussels sprouts, cut stems and halved (1/2 green)
- 1/4 cup parmesan cheese (1/2 healthy fat)
- 1 tbsp olive oil (1/4 condiment)
- 1/4 tsp garlic powder (1/4 condiment)
- Pepper (1/8 condiment) - Salt (1/8 condiment)

Directions:
1. Preheat the air fryer to 350 F.
2. Toss Brussels sprouts, oil, garlic powder, pepper, and salt into the bowl.
3. Situate Brussels sprouts into the air fryer basket and cook for 12 minutes. Top with cheese and serve.

Nutrition 132 Calories 7g Fat 7g Protein

524. Spicy Brussels sprouts

Preparation Time: 10 minutes
Cooking Time: 14 minutes
Servings: 2
Ingredients:
- 1/2 lb. Brussels sprouts, trimmed and halved (1 lean)
- 1/2 tsp chili powder (1/4 condiment)
- 1/4 tsp cayenne (1/4 condiment)
- 1/2 tbsp olive oil (1/4 condiment)
- 1/4 tsp smoked paprika (1/4 condiment)

Directions:
1. Mix all ingredients into the large bowl and toss well.
2. Add Brussels sprouts into the air fryer basket and cook at 370 F for 14 minutes.
3. Serve and enjoy.

Nutrition 82 Calories 4g Fat 4g Protein

525. Air Fried Tasty Eggplant

Preparation Time: 10 minutes
Cooking Time: 12 minutes
Servings: 2
Ingredients:
- 1 eggplant, cut into cubes (1 green)
- 1/4 tsp oregano (1/4 green)
- 1 tbsp olive oil (1/2 condiment)
- 1/2 tsp garlic powder (1/4 condiment)
- 1/4 tsp chili powder (1/4 condiment)

Directions:
1. Incorporate all ingredients into the huge bowl and toss well.
2. Transfer eggplant into the air fryer basket and cook at 390 F for 12 minutes. Stir halfway through.
3. Serve and enjoy.

Nutrition 120 Calories 7g Fat 2g Protein

526. Air Fryer Broccoli & Brussels Sprouts

Preparation Time: 10 minutes
Cooking Time: 30 minutes
Servings: 6
Ingredients:
- 1 lb. Brussels sprouts, cut ends (1 green)
- 1 lb. broccoli, cut into florets (1 green)
- 1 tsp paprika (1/4 condiment)
- 1 tsp garlic powder (1/4 condiment)
- 1/2 tsp pepper (1/4 condiment)
- 3 tbsp olive oil (1 healthy fat)
- 3/4 tsp salt (1/4 condiment)

Directions:
1. Add all ingredients into the bowl and toss well.
2. Add vegetable mixture into the air fryer basket and cook at 370 F for 30 minutes.
3. Serve and enjoy.

Nutrition 125 Calories 7.6g Fat 5g Protein

527. Spicy Asparagus Spears

Preparation Time: 10 minutes
Cooking Time: 15 minutes
Servings: 4
Ingredients:
- 35 asparagus spears, cut the ends (2 green)
- 1/2 tsp chili powder (1/4 condiment)
- 1/4 tsp paprika (1/4 condiment)
- 1 tbsp olive oil (1/4 condiment)
- Pepper (1/8 condiment) - Salt (1/8 condiment)

Directions:
1. Add asparagus into the large bowl. Drizzle with oil.
2. Sprinkle with paprika, chili powder, pepper, and salt. Toss well. Add asparagus into the air fryer basket and cook at 400 F for 15 minutes.
3. Serve and enjoy.

Nutrition 75 Calories 3.8g Fat 4.7g Protein

528. Stuffed Mushrooms

Preparation Time: 10 minutes
Cooking Time: 8 minutes
Servings: 16
Ingredients:
- 16 mushrooms, clean and chop stems (3 healthy fats)
- 2 garlic cloves, minced (1/2 condiment)
- 1/2 tsp chili powder (1/4 condiment)
- 1/4 cup cheddar cheese, shredded (1/2 healthy fat)
- 2 oz crab meat, chopped (1 lean)
- 8 oz cream cheese, softened (1/2 healthy fat)
- 1/4 tsp pepper (1/4 condiment)

Directions:
1. In a bowl, mix cheese, mushroom stems, chili powder, pepper, crabmeat, cream cheese, and garlic until well combined.
2. Stuff mushrooms with cheese mixture and place them into the air fryer basket and cook at 370 F for 8 minutes. Serve and enjoy.

Nutrition 65 Calories 5.3g Fat 2.6g Protein

529. Cheesy Broccoli Cauliflower

Preparation Time: 10 minutes
Cooking Time: 20 minutes
Servings: 6
Ingredients:
- 4 cups cauliflower florets (1 green)
- 4 cups broccoli florets (1 green)
- 2/3 cup parmesan cheese, shredded (1 healthy fat)
- 5 garlic cloves, minced (1/2 condiment)
- 1/3 cup olive oil (1/4 condiment)
- Pepper (1/8 condiment) - Salt (1/8 condiment)

Directions:
1. Add half cheese, broccoli, cauliflower, garlic, oil, pepper, and salt into the bowl and toss well.
2. Add broccoli and cauliflower to the air fryer basket and cook at 370 F for 20 minutes.
3. Add remaining cheese. Toss well.
4. Serve and enjoy.

Nutrition 165 Calories 13.6g Fat 6.4g Protein

530. Broccoli with Herbs and Cheese

Preparation Time: 8 minutes
Cooking Time: 17 minutes
Servings: 4
Ingredients:
- 1/3 cup grated yellow cheese (1/2 healthy fat)
- 1 large-sized head broccoli, stemmed and cut small florets (1 green)
- 2 1/2 tablespoons canola oil (1/8 condiment)
- 2 teaspoons dried rosemary (1/4 green)
- 2 teaspoons dried basil (1/4 green)
- Salt and ground black pepper to taste (1/8 condiment)

Directions:
1. Bring a medium pan filled with a lightly salted water to a boil. Then, boil the broccoli florets for about 3 minutes. Then, drain the broccoli florets well; toss them with canola oil, rosemary, basil, salt and black pepper. Set your oven to 390 degrees F; arrange the seasoned broccoli in the cooking basket; set the timer for 17 minutes. Toss the broccoli halfway through the cooking process.
2. Serve warm topped with grated cheese and enjoy!

Nutrition: 111 Calories 2.1g Fat 8.9g Protein

531. Almond Flour Battered 'n Crisped Onion Rings

Preparation Time: 10 minutes
Cooking Time: 15 minutes
Servings: 3
Ingredients:
- ½ cup almond flour (1/4 healthy fat)
- ¾ cup coconut milk (1/4 healthy fat)
- 1 big white onion, sliced into rings (1 green)
- 1 egg, beaten (1/4 healthy fat)
- 1 tablespoon baking powder (1/4 condiment)
- 1 tablespoon smoked paprika (1/4 condiment)
- Salt and pepper to taste (1/8 condiment)

Directions:
1. Preheat the air fryer for 5 minutes.
2. In a mixing bowl, mix the almond flour, baking powder, smoked paprika, salt and pepper.
3. In another bowl, combine the eggs and coconut milk.
4. Soak the onion slices into the egg mixture.
5. Dredge the onion slices in the almond flour mixture.
6. Place in the air fryer basket.
7. Close and cook for 15 minutes at 3250F.
8. Halfway through the cooking time, shake the fryer basket for even cooking.

Nutrition: 217 Calories 5.3g Protein 18g Fat

532. Spanish-Style Eggs with Manchego Cheese

Preparation Time: 10 minutes
Cooking Time: 38 minutes
Servings: 4
Ingredients:
- 1/3 cup grated Manchego cheese (1/2 healthy fat)
- 5 eggs (2 healthy fats)
- 2 green garlic stalks, peeled and finely minced (1 green)
- 1 ½ cups white mushrooms, chopped (1 healthy fat)
- 1 teaspoon dried basil (1/4 green)
- 1 ½ tablespoons olive oil (1/2 condiment)
- 3/4 teaspoon dried oregano (1/4 green)
- 1/2 teaspoon dried parsley flakes or 1 tablespoon fresh flat-leaf Italian parsley (1/4 green)
- 1 teaspoon porcini powder (1/8 condiment)
- Table salt and freshly ground black pepper to taste (1/8 condiment)

Directions:
1. Start by preheating your Air Fryer to 350 degrees F. Add the oil, mushrooms, and green garlic to the Air Fryer baking dish. Bake this mixture for 6 minutes or until it is tender.
2. Meanwhile, crack the eggs into a mixing bowl; beat the eggs until they're well whisked. Next, add the seasonings and mix again. Pause your Air Fryer and take the baking dish out of the basket.
3. Pour the whisked egg mixture into the baking dish with sautéed mixture. Top with the grated Manchego cheese.
4. Bake for about 32 minutes at 320 degrees F or until your frittata is set. Serve warm. Bon appétit!

Nutrition: 153 Calories 12g Fat 9g Protein

533. Tamarind Glazed Sweet Potatoes

Preparation Time: 2 minutes
Cooking Time: 22 minutes
Servings: 4
Ingredients:
- 1/3 teaspoon white pepper (1/8 condiment)
- 1 tablespoon butter, melted (1/4 healthy fat)
- 1/2 teaspoon turmeric powder (1/8 condiment)
- 5 garnet sweet potatoes, peeled and diced (2 healthy fat)
- A few drops liquid Stevia (1/8 condiment)
- 2 teaspoons tamarind paste (1/4 condiment)
- 1 1/2 tablespoons fresh lime juice (1/8 condiment)
- 1 1/2 teaspoon ground allspice (1/8 condiment)

Directions:
1. In a mixing bowl, toss all ingredients until sweet potatoes are well coated.
2. Air-fry them at 335 degrees F for 12 minutes.
3. Pause the Air Fryer and toss again. Increase the temperature to 390 degrees F and cook for an additional 10 minutes. Eat warm.

Nutrition: 103 Calories 9g Fat 1.9g Protein

534. Mediterranean style Eggs with Spinach

Preparation Time: 3 minutes
Cooking Time: 12 minutes
Servings: 2
Ingredients:
- 2 tablespoons olive oil, melted (1/4 condiment)
- 4 eggs, whisked (1 healthy fat)
- 5 ounces' fresh spinach, chopped (1 green)
- 1 medium-sized tomato, chopped (1 green)
- 1 teaspoon fresh lemon juice (1/4 condiment)
- 1/2 teaspoon coarse salt (1/8 condiment)
- 1/2 teaspoon ground black pepper (1/8 condiment)
- 1/2 cup of fresh basil, roughly chopped (1/4 green)

Directions:
1. Add the olive oil to an Air Fryer baking pan. Make sure to tilt the pan to spread the oil evenly.
2. Simply combine the remaining ingredients, except for the basil leaves; whisk well until everything is well incorporated.

3. Cook in the preheated oven for 8 to 12 minutes at 280 degrees F. Garnish with fresh basil leaves. Serve.

Nutrition: 274 Calories 23g Fat 14g Protein

535. Thai Roasted Veggies

Preparation Time: 20 minutes
Cooking Time: 6 to 8 hours
Servings: 8

Ingredients:
- 4 large carrots, peeled and cut into chunks (2 green)
- 6 garlic cloves, peeled and sliced (1/4 condiment)
- 2 parsnips, peeled and sliced (1/2 green)
- 2 jalapeño peppers, minced (1/2 green)
- 1/2 cup Roasted Vegetable Broth (1 condiment)
- 1/3 cup canned coconut milk (1/2 healthy fat)
- 3 tablespoons lime juice (1/8 condiment)
- 2 tablespoons grated fresh ginger root (1/4 condiment)
- 2 teaspoons curry powder (1/8 condiment)

Directions:
1. In a 6-quart slow cooker, mix the carrots, garlic, parsnips, and jalapeño peppers.
2. In a small bowl, mix the vegetable broth, coconut milk, lime juice, ginger root, and curry powder until well blended. Pour this mixture into the slow cooker.
3. Cover and cook on low for 6 to 8 hours, do it until the vegetables are tender when pierced with a fork.

Nutrition: 69 Calories 3g Fat 1g Protein

536. Spicy Zesty Broccoli with Tomato Sauce

Preparation Time: 5 minutes
Cooking Time: 15 minutes
Servings: 6

Ingredients:

For the Broccoli Bites:
- 1 medium-sized head broccoli, broken into florets (1 green)
- 1/2 teaspoon lemon zest, freshly grated (1/4 condiment)
- 1/3 teaspoon fine sea salt (1/8 condiment)
- 1/2 teaspoon hot paprika (1/8 condiment)
- 1 teaspoon shallot powder (1/8 condiment)
- 1 teaspoon porcini powder (1/8 condiment)
- 1/2 teaspoon granulated garlic (1/8 condiment)
- 1/3 teaspoon celery seeds (1/4 healthy fat)
- 1 ½ tablespoons olive oil (1/8 condiment)

For the Hot Sauce:
- 1/2 cup tomato sauce (1/2 healthy fat)
- 1 tablespoon balsamic vinegar (1/8 condiment)
- ½ teaspoon ground allspice (1/8 condiment)

Directions:
1. Toss all the ingredients for the broccoli bites in a mixing bowl, covering the broccoli florets on all sides.
2. Cook them in the preheated Air Fryer at 360 degrees for 13 to 15 minutes. In the meantime, mix all ingredients for the hot sauce.
3. Pause your Air Fryer, mix the broccoli with the prepared sauce and cook for a further 3 minutes. Bon appétit!

Nutrition: 70 Calories 4g Fat 2g Protein

537. Fried Squash Croquettes

Preparation Time: 5 minutes
Cooking Time: 17 minutes
Servings: 4

Ingredients:
- 1/3 cup all-purpose flour (1/4 condiment)
- 1/3 teaspoon freshly ground black pepper, or more to taste (1/4 condiment)
- 1/3 teaspoon dried sage (1/8 condiment)
- 4 cloves garlic, minced (1/4 condiment)
- 1 ½ tablespoons olive oil (1/4 condiment)
- 1/3 butternut squash, peeled and grated
- 2 eggs, well whisked (1 healthy fat)
- 1 teaspoon fine sea salt (1/8 condiment)
- A pinch of ground allspice (1/8 condiment)

Directions:
1. Thoroughly combine all ingredients in a mixing bowl.
2. Preheat your Air Fryer to 345 degrees and set the timer for 17 minutes; cook until your fritters are browned; serve right away.

Nutrition: 152 Calories 10g Fat 6g Protein

538. Cheese Stuffed Mushrooms with Horseradish Sauce

Preparation Time: 3 minutes
Cooking Time: 12 minutes
Servings: 5

Ingredients:
- 1/2 cup parmesan cheese, grated (1/4 healthy fat)
- 2 cloves garlic, pressed (1/4 condiment)
- 2 tablespoons fresh coriander, chopped (1/4 green)
- 1/3 teaspoon kosher salt (1/8 condiment)
- 1/2 teaspoon crushed red pepper flakes (1/8 condiment)
- 1 ½ tablespoons olive oil (1/4 condiment)
- 20 medium-sized mushrooms, cut off the stems (1 healthy fat)
- 1/2 cup Gorgonzola cheese, grated (1/2 healthy fat)
- 1/4 cup low-fat mayonnaise (1/4 healthy fat)
- 1 teaspoon prepared horseradish, well-drained (1/4 green)
- 1 tablespoon fresh parsley, finely chopped (1/4 green)

Directions:
1. Mix the parmesan cheese together with the garlic, coriander, salt, red pepper, and olive oil; mix to combine well.
2. Stuff the mushroom caps with the cheese filling. Top with grated Gorgonzola.
3. Place the mushrooms in the Air Fryer grill pan and slide them into the machine. Grill them at 380 degrees F for 8 to 12 minutes or until the stuffing is warmed through.

4. Meanwhile, prepare the horseradish sauce by mixing the mayonnaise, horseradish and parsley. Serve the horseradish sauce with the warm fried mushrooms. Enjoy!

Nutrition: 180 Calories 13.2g Fat 9g Protein

539. Creamy Spinach and Mushroom Lasagna

Preparation Time: 60 minutes
Cooking Time: 20 minutes
Servings: 6

Ingredients:
- 10 lasagna noodles (2 healthy fat)
- 1 package whole milk ricotta (1 healthy fat)
- 2 packages of frozen chopped spinach. (2 green)
- 4 cups mozzarella cheese (divided and shredded) (1 healthy fat)
- 3/4 cup grated fresh Parmesan (1/2 healthy fat)
- 3 tablespoons chopped fresh parsley leaves(optional) (1/4 green)

For the Sauce:
1. 1/4 cup butter(unsalted) (1/4 healthy fat)
2. 2 cloves garlic (1/8 condiment)
3. 1 pound of thinly sliced cremini mushroom (1/4 healthy fat)
4. 1 diced onion (1/8 condiment)
5. 1/4 cup flour (1/4 condiment)
6. 4 cups milk, kept at room temperature (1 healthy fat)
7. 1 teaspoon basil(dried) (1/8 green)
8. Pinch of nutmeg (1/8 condiment)

Directions:
1. Preheat oven to 352 degrees F.
2. To make the sauce, over a medium portion of heat, melt your butter, add garlic, mushrooms and onion. Cook and stir at intervals until it becomes tender at about 3-4 minutes.
3. Whisk in flour until lightly browned, it takes about 1 minute for it to become brown.
4. Next, whisk in the milk gradually, and cook, whisking always, about 2-3 minute till it becomes thickened. Stir in basil, oregano and nutmeg, season with salt and pepper for taste;
5. Then set aside.
6. In another pot of boiling salted water, cook lasagna noodles according to the package instructions.
7. Spread 1 cup mushroom sauce onto the bottom of a baking dish; top it with 4 lasagna noodles, 1/2 of the spinach, 1 cup mozzarella cheese and 1/4 cup Parmesan.
8. Repeat this process with remaining noodles, mushroom sauce, and cheeses.
9. Place into the oven and bake for 35-45 minutes, or until it starts bubbling. Then boil for 2-3 minutes until it becomes brown and translucent.
10. Let cool for 15 minutes.
11. Serve it with garnished parsley (Optional)

Nutrition: 488 Calories 19g Fats 25g Protein

540. Roasted Cauliflower with Pepper Jack Cheese

Preparation Time: 4 minutes
Cooking Time: 21 minutes
Servings: 2

Ingredients:
- 1/3 teaspoon shallot powder (1/4 condiment)
- 1 teaspoon ground black pepper (1/8 condiment)
- 1 ½ large-sized heads of cauliflower, broken into florets (1 green)
- 1/4 teaspoon cumin powder (1/8 condiment)
- ½ teaspoon garlic salt (1/8 condiment)
- 1/4 cup Pepper Jack cheese, grated (1/4 healthy fat)
- 1 ½ tablespoons vegetable oil (1/8 condiment)
- 1/3 teaspoon paprika (1/8 condiment)

Directions:
1. Boil cauliflower in a large pan of salted water for approximately 5 minutes. After that, drain the cauliflower florets; now transfer them to a baking dish.
2. Toss the cauliflower florets with the rest of the above ingredients.
3. Roast at 395 degrees F for 16 minutes, turn them halfway through the process. Enjoy!

Nutrition: 271 Calories 23g Fat Protein

541. Family Favorite Stuffed Mushrooms

Preparation Time: 4 minutes
Cooking Time: 12 minutes
Servings: 2

Ingredients:
- 2 teaspoons cumin powder (1/4 condiment)
- 4 garlic cloves, peeled and minced (1/4 condiment)
- 18 medium-sized white mushrooms (2 healthy fats)
- Fine sea salt and freshly ground black pepper to taste (1/8 condiment)
- A pinch ground allspice (1/8 condiment)
- 2 tablespoons olive oil (1/4 condiment)

Directions:
1. First, clean the mushrooms; remove the middle stalks from the mushrooms to prepare the "shells."
2. Grab a mixing dish and thoroughly combine the remaining items. Fill the mushrooms with the prepared mixture.
3. Cook the mushrooms at 345 degrees F heat for 12 minutes. Enjoy!

Nutrition: 179 Calories 15g Fat 6g Protein

542. Famous Fried Pickles

Preparation Time: 5 minutes
Cooking Time: 15 minutes
Servings: 6

Ingredients:
- 1/3 cup milk (1/2 healthy fat)
- 1 teaspoon garlic powder (1/8 condiment)
- 2 medium-sized eggs (1 healthy fat)
- 1 teaspoon fine sea salt (1/8 condiment)
- 1/3 teaspoon chili powder (1/4 condiment)
- 1/3 cup all-purpose flour (1/4 healthy fat)
- 1/2 teaspoon shallot powder (1/4 condiment)
- 2 jars sweet and sour pickle spears (1 healthy fat)

Directions:
1. Pat the pickle spears dry with a kitchen towel. Then take two mixing bowls.
2. Whisk the egg and milk in a bowl. In another bowl, combine all dry ingredients.
3. Firstly, dip the pickle spears into the dry mix; then coat each pickle with the egg/milk mixture; dredge them in the flour mixture again for additional coating.
4. Air fry battered pickles for 15 minutes at 385 degrees. Enjoy!

Nutrition: 58 Calories 2g Fat 3.2g Protein

543. Asian Stir Fry

Preparation Time: 15 minutes
Cooking Time: 10 minutes
Servings: 4

Ingredients:
- 1 tsp. Olive oil (1/8 condiment)
- 1 Tsp. Low Soy Sodium Sauce (1/8 condiment)
- 1 Lime Wedge (1/8 Lime) (1/8 condiment)
- Split into strips 7 ounces of boneless, skinless chicken breast (2 lean)
- C 3/4 Broccoli blossoms (1 green)
- 1/2 C. Sliced Chestnuts (1/2 healthy fat)
- 1/4 hp. Red bell pepper split (1/4 green)
- 1/4 hp. Freshwater (1/8 condiment)
- New ground potatoes, to taste (1/4 condiment)

Directions:
1. Prepare meat and veggies.
2. Add oil, soy sauce and lime wedge juice in a medium to large skillet.
3. Put on medium heat, then add chicken. Cook chicken over regularly, tossing or stirring.
4. Remove the chicken from the saucepan and put it aside.
5. Add water to the saucepan and stir until the water gets warm.
6. Next, add the vegetables and mix well to ensure that they are all eaten.
7. Cover and let cook for 5-7 minutes until almost tender vegetables.
8. Remove the cover and add the chicken, cook over medium-high to high heat until the vegetables are cooked, and the liquid is evaporated completely

Nutrition: 13g Carbohydrates 4g Protein 8g Fat

544. Cauliflower Crust Pizza

Preparation Time: 20 minutes
Cooking Time: 45 minutes
Servings: 4

Ingredients:
- 1 cauliflower (1 green)
- 1/4 grated parmesan cheese (1/2 healthy fat)
- 1 egg (1/4 healthy fat)
- 1Tsp Italian seasoning (1/8 condiment)
- 1/4 Tsp. kosher salt (1/8 condiment)
- 2 cups of freshly grated mozzarella (1/4 healthy fat)
- 1/4 cup of spicy pizza sauce (1/8 condiment)
- Basil leaves for garnishing (1/4 green)

Directions:
1. Begin by preheating your oven while using the parchment paper to rim the baking sheet.
2. Process the cauliflower into a fine powder, and then transfer to a bowl before putting it into the microwave.
3. Leave for about 5-6 minutes to get it soft.
4. Transfer the microwave cauliflower to a clean and dry kitchen towel.
5. Leave it to cool off.
6. When cold, use the kitchen towel to wrap the cauliflower and then get rid of all the moisture by wringing the towel.
7. Continue squeezing until the water is gone completely. Put the cauliflower, Italian seasoning, Parmesan, egg, salt, and mozzarella (1 cup).
8. Stir very well until well combined.
9. Transfer the combined mixture to the baking sheet previously prepared, pressing it into a 10-inch round shape.
10. Bake for 10-15 minutes until it becomes golden in color.
11. Take the baked crust out of the oven and use the spicy pizza sauce and mozzarella (the leftover 1 cup) to top it.
12. Bake again for 10 more minutes until the cheese melts and looks bubbly.
13. Garnish using fresh basil leaves.
14. You can also enjoy this with salad.

Nutrition: 74 Calories 6g Protein 4g Fat

545. Roasted Squash Puree

Preparation Time: 20 minutes
Cooking Time: 6 to 7 hours
Servings: 8
Ingredients:
- 1 (3-pound) butternut squash, peeled, seeded, and cut into 1-inch pieces (1 green)
- 3 (1-pound) acorn squash, peeled, seeded, and cut into 1-inch pieces (2 green)
- 3 garlic cloves, minced (1/4 condiment)
- 2 tablespoons olive oil (1/8 condiment)
- 1 teaspoon dried marjoram leaves (1/8 green)
- 1/2 teaspoon salt (1/8 condiment)
- 1/8 teaspoon freshly ground black pepper (1/8 condiment)

Directions:
1. In a 6-quart slow cooker, mix all of the ingredients.
2. Cover and cook on low for 6 to 7 hours, or until the squash is tender when pierced with a fork.
3. Use a potato masher to mash the squash right in the slow cooker.

Nutrition: 175 Calories 4g Fat 3g Protein

546. Kale Slaw and Strawberry Salad + Poppy seed Dressing

Preparation Time: 10 minutes
Cooking Time: 20 minutes
Servings: 2
Ingredients:
- Chicken breast; 8 ounces; sliced and baked (2 lean)
- Kale; 1 cup; chopped (1/4 green)
- Slaw mix; 1 cup (cabbage, broccoli slaw, carrots mixed) (1 green)
- Slivered almonds; 1/4 cup (1/4 healthy fat)
- Strawberries; 1 cup; sliced (1/4 healthy fat)

For the dressing:
1. Light mayonnaise; 1 tablespoon (1/8 healthy fat)
2. Dijon mustard (1/8 condiment)
3. Olive oil; 1 tablespoon (1/8 condiment)
4. Apple cider vinegar; 1 tablespoon (1/8 condiment)
5. Lemon juice; 1/2 teaspoon (1/8 condiment)
6. 1 tablespoon of Honey (1/8 condiment)
7. Onion powder; 1/4 teaspoon (1/8 condiment)
8. Garlic powder; 1/4 teaspoon (1/8 condiment)
9. Poppy seeds (1/8 healthy fat)

Directions:
1. Whisk the dressing ingredients together until well mixed, then leave to cool in the fridge.
2. Slice the chicken breasts.
3. Divide 2 bowls of spinach, slaw, and strawberries.
4. Cover with a sliced breast of chicken (4 oz. each), then scatter with almonds.
5. Divide the salad over the dressing and drizzle.

Nutrition: 340 Calories 14g Fats 6.2 g Protein

547. Tomato Bites with Creamy Parmesan Sauce

Preparation Time: 7 minutes
Cooking Time: 13 minutes
Servings: 4
Ingredients:
For the Sauce:
- 1/2 cup Parmigiano-Reggiano cheese, grated (1/4 healthy fat)
- 4 tablespoons pecans, chopped (1/2 healthy fat)
- 1 teaspoon garlic puree (1/8 condiment)
- 1/2 teaspoon fine sea salt (1/8 condiment)
- 1/3 cup extra-virgin olive oil (1/8 condiment)

For the Tomato Bites:
- 2 large-sized Roma tomatoes, cut into thin slices and pat them dry (1 green)
- 8 ounces Zaloumi cheese, cut into thin slices (1 healthy fat)
- 1 teaspoon dried basil (1/2 green)
- 1/4 teaspoon red pepper flakes, crushed (1/8 condiment)
- 1/8 teaspoon sea salt (1/8 condiment)

Directions:
1. Start by preheating your Air Fryer to 385 degrees F.
2. Make the sauce by mixing all ingredients, except the extra-virgin olive oil, in your food processor.
3. While the machine is running, slowly and gradually pour in the olive oil; puree until everything is well-blended.
4. Now, spread 1 teaspoon of the sauce over the top of each tomato slice. Place a slice of Halloumi cheese on each tomato slice. Top with onion slices. Sprinkle with basil, red pepper, and sea salt.
5. Transfer the assembled bites to the Air Fryer. Spray with non-stick cooking spray and cook for about 13 minutes.
6. Arrange these bites on a nice serving platter, garnish with the remaining sauce, and serve at room temperature. Bon appétit!

Nutrition: 428 Calories 38g Fat 18g Protein

548. Simple Green Beans with Butter

Preparation Time: 2 minutes
Cooking Time: 10 minutes
Servings: 4
Ingredients:
- 3/4-pound green beans, cleaned
- 1 tablespoon balsamic vinegar
- 1/4 teaspoon kosher salt
- 1/2 teaspoon mixed peppercorns, freshly cracked
- 1 tablespoon butter
- 2 tablespoons toasted sesame seeds to serve

Directions:
1. Set your Air Fryer to cook at 390 degrees F.
2. Mix the green beans with all of the above ingredients, apart from the sesame seeds. Set the timer for 10 minutes.

3. Meanwhile, toast the sesame seeds in a small-sized nonstick skillet; make sure to stir continuously.
4. Serve sautéed green beans on a nice serving platter sprinkled with toasted sesame seeds. Bon appétit!

Nutrition: 73 Calories 3g Fat 1.6g Protein

549. Creamy Cauliflower and Broccoli

Preparation Time: 4 minutes
Cooking Time: 16 minutes
Servings: 6
Ingredients:
- 1-pound cauliflower florets (1 green)
- 1-pound broccoli florets (1 green)
- 2 ½ tablespoons sesame oil (1/2 condiment)
- 1/2 teaspoon smoked cayenne pepper (1/4 condiment)
- 3/4 teaspoon sea salt flakes (1/4 condiment)
- 1 tablespoon lemon zest, grated (1/4 condiment)
- 1/2 cup Colby cheese, shredded (1/2 healthy fat)

Directions:
1. Prepare the cauliflower and broccoli using your favorite steaming method. Then, drain them well; add the sesame oil, cayenne pepper, and salt flakes.
2. Air-fry at 390 degrees F for approximately 16 minutes; make sure to check the vegetables halfway through the cooking time.
3. Afterward, stir in the lemon zest and Colby cheese; toss to coat well and serve immediately!

Nutrition: 133 Calories 9g Fat 6g Protein

550. Balsamic Artichokes

Preparation Time: 11 minutes
Cooking Time: 8 minutes
Servings: 4
Ingredients:
- 2 tsp. of balsamic vinegar
- Black pepper and salt
- ¼ cup of olive oil - 1 tsp. of oregano
- 4 big trimmed artichokes
- 2 tbsp. of lemon juice
- 2 cloves of garlic

Directions:
1. Sprinkle the artichokes with pepper and salt.
2. Brush oil over the artichokes and add lemon juice.
3. Place the artichokes on the PowerXL Air Fryer Grill.
4. Set the PowerXL Air Fryer Grill at Air Fryer/Grill, timer at 7 minutes at 360°F.
5. Mix garlic, lemon juice, pepper, vinegar, oil in a bowl.
6. Add oregano and salt. Mix well.
7. Serve the artichokes with balsamic vinaigrette.

Serving Suggestions: Serve with mint chutney.
Directions & Cooking Tips: Use fresh balsamic.
Nutrition:
Calories: 533, Fat: 29g, Carbs: 68g, Protein: 19 g.

551. Cheesy Artichokes

Preparation Time: 15 minutes
Cooking Time: 6 minutes
Servings: 5
Ingredients:
- 1 tsp. of onion powder - ½ cup of chicken stock
- 14 ounces of artichoke hearts
- 8 ounces of mozzarella - ½ cup of mayonnaise
- 8 ounces of cream cheese - 10 ounces of spinach
- 3 cloves of garlic
- 16 ounces of grated parmesan cheese
- ½ cup of sour cream

Directions:
1. Mix cream cheese, onion powder, chicken stock, and artichokes in a bowl.
2. Add sour cream, mayonnaise, and spinach to the bowl.
3. Transfer the mixture to the PowerXL Air Fryer Grill pan
4. Set the PowerXL Air Fryer Grill to the Air Fryer/Grill.
5. Set timer to 6 minutes at 350°F.
6. Serve immediately

Serving Suggestions: Serve with parmesan and mozzarella.
Directions & Cooking Tips: Rinse artichokes hearts well.
Nutrition:
Calories: 379, Fat: 19g, Carbs: 36g, Protein: 15 g.

552. Beet Salad with Parsley Dressing

Preparation Time: 15 minutes
Cooking Time: 15 minutes
Servings: 4
Ingredients:
- Black pepper and salt

- 1 clove of garlic
- 2 tbsp. of balsamic vinegar
- 4 beets
- 2 tbsp. of capers
- 1 bunch of chopped parsley
- 1 tbsp. of olive oil

Directions:
1. Place the beets on the PowerXL Air Fryer Grill pan.
2. Set the PowerXL Air Fryer Grill to the Air Fry function.
3. Set timer and temperature to 15 minutes and 360°F.
4. In another bowl, mix pepper, garlic, capers, salt, and olive oil. Mix well.
5. Remove the beets from the PowerXL Air Fryer Grill and place them on a flat surface.
6. Peel and put it in the salad bowl.
7. Serve with vinegar.

Serving Suggestions: Dress with parsley mixture.
Directions & Cooking Tips: Rinse beets before cooking.
Nutrition:
Calories: 185, Fat: 16g, Carbs: 11g, Protein: 8 g.

553. Blue Cheese Salad and Beets

Preparation Time: 15 minutes
Cooking Time: 15 minutes
Servings: 5
Ingredients:
- 1 tbsp. of olive oil
- Black pepper and salt
- 6 beets
- ¼ cup of blue cheese

Directions:
1. Set the beets on the PowerXL Air Fryer Grill pan.
2. Set the PowerXL Air Fryer Grill to the Air Fry function.
3. Set timer to 15 minutes.
4. Cook at 350°F.
5. Transfer it to a plate.
6. Add pepper, blue cheese, oil, and salt.
7. Serve immediately

Serving Suggestions: Serve with maple syrup.
Directions & Cooking Tips: Peel beets and cut them into quarters.
Nutrition:
Calories: 110, Fat: 11g, Carbs: 4g, Protein: 5 g.

554. Broccoli Salad

Preparation Time: 15 minutes
Cooking Time: 9 minutes
Servings: 4
Ingredients:
- 6 cloves of garlic
- 1 head of broccoli
- Black pepper and salt
- 1 tbsp. of Chinese rice wine vinegar
- 1 tbsp. of peanut oil

Directions:
1. Mix oil, salt, broccoli, and pepper.
2. Place the mixture on the PowerXL Air Fryer Grill pan.
3. Set the PowerXL Air Fryer Grill to the Air Fry function.
4. Cook for 9 minutes at 350°F.
5. Place the broccoli in the salad bowl and add peanuts oil, rice vinegar, and garlic.
6. Serve immediately.

Serving Suggestions: Toss the broccoli well in rice vinegar.
Directions & Cooking Tips: Separate the broccoli floret.
Nutrition:
Calories: 199, Fat: 14g, Carbs: 17g, Protein: 8 g.

555. Brussels Sprout with Tomatoes Mix

Preparation Time: 10 minutes
Cooking Time: 10 minutes
Servings: 3
Ingredients:
- 6 halved cherry tomatoes
- 1 tbsp. of olive oil
- 1 pound of Brussel sprouts
- Black pepper and salt
- ¼ cup of chopped green onions

Directions:
1. Sprinkle pepper and salt on the Brussels sprout.
2. Place it on the PowerXL Air Fryer Grill pan.
3. Set the PowerXL Air Fryer Grill to the Air Fry function.
4. Cook for 10 minutes at 350°F.
5. Place the cooked sprout in a bowl, add pepper, green onion, salt, olive oil, and cherry tomatoes.
6. Mix well and serve immediately

Serving Suggestions: Serve with tomato mix or ketchup.
Directions & Cooking Tips: Trim the Brussels sprout.
Nutrition:
Calories: 57, Fat: 1g, Carbs: 12g, Protein: 5 g.

556. Cheesy Brussels Sprout

Preparation Time: 10 minutes
Cooking Time: 8 minutes
Servings: 3
Ingredients:
- 1 lemon juice
- 2 tbsp. of butter
- 1 pound of Brussel sprout
- 3 tbsp. of grated parmesan
- Black pepper and salt

Directions:
1. Place the Brussel sprout on the PowerXL Air Fryer Grill pan.
2. Set the PowerXL Air Fryer Grill to the Air Fry function.
3. Cook for 8 minutes at 350°F.
4. Heat butter in a pan over medium fire. Add pepper, lemon juice, and salt.
5. Add Brussel sprout and parmesan.
6. Serve immediately.

Serving Suggestions: Serve with mint chutney.
Directions & Cooking Tips: Rinse the Brussel sprout well.
Nutrition:
Calories: 75, Fat: 5g, Carbs: 8g, Protein: 6 g.

557. Spicy Cabbage

Preparation Time: 10 minutes
Cooking Time: 8 minutes
Servings: 5
Ingredients:

- 1 grated carrot
- ½ tsp. of cayenne pepper
- ¼ cup of apple cider vinegar
- 1 cabbage
- 1 tsp. of red pepper flakes
- 1 tbsp. of sesame seed oil
- ¼ cups of apple juice

Directions:

1. Put carrot, cayenne, cabbage, and oil on the PowerXL Air Fryer Grill pan.
2. Add vinegar, pepper flakes, and apple juice.
3. Set the PowerXL Air Fryer Grill to the Air Fry function.
4. Cook for 8 minutes at 350°F
5. Serve immediately

Serving Suggestions: Serve with maple syrup.
Directions & Cooking Tips: Cut the cabbage into 8 wedges.
Nutrition:
Calories: 25, Fat: 0g, Carbs: 6g, Protein: 2 g.

558. Sweet Baby Carrots

Preparation Time: 15 minutes
Cooking Time: 10 minutes
Servings: 4
Ingredients:

- 1 tbsp. of brown sugar
- 2 cups of baby carrots
- ½ tbsp. of melted butter
- Black pepper and salt

Directions:

1. Mix butter, sugar, pepper, carrot, and salt in a bowl.
2. Transfer the mix to the PowerXL Air Fryer Grill pan.
3. Set the PowerXL Air Fryer Grill to the Air Fry function.
4. Cook for 10 minutes at 350°F.
5. Serve immediately.

Serving Suggestions: Serve with maple syrup.
Directions & Cooking Tips: Rinse the carrot before cooking.
Nutrition:
Calories: 77, Fat: 3g, Carbs: 15g, Protein: 3 g.

559. Zucchini Mix and Herbed Eggplant

Preparation Time: 10 minutes
Cooking Time: 8 minutes
Servings: 3
Ingredients:

- 1 tsp. of dried thyme
- 3 tbsp. of olive oil
- 1 eggplant
- 2 tbsp. of lemon juice
- 1 tsp. of dried oregano
- 3 cubed zucchinis
- Black pepper and salt

Directions:

1. Place the eggplants on the PowerXL Air Fryer Grill Pan, add thyme, zucchinis, olive oil, salt.
2. Add pepper, oregano, and lemon juice.
3. Set the PowerXL Air Fryer Grill to the Air Fry function.
4. Cook for 8 minutes at 360°F.
5. Serve immediately.

Nutrition:
Calories: 55, Fat: 1g, Carbs: 13g, Protein: 3 g.

560. Sweet Potato Toast

Preparation Time: 15 minutes
Cooking Time: 10 minutes
Servings: 2
Ingredients:

- 1 large sweet potato, cut
- 1 avocado/guacamole
- ½ cup Hummus
- 1 radish/tomato (optional)
- Salt and pepper to taste
- Lemon slices for garnish

Directions:

1. Toast the potatoes in the PowerXL Air Fryer Grill for 10 minutes on each side.
2. Spread mashed avocado, add seasoning, top it with radish slices and squeeze a lime over it.
3. Or, spread hummus, seasoning, and your choice of greens.

Nutrition:
Calories: 114, Carbs: 13g, Protein: 2g, Fat: 7 g.

561. Stuffed Portabella Mushroom

Preparation Time: 20 minutes
Cooking Time: 15 minutes
Servings: 2
Ingredients:

- 2 large portabella mushrooms
- Breadcrumbs
- Nutritional yeast (gives a cheesy, savory flavor)
- 1 cup tofu ricotta
- ½ cup canned marinara sauce
- 1 cup spinach
- ½ tsp. garlic powder
- 1 tsp. dry basil and 1 tsp. dry thyme
- Salt & pepper

Directions:

1. Make ricotta with tofu, lemon juice, nutritional yeast, salt, and pepper. Mix the tofu ricotta, spinach, thyme, basil, marinara sauce, and seasoning.
2. Brush marinara sauce on each mushroom and stuff the filling. Top it with breadcrumbs, nutritional yeast, and some olive oil.
3. Bake for 15 minutes at 230°C/ 450°F in your PowerXL Air Fryer Grill.

Nutrition:
Calories: 275, Carbs: 10.4 g, Protein: 23.0 g, Fat: 19.5 g.

562. Pumpkin Quesadillas

Preparation Time: 10 minutes
Cooking Time: 5 minutes
Servings: 3
Ingredients:
- ½ canned pumpkin (pure)
- 2 gluten-free tortillas
- ½ cup refried beans
- 1–2 tbsp. nutritional yeast
- 1 tsp. onion powder - 1 tsp. garlic powder
- Pinch of cayenne
- Salt & pepper

Directions:
1. Mix the pumpkin with nutritional yeast, onion powder, garlic powder, cayenne, salt, and pepper.
2. Spread the pumpkin paste mixture in one tortilla and the refried beans in another.
3. Sandwich them together and toast in the PowerXL Air Fryer Grill for 5 minutes

Nutrition:
Calories: 282, Carbs: 37 g, Protein: 13 g, Fat: 10 g.

563. Toasted-Baked Tofu cubes

Preparation Time: 10 minutes
Cooking Time: 30 minutes
Servings: 2
Ingredients:
- ½ block of tofu, cubed
- 1 tbsp. olive oil
- 1 tbsp. nutritional yeast
- 1 tbsp. flour
- ¼ tsp. black pepper
- 1 tsp. sea salt

Directions:
1. Combine all the ingredients with tofu.
2. Preheat the PowerXL Air Fryer Grill at 230°C/ 400°F.
3. Bake tofu on a lined baking tray for 15–30 minutes, turn it around every 10 minutes.

Nutrition:
Calories: 100, Carbs: 5 g, Protein: 8 g, Fat: 6 g.

564. Stuffed Squash

Preparation Time: 40 minutes
Cooking Time: 50 minutes
Servings: 4
Ingredients:
- Acorn squash, halved and deseeded
- 2 cups cooked quinoa
- ½ edamame (shelled)
- ½ corn kernels
- ¼ cranberries
- Some scallions, basil, and mint (thinly sliced)
- 2 tbsp. Olive oil
- Salt and pepper
- Lemon juice

Directions:
1. Brush squash pieces with olive oil, salt, and pepper.
2. Bake it at 176°C/ 350°F for 35 minutes in the PowerXL Air Fryer Grill.
3. Prepare the filling by mixing all the remaining ingredients. Stuff baked squash with filling and bake for another 15 minutes.

Nutrition:
Calories: 272, Carbs: 45 g, Protein: 7 g, Fat: 9 g.

565. Sriracha Roasted Potatoes

Preparation Time: 30 minutes
Cooking Time: 30 minutes
Servings: 3
Ingredients:
- 3 potatoes, diced
- 2–3 tsp. sriracha
- ¼ garlic powder
- Salt & pepper
- Olive oil
- Chopped fresh parsley

Directions:
1. Combine the potatoes with the remaining ingredients.
2. Preheat the PowerXL Air Fryer Grill at 230°C/ 450°F.
3. Line the pan with olive oil and spread the coated potatoes. Sprinkle parsley.
4. Bake for 30 minutes.

Nutrition:
Calories: 147, Carbs: 24.4 g, Protein: 3 g, Fat: 4.7 g.

566. Brussel Sprouts, Mango, Avocado Salsa Tacos

Preparation Time: 25 minutes
Cooking Time: 15 minutes
Servings: 4
Ingredients:
- 4 taco shells
- 8 ounces brussels sprouts, diced
- Half a mango, diced
- Half of an avocado, diced
- ½ cup black beans, cooked
- 2 tbsp. onions, chopped
- ¼ cup cilantro, chopped
- 1 tbsp. jalapeno, chopped
- Lime juice
- Olive oil
- 1 tbsp. taco seasoning
- Salt and pepper

Directions:
1. Preheat the PowerXL Air Fryer Grill at 230°C/ 400°F.
2. Mix the sprouts with taco seasoning, olive oil, salt, and pepper on the pan.
3. Roast for 15 minutes. Turn every 5 minutes.

4. To make the salsa, combine the mango, avocado, black beans, lime juice, cilantro, onion, jalapeno, salt, and pepper.
5. Cook taco shells and fill them with sprouts and salsa.

Nutrition:
Calories: 407, Carbs: 63.20g, Protein: 11.4g, Fat: 13.9g.

567. Spaghetti Squash Burrito Bowls

Preparation Time: 15 minutes
Cooking Time: 45 minutes
Servings: 2
Ingredients:
- 1 small spaghetti squash
- Zucchini, diced
- ¼ onion, diced
- Bell peppers, diced
- ¾ cup black beans, cooked
- ½ cup corn kernels
- ½ cup salsa
- 2 ounces cheese (optional)
- Olive oil
- ½ tsp. dried oregano

Directions:
1. Preheat the PowerXL Air Fryer Grill at 230°C/ 425°F on bake setting
2. Microwave the squash for 4 minutes and then cut it in half. Scoop out the seeds.
3. Rub oil, salt, and pepper all over the squash and bake it for 45 minutes.
4. Make the filling by stir-frying bell pepper, zucchini, oregano, corn, salt, and pepper for 10 minutes. Add the salsa and black beans.
5. Scrape squash flesh to make spaghetti and toss in the vegetables.
6. Bake them at 176°C/ 350°F for 10 minutes and then broil for 1–2 minutes.

Nutrition:
Calories: 390, Carbs: 51.4 g, Protein: 15.7 g, Fat: 17.1 g.

568. Baked Oatmeal

This wholesome breakfast is perfect to start your day.
Preparation Time: 15 minutes
Cooking Time: 25–35 minutes
Servings: 2
Ingredients:
- 1 cup original oats
- 1 banana
- ¼ cup pecans
- ½ cup milk
- 1 tbsp. flax meal
- 2 tsp. maple syrup
- ½ tsp. baking powder
- ½ tsp. ground cinnamon & salt
- ½ tsp. vanilla-extract

Directions:
1. Preheat the PowerXL Air Fryer Grill at 176°C/ 350°F on the baking setting.
2. Make a batter with mashed banana and all the ingredients.
3. Grease a 7x5-inch dish and pour your batter into it. Bake it for 25–35 minutes.

Nutrition:
Calories: 235, Carbs: 28.6 g, Protein: 4.9 g, Fat: 13.2 g.

569. Healthy Mixed Vegetables

Preparation Time: 10 minutes
Cooking Time: 10 minutes
Servings: 6
Ingredients:
- 2 cups mushrooms, cut in half
- 2 yellow squashes, sliced
- 2 medium zucchinis, sliced
- ¾ tsp. Italian seasoning
- ½ onion, sliced
- ½ cup olive oil
- ½ tsp. garlic salt

Directions:
1. Add vegetables and remaining ingredients into the mixing bowl and toss well.
2. Add vegetables into the Air Fryer basket and cook at 400°F for 10 minutes. Shake basket halfway through.
3. Serve and enjoy.

Nutrition:
Calories: 176, Fat: 17.3 g, Carbohydrates: 6.2 g, Sugar: 3.2 g, Protein: 2.5 g, Cholesterol: 0 mg.

570. Easy Roasted Vegetables

Preparation Time: 10 minutes
Cooking Time: 18 minutes
Servings: 6
Ingredients:
- ½ cup mushrooms, sliced
- ½ cup zucchini, sliced
- ½ cup yellow squash, sliced
- ½ cup baby carrots
- 1 cup cauliflower florets
- 1 cup broccoli florets
- ¼ cup parmesan cheese, grated
- 1 tsp. red pepper flakes
- 1 tbsp. garlic, minced
- 1 tbsp. olive oil
- ¼ cup balsamic vinegar
- 1 small onion, sliced
- 1 tsp. sea salt

Directions:
1. Preheat the Air Fryer to 400°F.
2. In a large mixing bowl, mix olive oil, garlic, vinegar, red pepper flakes, pepper, and salt.
3. Add vegetables and toss until well coated.
4. Add vegetables into the Air Fryer basket and cook for 8 minutes. Shake basket and cook for 8 minutes more.
5. Add parmesan cheese and cook for 2 minutes more.

6. Serve and enjoy.

Nutrition:
Calories: 59, Fat: 3.4 g, Carbohydrates: 5.3 g, Sugar: 2 g, Protein: 2.8 g, Cholesterol: 3 mg.

571. Easy & Crispy Brussels Sprouts
Preparation Time: 10 minutes
Cooking Time: 15 minutes
Servings: 4
Ingredients:
- 2 cups Brussels sprouts
- 2 tbsp. everything bagel seasoning
- ¼ cup almonds, crushed
- 2 tbsp. olive oil
- Salt

Directions:
1. Add Brussels sprouts into the saucepan with 2 cups of water. Cover and cook for 8–10 minutes.
2. Drain well and allow to cool completely. Sliced each Brussels sprouts in half.
3. Add Brussels sprouts and remaining ingredients into the mixing bowl and toss to coat.
4. Add Brussels sprout mixture into the Air Fryer basket and cook at 375°F for 12–15 minutes.
5. Serve and enjoy.

Nutrition:
Calories: 144, Fat: 11.5 g, Carbohydrates: 7.6 g, Sugar: 1.4 g, Protein: 5.1 g, Cholesterol: 4 mg.

572. Garlic Green Beans
Preparation Time: 10 minutes
Cooking Time: 8 minutes
Servings: 4
Ingredients:
- 1 lb. fresh green beans, trimmed
- 1 tsp. garlic powder
- 1 tbsp. olive oil
- Pepper - Salt

Directions:
1. Drizzle green beans with oil and season with garlic powder, pepper, and salt.
2. Place green beans into the Air Fryer basket and cook at 370°F for 8 minutes. Toss halfway through.
3. Serve and enjoy.

Nutrition:
Calories: 68, Fat: 3.7 g, Carbohydrates: 8.6 g, Sugar: 1.8 g, Protein: 2.2 g, Cholesterol: 0 mg.

573. Simple Vegan Broccoli
Preparation Time: 10 minutes
Cooking Time: 5 minutes
Servings: 2
Ingredients:
- 4 cups broccoli florets
- 1 tbsp. nutritional yeast
- 2 tbsp. olive oil
- Pepper
- Salt

Directions:
1. In a medium bowl, mix broccoli, nutritional yeast, oil, pepper, and salt.
2. Add broccoli florets into the Air Fryer basket and cook at 370°F for 5 minutes.
3. Serve and enjoy.

Nutrition:
Calories: 158, Fat: 14.3 g, Carbohydrates: 6.3 g, Sugar: 1 g, Protein: 4.3 g, Cholesterol: 0 mg.

574. Sesame Carrots
Preparation Time: 10 minutes
Cooking Time: 7 minutes
Servings: 4
Ingredients:
- 2 cups carrots, sliced
- 1 tsp. sesame seeds
- 1 tbsp. scallions, chopped
- 1 tsp. garlic, minced
- 1 tbsp. soy sauce

Directions:
1. In a medium bowl, mix carrots, garlic, soy sauce, ginger, and sesame oil.
2. Add carrots mixture into the Air Fryer basket and cook at 375 for 7 minutes. Shake basket halfway through.
3. Garnish with scallions and sesame seeds and serve.

Nutrition:
Calories: 95, Fat: 7.3 g, Carbohydrates: 7.2 g, Sugar: 2.9 g, Protein: 1 g, Cholesterol: 0 mg.

575. Asparagus with Almonds
Preparation Time: 10 minutes
Cooking Time: 5 minutes
Servings: 4
Ingredients:
- 12 asparagus spears
- 1/3 cup sliced almonds
- 2 tbsp. olive oil
- 2 tbsp. balsamic vinegar
- Pepper
- Salt

Directions:
1. Drizzle asparagus spears with oil and vinegar. Arrange asparagus spears into the Air Fryer basket and season with pepper and salt. Sprinkle sliced almond over asparagus spears.
2. Cook the asparagus at 350°F for 5 minutes. Shake the basket halfway through. Serve and enjoy.

Nutrition:
Calories: 122, Fat: 11.1 g, Carbohydrates: 4.6 g, Sugar: 1.7 g, Protein: 3.3 g, Cholesterol: 0 mg.

576. Easy Roasted Carrots
Preparation Time: 10 minutes
Cooking Time: 18 minutes
Servings: 4
Ingredients:
- 16 oz. carrots, peeled and cut into 2-inch chunks

- 1 tsp. olive oil
- Pepper
- Salt

Directions:
1. Preheat the Air Fryer to 360°F.
2. Toss the carrots with oil and season with pepper and salt.
3. Add carrots into the Air Fryer basket and cook for 15–18 minutes. Shake the basket 3–4 times. Serve and enjoy.

Nutrition:
Calories: 57, Fat: 1.2 g, Carbohydrates: 11.2 g, Sugar: 5.6 g, Protein: 0.9 g, Cholesterol: 0 mg.

577. Asian Broccoli
Preparation Time: 10 minutes
Cooking Time: 20 minutes
Servings: 4
Ingredients:
- 1 lb. broccoli florets
- 1 tsp. rice vinegar
- 2 tsp. sriracha
- 2 tbsp. soy sauce
- 1 tbsp. garlic, minced
- 1 ½ tbsp. sesame oil
- Salt

Directions:
1. Toss broccoli florets with garlic, sesame oil, and salt.
2. Add broccoli florets into the Air Fryer basket and cook at 400°F for 15–20 minutes. Shake the basket halfway through.
3. In a mixing bowl, mix rice vinegar, sriracha, and soy sauce. Add broccoli and toss well.
4. Serve and enjoy.

Nutrition:
Calories: 94, Fat: 5.5 g, Carbohydrates: 9.3 g, Sugar: 2.1 g, Protein: 3.8 g, Cholesterol: 0 mg.

578. Healthy Squash & Zucchini
Preparation Time: 10 minutes
Cooking Time: 25 minutes
Servings: 4
Ingredients:
- 1 lb. zucchini, cut into ½-inch half-moons
- 1 lb. yellow squash, cut into ½-inch half-moons
- 1 tbsp. olive oil
- Pepper
- Salt

Directions:
1. In a mixing bowl, add zucchini, squash, oil, pepper, and salt; toss well.
2. Add zucchini and squash mixture into the Air Fryer basket and cook at 400°F for 20 minutes. Shake basket halfway through.
3. Shake basket well and cook for 5 minutes more.
4. Serve and enjoy.

Nutrition:
Calories: 66, Fat: 3.9 g, Carbohydrates: 7.6 g, Sugar: 3.9 g, Protein: 2.7 g, Cholesterol: 0 mg.

579. Crunchy Fried Cabbage
Preparation Time: 10 minutes
Cooking Time: 10 minutes
Servings: 2
Ingredients:
- ½ cabbage head, sliced into 2-inch slices
- 1 tbsp. olive oil
- Pepper
- Salt

Directions:
1. Drizzle cabbage with olive oil and season with pepper and salt.
2. Add cabbage slices into the Air Fryer basket and cook at 375°F for 5 minutes.
3. Toss cabbage well and cook for 5 minutes more.
4. Serve and enjoy.

Nutrition:
Calories: 105, Fat: 7.2 g, Carbohydrates: 10.4 g, Sugar: 5.7 g, Protein: 2.3 g, Cholesterol: 0 mg.

580. Quick Vegetable Kebabs
Preparation Time: 10 minutes
Cooking Time: 10 minutes
Servings: 4
Ingredients:
- 2 bell peppers, cut into 1-inch pieces
- ½ onion, cut into 1-inch pieces
- 1 zucchini, cut into 1-inch pieces
- 1 eggplant, cut into 1-inch pieces
- Pepper
- Salt

Directions:
1. Thread vegetables onto the skewers and coat them with cooking spray. Season with pepper and salt.
2. Preheat the Air Fryer to 390°F.
3. Place skewers into the Air Fryer basket and cook for 10 minutes. Turn halfway through. Serve and enjoy.

Nutrition:
Calories: 48, Fat: 0.3 g, Carbohydrates: 11.2 g, Sugar: 5.9 g, Protein: 2.1 g, Cholesterol: 0 mg.

581. Easy Soy Garlic Mushrooms
Preparation Time: 10 minutes
Cooking Time: 12 minutes
Servings: 2
Ingredients:
- 8 oz. mushrooms, cleaned
- 1 tbsp. fresh parsley, chopped
- 1 tsp. soy sauce
- ½ tsp. garlic powder
- 1 tbsp. olive oil
- Pepper
- Salt

Directions:
1. Toss mushrooms with soy sauce, garlic powder, oil, pepper, and salt.

2. Add mushrooms into the Air Fryer basket and cook at 380°F for 10–12 minutes.
3. Garnish with parsley and serve.

Nutrition:
Calories: 89, Fat: 7.4 g, Carbohydrates: 4.6 g, Sugar: 2.2 g, Protein: 3.9 g, Cholesterol: 0 mg.

582. Spicy Edamame

Preparation Time: 10 minutes
Cooking Time: 18 minutes
Servings: 4
Ingredients:
- 16 oz. frozen edamame in shell, defrosted
- 1 lemon juice
- 1 lemon zest
- 1 tbsp. garlic, sliced
- 2 tsp. olive oil
- Salt

Directions:
1. Toss edamame with lemon zest, garlic, oil, chili powder, paprika, and salt.
2. Add edamame into the Air Fryer basket and cook at 400°F for 18 minutes. Shake basket twice.
3. Drizzle lemon juice over edamame and serve.

Nutrition:
Calories: 172, Fat: 8.5 g, Carbohydrates: 12.2 g, Sugar: 2.7 g, Protein: 12.3 g, Cholesterol: 0 mg.

583. Balsamic Mushrooms

Preparation Time: 10 minutes
Cooking Time: 8 minutes
Servings: 3
Ingredients:
- 8 oz. mushrooms
- 1 tsp. fresh parsley, chopped
- 2 tsp. balsamic vinegar
- ½ tsp. granulated garlic
- 1 tsp. olive oil
- Pepper - Salt

Directions:
1. Toss mushrooms with garlic, oil, pepper, and salt.
2. Add mushrooms into the Air Fryer basket and cook at 375°F for 8 minutes. Toss halfway through.
3. Toss mushrooms with parsley and balsamic vinegar.
4. Serve and enjoy.

Nutrition:
Calories: 32, Fat: 1.8 g, Carbohydrates: 2.9 g, Sugar: 1.4 g, Protein: 2.5 g, Cholesterol: 0 mg.

584. Mediterranean Vegetables

Preparation Time: 10 minutes
Cooking Time: 15 minutes
Servings: 2
Ingredients:
- 6 cherry tomatoes, cut in half
- 1 eggplant, diced
- 1 zucchini, diced
- 1 green bell pepper, diced
- 1 tsp. thyme
- Pepper
- Salt

Directions:
1. In a bowl, toss eggplant, zucchini, bell pepper, thyme, oregano, pepper, and salt.
2. Add vegetable mixture into the Air Fryer basket and cook at 360°F for 12 minutes.
3. Add cherry tomatoes and shake basket well and cook for 3 minutes more.
4. Serve and enjoy.

Nutrition:
Calories: 61, Fat: 0.3 g, Carbohydrates: 13.8 g, Sugar: 7.6 g, Protein: 2.8 g, Cholesterol: 0 mg.

585. Simple Roasted Okra

Preparation Time: 10 minutes
Cooking Time: 12 minutes
Servings: 1
Ingredients:
- ½ lb. okra, trimmed and sliced
- 1 tsp. olive oil
- Pepper
- Salt

Directions:
1. Preheat the Air Fryer to 350°F.
2. Mix okra, oil, pepper, and salt.
3. Add okra into the Air Fryer basket and cook for 10 minutes. Toss halfway through.
4. Toss well and cook for 2 minutes more.
5. Serve and enjoy.

Nutrition:
Calories: 176, Fat: 17.3 g, Carbohydrates: 6.2 g, Sugar: 3.2 g, Protein: 2.5 g, Cholesterol: 0 mg.

586. Air Fried Vegetables

Preparation Time: 10 minutes
Cooking Time: 8 minutes
Servings: 3
Ingredients:
- 2 tbsp. extra virgin olive oil
- 1 tbsp. minced garlic
- 1 large shallot, sliced
- 1 cup mushrooms, sliced
- 1 cup broccoli florets
- 1 cup artichoke hearts
- 1 bunch asparagus, sliced into 3-inch pieces
- 1 cup baby peas
- 1 cup cherry tomatoes, halved
- ½ tsp. sea salt

Vinaigrette
- 3 tbsp. white wine vinegar
- 6 tbsp. extra-virgin olive oil
- ½ tsp. sea salt
- 1 tsp. ground oregano

- handful fresh parsley, chopped

Directions:
1. Add oil to the pan of your Air Fryer toast oven set over medium heat. Stir in garlic and shallots and air fry for about 2 minutes.
2. Stir in mushrooms for about 3 minutes or until golden.
3. Stir in broccoli, artichokes, and asparagus and continue cooking for 3 more minutes. Stir in peas, tomatoes, and salt and transfer to the Air Fryer toast oven and cook for 5–8 more minutes.
4. Prepare vinaigrette: mix vinegar, oil, salt, oregano, and parsley in a bowl until well combined.

Nutrition:
Calories: 293, Carbs: 14.6 g, Fat: 27 g, Protein: 25 g.

587. Air Broiled Mushrooms

Preparation Time: 10 minutes
Cooking Time: 10 minutes
Servings: 4
Ingredients:
- 2 cups shiitake mushrooms
- 1 tbsp. balsamic vinegar
- ¼ cup extra virgin olive oil
- 1–2 garlic cloves, minced
- A handful of parsley
- 1 tsp. salt

Directions:
1. Rinse the mushroom and pat dry; put it in a foil and drizzle with balsamic vinegar and extra virgin olive oil.
2. Sprinkle the mushroom with garlic, parsley, and salt.
3. Broil for about 10 minutes in your Air Fryer toast oven at 350°F or until tender and cooked through. Serve warm.

Nutrition:
Calories: 260, Carbs: 11 g, Fat: 19.1 g, Protein: 22 g.

588. Hydrated Potato Wedges

Preparation Time: 5 minutes
Cooking Time: 30 minutes
Servings: 5
Ingredients:
- 2 medium Russet potatoes, diced into wedges
- 1 ½ tbsp. olive oil
- ½ tsp. chili powder
- ½ tsp. parsley
- ½ tsp. paprika
- 1/8 tsp. black pepper
- ½ tsp. sea salt

Directions:
1. In a large bowl, mix potato wedges, olive oil, chili, parsley, paprika, salt, and pepper until the potatoes are well coated.
2. Transfer half of the potatoes to a fryer basket and hydrate for 20 minutes.
3. Repeat with the remaining wedges. Serve hot with chilled orange juice.

Nutrition:
Calories: 129, Carbs: 10 g, Fat: 5.3 g, Protein: 2.3 g.

589. Crispy Baked Tofu

Preparation Time: 15 minutes
Cooking Time: 20 minutes
Servings: 4
Ingredients:
- 1 cup whole wheat flour
- 1 package (16-ounce) extra-firm tofu, chopped into 8 slices
- ¾ cup raw cashews
- 2 cups pretzel sticks
- 1 tbsp. extra virgin olive oil
- 2 tsp. chili powder
- 1 cup unsweetened almond milk

Directions:
1. Preheat your Air Fryer toast oven to 400°F.
2. Line a baking sheet with baking paper and set it aside.
3. In a food processor, pulse together the cashews and pretzel sticks until coarsely ground.
4. Combine garlic, onion, chili powder, lemon pepper, and salt in a small bowl.
5. In a large bowl, combine half of the spice mixture and flour.
6. Add almond milk to a separate bowl.
7. In another bowl, combine cashew mixture, salt, pepper, and olive oil; mix well.

Nutrition:
Calories: 332, Carbs: 23.3 g, Fat: 8.8 g, Protein: 12.9 g.

590. Spiced Tempeh

Preparation Time: 15 minutes
Cooking Time: 20 minutes
Servings: 4
Ingredients:
Tempeh Bits:
- ¼ cup vegetable oil 8 oz. tempeh
- 1 tsp. lemon pepper
- 1 tsp. chili powder
- 2 tsp. sweet paprika
- 2 tsp. garlic powder
- 1/8 tsp. cayenne pepper or more to taste

Dressing:
- 1 tbsp. freshly grated ginger
- ¼ cup low, Sodium: soy sauce
- 1/3 cup seasoned rice vinegar

Directions:
1. Blanch kale in a pot of salted boiling water for about 30 seconds and immediately run under cold water; drain and squeeze out excess water. Set aside.
2. Preheat your Air Fryer toast oven to 425°F.
3. In a small bowl, combine all the spices for tempeh. Add oil to a separate bowl. Slice tempeh into thin pieces.

Nutrition:
Calories: 308, Carbs: 19.2 g, Fat: 7.3 g, Protein: 9.8 g.

591. Steamed Broccoli

Preparation Time: 8 minutes
Cooking Time: 3 minutes
Servings: 2
Ingredients:
- 1 pound broccoli florets
- 1½ cups water
- Salt and pepper to taste
- 1 tsp. extra virgin olive oil

Directions:
1. Add water to the bottom of your Air Fryer toast oven and set the basket on top.
2. Toss the broccoli florets with, salt pepper, and olive oil until evenly combined; then transfer to the basket of your Air Fryer toast oven.
3. Select keep warm for 10 minutes.
4. Remove the basket and serve the broccoli.

Nutrition:
Calories: 160, Carbs: 6.1 g, Fat: 12 g, Protein: 13 g.

592. Air Fried Brussel Sprouts

Preparation Time: 10 minutes
Cooking Time: 10 minutes
Servings: 4
Ingredients:
- 2 pound Brussels sprouts, halved
- 1 tbsp. chopped almonds
- 1 tbsp. rice vinegar
- 2 tbsp. sriracha sauce
- ¼ cup gluten-free soy sauce
- 2 tbsp. sesame oil
- ½ tbsp. cayenne pepper
- 1 tbsp. smoked paprika

Directions:
1. Preheat your Air Fryer toast oven to 370°F.
2. Meanwhile, place your Air Fryer toast oven pan on medium heat and cook the almonds for 3 minutes; then add in all the remaining ingredients.
3. Place the pan in the Air Fryer toast oven and air fry for 8–10 minutes or until done to desire.
4. Serve hot over a bed of steamed rice.
5. Enjoy!

Nutrition:
Calories: 216, Carbs: 8.8 g, Fat: 18 g, Protein: 18 g.

CHAPTER 7: Rice And Grains Recipes

593. Rice and Calamari Mix
Preparation time: 10 minutes
Cooking time: 25 minutes
Servings: 4
Ingredients:
- 1 cup wild rice
- 2 cups fish stock
- ½ cup calamari rings
- ½ teaspoon sweet paprika
- ½ teaspoon curry powder
- A pinch of salt and black pepper
- 1 tablespoon parsley, chopped

Directions:
1. In the air fryer's pan, mix the rice with the stock, calamari and the other ingredients, toss, put the pan in the machine and cook for 25 minutes.
2. Divide into bowls and serve right away.

Nutrition: calories 394, fat 5, fiber 8, carbs 18, protein 4

594. Curry Rice
Preparation time: 10 minutes
Cooking time: 25 minutes
Servings: 4
Ingredients:
- 1 cup wild rice
- 2 tablespoons green curry paste
- 2 cups chicken stock
- Salt and black pepper to the taste
- ½ teaspoon curry powder
- 1 tablespoon chives, chopped

Directions:
1. In your air fryer's pan, mix the rice with the curry paste and the other ingredients, put the pan in the machine and cook at 360 degrees F for 25 minutes.
2. Divide the mix between plates and serve.

Nutrition: calories 182, fat 6, fiber 2, carbs 35, protein 3

595. Pesto Rice
Preparation time: 10 minutes
Cooking time: 20 minutes
Servings: 4
Ingredients:
- 2 tablespoons butter, melted
- 1 cup white rice
- 2 cups veggie stock
- 2 tablespoons basil pesto
- ½ teaspoon chili powder
- ½ teaspoon turmeric powder
- Salt and black pepper to the taste

Directions:
1. In the air fryer's pan, mix the melted butter with the rice, stock and the other ingredients, toss and cook at 380 degrees F for 20 minutes.
2. Divide the mix between plates and serve.

Nutrition: calories 251, fat 4, fiber 3, carbs 13, protein 6

596. Mango and Berries Rice
Preparation time: 10 minutes
Cooking time: 20 minutes
Servings: 4
Ingredients:
- 1 cup white rice - 2 cups coconut milk
- ½ cup mango, peeled and cubed
- ½ cup black berries, cubed
- 1 tablespoon sugar

Directions:
1. In a pan that fits your air fryer, mix the rice with the coconut milk and the other ingredients, put the pan in the fryer and cook at 360 degrees F for 20 minutes.
2. Divide into bowls and serve.

Nutrition: calories 200, fat 4, fiber 5, carbs 11, protein 4

597. Nutty Rice
Preparation time: 10 minutes
Cooking time: 25 minutes
Servings: 4
Ingredients:
- 1 cup wild rice - ½ cup peanuts, chopped
- ½ cup walnuts, chopped
- ½ cup spring onions, chopped
- 2 cups veggie stock
- A pinch of salt and black pepper

Directions:
1. In the air fryer's pan, mix the rice with the nuts and the other ingredients, toss, cook at 380 degrees F for 25 minutes, divide into bowls and serve.

Nutrition: calories 233, fat 12, fiber 4, carbs 5, protein 12

598. Pine Nuts Quinoa
Preparation time: 10 minutes
Cooking time: 25 minutes
Servings: 4
Ingredients:
- 1 cup quinoa
- ¼ cup pine nuts, toasted
- 1 tablespoon basil pesto

- 2 cups veggie stock
- 1 tablespoon lemon juice
- 1 teaspoon garlic powder

Directions:
1. In the air fryer's pan, combine quinoa with the pine nuts and the other ingredients, toss and cook at 350 degrees F for 25 minutes.
2. Divide between plates and serve.

Nutrition: calories 200, fat 4, fiber 4, carbs 16, protein 4

599. Beans and Corn

Preparation time: 10 minutes
Cooking time: 30 minutes
Servings: 4

Ingredients:
- 1 cup canned black beans, drained and rinsed
- 1 cup canned red kidney beans, drained and rinsed
- 1 cup corn
- 1 cup tomato sauce
- ½ cup cilantro, chopped
- 2 teaspoons chili powder
- 1 teaspoon garlic powder
- A pinch of salt and black pepper

Directions:
1. In the air fryer's pan, mix the beans with the corn and the other ingredients, toss, introduce in your fryer and cook at 350 degrees F for 30 minutes.
2. Divide between plates and serve.

Nutrition: calories 365, fat 12, fiber 6, carbs 22, protein 26

600. Corn and Pine Nuts Mix

Preparation time: 10 minutes
Cooking time: 20 minutes
Servings: 4

Ingredients:
- 2 cups corn
- ¼ cup pine nuts, toasted
- Juice of 1 lime
- Salt and black pepper to the taste
- 1 cup heavy cream
- 2 teaspoons olive oil

Directions:
1. In your air fryer's pan, mix the corn with the pine nuts and the other ingredients, toss, put the pan in the machine and cook at 380 degrees F for 25 minutes.
2. Divide on plates and serve as a side dish.

Nutrition: calories 152, fat 3, fiber 6, carbs 7, protein 4

601. Carrots Rice

Preparation time: 10 minutes
Cooking time: 25 minutes
Servings: 4

Ingredients:
- 1 cup wild rice
- 2 cups veggie stock
- 1 cup carrots, peeled and grated
- ½ teaspoon curry powder
- 2 tablespoons butter, melted
- ½ teaspoon cumin seeds
- Salt and black pepper the taste

Directions:
1. In the air fryer's pan, mix the rice with the stock, carrots and the other ingredients, toss, put the pan in the machine and cook at 370 degrees F for 25 minutes.
2. Divide between plates and serve.

Nutrition: calories 283, fat 4, fiber 8, carbs 34, protein 14

602. Ginger Rice

Preparation time: 10 minutes
Cooking time: 25 minutes
Servings: 4

Ingredients:
- 1 cup white rice
- 2 cups veggie stock
- 1 tablespoon butter, melted
- 1 tablespoon ginger, grated
- Salt and black pepper to the taste
- ¼ cup parsley, chopped

Directions:
1. In your air fryer's pan, mix the rice with the stock, butter and the other ingredients, toss, put the pan in the machine and cook at 370 degrees F for 25 minutes.
2. Divide between plates and serve hot.

Nutrition: calories 313, fat 12, fiber 14, carbs 27, protein 44

603. Rice and Radishes

Preparation time: 5 minutes
Cooking time: 25 minutes
Servings: 4

Ingredients:
- 1 cup white rice
- ½ cup radishes, cubed
- 2 cups veggie stock
- ½ cup spring onions, chopped
- A pinch of salt and black pepper

Directions:
1. In your air fryer's pan, mix the rice with the radishes and the other ingredients, stir, put the pan in the machine and cook at 360 degrees F for 25 minutes.
2. Divide the mix between plates and serve.

Nutrition: calories 251, fat 6, fiber 8, carbs 39, protein 12

604. Quinoa and Shrimp

Preparation time: 10 minutes
Cooking time: 20 minutes
Servings: 4

Ingredients:
- 1 cup quinoa
- ½ pound shrimp, peeled and deveined
- 1 tablespoon olive oil
- 1 cup fish stock
- ½ teaspoon chili powder

- 1 tablespoon lemon juice
- Salt and black pepper to the taste
- 1 tablespoon chives, chopped

Directions:
1. In your air fryer's pan, combine the quinoa with the shrimp, oil and the other ingredients, toss, put the pan in your air fryer and cook at 370 degrees F for 20 minutes, stirring halfway.
2. Divide into bowls and serve.

Nutrition: calories 300, fat 12, fiber 2, carbs 23, protein 25

605. Oregano Salsa Rice

Preparation time: 10 minutes
Cooking time: 30 minutes
Servings: 4

Ingredients:
- 2 teaspoons olive oil
- 1 cup white rice
- 2 cups veggie stock
- 1 tablespoon oregano, chopped
- ½ cup mild salsa
- A pinch of salt and black pepper
- ½ cup parmesan, grated

Directions:
1. In the air fryer's pan, mix the rice with the stock, oregano and the other ingredients, stir, put the pan in the machine and cook at 350 degrees F for 30 minutes.
2. Divide between plates and serve.

Nutrition: calories 142, fat 4, fiber 4, carbs 6, protein 4

606. Chestnut Rice

Preparation time: 10 minutes
Cooking time: 30 minutes
Servings: 4

Ingredients:
- 1 tablespoon olive oil
- 1 cup white rice
- 2 cups veggie stock
- Juice from ½ lemon
- 9 ounces' water chestnuts, drained
- ½ teaspoon curry powder
- ½ teaspoon cumin, ground
- A pinch of salt and black pepper

Directions:
1. In your air fryer's pan, mix the rice with the stock, oil and the other ingredients, stir, put the pan in the machine and cook at 360 degrees F for 30 minutes.
2. Divide between plates and serve.

Nutrition: calories 142, fat 3, fiber 2, carbs 6, protein 4

607. Beef Quinoa Mix

Preparation time: 10 minutes
Cooking time: 25 minutes
Servings: 4

Ingredients:
- 1 cup quinoa
- ½ cup beef stock
- ½ pound beef stew meat, ground
- 1 red onion, chopped
- ½ teaspoon coriander, ground
- ½ teaspoon sweet paprika
- 1 teaspoon olive oil
- 1 tablespoon tomato sauce

Directions:
1. In the air fry's pan, mix the quinoa with the stock, meat and the other ingredients, toss, put the pan in the machine and cook at 370 degrees F for 25 minutes.
2. Divide between plates and serve.

Nutrition: calories 240, fat 12, fiber 5, carbs 20, protein 13

608. Shallots Wild Rice

Preparation time: 10 minutes
Cooking time: 25 minutes
Servings: 4

Ingredients:
- 1 cup wild rice
- 2 cups chicken stock
- ½ cup shallots, chopped
- ½ teaspoon sweet paprika
- ½ teaspoon cumin, ground
- A pinch of salt and black pepper
- A drizzle of olive oil
- 1 tablespoon parsley, chopped

Directions:
1. In the air fryer's pan, mix the rice with the stock, shallots and the other ingredients, toss, put the pan in the machine and cook at 350 degrees F for 25 minutes.
2. Divide between plates and serve.

Nutrition: calories 142, fat 4, fiber 4, carbs 16, protein 4

609. Squash Quinoa

Preparation time: 5 minutes
Cooking time: 30 minutes
Servings: 4

Ingredients:
- 2 teaspoons avocado oil
- 1 red onion, chopped
- 1 cup quinoa
- ½ cup butternut squash, peeled and cubed
- 1 cup chicken stock
- A pinch of salt and black pepper

Directions:
1. In the air fryer's pan, mix the quinoa with the squash, oil and the other ingredients, put the pan in the machine and cook at 360 degrees F for 30 minutes.
2. Divide between plates and serve.

Nutrition: calories 261, fat 6, fiber 7, carbs 29, protein 4

610. Garlic Black Beans and Potatoes

Preparation time: 10 minutes

Cooking time: 30 minutes
Servings: 4
Ingredients:
- 2 cups canned black beans, drained and rinsed
- 1 pound sweet potatoes, peeled and cubed
- 1 teaspoon chili powder
- ¼ cup veggie stock
- 1 teaspoon curry powder
- 1 tablespoon olive oil
- Salt and white pepper to the taste

Directions:
1. In the air fryer's pan, mix the beans with the sweet potatoes and the other ingredients, toss, put the pan in the machine and cook at 370 degrees F for 30 minutes.
2. Divide between plates and serve.

Nutrition: calories 182, fat 3, fiber 6, carbs 8, protein 3

611. Parsley Beans

Preparation time: 10 minutes
Cooking time: 25 minutes
Servings: 4
Ingredients:
- 1 yellow onion, chopped
- 1 cup canned black beans, drained
- 1 cup white beans, drained
- ¼ cup tomato sauce
- 1 tablespoon avocado oil
- 1 teaspoon cumin, ground
- Salt and black pepper to the taste
- 2 tablespoons parsley, chopped

Directions:
1. In the air fryer's pan, mix the beans with the tomato sauce and the other ingredients, toss, put the pan in the machine and cook at 350 degrees F for 25 minutes.
2. Divide between plates and serve.

Nutrition: calories 200, fat 4, fiber 6, carbs 16, protein 4

612. Chili Beans and Quinoa

Preparation time: 10 minutes
Cooking time: 25 minutes
Servings: 4
Ingredients:
- 1 cup quinoa
- 1 cup canned black beans, drained
- 1 red chili pepper, chopped
- 1 teaspoon chili powder
- Salt and black pepper to the taste
- ½ teaspoon turmeric powder
- 1 tablespoon chives, chopped

Directions:
1. In the air fryer's pan, mix the quinoa with the beans, chili pepper and the other ingredients, put the pan in the air fryer and cook at 360 degrees F for 25 minutes.
2. Divide between plates and serve.

Nutrition: calories 171, fat 4, fiber 8, carbs 16, protein 7

613. Thyme Beans

Preparation time: 10 minutes
Cooking time: 20 minutes
Servings: 4
Ingredients:
- 1 cup canned red kidney beans, drained
- 1 cup canned white beans, drained
- 1 teaspoon olive oil
- 1 tablespoon thyme, chopped
- ¼ cup tomato sauce
- Salt and black pepper to the taste

Directions:
1. In a pan that fits your air fryer, mix the beans with the oil and the other ingredients, introduce in your air fryer and cook at 350 degrees F for 20 minutes.
2. Divide the mix between plates and serve.

Nutrition: calories 161, fat 4, fiber 6, carbs 15, protein 6

614. Millet Pudding

Preparation time: 10 minutes
Cooking time: 20 minutes
Servings: 4
Ingredients:
- 3 cups coconut milk
- ½ teaspoon nutmeg, ground
- ½ teaspoon cinnamon powder
- 1 tablespoon honey
- 1 cup millet
- ¼ cup raisins

Directions:
1. In the air fryer's pan, mix the millet with the coconut milk and the other ingredients, put the pan in the machine and cook at 380 degrees F for 20 minutes.
2. Divide into bowls and serve.

Nutrition: calories 231, fat 6, fiber 6, carbs 18, protein 6

615. Bulgur and Peas

Preparation time: 10 minutes
Cooking time: 25 minutes
Servings: 4
Ingredients:
- 1 cup bulgur
- 1 cup veggie stock
- ½ cup green peas
- 1 teaspoon sweet paprika
- 1 teaspoon coriander, ground

Directions:
1. In the air fryer's pan, mix the bulgur with the stock and the other ingredients, toss, put the pan in the machine and cook at 360 degrees F for 25 minutes.
2. Divide between plates and serve hot.

Nutrition: calories 313, fat 12, fiber 14, carbs 27, protein 44

616. Fennel and Peas Quinoa

Preparation time: 10 minutes

Cooking time: 25 minutes
Servings: 4
Ingredients:
- 1 cup quinoa
- 1 cup veggie stock
- 1 fennel bulb, sliced
- ½ cup peas
- 2 teaspoons avocado oil
- 2 scallions, chopped
- 2 garlic cloves, minced
- 1 tablespoon basil, chopped
- Salt and black pepper to the taste

Directions:
1. In the air fryer's pan, mix the quinoa with the stock and the other ingredients, toss, put the pan in the machine and cook at 370 degrees F for 25 minutes.
2. Divide the mix between plates and serve.

Nutrition: calories 264, fat 6, fiber 8, carbs 10, protein 5

617. Beans and Kale

Preparation time: 10 minutes
Cooking time: 25 minutes
Servings: 4
Ingredients:
- 1 cup canned red kidney beans, drained
- ½ pound baby kale
- ½ cup mild salsa
- 1 tablespoon olive oil
- ½ teaspoon sweet paprika
- Salt and black pepper to the taste

Directions:
1. In the air fryer's pan, mix the beans with the kale and the other ingredients, put the pan in the machine and cook at 370 degrees' f for 25 minutes.
2. Divide between plates and serve.

Nutrition: calories 200, fat 12, fiber 4, carbs 7, protein 6

618. Garlic Barley Mix

Preparation time: 10 minutes
Cooking time: 25 minutes
Servings: 4
Ingredients:
- 1 tablespoon olive oil - 3 garlic cloves, minced
- 2 cups pearl barley, rinsed
- 2 cups veggie stock
- 1 teaspoon sweet paprika
- Salt and black pepper to the taste
- 1 tablespoon parsley, chopped

Directions:
1. In the air fryer's pan, mix the barley with the garlic and the other ingredients, toss, put the pan in the machine and cook at 370 degrees F for 25 minutes.
2. Divide into bowls and serve.

Nutrition: calories 232, fat 5, fiber 4, carbs 12, protein 4

619. Quinoa and Broccoli Salad

Preparation time: 10 minutes
Cooking time: 20 minutes
Servings: 4
Ingredients:
- 1 cup quinoa - 2 cups veggie stock
- ½ cup broccoli florets
- 1 cup carrots, peeled and grated
- ¼ cup celery, chopped
- Salt and black pepper to the taste

Directions:
1. In the air fryer's pan, mix the quinoa with the stock, broccoli and the other ingredients, put the pan in the machine and cook at 370 degrees F for 20 minutes.
2. Divide into bowls and serve.

Nutrition: calories 200, fat 4, fiber 3, carbs 12, protein 5

620. Spring Onions and Tomatoes Beans

Preparation time: 10 minutes
Cooking time: 25 minutes
Servings: 4
Ingredients:
- 1 cup green beans, trimmed and halved
- 1 cup canned red kidney beans, drained
- 1 tablespoon olive oil
- ½ cup spring onions, chopped
- ½ cup cherry tomatoes, halved
- ½ cup kalamata olives, pitted and chopped

Directions:
1. In the air fryer's pan, mix the beans with the oil, spring onions and the other ingredients, put the pan in the machine and cook at 370 degrees F for 25 minutes.
2. Divide the mix into bowls and serve.

Nutrition: calories 200, fat 2, fiber 3, carbs 5, protein 4

621. Cracked What Mix

Preparation time: 10 minutes
Cooking time: 20 minutes
Servings: 4
Ingredients:
- ½ cup cracked whole wheat
- 1 cup veggie stock
- 1 cup white mushrooms, sliced
- ½ cup carrots, peeled and grated
- 1 cup cherry tomatoes, halved

Directions:
1. In the air fryer's pan, mix the wheat with the stock, mushrooms and the other ingredients, stir, put the pan in the machine and cook at 380 degrees F for 20 minutes.
2. Divide the mix between plates and serve.

Nutrition: calories 200, fat 12, fiber 3, carbs 4, protein 4

622. Creamy Beans Mix

Preparation time: 5 minutes
Cooking time: 25 minutes
Servings: 4
Ingredients:
- 2 cups canned white beans, drained
- 1 cup heavy cream
- ½ teaspoon turmeric powder
- 1 teaspoon fennel seeds
- ½ teaspoon garam masala
- A pinch of salt and black pepper

Directions:
1. In the air fryer's pan, mix the beans with the cream and the other ingredients, put the pan in the machine and cook at 380 degrees F for 25 minutes.
2. Divide between plates and serve.

Nutrition: calories 200, fat 12, fiber 3, carbs 5, protein 3

623. Walnuts Bulgur Mix

Preparation time: 5 minutes
Cooking time: 25 minutes
Servings: 4
Ingredients:
- 1 cup bulgur
- 2 teaspoons olive oil
- ½ cup walnuts, chopped
- 2 garlic cloves, minced
- 1 tablespoon chives, chopped

Directions:
1. In the air fryer's pan, mix the bulgur with the oil and the other ingredients, toss, put the pan in the fryer and cook at 370 degrees F for 25 minutes.
2. Divide everything between plates and serve.

Nutrition: calories 233, fat 3, fiber 4, carbs 12, protein 4

624. Minty Bulgur

Preparation time: 5 minutes
Cooking time: 25 minutes
Servings: 4
Ingredients:
- 1 red onion, chopped
- 1 cup bulgur
- 1 cup veggie stock
- 1 tablespoon mint, chopped
- Salt and black pepper to the taste
- ½ teaspoon ginger, grated
- ½ cup walnuts, toasted and chopped

Directions:
1. In your air fryer's pan, mix the bulgur with the onion, stock and the other ingredients, toss, put the pan in the machine and cook at 370 degrees F for 25 minutes.
2. Divide between plates and serve.

Nutrition: calories 263, fat 12, fiber 4, carbs 9, protein 4

625. Couscous and Veggies

Preparation time: 10 minutes
Cooking time: 20 minutes
Servings: 4
Ingredients:
- 1 cup couscous, cooked
- 1 red bell pepper, chopped
- 1 red onion, chopped
- ½ cup mushrooms, halved
- ½ cup eggplants, cubed
- ½ teaspoon chili powder

Directions:
1. In your air fryer's pan, combine the couscous with the bell pepper and the other ingredients, put the pan in the fryer, cook at 370 degrees F for 20 minutes, divide into bowls and serve.

Nutrition: calories 300, fat 12, fiber 3, carbs 12, protein 5

626. Coriander Couscous

Preparation time: 10 minutes
Cooking time: 20 minutes
Servings: 4
Ingredients:
- 2 spring onions, chopped
- 2 teaspoons olive oil
- 1 cup couscous, rinsed
- 2 cups veggie stock
- Salt and black pepper to the taste
- 1 tablespoon chives, chopped

Directions:
1. In the air fryer's pan, mix the couscous with the stock, onions and the other ingredients, toss, put the pan in the machine and cook at 360 degrees F for 20 minutes.
2. Divide the mix between plates and serve.

Nutrition: calories 200, fat 4, fiber 3, carbs 12, protein 6

627. Hydrated Kale Chips

Preparation Time: 5 minutes
Cooking Time: 5 minutes
Servings: 2
Ingredients:
- 4 cups loosely packed kale, stemmed
- 2 tsp. Ranch Seasoning
- 2 tbsp. olive oil
- 1 tbsp. nutritional yeast

Directions:
1. In a bowl, toss together kale pieces, oil, nutritional yeast, ranch seasoning, and salt until well coated.
2. Transfer to a fryer basket and hydrate for 15 minutes, shaking halfway through cooking.
3. Serve right away!

Nutrition:
Calories: 103, Carbs: 8.2 g, Fat: 7.1 g, Protein: 3.2 g.

CHAPTER 8 :
Appetizers and Snacks

628. Feta Tater Tots
Preparation Time: 15 minutes
Cooking Time: 25 minutes
Servings: 6
Ingredients:
- 2 pounds frozen tater tots
- ½ cup feta cheese, crumbled
- ½ cup tomato, chopped
- ¼ cup black olives, pitted and sliced
- ¼ cup red onion, chopped

Directions:
1. Arrange the tater tots in the basket.
2. Select "Air Fry" of Air Fryer Toaster Oven and then adjust the temperature to 450 degrees F.
3. Place the timer for 15 minutes and click "Start" to preheat.
4. After preheating, insert the basket in oven.
5. When cooking time is complete, remove the basket from oven and transfer tots into a large bowl.
6. Add the feta cheese, tomatoes, olives and onion and toss to coat well.
7. Now, place the mixture into a baking pan.
8. Select "Air Fry" of Air Fryer Toaster Oven and then adjust the temperature to 450 degrees F.
9. Place the timer for 10 minutes and click "Start" to preheat.
10. After preheating, insert the baking pan in oven.
11. When cooking time is finished, take away the baking pan from oven and serve warm.

Nutrition: Calories 322 Total Fat 17 g Saturated Fat 6 g Cholesterol 11 mg Sodium 784 mg Total Carbs 39 g Fiber 1 g Sugar 2 g Protein 5 g

629. Cauliflower Poppers
Preparation Time: 10 minutes
Cooking Time: 20 minutes
Servings: 6
Ingredients:
- 3 tablespoons olive oil - 1 teaspoon paprika
- ½ teaspoon ground cumin
- ¼ teaspoon ground turmeric
- Salt and ground black pepper, as required
- 1 medium head cauliflower, cut into florets

Directions:
1. In a bowl, place all ingredients and toss to coat well.
2. Place the cauliflower mixture in the greased baking pan. Select "Bake" of Air Fryer Toaster Oven and then adjust the temperature to 450 F.
3. Place the timer for 20 minutes and click "Start" to preheat. After preheating, put the baking pan in oven.
4. Flip the cauliflower mixture once halfway through.
5. When cooking time is finished, take away the pan from oven and serve warm.

Nutrition: Calories 73 Total Fat 1 g Saturated Fat 1 g Cholesterol 0 mg Sodium 41 mg Total Carbs 7 g Fiber 3 g Sugar 1 g Protein 1 g

630. Fish Nuggets
Preparation Time: 15 minutes
Cooking Time: 8 minutes
Servings: 5
Ingredients:
- 1 cup all-purpose flour
- 2 eggs
- ¾ cup seasoned breadcrumbs
- 2 tablespoons vegetable oil
- 1-pound boneless haddock fillet, cut into strips

Directions:
1. In a shallow dish, place the flour.
2. In a second dish, crack the eggs and beat well.
3. In a third dish, mix together the breadcrumbs and oil.
4. Coat the nuggets with flour, then dip into beaten eggs and finally, coat with the breadcrumbs.
5. Place the nuggets into the greased basket in a single layer.
6. Select "Air Fry" of Air Fryer Toaster Oven and then adjust the temperature to 390 degrees F.
7. Set the timer for 8 minutes and press "Start" to preheat.
8. After preheating, insert the basket in the center position of oven.
9. Flip the nuggets once halfway through.
10. When cooking time is complete, remove the basket from oven.
11. Serve warm.

Nutrition: Calories 311 Total Fat 14 g Saturated Fat 7 g Cholesterol 110 mg Sodium 312 mg Total Carbs 24 g Fiber 3 g Sugar 2 g Protein 26 g

631. Buffalo Chicken Wings
Preparation Time: 15 minutes
Cooking Time: 19 minutes
Servings: 4

Ingredients:
- 1½ pounds chicken wings
- 1 teaspoon olive oil
- Salt and ground black pepper, as required
- ¼ cup buffalo sauce

Directions:
1. In a large bowl, mix together the chicken wings, oil, salt and black pepper.
2. Arrange the wings into a greased baking pan.
3. Select "Air Fry" of Air Fryer Toaster Oven and then adjust the temperature to 360 degrees F.
4. Set the timer for 19 minutes and press "Start" to preheat.
5. After preheating, insert the baking pan in oven.
6. Flip the chicken wings once halfway through and coat with buffalo sauce.
7. When cooking time is finished, take away the pan from oven and serve immediately.

Nutrition: Calories 334 Total Fat 18 g Saturated Fat 6 g Cholesterol 151 mg Sodium 209 mg Total Carbs 1 g Fiber 0 g Sugar 0 g Protein 42 g

632. Bacon-Wrapped Shrimp

Preparation Time: 15 minutes
Cooking Time: 7 minutes
Servings: 6

Ingredients:
- 1-pound bacon, thinly sliced
- 1-pound shrimp, peeled and deveined

Directions:
1. Wrap each shrimp with one bacon slice.
2. Arrange the shrimp in a baking dish and refrigerate for about 20 minutes.
3. Now, place the shrimp into the greased basket.
4. Arrange the basket in the center of Air Fryer Oven.
5. Select "Air Fry" of Air Fryer Toaster Oven and then adjust the temperature to 390 degrees F.
6. Set the timer for 7 minutes and press "Start" to preheat.
7. After preheating, insert the baking pan in oven.
8. When cooking time is complete, remove the basket from oven. Serve warm.

Nutrition: Calories 499 Total Fat 39 g Saturated Fat 18 g Cholesterol 242 mg Sodium 1800 mg Total Carbs 2 g Fiber 0 g Sugar 0 g Protein 42 g

633. Crispy Coconut Prawns

Preparation Time: 20 minutes
Cooking Time: 12 minutes
Servings: 4

Ingredients:
- ½ cup flour - ¼ teaspoon paprika
- Salt and ground white pepper, as required
- 2 egg whites
- ¾ cup panko breadcrumbs
- ½ cup unsweetened coconut, shredded
- 2 teaspoons lemon zest, grated finely
- 1 pound prawns, peeled and deveined

Directions:
1. In a shallow plate, place the flour, paprika, salt and white pepper and mix well.
2. In a second shallow plate, add the egg whites and beat lightly.
3. In a third shallow plate, place the breadcrumbs, coconut and lemon zest and mix well.
4. Coat the prawns with flour mixture, then dip into egg whites and finally coat with the coconut mixture.
5. Place the prawns into a greased baking pan.
6. Select "Bake" of Air Fryer Toaster Oven and then adjust the temperature to 400 degrees F.
7. Set the timer for 12 minutes and press "Start" to preheat.
8. After preheating, insert the baking pan in oven.
9. Flip the cauliflower mixture once halfway through.
10. When cooking time is finished, take away the pan from oven and serve hot.

Nutrition: Calories 310 Total Fat 9 g Saturated Fat 1 g Cholesterol 239 mg Sodium 296 mg Total Carbs 17 g Fiber 5 g Sugar 9 g Protein 32 g

634. Pancetta Wrapped Shrimp

Preparation Time: 15 minutes
Cooking Time: 7 minutes
Servings: 6

Ingredients:
- 1-pound pancetta, thinly sliced
- 1-pound shrimp, peeled and deveined

Directions:
1. Wrap each shrimp with one pancetta slice.
2. Arrange the shrimp in a baking dish and refrigerate for about 20 minutes.
3. Now, place the shrimp into the greased air fryer basket.
4. Arrange the air fryer basket in the center of Instant Omni plus Toaster Oven.
5. Select "Air Fry" and then adjust the temperature to 390 degrees F.
6. Set the timer for 7 minutes and press "Start".
7. When the display shows "Turn Food" do nothing.
8. When cooking time is complete, remove the air fryer basket from Toaster Oven.
9. Serve warm.

Nutrition: Calories 499 Total Fat 39 g Saturated Fat 18 g Cholesterol 242 mg Sodium 1800 mg Total Carbs 2 g Fiber 0 g Sugar 0 g Protein 42 g

635. Haddock Nuggets

Preparation Time: 15 minutes
Cooking Time: 8 minutes
Servings: 5

Ingredients:
- 1 cup all-purpose flour
- 2 eggs
- ¾ cup seasoned breadcrumbs
- 2 tablespoons vegetable oil

- 1-pound boneless haddock fillet, cut into strips

Directions:
1. In a shallow dish, place the flour.
2. In a second dish, crack the eggs and beat well.
3. In a third dish, mix together the breadcrumbs and oil.
4. Coat the nuggets with flour, then dip into beaten eggs and finally, coat with the breadcrumbs.
5. Place the nuggets into the greased air fryer basket in a single layer.
6. Arrange the air fryer basket in the center of Instant Omni plus Toaster Oven.
7. Select "Air Fry" and then adjust the temperature to 390 degrees F.
8. Set the timer for 8 minutes and press "Start".
9. When the display shows "Turn Food" flip the wings.
10. When cooking time is complete, remove the air fryer basket from Toaster Oven.
11. Serve warm.

Nutrition: Calories 311 Total Fat 14 g Saturated Fat 7 g Cholesterol 110 mg Sodium 312 mg Total Carbs 24 g Fiber 3 g Sugar 2 g Protein 26 g

636. Taco Seasoned Kale Chips

Preparation Time: 5 minutes,
Cooking Time: 180 minutes;
Servings: 2

Ingredients:
- 3 whole Lacinato kale leaves, destemmed, cut into 2-inch squares - 1 tablespoon olive oil
- 1 tablespoon taco seasoning

Directions:
1. Mix olive oil and taco seasoning in a small bowl.
2. Toss taco seasoning mixture with kale leaves until all leaves are evenly coated.
3. Place kale leaves into the fry basket, then insert the fry basket at mid-position in the Air Fryer Toaster Oven.
4. Select the Dehydrate function, set time to 3 hours and temperature to 140°F, then press Start/Cancel.
5. Remove when done and serve.

Nutrition: Calories 125, Total Fat 7g, Total Carbs 15g, Protein 3g

637. Chili Beef Nachos

Preparation Time: 5 minutes,
Cooking Time: 5 minutes;
Servings: 2-3

Ingredients:
- 1 can chili (15 ounces) - ½ teaspoon cumin
- ¼ teaspoon oregano
- ¼ teaspoon taco seasoning
- A pinch of black pepper
- 1 bag tortilla chips (8 ounces)
- 1 bag Mexican blend shredded cheese (8 ounces)
- Mexican crema, for drizzling

Directions:
1. Combine chili, cumin, oregano, taco seasoning, and black pepper in a microwave-safe bowl.
2. Microwave the chili for 1 minute. Set aside.
3. Insert the wire rack at the top position in the Air Fryer Toaster Oven. Select the Broil function, set timer to 5 minutes, then press Start/Cancel to preheat.
4. Line the broiler pan with foil. Place half of the tortilla chips in the broiler pan, top them with half the chili, and then half the cheese. Repeat this process to add a second Layer of nachos.
5. Place the broiler pan on top of the wire rack in the preheated air fryer toaster oven and press Start/Cancel. Remove when done, drizzle with Mexican crema, and then serve.

Nutrition: Calories 466, Total Fat 37g, Total Carbs 30g, Protein 13g

638. Sausage Potato & Zucchini Skewers

Preparation Time: 10 minutes,
Cooking Time: 24 minutes;
Servings: 2

Ingredients:
- 2 Louisiana hot sausages or Andouille
- sausages, cut into ½-inch-thick slices
- 4 Yukon Gold potatoes, cut into ½-inch thick slices
- ½ zucchini, thinly sliced
- ½ teaspoon lemon pepper
- ½ teaspoon garlic powder
- ½ teaspoon onion powder
- ½ teaspoon black pepper
- ⅛ teaspoon kosher salt
- 1 tablespoon olive oil

Directions:
1. Combine all ingredients in a bowl until fully coated.
2. Skewer sausages, potatoes, and zucchini.
3. Select the Broil function on the Air Fryer Toaster Oven, set time to 24 minutes, then press Start/Cancel to preheat.
4. Set skewers onto the wire rack, then insert the rack at the top position in the preheated air fryer toaster oven. Press Start/Cancel.
5. Flip the skewers after 12 minutes of cook time.
6. Remove when done and serve immediately.

Nutrition: Calories 539, Total Fat 24g, Total Carbs 68g, Protein 11g

639. Salted Maple Pecan Granola

Preparation Time: 5 minutes,
Cooking Time: 40 minutes;
Servings: 4

Ingredients:
- 2 cups old fashioned oats
- 1 cup pecans, chopped
- 2 tablespoons dark brown sugar, packed
- ¾ teaspoon kosher salt
- 1 teaspoon ground cinnamon
- ¼ teaspoon ground nutmeg

- ¼ cup coconut oil, melted
- ½ cup maple syrup
- ½ teaspoon maple extract

Directions:
1. Mix all ingredients in a large bowl until well combined.
2. Line the food tray with parchment paper and spread the granola evenly on top. Set aside.
3. Select the Bake function on the Air Fryer Toaster Oven, set time to 40 minutes, then press Start/Cancel to preheat. Turn the convection fan on high speed for better airflow.
4. Insert the food tray at a low position in the preheated air fryer toaster oven, then press Start/Cancel.
5. Mix the granola every 10 minutes to ensure even baking.
6. Remove granola when done and allow to cool for 1 hour.
7. Break granola into chunks and enjoy immediately, or store in an airtight container for later.

Nutrition: Calories 577, Total Fat 24g, Total Carbs 86g, Protein 14g

640. Bacon-Wrapped Hot Dogs

Preparation Time: 5 minutes,
Cooking Time: 20 minutes;
Servings: 4

Ingredients:
- 4 strips thick-cut bacon
- 4 beef hot dogs
- 4 hot dog buns, slightly toasted

Directions:
1. Wrap 1 piece of bacon around each beef hot dog, allowing the edges of the bacon to overlap slightly. Set aside.
2. Select the Broil function on the Air Fryer Toaster Oven, set time to 20 minutes, then press Start/Cancel to preheat.
3. Line the food tray with foil, then set the wire rack on top of the food tray.
4. Place the bacon-wrapped hot dogs on the wire rack, then insert the rack and food tray at top position in the preheated air fryer toaster oven. Press Start/Cancel.
5. Flip the hot dogs halfway through cooking.
6. Remove when done and place each hot dog in a hot dog bun.
7. Serve with your choice of toppings.

Nutrition: Calories 265, Total Fat 13g, Total Carbs 24g, Protein 13g

641. Double-Baked Stuffed Potato

Preparation Time: 10 minutes,
Cooking Time: 75 minutes;
Servings: 2

Ingredients:
- 2 large russet potatoes
- 2 tablespoons butter
- ½ cup heavy whipping cream
- ¼ teaspoon kosher salt
- ¼ cup sour cream
- ¼ cup shredded cheddar cheese
- 2 slices cooked bacon, cut into bits
- 1 green onion, sliced

Directions:
1. Select the Bake function on the Air Fryer Toaster Oven, set time to 1 hour and temperature to 350°F, then press Start/Cancel to preheat.
2. Place potatoes on the wire rack and insert at mid-position in the preheated air fryer toaster oven. Press Start/Cancel.
3. Remove potatoes and cool for 5 minutes.
4. Make an incision in the middle of the potatoes and carefully scoop out the insides into a large bowl.
5. Add butter, heavy whipping cream, and kosher salt to the bowl and use a fork or masher to mash.
6. Place mashed potatoes back into the potato skins and put back in the air fryer toaster oven. Select the Bake function again, set time to 15 minutes and temperature to 350°F, then press Start/Cancel twice to forgo preheating.
7. Remove potatoes and garnish with sour cream, cheddar cheese, bacon bits, and green onion.
8. Remove when done and serve immediately.

Nutrition: Calories 694, Total Fat 47g, Total Carbs 61g Protein 16g

642. Garlic Bread

Preparation Time: 10 minutes,
Cooking Time: 75 minutes;
Servings: 2

Ingredients:
- Two 6-inch baguettes halved lengthwise
- 3 tablespoons unsalted butter, melted
- 3 cloves garlic, minced
- ¼ teaspoon salt
- 1 teaspoon dried parsley

Directions:
1. Mix melted butter, minced garlic, salt, and parsley.
2. Brush mixture over each baguette half.
3. Place baguettes on the Air Fryer Toaster Oven's wire rack and insert at mid position.
4. Select the Toast function, set to darkness level 6, and press Start/Cancel.
5. Remove when done and serve immediately

Nutrition: Calories 271, Total Fat 17g, Total Carbs 25g, Protein 5g

643. Butter Baked Mussels

Preparation Time: 15 minutes,
Cooking Time: 15 minutes;
Servings: 2

Ingredients
- 15 mussels - 10 grape tomatoes, halved
- ⅓ cup unsalted butter
- ⅛ cup parsley, chopped

- ¼ teaspoon crushed red peppers
- ¼ teaspoon kosher salt

Directions:
1. Soak mussels in cold salted water for 10 minutes.
2. Insert the wire rack at mid-position in the Air Fryer Toaster Oven. Select the Bake function, set timer to 15 minutes, then press Start/Cancel to preheat.
3. Place mussels, tomatoes, butter, parsley, crushed red peppers, and salt in the glass baking dish, then place the dish on top of the wire rack in the preheated air fryer toaster oven. Press Start/Cancel.
4. Remove when done and serve immediately.

Nutrition: Calories 507, Total Fat 35g, Carbs 28g, Protein 20g

644. Air Fried Zucchini Fries

Preparation Time: 15 minutes,
Cooking Time: 20 minutes;
Servings: 2-4

Ingredients
- 1 cup panko breadcrumbs
- ½ teaspoon cumin
- ½ teaspoon garlic powder
- ½ teaspoon onion powder
- ½ teaspoon smoked hot paprika
- ¼ teaspoon white pepper
- ½ teaspoon salt
- 2 eggs
- 2 zucchinis, halved and cut into
- wedges
- ⅓ cup flour
- Nonstick cooking spray
- Yogurt Sauce
- ½ cup yogurt
- ¼ cup sour cream
- ½ lemon, juiced

Directions:
1. Mix together breadcrumbs, cumin, garlic powder, onion powder, smoked hot paprika, white pepper, and salt.
2. Whisk the eggs in a separate dish.
3. Coat each piece of zucchini with flour, then dip in egg, then roll in breadcrumb mixture.
4. Select the Air Fry function on the Air Fryer Toaster Oven, set time to 20 minutes, then press Start/Cancel to preheat.
5. Place the zucchini fries into the fry basket.
6. Spray the zucchini with nonstick cooking spray, then insert the basket at mid-position in the preheated air fryer toaster oven. Press Start/Cancel.
7. Combine the ingredients for the yogurt sauce, then serve with the zucchini fries when done.

Nutrition: Calories 115, Total Fat 3g, Carbs 16g, Protein 6g

645. Blue Cheese Caesar Chicken Wings

Preparation Time: 15 minutes,
Cooking Time: 25 minutes;
Servings: 1-3

Ingredients
- 1½ pounds of chicken wings
- ½ teaspoon
- kosher salt
- 1 tablespoon cornstarch
- 1½ tablespoons Pecorino Romano cheese, shredded
- 1-ounce blue cheese
- ⅓ cup Caesar dressing
- Salt & pepper, to taste

Directions:
1. Select the Air Fry function on the Air Fryer Toaster Oven and press Start/Cancel to preheat.
2. Combine chicken wings, salt, cornstarch, and Pecorino Romano cheese in a bowl and mix well. Place chicken wings into the fry basket, then insert the rack at mid-position in the preheated air fryer toaster oven, then press Start/Cancel.
3. Combine blue cheese and Caesar dressing in a saucepan over medium heat. Cook for 3 minutes or until the blue cheese has melted into the Caesar dressing.
4. Take out the chicken wings when done, then toss the blue cheese dressing and chicken wings together.
5. Garnish with salt and pepper, then serve.

Nutrition: Calories 115, Total Fat 3g, Carbs 16g, Protein 6g

646. Sweet & Spicy Korean Chicken Wings

Preparation Time: 15 minutes,
Cooking Time: 35 minutes;
Servings: 4

Ingredients
- 2 pounds of chicken wings
- 2 tablespoons gochujang paste
- 2 tablespoons sambal chili paste
- ½ cup of water
- 2 tablespoons rice vinegar
- 1 teaspoon sesame oil
- 1 tablespoon fish sauce
- 2 tablespoons dark brown sugar
- 1 tablespoon ginger, grated
- ¼ teaspoon salt
- 1 tablespoon sesame seeds
- 1 green onion, sliced, for garnish

Directions:
1. Select the Air Fry function on the Air Fryer Toaster Oven, set time to 35 minutes, then press Start/Cancel to preheat.
2. Place chicken wings into the fry basket, then insert the basket at mid-position in the preheated air fryer toaster oven. Press Start/Cancel.
3. Combine gochujang paste, sambal chili paste, water, rice vinegar, sesame oil, fish sauce, dark brown sugar, ginger, and salt in a small saucepan and mix together.

4. Set the saucepan over medium-high heat and cook for 8 minutes, or until reduced by half.
5. Take out chicken wings when done, and put in a separate bowl.
6. Pour the sauce over the chicken wings, then toss to make sure they're well coated.
7. Sprinkle sesame seeds and sliced green onions to garnish, then serve.

Nutrition: Calories 483, Total Fat 19g, Carbs 11g, Protein 67g

647. Honey Mustard Chicken Legs

Preparation Time: 20 minutes,
Cooking Time: 35 minutes;
Servings: 3

Ingredients
- 6 chicken legs
- 1 lemon, juiced
- 2 tablespoons stone-ground mustard
- 2 tablespoons honey
- ¼ teaspoon kosher salt
- ¼ teaspoon black pepper

Directions:
1. Soak chicken legs in lemon juice for 15 minutes.
2. Select the Air Fry function on the Air Fryer Toaster Oven, set time to 30 minutes and temperature to 400°F, then press Start/Cancel to preheat.
3. Mix mustard and honey in a small bowl and set aside.
4. Sprinkle salt and pepper on both sides of the chicken legs.
5. Place the chicken legs in the fry basket, then insert the basket at mid-position in the preheated air fryer toaster oven. Press Start/Cancel.
6. Spoon half of the honey mustard mixture over the chicken legs. Set remaining honey mustard aside.
7. Insert the basket back into the air fryer toaster oven at mid position. Select the Air Fry function again, set time to 5 minutes and temperature to 400°F, then press Start/Cancel twice to skip preheating.
8. Allow chicken legs to rest for 5 minutes when done, then serve with the remaining honey mustard sauce.

Nutrition: Calories 497, Total Fat 29g, Carbs 16g, Protein 43g

648. Margherita Pizza

Preparation Time: 75 minutes,
Cooking Time: 15 minutes;
Servings: 4-6

Ingredients
- 12 ounces' pizza dough
- 2 tablespoons olive oil
- ¼ cup pizza sauce or tomato sauce
- 3 ounces' low-moisture mozzarella cheese
- 2 tablespoons grated Parmigiano Reggiano
- 1 teaspoon red pepper flakes
- 2 sprigs basil, for garnish

Directions:
1. Sprinkle flour onto a clean work surface and form the dough into a ball. Place a damp cloth over the dough and let it rest for 1 hour.
2. Insert wire rack at mid-position in the Air Fryer Toaster Oven. Select the Pizza function, then press Start/Cancel to preheat.
3. Pooch down the dough, then shape or roll the dough into a thin circle up to 12 inches in diameter. Transfer the dough onto a pizza pan.
4. Spread the olive oil onto the pizza dough evenly, making sure to brush the edges.
5. Spread pizza sauce evenly onto the dough, leaving a ½-inch border.
6. Sprinkle the mozzarella, Parmigiano Reggiano, and red pepper flakes evenly onto the pizza.
7. Place the pizza on top of the wire rack in the preheated air fryer toaster oven, then press Start/Cancel.
8. Remove pizza when done. Garnish with fresh basil leaves, then serve.

Nutrition: Calories 327, Total Fat 23g, Carbs 25g, Protein 5g

649. Pepperoni Pizza

Preparation Time: 85 minutes,
Cooking Time: 15 minutes;
Servings: 4

Ingredients
- 12 ounces' pizza dough
- 2 tablespoons olive oil
- ¼ cup tomato sauce
- 3 ounces' low-moisture mozzarella
- 2 tablespoons Parmesan, grated
- ¼ teaspoon kosher salt
- 2 ounces' pepperoni, sliced

Directions:
1. Sprinkle flour onto a clean work surface and form the pizza dough into a ball. Place a damp cloth over the dough and let it rest for 1 hour.
2. Punch down the dough, then shape or roll the dough into a thin circle up to 12 inches in diameter. Transfer the dough onto a pizza pan.
3. Spread the olive oil onto the pizza dough evenly, making sure to brush the edges.
4. Spread tomato sauce evenly onto the dough, leaving a ½-inch border.
5. Insert the wire rack at mid-position in the Air Fryer Toaster Oven. Select the Pizza function, set timer to 15 minutes, and press Start/Cancel to preheat.
6. Sprinkle mozzarella, Parmesan, and salt evenly onto the pizza. Top with pepperoni.
7. Place the pizza pan on top of the rack in the preheated air fryer toaster oven, then press Start/Cancel.
8. Remove when done and serve.

Nutrition: Calories 643, Total Fat 47g, Carbs 38g, Protein 17g

650. Avocado Baked Egg

Preparation Time: 5 minutes,
Cooking Time: 22 minutes;
Servings: 2

Ingredients:
- 1 large ripe avocado, halved and pitted
- 2 eggs
- ¼ teaspoon salt
- ¼ teaspoon black pepper
- 2 tablespoons grated Parmesan Cheese Finely chopped chives, for garnish

Directions:
1. Place the avocado halves on the corners of the baking sheet. The lip of the baking sheet will prevent them from rolling over.
2. Scoop out some of the flesh from the avocado halves to make a hole large enough for 1 egg.
3. Crack 1 egg into each of the halved avocados.
4. Season with salt and pepper.
5. Insert the wire rack at mid-position in the Air Fryer Toaster Oven. Select the Air Fry function, set timer to 22 minutes, then press Start/Cancel to preheat.
6. Place the baking sheet on top of the wire rack in the preheated air fryer toaster oven, then press Start/Cancel.
7. Sprinkle Parmesan cheese on the avocado halves after 12 minutes of cook time.
8. Remove the baked avocados when done and garnish with finely chopped chives, then serve.

Nutrition: Calories 377, Total Fat 30g, Total Carbs 12g, Protein 15g

651. Rotisserie Chicken

Preparation Time: 70 minutes,
Cooking Time: 70 minutes;
Servings: 3-5

Ingredients:
- 1 whole chicken (5 pounds)
- 1-gallon water
- ¾ cup kosher salt
- 3 tablespoons black pepper
- 2 bay leaves

Directions:
1. Mix water, salt, black pepper, and bay leaves to make a brine. Submerge the chicken in the brine and let it sit for 1 hour.
2. Pat chicken dry, then truss with butcher's twine to ensure the wings and legs are held together.
3. Insert the rotisserie shaft through the chicken, securing the chicken between the forks. Place the shaft into the designated ports in the Air Fryer Toaster Oven.
4. Select the Rotisserie function, set time to 1 hour 10 minutes and temperature to 380°F, then press Start/Cancel. Turn the convection fan on high speed for better crispness.
5. Remove rotisserie chicken with the rotisserie handle when done. Carve the chicken into desired portions, then serve.

Nutrition: Calories 82, Total Fat 8g, Total Carbs 3g, Protein 18g

652. Rustic Grilled Cheese

Preparation Time: 5 minutes,
Cooking Time: 14 minutes;
Servings: 2

Ingredients:
- 2 slices rustic bread
- 1 tablespoon butter
- ⅛ teaspoon salt
- 1 slice Swiss cheese
- ½ ounce smoked Gouda cheese, shredded
- ½ ounce Parmesan cheese, shredded
- ½ ounce mozzarella cheese, shredded

Directions:
1. Brush butter on both slices of bread and sprinkle salt.
2. Place bread slices on the wire rack. Insert rack at the top position in the Air Fryer Toaster Oven, select the Toast function, and set the darkness level to Press Start/Cancel.
3. Remove bread slices when done. Place all the cheeses on 1 of the bread slices and then top with the other bread slice.
4. Place sandwich on the wire rack in the air fryer toaster oven, select the Toast function again and set the darkness level to Press Start/Cancel.
5. Remove when done and serve immediately

Nutrition: Calories 242, Total Fat 16g, Total Carbs 14g, Protein 14g

653. Chicken Wraps

Preparation Time: 10 minutes
Cooking Time: 12 minutes
Servings: 4

Ingredients
- 2 skinless, boneless cooked chicken breasts, cubed
- 3 tbsp chopped onion
- 3 garlic cloves, peeled and minced
- 3/4 (8 oz.) package cream cheese
- 6 tbsp butter
- 3 (10 oz.) cans refrigerated crescent roll dough

Directions:
1. Heat oil in a skillet and add onion and garlic to sauté until soft.
2. Add cooked chicken, sautéed veggies, butter, and cream cheese to a blender.
3. Blend well until smooth. Spread the crescent dough over a flat surface.
4. Slice the dough into 12 rectangles.
5. Spoon the chicken mixture at the center of each rectangle.
6. Roll the dough to wrap the mixture and form a ball.
7. Divide these balls in the two Air Fryer baskets.

8. Return the Air Fryer Baskets to the Air Fryer.
9. Select the Air Fryer mode for Zone 1 with 390 degrees F temperature and 12 minutes cooking time.
10. Press the MATCH COOK button to copy the settings for Zone
11. Initiate cooking by pressing the START/PAUSE BUTTON.
12. Serve warm.

Nutrition: Calories 153 Total Fat 4 g Saturated Fat 3 g Cholesterol 21 mg Sodium 216 mg Total Carbs 18 g Fiber 3 g Sugar 2 g Protein 22 g

654. Chicken Mushroom Bites

Preparation Time: 10 minutes
Cooking Time: 15 minutes
Servings: 6
Ingredients
- 6 large fresh mushrooms, stems removed

Stuffing:
- ½ cup chicken meat, cubed
- 1 (4 oz.) package cream cheese, softened
- ¼ lb. imitation crabmeat, flaked
- 1 cup butter
- 1 garlic clove, peeled and minced
- Black pepper and salt to taste
- Garlic powder to taste
- Crushed red pepper to taste

Directions:
1. Melt and heat butter in a skillet over medium heat.
2. Add chicken and sauté for 5 minutes.
3. Add in all the remaining ingredients for the stuffing.
4. Cook for 5 minutes then turn off the heat.
5. Allow the mixture to cool. Stuff each mushroom with a tbsp of this mixture.
6. Divide the stuffed mushrooms in the two Air Fryer baskets.
7. Return the Air Fryer Baskets to the Air Fryer.
8. Select the Air Fryer mode for Zone 1 with 375 degrees F temperature and 15 minutes cooking time.
9. Press the MATCH COOK button to copy the settings for Zone
10. Initiate cooking by pressing the START/PAUSE BUTTON.
11. Serve warm.

Nutrition: Calories 129 Total Fat 17 g Saturated Fat 3 g Cholesterol 65 mg Sodium 391 mg Total Carbs 55 g Fiber 6 g Sugar 8 g Protein 14g

655. Potato Tater Tots

Preparation Time: 10 minutes
Cooking Time: 27 minutes
Servings: 4
Ingredients
- 2 potatoes, peeled
- 1/2 tsp Cajun seasoning
- Olive oil cooking spray
- Sea salt to taste

Directions:
1. Boil water in a cooking pot and cook potatoes in it for 15 minutes.
2. Drain and leave the potatoes to cool in a bowl.
3. Grate these potatoes and toss it with Cajun seasoning.
4. Make small tater tots out of this mixture.
5. Divide them in the two Air Fryer baskets and spray them with cooking oil.
6. Return the Air Fryer Baskets to the Air Fryer.
7. Select the Air Fryer mode for Zone 1 with 375 degrees F temperature and 27 minutes cooking time.
8. Press the MATCH COOK button to copy the settings for Zone Initiate cooking by pressing the START/PAUSE BUTTON. Flip them once cooked halfway through, and resume cooking. Serve warm.

Nutrition: Calories 152 Total Fat 14 g Saturated Fat 2 g Cholesterol 65 mg Sodium 220 mg Total Carbs 38 g Fiber 2 g Sugar 1 g Protein 6 g

656. Plantain Chips

Preparation Time: 10 minutes
Cooking Time: 20 minutes
Servings: 2
Ingredients
- 1 green plantain
- 1 tsp canola oil
- 1/2 tsp sea salt

Directions:
1. Peel and cut the plantains into long strips using a mandolin slicer.
2. Grease the Air Fryer basket with a ½ tsp with canola oil.
3. Toss the plantains with salt and remaining canola oil.
4. Divide these plantains in the two Air fryer baskets.
5. Return the Air Fryer Baskets to the Air Fryer.
6. Select the Air Fryer mode for Zone 1 with 350 degrees F temperature and 20 minutes cooking time.
7. Press the MATCH COOK button to copy the settings for Zone
8. Initiate cooking by pressing the START/PAUSE BUTTON.
9. Toss the plantains after 10 minutes and resume cooking.
10. Serve warm.

Nutrition: Calories 218 Total Fat 8 g Saturated Fat 1 g Cholesterol 153mg Sodium 339 mg Total Carbs 8 g Fiber 1 g Sugar 2 g Protein 3 g

657. Crispy Asparagus

Preparation Time: 10 minutes
Cooking Time: 16 minutes
Servings: 4
Ingredients
- 1 bunch of asparagus, trimmed
- Avocado or Olive Oil
- Himalayan salt, to taste
- Black pepper, to taste

Directions:

1. Divide the asparagus in the two Air Fryer baskets.
2. Toss the asparagus with salt, black pepper, and oil.
3. Return the Air Fryer Baskets to the Air Fryer.
4. Select the Air Fryer mode for Zone 1 with 390 degrees F temperature and 16 minutes cooking time.
5. Press the MATCH COOK button to copy the settings for Zone
6. Initiate cooking by pressing the START/PAUSE BUTTON.
7. Serve warm.

Nutrition: Calories 301 Total Fat 18 g Saturated Fat 7 g Cholesterol 75 mg Sodium 189 mg Total Carbs 37 g Fiber 3 g Sugar 1 g Protein 2 g

658. Breaded Ravioli

Preparation Time: 10 minutes
Cooking Time: 15 minutes
Servings: 4

Ingredients
- 1 package ravioli, frozen
- 1 cup bread crumbs
- 1/2 cup parmesan cheese
- 1 tbsp Italian seasoning
- 1 tbsp garlic powder
- 2 eggs, beaten
- Cooking spray

Directions:
1. Toss breadcrumbs with cheese, garlic powder, and Italian seasoning in a bowl.
2. Beat 2 eggs in another bowl and keep them aside.
3. Grease the Air Fryer's basket with cooking spray.
4. Dip ravioli first in egg mixture then coat it in the breadcrumb's mixture.
5. Divide the coated ravioli in the two Air fryer baskets.
6. Return the Air Fryer Baskets to the Air Fryer.
7. Select the Air Fryer mode for Zone 1 with 390 degrees F temperature and 15 minutes cooking time.
8. Press the MATCH COOK button to copy the settings for Zone
9. Initiate cooking by pressing the START/PAUSE BUTTON.
10. Flip the crispy ravioli once cooked halfway through, then resume cooking.
11. Serve warm.

Nutrition: Calories 231 Total Fat 21 g Saturated Fat 4 g Cholesterol 110 mg Sodium 941 mg Total Carbs 31 g Fiber 9 g Sugar 4 g Protein 6 g

659. Beef Enchilada Dip

Preparation Time: 5 minutes,
Cooking Time: 10 minutes,
Servings: 8

Ingredients:
- 2 lbs. ground beef
- ½ onion, chopped fine
- 2 cloves garlic, chopped fine
- 2 cups enchilada sauce
- 2 cups Monterrey Jack cheese, grated
- 2 tbsp. sour cream

Directions:
1. Place rack in position
2. Heat a large skillet over med-high heat. Add beef and cook until it starts to brown. Drain off fat.
3. Stir in onion and garlic and cook until tender, about 3 minutes. Stir in enchilada sauce and transfer mixture to a small casserole dish and top with cheese.
4. Set oven to convection bake on 325°F for 10 minutes. After 5 minutes, add casserole to the oven and bake 3-5 minutes until cheese is melted and mixture is heated through.
5. Serve warm topped with sour cream.

Nutrition: Calories 414, Total Fat 22g, Saturated Fat 10g, Total Carbs 15g, Net Carbs 11g, Protein 39g, Sugar 8g, Fiber 4g, Sodium 1155mg, Potassium 635mg, Phosphorus 385mg

660. Cheesy Stuffed Sliders

Preparation Time: 15 minutes,
Cooking Time: 50 minutes,
Servings: 10

Ingredients:
- 2 tbsp. garlic powder
- 1 ½ tsp salt
- 2 tsp pepper
- 2 lbs. ground beef
- 8 oz. mozzarella slices, cut in 20 small pieces
- 20 potato slider rolls

Directions:
1. Place baking pan in position
2. In a small bowl, combine garlic powder, salt, and pepper.
3. Use 1 ½ tablespoons ground beef per patty. Roll it into a ball and press an indentation in the ball with your thumb.
4. Place a piece of cheese into beef and fold over sides to cover it completely. Flatten to ½-inch thick by 3-inches wide. Season both sides with garlic mixture.
5. Place patties in fryer basket in a single layer and place on the baking pan. Set oven to air fry on 350°F for 10 minutes. Turn patties over halfway through cooking time. Repeat with any remaining patties.
6. Place patties on bottoms of rolls and top with your favorite toppings. Serve immediately.

Nutrition: Calories 402, Total Fat 14g, Saturated Fat 5g, Total Carbs 31g, Net Carbs 29g, Protein 38g, Sugar 3g, Fiber 2g, Sodium 835mg, Potassium 397mg, Phosphorus 400mg

661. Philly Egg Rolls

Preparation Time: 10 minutes,
Cooking Time: 25 minutes,
Servings: 6

Ingredients:
- Nonstick cooking spray
- ½ lb. lean ground beef
- ¼ tsp garlic powder
- ¼ tsp onion powder

- ¼ tsp salt
- ¼ tsp pepper
- ¾ cup green bell pepper, chopped
- ¾ cup onion, chopped
- 2 slices provolone cheese, torn into pieces
- 3 tbsp. cream cheese
- 6 square egg roll wrappers

Directions:
1. Place baking pan in position lightly spray fryer basket with cooking spray.
2. Heat a large skillet over med-high heat. Add beef, garlic powder, onion powder, salt and pepper. Stir to combine.
3. Add in bell pepper and onion and cook, stirring occasionally, until beef is no longer pink and vegetables are tender, about 6-8 minutes.
4. Remove from heat and drain fat. Add provolone and cream cheese and stir until melted and combined. Transfer to a large bowl.
5. Lay egg roll wrappers, one at a time, on a dry work surface. Spoon about 1/3 cup mixture in a row just below the center of the wrapper. Moisten edges with water. Fold the sides in towards the middle and roll up around filling.
6. Place egg rolls, seam side down in fryer basket. Spray lightly with cooking spray. Place the basket in the oven and set to air fry on 400°F for 10 minutes. Cook until golden brown, turning over halfway through cooking time. Serve immediately.

Nutrition: Calories 238, Total Fat 10g, Saturated Fat 5g, Total Carbs 21g, Net Carbs 20g, Protein 16g, Sugar 1g, Fiber 1g, Sodium 412mg, Potassium 206mg, Phosphorus 160mg

662. Mozzarella Cheese Sticks

Preparation Time: 10 minutes,
Cooking Time: 10 minutes,
Servings: 6

Ingredients:
- Nonstick cooking spray
- 12 Mozzarella cheese sticks, halved
- 2 eggs
- ½ cup flour
- 1 ½ cups Italian panko bread crumbs
- ½ cup marinara sauce

Directions:
1. Blot cheese sticks with paper towels to soak up excess moisture.
2. In a shallow dish, beat eggs.
3. Place flour in a separate shallow dish.
4. Place bread crumbs in a third shallow dish.
5. Line a baking sheet with parchment paper.
6. One at a time, dip cheese sticks in egg, then flour, back in egg and finally in bread crumbs. Place on prepared pan. Freeze 1-2 hours until completely frozen.
7. Place baking pan in position 2 of the oven. Lightly spray fryer basket with cooking spray.
8. Place cheese sticks in a single layer in the basket and place in oven. Set to air fry on 375°F for 8 minutes. Cook until nicely browned and crispy, turning over halfway through cooking time. Serve with marinara sauce for dipping.

Nutrition: Calories 199, Total Fat 3g, Saturated Fat 1g, Total Carbs 30g, Net Carbs 28g, Protein 13g, Sugar 3g, Fiber 2g, Sodium 368mg, Potassium 175mg, Phosphorus 220mg

663. Buffalo Quesadillas

Preparation Time: 5 minutes,
Cooking Time: 5 minutes,
Servings: 8

Ingredients:
- Nonstick cooking spray
- 2 cups chicken, cooked & chopped fine
- ½ cup Buffalo wing sauce
- 2 cups Monterey Jack cheese, grated
- ½ cup green onions, sliced thin
- 8 flour tortillas, 8-inch diameter
- ¼ cup blue cheese dressing

Directions:
1. Lightly spray the baking pan with cooking spray.
2. In a medium bowl, add chicken and wing sauce and toss to coat.
3. Place tortillas, one at a time on work surface. Spread ¼ of the chicken mixture over tortilla and sprinkle with cheese and onion. Top with a second tortilla and place on the baking pan.
4. Set oven to broil on 400°F for 8 minutes. After 5 minutes' place baking pan in position Cook quesadillas 2-3 minutes per side until toasted and cheese has melted. Repeat with remaining ingredients.
5. Cut quesadillas in wedges and serve with blue cheese dressing or other dipping sauce.

Nutrition: Calories 376, Total Fat 20g, Saturated Fat 8g, Total Carbs 27g, Net Carbs 26g, Protein 22g, Sugar 2g, Fiber 2g, Sodium 685mg, Potassium 201mg, Phosphorus 301mg

664. Crispy Sausage Bites

Preparation Time: 5 minutes,
Cooking Time: 15 minutes,
Servings: 12

Ingredients:
- Nonstick cooking spray
- 2 lbs. spicy pork sausage
- 1 ½ cups Bisquick
- 4 cups sharp cheddar cheese, grated
- ½ cup onion, diced fine
- 2 tsp pepper
- 2 tsp garlic, diced fine

Directions:
1. Lightly spray baking pan with cooking spray.
2. In a large bowl, combine all ingredients. Form into 1-inch balls and place on baking pan, these will need to be cooked in batches.

3. Set oven to bake on 375°F for 20 minutes. After 5 minutes, place baking pan in position 2 and cook 12-15 minutes or until golden brown. Repeat with remaining sausage bites. Serve immediately.

Nutrition: Calories 432, Total Fat 32g, Saturated Fat 13g, Total Carbs 14g, Net Carbs 14g, Protein 22g, Sugar 1g, Fiber 0g, Sodium 803mg, Potassium 286mg, Phosphorus 298mg

665. Puffed Asparagus Spears

Preparation Time: 20 minutes,
Cooking Time: 10 minutes,
Servings: 10

Ingredients:

- Nonstick cooking spray
- 3 oz. prosciutto, sliced thin & cut in 30 long strips
- 30 asparagus spears, trimmed
- 10 (14 x 9-inch) sheets phyllo dough, thawed

Directions:

1. Place baking pan in position 2 of the oven.
2. Wrap each asparagus spear with a piece of prosciutto, like a barber pole.
3. One at a time, place a sheet of phyllo on a work surface and cut into 3 4 1/2x9-inch rectangles.
4. Place an asparagus spear across a short end and roll up. Place in a single layer in the fryer basket. Spray with cooking spray.
5. Place the basket in the oven and set to air fry on 450°F for 10 minutes. Cook until phyllo is crisp and golden, about 8-10 minutes, turning over halfway through cooking time. Repeat with remaining ingredients. Serve warm.

Nutrition: Calories 74, Total Fat 2g, Saturated Fat 0g, Total Carbs 11g, Net Carbs 10g, Protein 3g, Sugar 0g, Fiber 1g, Sodium 189mg, Potassium 60mg, Phosphorus 33mg

666. Wonton Poppers

Preparation Time: 15 minutes,
Cooking Time: 10 minutes,
Servings: 10

Ingredients:

- Nonstick cooking spray
- 1 package refrigerated square wonton wrappers
- 1 8-ounce package cream cheese, softened
- 3 jalapenos, seeds and ribs removed, finely chopped
- 1/2 cup shredded cheddar cheese

Directions:

1. Place baking pan in position 2 of the oven. Lightly spray fryer basket with cooking spray.
2. In a large bowl, combine all ingredients except the wrappers until combined.
3. Lay wrappers in a single layer on a baking sheet. Spoon a teaspoon of filling in the center. Moisten the edges with water and fold wrappers over filling, pinching edges to seal. Place in a single layer in the basket.
4. Place the basket in the oven and set to air fry on 375°F for 10 minutes. Cook until golden brown and crisp, turning over halfway through cooking time. Repeat with remaining ingredients. Serve immediately.

Nutrition: Calories 287, Total Fat 11g, Saturated Fat 6g, Total Carbs 38g, Net Carbs 37g, Protein 9g, Sugar 1g, Fiber 1g, Sodium 485mg, Potassium 98mg, Phosphorus 104mg

667. Party Pull Apart

Preparation Time: 15 minutes,
Cooking Time: 20 minutes,
Servings: 10

Ingredients:

- 5 cloves garlic
- 1/3 cup fresh parsley
- 2 tbsp. olive oil
- 4 oz. mozzarella cheese, sliced
- 3 tbsp. butter
- 1/8 tsp salt
- 1 loaf sour dough bread

Directions:

1. Place the rack in position 1 of the oven.
2. In a food processor, add garlic, parsley, and oil and pulse until garlic is chopped fine.
3. Stack the mozzarella cheese and cut into 1-inch squares.
4. Heat the butter in a small saucepan over medium heat. Add the garlic mixture and salt and cook 2 minutes, stirring occasionally. Remove from heat.
5. Use a sharp, serrated knife to make 1-inch diagonal cuts across the bread being careful not to cut all the way through.
6. With a spoon, drizzle garlic butter into the cuts in the bread. Stack 3-4 cheese squares and place in each of the cuts.
7. Place the bread on a sheet of foil and fold up the sides. Cut a second piece of foil just big enough to cover the top.
8. Set oven to convection bake on 350°F for 25 minutes. After 5 minutes, place the bread in the oven and bake 10 minutes.
9. Remove the top piece of foil and bake 10 minutes more until the cheese has completely melted. Serve immediately.

Nutrition: Calories 173, Total Fat 7g, Saturated Fat 3g, Total Carbs 18g, Net Carbs 17g, Protein 7g, Sugar 2g, Fiber 1g, Sodium 337mg, Potassium 68mg, Phosphorus 112mg

668. Easy Cheesy Stuffed Mushrooms

Preparation Time: 10 minutes,
Cooking Time: 15 minutes,
Servings: 4

Ingredients:

- Nonstick cooking spray
- 1/3 cup cream cheese, soft
- 1 tbsp. parmesan cheese, grated
- ¼ tsp garlic salt
- 2 tbsp. spinach, thaw, press dry & chop
- 8 oz. mushrooms, rinsed & stems removed

- 1 tbsp. panko bread crumbs

Directions:
1. Lightly spray baking sheet with cooking spray.
2. In a medium bowl, combine cream cheese, parmesan, salt, and spinach, mix well.
3. Place mushrooms on baking sheet and fill with cheese mixture. Sprinkle bread crumbs over top.
4. Set oven to bake on 350°F for 20 minutes. After 5 minutes, place baking pan in position 2 of the oven and cook mushrooms 15 minutes until tops are lightly browned. Serve hot.

Nutrition: Calories 121, Total Fat 7g, Saturated Fat 4g, Total Carbs 8g, Net Carbs 7g, Protein 4g, Sugar 2g, Fiber 1g, Sodium 168mg, Potassium 225mg, Phosphorus 86mg

669. Roasted Peanuts

Preparation Time: 5 minutes
Cooking Time: 14 minutes
Servings: 6

Ingredients:
- 1½ cups raw peanuts
- Nonstick cooking spray

Directions:
1. Press "Power Button" of Air Fry Oven and turn the dial to select the "Air Fry" mode.
2. Press the Time button and again turn the dial to set the cooking time to 14 minutes.
3. Now push the Temp button and rotate the dial to set the temperature at 320 degrees F.
4. Press "Start/Pause" button to start.
5. When the unit beeps to show that it is preheated, open the lid.
6. Arrange the peanuts in "Air Fry Basket" and insert in the oven.
7. Toss the peanuts twice.
8. After 9 minutes of cooking, spray the peanuts with cooking spray.
9. Serve warm.

Nutrition: Calories 207 Total Fat 18 g Saturated Fat 5 g Cholesterol 0 mg Sodium 7 mg Total Carbs 9 g Fiber 1 g Sugar 5 g Protein 4 g

670. Roasted Cashews

Preparation Time: 5 minutes
Cooking Time: 5 minutes
Servings: 6

Ingredients:
- 1½ cups raw cashew nuts
- 1 teaspoon butter, melted
- Salt and freshly ground black pepper, as needed

Directions:
1. In a bowl, mix together all the ingredients.
2. Press "Power Button" of Air Fry Oven and turn the dial to select the "Air Fry" mode.
3. Press the Time button and again turn the dial to set the cooking time to 5 minutes.
4. Now push the Temp button and rotate the dial to set the temperature at 355 degrees F.
5. Press "Start/Pause" button to start.
6. When the unit beeps to show that it is preheated, open the lid.
7. Arrange the cashews in "Air Fry Basket" and insert in the oven.
8. Shake the cashews once halfway through.

Nutrition: Calories 202 Total Fat 15 g Saturated Fat 5 g Cholesterol 2 mg Sodium 37 mg Total Carbs 12 g Fiber 1 g Sugar 7 g Protein 3 g

671. French Fries

Preparation Time: 15 minutes
Cooking Time: 30 minutes
Servings: 4

Ingredients:
- 1 lb. potatoes, peeled and cut into strips
- 3 tablespoons olive oil
- ½ teaspoon onion powder
- ½ teaspoon garlic powder
- 1 teaspoon paprika

Directions:
1. In a large bowl of water, soak the potato strips for about 1 hour.
2. Drain the potato strips well and pat them dry with the paper towels.
3. In a large bowl, add the potato strips and the remaining ingredients and toss to coat well.
4. Press "Power Button" of Air Fry Oven and turn the dial to select the "Air Fry" mode.
5. Press the Time button and again turn the dial to set the cooking time to 30 minutes.
6. Now push the Temp button and rotate the dial to set the temperature at 375 degrees F.
7. Press "Start/Pause" button to start.
8. When the unit beeps to show that it is preheated, open the lid.
9. Arrange the potato fries in "Air Fry Basket" and insert in the oven.
10. Serve warm.

Nutrition: Calories 172 Total Fat 17 g Saturated Fat 5 g Cholesterol 0 mg Sodium 7 mg Total Carbs 16 g Fiber 3 g Sugar 6 g Protein 1 g

672. Spicy Carrot Fries

Preparation Time: 10 minutes
Cooking Time: 12 minutes
Servings: 2

Ingredients:
- 1 large carrot, peeled and cut into sticks
- 1 tablespoon fresh rosemary, chopped finely
- 1 tablespoon olive oil
- ¼ teaspoon cayenne pepper
- Salt and ground black pepper, as required

Directions:
1. In a bowl, add all the ingredients and mix well.
2. Press "Power Button" of Air Fry Oven and turn the dial to select the "Air Fry" mode.

3. Press the Time button and again turn the dial to set the cooking time to 12 minutes.
4. Now push the Temp button and rotate the dial to set the temperature at 390 degrees F.
5. Press "Start/Pause" button to start.
6. When the unit beeps to show that it is preheated, open the lid.

Arrange the carrot fries in "Air Fry Basket" and insert i
7. n the oven.
8. Serve warm.

Nutrition: Calories 81 Total Fat 3 g Saturated Fat 1 g Cholesterol 0 mg Sodium 36 mg Total Carbs 7 g Fiber 7 g Sugar 8 g Protein 4 g

673. Maple Carrot Fries

Preparation Time: 10 minutes
Cooking Time: 12 minutes
Servings: 6

Ingredients:
- 1 lb. carrots, peeled and cut into sticks
- 1 teaspoon maple syrup
- 1 teaspoon olive oil
- ½ teaspoon ground cinnamon
- Salt, to taste

Directions:
1. In a bowl, add all the ingredients and mix well.
2. Press "Power Button" of Air Fry Oven and turn the dial to select the "Air Fry" mode.
3. Press the Time button and again turn the dial to set the cooking time to 12 minutes.
4. Now push the Temp button and rotate the dial to set the temperature at 400 degrees F.
5. Press "Start/Pause" button to start.
6. When the unit beeps to show that it is preheated, open the lid.
7. Arrange the carrot fries in "Air Fry Basket" and insert in the oven.
8. Serve warm.

Nutrition: Calories 41 Total Fat 8 g Saturated Fat 1 g Cholesterol 0 mg Sodium 79 mg Total Carbs 3 g Fiber 2 g Sugar 4 g Protein 6 g

674. Squash Fries

Preparation Time: 10 minutes
Cooking Time: 35 minutes
Servings: 2

Ingredients:
- 14 oz. butternut squash, peeled, seeded and cut into strips
- 2 teaspoons olive oil
- ½ teaspoon ground cinnamon
- ½ teaspoon red chili powder
- ¼ teaspoon garlic salt
- Salt and freshly ground black pepper, as needed

Directions:
1. In a bowl, add all the ingredients and toss to coat well.
2. Press "Power Button" of Air Fry Oven and turn the dial to select the "Air Fry" mode.
3. Press the Time button and again turn the dial to set the cooking time to 30 minutes.
4. Now push the Temp button and rotate the dial to set the temperature at 400 degrees F.
5. Press "Start/Pause" button to start.
6. When the unit beeps to show that it is preheated, open the lid.
7. Arrange the squash fries in "Air Fry Basket" and insert in the oven.
8. Serve warm.

Nutrition: Calories 134 Total Fat 5 g Saturated Fat 7 g Cholesterol 0 mg Sodium 92 mg Total Carbs 23 g Fiber 5 g Sugar 5 g Protein 1 g

675. Dill Pickle Fries

Preparation Time: 15 minutes
Cooking Time: 15 minutes
Servings: 8

Ingredients:
- 1 (16-oz.) jar spicy dill pickle spears, drained and pat dried
- ¾ cup all-purpose flour
- ½ teaspoon paprika
- 1 egg, beaten
- ¼ cup milk
- 1 cup panko breadcrumbs
- Nonstick cooking spray

Directions:
1. In a shallow dish, mix together the flour, and paprika.
2. In a second dish, place the milk and egg and mix well.
3. In a third dish, put the breadcrumbs.
4. Coat the pickle spears with flour mixture, then dip into egg mixture and finally, coat evenly with the breadcrumbs.
5. Now, spray the pickle spears evenly with cooking spray.
6. Press "Power Button" of Air Fry Oven and turn the dial to select the "Air Fry" mode.
7. Press the Time button and again turn the dial to set the cooking time to 15 minutes.
8. Now push the Temp button and rotate the dial to set the temperature at 400 degrees F.
9. Press "Start/Pause" button to start.
10. When the unit beeps to show that it is preheated, open the lid.
11. Arrange the squash fries in "Air Fry Basket" and insert in the oven.
12. Serve warm.
13. Flip the fries once halfway through.
14. Serve warm.

Nutrition: Calories 110 Total Fat 9 g Saturated Fat 7 g Cholesterol 21 mg Sodium 697 mg Total Carbs 18 g Fiber 1 g Sugar 1 g Protein 7 g

676. Mozzarella Sticks

Preparation Time: 15 minutes
Cooking Time: 12 minutes
Servings: 3

Ingredients:
- ¼ cup white flour

- 2 eggs
- 3 tablespoons nonfat milk
- 1 cup plain breadcrumbs
- 1 lb. Mozzarella cheese block cut into 3x½-inch sticks

Directions:
1. In a shallow dish, add the flour.
2. In a second shallow dish, mix together the eggs, and milk.
3. In a third shallow dish, place the breadcrumbs.
4. Coat the Mozzarella sticks with flour, then dip into egg mixture and finally, coat evenly with the breadcrumbs.
5. Press "Power Button" of Air Fry Oven and turn the dial to select the "Air Fry" mode.
6. Press the Time button and again turn the dial to set the cooking time to 12 minutes.
7. Now push the Temp button and rotate the dial to set the temperature at 400 degrees F.
8. Press "Start/Pause" button to start.
9. When the unit beeps to show that it is preheated, open the lid.
10. Arrange the mozzarella sticks in "Air Fry Basket" and insert in the oven.
11. Serve warm

Nutrition: Calories 254 Total Fat 6 g Saturated Fat 4 g Cholesterol 114 mg Sodium 370 mg Total Carbs 32 g Fiber 9 g Sugar 2 g Protein 18 g

677. Apple Chips

Preparation Time: 10 minutes
Cooking Time: 8 minutes
Servings: 2

Ingredients:
- 1 apple, peeled, cored and thinly sliced
- 1 tablespoon sugar
- ½ teaspoon ground cinnamon
- Pinch of ground cardamom
- Pinch of ground ginger
- Pinch of salt

Directions:
1. In a bowl, add all the ingredients and toss to coat well.
2. Press "Power Button" of Air Fry Oven and turn the dial to select the "Air Fry" mode.
3. Press the Time button and again turn the dial to set the cooking time to 8 minutes.
4. Now push the Temp button and rotate the dial to set the temperature at 390 degrees F.
5. Press "Start/Pause" button to start.
6. When the unit beeps to show that it is preheated, open the lid. Arrange the apple chips in "Air Fry Basket" and insert in the oven.

Nutrition: Calories 83 Total Fat 2 g Saturated Fat 0 g Cholesterol 0 mg Sodium 79 mg Total Carbs 22 g Fiber 1 g Sugar 16 g Protein 3 g

678. Beet Chips

Preparation Time: 10 minutes
Cooking Time: 15 minutes
Servings: 6

Ingredients:
- 4 medium beetroots, peeled and thinly sliced
- 2 tablespoons olive oil
- ¼ teaspoon smoked paprika - Salt, to taste

Directions:
1. In a large bowl and mix together all the ingredients.
2. Press "Power Button" of Air Fry Oven and turn the dial to select the "Air Fry" mode.
3. Press the Time button and again turn the dial to set the cooking time to 15 minutes.
4. Now push the Temp button and rotate the dial to set the temperature at 325 degrees F.
5. Press "Start/Pause" button to start.
6. When the unit beeps to show that it is preheated, open the lid. Arrange the apple chips in "Air Fry Basket" and insert in the oven.
7. Toss the beet chips once halfway through.
8. Serve at room temperature.

Nutrition: Calories 70 Total Fat 8 g Saturated Fat 7 g Cholesterol 0mg Sodium 79 mg Total Carbs 7 g Fiber 4 g Sugar 3 g Protein 1 g

679. Potato Chips

Preparation Time: 15 minutes
Cooking Time: 30 minutes
Servings: 6

Ingredients:
- 4 small russet potatoes, thinly sliced
- 1 tablespoon olive oil
- 2 tablespoons fresh rosemary, finely chopped
- ¼ teaspoon salt

Directions:
1. In a large bowl of water, soak the potato slices for about 30 minutes, changing the water once halfway through.
2. Drain the potato slices well and pat them dry with the paper towels.
3. Press "Power Button" of Air Fry Oven and turn the dial to select the "Air Fry" mode.
4. Press the Time button and again turn the dial to set the cooking time to 25 minutes.
5. Now push the Temp button and rotate the dial to set the temperature at 350 degrees F.
6. Press "Start/Pause" button to start.
7. When the unit beeps to show that it is preheated, open the lid.
8. Arrange the potato chips in "Air Fry Basket" and insert in the oven.
9. Toss the potato chips once halfway through.

Nutrition: Calories 102 Total Fat 6 g Saturated Fat 4 g Cholesterol 0 mg Sodium 104 mg Total Carbs 15 g Fiber 2 g Sugar 3 g Protein 2 g

680. Buttered Corn

Preparation Time: 5 minutes
Cooking Time: 20 minutes
Servings: 2

Ingredients:
- 2 corn on the cob

- Salt and freshly ground black pepper, as needed
- 2 tablespoons butter, softened and divided

Directions:
1. Sprinkle the cobs evenly with salt and black pepper.
2. Then, rub with 1 tablespoon of butter.
3. With 1 piece of foil, wrap each cob.
4. Press "Power Button" of Air Fry Oven and turn the dial to select the "Air Fry" mode.
5. Press the Time button and again turn the dial to set the cooking time to 20 minutes.
6. Now push the Temp button and rotate the dial to set the temperature at 320 degrees F.
7. Press "Start/Pause" button to start.
8. When the unit beeps to show that it is preheated, open the lid.
9. Arrange the cobs in "Air Fry Basket" and insert in the oven.
10. Serve warm.

Nutrition: Calories 186 Total Fat 12 g Saturated Fat 4 g Cholesterol 31 mg Sodium 163 mg Total Carbs 21 g Fiber 5 g Sugar 2g Protein 9 g

681. Bread Sticks

Preparation Time: 15 minutes
Cooking Time: 6 minutes
Servings: 6

Ingredients:
- 1 egg
- 1/8 teaspoon ground cinnamon
- Pinch of ground nutmeg
- Pinch of ground cloves
- Salt, to taste
- 2 bread slices
- 1 tablespoon butter, softened
- Nonstick cooking spray
- 1 tablespoon icing sugar

Directions:
1. In a bowl, add the eggs, cinnamon, nutmeg, cloves and salt and beat until well combined.
2. Spread the butter over both sides of the slices evenly.
3. Cut each bread slice into strips.
4. Dip bread strips into egg mixture evenly.
5. Press "Power Button" of Air Fry Oven and turn the dial to select the "Air Fry" mode.
6. Press the Time button and again turn the dial to set the cooking time to 6 minutes.
7. Now push the Temp button and rotate the dial to set the temperature at 355 degrees F.
8. Press "Start/Pause" button to start.
9. When the unit beeps to show that it is preheated, open the lid.
10. Arrange the breadsticks in "Air Fry Basket" and insert in the oven.
11. After 2 minutes of cooking, spray the both sides of the bread strips with cooking spray.
12. Serve immediately with the topping of icing sugar.

Nutrition: Calories 41 Total Fat 8 g Saturated Fat 5 g Cholesterol 32 mg Sodium 72 mg Total Carbs 3 g Fiber 1 g Sugar 5 g Protein 2 g

682. Polenta Sticks

Preparation Time: 15 minutes
Cooking Time: 6 minutes
Servings: 4

Ingredients:
- 1 tablespoon oil
- 2½ cups cooked polenta
- Salt, to taste
- ¼ cup Parmesan cheese

Directions:
1. Place the polenta in a lightly greased baking pan.
2. With a plastic wrap, cover and refrigerate for about 1 hour or until set.
3. Remove from the refrigerator and cut into desired sized slices. Sprinkle with salt.
4. Press "Power Button" of Air Fry Oven and turn the dial to select the "Air Fry" mode.
5. Press the Time button and again turn the dial to set the cooking time to 6 minutes.
6. Now push the Temp button and rotate the dial to set the temperature at 350 degrees F.
7. Press "Start/Pause" button to start.
8. When the unit beeps to show that it is preheated, open the lid. Arrange the pan over the "Wire Rack" and insert in the oven. Top with cheese and serve.

Nutrition: Calories 397 Total Fat 6g Saturated Fat 3 g Cholesterol 4mg Sodium 127 mg Total Carbs 72 g Fiber 5 g Sugar 1 g Protein 1 g

683. Crispy Eggplant Slices

Preparation Time: 15 minutes
Cooking Time: 8 minutes
Servings: 4

Ingredients:
- 1 medium eggplant, peeled and cut into ½-inch round slices
- Salt, as required
- ½ cup all-purpose flour
- 2 eggs, beaten
- 1 cup Italian-style breadcrumbs
- ¼ cup olive oil

Directions:
1. In a colander, add the eggplant slices and sprinkle with salt. Set aside for about 45 minutes.
2. With paper towels, pat dry the eggplant slices.
3. In a shallow dish, place the flour.
4. Crack the eggs in a second dish and beat well.
5. In a third dish, mix together the oil, and breadcrumbs.
6. Coat each eggplant slice with flour, then dip into beaten eggs and finally, coat with the breadcrumbs mixture.
7. Press "Power Button" of Air Fry Oven and turn the dial to select the "Air Fry" mode.
8. Press the Time button and again turn the dial to set the cooking time to 8 minutes.
9. Now push the Temp button and rotate the dial to set the temperature at 390 degrees F.
10. Press "Start/Pause" button to start.

11. When the unit beeps to show that it is preheated, open the lid.
12. Arrange the eggplant slices in "Air Fry Basket" and insert in the oven.
13. Serve warm.

Nutrition: Calories 332 Total Fat 16 g Saturated Fat 8 g Cholesterol 82 mg Sodium 270 mg Total Carbs 33 g Fiber 7 g Sugar 3 g Protein 1 g

684. Simple Cauliflower Poppers

Preparation Time: 10 minutes
Cooking Time: 8 minutes
Servings: 4
Ingredients:
- ½ large head cauliflower, cut into bite-sized florets
- 1 tablespoon olive oil
- Salt and ground black pepper, as required

Directions:
1. In a bowl, add all the ingredients and toss to coat well.
2. Press "Power Button" of Air Fry Oven and turn the dial to select the "Air Fry" mode.
3. Press the Time button and again turn the dial to set the cooking time to 8 minutes.
4. Now push the Temp button and rotate the dial to set the temperature at 390 degrees F.
5. Press "Start/Pause" button to start.
6. When the unit beeps to show that it is preheated, open the lid.
7. Arrange the cauliflower florets in "Air Fry Basket" and insert in the oven.
8. Toss the cauliflower florets once halfway through.
9. Serve warm.

Nutrition: Calories 38 Total Fat 25 g Saturated Fat 5 g Cholesterol 0 mg Sodium 49 mg Total Carbs 8 g Fiber 8 g Sugar 8 g Protein 7 g

685. Crispy Cauliflower Poppers

Preparation Time: 10 minutes
Cooking Time: 20 minutes
Servings: 4
Ingredients:
- 1 egg white
- 1½ tablespoons ketchup
- 1 tablespoon hot sauce
- 1/3 cup panko breadcrumbs
- 2 cups cauliflower florets

Directions:
1. In a shallow bowl, mix together the egg white, ketchup and hot sauce.
2. In another bowl, place the breadcrumbs.
3. Dip the cauliflower florets in ketchup mixture and then coat with the breadcrumbs.
4. Press "Power Button" of Air Fry Oven and turn the dial to select the "Air Fry" mode.
5. Press the Time button and again turn the dial to set the cooking time to 20 minutes.
6. Now push the Temp button and rotate the dial to set the temperature at 320 degrees F.
7. Press "Start/Pause" button to start.
8. When the unit beeps to show that it is preheated, open the lid.
9. Arrange the cauliflower florets in "Air Fry Basket" and insert in the oven.
10. Toss the cauliflower florets once halfway through.
11. Serve warm.

Nutrition: Calories 55 Total Fat 7 g Saturated Fat 3g Cholesterol 0 mg Sodium 181 mg Total Carbs 6 g Fiber 3 g Sugar 6 g Protein 3 g

686. Broccoli Poppers

Preparation Time: 15 minutes
Cooking Time: 10 minutes
Servings: 4
Ingredients:
- 2 tablespoons plain yogurt
- ½ teaspoon red chili powder
- ¼ teaspoon ground cumin
- ¼ teaspoon ground turmeric
- Salt, to taste
- 1 lb. broccoli, cut into small florets
- 2 tablespoons chickpea flour

Directions:
1. In a bowl, mix together the yogurt, and spices.
2. Add the broccoli and coat with marinade generously.
3. Refrigerate for about 20 minutes.
4. Press "Power Button" of Air Fry Oven and turn the dial to select the "Air Fry" mode.
5. Press the Time button and again turn the dial to set the cooking time to 10 minutes.
6. Now push the Temp button and rotate the dial to set the temperature at 400 degrees F.
7. Press "Start/Pause" button to start.
8. When the unit beeps to show that it is preheated, open the lid.
9. Arrange the broccoli florets in "Air Fry Basket" and insert in the oven.
10. Toss the broccoli florets once halfway through.
11. Serve warm.

Nutrition: Calories 69 Total Fat 9 g Saturated Fat 1 g Cholesterol 0 mg Sodium 87 mg Total Carbs 12 g Fiber 2 g Sugar 2 g Protein 9 g

687. Cheesy Broccoli Bites

Preparation Time: 15 minutes
Cooking Time: 12 minutes
Servings: 5
Ingredients:
- 1 cup broccoli florets
- 1 egg, beaten
- ¾ cup cheddar cheese, grated
- 2 tablespoons Parmesan cheese, grated
- ¾ cup panko breadcrumbs
- Salt and freshly ground black pepper, as needed

Directions:
1. In a food processor, add the broccoli and pulse until finely crumbled.
2. In a large bowl, mix together the broccoli, and remaining ingredients.

3. Make small equal-sized balls from the mixture.
4. Press "Power Button" of Air Fry Oven and turn the dial to select the "Air Fry" mode.
5. Press the Time button and again turn the dial to set the cooking time to 12 minutes.
6. Now push the Temp button and rotate the dial to set the temperature at 350 degrees F.
7. Press "Start/Pause" button to start.
8. When the unit beeps to show that it is preheated, open the lid. Arrange the broccoli balls in "Air Fry Basket" and insert in the oven.
9. Serve warm.

Nutrition: Calories 153 Total Fat 2 g Saturated Fat 5g Cholesterol 52 mg Sodium 172 mg Total Carbs 4 g Fiber 5 g Sugar 5 g Protein 1 g

688. Mixed Veggie Bites

Preparation Time: 15 minutes
Cooking Time: 10 minutes
Servings: 5

Ingredients:
- ¾ lb. fresh spinach, blanched, drained and chopped
- ¼ of onion, chopped ½ of carrot, peeled and chopped
- 1 garlic clove, minced
- 1 American cheese slice, cut into tiny pieces
- 1 bread slice, toasted and processed into breadcrumbs
- ½ tablespoon corn flour
- ½ teaspoon red chili flakes
- Salt, as required

Directions:
1. In a bowl, add all the ingredients except breadcrumbs and mix until well combined.
2. Add the breadcrumbs and gently stir to combine.
3. Make 10 equal-sized balls from the mixture.
4. Press "Power Button" of Air Fry Oven and turn the dial to select the "Air Fry" mode.
5. Press the Time button and again turn the dial to set the cooking time to 10 minutes.
6. Now push the Temp button and rotate the dial to set the temperature at 355 degrees F.
7. Press "Start/Pause" button to start.
8. When the unit beeps to show that it is preheated, open the lid.
9. Arrange the veggie balls in "Air Fry Basket" and insert in the oven.
10. Serve warm.

Nutrition: Calories 43 Total Fat 4 g Saturated Fat 7 g Cholesterol 3 mg Sodium 155 mg Total Carbs 6 g Fiber 9 g Sugar 2 g Protein 1 g

689. Risotto Bites

Preparation Time: 15 minutes
Cooking Time: 10 minutes
Servings: 4

Ingredients:
- 1½ cups cooked risotto
- 3 tablespoons Parmesan cheese, grated
- ½ egg, beaten
- 1½ oz. mozzarella cheese, cubed
- 1/3 cup breadcrumbs

Directions:
1. In a bowl, add the risotto, Parmesan and egg and mix until well combined.
2. Make 20 equal-sized balls from the mixture.
3. Insert a mozzarella cube in the center of each ball.
4. With your fingers smooth the risotto mixture to cover the ball.
5. In a shallow dish, place the breadcrumbs.
6. Coat the balls with the breadcrumbs evenly.
7. Press "Power Button" of Air Fry Oven and turn the dial to select the "Air Fry" mode.
8. Press the Time button and again turn the dial to set the cooking time to 10 minutes.
9. Now push the Temp button and rotate the dial to set the temperature at 390 degrees F.
10. Press "Start/Pause" button to start.
11. When the unit beeps to show that it is preheated, open the lid. Arrange the balls in "Air Fry Basket" and insert in the oven. Serve warm.

Nutrition: Calories 340 Total Fat 3 g Saturated Fat 2 g Cholesterol 29 mg Sodium 173 mg Total Carbs 64 g Fiber 3 g Sugar 7 g Protein 13 g

690. Rice Flour Bites

Preparation Time: 15 minutes
Cooking Time: 12 minutes
Servings: 4

Ingredients:
- 6 tablespoons milk
- ½ teaspoon vegetable oil
- ¾ cup rice flour
- 1 oz. Parmesan cheese, shredded

Directions:
1. In a bowl, add milk, flour, oil and cheese and mix until a smooth dough forms.
2. Make small equal-sized balls from the dough.
3. Press "Power Button" of Air Fry Oven and turn the dial to select the "Air Fry" mode.
4. Press the Time button and again turn the dial to set the cooking time to 12 minutes.
5. Now push the Temp button and rotate the dial to set the temperature at 300 degrees F.
6. Press "Start/Pause" button to start.
7. When the unit beeps to show that it is preheated, open the lid.
8. Arrange the balls in "Air Fry Basket" and insert in the oven.
9. Serve warm.

Nutrition: Calories 148 Total Fat 3 g Saturated Fat 5 g Cholesterol 7 mg Sodium 77 mg Total Carbs 21 g Fiber 7 g Sugar 1 g Protein 8 g

691. Potato Croquettes

Preparation Time: 15 minutes
Cooking Time: 8 minutes
Servings: 4

Ingredients:
- 2 medium Russet potatoes, peeled and cubed

- 2 tablespoons all-purpose flour
- ½ cup Parmesan cheese, grated
- 1 egg yolk
- 2 tablespoons chives, minced
- Pinch of ground nutmeg
- Salt and freshly ground black pepper, as needed
- 2 eggs
- ½ cup breadcrumbs
- 2 tablespoons vegetable oil

Directions:
1. In a pan of a boiling water, add the potatoes and cook for about 15 minutes.
2. Drain the potatoes well and transfer into a large bowl.
3. With a potato masher, mash the potatoes and set aside to cool completely.
4. In the bowl of mashed potatoes, add the flour, Parmesan cheese, egg yolk, chives, nutmeg, salt, and black pepper and mix until well combined.
5. Make small equal-sized balls from the mixture.
6. Now, roll each ball into a cylinder shape.
7. In a shallow dish, crack the eggs and beat well.
8. In another dish, mix together the breadcrumbs, and oil.
9. Dip the croquettes in egg mixture and then coat with the breadcrumbs mixture.
10. Press "Power Button" of Air Fry Oven and turn the dial to select the "Air Fry" mode.
11. Press the Time button and again turn the dial to set the cooking time to 8 minutes.
12. Now push the Temp button and rotate the dial to set the temperature at 390 degrees F.
13. Press "Start/Pause" button to start.
14. When the unit beeps to show that it is preheated, open the lid.
15. Arrange the croquettes in "Air Fry Basket" and insert in the oven.
16. Serve warm.

Nutrition: Calories 283 Total Fat 14 g Saturated Fat 8 g Cholesterol 142 mg Sodium 263mg Total Carbs 29 g Fiber 3 g Sugar 3 g Protein 15 g

692. Bacon Croquettes

Preparation Time: 15 minutes
Cooking Time: 8 minutes
Servings: 8

Ingredients:
- 1-pound sharp cheddar cheese block
- 1-pound thin bacon slices
- 1 cup all-purpose flour
- 3 eggs
- 1 cup breadcrumbs
- Salt, as required
- ¼ cup olive oil

Directions:
1. Cut the cheese block into 1-inch rectangular pieces.
2. Wrap 2 bacon slices around 1 piece of cheddar cheese, covering completely.
3. Repeat with the remaining bacon and cheese pieces.
4. Arrange the croquettes in a baking dish and freeze for about 5 minutes.
5. In a shallow dish, place the flour.
6. In a second dish, crack the eggs and beat well.
7. In a third dish, mix together the breadcrumbs, salt, and oil.
8. Coat the croquettes with flour, then dip into beaten eggs and finally, coat with the breadcrumbs mixture.
9. Press "Power Button" of Air Fry Oven and turn the dial to select the "Air Fry" mode.
10. Press the Time button and again turn the dial to set the cooking time to 8 minutes.
11. Now push the Temp button and rotate the dial to set the temperature at 390 degrees F.
12. Press "Start/Pause" button to start.
13. When the unit beeps to show that it is preheated, open the lid.
14. Arrange the croquettes in "Air Fry Basket" and insert in the oven.
15. Serve warm.

Nutrition: Calories 723 Total Fat 53 g Saturated Fat 23 g Cholesterol 183 mg Sodium 1880 mg Total Carbs 23 g Fiber 1 g Sugar 3 g Protein 46 g

693. Chicken & Veggie Nuggets

Preparation Time: 20 minutes
Cooking Time: 10 minutes
Servings: 4

Ingredients:
- ½ of zucchini, roughly chopped
- ½ of carrot, roughly chopped
- 14 oz. chicken breast, cut into chunks
- ½ tablespoon mustard powder
- 1 tablespoon garlic powder
- 1 tablespoon onion powder
- Salt and freshly ground black pepper, as needed
- 1 cup all-purpose flour
- 2 tablespoons milk
- 1 egg
- 1 cup panko breadcrumbs

Directions:
1. In a food processor, add the zucchini, and carrot and pulse until finely chopped.
2. Add the chicken, mustard powder, garlic powder, onion powder, salt, and black pepper and pulse until well combined.
3. In a shallow dish, place the flour.
4. In a second dish, mix together the milk, and egg.
5. In a third dish, put the breadcrumbs.
6. Coat the nuggets with flour, then dip into egg mixture and finally, coat with the breadcrumbs.
7. Press "Power Button" of Air Fry Oven and turn the dial to select the "Air Fry" mode.
8. Press the Time button and again turn the dial to set the cooking time to 10 minutes.
9. Now push the Temp button and rotate the dial to set the temperature at 390 degrees F.
10. Press "Start/Pause" button to start.
11. When the unit beeps to show that it is preheated, open the lid.

12. Arrange the nuggets in "Air Fry Basket" and insert in the oven.
13. Serve warm.

Nutrition: Calories 371 Total Fat 4 g Saturated Fat 3 g Cholesterol 105 mg Sodium 118 mg Total Carbs 34 g Fiber 9 g Sugar 6 g Protein 29 g

694. Cod Nuggets

Preparation Time: 15 minutes
Cooking Time: 8 minutes
Servings: 5

Ingredients:
- 1 cup all-purpose flour
- 2 eggs
- ¾ cup breadcrumbs
- Pinch of salt
- 2 tablespoons olive oil
- 1 lb. cod, cut into 1x2½-inch strips

Directions:
1. In a shallow dish, place the flour.
2. Crack the eggs in a second dish and beat well.
3. In a third dish, mix together the breadcrumbs, salt, and oil.
4. Coat the nuggets with flour, then dip into beaten eggs and finally, coat with the breadcrumbs.
5. Press "Power Button" of Air Fry Oven and turn the dial to select the "Air Fry" mode.
6. Press the Time button and again turn the dial to set the cooking time to 8 minutes.
7. Now push the Temp button and rotate the dial to set the temperature at 390 degrees F.
8. Press "Start/Pause" button to start.
9. When the unit beeps to show that it is preheated, open the lid.
10. Arrange the nuggets in "Air Fry Basket" and insert in the oven.
11. Serve warm.

Nutrition: Calories 323 Total Fat 2 g Saturated Fat 7 g Cholesterol 115 mg Sodium 245 mg Total Carbs 39 g Fiber 4 g Sugar 2 g Protein 27 g

695. Crispy Prawns

Preparation Time: 15 minutes
Cooking Time: 8 minutes
Servings: 4

Ingredients:
- 1 egg - ½ pound nacho chips, crushed
- 12 prawns, peeled and deveined

Directions:
1. In a shallow dish, beat the egg.
2. In another shallow dish, place the crushed nacho chips. Coat the prawn into egg and then roll into nacho chips. Press "Power Button" of Air Fry Oven and turn the dial to select the "Air Fry" mode.
3. Press the Time button and again turn the dial to set the cooking time to 8 minutes.
4. Now push the Temp button and rotate the dial to set the temperature at 355 degrees F.
5. Press "Start/Pause" button to start.
6. When the unit beeps to show that it is preheated, open the lid. Arrange the prawns in "Air Fry Basket" and insert in the oven.
7. Serve immediately.

Nutrition: Calories 386 Total Fat 17 g Saturated Fat 9 g Cholesterol 182 mg Sodium 525 mg Total Carbs 31 g Fiber 6 g Sugar 2 g Protein 21 g

696. Breaded Shrimp

Preparation Time: 20 minutes
Cooking Time: 12 minutes
Servings: 4

Ingredients:
- 8 large shrimp, peeled and deveined
- Salt and ground black pepper, as required
- 8 ounces' coconut milk - ½ cup panko breadcrumbs
- ½ teaspoon cayenne pepper

Directions:
1. In a shallow dish, mix together salt, black pepper and coconut milk.
2. In another shallow dish, mix together breadcrumbs, cayenne pepper, salt and black pepper.
3. Dip the shrimp in coconut milk mixture and then roll into breadcrumbs mixture.
4. Press "Power Button" of Air Fry Oven and turn the dial to select the "Air Fry" mode.
5. Press the Time button and again turn the dial to set the cooking time to 12 minutes.
6. Now push the Temp button and rotate the dial to set the temperature at 350 degrees F.
7. Press "Start/Pause" button to start.
8. When the unit beeps to show that it is preheated, open the lid. Arrange the shrimp in "Air Fry Basket" and insert in the oven. Serve immediately.

Nutrition: Calories 193 Total Fat 17 g Saturated Fat 4 g Cholesterol 23 mg Sodium 74 mg Total Carbs 5 g Fiber 4 g Sugar 9 g Protein 2 g

697. Bacon Wrapped Shrimp

Preparation Time: 15 minutes
Cooking Time: 7 minutes
Servings: 6

Ingredients:
- 1 lb. bacon, sliced thinly
- 1 lb. shrimp, peeled and deveined

Directions:
1. Wrap one slice of bacon around each shrimp completely. Arrange the shrimp in a baking dish and refrigerate for about 20 minutes.
2. Press "Power Button" of Air Fry Oven and turn the dial to select the "Air Fry" mode.
3. Press the Time button and again turn the dial to set the cooking time to 6 minutes. Now push the Temp button and rotate the dial to set the temperature at 390 degrees F. Press "Start/Pause" button to start.
4. When the unit beeps to show that it is preheated, open the lid. Arrange the shrimp in "Air Fry Basket" and insert in the oven. Serve immediately.

Nutrition: Calories 499 Total Fat 39 g Saturated Fat 18 g Cholesterol 242 mg Sodium 1931 mg Total Carbs 2 g Fiber 0 g Sugar 0 g Protein 42 g

698. Mixed Berries Crisp

Preparation Time: 10 minutes
Cooking Time: 12 minutes
Servings: 4
Ingredients:
- ½ cup fresh blueberries
- ½ cup chopped fresh strawberries
- 1/3 cup frozen raspberries, thawed
- 1 tbsp. honey - 1 tbsp. freshly squeezed lemon juice
- ⅔ cup whole-wheat pastry flour
- 3 tbsp. packed brown sugar
- 2 tbsp. unsalted butter, melted

Directions:
1. Place the strawberries, blueberries, and raspberries in a baking pan and drizzle the honey and lemon juice over the top. Combine the pastry flour and brown sugar in a small mixing bowl.
2. Add the butter and whisk until the mixture is crumbly. Scatter the flour mixture on top of the fruit. Place the pan on the Bake position. Set time to 12 minutes.
3. When cooking is complete, the fruit should be bubbly and the topping should be golden brown.

Nutrition:
Calories: 170, Carbs: 8 g, Fat: 6 g, Protein: 16 g.

699. Duck, Fat: Roasted Red Potatoes

Preparation Time: 5 minutes
Cooking Time: 25 minutes
Servings: 4
Ingredients:
- 4 red potatoes, cut into wedges
- 1 tbsp. garlic powder - 2 tbsp. thyme, chopped
- 3 tbsp. duck fat, melted

Directions:
1. Preheat the Air Fryer to 380°F. In a bowl, mix duck, fat, garlic powder, salt, and pepper. Add the potatoes and shake to coat.
2. Place in the basket and bake for 12 minutes, remove the basket, shake and continue cooking for another 8–10 minutes until golden brown. Serve warm topped with thyme.

Nutrition:
Calories: 110, Carbs: 8 g, Fat: 5 g, Protein: 7 g.

700. Chicken Wings with Alfredo Sauce

Preparation Time: 5 minutes
Cooking Time: 20 minutes
Servings: 4
Ingredients:
- 1 ½ lb. chicken wings, pat-dried
- Salt to taste
- ½ cup Alfredo sauce

Directions:
3. Season the wings with salt. Arrange them in the greased Air Fryer basket, without touching, and Air Fry for 12 minutes until no longer pink in the center. Work in batches if needed. Flip them, increase the heat to 390°F and cook for 5 more minutes. Plate the wings and drizzle with Alfredo sauce to serve.

Nutrition:
Calories: 150, Carbs: 7 g, Fat: 5 g, Protein: 14 g.

701. Crispy Squash

Preparation Time: 5 minutes
Cooking Time: 20 minutes
Servings: 4
Ingredients:
- 2 cups butternut squash, cubed
- 2 tbsp. olive oil
- Salt and black pepper to taste
- ¼ tsp. dried thyme
- 1 tbsp. fresh parsley, finely chopped

Directions:
1. In a bowl, add squash, olive oil, salt, pepper, thyme, and toss to coat.
2. Place the squash in the Air Fryer and Air Fry for 14 minutes at 360°F, shaking once or twice. Serve sprinkled with fresh parsley.

Nutrition:
Calories: 100, Carbs: 5 g, Fat: 2 g, Protein: 3 g.

702. Classic French Fries

Preparation Time: 5 minutes
Cooking Time: 30 minutes
Servings: 4
Ingredients: 2 servings

- 2 Russet potatoes, cut into strips
- 2 tbsp. olive oil
- Kosher salt and black pepper to taste
- ½ cup aioli

Directions:

1. Preheat the fryer to 400°F. Coat the Air Fryer basket with cooking spray.
2. In a bowl, brush the strips with olive oil and season with salt and black pepper. Put it in the Air Fryer and cook for 20–22 minutes, turning once halfway through, until crispy. Serve with aioli.

Nutrition:
Calories: 120, Carbs: 7 g, Fat: 4 g, Protein: 6 g.

703. BBQ Chicken

Preparation Time: 5 minutes
Cooking Time: 30 minutes
Servings: 4
Ingredients:

- 1 whole small chicken, cut into pieces
- 1 tsp. salt
- 1 tsp. smoked paprika
- 1 tsp. garlic powder
- 1 cup BBQ sauce

Directions:

1. Mix salt, paprika, and garlic powder and coat the chicken pieces. Place them in the Air Fryer basket and bake for 18 minutes at 400°F. Remove to a plate and brush with barbecue sauce.
2. Wipe the fryer clean from the chicken fat. Return the chicken to the fryer, skin-side up, and bake for 5 more minutes at 340°F.

Nutrition:
Calories: 230, Carbs: 12 g, Fat: 9 g, Protein: 23 g.

704. Turkey Meatballs with Spaghetti Squash

Preparation Time: 15 minutes
Cooking Time: 35 minutes
Servings: 4
Ingredients:

- 1 lb. lean ground turkey
- 1 lb. spaghetti squash, halved and seeds removed
- 2 egg whites
- 1/3 cup green onions, diced fine
- ¼ cup onion, diced fine
- 2 ½ tbsp. flat-leaf parsley diced fine
- 1 tbsp. fresh basil diced fine

What you'll need from the store cupboard:

- 14 oz. can no-salt-added tomatoes, crushed
- 1/3 cup soft whole wheat bread crumbs
- ¼ cup low, Sodium: chicken broth
- 1 tsp. garlic powder
- 1 tsp. thyme
- 1 tsp. oregano
- ½ tsp. red pepper flakes
- ½ tsp. whole fennel seeds

Directions:

1. In a small bowl, combine bread crumbs, onion, garlic, parsley, pepper flakes, thyme, and fennel.
2. In a large bowl, combine turkey and egg whites. Add bread crumb mixture and mix well. Cover and chill for 10 minutes. Heat the oven to broil.
3. Place the squash, cut side down, in a glass baking dish. Add 3–4 tablespoons of water and microwave on high 10–12 minutes, or until fork-tender.
4. Make 20 meatballs from the turkey mixture and place them on a baking sheet. Broil 4–5 minutes, turn and cook 4 more minutes.
5. In a large skillet, combine tomatoes and broth; bring to a simmer over low heat. Add meatballs, oregano, basil, and green onions. Cook, stirring occasionally, 10 minutes or until heated through. Use a fork to scrape the squash into "strands" and arrange it on a serving platter. Top with meatballs and sauce and serve.

Nutrition:
Calories: 253, Total Carbs: 15 g, Net Carbs: 13 g, Protein: 27 g, Fat: 9 g, Sugar: 4 g, Fiber: 2 g.

705. Turkey & Mushroom Casserole

Preparation Time: 15 minutes
Cooking Time: 50 minutes
Servings: 8
Ingredients:

- 1 lb. cremini mushrooms, washed and sliced
- 1 onion, diced
- 6 cup cauliflower, grated
- 4 cup turkey, cooked and cut into bite-size pieces
- 2 cups reduced-fat Mozzarella, grated, divided
- 1 cup fat-free sour cream
- ½ cup lite mayonnaise
- ¼ cup reduced-fat parmesan cheese
- 2 tbsp. olive oil, divided
- 2 tbsp. Dijon mustard
- 1 ½ tsp. thyme
- 1 ½ tsp. poultry seasoning

Directions:

1. Heat oven to 375°F. Grease a 9x13-inch baking dish with cooking spray.
2. In a medium bowl, stir together sour cream, mayonnaise, mustard, ½ teaspoon of each thyme and poultry seasoning, 1 cup of mozzarella, and parmesan cheese.
3. Heat 2 teaspoons of oil in a large skillet over a med-high fire. Add mushrooms and sauté until they start to brown and all liquid is evaporated. Transfer them to the baking dish.

4. Add 2 more teaspoons of oil to the skillet along with the onion and sauté until soft and they start to brown. Add the onions to the mushrooms.
5. Add 2 teaspoons of oil to the skillet with the cauliflower. Cook, stirring frequently, until it starts to get soft, about 3–4 minutes. Add the remaining thyme and poultry seasoning and cook for 1 more minute.
6. Season with salt and pepper and add to baking dish. Place the turkey over the vegetables and stir everything together.
7. Spread the sauce mixture over the top and stir to combine. Sprinkle the remaining mozzarella over the top and bake for 40 minutes, or until bubbly and cheese is golden brown. Let cool for 5 minutes, then cut and serve.

Nutrition:
Calories: 351, Total Carbs: 13 g, Net Carbs: 10 g, Protein: 37 g, Fat: 16 g, Sugar: 5 g, Fiber: 3 g.

706. Prosciutto-Wrapped Asparagus

Preparation Time: 10 minutes
Cooking Time: 12 minutes
Servings: 6
Ingredients:
- 12 spears asparagus, trimmed
- 2 tsp. olive oil
- Salt and freshly ground black pepper, to taste
- 12 prosciutto slices

Directions:
1. Drizzle the asparagus spears with oil and then sprinkle with salt and black pepper.
2. Wrap one prosciutto slice around each asparagus spear from top to bottom.
3. Turn the "Temperature Knob" of the PowerXL Air Fryer Grill to line the temperature to 300°F.
4. Turn the "Function Knob" to settle on "Air Fry."
5. Turn the "timer Knob" to line the time for 10 minutes.
6. After preheating, arrange the asparagus spears into the greased air fry basket.
7. Insert the air fry basket at position 2 of the Air Fryer Grill.
8. Flip the asparagus spears once halfway through.
9. When the cooking time is over, transfer the asparagus spears onto a platter. Serve hot.

Nutrition:
Calories: 144, Fat: 8.7 g, Carbs: 1.9 g, Protein: 16 g.

707. Coconut Shrimp

Preparation Time: 15 minutes
Cooking Time: 8 minutes
Servings: 3
Ingredients:
- ¼ cup almond flour
- ½ tsp. garlic powder, divided
- ½ tsp. paprika, divided
- Salt and freshly ground black pepper, to taste
- 2 large eggs, beaten
- 1 tbsp. unsweetened almond milk
- ½ cup unsweetened flaked coconut
- ¼ cup pork rinds, crushed
- ½ pound large shrimp, peeled and deveined
- Nonstick cooking spray

Directions:
1. Place the flour, half the spices, salt, and black pepper in a shallow dish and blend well.
2. Place the eggs and almond milk in a second shallow dish and beat well.
3. Place the coconut, pork rinds, remaining spices, salt, and black pepper and blend well.
4. Coat shrimp with flour mixture, then the egg mixture and eventually coat with the coconut mixture.
5. Again, dip in the egg mixture and coat with the coconut mixture. Turn the "Temperature Knob" of the PowerXL Air Fryer Grill to line the temperature to 380°F.
6. Turn the "Function Knob" to settle on "Air Fry."
7. Turn the "timer Knob" to line the time for 8 minutes.
8. After preheating, arrange the shrimp into the greased air fry basket. Insert the air fry basket at position 2 of the Air Fryer Grill.
9. Flip the shrimp once halfway through.
10. When the cooking time is over, transfer the shrimp onto a platter. Serve immediately.

Nutrition:
Calories: 234, Fat: 13.8 g, Carbs: 5.9 g, Protein: 20 g.

708. Rice Bites

Preparation Time: 10 minutes
Cooking Time: 10 minutes
Servings: 4
Ingredients:
- 3 cups cooked risotto
- 1/3 cup Parmesan cheese, grated
- 1 egg, beaten
- 3 ounces mozzarella cheese, cubed
- ¾ cup breadcrumbs

Directions:
1. In a bowl, mix the risotto, Parmesan cheese, and egg.
2. Make 20 equal-sized balls from the mixture.
3. Insert a mozzarella cube in the center of every ball.
4. With your fingers, smooth the risotto mixture to hide the mozzarella.
5. In a shallow dish, add the breadcrumbs.
6. Coat the balls with breadcrumbs.
7. Turn the "Temperature Knob" of the PowerXL Air Fryer Grill to line the temperature to 390°F.
8. Turn the "Function Knob" to settle on "Air Fry."
9. Turn the "timer Knob" to line the time for 10 minutes.
10. After preheating, arrange the balls in the Air Fryer basket in a single layer.
11. Insert the Air Fryer basket at position 2 of the Air Fryer Grill.
12. When the cooking time is over, transfer the balls onto a platter.
13. Serve warm.

Nutrition:
Calories: 241, Fat: 5.2 g, Carbs: 36.9 g, Protein: 10 g.

709. Grilled Tomato Salsa

Preparation Time: 15 minutes
Cooking Time: 10 minutes
Servings: 4 to 8

Ingredients:
- 1 onion, sliced
- 1 jalapeño pepper, sliced in half
- 5 tomatoes, sliced
- 2 tbsp. oil
- Salt and pepper to taste
- 1 cup cilantro, trimmed and sliced
- 1 tbsp. lime juice
- 1 tsp. lime zest
- 2 tbsp. ground cumin
- 3 cloves garlic, peeled and sliced

Directions:
1. Coat onion, jalapeño pepper, and tomatoes with oil.
2. Season with salt and pepper.
3. Add grill grate to your PowerXL Grill.
4. Press grill setting.
5. Choose max temperature and set it to 10 minutes.
6. Press Start to preheat.
7. Add vegetables to the grill.
8. Cook for 5 minutes per side.
9. Transfer to a plate and let cool.
10. Add vegetable mixture to a food processor.
11. Stir in the remaining ingredients.
12. Pulse until smooth.

Nutrition:
Calories: 369, Fat: 16 g, Carbohydrates: 37 g, Fiber: 5 g, Protein: 14 g.

710. Parmesan French Fries
Preparation Time: 15 minutes
Cooking Time: 15 minutes
Servings: 6
Ingredients:
- 1 lb. French fries
- ½ cup mayonnaise
- 2 cloves garlic, minced
- 1 tbsp. oil
- Salt and pepper to taste
- 1 tsp. garlic powder
- ½ cup Parmesan cheese, grated
- 1 tsp. lemon juice

Directions:
1. Add a crisper basket to your PowerXL Grill.
2. Select the air fry function.
3. Set it to 375°F for 22 minutes.
4. Press Start to preheat.
5. Add fries to the basket.
6. Cook for 10 minutes.
7. Shake and cook for another 5 minutes.
8. Toss in oil and sprinkle with Parmesan cheese. Mix the remaining ingredients in a bowl. Serve fries with this sauce.

Nutrition:
Calories: 445, Fat: 27 g, Carbohydrates: 25 g, Fiber: 2 g, Protein: 20 g.

711. Fish Sticks
Preparation Time: 15 minutes
Cooking Time: 15 minutes
Servings: 8
Ingredients:
- 16 oz. tilapia fillets, sliced into strips
- 1 cup all-purpose flour
- 2 eggs - 1 ½ cups breadcrumbs
- Salt to taste

Directions:
1. Dip fish strips in flour and then in eggs.
2. Mix breadcrumbs and salt.
3. Coat fish strips with breadcrumbs.
4. Add fish strips to a crisper plate.
5. Place crisper plate inside the basket.
6. Choose Air Fry setting.
7. Cook fish strips at 390°F for 12 to 15 minutes, flipping once halfway through.

Nutrition:
Calories: 324, Fat: 21.5 g, Saturated Fat: 4 g, Trans Fat: 0 g, Carbohydrates: 7.5 g, Fiber: 2 g, Sodium: 274 mg, Protein: 20 g.

712. Homemade Fries
Preparation Time: 15 minutes
Cooking Time: 45 minutes
Servings: 6
Ingredients:
- 1 lb. large potatoes, sliced into strips
- 2 tbsp. vegetable oil
- Salt to taste

Directions:
1. Toss potato strips in oil.
2. Add crisper plate to the Air Fryer basket inside the PowerXL Grill.
3. Choose air fry function. Set it to 390°F for 3 minutes.
4. Press Start to preheat.
5. Add potato strips to the crisper plate.
6. Cook for 25 minutes.
7. Stir and cook for another 20 minutes.

Nutrition:
Calories: 183, Fat: 7.4 g, Carbohydrates: 5.4 g, Fiber: 1 g, Protein: 22.3 g.

713. Fried Garlic Pickles
Preparation Time: 20 minutes
Cooking Time: 15 minutes
Servings: 6
Ingredients:
- ¼ cup all-purpose flour
- Pinch baking powder
- 2 tbsp. water
- Salt to taste
- 20 dill pickle slices
- 2 tbsp. cornstarch
- 1 ½ cups panko bread crumbs
- 2 tsp. garlic powder
- 2 tbsp. canola oil

Directions:
1. In a bowl, combine flour, baking powder, water, and salt.

2. Add more water if the batter is too thick.
3. Put the cornstarch in a second bowl, and mix breadcrumbs and garlic powder in a third bowl.
4. Dip pickles in cornstarch, then in the batter, and finally dredge with breadcrumb mixture.
5. Add crisper plate to the Air Fryer basket inside the PowerXL Grill.
6. Press Air Fry setting.
7. Set it to 360°F for 3 minutes.
8. Press Start to preheat.
9. Add pickles to the crisper plate.
10. Brush with oil. Air fry for 10 minutes.
11. Flip, brush with oil and cook for another 5 minutes.

Nutrition:
Calories: 112, Fat: 4.6 g, Carbohydrates: 18.6 g, Fiber: 2 g, Protein: 1.7 g.

714. Zucchini Strips with Marinara Dip

Preparation Time: 1 hour and 10 minutes
Cooking Time: 30 minutes
Servings: 8
Ingredients:
- 2 zucchinis, sliced into strips
- Salt to taste
- 1 ½ cups all-purpose flour
- 2 eggs, beaten
- 2 cups bread crumbs
- 2 tsp. onion powder
- 1 tbsp. garlic powder
- ¼ cup Parmesan cheese, grated
- ½ cup marinara sauce

Directions:
1. Season zucchini with salt.
2. Let it sit for 15 minutes.
3. Pat dry with paper towels.
4. Add flour to a bowl.
5. Add eggs to another bowl.
6. Mix remaining ingredients except for the marinara sauce in a third bowl.
7. Dip zucchini strips in the first, second, and third bowls.
8. Cover with foil and freeze for 45 minutes.
9. Add crisper plate to the Air Fryer basket inside the PowerXL Grill.
10. Select the air fry function.
11. Preheat to 360°F for 3 minutes.
12. Add zucchini strips to the crisper plate.
13. Air fry for 20 minutes.
14. Flip and cook for another 10 minutes.
15. Serve with marinara dip.

Nutrition:
Calories: 364, Fat: 35 g, Saturated Fat: 17 g, Trans Fat: 0 g, Carbohydrates: 8 g, Fiber: 1.5g, Sodium: 291 mg, Protein: 8 g.

715. Greek Potatoes

Preparation Time: 20 minutes
Cooking Time: 30 minutes
Servings: 4
Ingredients:
- 1 lb. potatoes, sliced into wedges
- 2 tbsp. olive oil
- 1 tsp. paprika
- 2 tsp. dried oregano
- Salt and pepper to taste
- ¼ cup onion, diced
- 2 tbsp. lemon juice
- 1 tomato, diced
- ¼ cup black olives, sliced
- ½ cup feta cheese, crumbled

Directions:
1. Add crisper plate to the Air Fryer basket inside the PowerXL Grill.
2. Choose Air Fry setting.
3. Set it to 390°F.
4. Preheat for 3 minutes.
5. While preheating, toss potatoes in oil.
6. Sprinkle with paprika, oregano, salt, and pepper.
7. Add potatoes to the crisper plate.
8. Air fry for 18 minutes.
9. Toss and cook for another 5 minutes.
10. Add onion and cook for 5 minutes.
11. Transfer to a bowl.
12. Stir in the rest of the ingredients.

Nutrition:
Calories: 368, Fat: 24.2g, Carbohydrates: 21g, Fiber: 4.1g, Protein: 17.6g

716. Ranch Chicken Fingers

Preparation Time: 15 minutes
Cooking Time: 20 minutes
Servings: 4
Ingredients:
- 2 lb. chicken breast fillet, sliced into strips
- 1 tbsp. olive oil
- 1 oz. ranch dressing seasoning mix
- 4 cups breadcrumbs
- Salt to taste

Directions:
1. Coat chicken strips with olive oil.
2. Sprinkle all sides with ranch seasoning.
3. Cover with foil and refrigerate for 1 to 2 hours.
4. In a bowl, mix breadcrumbs and salt.
5. Dredge the chicken strips with seasoned breadcrumbs.
6. Add crisper plate to the Air Fryer basket inside the PowerXL Grill.
7. Choose Air Fry setting.
8. Set it to 390°F.
9. Preheat for 3 minutes.
10. Add chicken strips to the crisper plate.
11. Cook for 15 to 20 minutes, flipping halfway through.

Nutrition:
Calories: 188, Fat: 3.2 g, Carbohydrates: 28.5 g, Fiber: 6.2 g, Protein: 29.4 g.

717. Crunchy Parmesan Asparagus

Preparation Time: 10 minutes
Cooking Time: 10 minutes
Servings: 4

Ingredients:
- ¼ cup all-purpose flour
- Salt to taste
- 2 eggs, beaten
- ¼ cup Parmesan cheese, grated
- ½ cup breadcrumbs
- 1 cup asparagus, trimmed
- Cooking spray

Directions:
1. Mix flour and salt in a bowl.
2. Add eggs to a second bowl.
3. Combine Parmesan cheese and breadcrumbs in a third bowl.
4. Dip asparagus spears in the first, second and third bowls.
5. Spray with oil.
6. Add crisper plate to the Air Fryer basket inside the PowerXL Grill.
7. Set it to Air Fry.
8. Preheat at 390°F for 3 minutes.
9. Add asparagus to the plate.
10. Air fry for 5 minutes per side.

Nutrition:
Calories: 243, Fat: 10.5 g, Saturated Fat: 3 g, Trans Fat: 0 g, Carbohydrates: 10 g, Fiber: 3 g, Sodium: 824 mg, Protein: 35 g.

718. Bacon Bell Peppers

Preparation Time: 10 minutes
Cooking Time: 5 minutes
Servings: 16
Ingredients:
- 1 pack bacon slices
- 12 bell peppers, sliced in half
- 8 oz. cream cheese

Directions:
1. Stuff bell pepper halves with cream cheese.
2. Wrap with bacon slices.
3. Preheat PowerXL Grill to 500°F.
4. Add bell peppers to the grill.
5. Grill for 3 to 5 minutes.

Nutrition:
Calories: 482, Fat: 42 g, Carbohydrates: 14 g, Fiber: 5 g, Protein: 28 g.

719. Corn & Carrot Fritters

Preparation Time: 8 to 10 minutes
Cooking Time: 12 minutes
Servings: 4 to 5
Ingredients:
- 4 ounces canned sweet corn kernels, drained
- 1 tsp. sea salt flakes
- 1 tbsp. cilantro, chopped
- 1 carrot, grated
- 1 yellow onion, finely chopped
- 1 medium-sized egg, whisked
- ¼ cup of self-rising flour
- 1/3 tsp. baking powder
- 2 tbsp. milk
- 1 cup Parmesan cheese, grated
- 1/3 tsp. brown sugar

Directions:
1. Place your Air Fryer on a flat kitchen surface; plug it and turn it on. Set temperature to 350°F and let it preheat for 4–5 minutes.
2. Press the carrot in the colander to remove excess liquid. Arrange the carrot between several sheets of kitchen towels and pat it dry.
3. Then, mix the carrots with the remaining ingredients in a big bowl. Make small balls from the mixture.
4. Gently flatten them with your hand. Spitz the balls with nonstick cooking oil. Add the balls to the basket.
5. Push the air-frying basket in the Air Fryer. Cook for 8–10 minutes. Slide out the basket; serve warm!

Nutrition:
Calories: 274, Fat: 8.3 g, Carbohydrates: 38.8 g, Fiber: 2.3 g, Protein: 15.6 g.

720. Butter Baked Nuts

Preparation Time: 10 minutes
Cooking Time: 15 minutes
Servings: 4
Ingredients:
- 1 cup raw almonds or pistachios
- 1 cup raw peanuts
- 1 tbsp. butter, melted
- ½ cup raw cashew nuts
- Salt to taste

Directions:
1. Take PowerXL multi-cooker, arrange it over a cooking platform, and open the top lid.
2. In the pot, arrange a reversible rack and place the Crisping Basket over the rack.
3. In the basket, add the nuts.
4. Seal the multi-cooker by locking it with the crisping lid; ensure to keep the pressure release valve locked/sealed.
5. Select the "AIR CRISP" mode and adjust the 350°F temperature level. Then, set the timer to 10 minutes and press "STOP/START"; it will start the cooking process by building up pressure inside.
6. When the timer goes off, quick release pressure by adjusting the pressure valve to the VENT.
7. After pressure gets released, open the pressure lid.
8. Add the butter on top and season with some salt; shake well.
9. Seal the multi-cooker by locking it with the crisping lid; ensure to keep the pressure release valve locked/sealed.
10. Select "BAKE/ROAST" mode and adjust the 350°F temperature level. Then, set the timer to 5 minutes and press "STOP/START"; it will start the cooking process by building up inside pressure.
11. When the timer goes off, quick release pressure by adjusting the pressure valve to the VENT. After pressure gets released, open the pressure lid.
12. Serve warm and enjoy!

Nutrition:

Calories: 192, Fat: 16 g, Saturated Fat: 2 g, Trans Fat: 0 g, Carbohydrates: 6.5 g, Fiber: 3 g, Sodium: 64mg, Protein: 7.5 g.

721. Eggs Spinach Side

Preparation Time: 5 minutes
Cooking Time: 12 minutes
Servings: 2 to 3
Ingredients:
- 1 medium-sized tomato, chopped
- 1 tsp. lemon juice - ½ tsp. coarse salt
- 2 tbsp. olive oil - 4 eggs, whisked
- 5 ounces spinach, chopped
- ½ tsp. black pepper
- ½ cup basil, roughly chopped

Directions:
1. Place your Air Fryer on a flat kitchen surface; plug it and turn it on. Set temperature to 280°F and let it preheat for 4–5 minutes.
2. Take out the air-frying basket and gently coat it using olive oil. In a bowl of medium size, thoroughly mix the ingredients except for the basil leaves.
3. Add the mixture to the basket. Push the air-frying basket in the Air Fryer. Cook for 10–12 minutes. Slide out the basket; top with basil and serve warm with sour cream!

Nutrition:
Calories: 272, Fat: 23 g, Carbohydrates: 5.4 g, Fiber: 2 g, Protein: 13.2 g.

722. Squash and Cumin Chili

Preparation Time: 10 minutes
Cooking Time: 25 minutes
Servings: 4
Ingredients:
- 1 medium butternut squash
- 1 tsp. cumin seed
- 1 large pinch of chili flakes
- 1 tbsp. olive oil
- 1 and ½ ounces pine nuts
- 1 small bunch of fresh coriander, chopped

Directions:
1. Take the squash and slice it.
2. Remove seeds and cut them into smaller chunks.
3. Take a bowl and add chunked squash, spice, and oil.
4. Mix well.
5. Preheat your Fryer to 360°F and add the squash to the cooking basket.
6. Roast for 20 minutes. Ensure to shake the basket from time to time to avoid burning.
7. Take a pan and place it over medium heat, add pine nuts to the pan, and dry toast for 2 minutes. Sprinkle nuts on top of the squash and serve.
8. Enjoy!

Nutrition:
Calories: 414, Fat: 15 g, Carbohydrates: 10 g, Protein: 16 g.

723. Fried Up Avocados

Preparation Time: 10 minutes
Cooking Time: 20 minutes
Servings: 6
Ingredients:
- ½ cup almond meal
- ½ tsp. salt
- 1 Hass avocado, peeled, pitted, and sliced
- Aquafaba from one bean can (bean liquid)

Directions:
1. Take a shallow bowl and add almond meal and salt. Pour aquafaba into another bowl. Dredge avocado slices in aquafaba, and then into the crumbs to get a nice coating.
2. Assemble them in a single layer in your Air Fryer cooking basket; don't overlap.
3. Cook for 10 minutes at 390°F, give the basket a shake and cook for 5 minutes more.
4. Serve and enjoy!

Nutrition:
Calories: 356, Fat: 14 g, Carbohydrates: 8 g, Protein: 23 g.

724. Hearty Green Beans

Preparation Time: 5 minutes
Cooking Time: 10 to 15 minutes
Servings: 6
Ingredients:
- 1-pound green beans washed and de-stemmed
- 1 lemon
- Pinch of salt
- ¼ tsp. oil

Directions:
1. Add beans to your Air Fryer cooking basket.
2. Squeeze a few drops of lemon.
3. Season with salt and pepper.
4. Drizzle olive oil on top.
5. Cook for 10–12 minutes at 400°F.
6. Once done, serve and enjoy!

Nutrition:
Calories: 84, Fat: 5 g, Carbohydrates: 7 g, Protein: 2 g.

725. Parmesan Cabbage Wedges

Preparation Time: 5 minutes
Cooking Time: 20 minutes
Servings: 4
Ingredients:
- ½ a head cabbage
- 2 cups parmesan
- 4 tbsp. melted butter
- Salt and pepper to taste

Directions:
1. Preheat your Air Fryer to 380°F.
2. In a container, add melted butter and season with salt and pepper.
3. Cover cabbages with your melted butter.
4. Coat the cabbages with parmesan.
5. Transfer the coated cabbages to your Air Fryer and bake for 20 minutes.
6. Serve with cheesy sauce and enjoy!

Nutrition:
Calories: 108, Fat: 7 g, Carbohydrates: 11 g, Protein: 2 g.

726. Extreme Zucchini Fries

Preparation Time: 10 minutes
Cooking Time: 15 to 20 minutes
Servings: 4
Ingredients:

- 3 medium zucchinis, sliced
- 2 egg whites
- ½ cup seasoned almond meal
- 2 tbsp. grated parmesan cheese
- ¼ tsp. garlic powder

Directions:

1. Preheat your Fryer to 425°F.
2. Take the Air Fryer cooking basket and place a cooling rack.
3. Coat the rack with cooking spray.
4. Take a bowl, add egg whites, beat it well, and season with some pepper and salt.
5. Take another bowl and add garlic powder, cheese, and almond meal
6. Take the Zucchini sticks, dredge them in the egg, and finally breadcrumbs.
7. Transfer the Zucchini to your cooking basket and spray a bit of oil.
8. Bake for 20 minutes and serve with Ranch sauce. Enjoy!

Nutrition:
Calories: 367, Fat: 28 g, Carbohydrates: 5 g, Protein: 4 g.

727. Easy Fried Tomatoes

Preparation Time: 5 minutes
Cooking Time: 10 minutes
Servings: 3
Ingredients:

- 1 green tomato
- ¼ tbsp. Creole seasoning
- Salt and pepper to taste
- ¼ cup almond flour
- ½ cup buttermilk

Directions:

1. Add flour to your plate; take another plate and add buttermilk.
2. Cut tomatoes and season with salt and pepper.
3. Make a mix of Creole seasoning and crumbs.
4. Take tomato slice and cover with flour, place in buttermilk, and then into crumbs.
5. Repeat with all tomatoes.
6. Preheat your fryer to 400°F.
7. Cook the tomato slices for 5 minutes.
8. Serve with basil and enjoy!

Nutrition:
Calories: 166, Fat: 12 g, Carbohydrates: 11 g, Protein: 3 g.

728. Roasted Up Brussels

Preparation Time: 10 minutes
Cooking Time: 15 minutes
Servings: 4
Ingredients:

- 1 block Brussels sprouts
- ½ tsp. garlic
- 2 tsp. olive oil
- ½ tsp. pepper
- Salt as needed

Directions:

1. Preheat your Fryer to 390°F.
2. Remove leaves off the chokes, leaving only the head.
3. Wash and dry the sprouts well.
4. Make a mixture of olive oil, salt, and pepper with garlic.
5. Cover sprouts with the marinade and let them rest for 5 minutes.
6. Transfer coated sprouts to the Air Fryer and cook for 15 minutes.
7. Serve and enjoy!

Nutrition:
Calories: 43, Fat: 2 g, Carbohydrates: 5 g, Protein: 2 g.

729. Roasted Brussels and Pine Nuts

Preparation Time: 10 minutes
Cooking Time: 35 minutes
Servings: 6
Ingredients:

- 15 ounces Brussels sprouts
- 1 tbsp. olive oil
- 1 and ¾ ounces raisins, drained
- Juice of 1 orange
- 1 and ¾ ounces toasted pine nuts

Directions:

1. Take a pot of boiling water, then add sprouts and boil them for 4 minutes.
2. Transfer the sprouts to cold water and drain them well.
3. Place them in a freezer and cool them.
4. Take your raisins and soak them in orange juice for 20 minutes.
5. Warm your Air Fryer to a temperature of 392°F. Take a pan and pour oil, and stir the sprouts.
6. Take the sprouts and transfer them to your Air Fryer. Roast for 15 minutes.
7. Serve the sprouts with pine nuts, orange juice, and raisins!

Nutrition:
Calories: 260, Fat: 20 g, Carbohydrates: 10 g, Protein: 7 g.

730. Low-Calorie Beets Dish

Preparation Time: 10 minutes
Cooking Time: 10 minutes
Servings: 2
Ingredients:

- 4 whole beets
- 1 tbsp. balsamic vinegar
- 1 tbsp. olive oil
- Salt and pepper to taste
- 2 springs rosemary

Directions:

1. Wash your beets and peel them.
2. Cut beets into cubes.
3. Take a bowl and mix in rosemary, pepper, salt, and vinegar.
4. Cover the beets with the sauce.
5. Coat the beets with olive oil.

6. Preheat your Fryer to 400°F.
7. Transfer beets to the Air Fryer cooking basket and cook for 10 minutes.
8. Serve with your cheese sauce and enjoy!

Nutrition:
Calories: 149, Fat: 1 g, Carbohydrates: 5 g, Protein: 30 g.

731. Broccoli and Parmesan Dish
Preparation Time: 5 minutes
Cooking Time: 20 minutes
Servings: 4
Ingredients:
- 1 fresh head broccoli
- 1 tbsp. olive oil
- 1 lemon, juiced
- Salt and pepper to taste
- 1-ounce parmesan cheese, grated

Directions:
1. Wash broccoli thoroughly and cut them into florets.
2. Add the listed ingredients to your broccoli and mix well.
3. Preheat your fryer to 365°F.
4. Air fry broccoli for 20 minutes.
5. Serve and enjoy!

Nutrition:
Calories: 114, Fat: 6 g, Carbohydrates: 10 g, Protein: 7 g.

732. Bacon and Asparagus Spears
Preparation Time: 15 minutes
Cooking Time: 8 minutes
Servings: 4
Ingredients:
- 20 spears asparagus
- 4 bacon slices
- 1 tbsp. olive oil
- 1 tbsp. sesame oil
- 1 garlic clove, crushed

Directions:
1. Warm your Air Fryer to 380°F.
2. Take a small bowl and add oil, crushed garlic, and mix.
3. Separate asparagus into four bunches and wrap them in bacon.
4. Brush wraps with oil and garlic mix and transfer to your Air Fryer basket.
5. Cook for 8 minutes.
6. Serve and enjoy!

Nutrition:
Calories: 175, Fat: 15 g, Carbohydrates: 6 g, Protein: 5 g.

733. Healthy Low Carb Fish Nugget
Preparation Time: 5 minutes
Cooking Time: 10 minutes
Servings: 4
Ingredients:
- 1-pound fresh cod
- 2 tbsp. olive oil
- ½ cup almond flour
- 2 larges finely beaten eggs
- 1–2 cups almond meal

Directions:
1. Preheat your Air Fryer to 388°F.
2. Take a food processor and add olive oil, almond meal, salt, and blend.
3. Take three bowls and add almond flour, almond meal, beaten eggs individually.
4. Take the cods and cut them into slices of 1-inch thickness and 2-inch length.
5. Dredge slices into flour and eggs.
6. Transfer nuggets to the Air Fryer cooking basket and cook for 10 minutes until golden.
7. Serve and enjoy!

Nutrition:
Calories: 196, Fat: 14 g, Carbohydrates: 6 g, Protein: 14 g.

734. Fried Up Pumpkin Seeds
Preparation Time: 10 minutes
Cooking Time: 60 minutes
Servings: 2
Ingredients:
- 1 and ½ cups pumpkin seeds
- Olive oil as needed
- 1 and ½ tsp. salt
- 1 tsp. smoked paprika

Directions:
1. Cut pumpkin and scrape out seeds and flesh.
2. Separate flesh from seeds and rinse the seeds under cold water.
3. Bring two-quarter of salted water to boil and add seeds, boil for 10 minutes.
4. Drain seeds and spread them on a kitchen towel.
5. Dry for 20 minutes.
6. Preheat your fryer to 350°F.
7. Take a bowl and add seeds, smoked paprika, and olive oil.
8. Season with salt and transfer to your Air Fryer cooking basket.
9. Cook for 35 minutes, enjoy it!

Nutrition:
Calories: 237, Fat: 21 g, Carbohydrates: 4 g, Protein: 12 g.

735. Decisive Tiger Shrimp Platter
Preparation Time: 5 minutes
Cooking Time: 10 minutes
Servings: 6
Ingredients:
- 1 ¼ pound tiger shrimp, or a count of about 16 to 20
- ¼ tsp. cayenne pepper
- ½ tsp. old bay seasoning
- ¼ tsp. smoked paprika
- 1 tbsp. olive oil

Directions:
1. Preheat your Fryer to 390°F
2. Take a bowl and add the listed ingredients.
3. Mix well.

4. Transfer the shrimp to your fryer cooking basket and cook for 5 minutes.
5. Remove and serve the shrimp over cauliflower rice if preferred.
6. Enjoy!

Nutrition:
Calories: 251, Carbohydrate: 3 g, Protein: 17 g, Fat: 19 g.

736. Air Fried Olives

Preparation Time: 5 minutes
Cooking Time: 8 minutes
Servings: 4
Ingredients:
- 1 (5½ -ounce / 156-g) jar pitted green olives
- ½ cup all-purpose flour
- Salt and pepper, to taste
- ½ cup bread crumbs
- One egg

Directions:
1. Preheat the Air Fryer oven to 400°F (204°C).
2. Take away the olives from the jar and dry thoroughly with paper towels.
3. In a small bowl, combine the flour with salt and pepper to taste. Place the bread crumbs in another small container. In a third small bowl, beat the egg.
4. Grease the basket with cooking spray.
5. Drench the olives in the flour, then the egg, and then the bread crumbs.
6. Place the breaded olives in the Air Fryer basket. It is okay to stack them. Spray the olives with cooking spray.
7. Place the Air Fryer basket onto the warming pan.
8. Slide into Rack Position 2.

Nutrition:
Calories: 188, Fat: 6.8 g, Carbs: 1.9 g, Protein: 30.3 g.

737. Bacon-Wrapped Dates

Preparation Time: 10 minutes
Cooking Time: 6 minutes
Servings: 6
Ingredients:
- 12 dates, pitted
- Six slices of high-quality bacon, cut in half
- Cooking spray

Directions:
1. Preheat the Air Fryer oven to 360°F (182°C).
2. Cover each date with half a bacon slice and secure with a toothpick.
3. Grease the Air Fryer basket with cooking spray, then place bacon-wrapped dates in the basket.
4. Place the Air Fryer basket onto the baking pan.
5. Slide into Rack Position 2, select Air Fry, set time to 6 minutes, or wait until the bacon is crispy.
6. Remove the dates and allow them to cool on a wire rack for 5 minutes before serving.

Nutrition:
Calories: 246, Protein: 14.4 g, Fiber: 0.6 g, Net Carbohydrates: 2.0 g, Fat: 17.9 g, Sodium: 625 mg, Carbohydrates: 2.6 g.

738. Bacon-Wrapped Shrimp and Jalapeño

Preparation Time: 20 minutes
Cooking Time: 13 minutes
Servings: 8
Ingredients:
- 24 large shrimp, peeled and deveined, about ¾ pound (340 g)
- Five tbsp. barbecue sauce, divided
- 12 strips bacon, cut in half
- 24 small pickled jalapeño slices

Directions:
1. Toss together the shrimp and three tablespoons of the barbecue sauce. Let it stand for 15 minutes. Soak 24 wooden toothpicks in water for 10 minutes. Wrap 1-piece bacon around the shrimp and jalapeño slice, then secure with a toothpick.
2. Preheat the Air Fryer oven to 350°F (177°C).
3. Position the shrimp in the Air Fryer basket, spacing them ½ inch apart.
4. Place the Air Fryer basket onto the baking pan.
5. Slide into Rack Position 2, select Air Fry, and time to 10 minutes.
6. Turn shrimp over with tongs and air fry for 3 minutes more, or until bacon is golden brown and shrimp are cooked through.
7. Brush with the remaining barbecue sauce and serve.

Nutrition:
Calories: 246, Protein: 14.4 g, Fiber: 0.6 g, Net Carbohydrates: 2.0 g, Fat: 17.9 g, Sodium: 625 mg, Carbohydrates: 2.6 g.

739. Breaded Artichoke Hearts

Preparation Time: 5 minutes
Cooking Time: 8 minutes
Servings: 14
Ingredients:
- 14 whole artichoke hearts, packed in water
- One egg
- ½ cup all-purpose flour
- 1/3 cup panko bread crumbs
- One tsp. Italian seasoning

Directions:
1. Preheat the Air Fryer oven to 380°F (193°C).
2. Squeeze excess water from the artichoke hearts and place them on paper towels to dry.
3. In a small bowl, beat the egg.
4. In another small bowl, place the flour.
5. In a third small bowl, blend the bread crumbs and Italian seasoning; stir.
6. Spritz the Air Fryer basket with cooking spray.
7. Drench the artichoke hearts in the flour, then the egg, and then the bread crumb mixture.
8. Place the breaded artichoke hearts in the Air Fryer basket. Coat them with cooking spray.
9. Place the Air Fryer basket onto the baking pan.

Nutrition:
Calories: 149, Fat: 1 g, Carbohydrates: 5 g, Protein: 30 g.

740. Bruschetta with Basil Pesto

Preparation Time: 10 minutes
Cooking Time: 5 to 7 minutes
Servings: 4
Ingredients:
- 8 slices French bread, ½ inch thick
- 2 tbsp. softened butter
- 1 cup shredded Mozzarella cheese
- ½ cup basil pesto
- 1 cup chopped grape tomatoes

Directions:
1. Preheat the Air Fryer oven to 350°F (177°C).
2. Spread the bread with the butter and put it butter-side up in a baking pan.
3. Slide the baking pan into Rack Position 1, select Convection Bake, set time to 4 minutes, or wait until the bread is light golden brown.
4. Remove the bread from the oven and top each piece with some of the cheese.
5. Back to the oven and bake for 1 to 3 minutes more, or until the cheese melts.
6. In the meantime, combine the pesto, tomatoes, and green onions in a small bowl.

Nutrition:
Calories: 251, Carbohydrate: 3 g, Protein: 17 g, Fat: 19 g.

741. Cajun Zucchini Chips

Preparation Time: 5 minutes
Cooking Time: 16 minutes
Servings: 4
Ingredients:
- 2 large zucchinis, cut into 1/8-inch-thick slices
- 2 tsp. Cajun seasoning
- Cooking spray

Directions:
1. Preheat the Air Fryer oven to 370°F (188°C).
2. Grease the Air Fryer basket lightly with cooking spray.
3. Put the zucchini slices in a medium bowl and coat them generously with cooking spray.
4. Sprinkle the Cajun seasoning over the zucchini and stir to make sure they are evenly coated with oil and seasoning.
5. Position the slices in a single layer in the Air Fryer basket, making sure not to overcrowd.
6. Place the Air Fryer basket onto the baking pan.
7. Slide into Rack Position 2
8. Select Air Fry and set the time to 8 minutes.

Nutrition:
Calories: 367, Fat: 28 g, Carbohydrates: 5 g, Protein: 4 g.

742. Cheesy Apple Roll-Ups

Preparation Time: 5 minutes
Cooking Time: 5 minutes
Servings: 8
Ingredients:
- 8 slices whole-wheat sandwich bread
- 4 ounces (113 g) Colby Jack cheese, grated
- ½ small apple, chopped
- 2 tbsp. butter, melted

Directions:
1. Preheat the Air Fryer oven to 390°F (199°C).
2. Take away the crusts from the bread and flatten the slices with a rolling pin. Don't be gentle. Press hard so that the bread will be fragile.
3. Top bread slices with cheese and chopped apple, dividing the ingredients evenly.
4. Roll up each slice tightly and secure each with one or two toothpicks.
5. Brush outside of rolls with melted butter. Place them in the Air Fryer basket.
6. Place the Air Fryer basket onto the baking pan.

Nutrition:
Calories: 147, Fat: 9.5 g, Carbohydrates: 13.8 g, Sugar: 2.1 g, Protein: 1.9 g, Sodium: 62mg.

743. Cheesy Jalapeño Poppers

Preparation Time: 5 minutes
Cooking Time: 10 minutes
Servings: 4
Ingredients:
- 8 jalapeño peppers
- ½ cup whipped cream cheese
- ¼ cup shredded Cheddar cheese

Directions:
1. Preheat the Air Fryer oven to 360°F (182°C).
2. Use a paring knife to carefully cut off the jalapeño tops, then scoop out the ribs and seeds. Set aside.
3. In a medium bowl, combine the whipped cream cheese and shredded Cheddar cheese. Place the mixture in a sealable plastic bag, and using a pair of scissors, cut off one corner from the bag. Gently squeeze some cream cheese mixture into each pepper until almost full.
4. Place a piece of parchment paper on the bottom of the Air Fryer basket and place the poppers on top, distributing evenly.
5. Place the Air Fryer basket onto the baking pan.

Nutrition:
Calories: 456, Fat: 60 g, Carbohydrates: 7 g, Protein: 15 g.

744. Cheesy Steak Fries

Preparation Time: 5 minutes
Cooking Time: 20 minutes
Servings: 5
Ingredients:
- 1 (28-ounce / 794-g) bag frozen steak fries
- Cooking spray
- ½ cup beef gravy
- 1 cup shredded Mozzarella cheese
- 2 scallions, green parts only, chopped

Directions:
1. Preheat the Air Fryer oven to 400°F (204°C).
2. Place the frozen steak fries in the Air Fryer basket.
3. Place the Air Fryer basket onto the baking pan.
4. Slide into Rack Position 2, select Air Fry, and time to 10 minutes.

5. Shake the basket and spritz the fries with cooking spray. Sprinkle with salt and pepper. Air fry for an additional 8 minutes.
6. Pour the beef gravy into a medium, microwave-safe bowl. Microwave for 30 seconds, or until the sauce is warm.

Nutrition:
Calories: 1536, Fat: 123.7 g, Protein: 103.4 g.

745. Crispy Breaded Beef Cubes

Preparation Time: 10 minutes
Cooking Time: 8 minutes
Servings: 4
Ingredients:
- 1-pound (454 g) sirloin tip, cut into 1-inch cubes
- 1 cup cheese pasta sauce
- 1½ cups soft bread crumbs
- 2 tbsp. olive oil
- ½ tsp. dried marjoram

Directions:
1. Preheat the Air Fryer oven to 360°F (182°C).
2. In a medium container, toss the beef with the pasta sauce to coat.
3. In a shallow bowl, blend the bread crumbs, oil, and marjoram; stir completely. Put the beef cubes, one at a time, into the bread crumb mixture to coat methodically. Transfer the beef to the Air Fryer basket.
4. Place the Air Fryer basket onto the baking pan.
5. Slide into Rack Position 2, select Air Fry, set time to 8 minutes, or until the beef is at least 145°F (63°C), and the outside is crisp and brown. Shake the basket once during cooking time.
6. Serve hot.

Nutrition:
Calories: 262, Total Fat: 9.4 g, Carbs: 8.2 g, Protein: 16.2 g.

746. Coriander Artichokes

Preparation Time: 5 minutes
Cooking Time: 20 minutes
Servings: 4
Ingredients:
- 12 oz. artichoke hearts
- 1 tbsp. lemon juice
- 1 tsp. coriander, ground
- ½ tsp. cumin seeds
- ½ tsp. olive oil

Directions:
1. Mix all the ingredients, toss.
2. Introduce the pan in the fryer and cook at 370°F for 15 minutes.
3. Divide the mix between plates and serve as a side dish.

Nutrition:
Calories: 200, Fat: 7 g, Fiber: 2 g, Carbs: 5 g, Protein: 8 g.

747. Spinach and Artichokes Sauté

Preparation Time: 5 minutes
Cooking Time: 20 minutes
Servings: 4
Ingredients:
- 10 oz. artichoke hearts; halved
- 2 cups baby spinach
- Three garlic cloves
- ¼ cup veggie stock - 2 tsp. lime juice
- Salt and black pepper to taste.

Directions:
1. Mix all the ingredients, toss, introduce in the fryer and cook at 370°F for 15 minutes
2. Divide between plates and serve.

Nutrition:
Calories: 209, Fat: 6 g, Fiber: 2 g, Carbs: 4 g, Protein: 8 g.

748. Green Beans

Preparation Time: 5 minutes
Cooking Time: 25 minutes
Servings: 4
Ingredients:
- 6 cups green beans; trimmed
- 1 tbsp. hot paprika
- 2 tbsp. olive oil
- A pinch of salt and black pepper

Directions:
1. Take a bowl and mix the green beans with the other ingredients, toss, put them in the Air Fryer's basket and cook at 370°F for 20 minutes
2. Divide among plates and serve as a side dish.

Nutrition:
Calories: 120, Fat: 5 g, Fiber: 1 g, Carbs: 4 g, Protein: 2 g.

749. Bok Choy and Butter Sauce

Preparation Time: 5 minutes
Cooking Time: 20 minutes
Servings: 4
Ingredients:
- Two bok choy heads; trimmed and cut into strips
- 1 tbsp. butter; melted
- 2 tbsp. chicken stock
- 1 tsp. lemon juice
- 1 tbsp. olive oil

Directions:
1. Mix all the ingredients, toss, introduce the pan to the Air Fryer, and then cook at 380°F for 15 minutes.
2. Split between plates and serve as a side dish.

Nutrition:
Calories: 141, Fat: 3 g, Fiber: 2 g, Carbs: 4 g, Protein: 3 g.

750. Turmeric Mushroom

Preparation Time: 5 minutes
Cooking Time: 20 minutes
Servings: 4
Ingredients:
- 1 lb. brown mushrooms
- 4 garlic cloves; minced
- ¼ tsp. cinnamon powder
- 1 tsp. olive oil
- ½ tsp. turmeric powder

Directions:
1. Mix all the ingredients and toss.
2. Put the mushrooms in your Air Fryer's basket and cook at 370°F for 15 minutes.
3. Divide the mix between plates and serve as a side dish.

Nutrition:
Calories: 208, Fat: 7 g, Fiber: 3 g, Carbs: 5 g, Protein: 7 g.

751. Creamy Fennel

Preparation Time: 5 minutes
Cooking Time: 17 minutes
Servings: 4
Ingredients:
- 2 big fennel bulbs; sliced
- ½ cup coconut cream
- 2 tbsp. butter; melted
- Salt and black pepper to taste.

Directions:
1. In a pan that fits the Air Fryer, combine all the ingredients, toss, introduce in the machine and cook at 370°F for 12 minutes.
2. Divide between plates and serve as a side dish.

Nutrition:
Calories: 151, Fat: 3 g, Fiber: 2 g, Carbs: 4 g, Protein: 6 g.

752. Air Fried Green Tomatoes

Preparation Time: 5 minutes
Cooking Time: 8 minutes
Servings: 4
Ingredients:
- 2 medium green tomatoes
- 1/3 cup grated Parmesan cheese.
- ¼ cup blanched finely ground almond flour.
- One large egg.

Directions:
1. Cut the tomatoes into ½-inch-thick slices. In a medium bowl, whisk the egg. In a large bowl, mix the almond flour and Parmesan.
2. Dip each tomato slice into the egg, then scour in the almond flour mixture. Put the slices into the Air Fryer basket.
3. Adjust the temperature to 400°F and set the timer for 7 minutes. Flip the slices midway over the cooking time. Serve immediately.

Nutrition:
Calories: 106, Protein: 6.2 g, Fiber: 1.4 g, Fat: 6.7 g, Carbs: 5.9 g.

753. Seasoned Potato Wedges

Preparation Time: 10 minutes
Cooking Time: 20 minutes
Servings: 4
Ingredients:
- 4 russet potatoes
- 1 tbsp. bacon fat
- 1 tsp. paprika
- 1 tsp. chili powder
- 1 tsp. salt

Directions:
1. Wash potatoes and portion them into eight slices.
2. Warm bacon fat in the microwave for 10 seconds.
3. Combine all of your dry seasonings in a bowl and toss to mix.
4. Add bacon fat to the bowl and stir.
5. Toss the wedges in the bowl and transfer them to the basket.
6. Cook for 20 minutes, tossing halfway through.

Nutrition:
Calories: 171, Sodium: 684 mg, Dietary Fiber: 5.6 g, Fat: 1.9 g, Carbs: 34.3 g, Protein: 5.1 g.

754. Honey Roasted Carrots

Preparation Time: 5 minutes
Cooking Time: 10 minutes
Servings: 4
Ingredients:
- 1 tbsp. olive oil
- 3 cups baby carrots
- 1 tbsp. honey
- salt and pepper to taste

Directions:
1. In a container, put the carrots, then using oil and honey, drizzle it.
2. Sprinkle on salt and pepper, then using a wooden spoon, blend it entirely.
3. Put the carrots in the basket, then cook at 400°F or 10 minutes.
4. For best results, serve immediately.

Nutrition:
Calories: 83, Sodium: 74 mg, Dietary Fiber: 2.5 g, Fat: 3.5 g, Carbs: 13 g, Protein: 1.3 g.

755. Onion Rings

Preparation Time: 7 minutes
Cooking Time: 7 minutes
Servings: 4
Ingredients:
- 1 tsp. baking powder
- 1 cup panko breadcrumbs
- 2 eggs
- 1 large Vidalia onion
- 1 cup all-purpose flour

Directions:
1. Peel, core, and cut the onion into rings.
2. Combine the flour, salt, and baking powder in a bag and shake well to combine.
3. Add the onions to the bag and toss to coat.
4. Beat the eggs in a shallow bowl.
5. Spread the panko crumbs over a plate.
6. Remove one ring at a time, shake off any extra flour, dip in the egg, and then dredge through the bread crumb.
7. Add 5 to 7 rings to the fryer and cook at 400°F or 7 minutes.
8. Flip the rings halfway through and serve hot.

Nutrition:
Calories: 186, Sodium: 615 mg, Dietary Fiber: 1.8 g, Fat: 2.6 g, Carbs: 33.3 g, Protein: 7.1 g.

756. Chicken Kebab

Preparation Time: 15 minutes
Cooking Time: 15 minutes
Servings: 6
Ingredients:
- 1.5 lb. boneless chicken breast cut into large, bite-sized pieces
- ½ tsp. smoked paprika
- 1 tsp. turmeric
- ½ tsp. ground black pepper
- ¼ cup plain Greek yogurt

Directions:
1. Place chicken into a large bowl.
2. Place Greek yogurt, smoked paprika, black pepper, and turmeric in a small blender container and process till you get a smooth mixture.
3. Pour the blend over the chicken and coat it evenly.
4. Allow the chicken to marinate for 15 minutes.
5. Put the chicken inside the basket of the Air Fryer.
6. Set the Air Fryer to 370°F and cook for 15 minutes.
7. After 8 minutes, flip the chicken over and continue cooking.
8. Once done, let it sit for several minutes and serve.

Nutrition:
Calories: 150, Fats: 2 g, Protein: 20 g, Carbs: 0.5 g.

757. Mac and Cheese Balls

Preparation Time: 20 minutes
Cooking Time: 25 minutes
Servings: 6
Ingredients:
- ½ shredded pound mozzarella cheese
- 2 eggs
- 3 cup seasoned panko breadcrumbs
- Salt
- 2 tbsp. all-purpose flour
- 1 lb. grated cheddar cheese
- 1 lb. elbow macaroni
- 2 cup heated cream
- Pepper
- 2 tbsp. unsalted butter
- 2 tbsp. egg wash
- ½ lb. shredded parmesan cheese

Directions:
1. Prepare the macaroni to the directions on the package.
2. Rinse with cold water and drain. Transfer to a bowl and set it aside.
3. Melt butter in a saucepan over medium flame. Add flour and whisk for a couple of minutes. Stir the heated cream until there are no more lumps. Cook until thick. Remove from the stove. Stir in the cheeses until melted. Season with salt and pepper.
4. Top the cheese mixture onto the cooked macaroni. Gently fold until combined. Transfer to a shallow pan and refrigerate for 2 hours.
5. Use your hands to form meatball-sized balls from the mixture. Arrange them in a tray lined with wax paper. Freeze overnight.
6. Prepare the egg wash by combining 2 tablespoons of cream and eggs in a shallow bowl.
7. Dip the frozen mac and cheese balls in the egg wash and coat them with panko breadcrumbs. Gently press to make the coating stick.
8. Arrange them in the cooking basket. Cook for 8 minutes at 400°F.

Nutrition:
Calories: 907, Fat: 423 g, Carbs: 874 g, Protein: 499 g.

758. Cauliflower Fritters

Preparation Time: 2 minutes
Cooking Time: 13 minutes
Servings: 4
Ingredients:
- 4 cups. cauliflower florets
- 1 cup bread crumbs
- 1 tsp. salt
- ¼ cup butter, melted.
- ¼ cup buffalo sauce

Directions:
1. Twitch by melting the butter in the microwave for 10 seconds.
2. Add the buffalo sauce into the butter and whisk well.
3. Hold each cauliflower by its stem and dip it into the mixture.
4. Next, coat the cauliflower into the bread crumbs.
5. Place the coated cauliflowers into the Air Fryer.
6. Cook at 400°F for 12 minutes.
7. After 7 minutes, toss the cauliflowers and cook for another 6 minutes.
8. Once done, serve hot and enjoy or with your favorite dip.

Nutrition:
Calories: 80, Fats: 6 g, Protein: 6 g, Carbs: 1 g.

759. Loaded Tater Tot Bites

Preparation Time: 5 minutes
Cooking Time: 20 minutes
Servings: 6
Ingredients:
- 24 tater tots, frozen
- 1 cup Swiss cheese, grated
- Six tbsp. Canadian bacon, cooked and chopped
- ¼ cup Ranch dressing

Directions:
1. Spritz the silicone muffin cups with non-stick cooking spray. Now, press the tater tots down into each cup.
2. Divide the cheese, bacon, and Ranch dressing between tater tot cups.
3. Cook in the preheated Air Fryer at 395° for 10 minutes. Serve in paper cake cups. Bon appétit!

Nutrition:
Calories: 164, Fat: 7 g, Carbs: 2 g, Protein: 3 g, Sugar: 8 g.

760. Italian-Style Tomato-Parmesan Crisps

Preparation Time: 5 minutes
Cooking Time: 20 minutes
Servings: 4
Ingredients:
- 4 Roma tomatoes, sliced
- Two tbsp. olive oil
- Sea salt and white pepper, to taste
- One tsp. Italian seasoning mix
- Four tbsp. Parmesan cheese, grated

Directions:
1. Begin by preheating your Air Fryer, then set it to 350°F. Generously grease the Air Fryer basket with nonstick cooking oil.
2. Toss the sliced tomatoes with the remaining ingredient. Transfer them to the cooking basket without overlapping.
3. Cook in the warmed Air Fryer for 5 minutes. Shake the cooking basket and cook for an additional 5 minutes. Work in batches.
4. Serve with Mediterranean aioli for dipping, if desired. Bon appétit!

Nutrition:
Calories: 90, Fat: 2 g, Carbs: 7 g, Protein: 8 g, Sugar: 1 g.

761. Baked Cheese Crisps

Preparation Time: 5 minutes
Cooking Time: 15 minutes
Servings: 4
Ingredients:
- ½ cup Parmesan cheese, shredded
- 1 cup Cheddar cheese, shredded
- One tsp. Italian seasoning
- ½ cup marinara sauce

Directions:
1. Begin by preheating your Air Fryer and set it to 350°F. Place a piece of parchment paper in the cooking basket.
2. Mix the cheese with the Italian seasoning.
3. Add around one tablespoon of the cheese mixture (per crisp to the basket, making sure they are not touching). Bake for 6 minutes or until browned to your liking.
4. Work in batches and place them on a large tray to cool slightly. Serve with marinara sauce. Bon appétit!

Nutrition:
Calories: 198, Fat: 17 g, Carbs: 7 g, Protein: 12 g, Sugar: 4 g.

762. Puerto Rican Tostones

Preparation Time: 5 minutes
Cooking Time: 15 minutes
Servings: 2
Ingredients:
- 1 ripe plantain, sliced
- 1 tbsp. sunflower oil
- A pinch of grated nutmeg
- A pinch of kosher salt

Directions:
1. Toss the plantains with the oil, nutmeg, and salt in a bowl.
2. Cook in the preheated Air Fryer at 400°F for 10 minutes, shaking the cooking basket halfway through the cooking time.
3. Regulate the seasonings to taste and serve immediately.

Nutrition:
Calories: 151, Fat: 1 g, Carbs: 29 g, Protein: 6g, Sugar: 17 g.

763. Cajun Cheese Sticks

Preparation Time: 5 minutes
Cooking Time: 15 minutes
Servings: 4
Ingredients:
- ½ cup all-purpose flour
- Two eggs
- ½ cup parmesan cheese, grated
- One tbsp. Cajun seasonings
- Eight cheese sticks, kid-friendly

Directions:
1. To begin, set up your breading station. Place the all-purpose flour in a dish. In a separate dish, whisk the eggs.
2. Finally, mix the parmesan cheese and Cajun seasoning in a third dish. Start by dredging the cheese sticks in the flour; then, dip them into the egg. Press the cheese sticks into the parmesan mixture, coating evenly.
3. Place the breaded cheese sticks in the lightly greased Air Fryer basket. Cook with settings at 380°F for 6 minutes.
4. Serve with ketchup and enjoy!

Nutrition:
Calories: 372, Fat: 27 g, Carbs: 15 g, Protein: 28g, Sugar: 8 g.

764. Classic Deviled Eggs

Preparation Time: 5 minutes
Cooking Time: 20 minutes
Servings: 3
Ingredients:
- Five eggs - 2 tbsp. mayonnaise
- 2 tbsp. sweet pickle relish - Sea salt, to taste
- ½ tsp. mixed peppercorns, crushed

Directions:
1. Put the wire rack in the Air Fryer basket; lower the eggs onto the wire rack. Cook at 270°F for 15 minutes.
2. Remove from heat and put them under an ice-cold water bath to stop the cooking.
3. Peel the eggs underneath cold running water; slice them into halves. Puree the egg yolks with the mayo, sweet pickle relish, salt; spoon yolk mixture into egg whites. Assemble on a nice serving platter and garnish with the mixed peppercorns. Bon appétit!

Nutrition:
Calories: 261, Fat: 12 g, Carbs: 5 g, Protein: 15 g, Sugar: 1 g.

765. Barbecue Little Smokies

Preparation Time: 5 minutes
Cooking Time: 20 minutes
Servings: 6
Ingredients:
- 1-pound beef cocktail wieners
- 10 ounces barbecue sauce

Directions:
1. Preheat your Air Fryer to 380°F.
2. Prick holes into your sausages using a fork and transfer them to the baking pan.
3. Cook for 13 minutes. Spoon the barbecue sauce into the pan and cook for an additional 2 minutes.
4. Serve with toothpicks. Bon appétit!

Nutrition:
Calories: 182, Fat: 6 g, Carbs: 12 g, Protein: 19 g, Sugar: 17 g.

766. Paprika Potato Chips

Preparation Time: 5 minutes
Cooking Time: 45 minutes
Servings: 3

Ingredients:
- 3 potatoes, thinly sliced
- 1 tsp. sea salt
- 1 tsp. garlic powder
- 1 tsp. paprika
- ¼ cup ketchup

Directions:
1. Add the sliced potatoes to a bowl with salted water. Let them soak for 30 minutes. Drain and rinse your potatoes.
2. Pat dry and toss with salt.
3. Cook in the preheated Air Fryer set at 400°F for 15 minutes, occasionally shaking the basket.
4. Work in batches. Toss with garlic powder and paprika. Serve with ketchup. Enjoy!

Nutrition:
Calories: 190, Fat: 3 g, Carbs: 48 g, Protein: 7g, Sugar: 1 g.

767. Cheddar Dip

Preparation Time: 5 minutes
Cooking Time: 15 minutes
Servings: 6

Ingredients:
- 8 oz. cheddar cheese; grated
- 12 oz. coconut cream
- 2 tsp. hot sauce

Directions:
1. In a ramekin, mix the cream with hot sauce and cheese; whisk.
2. Put the ramekin in the fryer and cook at 390°F for 12 minutes. Whisk, divide into bowls and serve as a dip

Nutrition:
Calories: 170, Fat: 9 g, Fiber: 2 g, Carbs: 4 g, Protein: 12 g.

768. Coated Avocado Tacos

Preparation Time: 10 minutes
Cooking Time: 20 minutes
Servings: 12

Ingredients:
- 1 avocado
- Tortillas and toppings
- ½ cup panko breadcrumbs
- 1 egg
- Salt

Directions:
1. Scoop out the meat from each avocado shell and slice them into wedges.
2. Beat the egg in a shallow bowl and put the breadcrumbs in another bowl.
3. Dip the avocado wedges in the beaten egg and coat them with breadcrumbs. Sprinkle them with a bit of salt. Arrange them in the cooking basket in a single layer.
4. Cook for 15 minutes at 392°F. Shake the basket halfway through the cooking process.
5. Put the cooked avocado wedges in tortillas and add your preferred toppings.

Nutrition:
Calories: 179, Fat: 07 g, Carbs: 229 g, Protein: 94 g.

769. Roasted Corn with Butter and Lime

Preparation Time: 2 minutes
Cooking Time: 20 minutes
Servings: 4

Ingredients:
- 4 corns
- ½ tsp. pepper
- 1 tsp. lime juice
- 1 tbsp. chopped parsley
- 1 tbsp. butter
- ¼ tsp. salt

Directions:
1. Preheat the Air Fryer to a temperature of 400°F.
2. Remove husk, transfer corns into the Air Fryer and cook for 20 minutes.
3. After every 5 minutes, shake the fryer basket.
4. When done, rub butter. Sprinkle parsley, pepper, and salt. Drizzle lime juice on top. Serve!

Nutrition:
Calories: 114, Protein: 4 g, Fat: 26 g, Carbs: 124 g.

770. Batter-Fried Scallions

Preparation Time: 5 minutes
Cooking Time: 5 minutes
Servings: 4

Ingredients:
- Trimmed scallion bunches
- 1 cup white wine - 1 tsp. salt
- 1 cup flour - 1 tsp. black pepper

Directions:
1. Preheat the Air Fryer to 390°F. Using a bowl, mix the white wine and flour and stir until it gets smooth. Add salt and black pepper and mix again. Dip each scallion into the flour mixture until it is properly covered and remove any excess batter. Grease your Air Fryer basket with nonstick cooking spray and add the scallions. You may need to work in batches.
2. Leave the scallions to cook for 5 minutes or until it has a golden-brown color and crispy texture, while still shaking it after every 2 minutes. Carefully remove it from your Air Fryer and check if it's properly done.

3. Then allow it to cool before serving. Serve and enjoy.

Nutrition:
Calories: 179, Fat: 07 g, Carbs: 229 g, Protein: 94 g.

771. Heirloom Tomato with Baked Feta
Preparation Time: 20 minutes
Cooking Time: 14 minutes
Servings: 4
Ingredients:
- 8 oz. feta cheese
- Salt
- 2 heirloom tomatoes
- ½ cup sliced red onions
- 1 tbsp. olive oil
- For the basil pesto
- ½ cup grated parmesan cheese
- Salt
- ½ cup olive oil
- 3 tbsp. toasted pine nuts
- ½ cup chopped basil
- 1 garlic clove
- ½ cup chopped parsley

Directions:
1. Put the toasted pine nuts, garlic, salt, basil, and parmesan in a food processor. Process until combined.
2. Gradually add oil as you mix. Process until everything is blended.
3. Transfer to a bowl and cover. Refrigerate until ready to use.
4. Slice the feta and tomato into round slices with half an inch thickness. Use paper towels to pat them dry.
5. Spread 1 tablespoon of pesto on top of each tomato slice.
6. Top with a slice of feta.
7. In a small bowl, mix 1 tablespoon of olive oil and red onions.
8. Scoop the mixture on top of the feta layer. Arrange them in the cooking basket. Cook for 14 minutes at 390°F.
9. Transfer to a platter and add 1 tablespoon of basil pesto on top of each. Sprinkle them with a bit of salt before serving.

Nutrition:
Calories: 493, Fat: 423 g, Carbs: 61 g, Protein: 169 g.

772. Crispy Potato Skins
Preparation Time: 5 minutes
Cooking Time: 55 minutes
Servings: 2
Ingredients:
- 2 Yukon gold potatoes
- ¼ tsp. sea salt
- ½ tsp. olive oil
- 2 minced green onions, 4 bacon strips
- ¼ cup shredded cheddar cheese
- 1/3 cup sour cream

Directions:
1. Rinse and scrub the potatoes until clean. Rub with oil and sprinkle with salt. Put them in the cooking basket. Cook for 35 minutes at 400°F. Transfer the cooked potatoes to a platter. Put the bacon strip in the cooking basket. Cook for 5 minutes at 400°F.
2. Move to a plate and leave to cool. Crumble into bits.
3. Slice the potatoes in half.
4. Scoop out most of the meat. Arrange the potato skins with the skin facing side up in the cooking basket. Spray them with oil. Cook for 3 minutes at 400°F. Flip the potato skins. Fill each piece with cheese and crumbled bacon. Continue cooking for 2 more minutes. Transfer to a platter. Add a bit of sour cream on top. Sprinkle with minced onion and serve while warm.

Nutrition:
Calories: 483, Fat: 73 g, Carbs: 98 g, Protein: 152 g.

773. Beets and Carrots
Preparation Time: 1 minute
Cooking Time: 12 minutes
Servings: 4
Ingredients:
- 4 carrots
- 4 sliced young beetroots
- ¼ tsp. black pepper
- 1 tsp. olive oil - ¼ tsp. salt
- 1 tbsp. lemon juice

Directions:
1. Preheat the Air Fryer to 400°F (200°c).
2. Transfer beetroots and carrots to the Air Fryer basket and sprinkle salt and pepper. Drizzle olive oil and toss to combine.
3. Let cook for 12 minutes. Shake the basket after half of the time. Remove from the Air Fryer and drizzle lemon juice. Serve and enjoy!

Nutrition:
Calories: 71, Protein: 92 g, Fat: 43 g, Carbs: 106 g.

774. Broccoli Crisps
Preparation Time: 10 minutes
Cooking Time: 12 minutes
Servings: 4
Ingredients:
- Large chopped broccoli head
- 1 tsp. salt - 2 tbsp. olive oil
- 1 tsp. black pepper

Directions:
1. Preheat the Air Fryer to 360°F.
2. Using a bowl, add and toss the broccoli florets with olive oil, salt, and black pepper.
3. Add the broccoli florets and cook for 12 minutes, then shake after 6 minutes. Carefully remove it from your Air Fryer and allow it to cool. Serve and enjoy!

Nutrition:
Calories: 120, Fat: 19 g, Protein: 5 g, Carbs: 3 g.

775. Maple Syrup Bacon
Preparation Time: 5 minutes
Cooking Time: 10 minutes
Servings: 2
Ingredients:
- Maple syrup.

- 1 Thick bacon slices

Directions:
1. Preheat your Air Fryer to 400°F.
2. Place the bacon on the flat surface and brush with the maple syrup.
3. Move to the Air Fryer to cook for 10 minutes.
4. Serve and enjoy!

Nutrition:
Calories: 91, Carbs: 0 g, Protein: 8 g, Fat: 2 g.

776. Low-Carb Pizza Crust

Preparation Time: 10 minutes
Cooking Time: 20 minutes
Servings: 4
Ingredients:
- 1 tbsp. full-fat cream cheese
- ½ cup whole-milk mozzarella cheese, shredded
- 2 tbsp. flour
- 1 egg white

Directions:
1. Prepare the cream cheese, mozzarella, and flour in a microwaveable bowl and heat in the microwave for half a minute. Mix well to create a smooth consistency. Add in the egg white and stir to form a soft ball of dough.
2. With slightly wet hands, press the dough into a pizza crust about six inches in diameter.
3. Arrange a sheet of parchment paper in the bottom of your fryer and lay the crust on top. Cook for ten minutes at 350°F, turning the crust over halfway through the cooking time.
4. Top the pizza base with the toppings of your choice and enjoy!

Nutrition:
Calories: 260, Fat: 21 g, Carbs: 6 g, Protein: 9 g.

777. Colby Potato Patties

Preparation Time: 5 minutes
Cooking Time: 15 minutes
Servings: 8
Ingredients:
- 2 lb. white potatoes, peeled and grated
- ½ cup scallions, finely chopped
- ½ tsp. freshly ground black pepper
- 1 tbsp. fine sea salt
- ½ tsp. hot paprika
- 2 cups Colby cheese, shredded
- ¼ cup canola oil
- 1 cup crushed crackers

Directions:
1. Boil the potatoes until soft. Dry them off and peel them before mashing thoroughly, leaving no lumps.
2. Combine the mashed potatoes with scallions, pepper, salt, paprika, and cheese.
3. Shape mixture into balls with your hands and press with your palm to flatten them into patties.
4. In a shallow dish, combine the canola oil and crushed crackers. Coat the patties in the crumb mixture.
5. Cook the patties at 360°F for about 10 minutes, in multiple batches, if necessary.
6. Serve with Tabasco mayo or the sauce of your choice.

Nutrition:
Calories: 130, Fat: 7 g, Carbs: 17 g, Protein: 1 g.

778. Turkey Garlic Potatoes

Preparation Time: 10 minutes
Cooking Time: 45 minutes
Servings: 2
Ingredients:
- unsmoked turkey strips
- 2 small potatoes
- 1 tsp. garlic, minced
- 2 tsp. olive oil - Salt to taste
- Pepper to taste

Directions:
1. Peel the potatoes and cube them finely.
2. Coat in 1 teaspoon of oil and cook in the Air Fryer for 10 minutes at 350°F.
3. In a separate bowl, slice the turkey finely and combine with the garlic, oil, salt, and pepper. Pour the potatoes into the bowl and mix well.
4. Lay the mixture on some silver aluminum foil, transfer to the fryer and cook for about 10 minutes. Serve with raita.

Nutrition:
Calories: 210, Fat: 4 g, Carbs: 22 g, Protein: 22 g.

779. Creamy Scrambled Eggs

Preparation Time: 5 minutes
Cooking Time: 15 minutes
Servings: 2
Ingredients:
- 2 tbsp. olive oil, melted
- 2 eggs, whisked
- oz. fresh spinach, chopped
- 1 medium-sized tomato, chopped
- 1 tsp. fresh lemon juice
- ½ tsp. coarse salt
- ½ tsp. ground black pepper
- ½ cup of fresh basil, roughly chopped

Directions:
1. Grease the Air Fryer baking pan with the oil, tilting it to spread the oil around. Preheat the fryer at 280°F.
2. Mix the remaining ingredients, apart from the basil leaves, whisking well until everything is completely combined.
3. Cook in the fryer for 8–12 minutes.
4. Top with fresh basil leaves before serving with little sour cream if desired.

Nutrition:
Calories: 140, Fat: 10 g, Carbs: 2 g, Protein: 12 g.

780. Bacon-Wrapped Onion Rings

Preparation Time: 10 minutes
Cooking Time: 15 minutes
Servings: 8
Ingredients:
- 1 large onion, peeled

- slices sugar-free bacon
- 1 tbsp. sriracha

Directions:
1. Chop up the onion into slices a quarter-inch thick. Gently pull apart the rings. Take a slice of bacon and wrap it around an onion ring. Repeat with the rest of the ingredients.
2. Place each onion ring in your fryer.
3. Cut the onion rings at 350°F for ten minutes, turning them halfway through to ensure the bacon crisps up.
4. Serve hot with the sriracha.

Nutrition:
Calories: 280, Fat: 19 g, Carbs: 25 g, Protein: 3 g.

781. Grilled Cheese

Preparation Time: 5 minutes
Cooking Time: 5 minutes
Servings: 2
Ingredients:
- 4 slices of bread
- ½ cup sharp cheddar cheese
- ¼ cup butter, melted

Directions:
1. Preheat the Air Fryer at 360°F.
2. Put cheese and butter in separate bowls.
3. Apply the butter to each side of the bread slices with a brush.
4. Spread the cheese across two of the slices of bread and make two sandwiches. Transfer both to the fryer.
5. Cook for 5–7 minutes or until a golden-brown color is achieved and the cheese is melted.

Nutrition:
Calories: 170, Fat: 8 g, Carbs: 17 g, Protein: 5 g.

782. Peppered Puff Pastry

Preparation Time: 10 minutes
Cooking Time: 25 minutes
Servings: 4
Ingredients:
- 1 ½ tbsp. sesame oil
- 1 cup white mushrooms, sliced
- 2 cloves garlic, minced
- 1 bell pepper, seeded and chopped
- ¼ tsp. sea salt
- ¼ tsp. dried rosemary
- ½ tsp. ground black pepper, or more to taste
- oz. puff pastry sheets
- ½ cup crème Fraiche
- 1 egg, well whisked
- ½ cup parmesan cheese, preferably freshly grated

Directions:
1. Preheat your Air Fryer to 400°F.
2. Heat the sesame oil over moderate temperature and fry the mushrooms, garlic, and pepper until soft and fragrant.
3. Sprinkle on the salt, rosemary, and pepper.
4. In the meantime, unroll the puff pastry and slice it into 4-inch squares.
5. Spread the crème Fraiche across each square.
6. Spoon equal amounts of the vegetables into the puff pastry squares. Enclose each square around the filling in a triangle shape, pressing the edges with your fingertips.
7. Brush each triangle with some whisked egg and cover with grated Parmesan.
8. Cook for 22–25 minutes.

Nutrition:
Calories: 259, Fat: 18 g, Carbs: 21 g, Protein: 3 g.

783. Horseradish Mayo & Gorgonzola Mushrooms

Preparation Time: 10 minutes
Cooking Time: 15 minutes
Servings: 5
Ingredients:
- ½ cup of breadcrumbs
- 2 cloves garlic, pressed
- 2 tbsp. fresh coriander, chopped
- 1/3 tsp. kosher salt
- ½ tsp. crushed red pepper flakes
- 1 ½ tbsp. olive oil
- 2 medium-sized mushrooms, stems removed
- ½ cup Gorgonzola cheese, grated
- ¼ cup low-fat mayonnaise
- 1 tsp. horseradish, well-drained
- 1 tbsp. fresh parsley, finely chopped

Directions:
1. Combine the breadcrumbs with garlic, coriander, salt, red pepper, and olive oil.
2. Take equal-sized amounts of the bread crumb mixture and use them to stuff the mushroom caps. Add the grated Gorgonzola on top of each.
3. Put the mushrooms in the Air Fryer grill pan and transfer them to the fryer.
4. Grill them at 380°F for 8–12 minutes, ensuring the stuffing is warm throughout.
5. In the meantime, prepare the horseradish mayo. Mix the mayonnaise, horseradish, and parsley.
6. When the mushrooms are ready, serve with the mayo.

Nutrition:
Calories: 140, Fat: 13 g, Carbs: 6 g, Protein: 0 g.

784. Crumbed Beans

Preparation Time: 5 minutes
Cooking Time: 10 minutes
Servings: 4
Ingredients:
- ½ cup flour
- 1 tsp. smoky chipotle powder
- ½ tsp. ground black pepper
- 1 tsp. sea salt flakes
- 2 eggs, beaten
- ½ cup crushed saltines
- 20 oz. wax beans

Directions:
1. Combine the flour, chipotle powder, black pepper, and salt in a bowl. Put the eggs in the second bowl. Place the crushed saltines in the third bowl.
2. Wash the beans with cold water and discard any tough strings.
3. Coat the beans with the flour mixture, before dipping them into the beaten egg. Lastly, cover them with the crushed saltines.
4. Spritz the beans with cooking spray.
5. Air-fry at 360°F for 4 minutes. Give the cooking basket a good shake and continue to cook for 3 minutes. Serve hot.

Nutrition:
Calories: 200, Fat: 8 g, Carbs: 27 g, Protein: 4 g.

785. Croutons
Preparation Time: 5 minutes
Cooking Time: 10 minutes
Servings: 4
Ingredients:
- 2 slices friendly bread
- 1 tbsp. olive oil

Directions:
1. Cut the slices of bread into medium-sized chunks.
2. Coat the inside of the Air Fryer with the oil. Set it to 390°F and allow it to heat up.
3. Place the chunks inside and shallow fry for at least 8 minutes.
4. Serve with hot soup.

Nutrition:
Calories: 186, Fat: 7 g, Carbs: 25 g, Protein: 4 g.

786. Cheese Lings
Preparation Time: 5 minutes
Cooking Time: 5 minutes
Servings: 6
Ingredients:
- 1 cup flour
- small cubes cheese, grated
- ¼ tsp. chili powder
- 1 tsp. butter
- Salt to taste
- 1 tsp. baking powder

Directions:
1. Put all ingredients to form a dough, along with a small amount of water as necessary.
2. Divide the dough into equal portions and roll each one into a ball. Preheat the Air Fryer at 360°F.
3. Transfer the balls to the fryer and air fry for 5 minutes, stirring periodically.

Nutrition:
Calories: 489, Fat: 20 g, Carbs: 69 g, Protein: 8 g.

787. Sweet Potato Wedges
Preparation Time: 10 minutes
Cooking Time: 20 minutes
Servings: 4
Ingredients:
- 2 sweet potatoes, sliced into wedges
- 1 tbsp. vegetable oil
- 1 tsp. smoked paprika
- 1 tbsp. honey
- Salt and pepper to taste

Directions:
1. Add Air Fryer basket to your PowerXL Grill.
2. Choose Air Fry setting.
3. Preheat at 390°F for 5 minutes.
4. Add sweet potato wedges to the basket.
5. Cook for 10 minutes.
6. Stir and cook for another 10 minutes.
7. Toss in paprika and honey.
8. Sprinkle with salt and pepper.

Nutrition:
Calories: 368, Fat: 24.2 g, Carbohydrates: 21 g, Fiber: 4.1 g, Protein: 17.6 g.

788. Spiced Almonds
Preparation Time: 5 minutes
Cooking Time: 15 minutes
Servings: 4
Ingredients:
- ½ tsp. ground cinnamon
- ½ tsp. smoked paprika
- 1 cup almonds
- 1 egg white

Directions:
1. Preheat the Air Fryer to 310°F. Grease the Air Fryer basket with cooking spray. In a bowl, beat the egg white with cinnamon and paprika and stir in almonds.
2. Spread the almonds on the bottom of the frying basket and Air Fry for 12 minutes, shaking once or twice. Remove and sprinkle with sea salt to serve.

Nutrition:
Calories: 90, Carbs: 3 g, Fat: 2 g, Protein: 5 g.

789. Crispy Cauliflower Bites
Preparation Time: 5 minutes
Cooking Time: 15 minutes
Servings: 4
Ingredients:
- 1 tbsp. Italian seasoning
- 1 cup flour
- 1 cup milk
- 1 egg, beaten
- 1 head cauliflower, cut into florets

Directions:
1. Preheat the Air Fryer to 390°F. Grease the Air Fryer basket with cooking spray. In a bowl, mix the flour, milk, egg, and Italian seasoning. Coat the cauliflower in the mixture and drain the excess liquid.
2. Place the florets in the frying basket. Spray them with cooking spray and Air Fry for 7 minutes. Shake and continue cooking for another 5 minutes. Allow cooling before serving.

Nutrition:
Calories: 70, Carbs: 2 g, Fat: 1 g, Protein: 3 g.

790. Roasted Coconut Carrots

Preparation Time: 5 minutes
Cooking Time: 15 minutes
Servings: 4
Ingredients:

- 1 tbsp. coconut oil, melted
- 1 lb. horse carrots, sliced
- ½ tsp. chili powder

Directions:

1. Preheat the Air Fryer to 400°F.
2. In a bowl, mix the carrots with coconut oil, chili powder, salt, and pepper. Place it in the Air Fryer and Air Fry for 10 minutes. Shake the basket and cook for another 5 minutes until golden brown. Serve.

Nutrition:
Calories: 80, Carbs: 3 g, Fat: 1 g, Protein: 4 g.

791. Spicy Grilled Turkey Breast

Preparation Time: 10 minutes
Cooking Time: 40 minutes
Servings: 14
Ingredients:

- 5 lb. turkey breast, bone-in

What you'll need from the store cupboard:

- 1 cup low, sodium: chicken broth
- ¼ cup vinegar
- ¼ cup jalapeno pepper jelly
- 2 tbsp. Splenda brown sugar
- 2 tbsp. olive oil
- 2 tsp. cinnamon
- 1 tsp. cayenne pepper
- ½ tsp. ground mustard
- Nonstick cooking spray

Directions:

1. Heat grill to medium fire. Grease rack with cooking spray. Place a drip pan on the grill for indirect heat.
2. In a small bowl, combine Splenda brown sugar with seasonings.
3. Carefully loosen the skin on the turkey from both sides with your fingers. Spread half the spice mix on the turkey. Secure the skin to the underneath with toothpicks and spread the remaining spice mix on the outside.
4. Place the turkey over the drip pan and grill for 30 minutes.
5. In a small saucepan over medium heat, combine broth, vinegar, jelly, and oil. Cook and stir for 2 minutes until jelly is completely melted. Reserve ½ cup of the mixture.
6. Baste turkey with some of the jelly mixture. Cook 1–1 ½ hour, basting every 15 minutes until done when the thermometer reaches 170°F.
7. Cover and let it rest for 10 minutes. Discard the skin. Brush with reserved jelly mixture and slice and serve.

Nutrition:
Calories: 314, Total Carbs: 5 g, Protein: 35 g, Fat: 14 g, Sugar: 5 g, Fiber: 0 g.

792. Teriyaki Turkey Bowls

Preparation Time: 10 minutes
Cooking Time: 15 minutes
Servings: 4
Ingredients:

- 1 lb. lean ground turkey
- 1 medium head cauliflower, separated into small florets

What you'll need from the store cupboard:

- 1 cup water, divided
- ¼ cup + 1 tbsp. soy sauce
- 2 tbsp. Hoisin sauce
- 2 tbsp. honey
- 1 ½ tbsp. cornstarch
- 1 tsp. crushed red pepper flakes
- 1 tsp. garlic powder

Directions:

1. In a medium nonstick skillet, cook turkey over med-high heat until brown.
2. In a medium saucepan, combine ¾ cup water, ¼ cup soy sauce, hoisin, pepper flakes, honey, and garlic powder; cook over medium heat, stirring occasionally, until it starts to bubble.
3. In a small bowl whisk together ¼ cup water and cornstarch and add to the saucepan. Bring mixture to a full boil, stirring occasionally. Once it starts to boil, remove from heat and add the turkey. Stir to combine.
4. Place the cauliflower florets in a food processor and pulse until it resembles rice.
5. Grease a nonstick skillet with cooking spray. Add the cauliflower and 1 tablespoon of soy sauce and cook until cauliflower starts to get soft, about 5–7 minutes.
6. To serve, spoon cauliflower evenly into four bowls, top with turkey mixture, and garnish with

Nutrition:
Calories: 267, Total Carbs: 24 g, Net Carbs: 20 g, Protein: 26 g, Fat: 9 g, Sugar: 15 g, Fiber: 4 g.

793. Thai Turkey Stir Fry

Preparation Time: 5 minutes
Cooking Time: 15 minutes
Servings: 6
Ingredients:

- 1 ½ lb. lean ground turkey
- 1–2 cups Thai basil, chopped
- 1 onion, cut in slivers
- 1 red bell pepper, cut in thin strips
- 2 tbsp. fresh lime juice

What you'll need from the store cupboard:

- 2–3 large cloves garlic, peeled and sliced
- 1 tbsp. + 1 tsp. peanut oil
- 1 tbsp. fish sauce
- 1 tbsp. Sriracha Sauce
- 1 tbsp. soy sauce
- 1 tbsp. honey

Directions:
1. In a small bowl, whisk together lime juice, fish sauce, Sriracha, soy sauce, and honey.
2. Place a large wok or heavy skillet over high heat. Once the pan gets hot, add 1 tablespoon of oil and let it get hot. Add garlic and cook just until fragrant, about 30 seconds. Remove the garlic and discard.
3. Add the onion and bell pepper and cook, stirring frequently 1–2 minutes, or until they start to get soft, transfer to a bowl.
4. Add the remaining oil, if it's needed, and cook the turkey, breaking it up as it cooks, until it starts to brown and the liquid has evaporated.
5. Add the vegetables back to the pan along with the basil and cook another minute more. Stir in the sauce until all ingredients are mixed well. Cook, stirring 2 minutes, or until most of the sauce is absorbed.

Nutrition:
Calories: 214, Total Carbs: 7 g, Net Carbs: 6 g, Protein: 23 g, Fat: 11 g, Sugar: 5 g, Fiber: 1 g.

794. Turkey Enchiladas
Preparation Time: 15 minutes
Cooking Time: 35 minutes
Servings: 8
Ingredients:
- 3 cup turkey, cooked and cut into pieces
- 1 onion, diced
- 1 bell pepper, diced
- 1 cup, Fat: free sour cream
- 1 cup reduced-fat cheddar cheese, grated

What you'll need from the store cupboard:
- 8 6-inch flour tortillas
- 14 ½ oz. low, Sodium: chicken broth
- ¾ cup salsa - 3 tbsp. flour
- 2 tsp. olive oil
- 1 ¼ tsp. coriander
- Nonstick cooking spray

Directions:
1. Grease a large saucepan with cooking spray and heat oil over med-high fire. Add onion and bell pepper and cook until tender.
2. Sprinkle with flour, coriander, and pepper and stir until blended. Slowly stir in broth. Bring to a boil and cook, stirring, 2 minutes or until thickened.
3. Remove from heat and stir in sour cream and ¾ cup cheese. Heat the oven to 350°F. Grease a 13x9-inch pan with cooking spray.
4. In a large bowl, combine turkey, salsa, and 1 cup of cheese mixture. Spoon 1/3 cup mixture down the middle of each tortilla and roll up. Place seam side down in dish.
5. Pour the remaining cheese mixture over top of enchiladas. Cover and bake for 20 minutes. Uncover and sprinkle with remaining cheese. Bake another 5–10 minutes until cheese is melted and starts to brown.

Nutrition:
Calories: 304, Total Carbs: 29 g, Net Carbs: 27 g, Protein: 23 g, Fat: 10 g, Sugar: 5 g, Fiber: 2 g.

795. Baked Potatoes with Bacon
Preparation Time: 5 minutes
Cooking Time: 20 minutes
Servings: 4
Ingredients:
- 4 potatoes, scrubbed, halved, cut lengthwise
- 1 tbsp. olive oil
- Salt and black pepper to taste
- 4 oz. bacon, chopped

Directions:
1. Preheat the Air Fryer to 390°F. Brush the potatoes with olive oil and season with salt and pepper. Arrange them in the greased frying basket, cut-side down.
2. Bake for 15 minutes, flip them, top with bacon and bake for 12–15 minutes or until potatoes are golden and bacon is crispy. Serve warm.

Nutrition:
Calories: 150, Carbs: 9 g, Fat: 7 g, Protein: 12 g.

796. Walnut & Cheese Filled Mushrooms
Preparation Time: 5 minutes
Cooking Time: 10 minutes
Servings: 4
Ingredients:
- 4 large Portobello mushroom caps
- 1/3 cup walnuts, minced
- 1 tbsp. canola oil
- ½ cup mozzarella cheese, shredded
- 2 tbsp. fresh parsley, chopped

Directions:
1. Preheat the Air Fryer to 350°F. Grease the Air Fryer basket with cooking spray.
2. Rub the mushrooms with canola oil and fill them with mozzarella cheese. Top with minced walnuts and arrange on the bottom of the greased Air Fryer basket. Bake for 10 minutes or until golden on top. Remove, let it cool for a few minutes and sprinkle with freshly chopped parsley to serve.

Nutrition:
Calories: 110, Carbs: 6 g, Fat: 5 g, Protein: 8 g.

797. Air-Fried Chicken Thighs
Preparation Time: 5 minutes
Cooking Time: 15 minutes
Servings: 4
Ingredients:
- 1 ½ lb. chicken thighs
- 2 eggs, lightly beaten
- 1 cup seasoned breadcrumbs
- ½ tsp. oregano
- Salt and black pepper, to taste

Directions:
1. Preheat the Air Fryer to 390°F. Season the chicken with oregano, salt, and pepper. In a bowl, add the beaten eggs. In a separate bowl, add the breadcrumbs. Dip chicken

thighs in the egg wash, then roll them in the breadcrumbs and press firmly so the breadcrumbs stick well.
2. Coat the chicken with cooking spray and arrange the frying basket in a single layer, skin-side up. Air Fry for 12 minutes, turn the chicken thighs over, and continue cooking for 6–8 more minutes. Serve.

Nutrition:
Calories: 190, Carbs: 11 g, Fat: 8 g, Protein: 16 g.

798. Simple Buttered Potatoes
Preparation Time: 5 minutes
Cooking Time: 30 minutes
Servings: 4
Ingredients:
- 1 pound potatoes, cut into wedges
- 2 garlic cloves, grated
- 1 tsp. fennel seeds
- 2 tbsp. butter, melted
- Salt and black pepper to taste

Directions:
1. In a bowl, mix the potatoes, butter, garlic, fennel seeds, salt, and black pepper until they are well-coated. Set up the potatoes in the Air Fryer basket.
2. Bake at 360°F for 25 minutes, shaking once during cooking until crispy on the outside and tender on the inside. Serve warm.

Nutrition:
Calories: 100, Carbs: 8 g, Fat: 4 g, Protein: 7 g.

799. Homemade Peanut Corn Nuts
Preparation Time: 5 minutes
Cooking Time: 20 minutes
Servings: 4
Ingredients:
- 6 oz. dried hominy, soaked overnight
- 3 tbsp. peanut oil
- 2 tbsp. old bay seasoning
- Salt to taste

Directions:
1. Pat dry hominy and season with salt and old bay seasoning.
2. Drizzle with oil and toss to coat.
3. Spread in the Air Fryer basket and Air Fry for 10–12 minutes.
4. Remove to shake up and return to cook for 10 more minutes until crispy. Transfer to a towel-lined plate to soak up the excess fat. Let it cool and serve.

Nutrition:
Calories: 100, Carbs: 3 g, Fat: 3 g, Protein: 5 g.

800. Corn-Crusted Chicken Tenders
Preparation Time: 5 minutes
Cooking Time: 15 minutes
Servings: 4
Ingredients:
- 2 chicken breasts, cut into strips
- Salt and black pepper to taste
- 2 eggs
- 1 cup ground cornmeal

Directions:
1. In a bowl, mix ground cornmeal, salt, and black pepper.
2. In another bowl, beat the eggs season with salt and pepper.
3. Dip the chicken in the eggs and then coat in cornmeal.
4. Coat the sticks with cooking spray and place them in the Air Fryer basket in a single layer.
5. Air Fry for 6 minutes. Slide the basket out and flip the sticks, cook for 6–8 more minutes until golden brown.

Nutrition:
Calories: 170, Carbs: 8 g, Fat: 6 g, Protein: 16 g.

801. Choco Hazelnut Croissant
Preparation Time: 15 minutes
Cooking Time: 10 minutes
Servings: 2
Ingredients:
- 1 oz. canned crescent rolls
- 8 tsp. chocolate hazelnut spread

Directions:
1. Separate crescent dough into triangles.
2. Spread top with chocolate hazelnut spread.
3. Roll up the triangles to form a crescent shape. Place these in the Air Fryer.
4. Select Bake setting.
5. Cook at 320°F for 8 to 10 minutes or until golden.

Nutrition:
Calories: 101, Fat: 8.9 g, Carbohydrates: 3.6 g, Sugar: 0.5 g, Protein: 3.2 g, Cholesterol: 60 mg.

802. Blueberry Muffin Surprise
Preparation Time: 10 minutes
Cooking Time: 20 minutes
Servings: 12
Ingredients:
- 2 eggs
- ½ tsp. vanilla
- ½ cups Swerve
- 16 oz. cream cheese
- ¼ cup almonds, sliced
- ¼ cup blueberries

Directions:
1. Preheat the Air Fryer to 350°F.
2. In a mixing bowl, beat cream cheese until smooth.
3. Add eggs, vanilla, and sweetener and beat until well combined.
4. Add almonds and blueberries and fold well.
5. Spoon mixture into the silicone muffin molds. Place molds in the Air Fryer basket and cook for 20 minutes. Cook in batches.

Nutrition:
Calories: 156, Fat: 14.9 g, Carbohydrates: 2 g, Sugar: 0.5 g, Protein: 4.2 g, Cholesterol: 69 mg.

803. Blueberry Crumble
Preparation Time: 15 minutes
Cooking Time: 15 minutes
Servings: 4
Ingredients:
- ½ cup blueberries, sliced

- 1 apple, diced
- 2 tbsp. butter
- 2 tbsp. Sugar
- ¼ cup rice flour
- ½ tsp. cinnamon powder

Directions:
1. Mix all the ingredients in a small baking pan.
2. Place them inside the Air Fryer.
3. Choose bake setting.
4. Set it to 350°F. Cook for 15 minutes.

Nutrition:
Calories: 93, Fat: 8.8 g, Carbohydrates: 1 g, Sugar: 0.2 g, Protein: 2.8 g, Cholesterol: 58 mg.

804. Golden Caramelized Pear Tart
Preparation Time: 15 minutes
Cooking Time: 25 minutes
Servings: 8
Ingredients:
- Juice of 1 lemon
- 4 cups water
- 3 medium or 2 large ripe or almost ripe pears (preferably Bosc or Anjou), peeled, stemmed, and halved lengthwise
- 1 sheet (½ package) frozen puff pastry, thawed
- All-purpose flour, for dusting
- 4 tbsp. caramel sauce such as Smucker's Salted Caramel, divided

Directions:
1. Combine the lemon juice and water in a large bowl.
2. Remove the seeds from the pears with a melon baller and cut out the blossom end. Remove any tough fibers between the stem end and the center. As you work, place the pear halves in the acidulated water.
3. On a lightly floured cutting board, unwrap and unfold the puff pastry, roll it very lightly with a rolling pin to press the folds together. Place it on the sheet pan.
4. Roll about ½ inch of the pastry edges up to form a ridge around the perimeter. Crimp the corners together to create a solid rim around the pastry to hold in the liquid as the tart cooks.
5. Brush 2 tablespoons of caramel sauce over the bottom of the pastry.
6. Remove the pear halves from the water and blot off any remaining water with paper towels.
7. Place one of the halves on the board cut-side down and cut ¼-inch-thick slices radially. Repeat with the remaining halves. Arrange the pear slices over the pastry. Drizzle the remaining 2 tablespoons of caramel sauce over the top.
8. Place the basket on the Bake position.
9. Select Bake, set the temperature to 350°F (180°C), and time to 25 minutes.
10. After 15 minutes, check the tart, rotating the pan if the crust is not browning evenly. Continue cooking for another 10 minutes, or until the pastry is golden brown, the pears are soft, and the caramel is bubbling.
11. When done, remove the pan from the Air Fryer grill and allow it to cool for about 10 minutes.
12. Serve warm.

Nutrition:
Calories: 83, Fat: 7.8 g, Carbohydrates: 1 g, Sugar: 0.3 g, Protein: 2.9 g, Cholesterol: 58 mg.

805. Middle East Baklava
Preparation Time: 10 minutes
Cooking Time: 16 minutes
Servings: 10
Ingredients:
- 1 cup walnut pieces
- 1 cup shelled raw pistachios
- ½ cup unsalted butter, melted
- ¼ cup plus 2 tbsp. honey, divided
- 3 tbsp. granulated sugar
- 1 tsp. ground cinnamon
- 2 (1.9-ounce) packages frozen miniature phyllo tart shells

Directions:
1. Place the walnuts and pistachios in the Air Fry basket in an even layer.
2. Place the basket on the Air Fry position.
3. Select Air Fry, set the temperature to 350°F (180°C) and set the timer for 4 minutes.
4. After 2 minutes, remove the basket and stir the nuts. Transfer the basket back to the Air Fryer grill and cook for another 1 to 2 minutes until the nuts are golden brown and fragrant.
5. Meanwhile, stir together the butter, sugar, cinnamon, and ¼ cup of honey in a medium bowl.
6. When done, remove the basket from the Air Fryer grill, place the nuts on a cutting board and allow them to cool for 5minutes. Finely chop the nuts. Add the chopped nuts and all the "nut dust" to the butter mixture and stir well.
7. Arrange the phyllo cups on the basket. Evenly fill the phyllo cups with the nut mixture, mounding it up. As you work, stir the nuts in the bowl frequently so that the syrup is evenly distributed throughout the filling.
8. Place the basket on the Bake position.
9. Select Bake, set the temperature to 350°F (180°C), and time to 12 minutes. After about 8 minutes, check the cups. Continue cooking until the cups are golden brown and the syrup is bubbling.
10. When cooking is complete, remove the baklava from the Air Fryer grill, drizzle each cup with about 1/8 teaspoon of the remaining honey over the top.
11. Allow cooling for 5 minutes before serving.

Nutrition:
Calories: 95, Fat: 7.8 g, Carbohydrates: 2 g, Sugar: 0.2 g, Protein: 3.8 g, Cholesterol: 50 mg.

806. Chocolate Donuts
Preparation Time: 5 minutes
Cooking Time: 20 minutes
Servings: 8–10
Ingredients:
- (8-ounce) can jumbo biscuits
- cooking oil
- chocolate sauce, such as Hershey's

Directions:
1. Separate the biscuit dough into 8 pieces and place them on a flat work surface. Use a small circle cookie cutter or a biscuit cutter to cut a hole in each biscuit center. You can also cut the holes using a knife.
2. Grease the basket with cooking oil.
3. Place 4 donuts in the Air Fryer oven. Do not stack. Spray with cooking oil. Cook for 4 minutes.
4. Open the Air Fryer and flip the donuts. Cook for an additional 4 minutes.
5. Remove the cooked donuts from the Air Fryer Oven, then repeat for the remaining 4 donuts.
6. Drizzle chocolate sauce over the donuts and enjoy while warm.

Nutrition:
Calories: 181, Protein: 3 g, Fat: 98 g, Carbs: 42 g.

807. Coconut Pancake

Preparation Time: 10 minutes
Cooking Time: 20 minutes
Servings: 4
Ingredients:
- 2 cups self-rising flour
- 2 tbsp. Sugar
- 2 eggs
- 1 and ½ cups coconut milk
- A drizzle of olive oil

Directions:
1. In a bowl, mix eggs with sugar, milk, flour, and whisk until you obtain a batter.
2. Grease your Air Fryer with the oil, add the batter, spread into the pot, cover, and cook on Low for 20 minutes.
3. Slice pancake, divide between plates and serve cold.

Nutrition:
Calories: 162, Protein: 8 g, Fat: 3 g, Carbs: 7 g.

808. Cinnamon Rolls

Preparation Time: 2 hours
Cooking Time: 15 minutes
Servings: 8
Ingredients:
- 1-pound vegan bread dough
- ¾ cup coconut sugar
- 1 and ½ tbsp. cinnamon powder
- 2 tbsp. vegetable oil

Directions:
1. Roll the dough on a floured working surface, shape a rectangle, and brush with the oil.
2. In a bowl, mix cinnamon with sugar. Stir, sprinkle this over dough, roll into a log, seal well and cut into 8 pieces.
3. Leave rolls to rise for 2 hours
4. Place them in your Air Fryer's basket, cook at 350°F for 5 minutes, flip them, cook for 4 minutes more and transfer to a platter.
5. Enjoy!

Nutrition:
Calories: 170, Protein: 6 g, Fat: 1 g, Carbs: 7 g.

CHAPTER 9: Sweets and Desserts

809. Easy Baked Chocolate Mug Cake
Preparation Time: 5 Minutes
Cooking Time: 15 Minutes
Servings: 3
Ingredients
- ½ cup cocoa powder
- ½ cup stevia powder
- 1 cup coconut cream
- 1 package cream cheese, room temperature
- 1 tablespoon vanilla extract
- 1 tablespoons butter

Directions:
1. Preheat the Smart Air Fryer Oven for 5 minutes.
2. In a mixing bowl, combine all ingredients.
3. Use a hand mixer to mix everything until fluffy.
4. Pour into greased mugs.
5. Place the mugs in the fryer basket.
6. Bake for 15 minutes at 350°F.
7. Place in the fridge to chill before serving.

Nutrition: CALORIES: 744; FAT: 67G; PROTEIN: 19G; SUGAR: 4G

810. Angel Food Cake
Preparation Time: 5 Minutes
Cooking Time: 30 Minutes
Servings: 12
Ingredients
- ¼ cup butter, melted
- 1 cup powdered erythritol
- 1 teaspoon strawberry extract
- 12 egg whites
- 2 teaspoons cream of tartar
- A pinch of salt

Directions:
1. Preheat the Smart Air Fryer Oven for 5 minutes.
2. Mix the egg whites and cream of tartar.
3. Use a hand mixer and whisk until white and fluffy.
4. Add the rest of the ingredients except for the butter and whisk for another minute.
5. Pour into a baking dish.
6. Place in the air fryer basket and cook for 30 minutes at 400°F or if a toothpick inserted in the middle comes out clean.
7. Drizzle with melted butter once cooled.

Nutrition: CALORIES: 65; FAT: 5G; PROTEIN: 1G; FIBER: 1G

811. Fried Peaches
Preparation Time: 2 Hours 10 Minutes
Cooking Time: 15 Minutes
Servings: 4
Ingredients
- 4 ripe peaches (1/2 a peach = 1 serving)
- 1 1/2 cups flour
- 1 teaspoon Salt
- 2 egg yolks
- 3/4 cups cold water
- 1 1/2 tablespoons olive oil
- 2 tablespoons brandy
- 4 egg whites
- 2 teaspoon Cinnamon/sugar mix

Directions:
1. Mix flour, egg yolks, and salt in a mixing bowl. Slowly mix in water, then add brandy. Set the mixture aside for 2 hours and go do something for 1 hour 45 minutes.
2. Boil a large pot of water and cut and X at the bottom of each peach. While the water boils fill another large bowl with water and ice. Boil each peach for about a minute, then plunge it in the ice bath. Now the peels should basically fall off the peach. Beat the egg whites and mix into the batter mix. Dip each peach in the mix to coat.
3. Pour the coated peach into the Oven rack/basket. Place the Rack on the middle-shelf of the Smart Air Fryer Oven. Set temperature to 360°F, and set time to 10 minutes.
4. Prepare a plate with cinnamon/sugar mix, roll peaches in mix and serve.

Nutrition: CALORIES: 306; FAT: 3G; PROTEIN: 10G; FIBER: 7G

812. Apple Dumplings
Preparation Time: 10 Minutes
Cooking Time: 25 Minutes
Servings: 4
Ingredients
- 2 tbsp. melted coconut oil
- 2 puff pastry sheets
- 1 tbsp. brown sugar
- 2 tbsp. raisins
- 2 small apples of choice

Directions:
1. Ensure your Smart Air Fryer Oven is preheated to 356 degrees.
2. Core and peel apples and mix with raisins and sugar.

3. Place a bit of apple mixture into puff pastry sheets and brush sides with melted coconut oil.
4. Place into the air fryer. Cook 25 minutes, turning halfway through. Will be golden when done.

Nutrition: CALORIES: 367; FAT: 7G; PROTEIN: 2G; SUGAR: 5G

813. Apple Pie in Air Fryer

Preparation Time: 5 Minutes
Cooking Time: 35 Minutes
Servings: 4

Ingredients

- ½ teaspoon vanilla extract
- 1 beaten egg - 1 large apple, chopped
- 1 Pillsbury Refrigerator pie crust
- 1 tablespoon butter
- 1 tablespoon ground cinnamon
- 1 tablespoon raw sugar - 1 tablespoon sugar
- 1 teaspoons lemon juice
- Baking spray

Directions:

1. Lightly grease baking pan of Smart Air Fryer Oven with cooking spray. Spread pie crust on bottom of pan up to the sides.
2. In a bowl, mix vanilla, sugar, cinnamon, lemon juice, and apples. Pour on top of pie crust. Top apples with butter slices.
3. Cover apples with the other pie crust. Pierce with knife the tops of pie.
4. Spread beaten egg on top of crust and sprinkle sugar.
5. Cover with foil.
6. For 25 minutes, cook on 390°F.
7. Remove foil cook for 10 minutes at 330oF until tops are browned.
8. Serve and enjoy.

Nutrition: CALORIES: 372; FAT: 19G; PROTEIN: 2G; SUGAR: 5G

814. Raspberry Cream Roll-Ups

Preparation Time: 10 Minutes
Cooking Time: 25 Minutes
Servings: 4

Ingredients

- 1 cup of fresh raspberries, rinsed and patted dry
- ½ cup of cream cheese, softened to room temperature
- ¼ cup of brown sugar
- ¼ cup of sweetened condensed milk
- 1 egg
- 1 teaspoon of corn starch
- 6 spring roll wrappers (any brand will do, we like Blue Dragon or Tasty Joy, both available through Target or Walmart, or any large grocery chain)
- ¼ cup of water

Directions:

1. Cover the basket of the Smart Air Fryer Oven with a lining of tin foil, leaving the edges uncovered to allow air to circulate through the basket. Preheat the Smart Air Fryer Oven to 350 degrees.
2. In a mixing bowl, combine the cream cheese, brown sugar, condensed milk, cornstarch, and egg. Beat or whip thoroughly, until all ingredients are completely mixed and fluffy, thick and stiff.
3. Spoon even amounts of the creamy filling into each spring roll wrapper, then top each dollop of filling with several raspberries.
4. Roll up the wraps around the creamy raspberry filling, and seal the seams with a few dabs of water.
5. Place each roll on the foil-lined air fryer basket, seams facing down.
6. Set the Smart Air Fryer Oven timer to 10 minutes. During cooking, shake the handle of the fryer basket to ensure a nice even surface crisp.
7. After 10 minutes, when the Smart Air Fryer Oven shuts off, the spring rolls should be golden brown and perfect on the outside, while the raspberries and cream filling will have cooked together in a glorious fusion. Remove with tongs and serve hot or cold.

Nutrition: CALORIES: 124; FAT: 2G; PROTEIN: 0G; SUGAR: 4G

815. Air Fryer Chocolate Cake

Preparation Time: 5 Minutes
Cooking Time: 35 Minutes
Servings: 8-10

Ingredients

- ½ C. hot water
- 1 tsp. vanilla
- ¼ C. olive oil
- ½ C. almond milk
- 1 egg
- ½ tsp. salt
- ¾ tsp. baking soda
- ¾ tsp. baking powder
- ½ C. unsweetened cocoa powder
- 2 C. almond flour
- 1 C. brown sugar

Directions:

1. Preheat your Smart Air Fryer Oven to 356 degrees.
2. Stir all dry ingredients together. Then stir in wet ingredients. Add hot water last.
3. The batter will be thin, no worries.
4. Pour cake batter into a pan that fits into the fryer. Cover with foil and poke holes into the foil.
5. Bake 35 minutes.
6. Discard foil and then bake another 10 minutes.

Nutrition: CALORIES: 378; FAT: 9G; PROTEIN: 4G; SUGAR: 5G

816. Banana-Choco Brownies

Preparation Time: 5 Minutes
Cooking Time: 30 Minutes
Servings: 12

Ingredients

- 2 cups almond flour
- 2 teaspoons baking powder
- ½ teaspoon baking powder
- ½ teaspoon baking soda

- ½ teaspoon salt
- 1 over-ripe banana
- 3 large eggs
- ½ teaspoon stevia powder
- ¼ cup coconut oil
- 1 tablespoon vinegar
- 1/3 cup almond flour
- 1/3 cup cocoa powder

Directions:
1. Preheat the Smart Air Fryer Oven for 5 minutes.
2. Combine all ingredients in a food processor and pulse until well-combined.
3. Pour into a baking dish that will fit in the air fryer.
4. Place in the air fryer basket and cook for 30 minutes at 350°F or if a toothpick inserted in the middle comes out clean.

Nutrition: CALORIES: 75; FAT: 5G; PROTEIN: 7G; SUGAR: 2G

817. Chocolate Donuts

Preparation Time: 5 Minutes
Cooking Time: 20 Minutes
Servings: 8-10

Ingredients
- (8-ounce) can jumbo biscuits
- Cooking oil
- Chocolate sauce, such as Hershey's

Directions:
1. Separate the biscuit dough into 8 biscuits and place them on a flat work surface. Use a small circle cookie cutter or a biscuit cutter to cut a hole in the center of each biscuit. You can also cut the holes using a knife.
2. Spray the air fryer basket with cooking oil.
3. Place 4 donuts in the Smart Air Fryer Oven. Do not stack. Spray with cooking oil. Cook for 4 minutes.
4. Open the air fryer and flip the donuts. Cook for an additional 4 minutes.
5. Remove the cooked donuts from the Smart Air Fryer Oven, then repeat for the remaining 4 donuts.
6. Drizzle chocolate sauce over the donuts and enjoy while warm.

Nutrition: CALORIES: 181; FAT: 98G; PROTEIN: 3G; FIBER: 1G

818. Air Fryer Cinnamon Rolls

Preparation Time: 15 Minutes
Cooking Time: 5 Minutes
Servings: 8

Ingredients
- 1½ tbsp. Cinnamon - ¾ C. brown sugar
- ¼ C. melted coconut oil
- 1 pound frozen bread dough, thawed

Glaze:
- ½ tsp. Vanilla - 1 ¼ C. powdered erythritol
- 2 tbsp. softened ghee
- 3 ounces softened cream cheese

Directions:
1. Lay out bread dough and roll out into a rectangle. Brush melted ghee over dough and leave a 1-inch border along edges.
2. Mix cinnamon and sweetener together and then sprinkle over dough.
3. Roll dough tightly and slice into 8 pieces. Let sit 1-2 hours to rise.
4. To make the glaze, simply mix ingredients together till smooth. Once rolls rise, place into air fryer and cook 5 minutes at 350 degrees.
5. Serve rolls drizzled in cream cheese glaze. Enjoy!

Nutrition: CALORIES: 390; FAT: 8G; PROTEIN: 1G; SUGAR: 7G

819. Easy Air Fryer Donuts

Preparation Time: 5 Minutes
Cooking Time: 5 Minutes
Servings: 8

Ingredients
- Pinch of allspice
- 4 tbsp. dark brown sugar
- ½ - 1 tsp. cinnamon
- 1/3 C. granulated sweetener
- 3 tbsp. melted coconut oil
- 1 can of biscuits

Directions:
1. Mix allspice, sugar, sweetener, and cinnamon together.
2. Take out biscuits from can and with a circle cookie cutter, cut holes from centers and place into air fryer.
3. Cook 5 minutes at 350 degrees. As batches are cooked, use a brush to coat with melted coconut oil and dip each into sugar mixture.
4. Serve warm!

Nutrition: CALORIES: 209; FAT: 4G; PROTEIN: 0G; SUGAR: 3G

820. Chocolate Soufflé for Two

Preparation Time: 5 Minutes
Cooking Time: 14 Minutes
Servings: 2

Ingredients
- 2 tbsp. almond flour
- ½ tsp. vanilla
- 3 tbsp. sweetener
- 2 separated eggs
- ¼ C. melted coconut oil
- 3 ounces of semi-sweet chocolate, chopped

Directions:
1. Brush coconut oil and sweetener onto ramekins.
2. Melt coconut oil and chocolate together.
3. Beat egg yolks well, adding vanilla and sweetener. Stir in flour and ensure there are no lumps.
4. Preheat the Smart Air Fryer Oven to 330 degrees.
5. Whisk egg whites till they reach peak state and fold them into chocolate mixture.
6. Pour batter into ramekins and place into the Smart Air Fryer Oven.
7. Cook 14 minutes.

8. Serve with powdered sugar dusted on top.

Nutrition: CALORIES: 238; FAT: 6G; PROTEIN: 1G; SUGAR: 4G

821. Fried Bananas with Chocolate Sauce

Preparation Time: 10 Minutes
Cooking Time: 10 Minutes
Servings: 2

Ingredients

- 1 large egg
- ¼ cup cornstarch
- ¼ cup plain bread crumbs
- 3 bananas, halved crosswise
- Cooking oil
- Chocolate sauce

Directions:

1. In a small bowl, beat the egg. In another bowl, place the cornstarch. Place the bread crumbs in a third bowl. Dip the bananas in the cornstarch, then the egg, and then the bread crumbs.
2. Spray the air fryer basket with cooking oil. Place the bananas in the basket and spray them with cooking oil.
3. Cook for 5 minutes. Open the air fryer and flip the bananas. Cook for an additional 2 minutes. Transfer the bananas to plates.
4. Drizzle the chocolate sauce over the bananas, and serve.
5. You can make your own chocolate sauce using 2 tablespoons milk and ¼ cup chocolate chips. Heat a saucepan over medium-high heat. Add the milk and stir for 1 to 2 minutes. Add the chocolate chips. Stir for 2 minutes, or until the chocolate has melted.

Nutrition: CALORIES: 203; FAT: 6G; PROTEIN: 3G; FIBER: 3G

822. Apple Hand Pies

Preparation Time: 5 Minutes
Cooking Time: 8 Minutes
Servings: 6

Ingredients

- 15-ounces no-sugar-added apple pie filling
- 1 store-bought crust

Directions:

1. Lay out pie crust and slice into equal-sized squares.
2. Place 2 tbsp. filling into each square and seal crust with a fork.
3. Pour into the Oven rack/basket. Place the Rack on the middle-shelf of the Smart Air Fryer Oven. Set temperature to 390°F, and set time to 8 minutes until golden in color.

Nutrition: CALORIES: 278; FAT: 10G; PROTEIN: 5G; SUGAR: 4G

823. Chocolaty Banana Muffins

Preparation Time: 5 Minutes
Cooking Time: 25 Minutes
Servings: 12

Ingredients

- ¾ cup whole wheat flour
- ¾ cup plain flour
- ¼ cup cocoa powder
- ¼ teaspoon baking powder
- 1 teaspoon baking soda
- ¼ teaspoon salt
- 2 large bananas, peeled and mashed
- 1 cup sugar
- 1/3 cup canola oil
- 1 egg
- ½ teaspoon vanilla essence
- 1 cup mini chocolate chips

Directions:

1. In a large bowl, mix together flour, cocoa powder, baking powder, baking soda and salt.
2. In another bowl, add bananas, sugar, oil, egg and vanilla extract and beat till well combined.
3. Slowly, add flour mixture in egg mixture and mix till just combined.
4. Fold in chocolate chips.
5. Preheat the Smart Air Fryer Oven to 345 degrees F. Grease 12 muffin molds.
6. Transfer the mixture into prepared muffin molds evenly and cook for about 20-25 minutes or till a toothpick inserted in the center comes out clean.
7. Remove the muffin molds from Air fryer and keep on wire rack to cool for about 10 minutes. Carefully turn on a wire rack to cool completely before serving.

Nutrition: CALORIES: 124; FAT: 2G; PROTEIN: 0G; SUGAR: 4G

824. Bread Pudding with Cranberry

Preparation Time: 5 Minutes
Cooking Time: 45 Minutes
Servings: 4

Ingredients

- 1-1/2 cups milk
- 2-1/2 eggs
- 1/2 cup cranberries1 teaspoon butter
- 1/4 cup and 2 tablespoons white sugar
- 1/4 cup golden raisins
- 1/8 teaspoon ground cinnamon
- 3/4 cup heavy whipping cream
- 3/4 teaspoon lemon zest
- 3/4 teaspoon kosher salt
- 3/4 French baguettes, cut into 2-inch slices
- 3/8 vanilla bean, split and seeds scraped away

Directions:

1. Lightly grease baking pan of air fryer with cooking spray. Spread baguette slices, cranberries, and raisins.
2. In blender, blend well vanilla bean, cinnamon, salt, lemon zest, eggs, sugar, and cream. Pour over baguette slices. Let it soak for an hour.
3. Cover pan with foil.
4. For 35 minutes, cook on 330°F.
5. Let it rest for 10 minutes.
6. Serve and enjoy.

Nutrition: CALORIES: 581; FAT: 28G; PROTEIN: 18G; SUGAR: 7G

825. Black and White Brownies

Preparation Time: 10 Minutes
Cooking Time: 20 Minutes
Servings: 8

Ingredients
- 1 egg
- ¼ cup brown sugar
- 2 tablespoons white sugar
- 2 tablespoons safflower oil
- 1 teaspoon vanilla
- ¼ cup cocoa powder
- ⅓ cup all-purpose flour
- ¼ cup white chocolate chips
- Nonstick baking spray with flour

Directions:
1. In a medium bowl, beat the egg with the brown sugar and white sugar. Beat in the oil and vanilla.
2. Add the cocoa powder and flour, and stir just until combined. Fold in the white chocolate chips.
3. Spray a 6-by-6-by-2-inch baking pan with nonstick spray. Spoon the brownie batter into the pan.
4. Pour the pan into the Oven rack/basket. Place the Rack on the middle-shelf of the Smart Air Fryer Oven. Set temperature to 390°F, and set time to 20 minutes. Bake for 20 minutes or until the brownies are set when lightly touched with a finger. Let cool for 30 minutes before slicing to serve.

Nutrition: CALORIES: 81; FAT: 4G; PROTEIN: 1G; FIBER: 1G

826. Sweet Cream Cheese Wontons

Preparation Time: 5 Minutes
Cooking Time: 5 Minutes
Servings: 16

Ingredients
- egg mixed with a bit of water
- Wonton wrappers
- ½ C. powdered erythritol
- 8 ounces softened cream cheese
- Olive oil

Directions:
1. Mix sweetener and cream cheese together.
2. Lay out 4 wontons at a time and cover with a dish towel to prevent drying out.
3. Place ½ of a teaspoon of cream cheese mixture into each wrapper.
4. Dip finger into egg/water mixture and fold diagonally to form a triangle. Seal edges well.
5. Repeat with remaining ingredients.
6. Place filled wontons into the Smart Air Fryer Oven and cook 5 minutes at 400 degrees, shaking halfway through cooking.

Nutrition: CALORIES: 303; FAT: 3G; PROTEIN: 5G; SUGAR: 4G

827. Baked Apple

Preparation Time: 5 Minutes
Cooking Time: 20 Minutes
Servings: 4

Ingredients
- ¼ C. water
- ¼ tsp. nutmeg
- ¼ tsp. cinnamon
- 1 ½ tsp. melted ghee
- 2 tbsp. raisins
- 2 tbsp. chopped walnuts
- 1 medium apple

Directions:
1. Preheat your air fryer to 350 degrees.
2. Slice apple in half and discard some of the flesh from the center.
3. Place into frying pan.
4. Mix remaining ingredients together except water. Spoon mixture to the middle of apple halves.
5. Pour water over filled apples.
6. Place pan with apple halves into the Smart Air Fryer Oven, bake 20 minutes.

Nutrition: CALORIES: 199; FAT: 9G; PROTEIN: 1G; SUGAR: 3G

828. Coffee and Blueberry Cake

Preparation Time: 5 Minutes
Cooking Time: 35 Minutes
Servings: 6

Ingredients
- cup white sugar
- 1 egg
- 1/2 cup butter, softened
- 1/2 cup fresh or frozen blueberries
- 1/2 cup sour cream
- 1/2 teaspoon baking powder
- 1/2 teaspoon ground cinnamon
- 1/2 teaspoon vanilla extract
- 1/4 cup brown sugar
- 1/4 cup chopped pecans
- 1/8 teaspoon salt
- 1-1/2 teaspoons confectioners' sugar for dusting
- 3/4 cup and 1 tablespoon all-purpose flour

Directions:
1. In a small bowl, whisk well pecans, cinnamon, and brown sugar.
2. In a blender, blend well all wet Ingredients. Add dry Ingredients except for confectioner's sugar and blueberries. Blend well until smooth and creamy.
3. Lightly grease baking pan of air fryer with cooking spray.
4. Pour half of batter in pan. Sprinkle half of pecan mixture on top. Pour the remaining batter. And then topped with remaining pecan mixture.
5. Cover pan with foil.
6. For 35 minutes, cook on 330°F.
7. Serve and enjoy with a dusting of confectioner's sugar.

Nutrition: CALORIES: 471; FAT: 24G; PROTEIN: 1G; SUGAR: 6G

829. Cinnamon Sugar Roasted Chickpeas

Preparation Time: 5 Minutes
Cooking Time: 10 Minutes
Servings: 2
Ingredients

- 1 tbsp. sweetener
- 1 tbsp. cinnamon
- 1 chickpeas

Directions:
1. Preheat Smart Air Fryer Oven to 390 degrees.
2. Rinse and drain chickpeas.
3. Mix all ingredients together and add to air fryer.
4. Pour into the Oven rack/basket. Place the Rack on the middle-shelf of the Smart Air Fryer Oven. Set temperature to 390°F, and set time to 10 minutes.

Nutrition: CALORIES: 111; FAT: 19G; PROTEIN: 16G; SUGAR: 5G

830. Cherry-Choco Bars

Preparation Time: 5 Minutes
Cooking Time: 15 Minutes
Servings: 8
Ingredients

- ¼ teaspoon salt
- ½ cup almonds, sliced
- ½ cup chia seeds
- ½ cup dark chocolate, chopped
- ½ cup dried cherries, chopped
- ½ cup prunes, pureed
- ½ cup quinoa, cooked
- ¾ cup almond butter
- 1/3 cup honey
- 2 cups old-fashioned oats
- 2 tablespoon coconut oil

Directions:
1. Preheat the Smart Air Fryer Oven to 375°F.
2. In a mixing bowl, combine the oats, quinoa, chia seeds, almond, cherries, and chocolate.
3. In a saucepan, heat the almond butter, honey, and coconut oil.
4. Pour the butter mixture over the dry mixture. Add salt and prunes.
5. Mix until well combined.
6. Pour over a baking dish that can fit inside the air fryer.
7. Cook for 15 minutes.
8. Let it cool for an hour before slicing into bars.

Nutrition: CALORIES: 321; FAT: 17G; PROTEIN: 7G; SUGAR: 5G

831. Cinnamon Fried Bananas

Preparation Time: 5 Minutes
Cooking Time: 10 Minutes
Servings: 2-3
Ingredients

- 1 C. panko breadcrumbs
- 3 tbsp. cinnamon
- ½ C. almond flour
- 3 egg whites
- 8 ripe bananas
- 3 tbsp. vegan coconut oil

Directions:
1. Heat coconut oil and add breadcrumbs. Mix around 2-3 minutes until golden. Pour into bowl.
2. Peel and cut bananas in half. Roll each bananas half into flour, eggs, and crumb mixture.
3. Place into the Smart Air Fryer Oven. Cook 10 minutes at 280 degrees.
4. A great addition to a healthy banana split!

Nutrition: CALORIES: 219; FAT: 10G; PROTEIN: 3G; SUGAR: 5G

832. Coconutty Lemon Bars

Preparation Time: 5 Minutes
Cooking Time: 25 Minutes
Servings: 12
Ingredients

- ¼ cup cashew
- ¼ cup fresh lemon juice, freshly squeezed
- ¾ cup coconut milk
- ¾ cup erythritol
- 1 cup desiccated coconut
- 1 teaspoon baking powder
- 2 eggs, beaten
- 2 tablespoons coconut oil
- air fryer of salt

Directions:
1. Preheat the Smart Air Fryer Oven for 5 minutes. In a mixing bowl, combine all ingredients. Use a hand mixer to mix everything. Pour into a baking dish that will fit in the air fryer.
2. Bake for 25 minutes at 350°F or until a toothpick inserted in the middle comes out clean.

Nutrition: CALORIES: 118; FAT: 10G; PROTEIN: 6G; SUGAR: 5G

833. Awesome Chinese Doughnuts

Preparation Time: 10 minutes
Cooking Time: 8 minutes
Servings: 8
Ingredients:

- 1 tbsp. baking powder
- 6 tbsps. coconut oil
- ¾ c. of coconut milk
- 2 tsps. sugar
- 2 c. all-purpose flour
- ½ tsp. sea salt

Directions:
1. Preheat the air fryer to 3500F.
2. Mix baking powder, flour, sugar, and salt in a bowl.
3. Add coconut oil and mix well. Add coconut milk and mix until well combined.
4. Knead dough for 3-4 minutes.

5. Roll dough half inch thick and using cookie cutter cut doughnuts.
6. Place doughnuts in cake pan and brush with oil. Place cake pan in air fryer basket and air fry doughnuts for 5 minutes. Turn doughnuts to other side and air fry for 3 minutes more.
7. Serve and enjoy.

Nutrition: Calories: 259 Fat: 19 g Carbs: 27 g Protein: 8 g

834. Banana and Walnuts Muffins

Preparation Time: 10 minutes
Cooking Time: 10 minutes
Servings: 2

Ingredients:
- ¼ c. flour
- ½ tsp. baking powder
- ¼ c. mashed banana
- ¼ c. butter
- 1 tbsp. chopped walnuts
- ¼ c. oats

Directions:
1. Spray four muffin molds with cooking spray and set aside.
2. In a bowl, mix together mashed banana, walnuts, sugar, and butter.
3. In another bowl, mix oat, flour, and baking powder.
4. Combine the flour mixture to the banana mixture.
5. Pour batter into the prepared muffin mold.
6. Place in air fryer basket and cook at 320 F/ 160 C for 10 minutes.
7. Remove muffins from air fryer and allow to cool completely.
8. Serve and enjoy.

Nutrition: Calories: 192 Fat: 13 g Carbs: 14 g Protein: 9 g

835. Vanilla Spiced Soufflé

Preparation Time: 20 minutes
Cooking Time: 32 minutes
Servings: 6

Ingredients:
- 1 tsp. cream of tartar
- 1 vanilla bean
- 4 egg yolks
- ¼ c. all-purpose flour
- 1 c. whole milk
- 2 tsps. vanilla extract
- 1-oz. sugar
- ¼ c. softened butter
- ¼ c. sugar
- 5 egg whites

Directions:
1. Combine flour and the butter in a bowl until the mixture becomes a smooth paste.
2. Set the pan over medium flame to heat the milk. Add sugar and stir until dissolved.
3. Mix in the vanilla bean and bring to a boil.
4. Beat the mixture using a wire whisk as you add the butter and flour mixture.
5. Lower the heat to simmer until thick. Discard the vanilla bean. Turn off the heat.
6. Place them on an ice bath and allow to cool for 10 minutes. Grease 6 ramekins with butter. Sprinkle each with a bit of sugar.
7. Beat the egg yolks in a bowl. Add the vanilla extract and milk mixture. Mix until combined.
8. Whisk together the tartar cream, egg whites, and sugar until it forms medium stiff peaks.
9. 1Gradually fold the egg whites into the soufflé base. Transfer the mixture to the ramekins.
10. 1Put 3 ramekins in the cooking basket at a time. Cook for 16 minutes at 330 degrees. Move to a wire rack for cooling and cook the rest.
11. 1Sprinkle powdered sugar on top and drizzle with chocolate sauce before serving.

Nutrition: Calories: 215 Fat: 12g Carbs: 198g Protein: 66g

836. Apricot Blackberry Crumble

Preparation Time: 10 minutes
Cooking Time: 20 minutes
Servings: 8

Ingredients:
- 1 c. flour
- 18 oz. fresh apricots
- 5 tbsps. cold butter
- ½ c. sugar
- 5½ oz. fresh blackberries
- Salt
- 2 tbsps. lemon juice

Directions:
1. Put the apricots and blackberries in a bowl. Add lemon juice and 2 tbsps. of sugar. Mix until combined.
2. Transfer the mixture to a baking dish.
3. Put flour, the rest of the sugar, and a pinch of salt in a bowl. Mix well. Add a tbsp. of cold butter.
4. Combine the mixture until it becomes crumbly. Put this on top of the fruit mixture and press it down lightly.
5. Set the baking tray in the cooking basket.
6. Cook for 20 minutes at 390 degrees.
7. Allow to cool before slicing and serving.

Nutrition: Calories: 217 Fat: 44g Carbs: 32g Protein: 3g

837. Roasted Pineapples with Vanilla Zest

Preparation Time: 5 minutes
Cooking Time: 8 minutes
Servings: 4

Ingredients:
- 2 anise stars
- ¼ c. orange juice
- 1 tsp. lime juice
- g1 vanilla pod
- 2 tbsps. caster sugar
- ¼ c. pineapple juice
- 1 lb. pineapple slice

Directions:
1. Preheat Air Fryer to a temperature of 350°F (180°C).

2. Take a baking pan that can fit into Air Fryer basket.
3. Now add pineapple juice, sugar, orange juice, anise stars, and vanilla pod into a pan and mix well.
4. Place in pineapple slices evenly and transfer pan into Air Fryer basket.
5. Cook for 8 minutes.
6. Serve!

Nutrition: Calories: 90 Protein: 79 g Fat: 17 g Carbs: 222 g

838. Chocolate Cup cakes

Preparation Time: 5 minutes
Cooking Time: 12 minutes
Servings: 6
Ingredients:
- 3 eggs
- ¼ c. caster sugar
- ¼ c. cocoa powder
- 1 tsp. baking powder
- 1 c. milk
- ¼ tsp. vanilla essence
- 2 c. all-purpose flour
- 4 tbsps. butter

Directions:
1. Preheat your Air Fryer to a temperature of 400°F (200°C).
2. Beat eggs with sugar in a bowl until creamy.
3. Add butter and beat again for 1-2 minutes.
4. Now add flour, cocoa powder, milk, and baking powder, and vanilla essence, mix with a spatula.
5. Fill ¾ of muffin tins with the mixture and place them into Air Fryer basket.
6. Let to cook for 12 minutes.
7. Serve!

Nutrition: Calories: 289 Protein: 72 g Fat: 15 g Carbs: 394 g

839. Crispy Bananas

Preparation Time: 10 minutes
Cooking Time: 10 minutes
Servings: 4
Ingredients:
- ½ c. breadcrumbs
- ½ tbsps. cinnamon sugar
- 1 tbsp. almond meal
- 1 ½ tbsps. coconut oil
- 4 sliced ripe bananas
- 1 beaten egg
- 1 tbsp. crushed cashew
- ¼ c. corn flour

Directions:
1. Set the pan on fire to heat the coconut oil over medium heat and add breadcrumbs in the pan and stir for 3-4 minutes.
2. Remove pan from heat and transfer breadcrumbs in a bowl.
3. Add almond meal and crush cashew in breadcrumbs and mix well.
4. Dip banana half in corn flour then in egg and finally coat with breadcrumbs.
5. Place coated banana in air fryer basket. Sprinkle with Cinnamon Sugar.
6. Air fry at 350 F/ 176 C for 10 minutes.
7. Serve and enjoy.

Nutrition: Calories: 282 Fat: 9 g Carbs: 46 g Protein: 5 g

840. Stuffed Baked Apples

Preparation Time: 3 minutes
Cooking Time: 12 minutes
Servings: 4
Ingredients:
- 4 tbsps. honey
- ¼ c. brown sugar
- ½ c. raisins
- ½ c. crushed walnuts
- 4 large apples

Directions:
1. Preheat Air Fryer to a temperature of 350°F (180°C).
2. Cut the apples from the stem and remove the inner using spoon.
3. Now fill each apple with raisins, walnuts, honey, and brown sugar.
4. Transfer apples in a pan and place in Air Fryer basket, cook for 12 minutes.
5. Serve.

Nutrition: Calories: 324 Protein: 8 g Fat: 99 g Carbs: 731 g

841. Cinnamon Apple Chips

Preparation Time: 10 minutes
Cooking Time: 8 minutes
Servings: 6
Ingredients:
- 3 granny smith apples, wash, core, and thinly slice
- 1 tsp. ground cinnamon pinch of salt

Directions:
1. Rub apple slices with cinnamon and salt and place them into the Air Fryer basket.
2. Cook at 390°F for 8 minutes. Turn halfway through.
3. Serve and enjoy.

Nutrition:
Calories: 170, Protein: 4 g, Fat: 1g, Carbs: 6 g.

842. Apple Chips with Dip

Preparation Time: 10 minutes
Cooking Time: 12 minutes
Servings: 4
Ingredients:
- 1 apple, thinly slice using a mandolin slicer
- 1 tbsp. almond butter
- ¼ cup plain yogurt
- 2 tsp. olive oil
- 1 tsp. ground cinnamon
- Drops liquid stevia

Directions:
1. Add apple slices, oil, and cinnamon to a large bowl and toss well.
2. Grease air the fryer basket with cooking spray.
3. Place apple slices in an Air Fryer basket and cook at 375°F for 12 minutes. Turn after every 4 minutes.
4. Meanwhile, in a small bowl, mix almond butter, yogurt, and sweetener.
5. Serve apple chips with dip and enjoy.

Nutrition:
Calories: 253, Total Carbs: 15 g, Net Carbs: 13 g, Protein: 27 g, Fat: 9 g, Sugar: 4 g, Fiber: 2 g.

843. Delicious Spiced Apples

Preparation Time: 10 minutes
Cooking Time: 10 minutes
Servings: 6
Ingredients:
- Small apples, sliced
- 1 tsp. apple pie spice
- ½ cup erythritol
- 2 tbsp. coconut oil, melted

Directions:
1. Add apple slices in a mixing bowl and sprinkle sweetener, apple pie spice, and coconut oil over the apple and toss to coat.
2. Transfer apple slices in an Air Fryer dish. Place dish in the Air Fryer basket and cook at 350°F for 10 minutes.
3. Serve and enjoy.

Nutrition:
Calories: 234, Fat: 13.8 g, Carbs: 5.9 g, Protein: 20 g.

844. Tasty Cheese Bites

Preparation Time: 10 minutes
Cooking Time: 2 minutes
Servings: 16
Ingredients:
- 8 oz. cream cheese, softened
- 2 tbsp. erythritol
- ½ cup almond flour
- ½ tsp. vanilla
- 4 tbsp. heavy cream
- ½ cup erythritol

Directions:
1. Add cream cheese, vanilla, ½ cup erythritol, and 2 tablespoons of heavy cream in a stand mixer and mix until smooth.
2. Scoop cream cheese mixture onto the parchment-lined plate and place it in the refrigerator for 1 hour.
3. In a small bowl, mix almond flour and 2 tablespoons of erythritol.
4. Dip cheesecake bites in remaining heavy cream and coat with almond flour mixture.
5. Place cheesecake bites in the Air Fryer basket and air fry for 2 minutes at 350°F.
6. Make sure cheesecake bites are frozen before air fry otherwise they will melt.
7. Drizzle with chocolate syrup and serve.

Nutrition:
Calories: 383, Fat: 19.8 g, Carbs: 28 g, Protein: 23 g.

845. Apple Chips

Preparation Time: 10 minutes
Cooking Time: 20 minutes
Servings: 2
Ingredients:
- 1 apple, sliced thinly
- Salt to taste
- ¼ tsp. ground cinnamon

Directions:
1. Preheat the Air Fryer to 350°F.
2. Toss the apple slices in salt and cinnamon.
3. Add to the Air Fryer.
4. Let it cool before serving.

Nutrition:
Calories: 59, Protein: 0.3 g, Fat: 0.2 g, Carbs: 15.6 g.

846. Gooey Cinnamon Smores

Preparation Time: 5 minutes
Cooking Time: 3 minutes
Servings: 12 or more
Ingredients:
- 12 whole cinnamon graham crackers, halved
- 2 (1.55-ounce) chocolate bars, cut into 12 pieces
- 12 marshmallows

Directions:
1. Arrange 12 graham cracker squares in the Air Fry basket in a single layer.
2. Top each square with a piece of chocolate.
3. Place the basket on the Bake position.
4. Select Bake, set the temperature to 350°f (180°c), and time to 3 minutes.
5. After 2 minutes, remove the basket and place a marshmallow on each piece of melted chocolate. Return the basket to the Air Fryer grill and continue to cook for another 1 minute.
6. Remove from the Air Fryer grill to a serving plate.
7. Serve topped with the remaining graham cracker squares.

Nutrition:
Calories: 234, Fat: 13.8 g, Carbs: 5.9 g, Protein: 20 g.

847. Sweetened Plantains

Preparation Time: 5 minutes
Cooking Time: 8 minutes
Servings: 4
Ingredients:
- 2 ripe plantains, sliced
- 2 tsp. avocado oil
- Salt to taste
- Maple syrup

Directions:
1. Toss the plantains in oil.
2. Season with salt.
3. Cook in the Air Fryer basket at 400°F for 10 minutes, shaking after 5 minutes.
4. Drizzle with maple syrup before serving.

Nutrition:
Calories: 125, Protein: 1.2 g, Fat: 0.6 g, Carbs: 32 g.

848. Pear Crisp

Preparation Time: 10 minutes
Cooking Time: 25 minutes
Servings: 2
Ingredients:
- 1 cup flour
- 1 stick vegan butter
- 1 tbsp. cinnamon
- ½ cup sugar
- 2 pears, cubed

Directions:
1. Mix flour and butter to form a crumbly texture.
2. Add cinnamon and sugar.
3. Put the pears in the Air Fryer.
4. Pour and spread the mixture on top of the pears.
5. Cook at 350°F for 25 minutes.

Nutrition:
Calories: 544, Protein: 7.4 g, Fat: 0.9 g, Carbs: 132.3 g.

849. Easy Pears Dessert

Preparation Time: 10 minutes
Cooking Time: 25 minutes
Servings: 12
Ingredients:
- 6 big pears, cored and chopped
- ½ cup raisins
- 1 tsp. ginger powder
- ¼ cup coconut sugar
- 1 tsp. lemon zest, grated

Directions:
1. In a container that fits your Air Fryer, mix pears with raisins, ginger, sugar, and lemon zest, and stir, introduce in the fryer and cook at 350°F for 25 minutes.
2. Divide into bowls and serve cold.
3. Enjoy!

Nutrition:
Calories: 200, Protein: 6 g, Fat: 3 g, Carbs: 6 g.

850. Vanilla Strawberry Mix

Preparation Time: 10 minutes
Cooking Time: 20 minutes
Servings: 10
Ingredients:
- 2 tbsp. lemon juice
- 2 pounds strawberries
- 4 cups coconut sugar
- 1 tsp. cinnamon powder
- 1 tsp. vanilla extract

Directions:
1. In a pot that fits your Air Fryer, mix strawberries with coconut sugar, lemon juice, cinnamon, and vanilla. Stir gently, introduce in the fryer and cook at 350°F for 20 minutes
2. Divide into bowls and serve cold.
3. Enjoy!

Nutrition:
Calories: 140, Protein: 2 g, Fat: 0 g, Carbs: 5 g.

851. Sweet Bananas and Sauce

Preparation Time: 10 minutes
Cooking Time: 20 minutes
Servings: 4
Ingredients:
- Juice of ½ lemon - 3 tbsp. agave nectar
- 1 tbsp. coconut oil
- 4 bananas, peeled and sliced diagonally
- ½ tsp. cardamom seeds

Directions:
1. Arrange bananas in a pan that fits your Air Fryer. Add agave nectar, lemon juice, oil, and cardamom. Introduce in the fryer and cook at 360°F for 20 minutes.

2. Divide bananas and sauce between plates and serve.
3. Enjoy!

Nutrition:
Calories: 210, Protein: 3 g, Fat: 1 g, Carbs: 8 g.

852. Cinnamon Apples and Mandarin Sauce

Preparation Time: 10 minutes
Cooking Time: 20 minutes
Servings: 4
Ingredients:

- 4 apples, cored, peeled, and cored
- 2 cups mandarin juice
- ¼ cup maple syrup - 2 tsp. cinnamon powder
- 1 tbsp. ginger, grated

Directions:

1. In a pot that fits your Air Fryer, mix apples with mandarin juice, maple syrup, cinnamon, and ginger. Introduce it in the fryer and cook at 365°F for 20 minutes.
2. Divide apples mix between plates and serve warm.
3. Enjoy!

Nutrition:
Calories: 170, Protein: 4 g, Fat: 1 g, Carbs: 6 g.

853. Cocoa Berries Cream

Preparation Time: 10 minutes
Cooking Time: 10 minutes
Servings: 4
Ingredients:

- 3 tbsp. cocoa powder
- 14 ounces coconut cream
- 1 cup blackberries
- 1 cup raspberries - 2 tbsp. stevia

Directions:

1. In a bowl, whisk cocoa powder with stevia and cream; stir.
2. Add raspberries and blackberries. Toss gently, transfer to a pan that fits your Air Fryer, introduce in the fryer and cook at 350°F for 10 minutes.
3. Divide into bowls and serve cold. Enjoy!

Nutrition:
Calories: 205, Protein: 2 g, Fat: 34 g, Carbs: 6 g.

854. Sweet Vanilla Rhubarb

Preparation Time: 10 minutes
Cooking Time: 10 minutes
Servings: 4
Ingredients:

- 5 cups rhubarb, chopped
- 2 tbsp. coconut butter, melted
- 1/3 cup water - 1 tbsp. stevia
- 1 tsp. vanilla extract

Directions:

1. Put rhubarb, ghee, water, stevia, and vanilla extract in a pan that fits your Air Fryer. Introduce it in the fryer and cook at 365°F for 10 minutes.
2. Divide into small bowls and serve cold.
3. Enjoy!

Nutrition:
Calories: 103, Protein: 2 g, Fat: 2 g, Carbs: 6 g.

855. Cherries and Rhubarb Bowls

Preparation Time: 10 minutes
Cooking Time: 35 minutes
Servings: 4
Ingredients:

- 2 cups cherries, pitted and halved
- 1 cup rhubarb, sliced - 1 cup apple juice
- 2 tbsp. sugar - ½ cup raisins.

Directions:

1. In a pot that fits your Air Fryer, combine the cherries with the rhubarb and the other ingredients. Toss, cook at 330°F for 35 minutes, divide into bowls, cool down, and serve.

Nutrition:
Calories: 212, Protein: 7 g, Fat: 8 g, Carbs: 13 g.

856. Pumpkin Bowls

Preparation Time: 10 minutes
Cooking Time: 15 minutes
Servings: 4
Ingredients:

- 2 cups pumpkin flesh, cubed
- 1 cup heavy cream
- 1 tsp. cinnamon powder
- 3 tbsp. sugar
- 1 tsp. nutmeg, ground

Directions:

1. In a pot that fits your Air Fryer, combine the pumpkin with the cream and the other ingredients. Introduce it in the fryer and cook at 360°F for 15 minutes.
2. Divide into bowls and serve.

Nutrition:
Calories: 212, Protein: 7 g, Fat: 5 g, Carbs: 15 g.

857. Buttery Fennel and Garlic

Preparation Time: 10 minutes
Cooking Time: 5 minutes
Servings: 4
Ingredients:

- ½ stick butter
- 2 garlic cloves, sliced
- ½ tsp. salt
- 1 and ½ pounds fennel bulb., cut into wedges
- ¼ tsp. ground black pepper
- ½ tsp. cayenne
- ¼ tsp. dried dill weed
- 1/3 cup dry white wine
- 2/3 cup stock

Directions:

1. Set your PowerXL Deluxe to Sauté mode and add butter, let it heat.
2. Add garlic and cook for 30 seconds.
3. Add the rest of the ingredients.
4. Lock lid and cook on LOW pressure for 3 minutes.
5. Remove the lid and serve.
6. Enjoy!

Nutrition:
Calories: 111, Fat: 6 g, Saturated Fat: 2 g, Carbohydrates: 2 g, Fiber: 2 g, Sodium: 317 mg, Protein: 2 g.

858. Lemon Mousse

Preparation Time: 10 minutes
Cooking Time: 12 minutes
Servings: 2
Ingredients:
- 4 ounces cream cheese, softened
- ½ cup heavy cream
- 2 tbsp. fresh lemon juice
- 2 tbsp. honey
- Pinch of salt

Directions:
1. In a bowl, add all the ingredients and mix until well combined.
2. Transfer the mixture into 2 ramekins.
3. Select "Bake" of Kalorik Maxx Air Fryer Oven and then adjust the temperature to 350°F.
4. Set the timer for 12 minutes and press "Start/Stop" to begin cooking.
5. When the unit beeps to show that it is preheated, place the ramekins over the air rack and insert them in the Kalorik Oven.
6. When cooking time is complete, remove the ramekin from Kalorik Oven and place it onto a wire rack to cool completely.
7. Refrigerate the ramekins for at least 3 hours before serving.

Nutrition:
Calories: 369, Total Fat: 31 g, Saturated Fat: 19.5 g, Cholesterol: 103mg, Sodium: 261mg, Total Carbohydrates: 20 g, Fiber: 0.1 g, Sugar: 17.7 g, Protein: 5.1 g.

859. Glazed Banana

Preparation Time: 10 minutes
Cooking Time: 10 minutes
Servings: 4
Ingredients:
- 2 ripe bananas, peeled and sliced lengthwise
- 1 tsp. fresh lime juice
- 4 tsp. maple syrup
- 1/8 tsp. ground cinnamon

Directions:
1. Coat each banana half with lime juice.
2. Arrange the banana halves onto a greased baking pan, cut sides up.
3. Drizzle the banana halves with maple syrup and sprinkle with cinnamon.
4. Select "Air Fry" of Kalorik Maxx Air Fryer Oven and then adjust the temperature to 350°F.
5. Set the timer for 10 minutes and press "Start/Stop" to begin cooking.
6. When the unit beeps to show that it is preheated, insert the baking pan in the Kalorik Oven.
7. When cooking time is complete, remove the baking pan from Kalorik Oven and serve immediately.

Nutrition:
Calories: 70, Total Fat: 0.2 g, Saturated Fat: 0.1 g, Cholesterol: 0mg, Sodium: 1mg, Total Carbohydrates: 18 g, Fiber: 1.6 g, Sugar: 11.2 g, Protein: 0.6 g.

860. Raspberry Danish

Preparation Time: 20 minutes
Cooking Time: 25 minutes
Servings: 6
Ingredients:
- 1 tube full-sheet crescent roll dough
- 4 ounces cream cheese, softened
- ¼ cup raspberry jam
- ½ cup fresh raspberries, chopped
- 1 cup powdered sugar
- 2–3 tbsp. heavy whipping cream

Directions:
1. Place the sheet of crescent roll dough onto a flat surface and unroll it.
2. In a microwave-safe bowl, add the cream cheese and microwave for about 20–30 seconds.
3. Remove from microwave and stir until creamy and smooth.
4. Spread the cream cheese over the dough sheet, followed by the strawberry jam.
5. Now, place the raspberry pieces evenly across the top.
6. From the short side, roll the dough and pinch the seam to seal.
7. Arrange a greased parchment paper onto the steak tray of the oven.
8. Carefully, curve the rolled pastry into a horseshoe shape and arrange it onto the tray.
9. Select "Air Fry" of Kalorik Maxx Air Fryer Oven and then adjust the temperature to 350°F.
10. Set the timer for 25 minutes and press "Start/Stop" to begin cooking.
11. When the unit beeps to show that it is preheated, insert the tray in the Kalorik Oven.
12. When cooking time is complete, remove the tray from Kalorik Oven and place it onto a rack to cool.
13. Meanwhile, in a bowl, mix the powdered sugar and cream.
14. Drizzle the cream mixture over cooled Danish and serve.

Nutrition:
Calories: 335, Total Fat: 15.3 g, Saturated Fat: 8 g, Cholesterol: 28mg, Sodium: 342 mg, Total Carbohydrates: 45.3 g, Fiber: 0.7 g, Sugar: 30.1 g, Protein: 4.4 g.

861. Blueberry Muffins

Preparation Time: 15 minutes
Cooking Time: 15 minutes
Servings: 8
Ingredients:
- ¼ cup unsweetened coconut milk
- 2 large eggs
- ½ tsp. vanilla extract
- 1½ cups almond flour
- ¼ cup Swerve
- 1 tsp. baking powder
- ¼ tsp. ground cinnamon

- Pinch of ground cloves
- Pinch of ground nutmeg
- 1/8 tsp. salt
- ½ cup fresh blueberries
- ¼ cup pecans, chopped

Directions:
1. In a blender, add the almond milk, eggs, and vanilla extract; pulse for about 20–30 seconds.
2. Add the almond flour, Swerve, baking powder, spices, and salt; pulse for about 30–45 seconds until well blended.
3. Transfer the mixture into a bowl
4. Gently, fold in half of the blueberries and pecans.
5. Place the mixture into 8 silicone muffin cups and top each with remaining blueberries.
6. Select "Air Fry" of Kalorik Maxx Air Fryer Oven and then adjust the temperature to 325°F.
7. Set the timer for 15 minutes and press "Start/Stop" to begin cooking.
8. When the unit beeps to show that it is preheated, place the cups over the air rack and insert them in the Kalorik Oven.
9. When cooking time is complete, remove the cups from Kalorik Oven and place them onto a wire rack to cool for about 10 minutes.
10. Carefully, invert the muffins onto the wire rack to completely cool before serving.

Nutrition:
Calories: 191, Total Fat: 16.5 g, Saturated Fat: 3 g, Cholesterol: 47 mg, Sodium: 54 mg; Total Carbohydrates: 14.8 g, Fiber: 3.2 g, Sugar: 9.7 g, Protein: 6.8 g.

862. Cranberry Cupcakes
Preparation Time: 15 minutes
Cooking Time: 15 minutes
Servings: 10
Ingredients:
- 4½ ounces self-rising flour
- ½ tsp. baking powder
- Pinch of salt
- ½ ounce cream cheese, softened
- 4¾ ounces butter, softened
- 4¼ ounces caster sugar
- 2 eggs
- 2 tsp. fresh lemon juice
- ½ cup fresh cranberries

Directions:
1. In a bowl, mix the flour, baking powder, and salt.
2. In another bowl, mix the cream cheese, and butter.
3. Add the sugar and beat until fluffy and light.
4. Add the eggs, one at a time, and whisk until just combined.
5. Add the flour mixture and stir until well combined.
6. Stir in the lemon juice.
7. Place the mixture into silicone cups and top each with cranberries evenly, pressing slightly.
8. Select "Air Fry" of Kalorik Maxx Air Fryer Oven and then adjust the temperature to 365°F. Set the timer for 15 minutes and press "Start/Stop" to begin cooking.
9. When the unit beeps to show that it is preheated, place the cups over the air rack and insert them in the Kalorik Oven.
10. When cooking time is complete, remove the cups from Kalorik Oven and place them onto a wire rack to cool for about 10 minutes. Carefully, invert the cupcakes onto the wire rack to completely cool before serving.

Nutrition:
Calories: 209, Total Fat: 12.4 g, Saturated Fat: 7.5 g, Cholesterol: 63mg, Sodium: 110mg. Total Carbohydrates: 22.6 g, Fiber: 0.6 g, Sugar: 12.4 g, Protein: 2.7 g.

863. Zucchini Mug Cake
Preparation Time: 10 minutes
Cooking Time: 20 minutes
Servings: 1
Ingredients:
- ¼ cup whole-wheat pastry flour
- 1 tbsp. sugar
- ¼ tsp. baking powder
- ¼ tsp. ground cinnamon
- Pinch of salt
- 2 tbsp. plus 2 tsp. milk
- 2 tbsp. zucchini, grated and squeezed
- 2 tbsp. almonds, chopped
- 1 tbsp. raisins
- 2 tsp. maple syrup

Directions:
1. In a bowl, mix the flour, sugar, baking powder, cinnamon, and salt.
2. Add the remaining ingredients and mix until well combined.
3. Place the mixture into a lightly greased ramekin.
4. Select "Bake" of Kalorik Maxx Air Fryer Oven and then adjust the temperature to 350°F.
5. Set the timer for 20 minutes and press "Start/Stop" to begin cooking.
6. When the unit beeps to show that it is preheated, place the ramekin over the air rack and insert it in the Kalorik Oven.
7. When cooking time is complete, remove the ramekin from Kalorik Oven and place it onto a wire rack to cool slightly before serving.

Nutrition:
Calories: 310, Total Fat: 7 g, Saturated Fat: 0.9 g, Cholesterol: 3 mg, Sodium: 175 mg, Total Carbohydrates: 57.5 g, Fiber: 3.2 g, Sugar: 27.5g, Protein: 7.2 g.

864. Chocolate Brownies
Preparation Time: 15 minutes
Cooking Time: 15 minutes
Servings: 4
Ingredients:
- ½ cup all-purpose flour
- ¾ cup sugar
- 6 tbsp. cacao powder
- ¼ tsp. baking powder
- ¼ tsp. salt
- ¼ cup butter, melted
- 2 large eggs
- 1 tbsp. olive oil

- ½ tsp. pure vanilla extract

Directions:
1. Grease a 7-inch baking dish generously. Set aside.
2. In a bowl, add all the ingredients and mix until well combined. Place the mixture into the baking dish and with the back of a spoon, smooth the top surface.
3. Arrange the baking pan of the oven in the bottom of the Kalorik Digital Air Fryer Oven.
4. Select "Air Fry" of Kalorik Maxx Air Fryer Oven and then adjust the temperature to 320°F.
5. Set the timer for 30 minutes and press "Start/Stop" to begin cooking. When the unit beeps to show that it is preheated, place the baking dish over the baking pan and insert it in the Kalorik Oven. When cooking time is complete, remove the pan from Kalorik Oven and place it onto a wire rack to cool completely before cutting.
6. Cut the brownie into desired-sized squares and serve.

Nutrition:
Calories: 367, Total Fat: 19.2 g, Saturated Fat: 9.5 g, Cholesterol: 124 mg, Sodium: 265 mg, Total Carbohydrates: 53.6 g, Fiber: 2.7 g, Sugar: 37.8 g, Protein: 6.4 g.

865. Apple Crisp
Preparation Time: 15 minutes
Cooking Time: 40 minutes
Servings: 2
Ingredients:
- 1½ cups apple, peeled, cored, and sliced
- ¼ cup sugar, divided
- 1½ tsp. cornstarch
- 3 tbsp. all-purpose flour
- ¼ tsp. ground cinnamon
- Pinch of salt
- 1½ tbsp. cold butter, chopped
- 3 tbsp. rolled oats

Directions:
1. In a bowl, place apple slices, 1 tablespoon of sugar, and cornstarch; toss to coat well.
2. Divide the plum mixture into lightly greased 2 (8-ounce) ramekins.
3. In a bowl, mix the flour, remaining sugar, cinnamon, and salt.
4. With 2 forks, blend in the butter until a crumbly mixture forms.
5. Add the oats and gently stir to combine.
6. Place the oat mixture over apple slices into each ramekin.
7. Select "Bake" of Kalorik Maxx Air Fryer Oven and then adjust the temperature to 350°F.
8. Set the timer for 40 minutes and press "Start/Stop" to begin cooking.
9. When the unit beeps to show that it is preheated, place the ramekins over the air rack and insert them in the Kalorik Oven.
10. When cooking time is complete, remove the ramekins from Kalorik Oven and place them onto a wire rack to cool for about 10 minutes before serving.

Nutrition:
Calories: 337, Total Fat: 9.6 g, Saturated Fat: 5.6 g, Cholesterol: 23mg, Sodium: 141mg, Total Carbohydrates: 64.3 g, Fiber: 5.3 g, Sugar: 42.5 g, Protein: 2.8 g.

866. Banana and Walnut Cake
Preparation Time: 10 minutes
Cooking Time: 25 minutes
Servings: 6
Ingredients:
- 1 pound (454g) bananas, mashed
- 8 ounces (227g) flour
- 6 ounces (170g) sugar
- 3.5 ounces (99g) walnuts, chopped
- 3 ounces (71g) butter, melted
- 2 eggs, lightly beaten
- ¼ tsp. baking soda

Directions:
1. Select the Bake function and preheat Maxx to 355°F (179°C).
2. In a bowl, combine the sugar, butter, egg, flour, and baking soda with a whisk. Stir in the bananas and walnuts.
3. Transfer the mixture to a greased baking dish. Put the dish in the Air Fryer oven and bake for 10 minutes.
4. Reduce the temperature to 330°F (166°C) and bake for another 15 minutes. Serve hot.

Nutrition:
Calories: 70, Total Fat: 0.2 g, Saturated Fat: 0.1 g, Cholesterol: 0mg, Sodium: 1 mg, Total Carbohydrates: 18 g, Fiber: 1.6 g, Sugar: 11.2 g, Protein: 0.6 g.

867. Perfect Cinnamon Toast
Preparation Time: 10 minutes
Cooking Time: 5 minutes
Servings: 6
Ingredients:
- 2 tsp. pepper
- 1 ½ tsp. vanilla extract
- 1 ½ tsp. cinnamon
- ½ cup sweetener of choice
- 1 cup coconut oil
- 12 slices whole-wheat bread

Directions:
1. Melt coconut oil and mix with sweetener until dissolved. Mix in remaining ingredients except for bread till incorporated.
2. Spread mixture onto bread, covering all area.
3. Pour the coated pieces of bread into the oven rack/basket. Place the rack on the middle shelf of the Air Fryer oven. Set temperature to 400°F, and time to 5 minutes.
4. Remove and cut diagonally. Enjoy!

Nutrition:
Calories: 124, Fat: 2 g, Protein: 0 g, Sugar: 4 g.

868. Apple Pie in Air Fryer
Preparation Time: 5 minutes
Cooking Time: 35 minutes
Servings: 4
Ingredients:

- ½ tsp. vanilla extract
- 1 beaten egg
- 1 large apple, chopped
- 1 Pillsbury Refrigerator pie crust
- 1 tbsp. butter
- 1 tbsp. ground cinnamon
- 1 tbsp. raw sugar
- 2 tbsp. sugar
- 2 tsp. lemon juice
- Baking spray

Directions:
1. Lightly grease the baking pan of the Air Fryer oven with cooking spray. Spread pie crust on the bottom of the pan up to the sides.
2. In a bowl, mix vanilla, sugar, cinnamon, lemon juice, and apples. Pour on top of pie crust. Top apples with butter slices.
3. Cover apples with the other pie crust. Pierce with a knife the tops of pie.
4. Spread beaten egg on top of crust and sprinkle sugar.
5. Cover with foil.
6. For 25 minutes, cook on 390°F.
7. Remove foil and cook for 10 minutes at 330F or until tops are browned.
8. Serve and enjoy.

Nutrition:
Calories: 372, Fat: 19 g, Protein: 4.2 g, Sugar: 5 g.

869. Banana Brownies

Preparation Time: 5 minutes
Cooking Time: 30 minutes
Servings: 12
Ingredients:
- 2 cups almond flour
- 2 tsp. baking powder
- ½ tsp. baking powder
- ½ tsp. baking soda
- ½ tsp. salt
- 1 over-ripe banana
- 3 large eggs
- ½ tsp. stevia powder
- ¼ cup coconut oil
- 1 tbsp. vinegar
- 1/3 cup almond flour
- 1/3 cup cocoa powder

Directions:
1. Preheat the Air Fryer oven for 5 minutes.
2. Combine all ingredients in a food processor and pulse until well-combined.
3. Pour into a baking dish that will fit in the Air Fryer.
4. Place it in the Air Fryer basket and cook for 30 minutes at 350°F or if a toothpick inserted in the middle comes out clean.

Nutrition:
Calories: 75, Fat: 6.5 g, Protein: 1.7 g, Sugar: 2 g.

870. Chocolate Soufflé for Two

Preparation Time: 5 minutes
Cooking Time: 14 minutes
Servings: 2
Ingredients:
- 2 tbsp. almond flour
- ½ tsp. vanilla
- 3 tbsp. sweetener
- 2 eggs
- ¼ cup melted coconut oil
- 3 ounces of semi-sweet chocolate, chopped

Directions:
1. Brush coconut oil and sweetener onto ramekins.
2. Melt coconut oil and chocolate together.
3. Beat egg yolks well, adding vanilla and sweetener. Stir in flour and ensure there are no lumps.
4. Preheat the Air Fryer oven to 330°F.
5. Whisk egg whites till they reach peak state and fold them into chocolate mixture.
6. Pour batter into ramekins and place into the Air Fryer oven.
7. Cook 14 minutes.
8. Serve with powdered sugar dusted on top.

Nutrition:
Calories: 238, Fat: 6 g, Protein: 1 g, Sugar: 4 g.

871. Blueberry Lemon Muffins

Preparation Time: 5 minutes
Cooking Time: 10 minutes
Servings: 12
Ingredients:
- 1 tsp. vanilla
- Juice and zest of 1 lemon
- 2 eggs
- 1 cup blueberries
- ½ cup cream
- ¼ cup avocado oil
- ½ cup monk fruit
- 2 ½ cup almond flour

Directions:
1. Mix monk fruit and flour.
2. In another bowl, mix vanilla, egg, lemon juice, and cream. Combine mixtures and blend well.
3. Spoon batter into cupcake holders.
4. Place it in the Air Fryer oven. Bake for 10 minutes at 320°F, checking at 6 minutes to ensure you don't overbake them.

Nutrition:
Calories: 317, Fat: 11 g, Protein: 3 g, Sugar: 5 g.

872. Raspberry Cream Roll-Ups

Preparation Time: 10 minutes
Cooking Time: 25 minutes
Servings: 4
Ingredients:
- 1 cup of fresh raspberries rinsed and patted dry

- ½ cup of cream cheese softened to room temperature
- ¼ cup of brown sugar
- ¼ cup of sweetened condensed milk
- 1 egg
- 1 tsp. of corn starch
- 6 spring roll wrappers (any brand will do, we like Blue Dragon or Tasty Joy, both available through Target or Walmart, or any large grocery chain)
- ¼ cup of water

Directions:
1. Prepare the ingredients. Cover the basket of the Kalorik Maxx Air Fryer with a lining of tin foil, leaving the edges uncovered to allow air to circulate through the basket. Preheat the Kalorik Maxx Air Fryer to 350°F.
2. In a mixing bowl, combine the cream cheese, brown sugar, condensed milk, cornstarch, and egg. Beat or whip thoroughly, until all ingredients are completely mixed and fluffy, thick, and stiff.
3. Spoon even amounts of the creamy filling into each spring roll wrapper, then top each dollop of filling with several raspberries.
4. Roll up the wraps around the creamy raspberry filling, and seal the seams with a few dabs of water.
5. Place each roll on the foil-lined Kalorik Maxx Air Fryer basket, seams facing down.
6. Air Frying. Set the Kalorik Maxx Air Fryer timer to 10 minutes. During cooking, shake the handle of the fryer basket to ensure a nice even surface crisp.
7. After 10 minutes, when the Kalorik Maxx Air Fryer shuts off, the spring rolls should be golden brown and perfect on the outside, while the raspberries and cream filling will have cooked together in a glorious fusion. Remove with tongs and serve hot or cold.

Nutrition:
Calories: 335, Total Fat: 15.3 g, Saturated Fat: 8 g, Cholesterol: 28 mg, Sodium: 342 mg, Total Carbohydrates: 45.3 g, Fiber: 0.7 g, Sugar: 30.1 g, Protein: 4.4 g.

873. Black and White Brownies
Preparation Time: 10 minutes
Cooking Time: 20 minutes
Servings: 8
Ingredients:
- 1 egg
- ¼ cup brown sugar
- 2 tbsp. white sugar
- 2 tbsp. safflower oil
- 1 tsp. vanilla
- ¼ cup cocoa powder
- ⅓ cup all-purpose flour
- ¼ cup white chocolate chips
- Nonstick baking spray with flour

Directions:
1. Prepare the ingredients. In a medium bowl, beat the egg with brown sugar and white sugar. Beat in the oil and vanilla.
2. Add the cocoa powder and flour, and stir just until combined. Fold in the white chocolate chips.
3. Spray a 6-by-6-by-2-inch baking pan with nonstick spray. Spoon the brownie batter into the pan.
4. Bake for 20 minutes or until the brownies are set when lightly touched with a finger. Let cool for 30 minutes before slicing to serve.

Nutrition:
Calories: 81, Fat: 4 g, Protein: 1 g, Fiber: 1 g.

874. Baked Apple
Preparation Time: 5 minutes
Cooking Time: 20 minutes
Servings: 4
Ingredients:
- ¼ cup water
- ¼ tsp. nutmeg
- ¼ tsp. cinnamon
- 1 ½ tsp. melted ghee
- 2 tbsp. raisins
- 2 tbsp. chopped walnuts
- 1 medium apple

Directions:
1. Prepare the ingredients. Preheat your Air Fryer to 350°F.
2. Slice an apple in half and discard some of the flesh from the center.
3. Place it into the frying pan.
4. Mix the remaining ingredients except for water. Spoon the mixture to the middle of apple halves.
5. Pour water over the filled apples.
6. Place pan with apple halves into the Kalorik Maxx Air Fryer, bake 20 minutes.

Nutrition:
Calories: 199, Fat: 9 g, Protein: 1 g, Sugar: 3 g.

875. Cinnamon Fried Bananas
Preparation Time: 5 minutes
Cooking Time: 10 minutes
Servings: 2–3
Ingredients:
- 1 cup panko breadcrumbs
- 3 tbsp. cinnamon
- ½ cup almond flour
- 3 egg whites
- 8 ripe bananas
- 3 tbsp. vegan coconut oil

Directions:
1. Prepare the ingredients. Heat coconut oil and add breadcrumbs. Mix around 2–3 minutes until golden. Pour into a bowl.
2. Peel and cut bananas in half. Roll half of each banana into flour, eggs, and crumb mixture.
3. Place it into the Kalorik Maxx Air Fryer. Cook for 10 minutes at 280°F.
4. A great addition to a healthy banana split!

Nutrition:
Calories: 219, Fat: 10 g, Protein: 3 g, Sugar: 5 g.

876. Awesome Chinese Doughnuts

Preparation Time: 10 minutes
Cooking Time: 8 minutes
Servings: 8
Ingredients:
- 1 tbsp. baking powder
- 1 tbsp. coconut oil
- ¾ cup of coconut milk
- 6 tsp. sugar
- 2 cup all-purpose flour
- ½ tsp. sea salt

Directions:
1. Preheat the Air Fryer to 350°F.
2. Mix baking powder, flour, sugar, and salt in a bowl.
3. Add coconut oil and mix well. Add coconut milk and mix until well combined.
4. Knead the dough for 3–4 minutes.
5. Roll dough half-inch thick and using a cookie cutter cut doughnuts.
6. Place doughnuts in a cake pan and brush with oil. Place the cake pan in the Air Fryer basket and air fry doughnuts for 5 minutes. Turn doughnuts to the other side and air fry for 3 minutes more. Serve and enjoy.

Nutrition:
Calories: 259, Fat: 15.9 g, Carbohydrates: 27 g, Protein: 3.8 g.

877. Crispy Bananas

Preparation Time: 10 minutes
Cooking Time: 10 minutes
Servings: 4
Ingredients:
- 4 sliced ripe bananas
- 1 egg
- ½ cup breadcrumbs
- 1 ½ tbsp. cinnamon sugar
- 1 tbsp. almond meal
- 1 ½ tbsp. coconut oil
- 1 tbsp. crushed cashew
- ¼ cup cornflour

Directions:
1. Set the pan on fire to heat the coconut oil over medium fire. Add breadcrumbs to the pan and stir for 3–4 minutes.
2. Remove the pan from heat and transfer breadcrumbs to a bowl.
3. Add almond meal and crush cashew in breadcrumbs; mix well.
4. Dip the banana half in cornflour, then in egg, and finally coat with breadcrumbs.
5. Place the coated banana in the Air Fryer basket. Sprinkle with cinnamon sugar.
6. Air fry at 350°F/ 176°C for 10 minutes.
7. Serve and enjoy.

Nutrition:
Calories: 282, Fat: 9 g, Carbohydrates: 46 g, Protein: 5 g.

878. Air Fried Banana and Walnuts Muffins

Preparation Time: 10 minutes
Cooking Time: 10 minutes
Servings: 2
Ingredients:
- ¼ cup flour
- ½ tsp. baking powder
- ¼ cup mashed banana
- ¼ cup butter
- 1 tbsp. chopped walnuts
- ¼ cup oats

Directions:
1. Grease four muffin molds with cooking spray and set them aside.
2. In a bowl, mix mashed bananas, walnuts, sugar, and butter.
3. In another bowl, mix oat flour, and baking powder.
4. Combine the flour mixture with the banana mixture.
5. Pour the batter into the muffin mold.
6. Place it in the Air Fryer basket and cook at 320°F/ 160°C for 10 minutes.
7. Remove the muffins from the Air Fryer and allow them to cool completely.
8. Serve and enjoy.

Nutrition:
Calories: 192, Fat: 12.3 g, Carbohydrates: 19.4 g, Protein: 1.9 g.

879. Nutty Mix

Preparation Time: 5 minutes
Cooking Time: 4 minutes
Servings: 6
Ingredients:
- 2 cup mix nuts
- 1 tsp. ground cumin
- 1 tsp. chili powder
- 1 tbsp. melted butter
- 1 tsp. salt
- 1 tsp. pepper

Directions:
1. Set all ingredients in a large bowl and toss until well coated.
2. Preheat the Air Fryer at 350°F for 5 minutes.
3. Add mix nuts in the Air Fryer basket and air fry for 4 minutes. Shake basket halfway through. Serve and enjoy.

Nutrition:
Calories: 316, Fat: 29 g, Carbohydrates: 11.3 g, Protein: 7.6 g.

880. Vanilla Spiced Soufflé

Preparation Time: 20 minutes
Cooking Time: 32 minutes
Servings: 6
Ingredients:
- ¼ cup all-purpose flour
- 1 cup whole milk
- 2 tsp. vanilla extract
- 1 tsp. cream of tartar
- 1 vanilla bean

- 4 egg yolks
- 1-oz. sugar
- ¼ cup softened butter
- ¼ cup sugar - 5 egg whites

Directions:
1. Combine flour and butter in a bowl until the mixture becomes a smooth paste.
2. Set the pan over medium flame to heat the milk. Add sugar and stir until dissolved.
3. Mix in the vanilla bean and bring to a boil.
4. Beat the mixture using a wire; whisk as you add the butter and flour mixture.
5. Lower the heat to simmer until thick. Discard the vanilla bean. Turn off the heat.
6. Place the mixture on an ice bath and allow them to cool for 10 minutes.
7. Grease 6 ramekins with butter. Sprinkle each with a bit of sugar.
8. Beat the egg yolks in a bowl. Add the vanilla extract and milk mixture. Mix until combined. Whisk together the tartar cream, egg whites, and sugar until it forms medium-stiff peaks.
9. Gradually fold egg whites into the soufflé base. Transfer the mixture to the ramekins.
10. Put 3 ramekins in the cooking basket at a time. Cook for 16 minutes at 330°F. Move to a wire rack for cooling and cook the rest.
11. Sprinkle powdered sugar on top and drizzle with chocolate sauce before serving.

Nutrition:
Calories: 215, Fat: 12.2 g, Carbohydrates: 18.98 g, Protein: 6.66 g.

881. Chocolate Cup Cakes
Preparation Time: 5 minutes
Cooking Time: 12 minutes
Servings: 6
Ingredients:
- 3 eggs
- ¼ cup caster sugar
- ¼ cup cocoa powder
- 1 tsp. baking powder
- 1 cup milk
- ¼ tsp. vanilla essence
- 2 cup all-purpose flour
- 4 tbsp. butter

Directions:
1. Preheat your Air Fryer to a temperature of 400°F (200°C).
2. Beat eggs with sugar in a bowl until creamy.
3. Add butter and beat again for 1–2 minutes.
4. Now add flour, cocoa powder, milk, baking powder, and vanilla essence, mix with a spatula.
5. Fill ¾ of muffin tins with the mixture and place them into the Air Fryer basket.
6. Let cook for 12 minutes.
7. Serve!

Nutrition:
Calories: 289, Fat: 11.5 g, Carbohydrates: 38.94 g, Protein: 8.72 g.

882. Air Baked Cheesecake
Preparation Time: 20 minutes
Cooking Time: 20 minutes
Servings: 8–12
Ingredients:
Crust
- ½ cup dates, chopped, soaked in water for at least 15 min, soaking liquid reserved
- ½ cup walnuts
- 1 cup quick oats

Filling
- ½ cup vanilla almond milk
- ¼ cup coconut palm sugar
- ½ cup coconut flour
- 1 cup cashews, soaked in water for at least 2 hours
- 1 tsp. vanilla extract
- 2 tbsp. lemon juice
- 1 to 2 tsp. grated lemon zest
- ½ cup fresh berries or 6 figs, sliced
- 1 tbsp. arrowroot powder

Directions:
1. Make the crust: in a food processor, process together with all the crust ingredients until smooth and press the mixture into the bottom of a springform pan.
2. Make the filling: add cashews along with soaking liquid to a blender and process until very smooth; add milk, palm sugar, coconut flour, lemon juice, lemon zest, and vanilla and blend until well combined; add arrowroot and continue blending until mixed and pour into the crust. Smooth the top and cover the springform pan with foil.
3. Place the pan in your air fry toaster oven and bake at 375°F for 20 minutes.
4. Carefully remove the pan from the fryer and remove the foil; let the cake cool completely and top with fruit to serve.

Nutrition:
Calories: 423, Fat: 3.1 g, Carbohydrates: 33.5 g, Protein: 1.2 g.

883. Air Roasted Nuts
Preparation Time: 10 minutes
Cooking Time: 20 minutes
Servings: 8
Ingredients:
- 1 cup raw peanuts
- ½ tsp. cayenne pepper
- 3 tsp. seafood seasoning
- 2 tbsp. olive oil
- salt

Directions:
1. Preheat your Air Fryer toast oven to 320°F.
2. In a bowl, whisk together cayenne pepper, olive oil, and seafood seasoning; stir in peanuts until well coated.
3. Transfer to the fryer basket and air roast for 10 minutes; toss well and then cook for another 10 minutes.

4. Transfer the peanuts to a dish and season with salt. Let it cool before serving.

Nutrition:
Calories: 193, Fat: 17.4 g, Carbohydrates: 4.9 g, Protein: 7.4 g.

884. Air Fried White Corn

Preparation Time: 10 minutes
Cooking Time: 40 minutes
Servings: 8
Ingredients:
- 2 cups giant white corn
- 3 tbsp. olive oil
- 1½ tsp. sea salt

Directions:
1. Soak the corn in a bowl of water for at least 8 hours or overnight; drain and spread it in a single layer on a baking tray; pat dry with paper towels.
2. Preheat your Air Fryer toast oven to 400°F.
3. In a bowl, mix corn, olive oil, and salt and toss to coat well.
4. Air fry corn in batches in the preheated Air Fryer toast oven for 20 minutes, shaking the basket halfway through cooking.
5. Let the corn cool for at least 20 minutes or until crisp.

Nutrition:
Calories: 225, Fat: 7.4 g, Carbohydrates: 35.8 g, Protein: 5.9 g.

885. Fruit Cake

Preparation Time: 5 minutes
Cooking Time: 45 minutes
Servings: 4–6
Ingredients:
Dry Ingredients:
- 1/8 tsp. sea salt
- ½ tsp. baking powder
- ½ tsp. baking soda
- ½ tsp. ground cardamom
- 1¼ cup whole wheat flour

Wet Ingredients:
- 2 tbsp. coconut oil
- ½ cup unsweetened nondairy milk
- 2 tbsp. ground flax seeds
- ¼ cup agave
- 1½ cups water
- Mix-Ins
- ½ cup chopped cranberries
- 1 cup chopped pear

Directions:
1. Grease a Bundt pan; set it aside.
2. In a bowl, mix all dry ingredients. In another bowl, combine the wet ingredients; whisk the wet ingredients into the dry until smooth.
3. Fold in the add-ins and spread the mixture into the pan; cover with foil.
4. Place pan in your Air Fryer toast oven and add water in the bottom and bake at 370°F for 35 minutes.
5. When done, use a toothpick to check for doneness. If it comes out clean, then the cake is ready, if not, bake for 5–10 more minutes, checking frequently to avoid burning.
6. Remove the cake and let it stand for 10 minutes before transferring from the pan.
7. Enjoy!

Nutrition:
Calories: 309, Fat: 27 g, Carbohydrates: 14.7 g, Protein: 22.6 g.

886. Hydrated Apples

Preparation Time: 5 minutes
Cooking Time: 20 minutes
Servings: 6
Ingredients:
- 3 apples, cored
- 1 tsp. cinnamon powder
- ½ cup sugar
- 1 cup red wine
- ¼ cup raisins

Directions:
1. Add apples to your Air Fryer toast oven pan and then add wine, cinnamon powder, sugar, and raisins.
2. Hydrate for 20 minutes and remove from air fry toaster oven. Serve the apples in small serving bowls drizzled with lots of cooking juices. Enjoy!

Nutrition:
Calories: 229, Fat: 0.4 g, Carbohydrates: 53.3 g, Protein: 0.8 g.

887. Nutty Slice

Preparation Time: 10 minutes
Cooking Time: 30 minutes
Servings: 4
Ingredients:
- 4 cups fresh or frozen mixed berries
- 1 cup almond meal
- ½ cup almond butter
- 1 cup oven roasted walnuts, sunflower seeds, pistachios.
- ½ tsp. ground cinnamon

Directions:
1. Preheat the Air Fryer toast oven to 375°F.
2. Crush the nuts using a mortar and pestle.
3. In a bowl, combine the nut mix, almond meal, cinnamon, and ghee and combine well.
4. In a pie dish, spread half the nut mixture over the bottom of the dish, then top with the berries and finish with the rest of the nut mixture.
5. Bake for 30 minutes. Slice and serve warm with natural vanilla yogurt.
6. Yum!

Nutrition:
Calories: 278, Fat: 15.7 g, Carbohydrates: 10.3 g, Protein: 13.8 g.

888. Energy Brownies

Preparation Time: 10 minutes
Cooking Time: 35 minutes
Servings: 10
Ingredients:

- 1½ cups unsweetened shredded coconut
- ½ cup dried cranberries
- ½ cup golden flax meal
- ½ cup coconut butter
- 1 cup hemp seeds
- A good pinch of sea salt

Directions:
1. Combine the cranberries, flax, and hemp seeds in the bowl of your food processor and pulse until well-ground.
2. Add the shredded coconut, coconut butter, stevia, and salt and pulse until it forms a thick dough.
3. Transfer the dough to a baking dish and bake for 10 minutes in your Air Fryer toast oven at 370°F, then remove from heat.
4. Let it cool completely, then chill in the fridge to firm up. Slice it into bars and enjoy!

Nutrition:
Calories: 314, Fat: 10.1 g, Carbohydrates: 19.8 g, Protein: 7.8 g.

889. Air Fry Toaster Oven Bars
Preparation Time: 5 minutes
Cooking Time: 25 minutes
Servings: 4
Ingredients:
- 1 cup chopped chocolate
- 2 ripe avocados
- 1 tsp. raw honey
- 2 tsp. vanilla extract
- 4 eggs
- 1 cup ground almonds
- ½ cup cocoa powder
- ¼ tsp. salt

Directions:
1. Prepare an 8-inch baking pan by lining it with foil and then coating it with non-stick cooking spray.
2. Add chocolate to a bowl and place it over a large saucepan of boiling water.
3. Stir until chocolate is melted. Remove from heat and let cool.
4. Meanwhile, prepare the batter: In a bowl, mash the avocados; add honey and stir to combine.
5. Whisk in vanilla extract and eggs until well blended. Gradually whisk in the chocolate until well incorporated.
6. Stir in ground almonds, cocoa powder, and salt until well blended.
7. Transfer the batter to the baking pan, cover with a paper towel, and then with aluminum foil.
8. Place the pan in your Air Fryer toast oven and bake at 375°F for 30 minutes or until done to desire.
9. Let cool completely before cutting into squares. These brownies are best served chilled.

Nutrition:
Calories: 512, Fat: 12.3 g, Carbohydrates: 31.2 g, Protein: 14.4 g.

890. Self-Saucing Banana Pudding
Preparation Time: 5 minutes
Cooking Time: 60 minutes
Servings: 6–8
Ingredients:
- 1 cup caster sugar
- 1 ½ cups self-rising flour, sifted
- 1/3 cup butter, melted and cooled
- 1 tsp. vanilla extract
- ¼ cup mashed banana
- 1 egg, lightly beaten
- ¾ cups milk
- ½ cup packed brown sugar
- 1/8 tsp. nutmeg - 1 tsp. cinnamon
- ½ cups boiling water
- ice cream, to serve

Directions:
1. Preheat the Air Fryer oven for 10 minutes.
2. Grease the Air Fryer oven pan with butter using wax paper.
3. Combine the first 7 ingredients above in a large mixing bowl; whisk until well-combined.
4. Fold into the Air Fryer oven pan. Sift sugar, nutmeg, and cinnamon over the pudding mix. Spoon the boiling water gently and evenly over the mixture.
5. Lock lid in place and cook for 1 hour.
6. Serve hot with a scoop of ice cream on top!

Nutrition:
Calories: 307, Sodium: 76mg, Dietary Fiber: 0.9g, Fat: 9g, Carbohydrates: 54.3g, Protein: 4 g.

891. Chocolate Lava Cake
Preparation Time: 5 minutes
Cooking Time: 1 hour 10 minutes
Servings: 6–8
Ingredients:
- 1 box of Devil's Food Chocolate Cake mix, according to box instructions
- 1 (15 oz.) can of milk chocolate frosting, divided
- Non-stick cooking spray

Directions:
1. Coat the Air Fryer oven pan with cooking spray. Add cake batter as instructed on the box. Spoon half of the chocolate frosting into the middle of the cake batter.
2. Cook for 1 hour.
3. Flip the Air Fryer oven pan upside down over a cake plate. Heat the remaining frosting in a microwave for 25 seconds, pour over the warm cake, and serve.

Nutrition:
Calories: 172, Sodium: 91mg, Dietary Fiber: 0.7g, Fat: 7.6g, Carbohydrates: 27g, Protein: 0.3g

892. Banana and Walnut Bread
Preparation Time: 5 minutes
Cooking Time: 1 hour 10 minutes
Servings: 6–8
Ingredients:
- 1 ½ cup unbleached flour
- ½ cup sugar or sugar substitute
- 2 tsp. baking powder
- ½ tsp. baking soda

- ½ tsp. vanilla extract
- ½ tsp. sea salt
- 1 cup ripe bananas, mashed
- 1/3 cup softened butter
- ¼ cup milk - 1 egg
- ¼ cup walnuts chopped

Directions:
1. Combine the flour, sugar, baking powder, baking soda, and salt in a large mixing bowl; whisk until the ingredients are well mixed.
2. Fold in the bananas, butter, milk, egg, and vanilla extract. Use an electric mixer to mix until the batter has a uniform thick consistency. Fold in chopped walnuts.
3. Grease the bottom of the Air Fryer oven pan with non-stick cooking spray. Pour batter into Air Fryer oven pan and cook for 1 hour. Transfer to plate and let it cool for one hour before serving.

Nutrition:
Calories: 255, Sodium: 211mg, Dietary Fiber: 1.4 g, Fat: 11 g, Carbohydrates: 36.1 g, Protein: 4.6 g.

893. Choco-Peanut Mug Cake

Preparation Time: 5 minutes
Cooking Time: 20 minutes
Servings: 1
Ingredients:
- 1 tsp. softened butter
- 1 egg
- 1 tsp. butter
- 1 tsp. vanilla extract
- 2 tbsp. erythritol
- 2 tbsp. unsweetened cocoa powder
- ¼ tsp. baking powder
- 1 tbsp. heavy cream

Directions:
1. Preheat the Air Fryer for 5 minutes.
2. Combine all ingredients in a mixing bowl.
3. Pour the mixture into a greased mug.
4. Set in the Air Fryer basket and cook for 20 minutes at 400°F

Nutrition:
Calories: 293, Protein: 12.4 g, Fat: 23.3 g, Carbohydrates: 8.5 g.

894. Raspberry-Coco Desert

Preparation Time: 5 minutes
Cooking Time: 20 minutes
Servings: 12
Ingredients:
- 1 tsp. vanilla bean
- 1 cup pulsed raspberries
- 1 cup coconut milk
- 3cups desiccated coconut
- ¼ cup coconut oil
- 1/3 cup Erythritol powder

Directions:
1. Preheat the Air Fryer for 5 minutes.
2. Combine all the ingredients in a mixing bowl.
3. Pour the mixture into a greased baking dish.
4. Bake in the Air Fryer for 20 minutes at 375°F.

Nutrition:
Calories: 132, Protein: 1.5 g, Fat: 9.7 g, Carbohydrates: 9.7 g.

895. Almond Cherry Bars

Preparation Time: 5 minutes
Cooking Time: 35 minutes
Servings: 12
Ingredients:
- 1 tbsp. Xanthan gum
- 1 ½ cup almond flour
- ½ tsp. salt
- 1 cup pitted fresh cherries
- ½ cup softened butter
- 2eggs
- ¼ cup water
- ½ tsp. vanilla
- 1 cup Erythritol

Directions:
1. Combine almond flour, softened butter, salt, vanilla, eggs, and erythritol in a large bowl until you form a dough.
2. Press the dough in a baking dish that will fit in the Air Fryer.
3. Set in the Air Fryer and bake for 10 minutes at 375°F.
4. Meanwhile, mix the cherries, water, and xanthan gum in a bowl.
5. Take the dough out and pour over the cherry mixture. Cook again for 25 minutes more at 375°F in the Air Fryer.

Nutrition:
Calories: 99, Protein: 1.8 g, Fat: 9.3g, Carbohydrates: 2.1 g.

896. Coffee Flavored Doughnuts

Preparation Time: 5 minutes
Cooking Time: 6 minutes
Servings: 6
Ingredients:
- 1 tsp. baking powder
- ½ tsp. salt
- 1 tbsp. sunflower oil
- ¼ cup coffee
- ¼ cup coconut sugar
- 1 cup white all-purpose flour
- 2 tbsp. Aquafaba

Directions:
1. Combine sugar, flour, baking powder, and salt in a mixing bowl.
2. In another bowl, combine the aquafaba, sunflower oil, and coffee.
3. Mix to form a dough.
4. Let the dough rest inside the fridge.
5. Preheat the Air Fryer to 400°F.
6. Knead the dough and create doughnuts.
7. Arrange it inside the Air Fryer in a single layer and cook for 6 minutes.
8. Do not shake so that the donut maintains its shape.

Nutrition:
Calories: 113, Protein: 21.6 g, Fat: 2.54 g, Carbohydrates: 20.45 g.

897. Simple Strawberry Cobbler

Preparation Time: 10 minutes
Cooking Time: 25 minutes
Servings: 4
Ingredients:

- ¼ cup heavy whipping cream
- 1 ½ tsp. cornstarch
- 1 ½ tsp. white sugar
- ½ cup water
- ¼ tsp. salt
- 2 tsp. butter
- 1 ½ cup hulled strawberries
- 1 ½ tsp. white sugar
- 1 tbsp. diced butter
- 1 tbsp. butter
- ½ cup all-purpose flour
- ¾ tsp. baking powder

Directions:

1. Lightly grease the baking pan of the Air Fryer with cooking spray. Add water, cornstarch, and sugar. Cook for 10 minutes at 390°F or until hot and thick. Add strawberries and mix well. Dot tops with 1 teaspoon of butter.
2. In a bowl, mix well salt, baking powder, sugar, and flour. Cut in 2 teaspoons of butter. Mix in cream. Spoon on top of berries.
3. Cook for 15 minutes at 390°F, until tops are lightly browned. Serve and enjoy.

Nutrition:
Calories: 255, Protein: 2.4 g, Fat: 13 g, Carbohydrates: 32 g.

898. Easy Pumpkin Pie

Preparation Time: 5 minutes
Cooking Time: 35 minutes
Servings: 8
Ingredients:

- 2 egg yolks
- 1 large egg
- ½ tsp. ground ginger
- ½ tsp. fine salt
- 1/8 tsp. Chinese 5-spice powder
- 19-inch unbaked pie crust
- ¼ tsp. freshly grated nutmeg
- 14 oz. sweetened condensed milk
- 15 oz. pumpkin puree
- 1 tsp. ground cinnamon

Directions:

1. Lightly grease the baking pan of the Air Fryer with cooking spray. Press pie crust on the bottom of the pan, stretching up to the sides of the pan. Pierce all over with a fork.
2. In a blender, blend well egg, egg yolks, and pumpkin puree. Add Chinese 5-spice powder, nutmeg, salt, ginger, cinnamon, and condensed milk. Pour on top of pie crust.
3. Cover the pan with foil.
4. For 15 minutes, cook on preheated 390°F Air Fryer.
5. Cook for 20 more minutes at 330°F without the foil until the middle is set.
6. Allow cooling in the Air Fryer completely.
7. Serve and enjoy.

Nutrition:
Calories: 326, Protein: 7.6 g, Fat: 14.2 g, Carbohydrates: 41.9 g.

899. Simple Cheesecake

Preparation Time: 10 minutes
Cooking Time: 19 minutes
Servings: 5
Ingredients:

- 1 cup crumbled graham crackers
- ½ tsp. vanilla extract
- 4 tbsp. sugar
- 2 tbsp. butter
- 1 lb. cream cheese
- 2 eggs

Directions:

1. Mix crackers with the butter in a bowl.
2. Press crackers mixture on the bottom of a lined cake pan.
3. Transfer to the Air Fryer to cook at 350°F for 4 minutes.
4. Meanwhile, in a bowl, mix eggs, cream cheese, sugar, and vanilla; whisk well.
5. Spread filling over crackers crust and cook in the Air Fryer at 310°F for 15 minutes.
6. Cool and keep in the refrigerator for 3 hours.
7. Slice and serve.

Nutrition:
Calories: 245, Protein: 3 g, Fat: 12 g, Carbohydrates: 20 g.

900. Strawberry Donuts

Preparation Time: 10 minutes
Cooking Time: 15 minutes
Servings: 4
Ingredients:

- 4 oz. whole milk
- 1 egg
- 1 tsp. baking powder
- 1 tbsp. brown sugar
- 1 tbsp. white sugar
- 8 oz. flour
- ½ tbsp. butter
- for the strawberry icing:
- 1 tbsp. whipped cream
- ½ tsp. pink coloring
- 2 tbsp. butter
- ¼ cup chopped strawberries

Directions:

1. In a bowl, mix flour, 1 tablespoon of white sugar, 1 tablespoon of brown sugar and butter, and stir.
2. Stir together the egg with milk, and 1 ½ tablespoon of butter in another bowl.
3. Combine the 2 mixtures, stir, then shape donuts from this mix.

4. Cook the doughnuts in the Air Fryer at 360°F for 15 minutes.
5. Mix strawberry puree, whipped cream, food coloring, icing, sugar, and 1 tablespoon of butter, and whisk well.
6. Arrange donuts on a platter and serve with strawberry icing on top.

Nutrition:
Calories: 250, Protein: 4 g, Fat: 12 g, Carbohydrates: 32 g.

901. Apricot Blackberry Crumble

Preparation Time: 10 minutes
Cooking Time: 20 minutes
Servings: 8
Ingredients:

- 1 cup flour
- 2 tbsp. lemon juice
- 2 oz. cubed and deseeded fresh apricots
- ½ cup sugar
- 2 tbsp. cold butter
- 5.5 oz. fresh blackberries
- salt.

Directions:

1. Put the apricots and blackberries in a bowl. Add lemon juice and 2 tablespoons of sugar. Mix until combined. Transfer the mixture to a baking dish.
2. Mix flour, the rest of the sugar, and a pinch of salt in a bowl.
3. Add 1 tablespoon of cold butter. Combine the mixture until it becomes crumbly. Put this on top of the fruit mixture and press it down lightly.
4. Move the baking dish to the cooking basket. Cook for 20 minutes at 390°F.
5. Allow cooling before slicing and serving.

Nutrition:
Calories: 217, Protein: 2.3 g, Fat: 7.44 g, Carbohydrates: 36.2 g.

902. Ginger Cheesecake

Preparation Time: 2 hours 10 minutes
Cooking Time: 20 minutes
Servings: 6
Ingredients:

- ½ tsp. ground nutmeg
- oz. soft cream cheese
- 1 tsp. rum
- ½ cup crumbled ginger cookies
- ½ tsp. vanilla extract
- tsp. melted butter
- 6 eggs - ½ cup sugar

Directions:

1. Grease a pan with butter and spread cookie crumbs on the bottom.
2. In a bowl, beat cream cheese, eggs, rum, vanilla, and nutmeg. Whisk well and spread over the cookie crumbs.
3. Place them in the Air Fryer and cook at 340°F for 20 minutes.
4. Cool and keep in the refrigerator.
5. Slice and serve.

Nutrition:
Calories: 412, Protein: 6 g, Fat: 12 g, Carbohydrates: 20 g.

903. Coconut Donuts

Preparation Time: 5 minutes
Cooking Time: 15 minutes
Servings: 4
Ingredients:

- 8 ounces coconut flour - 1 egg, whisked
- 2 and ½ tbsp. butter, melted
- 4 ounces coconut milk
- 1 tsp. baking powder

Directions:

1. In a bowl, put all of the ingredients and mix well.
2. Shape donuts from this mix, place them in your Air Fryer's basket and cook at 370°F for 15 minutes.
3. Serve warm.

Nutrition:
Calories: 190, Protein: 6 g, Fat: 12 g, Carbohydrates: 4 g.

904. Blueberry Cream

Preparation Time: 4 minutes
Cooking Time: 20 minutes
Servings: 6
Ingredients:

- 2 cups blueberries
- Juice of ½ lemon
- 2 tbsp. water
- 1 tsp. vanilla extract
- 2 tbsp. swerve

Directions:

1. In a large bowl, put all ingredients and mix well.
2. Divide this into 6 ramekins, put them in the Air Fryer, and cook at 340°F for 20 minutes.
3. Cool down and serve.

Nutrition:
Calories: 123, Protein: 3 g, Fat: 2 g, Carbohydrates: 4 g.

905. Blackberry Chia Jam

Preparation Time: 10 minutes
Cooking Time: 30 minutes
Servings: 12
Ingredients:

- 3 cups blackberries
- ¼ cup swerve
- 4 tbsp. lemon juice
- 4 tbsp. chia seeds

Directions:

1. In a pan that suits the Air Fryer, combine all the ingredients and toss.
2. Put the pan in the fryer and cook at 300°F for 30 minutes.
3. Divide into cups and serve cold.

Nutrition:
Calories: 100, Protein: 1 g, Fat: 2 g, Carbohydrates: 3 g.

906. Mixed Berries Cream

Preparation Time: 5 minutes
Cooking Time: 30 minutes
Servings: 6

Ingredients:
- 12ounces blackberries
- 6ounces raspberries
- 12ounces blueberries
- ¾ cup swerve
- 2ounces coconut cream

Directions:
1. In a bowl, put all the ingredients and mix well.
2. Divide this into 6 ramekins, put them in your Air Fryer, and cook at 320°F for 30 minutes.
3. Cool down and serve it.

Nutrition:
Calories: 100, Protein: 2 g, Fat: 1 g, Carbohydrates: 2 g.

907. Cinnamon-Spiced Acorn Squash

Preparation Time: 5 minutes
Cooking Time: 15 minutes
Servings: 2

Ingredients:
- 1 medium acorn squash, halved crosswise and deseeded
- 1 tsp. coconut oil
- 1 tsp. light brown sugar
- Few dashes of ground cinnamon
- Few dashes of ground nutmeg

Directions:
1. On a clean work surface, rub the cut sides of the acorn squash with coconut oil. Scatter with brown sugar, cinnamon, and nutmeg.
2. Put the squash halves in the Air Fryer basket, cut-side up.
3. Put in the Air Fryer basket and cook at 325°F for 15 minutes.
4. When cooking is complete, the squash halves should be just tender when pierced in the center with a paring knife. Remove from the oven. Rest for 5 to 10 minutes and serve warm.

Nutrition:
Calories: 172, Protein: 3.9 g, Fat: 9.8 g, Carbohydrates: 17.5 g.

908. Pear Sauce

Preparation Time: 10 minutes
Cooking Time: 15 minutes
Servings: 6

Ingredients:
- 10pears, sliced
- 1 cup apple juice
- 1 ½ tsp. cinnamon
- ¼ tsp. nutmeg

Directions:
1. Put all of the ingredients in the Air Fryer and stir well.
2. Seal pot and cook on High for 15 minutes.
3. Once done, allow to release pressure naturally for 10 minutes, then release remaining using quick release. Remove lid.
4. Blend the pear mixture using an immersion blender until smooth. Serve and enjoy.

Nutrition:
Calories: 222, Protein: 1.3 g, Fat: 0.6 g, Carbohydrates: 58.2 g.

909. Brownie Muffins

Preparation Time: 10 minutes
Cooking Time: 10 minutes
Servings: 12

Ingredients:
- 1 package Betty Crocker fudge brownie mix
- ¼ cup walnuts, chopped
- 1 egg
- 1/3 cup vegetable oil
- 2 tsp. water

Directions:
1. Grease 12 muffin molds. Set aside.
2. In a bowl, put all ingredients together.
3. Place the mixture into the muffin molds.
4. Press the "Power Button" of the Air Fryer and turn the dial to select the "Air Fry" mode.
5. Press the time button and again turn the dial to set the cooking time to 10 minutes.
6. Now push the Temp button and rotate the dial to set the temperature at 300°F.
7. Press the "Start/Pause" button to start.
8. When the unit beeps to show that it is preheated, open the lid.
9. Arrange the muffin molds in the "Air Fry Basket" and insert them in the oven.
10. Place the muffin molds onto a wire rack to cool for about 10 minutes.
11. Carefully, invert the muffins onto the wire rack to completely cool before serving.

Nutrition:
Calories: 168, Protein: 2 g, Fat: 8.9 g, Carbohydrates: 20.8 g.

910. Chocolate Mug Cake

Preparation Time: 7 minutes
Cooking Time: 13 minutes
Servings: 3

Ingredients:
- ½ cup of cocoa powder
- ½ cup stevia powder
- 1 cup coconut cream
- 1 package cream cheese, room temperature
- 1 tbsp. vanilla extract
- 1 tbsp. butter

Directions:
1. Preheat the Smart Air Fryer Oven for 5 minutes at 350°F.
2. In a mixing bowl, combine all the listed ingredients using a hand mixer until fluffy.
3. Pour into greased mugs.
4. Place the mugs in the fryer basket and bake for 13 minutes at 350°F. Serve when cool.

Nutrition:
Calories: 100, Protein: 3 g, Fat: 0 g, Carbohydrates: 21 g.

911. Chocolate Soufflé

Preparation Time: 7 minutes
Cooking Time: 12 minutes
Servings: 2

Ingredients:
- 2 tbsp. almond flour
- ½ tsp. vanilla - 2 tbsp. sweetener
- 2 separated eggs
- ¼ cups melted coconut oil
- 2oz. of semi-sweet chocolate, chopped

Directions:
1. Preheat the Smart Air Fryer Oven to 330°F.
2. Brush coconut oil and sweetener onto ramekins.
3. Melt coconut oil and chocolate together.
4. Beat egg yolks well, adding vanilla and sweetener.
5. Stir in flour and ensure there are no lumps.
6. Whisk egg whites till they reach peak state and fold them into chocolate mixture.
7. Pour batter into ramekins and place into the Smart Air Fryer Oven, then cook for 12 minutes. Serve with powdered sugar dusted on top.

Nutrition:
Calories: 378, Protein: 4 g, Fat: 9 g, Carbohydrates: 5 g.

912. Chocolate Cake

Preparation Time: 6 minutes
Cooking Time: 35 minutes
Servings: 9
Ingredients:
- ½ cups hot water
- 1 tsp. vanilla
- ¼ cups olive oil
- ½ cups almond milk
- 1 egg
- ½ tsp. salt
- ¾ tsp. baking soda
- ¾ tsp. baking powder
- ½ cups unsweetened cocoa powder
- 2 cups almond flour
- 1 cup brown sugar

Directions:
1. Preheat your Smart Air Fryer Oven to 356°F.
2. Stir all dry ingredients together and then stir in wet ingredients.
3. Add hot water last.
4. The batter should be thin.
5. Pour cake batter into a pan that fits into the fryer.
6. Bake for 35 minutes.

Nutrition:
Calories: 378, Protein: 4 g, Fat: 9 g, Carbohydrates: 5 g.

913. Chocolate Chip Air Fryer Cookies

Preparation Time: 10 minutes
Cooking Time: 16 minutes
Servings: 3
Ingredients:
- 75g (2oz.) self-rising flour
- 100g (2.83oz.) butter
- 75g (2oz.) brown sugar
- 75g (2oz.) milk chocolate
- 30 milliliters honey
- 30 milliliters whole milk

Directions:
1. Beat the butter until smooth and fluffy. Add the butter to the sugar and beat together in a smooth mixture.
2. Now add and mix in the milk, sugar, chocolate (broken into small chunks/chips), and flour. Preheat your Air Fryer to 360°F.
3. Shape the mixture into cookie shapes and put them on a baking sheet that will sit 16 minutes or until cooked through in the Air Fryer Bake.

Nutrition:
Calories: 515, Protein: 4 g, Fat: 9 g, Carbohydrates: 5 g.

914. Doughnuts

Preparation Time: 35 minutes
Cooking Time: 60 minutes
Servings: 8
Ingredients:
- ¼ cup warm water, warmed (100°F to 110°F)
- 1 tbsp. active yeast
- ¼ cup, plus half tsp. granulated sugar, divided
- 2 cups (about 8 ½ oz.) all-purpose flour
- ¼ tsp. kosher salt
- ¼ cup whole milk, at room temperature
- 2 tbsp. unsalted butter, melted
- 1 large egg, beaten
- 1 cup (about 4 oz.) powdered sugar
- 4 tsp. tap water

Directions:
1. Mix water, yeast, and ½ teaspoon of the granulated sugar in a small bowl; let it stand until foamy, around five minutes. Combine flour, salt, and the remaining ¼ cup of granulated sugar in a medium bowl. Add yeast mixture, milk, butter, and egg; stir it with a wooden spoon until a soft dough comes together. Turn dough out onto a lightly floured surface and knead until smooth, 1 to 2 minutes. Switch dough to a lightly greased tub. Cover and let rise in a warm place until doubled in volume, around 1 hour.
2. Turn dough out onto a lightly floured surface. Gently roll to ¼-inch thickness. Cut out eight doughnuts using a 3-inch round cutter and a 1-inch round cutter to delete core: place doughnuts and doughnuts holes on a lightly floured surface. Cover loosely with plastic wrap and let it stand for about 30 minutes until doubled in volume.
3. Place two doughnuts and two doughnuts holes in a single layer in an Air Fryer pan, and cook at 350°F until golden brown, 4 to 5 minutes. Continue with doughnuts and holes remaining on.
4. Whisk powdered sugar together and tap water until smooth in a medium bowl. In a glaze, dip doughnuts and doughnut holes, place them on a wire rack set above a rimmed baking sheet to allow excess glaze to drip off. Let it stand for about 10 minutes until the glaze hardens.

Nutrition:
Calories: 378, Protein: 4 g, Fat: 9 g, Carbohydrates: 5 g.

915. Cherry-Choco Bars

Preparation Time: 7 minutes
Cooking Time: 15 minutes
Servings: 8
Ingredients:
- ¼ tsp. salt - ½ cup almonds, sliced
- ½ cup chia seeds
- ½ cup dark chocolate, chopped
- ½ cup dried cherries, chopped
- ½ cup prunes, pureed
- ½ cup quinoa, cooked
- ¾ cup almond butter
- 1/3 cup honey - 2cups oats
- 2 tbsp. coconut oil

Directions:
1. Preheat the Kalorik Maxx Air Fryer Oven to 375°F.
2. In a bowl, combine the oats, quinoa, chia seeds, almond, cherries, and chocolate.
3. In a saucepan, heat the almond butter, honey, and coconut oil.
4. Pour the butter mixture over the dry mix, then add salt and prunes and mix until well combined.
5. Pour over a baking dish that can fit inside the Air Fryer.
6. Bake for 15 minutes.
7. Let it cool before slicing into bars.

Nutrition:
Calories: 378, Protein: 4 g, Fat: 9 g, Carbohydrates: 5 g.

916. Crusty Apple Hand Pies

Preparation Time: 7 minutes
Cooking Time: 8 minutes
Servings: 6
Ingredients:
- 15-oz. no-sugar-added apple pie filling
- 1 store-bought crust

Directions:
1. Lay out the pie crust and slice it into equal-sized squares.
2. Place 2 tablespoons of filling into each square and seal crust with a fork
3. Pour into the oven rack/basket.
4. Place the rack on the middle shelf of the Smart Air Fryer Oven.
5. Set temperature to 390°F and time to 8 minutes until golden in color.

Nutrition:
Calories: 378, Protein: 4 g, Fat: 9 g, Carbohydrates: 5 g.

917. Pancakes Nutella-Stuffed

Preparation Time: 15 minutes
Cooking Time: 20 minutes
Servings: 12
Ingredients:
- 4 tsp. of chocolate-hazelnut spread, such as Nutella ®, at room temperature
- ¼ cup vegetable oil, plus
- ¼ cup grid all-purpose flour
- 1 ¼ cup buttermilk
- ¼ cup of granulated sugar
- 1 tsp. baking soda
- 1 tsp. baking soda
- 1 egg
- A pinch of salt
- sugar for dusting
- Maple syrup for serving

Directions:
1. Line a parchment baking sheet and drop 12 different teaspoons of mounds of chocolate hazelnut spread over it. Place the baking sheet on a counter to flatten the dollops and freeze for about 15 minutes until firm.
2. In the meantime, preheat a griddle over low heat and brush with oil lightly.
3. In a large bowl, whisk together the flour, buttermilk, oil, granulated sugar, baking powder, baking soda, egg, and a pinch of salt until smooth.
4. Pour batter pools on the hot griddle and cook until bubbles just start forming on the pancake's surface and the bottoms are golden, 1 to 2 minutes. Place a frozen chocolate-hazelnut dish spread on 4 of the pancakes and flip the remaining four pancakes on top of those, so that the wet batter envelopes the disks. Put the rest of the discs back into the freezer. Continue cooking the pancakes for about 1 minute, flipping halfway, until the edges are set. Repeat with the remaining batters and disks, oiling the grid lightly in between lots.
5. Stub the pancakes with the sugar of the confectioners and serve warmly with syrup.

Nutrition:
Calories: 151, Protein: 4 g, Fat: 9 g, Carbohydrates: 5 g.

918. Spiced Pear Sauce

Preparation Time: 10 minutes
Cooking Time: 6 hours
Servings: 12
Ingredients:
- 8 pears, cored and diced
- ½ tsp. ground cinnamon
- ¼ tsp. ground nutmeg
- ¼ tsp. ground cardamom
- 1 cup of water

Directions:
1. Put all of the ingredients in the Air Fryer and stir well.
2. Seal the pot with a lid, select slow cook mode and cook on low for 6 hours.
3. Mash the sauce using a potato masher.
4. Pour into the container and store.

Nutrition:
Calories: 81, Protein: 0.5 g, Fat: 0.2 g, Carbohydrates: 21.4 g.

919. Saucy Fried Bananas

Preparation Time: 7 minutes
Cooking Time: 10 minutes
Servings: 2
Ingredients:
- 1 large egg

- ¼ cup cornstarch
- ¼ cup plain breadcrumbs
- 2 bananas, halved crosswise
- Cooking oil
- Chocolate sauce

Directions:
1. Preheat your Kalorik Maxx Air Fryer Oven to 350°F.
2. In a small bowl, beat the egg.
3. In another bowl, place the cornstarch.
4. Place the breadcrumbs in a different bowl.
5. Dip the bananas in the cornstarch, then the egg, and then the breadcrumbs.
6. Spray the basket with cooking oil. Place the bananas in the basket and spray them with cooking oil.
7. Cook for 5 minutes.
8. Open the Air Fryer and flip the bananas then cook for an additional 2 minutes.
9. Transfer the bananas to plates.
10. Drizzle the chocolate sauce over the bananas and serve.

Nutrition:
Calories: 378, Protein: 4 g, Fat: 9 g, Carbohydrates: 5 g.

920. Macaroons

Preparation Time: 10 minutes
Cooking Time: 8 minutes
Servings: 20
Ingredients:
- 2 tbsp. sugar
- 2 cup coconut, shredded
- 4 egg whites
- 1 tsp. Vanilla extract

Directions:
1. In a bowl, mix egg whites with stevia and beat using your mixer
2. Add coconut and vanilla extract, whisk again. Shape small balls out of this mix, put them in your Air Fryer, and cook at 340°F for 8 minutes.
3. Serve macaroons cold

Nutrition:
Calories: 55, Fats: 6 g, Carbs: 2 g, Protein: 1 g.

921. Orange Cake

Preparation Time: 10 minutes
Cooking Time: 16 minutes
Servings: 12
Ingredients:
- 1 orange, peeled, and cut into quarters
- 1 tsp. vanilla extract
- 6 eggs
- 2 tbsp. orange zest
- 4 oz. cream cheese
- 1 tsp. baking powder
- 9 oz. flour
- 2 oz. sugar+ 2 tbsp.
- 4 oz. Yogurt

Directions:
4. In your food processor, pulse orange very well
5. Add flour, 2 tablespoons of sugar, eggs, baking powder, and vanilla extract; pulse well again.
6. Transfer this into 2 pans. Introduce each in your fryer and cook at 330°F, for 16 minutes
7. Mix cream cheese with orange zest, yogurt, and the rest of the sugar and stir well.
8. Add half of the cream cheese mix, add the other cake layer, and top with the rest of the cream cheese mix.
9. Spread it well, slice, and serve.

Nutrition:
Calories: 200, Fats: 13 g, Carbs: 9 g, Protein: 8 g.

922. Carrot Cake

Preparation Time: 10 minutes
Cooking Time: 45 minutes
Servings: 6
Ingredients:
- 5 oz. flour
- ¾ tsp. baking powder
- ¼ tsp. nutmeg ground
- ½ tsp. baking soda
- ½ tsp. cinnamon powder
- ½ cup sugar
- 1/3 cup carrots, grated
- 1/3 cup pecans, toasted and chopped.
- ¼ cup pineapple juice
- ½ tsp. allspice
- 1 egg
- 3 tbsp. yogurt
- 4 tbsp. sunflower oil
- 1/3 cup coconut flakes; shredded
- Cooking spray

Directions:
1. In a bowl, mix flour with baking soda and powder, salt, allspice, cinnamon, and nutmeg and stir. In another bowl, mix egg with yogurt, sugar, pineapple juice, oil, carrots, pecans, and coconut flakes; stir well
2. Combine the two mixtures and stir well, pour this into a springform pan that fits your Air Fryer previously greased with some cooking spray; transfer to your Air Fryer and cook on 320°F for 45 minutes.
3. Leave the cake to cool down, then cut and serve it.

Nutrition:
Calories: 200, Fats: 6g, Carbs: 22g, Protein: 4 g

923. Easy Baked Chocolate Mug Cake

Preparation Time: 5 minutes
Cooking Time: 15 minutes
Servings: 3
Ingredients:
- ½ cup cocoa powder
- ½ cup stevia powder
- 1 cup coconut cream
- 1 package cream cheese, room temperature
- 1 tbsp. vanilla extract
- 1 tbsp. butter

Directions:
1. Preheat the Air Fryer oven for 5 minutes.
2. In a mixing bowl, combine all ingredients.
3. Use a hand mixer to mix everything until fluffy.
4. Pour into greased mugs.
5. Place the mugs in the fryer basket.
6. Bake for 15 minutes at 350°F.
7. Place them in the fridge to chill before serving.

Nutrition:
Calories: 744, Fat: 69.7 g, Protein: 13.9 g, Sugar: 4 g.

924. Fried Peaches

Preparation Time: 2 hours 10 minutes
Cooking Time: 15 minutes
Servings: 4
Ingredients:
- 4 ripe peaches (½ a peach = 1 serving)
- 1 ½ cups flour
- Salt
- 2 egg yolks
- ¾ cups cold water
- 1 ½ tbsp. olive oil
- 2 tbsp. brandy
- 4 egg whites
- Cinnamon/sugar mix

Directions:
1. Mix flour, egg yolks, and salt in a mixing bowl. Slowly mix in water, then add brandy. Set the mixture aside for 2 hours and go do something for 1 hour 45 minutes.
2. Boil a large pot of water and cut and x at the bottom of each peach. While the water boils, fill another large bowl with water and ice. Boil each peach for about a minute, then plunge them in the ice bath. Now the peels should fall off the peach. Beat the egg whites and mix into the batter mix. Dip each peach in the mix to coat.
3. Pour the coated peach into the oven rack/basket. Place the rack on the middle shelf of the Air Fryer oven. Set temperature to 360°F, and time to 10 minutes.
4. Prepare a plate with cinnamon/sugar mix, roll peaches in the mix and serve.

Nutrition:
Calories: 306, Fat: 3 g, Protein: 10 g, Fiber: 2.7 g.

925. Apple Dumplings

Preparation Time: 10 minutes
Cooking Time: 25 minutes
Servings: 4
Ingredients:
- 2 tbsp. melted coconut oil
- 2 puff pastry sheets
- 1 tbsp. brown sugar
- 2 tbsp. raisins
- 2 small apples of choice

Directions:
1. Ensure your Air Fryer oven is preheated to 356°F.
2. Core and peel apples and mix with raisins and sugar.
3. Place a bit of apple mixture into puff pastry sheets and brush sides with melted coconut oil.
4. Place them into the Air Fryer. Cook for 25 minutes, turning halfway through. They will be golden when done.

Nutrition:
Calories: 367, Fat: 7 g, Protein: 2 g, Sugar: 5 g.

926. Air Fryer Chocolate Cake

Preparation Time: 5 minutes
Cooking Time: 45 minutes
Servings: 8–10
Ingredients:
- ½ c. hot water
- 1 tsp. vanilla
- ¼ c. olive oil
- ½ c. almond milk
- 1 egg - ½ tsp. salt
- ¾ tsp. baking soda
- ¾ tsp. baking powder
- ½ c. unsweetened cocoa powder
- 2 c. almond flour - 1 c. brown sugar

Directions:
1. Preheat your Air Fryer oven to 356°F.
2. Stir all dry ingredients together. Then stir in wet ingredients. Add hot water last.
3. The batter will be thin, no worries.
4. Pour cake batter into a pan that fits into the fryer. Cover with foil and poke holes into the foil.
5. Bake for 35 minutes.
6. Discard foil and then bake another 10 minutes.

Nutrition:
Calories: 378, Fat: 9 g, Protein: 4 g, Sugar: 5 g.

927. Banana-Choco Brownies

Preparation Time: 5 minutes
Cooking Time: 30 minutes
Servings: 12
Ingredients:
- 2 cups almond flour
- 2 tsp. baking powder
- ½ tsp. baking powder
- ½ tsp. baking soda
- ½ tsp. salt
- 1 over-ripe banana
- 3 large eggs
- ½ tsp. stevia powder
- ¼ cup coconut oil
- 1 tbsp. vinegar
- 1/3 cup almond flour
- 1/3 cup cocoa powder

Directions:
1. Preheat the Air Fryer oven for 5 minutes.
2. Combine all ingredients in a food processor and pulse until well-combined.
3. Pour the mixture into a baking dish that will fit in the Air Fryer.

4. Place it in the Air Fryer basket and cook for 30 minutes at 350°F or if a toothpick inserted in the middle comes out clean.

Nutrition:
Calories: 75, Fat: 6.5 g, Protein: 1.7 g, Sugar: 2 g.

928. Easy Air Fryer Donuts

Preparation Time: 5 minutes
Cooking Time: 5 minutes
Servings: 8
Ingredients:
- Pinch of allspice - 4 tbsp. dark brown sugar
- ½–1 tsp. cinnamon
- 1/3 c. granulated sweetener
- 3 tbsp. melted coconut oil
- 1 can of biscuits

Directions:
1. Mix allspice, sugar, sweetener, and cinnamon.
2. Take out biscuits from the can. With a circle cookie cutter, cut holes from centers, and place them into the Air Fryer.
3. Cook for 5 minutes at 350°F. As batches are cooked, use a brush to coat with melted coconut oil and dip each into a sugar mixture.
4. Serve warm!

Nutrition:
Calories: 209, Fat: 4 g, Protein: 0 g, Sugar: 3 g.

929. Fried Bananas with Chocolate Sauce

Preparation Time: 10 minutes
Cooking Time: 10 minutes
Servings: 2
Ingredients:
- 1 large egg
- ¼ cup cornstarch
- ¼ cup plain bread crumbs
- 3 bananas, halved crosswise
- Cooking oil
- Chocolate sauce

Directions:
1. In a small bowl, beat the egg. In another bowl, place the cornstarch. Place the bread crumbs in a third bowl. Dip the bananas in the cornstarch, then the egg, and then the bread crumbs.
2. Spray the Air Fryer basket with cooking oil. Place the bananas in the basket and spray them with cooking oil.
3. Set temperature to 360°F and cook for 5 minutes. Open the Air Fryer and flip the bananas. Cook for an additional 2 minutes. Transfer the bananas to plates.
4. Drizzle the chocolate sauce over the bananas, and serve.
5. You can make your chocolate sauce using 2 tablespoons of milk and ¼ cup chocolate chips. Heat a saucepan over medium-high fire. Add the milk and stir for 1 to 2 minutes. Add the chocolate chips. Stir for 2 minutes, or until the chocolate has melted.

Nutrition:
Calories: 203, Fat: 6 g, Protein: 3 g, Fiber: 3 g.

930. Chocolaty Banana Muffins

Preparation Time: 5 minutes
Cooking Time: 25 minutes
Servings: 12
Ingredients:
- ¾ cup whole wheat flour
- ¾ cup plain flour
- ¼ cup cocoa powder
- ¼ tsp. baking powder
- 1 tsp. baking soda
- ¼ tsp. salt
- 2 large bananas, peeled and mashed
- 1 cup sugar
- 1/3 cup canola oil
- 1 egg
- ½ tsp. vanilla essence
- 1 cup mini chocolate chips

Directions:
1. In a large bowl, mix flour, cocoa powder, baking powder, baking soda, and salt.
2. In another bowl, add bananas, sugar, oil, egg, and vanilla extract; beat till well combined.
3. Slowly, add flour mixture in egg mixture and mix till just combined.
4. Fold in chocolate chips.
5. Preheat the Air Fryer oven to 345°F. Grease 12 muffin molds.
6. Transfer the mixture into the muffin molds evenly and cook for about 20–25 minutes or till a toothpick inserted in the center comes out clean.
7. Remove the muffin molds from the Air Fryer and keep them on a wire rack to cool for about 10 minutes. Carefully turn on a wire rack to cool completely before serving.

Nutrition:
Calories: 203, Fat: 6 g, Protein: 3 g, Fiber: 3 g.

931. Sweet Cream Cheese Wontons

Preparation Time: 5 minutes
Cooking Time: 5 minutes
Servings: 16
Ingredients:
- 1 egg mixed with a bit of water
- Wonton wrappers
- ½ c. powdered Erythritol
- 8 ounces softened cream cheese
- Olive oil

Directions:
1. Mix sweetener and cream cheese together.
2. Lay out 4 wontons at a time and cover with a dish towel to prevent drying out.
3. Place ½ of a teaspoon of cream cheese mixture into each wrapper.
4. Dip finger into egg/water mixture and fold diagonally to form a triangle. Seal edges well.
5. Repeat with remaining ingredients.

6. Place filled wontons into the Air Fryer oven and cook for 5 minutes at 400°F, shaking halfway through cooking.

Nutrition:
Calories: 303, Fat: 3 g, Protein: 0.5 g, Sugar: 4 g.

932. Air Fryer Cinnamon Rolls

Preparation Time: 15 minutes
Cooking Time: 5 minutes
Servings: 8
Ingredients:

- 1 ½ tbsp. cinnamon
- ¾ c. brown sugar
- ¼ c. melted coconut oil
- 1 pound frozen bread dough, thawed

Glaze:

- ½ tsp. vanilla
- 1 ¼ c. powdered Erythritol
- 2 tbsp. softened ghee
- Ounces softened cream cheese

Directions:

1. Lay out bread dough and roll it out into a rectangle. Brush melted ghee over the dough and leave a 1-inch border along the edges.
2. Mix cinnamon and sweetener together and then sprinkle over dough.
3. Roll dough tightly and slice into 8 pieces. Let it sit 1–2 hours to rise.
4. To make the glaze, simply mix ingredients till smooth.
5. Once rolls rise, place them into the Air Fryer and cook for 5 minutes at 350°F.
6. Serve rolls drizzled in cream cheese glaze. Enjoy!

Nutrition:
Calories: 390, Fat: 8 g, Protein: 1 g, Sugar: 7 g.

933. Bread Pudding with Cranberry

Preparation Time: 5 minutes
Cooking Time: 45 minutes
Servings: 4
Ingredients:

- 1½ cups milk
- 2½ eggs
- ½ cup cranberries1 tsp. butter
- ¼ cup and 2 tbsp. white sugar
- ¼ cup golden raisins
- 1/8 tsp. ground cinnamon
- ¾ cup heavy whipping cream
- ¾ tsp. lemon zest
- ¾ tsp. kosher salt
- ¾ French baguettes, cut into 2-inch slices
- 3/8 vanilla bean, split and seeds scraped away

Directions:

1. Lightly grease the baking pan of the Air Fryer with cooking spray. Spread baguette slices, cranberries, and raisins.
2. In a blender, blend well vanilla bean, cinnamon, salt, lemon zest, eggs, sugar, and cream. Pour over baguette slices. Let it soak for an hour. Cover pan with foil.
3. For 35 minutes, cook at 330°F.
4. Let it rest for 10 minutes. Serve and enjoy.

Nutrition:
Calories: 581, Fat: 23.8 g, Protein: 15.8 g, Sugar: 7 g.

CHAPTER 10:
Bread Recipes

934. Mini Pizza

Preparation Time: 10 minutes
Cooking Time: 20 minutes
Servings: 4
Ingredients:
- 1 tsp. of Italian herb seasoning
- ¼ cup of minced onion
- 6 toasted and split muffins
- 3 tbsp. of steak sauce
- 2 cups of mozzarella cheese
- ¼ cup of sliced green onion
- 1 can of tomato paste - ¾ pound of ground beef
- 2 cups of parmesan cheese

Directions:
1. Crumble meat in a bowl. Add onion, tomato paste, Italian herb, and steak sauce.
2. Stir well.
3. Spread the mixture on muffins and transfer to the PowerXL Air Fryer Grill pan.
4. Set the PowerXL Air Fryer Grill to the Pizza function.
5. Cook for about 20 minutes on both sides at 350°F.
6. Serve immediately with green onions and cheese.

Serving Suggestions: Serve with tomato ketchup.
Directions & Cooking Tips: Mix the ingredients well.
Nutrition:
Calories: 273, Fat: 27 g, Carbs: 23 g, Protein: 21 g.

935. Artichoke with Red Pepper Pizza

Preparation Time: 10 minutes
Cooking Time: 20 minutes
Servings: 1
Ingredients:
- 1 tsp. of dried basil
- 1 can of artichoke hearts
- 1½ cup of mozzarella cheese
- 1 cup of red bell pepper - 5 cloves of garlic
- Cracked pepper - 1 tbsp. of olive oil
- 1 pizza shell - 1 tsp. of oregano
- 1 jar of sliced mushroom

Directions:
1. Mix artichoke hearts, basil, bell pepper, garlic, and cracked pepper in a bowl.
2. Add oregano, mushroom, and olive oil.
3. Place the mixture on the pizza shell.
4. Transfer the pizza shell to PowerXL Air Fryer Grill pan.
5. Set the PowerXL Air Fryer Grill to the Pizza function.
6. Cook for about 20 minutes at 350°F.
7. Serve immediately.

Serving Suggestions: Serve with tomato ketchup.
Directions & Cooking Tips: Rinse the artichoke well.
Nutrition:
Calories: 359, Fat: 18 g, Carbs: 43 g, Protein: 12 g.

936. Flatbread

Preparation Time: 5 minutes
Cooking Time: 7 minutes
Servings: 2
Ingredients:
- 1 cup shredded mozzarella cheese
- ¼ cup almond flour
- 1-ounce full-fat cream cheese softened

Directions:
7. Melt mozzarella in the microwave for 30 seconds. Stir in almond flour until smooth.

8. Add cream cheese. Continue mixing until dough forms. Knead with wet hands if necessary.
9. Divide the dough into two pieces and roll out to ¼-inch thickness between two pieces of parchment.
10. Cover the air fryer basket with parchment and place the flatbreads into the air fryer basket. Work in batches if necessary.
11. Cook at 320F for 7 minutes. Flip once at the halfway mark.
12. Serve.

Nutrition: Calories: 296 Fat: 22.6g Carb: 3.3g Protein: 16.3g

937. Artichoke Turkey Pizza

Preparation Time: 10minutes
Cooking Time: 10 minutes
Servings: 2
Ingredients:
- 2 cups of chopped cooked turkey
- 1½ cup of mozzarella cheese
- 2 baked pizza crust
- 1 can of black olives
- 1 can of diced tomatoes with garlic, oregano, and basil
- ½ cup of shredded parmesan cheese
- 1 can of artichoke hearts

Directions:
1. Place the pizza crusts on a working surface.
2. Place turkey, olive, tomatoes mix, parmesan cheese, olives, and artichokes on them.
3. Transfer the pizza crusts to the PowerXL Air Fryer Grill pan.
4. Set the PowerXL Air Fryer Grill to the Pizza function.
5. Cook for 10 minutes at 450°F
6. Serve immediately.

Serving Suggestions: Top with mozzarella cheese while serving.
Directions & Cooking Tips: Drain the heart of the artichoke.
Nutrition:
Calories: 196, Fat: 7 g, Carbs: 28 g, Protein: 8 g.

938. Bacon Cheeseburger Pizza

Preparation Time: 10 minutes
Cooking Time: 10 minutes
Servings: 2
Ingredients:
- 6 bacon strips
- ½ pound of ground beef
- 1 tsp. of pizza seasoning
- 2 cups of mozzarella cheese
- 2 baked-bread crusts
- 20 slices of dill pickles
- 1 chopped small onion
- 2 cups of shredded cheddar cheese
- 8 ounces of pizza sauce

Directions:
1. Cook onion and beef over medium heat for about 5 minutes.
2. Drain the meat.
3. Add bacon, seasonings, sauce, cheeses, and pickles.
4. Place the bread crusts on a working surface.
5. Place the ingredients on them.
6. Transfer them to the PowerXL Air Fryer Grill pan.
7. Set the PowerXL Air Fryer Grill to the Pizza function.
8. Cook for 10 minutes at 450°F.

Serving Suggestions: Serve with ketchup.
Directions & Cooking Tips: Rinse the beef and bacon well.
Nutrition:
Calories: 322, Fat: 12 g, Carbs: 42 g, Protein: 17 g.

939. Bacon Lettuce Tomato Pizza

Preparation Time: 10 minutes
Cooking Time: 17 minutes
Servings: 2
Ingredients:
- 6 slices of plum tomatoes
- 1 cup of torn Romaine lettuce
- 1/3 cup of mayonnaise
- 8 sliced of bacon
- 2 bread shell
- 1 cup of mozzarella cheese

Directions:
1. Spread the bread shell on a working surface.
2. Put mayonnaise, cheese, bacon, and tomatoes on the bread shells.
3. Transfer it to the PowerXL Air Fryer Grill pan.
4. Set the PowerXL Air Fryer Grill to the Pizza function.
5. Cook for 17 minutes at 450°F.
6. Serve immediately.

Serving Suggestions: serve with lettuce
Directions & Cooking Tips: cooked and quartered bacon should be used
Nutrition:
Calories: 132, Fat: 8 g, Carbs: 9 g, Protein: 8 g.

940. Breakfast Pizza

Preparation Time: 10 minutes
Cooking Time: 15 minutes
Servings: 5
Ingredients:
- 1 pound of bacon
- 8 ounces of crescent dinner rolls
- 1 cup of cheddar cheese
- 6 eggs

Directions:
1. Place the rolls on the pizza pan.

2. Mix cheese, eggs, and bacon in a bowl.
3. Pour the mixture over the crust.
4. Place the pan in the PowerXL Air Fryer Grill.
5. Set the PowerXL Air Fryer Grill to the Pizza function.
6. Cook for 15 minutes at 370°F.
7. Serve immediately.

Serving Suggestions: Serve with ketchup.
Directions & Cooking Tips: Cooked bacon should be used.
Nutrition:
Calories: 311, Fat: 11 g, Carbs: 43 g, Protein: 15 g.

941. French Bread Pizza

Preparation Time: 10 minutes
Cooking Time: 10 minutes
Servings: 4
Ingredients:

- 1 tsp. of dried oregano
- ½ cup of fresh mushrooms
- 1 loaf of French bread
- ¼ cup of parmesan cheese
- 1 cup of mozzarella cheese
- ½ green pepper
- ¾ cup of spaghetti sauce

Directions:

1. Put the spaghetti sauce on the French bread.
2. Add green pepper, cheeses, mushroom, and oregano. Place it on the PowerXL Air Fryer Grill pan.
3. Set the PowerXL Air Fryer Grill to the Pizza function.
4. Cook for 15 minutes at 370°F.

Serving Suggestions: Serve with cheese.
Directions & Cooking Tips: Shred the mozzarella cheese before using.
Nutrition:
Calories: 303, Fat: 7 g, Carbs: 51 g, Protein: 13 g.

942. Vegetable Pizza Pan Supreme

Preparation Time: 30 minutes
Cooking Time: 20 minutes
Servings: 2
Ingredients:

- 1 pizza dough
- 2 tbsp. of olive oil
- 8 creaming mushrooms
- 8 slices of white onion
- 4 tbsp. of pesto
- 1.5 cup grated mozzarella
- 0.5 green pepper
- 1 cup of spinach
- 12 tomato slices

Directions:

1. Roll the pizza dough halves until each is the size of the airflow shelves.
2. Lightly grease both sides of each dough with olive oil.
3. Place each pizza on a rack. Place the racks on the top and bottom shelves of the Power Air Fryer.
4. Press the On/Off button, then the French Fries button (400°F), and reduce the cooking time to 13 minutes.
5. After 5 minutes, turn the dough on the top shelf and rotate the racks.
6. After 4 minutes, turn the dough onto the top shelf.
7. Remove both racks and the top pizzas with toppings.
8. Place the racks on the top and bottom shelves of the electric fryer.
9. Press the power button and then the French Fries button (400°F) and reduce the cooking time to 7 minutes.
10. Turn the pizza after 4 minutes.
11. As soon as the pizzas are ready, let them rest for 4 minutes before cutting.

Nutrition:
Calories: 183, Carbs: 32.7 g, Protein: 9.4 g, Fat: 2 g.

943. Garlic Bread Pizza

Preparation Time: 10 minutes
Cooking Time: 10 minutes
Servings: 4
Ingredients:

- 4 pieces baguette, cut in half
- Mint leaves, chopped - 2–3 tsp. butter
- 2–3 garlic cloves, minced

Directions:

1. Mix butter, mint, and garlic.
2. Spread mixture on every slice.
3. Bake at 200°C/ 400°F in the PowerXL Air Fryer Grill for 5–6 minutes.

Nutrition:
Calories: 160, Carbs: 18 g, Protein: 3.6 g, Fat: 7.1 g.

944. Cheesy Pepperoni Pizza Bites

Preparation Time: 5 minutes
Cooking Time: 12 minutes
Servings: 8
Ingredients:

- 1 cup finely shredded Mozzarella cheese
- ½ cup chopped pepperoni
- ¼ cup marinara sauce
- 1 (8-ounce) can crescent roll dough
- All-purpose flour, for dusting

Directions:

1. In a small bowl, stir together the cheese, pepperoni, and marinara sauce.
2. Lay the dough on a lightly floured work surface. Separate it into 4 rectangles. Firmly pinch the perforations together and pat the dough pieces flat.
3. Divide the cheese mixture evenly between the rectangles and spread it out over the dough, leaving a ¼-inch border. Roll a rectangle up tightly, starting with the short end. Pinch the edge down to seal the roll. Repeat with the remaining rolls.
4. Slice the rolls into 4 or 5 even slices. Place the slices on the sheet pan, leaving a few inches between each slice.
5. Place the pan on the toast position.
6. Select Toast, set the temperature to 350°F (180°C), and time to 12 minutes.
7. After 6 minutes, rotate the pan and continue cooking.

8. When cooking is complete, the rolls will be golden brown with crisp edges. Remove the pan from the Air Fryer grill. Serve hot.

Nutrition:
Calories: 207, Carbs: 17 g, Protein: 9 g, Fat: 12 g.

945. Cheesy BBQ Chicken Pizza

Preparation Time: 5 minutes
Cooking Time: 8 minutes
Servings: 1
Ingredients:
- 1 piece naan bread
- ¼ cup Barbecue sauce
- ¼ cup shredded Monterrey Jack cheese
- ¼ cup shredded Mozzarella cheese
- ½ chicken herby sausage, sliced
- 2 tbsp. red onion, thinly sliced
- Chopped cilantro or parsley, for garnish
- Cooking spray

Directions:
1. Spritz the bottom of naan bread with cooking spray, then transfer to the air fry basket.
2. Brush with the Barbecue sauce. Top with the sausage, cheeses, and finish with the red onion.
3. Place the basket on the Air Fry position.
4. Select Air Fry, set the temperature to 400°F (205°C), and time to 8 minutes.
5. When cooking is complete, the cheese should be melted. Remove the basket from the Air Fryer grill.
6. Garnish with chopped cilantro or parsley before slicing to serve.

Nutrition:
Calories: 227, Carbs: 18 g, Protein: 11 g, Fat: 22 g.

946. Eggplant Pizza

Preparation Time: 15 minutes
Cooking Time: 30 minutes
Servings: 2
Ingredients:
- 1 eggplant (sliced ¼ -inch)
- 1 gluten-free pizza dough
- 1 cup of pizza sauce
- 1 tbsp fresh rosemary and basil
- 1 cup cheese
- 2 garlic cloves, chopped
- 1 red pepper, salt, and pepper
- 1 tbsp olive oil

Directions:
1. Rub eggplant slices with vegetable oil and rosemary, salt and pepper, and bake for 25 minutes at 218°C/ 425°F in the PowerXL Air Fryer Grill.
2. Roll the dough round and spread the remaining ingredients on top.
3. Preheat the PowerXL Air Fryer Grill at 230°C/ 450°F at pizza setting and bake the pizza for 10 minutes.

Nutrition:
Calories: 260, Carbs: 24 g, Protein: 9 g, Fat: 14 g.

947. Veggie Pizza

Preparation Time: 10 minutes
Cooking Time: 10 minutes
Servings: 2
Ingredients:
- 1 cup of tomatoes, sliced
- Capsicum, sliced
- 4 baby corns
- 1–2 tsp. pizza sauce
- 1 cup of mozzarella cheese
- 3.5 cup of all-purpose flour
- 1.5 tsp. oregano seasoning
- Salt
- 1.5 tsp. yeast
- 2–3 tsp. oil
- 1.5 cup of water

Directions:
1. Make pizza dough with all-purpose flour adding oil, salt, yeast, and water.
2. Spread the remaining ingredients on the pizza base made from dough.
3. Preheat the PowerXL Air Fryer Grill and bake for 10 minutes.

Nutrition:
Calories: 300, Carbs: 37.5 g, Protein: 15 g, Fat: 10 g.

948. Grill Pizza Sandwiches

Preparation Time: 5 minutes
Cooking Time: 5 minutes
Servings: 1
Ingredients:
- 1 French bread sandwich roll, sliced
- 5 tsp. pizza sauce
- 15–20 slices pepperoni
- 1 cup mozzarella cheese, shredded

Directions:
1. Preheat the PowerXL Air Fryer Grill to 250°C/ 482°F.
2. Spread pizza sauce on the bread.
3. Add toppings, cheese, and pepperoni to each slice of bread.
4. Toast it until the cheese melts.

Nutrition:
Calories: 752.1, Carbs: 33.5 g, Protein: 35.2 g, Fat: 15.7 g.

949. Basil Pizza

Preparation Time: 10 minutes
Cooking Time: 7 minutes
Servings: 2
Ingredients:
- 1 pizza dough
- ½ tbsp. olive oil
- 1 cup pizza sauce

- 1½ cups part-skim mozzarella cheese, shredded
- 1½ cups part-skim provolone cheese, shredded
- 10 fresh basil leaves

Directions:
1. Place the water tray in the bottom of the PowerXL Smokeless Electric Grill.
2. Place about 2 cups of lukewarm water into the water tray.
3. Place the drip pan over the water tray and then arrange the heating element.
4. Now, place the grilling pan over the heating element.
5. Plug in the PowerXL Smokeless Electric Grill and press the "Power" button to turn it on.
6. Then press the "Fan" button.
7. Set the temperature settings according to the manufacturer's directions.
8. Cover the grill with a lid and let it preheat.
9. With your hands, stretch the dough into the size that will fit into the grilling pan.
10. After preheating, remove the lid and grease the grilling pan.
11. Place the dough over the grilling pan.
12. cover with the lid and cook for about 2–3 minutes.
13. Remove the lid and with a heat-safe spatula, flip the dough.
14. Cover with the lid and cook for about 2 minutes.
15. Remove the lid and flip the crust.
16. Immediately, spread the pizza sauce over the crust and sprinkle with both kinds of cheese.
17. Cover with the lid and cook for about 1 minute.
18. Remove the lid and cook for about 1 minute or until the cheese is melted.
19. Remove from the grill and immediately top the pizza with basil leaves.
20. Cut into desired-sized wedges and serve.

Nutrition:
Calories: 707, Total Fat: 47.5 g, Saturated Fat: 23.1 g, Cholesterol: 80mg, Sodium: 1000mg, Total Carbs: 34.9 g, Fiber: 3.5 g, Sugar: 4.6 g, Protein: 35.8 g.

950. PowerXL Air Fryer Grill-baked Grilled Cheese

Preparation Time: 10 minutes
Cooking Time: 5 minutes
Servings: 1
Ingredients:
- 2 slices bread
- 1–2 tsp. mayonnaise
- 2–3 tsp. cheddar cheese
- Fresh spinach

Directions:
1. Preheat the PowerXL Air Fryer Grill to 200°C/ 400°F.
2. Spread mayonnaise and cheese on the bread.
3. Bake for 5–7 minutes. Add the spinach.

Nutrition:
Calories: 353, Carbs: 42.1 g, Protein: 18.9 g, Fat: 7.8 g.

951. Cheese Chili Toast

Preparation Time: 5 minutes
Cooking Time: 10 minutes
Servings: 2
Ingredients:
- 2–4 slices bread
- Capsicum, chopped
- Salt & pepper
- 1–2 Chilies
- 20gm cheese, grated
- 10gm cream
- Oil

Directions:
1. Place the bread on the baking pan.
2. Make a mixture of oil, capsicums, peppers, salt, and chilies.
3. Apply the mixture on bread and grated cheese.
4. Bake at 350°F or 177°C for 5–7 minutes in the PowerXL Air Fryer Grill. You're all set.

Nutrition:
Calories: 135, Carbs: 11.6 g, Protein: 7.1 g, Fat: 6.5 g.

952. Cheese Pizza

Preparation Time: 10 minutes
Cooking Time: 10 minutes
Servings: 4
Ingredients:
- Readymade pizza base
- 2–3 tsp. tomato ketchup
- 100g (3.52oz.) cheese, shredded
- Salt & pepper
- 2 ounces mushroom
- Capsicum, onions, tomatoes

Directions:
1. Preheat the PowerXL Air Fryer Grill to 250°C/ 482°F.
2. Spread ketchup on the pizza base and then toppings and cheese.
3. Bake for 10–12 minutes.

Nutrition:
Calories: 306, Carbs: 40 g, Protein: 15 g, Fat: 11 g.

953. Garlic Bread

Preparation Time: 10 minutes
Cooking Time: 5 minutes
Servings: 4
Ingredients:
- 4 pieces baguette, cut in half
- Mint leaves, chopped
- 2–3 tsp. butter
- 2–3 garlic cloves, minced

Directions:
1. Mix butter, mint, and garlic.
2. Spread the mixture on every piece of baguette.
3. Bake at 200°C/ 400°F in the PowerXL Air Fryer Grill for 5–6 minutes

Nutrition:
Calories: 160, Carbs: 18 g, Protein: 3.6 g, Fat: 7.1 g.

954. Pepperoni Pizza

Preparation Time: 10 minutes
Cooking Time: 10 minutes

Servings: 8
Ingredients:
- 1 pepperoni, sliced
- 1 cup pizza sauce
- 1 cup mozzarella cheese
- 1 readymade pizza dough
- 1 cup Parmesan cheese, grated

Directions:
1. Arrange toppings on pizza dough.
2. Preheat the PowerXL Air Fryer Grill to 177°C/ 350°F.
3. Bake for 25 minutes.

Nutrition:
Calories: 235, Carbs: 35.6 g, Protein: 11 g, Fat: 11 g.

955. Egg Sandwich

Preparation Time: 10 minutes
Cooking Time: 16 minutes
Servings: 4
Ingredients:
- 4 eggs
- 1 cup light mayonnaise
- 1 tbsp. chopped chives
- Pepper to taste
- 8 slices loaf bread

Directions:
1. Add the eggs to the Air Fryer rack.
2. Select the air fry function.
3. Set it to 250°F.
4. Cook for 16 minutes.
5. Place the eggs in a bowl with ice water.
6. Peel and transfer to another bowl.
7. Mash the eggs with a fork.
8. Stir in the mayo, chives, and pepper.
9. Spread mixture on bread and top with another bread to make a sandwich.

Nutrition:
Calories: 121, Fat: 20 g, Protein: 9 g.

956. Grilled Cheese Sandwich

Preparation Time: 5 minutes
Cooking Time: 8 minutes
Servings: 1
Ingredients:
- 2 slices bread
- 1 tbsp. butter
- 2 slices cheddar cheese

Directions:
10. Spread one side of bread slices with butter.
11. Situate the cheese between the two bread slices.
12. Choose grill setting in your Air Fryer.
13. Cook at 350°F for 5 minutes.
14. Flip and cook for another 3 minutes.

Nutrition:
Calories: 133, Fat: 19 g, Protein: 8 g.

957. Beef and Seeds Burgers

Preparation Time: 15 minutes
Cooking Time: 10 minutes
Servings: 4
Ingredients:
- 1 tsp. cumin seeds
- 1 tsp. mustard seeds
- 1 tsp. coriander seeds
- 1 tsp. dried minced garlic
- 1 tsp. dried red pepper flakes
- 1 tsp. kosher salt
- 2 tsp. ground black pepper
- 1 pound (454 g) 85% lean ground beef
- 2 tbsp. Worcestershire sauce
- 4 hamburger buns
- Mayonnaise, for serving
- Cooking spray

Directions:
1. Spritz the air fry basket with cooking spray.
2. Put the garlic, seeds, salt, red pepper flakes, and ground black pepper in a food processor. Pulse to ground the mixture coarsely.
3. Put the ground beef in a large bowl. Pour in the seed mixture and drizzle with Worcestershire sauce. Stir to mix well.
4. Divide the mixture into four parts, shape each piece into a ball, and then bash each ball into a patty. Arrange the patties in the basket.
5. Place the basket on the Air Fry position.
6. Select Air Fry, set the temperature to 350°F (180°C), and time to 10 minutes. Flip the patties with tongs halfway through the cooking time.
7. When cooked, the patties will be well browned.
8. Assemble the buns with the patties, then drizzle the mayo over the patties to make the burgers. Serve immediately.

Nutrition:
Calories: 133, Fat: 19 g, Protein: 8 g.

958. Thai Pork Burgers

Preparation Time: 10 minutes
Cooking Time: 14 minutes
Servings: 6
Ingredients:
- 1 pound (454 g) ground pork
- 1 tbsp. Thai curry paste
- 1½ tbsp. fish sauce
- ¼ cup thinly sliced scallions, white and green parts
- 2 tbsp. minced peeled fresh ginger
- 1 tbsp. light brown sugar
- 1 tsp. ground black pepper
- 6 slider buns, split open lengthwise, warmed
- Cooking spray

Directions:
1. Spritz the air fry basket with cooking spray.
2. Combine all the ingredients except for the buns in a large bowl. Stir to mix well.
3. Divide and shape the mixture into six balls, then bash the balls into six 3-inch-diameter patties.

4. Arrange the patties in the basket and spritz with cooking spray.
5. Place the basket on the Air Fry position.
6. Select Air Fry, set the temperature to 375°F (190°C), and time to 14 minutes. Flip the patties halfway through the cooking time.
7. When cooked, the patties should be well browned.
8. Assemble the buns with patties to make the sliders and serve immediately.

Nutrition:
Calories: 161, Protein: 8 g, Fat: 88 g, Carbs: 32 g.

959. Cheesy Philly Steaks

Preparation Time: 20 minutes
Cooking Time: 20 minutes
Servings: 2
Ingredients:
- 12 ounces (340 g) boneless rib-eye steak, sliced thinly
- ½ tsp. Worcestershire sauce
- ½ tsp. soy sauce
- Kosher salt and ground black pepper, to taste
- ½ green bell pepper, stemmed, deseeded, and thinly sliced
- ½ small onion, halved and thinly sliced
- 1 tbsp. vegetable oil
- 2 soft hoagie rolls, split three-fourths of the way through
- 1 tbsp. butter, softened
- 2 slices provolone cheese, halved

Directions:
1. Combine the steak, soy sauce, salt, ground black pepper, and Worcestershire sauce in a large bowl. Toss to coat well. Set aside.
2. Combine the bell pepper, onion, vegetable oil, salt, and ground black pepper in a separate bowl. Toss to coat the vegetables well.
3. Pour the steak and vegetables into the air fry basket.
4. Place the basket on the Air Fry position.
5. Select Air Fry, set the temperature to 400°F (205°C), and time to 15 minutes.
6. When cooked, the steak will be browned and the vegetables will be tender. Transfer them to a plate. Set aside.
7. Brush the hoagie rolls with butter and place them in the basket.
8. Select Toast and set the time to 3 minutes. Place the basket on the toast position. When done, the rolls should be lightly browned.
9. Transfer the rolls to a clean work surface and divide the steak and vegetable mixture between the rolls. Spread with cheese. Place the stuffed rolls back in the basket.
10. Place the basket on the Air Fry position.
11. Select Air Fry and set the time to 2 minutes. When done, the cheese should be melted.
12. Serve immediately.

Nutrition:
Calories: 1564, Carbs: 9 g, Fat: 3.5 g, Protein: 8.6 g.

960. Cheese & Egg Breakfast Sandwich

Preparation Time: 3 minutes
Cooking Time: 6 minutes
Servings: 1
Ingredients:
- 1 egg
- 2 slices of cheddar or Swiss cheese
- A bit of butter
- 1 roll either an English muffin or Kaiser bun halved

Directions:
1. Butter the sliced rolls on both sides.
2. Whisk the eggs in an oven-safe dish.
3. Place the cheese, egg dish, and rolls into the Air Fryer. Make sure the buttered sides of the roll are facing upwards.
4. Adjust the Air Fryer to 390°F. Cook for 6 minutes.
5. Place the egg and cheese between the pieces of roll. Serve warm.

Nutrition:
Calories: 212, Total Fat: 11.2 g, Carbs: 9.3 g, Protein: 12.4 g.

961. Peanut Butter & Banana Sandwich

Preparation Time: 4 minutes
Cooking Time: 6 minutes
Servings: 1
Ingredients:
- 2 slices whole-wheat bread
- 1 tsp. sugar-free maple syrup
- 1 sliced banana
- 2 tbsp. peanut butter

Directions:
1. Evenly coat each side of the sliced bread with peanut butter.
2. Add the sliced banana and drizzle with some sugar-free maple syrup.
3. Adjust the Air Fryer to 330°F, then cook for 6 minutes. Serve warm.

Nutrition:
Calories: 211, Total Fat: 8.2 g, Carbs: 6.3 g, Protein: 11.2 g.

962. Super Cheesy Sandwiches

Preparation Time: 10 minutes
Cooking Time: 6 minutes
Servings: 4 to 8
Ingredients:
- 8 ounces Brie
- 8 slices oat nut bread
- 1 large ripe pear, cored and cut into ½-inch-thick slices
- 2 tbsp. butter, melted

Directions:
1. Make the sandwiches: Spread each of 4 slices of bread with ¼ of the Brie. Top the Brie with the pear slices and the remaining 4 bread slices.
2. Brush the melted butter lightly on both sides of each sandwich.
3. Arrange the sandwiches in the Air Fry basket.
4. Place the basket on the Bake position.
5. Select Bake, set the temperature to 360°F (182°C), and time to 6 minutes.

6. When cooking is complete, the cheese should be melted. Remove the basket from the Air Fryer grill and serve warm.

Nutrition:
Calories: 154, Carbs: 9 g, Fat: 2.5 g, Protein: 8.6 g.

963. Simple Cuban Sandwiches

Preparation Time: 20 minutes
Cooking Time: 8 minutes
Servings: 4 sandwiches
Ingredients:

- 4 slices ciabatta bread, about ¼-inch thick
- Cooking spray
- 1 tbsp. brown mustard

Toppings:

- 6 to 8 ounces thinly sliced leftover roast pork
- 4 ounces thinly sliced deli turkey
- ⅓ cup bread and butter pickle slices
- 2 to 3 ounces Pepper Jack cheese slices

Directions:

1. On a clean work surface, spray one side of each coat of bread with cooking spray. Spread the other side of each slice of bread evenly with brown mustard.
2. Top 4 of the bread slices with the turkey, roast pork, pickle slices, cheese, and finish with the remaining bread slices. Transfer to the air fry basket.
3. Place the basket on the Air Fry position.
4. Select Air Fry, set the temperature to 390°F (199°C), and time to 8 minutes.
5. When cooking is complete, remove the basket from the Air Fryer grill. Cool for 5 minutes and serve warm.

Nutrition:
Calories: 164, Carbs: 10 g, Fat: 4.5 g, Protein: 8.7 g.

964. Hot Ham and Cheese Sandwich

Preparation Time: 5 minutes
Cooking Time: 10 minutes
Servings: 2
Ingredients:

- 2–4 sandwich bread
- Olive oil
- ¼ tsp. oregano & basil
- 4 ounces ham, sliced
- 4 ounces cheese, sliced

Directions:

1. Preheat the PowerXL Air Fryer Grill to 200°C/ 400°F.
2. Apply vegetable oil and sprinkle oregano on each side of the bread slices.
3. Put the ham, spread cheese over one bread slice, and place the opposite on the sheet.
4. Bake for 10 minutes.

Nutrition:
Calories: 245, Carbs: 28 g, Protein: 16.18 g, Fat: 18.53 g.

965. Philly Cheesesteak Sandwiches

Preparation Time: 15 minutes
Cooking Time: 15 minutes
Servings: 6
Ingredients:

- 1–2 pounds steak
- 1 tsp. Worcestershire sauce
- Salt & pepper
- 2 tsp. butter
- 1 green bell pepper
- Cheese slices
- Bread rolls

Directions:

1. Marinate the steak with sauce, pepper, and salt. Cook the steak in a pan with butter until brown.
2. Cook veggies for 2–3 minutes.
3. Slice the steak and place it on the bread rolls with veggies, sliced cheese, and bell peppers.
4. Bake for a quarter-hour in the PowerXL Air Fryer Grill.

Nutrition:
Calories: 476, Carbs: 15 g, Protein: 37 g, Fat: 35 g.

966. Chicken Focaccia Bread Sandwiches

Preparation Time: 15 minutes
Cooking Time: 25 minutes
Servings: 6
Ingredients:

- Flatbread or focaccia, halved
- 2 cups of chicken, sliced
- Fresh basil leaves
- 1 cup of sweet pepper, roasted

Directions:

1. Roast the chicken at 177°C/ 350°F in the PowerXL Air Fryer Grill for 25 minutes to a half-hour.
2. Spread mayonnaise on the bread and put the remaining ingredients on top.

Nutrition:
Calories: 263cal, Carbs: 26.9 g, Protein: 19 g, Fat: 10 g.

967. Guacamole Turkey Burgers

Preparation Time: 10 minutes
Cooking Time: 30 minutes
Servings: 3
Ingredients:

- 12 oz. turkey, ground
- 1½ avocados
- 2 tsp. of juice from a lime
- ½ tsp. cumin
- 1 red chili, chopped
- ½ tsp. garlic powder
- ½ tsp. onion powder
- 3 tsp. of olive oil
- ½ tsp. salt

Directions:

1. Mix the turkey with the cumin, chili, salt, garlic powder, and onion powder in a medium-sized bowl.
2. Create 3 patties
3. Pour 3 teaspoons of olive oil into a skillet and heat over medium fire.

4. Now cook your patties. Make sure that both sides are brown.
5. Make the guacamole in the meantime.
6. Mash together the garlic powder, juice from the lime, and avocados in a bowl.
7. Add salt for seasoning.
8. Serve the burgers with guacamole on the patties.

Nutrition:
Calories: 316, Carbohydrates: 9 g, Fiber 8 g, Sugar: 0 g, Cholesterol: 80 mg, Total Fat: 21 g, Protein: 24 g.

968. Bread Pudding

Preparation Time: 10 minutes
Cooking Time: 1 hour
Servings: 8
Ingredients:
- 3 eggs
- 2 tbsp. vanilla
- 3 cups whole milk
- 3 egg yolks
- 2 tsp. cinnamon
- 8 tbsp. butter
- 1 cup cubed French bread
- 2 cups granulated sugar
- ¼ pyrex bowl

Directions:
1. Mix milk and butter in a bowl and heat in the microwave.
2. Break the egg into another bowl and whisk.
3. Add cinnamon, sugar, eggs, and vanilla.
4. Add the milk mix.
5. Add dried bread, mix until the bread is soaked.
6. Put the mixture in a pyrex bowl.
7. Place the pyrex bowl on the PowerXL Air Fryer Grill pan.
8. Set the PowerXL Air Fryer Grill to bagel/toast.
9. Cook 60 minutes at 270°F.
10. Allow cooling before serving

Serving Suggestions: Serve with Cointreau sauce.
Directions & Cooking Tips: Dried bread should be used.
Nutrition:
Calories: 379, Fat: 8 g, Carbs: 70 g, Protein: 9 g.

969. Cheesy Bread Pudding

Preparation Time: 10 minutes
Cooking Time: 8 minutes
Servings: 4
Ingredients:
- 4 cloves of garlic
- 1 cup of mozzarella cheese
- 8 slices of bread
- 6 tsp. of sun-dried tomatoes
- 5 tbsp. of melted butter

Directions:
1. Place the bread slices on a flat surface.
2. Put butter on it, garlic, and tomato paste.
3. Add cheese
4. Place the bread on the PowerXL Air Fryer Grill pan.
5. Set the PowerXL Air Fryer Grill to toast/bagel function.
6. Cook for 8 minutes a 350°F.

Serving Suggestions: Can be served with orange juice.
Cooking Tips: Prepare with tomato paste.
Nutrition:
Calories: 226, Fat: 8 g, Carbs: 32 g, Protein: 8 g.

970. Chocolate Bread Pudding

Preparation Time: 10 minutes
Cooking Time: 10 minutes
Servings: 8
Ingredients:
- 1 egg
- 1 egg yolk
- ¾ cup chocolate milk
- 3 tbsp. brown sugar
- 3 tbsp. peanut butter
- 2 tbsp. cocoa powder
- 1 tsp. vanilla
- 5 slices firm white bread, cubed
- Nonstick cooking spray

Directions:
1. Spritz a baking pan with nonstick cooking spray.
2. Whisk together the egg yolk, egg, peanut butter, chocolate milk, cocoa powder, brown sugar, and vanilla until well combined.
3. Fold in the bread cubes and stir to mix well. Allow the bread to soak for 10 minutes.
4. When ready, transfer the egg mixture to the baking pan.
5. Place the pan on the Bake position.
6. Select Bake, set the temperature to 330°F (166°C), and time to 10 minutes.
7. When done, the pudding should be just firm to the touch.
8. Serve at room temperature.

Nutrition:
Calories: 164, Protein: 2 g, Fat: 22 g, Carbs: 4 g.

971. Fast Pumpkin Pudding

Preparation Time: 10 minutes
Cooking Time: 15 minutes
Servings: 4
Ingredients:
- 1 cup canned no-salt-added pumpkin purée (not pumpkin pie filling)
- ¼ cup packed brown sugar
- 3 tbsp. all-purpose flour
- 1 egg, whisked
- 2 tbsp. milk
- 1 tbsp. unsalted butter, melted
- 1 tsp. pure vanilla extract
- 4 low-fat vanilla wafers, crumbled
- Cooking spray

Directions:
1. Coat a baking pan with cooking spray. Set aside.
2. Mix the pumpkin purée, flour, brown sugar, whisked egg, melted butter, milk, and vanilla in a medium bowl; whisk to combine. Transfer the mixture to the baking pan.
3. Place the pan on the Bake position.

4. Select Bake, set the temperature to 350°F (180°C), and time to 15 minutes.
5. When cooking is complete, the pudding should be set.
6. Remove the pudding from the Air Fryer grill to a wire rack to cool.
7. Divide the pudding into four bowls and serve with the vanilla wafers sprinkled on top.

Nutrition:
Calories: 184, Protein: 2 g, Fat: 12 g, Carbs: 3 g.

972. Coconut Berry Pudding

Preparation Time: 10 minutes
Cooking Time: 15 minutes
Servings: 6
Ingredients:
- 2 cups coconut cream
- 1 lime zest, grated
- 3 tbsp. erythritol
- ¼ cup blueberries
- 1/3 cup blackberries

Directions:
1. Add all ingredients into the blender and blend until well combined.
2. Spray 6 ramekins with cooking spray.
3. Pour blended mixture into the ramekins and place in the Air Fryer.
4. Cook at 340°F for 15 minutes.
5. Serve and enjoy.

Nutrition:
Calories: 164, Protein: 2 g, Fat: 22 g, Carbs: 4 g.

973. Pineapple Pudding

Preparation Time: 10 minutes
Cooking Time: 5 minutes
Servings: 8
Ingredients:
- 1 tbsp. avocado oil
- 1 cup rice
- 14 ounces milk
- Sugar to the taste
- 8 ounces canned pineapple, chopped

Directions:
1. In your Air Fryer, mix oil, milk, and rice, stir, cover and cook on High for 3 minutes.
2. Add sugar and pineapple, stir, cover and cook on High for 2 minutes more.
3. Divide into dessert bowls and serve.

Nutrition:
Calories: 154, Protein: 8 g, Fat: 4 g, Carbs: 14 g.

974. Cocoa Pudding

Preparation Time: 10 minutes
Cooking Time: 20 minutes
Servings: 2
Ingredients:
- 2 tbsp. water - ½ tbsp. agar
- 4 tbsp. stevia - 4 tbsp. cocoa powder
- 2 cups coconut milk, hot

Directions:
1. In a bowl, mix milk with stevia and cocoa powder and stir well.
2. In a bowl, mix agar with water, stir well, add to the cocoa mix, stir and transfer to a pudding pan that fits your Air Fryer.
3. Introduce in the fryer and cook at 356°F for 20 minutes.
4. Serve the pudding cold.
5. Enjoy!

Nutrition:
Calories: 170, Protein: 3 g, Fat: 2 g, Carbs: 4 g.

975. Cauliflower Pudding

Preparation Time: 10 minutes
Cooking Time: 30 minutes
Servings: 4
Ingredients:
- 2½ cups water
- 1 cup coconut sugar
- 2 cups cauliflower rice
- 2 cinnamon sticks
- ½ cup coconut, shredded

Directions:
1. In a pot that fits your Air Fryer, mix water with coconut sugar, cauliflower rice, cinnamon, and coconut. Stir, introduce in the fryer and cook at 365°F for 30 minutes.
2. Divide pudding into cups and serve cold. Enjoy!

Nutrition:
Calories: 203, Protein: 4 g, Fat: 4 g, Carbs: 9 g.

976. Tuna and Lettuce Wraps

Preparation Time: 10 minutes
Cooking Time: 4 to 7 minutes
Servings: 4
Ingredients:
- 1 pound (454 g) fresh tuna steak, cut into 1-inch cubes
- 1 tbsp. grated fresh ginger
- 2 garlic cloves, minced
- ½ tsp. toasted sesame oil
- 2 low-Sodium whole-wheat tortillas
- ¼ cup low-fat mayonnaise
- 1 cups shredded romaine lettuce
- 1 red bell pepper, thinly sliced

Directions:
1. In a medium bowl, mix the tuna, ginger, garlic, and sesame oil. Let it stand for 10 minutes.
2. Transfer the tuna to the Air Fryer basket.
3. Select the Air Fry function and cook at 390°F (199°C) for 4 to 7 minutes, or until lightly browned.
4. Make the wraps with tuna, tortillas, mayonnaise, lettuce, and bell pepper.
5. Serve immediately.

Nutrition:
Calories: 485 Carbohydrates: 6.3 g, Protein: 47.6 g, Fat: 29.9 g

977. Crunchy Chicken Egg Rolls

Preparation Time: 10 minutes
Cooking Time: 24 minutes

Servings: 4
Ingredients:
- 1 pound (454 g) ground chicken
- 2 tsp. olive oil
- 2 garlic cloves, minced
- 1 tsp. grated fresh ginger
- 2 cups white cabbage, shredded
- 1 onion, chopped
- ¼ cup soy sauce
- 8 egg roll wrappers
- 1 egg, beaten
- Cooking spray

Directions:
1. Spritz the air fry basket with cooking spray.
2. Heat olive oil in a saucepan over medium fire. Sauté the garlic and ginger in the olive oil for 1 minute, or until fragrant. Add the ground chicken to the saucepan. Sauté for 5 minutes, or until the chicken is cooked through. Add the cabbage, onion, and soy sauce and sauté for 5 to 6 minutes, or until the vegetables become soft. Remove the saucepan from the heat.
3. Unfold the egg roll wrappers on a clean work surface. Divide the chicken mixture among the wrappers and brush the edges of the wrappers with the beaten egg. Tightly roll up the egg rolls, enclosing the filling. Arrange the rolls in the basket.
4. Place the basket on the Air Fry position.
5. Select Air Fry, set the temperature to 370°F (188°C), and time to 12 minutes. Flip the rolls halfway through the cooking time.
6. When cooked, the rolls will be crispy and golden brown.
7. Transfer to a platter and let cool for 5 minutes before serving.

Nutrition:
Calories: 181, Protein: 3 g, Fat: 98 g, Carbs: 42 g.

978. Golden Cabbage and Mushroom Spring Rolls

Preparation Time: 20 minutes
Cooking Time: 14 minutes
Servings: 14
Ingredients:
- 2 tbsp. vegetable oil
- 4 cups sliced Napa cabbage
- 5 ounces (142 g) shiitake mushrooms, diced
- 3 carrots, cut into thin matchsticks
- 1 tbsp. minced fresh ginger
- 1 tbsp. minced garlic
- 1 bunch scallions, white and light green parts only, sliced
- 2 tbsp. soy sauce
- 1 (4-ounce / 113-g) package cellophane noodles
- ¼ tsp. cornstarch
- 1 (12-ounce / 340-g) package frozen spring roll wrappers, thawed
- Cooking spray

Directions:
1. Heat the olive oil in a nonstick skillet over medium-high heat until shimmering.
2. Add the cabbage, carrots, mushrooms, and sauté for 3 minutes or until tender.
3. Add the garlic, scallions, and ginger and sauté for 1 minute or until fragrant.
4. Mix in the soy sauce and turn off the heat. Discard any liquid that remains in the skillet and allow it to cool for a few minutes.
5. Bring a pot of water to a boil, then turn off the heat and pour in the noodles. Let sit for 10 minutes or until the noodles are al dente. Transfer 1 cup of the noodles to the skillet and toss with the cooked vegetables. Reserve the remaining noodles for other use.
6. Dissolve the cornstarch in a small water dish, then place the wrappers on a clean work surface. Dab the edges of the wrappers with cornstarch.
7. Scoop up 3 tablespoons of filling in the center of each wrapper, then fold the corner in front of you over the filling. Tuck the wrapper under the filling, then fold the corners on both sides into the center. Keep rolling to seal the wrapper. Repeat with remaining wrappers. Spritz the air fry basket with cooking spray. Arrange the wrappers in the basket and spritz with cooking spray.
8. Place the basket on the Air Fry position.
9. Select Air Fry, set the temperature to 400°F (205°C), and time to 10 minutes. Flip the wrappers halfway through the cooking time.
10. When cooking is complete, the wrappers will be golden brown.
11. Serve immediately.

Nutrition:
Calories: 161, Protein: 8 g, Fat: 88 g, Carbs: 32 g.

979. Korean Beef and Onion Tacos

Preparation Time: 1 hour 15 minutes
Cooking Time: 12 minutes
Servings: 6
Ingredients:
- 2 tbsp. gochujang
- 1 tbsp. soy sauce
- 2 tbsp. sesame seeds
- 2 tsp. minced fresh ginger
- 2 cloves garlic, minced
- 2 tbsp. toasted sesame oil
- 2 tsp. sugar
- ½ tsp. kosher salt
- 1½ pounds (680 g) thinly sliced beef chuck
- 1 medium red onion, sliced
- 6 corn tortillas, warmed
- ¼ cup chopped fresh cilantro
- ½ cup kimchi
- ½ cup chopped green onions

Directions:
1. Combine the ginger, garlic, gochujang, sesame seeds, soy sauce, sesame oil, salt, and sugar in a large bowl. Stir to mix well.

2. Dunk the beef chunk in the large bowl. Press to submerge, then wrap the bowl in plastic and refrigerate to marinate for at least 1 hour.
3. Remove the beef chunk from the marinade and transfer it to the air fry basket. Add the onion to the basket.
4. Place the basket on the Air Fry position.
5. Select Air Fry, set the temperature to 400°F (205°C), and time to 12 minutes. Stir the mixture halfway through the cooking time.
6. When cooked, the beef will be well browned.
7. Unfold the tortillas on a clean work surface, divide the fried beef and onion on the tortillas. Spread the green onions, kimchi, and cilantro on top.
8. Serve immediately.

Nutrition:
Calories: 181, Protein: 3 g, Fat: 98 g, Carbs: 42 g.

980. Cheesy Sweet Potato and Bean Burritos

Preparation Time: 15 minutes
Cooking Time: 30 minutes
Servings: 6
Ingredients:

- 2 sweet potatoes, peeled and cut into a small dice
- 1 tbsp. vegetable oil
- Kosher salt and ground black pepper, to taste
- 6 large flour tortillas
- 1 (16-ounce / 454-g) can refry black beans, divided
- 1½ cups baby spinach, divided
- 6 eggs, scrambled
- ¾ cup grated Cheddar cheese, divided
- ¼ cup salsa
- ¼ cup sour cream
- Cooking spray

Directions:

1. Put the sweet potatoes in a large bowl, then drizzle with vegetable oil and sprinkle with salt and black pepper. Toss to coat well.
2. Place the potatoes in the Air Fry basket.
3. Place the basket on the Air Fry position.
4. Select Air Fry, set the temperature to 400°F (205°C), and time to 10 minutes. Flip the potatoes halfway through the cooking time.
5. When done, the potatoes should be lightly browned. Remove the potatoes from the Air Fryer grill.
6. Unfold the tortillas on a clean work surface. Divide the air-fried sweet potatoes, black beans, spinach, scrambled eggs, and cheese on top of the tortillas.
7. Fold the long side of the tortillas over the filling, then fold in the shorter side to wrap the filling to make the burritos.
8. Wrap the burritos in aluminum foil and put them in the basket.
9. Place the basket on the Air Fry position.
10. Select Air Fry, set the temperature to 350°F (180°C), and time to 20 minutes. Flip the burritos halfway through the cooking time.
11. Remove the burritos from the Air Fryer grill and spread with sour cream and salsa. Serve immediately.

Nutrition:
Calories: 133, Fat: 19 g, Protein: 8 g.

981. Golden Chicken and Yogurt Taquitos

Preparation Time: 15 minutes
Cooking Time: 12 minutes
Servings: 4
Ingredients:

- 1 cup cooked chicken, shredded
- ¼ cup Greek yogurt
- ¼ cup salsa
- 1 cup shredded Mozzarella cheese
- Salt and ground black pepper, to taste
- 4 flour tortillas
- Cooking spray

Directions:

1. Spritz the air fry basket with cooking spray.
2. Combine all the ingredients except for the tortillas, in a large bowl. Stir to mix well.
3. Make the taquitos: Unfold the tortillas on a clean work surface, then scoop up 2 tablespoons of the chicken mixture in the middle of each tortilla. Roll the tortillas up to wrap the filling.
4. Arrange the taquitos in the basket and spritz with cooking spray.
5. Place the basket on the Air Fry position.
6. Select Air Fry, set the temperature to 380°F (193°C), and time to 12 minutes. Flip the taquitos halfway through the cooking time.
7. When cooked, the taquitos should be golden brown and the cheese should be melted.
8. Serve immediately.

Nutrition:
Calories: 153, Fat: 15 g, Protein: 9 g.

982. Cod Tacos with Salsa

Preparation Time: 5 minutes
Cooking Time: 15 minutes
Servings: 4
Ingredients:

- 2 eggs
- 1¼ cups Mexican beer
- 1½ cups coconut flour
- 1½ cups almond flour
- ½ tbsp. chili powder
- 1 tbsp. cumin
- Salt, to taste
- 1 pound (454 g) cod fillet, slice into large pieces
- 4 toasted corn tortillas
- 4 large lettuce leaves, chopped
- ¼ cup salsa
- Cooking spray

Directions:

1. Spritz the air fry basket with cooking spray.

2. Break the eggs in a bowl, then pour in the beer. Whisk to combine well.
3. Combine the almond flour, coconut flour, cumin, chili powder, and salt in a separate bowl. Stir to mix well.
4. Dunk the cod pieces in the egg mixture, then shake the excess off and dredge into the flour mixture to coat well. Arrange the cod in the basket.
5. Place the basket on the Air Fry position.
6. Select Air Fry, set the temperature to 375°F (190°C), and time to 15 minutes. Flip the cod halfway through the cooking time.
7. When cooking is complete, the cod should be golden brown.
8. Unwrap the toasted tortillas on a large plate, then divide the cod and lettuce leaves on top. Baste with salsa and wrap to serve.

Nutrition:
Calories: 133, Fat: 19 g, Protein: 8 g.

983. Golden Spring Rolls

Preparation Time: 10 minutes
Cooking Time: 18 minutes
Servings: 4
Ingredients:

- 4 spring roll wrappers
- ½ cup cooked vermicelli noodles
- 1 tsp. sesame oil
- 1 tbsp. freshly minced ginger
- 1 tbsp. soy sauce
- 1 clove garlic, minced
- ¼ cup chopped scallions
- Cooking spray

Directions:
1. Spritz the air fry basket with cooking spray and set it aside.
2. Heat the sesame oil in a saucepan on medium heat.
3. Sauté the garlic and ginger in the sesame oil for 1 minute, or until fragrant. Add soy sauce, carrot, red bell pepper, mushrooms, and scallions. Sauté for 5 minutes or until the vegetables become tender.
4. Mix in vermicelli noodles. Turn off the heat and remove them from the saucepan. Allow cooling for 10 minutes.
5. Lay out one spring roll wrapper with a corner pointed toward you. Scoop the noodle mixture on the spring roll wrapper and fold the corner up over the mixture. Fold left and right corners toward the center and continue to roll to make firmly sealed rolls.
6. Arrange the spring rolls in the basket and spritz with cooking spray.
7. Place the basket on the Air Fry position.
8. Select Air Fry, set the temperature to 340°F (171°C), and time to 12 minutes. Flip the spring rolls halfway through the cooking time.
9. When done, the spring rolls will be golden brown and crispy. Serve warm.

Nutrition:
Calories: 137, Fat: 15 g, Protein: 10 g.

984. Fast Cheesy Bacon and Egg Wraps

Preparation Time: 15 minutes
Cooking Time: 10 minutes
Servings: 3
Ingredients:

- 3 corn tortillas
- 3 slices bacon, cut into strips
- 2 scrambled eggs
- 3 tbsp. salsa
- 1 cup grated Pepper Jack cheese
- 3 tbsp. cream cheese, divided
- Cooking spray

Directions:
1. Spritz the air fry basket with cooking spray.
2. Unfold the tortillas on a clean work surface, divide the bacon and eggs in the middle of the tortillas, and then spread with salsa and cheeses. Fold the tortillas over.
3. Arrange the tortillas in the basket.
4. Place the basket on the Air Fry position.
5. Select Air Fry, set the temperature to 390°F (199°C), and time to 10 minutes. Flip the tortillas halfway through the cooking time.
6. When cooking is complete, the cheeses will be melted and the tortillas will be lightly browned.
7. Serve immediately.
8. **Nutrition:**
Calories: 133, Fat: 19 g, Protein: 8 g.

985. Chicken-Lettuce Wraps

Preparation Time: 15 minutes
Cooking Time: 12 to 16 minutes
Servings: 2 to 4
Ingredients:

- 1 pound (454 g) boneless, skinless chicken thighs, trimmed
- 1 tsp. vegetable oil
- tbsp. lime juice
- 1 shallot, minced
- 1 tbsp. fish sauce, plus extra for serving
- 1 tsp. packed brown sugar
- 1 garlic clove, minced
- 1/8 tsp. red pepper flakes
- 1/3 cup chopped fresh Thai basil
- 1 head Bibb lettuce, leaves separated (8 ounces/227 g)
- ¼ cup chopped dry-roasted peanuts
- Thai chiles, stemmed and sliced thin

Directions:
1. Pat the chicken dry with paper towels and rub with oil. Place the chicken in the Air Fryer basket.
2. Select the Air Fry function and cook at 400°F (204°C) for 12 to 16 minutes, or until the chicken registers 175°F (79°C), flipping and rotating chicken halfway through cooking.
3. Meanwhile, whisk lime juice, shallot, fish sauce, sugar, garlic, and pepper flakes together in a large bowl; set it aside.
4. Transfer the chicken to a cutting board, let it cool slightly, then shred into bite-size pieces using 2 forks.

5. Add the shredded chicken, mango, mint, cilantro, and basil to a bowl with dressing and toss to coat.
6. Serve the chicken in the lettuce leaves, passing peanuts, Thai chiles, and extra fish sauce separately.

Nutrition:
Calories: 311, Fat: 11 g, Carbohydrate 22 g, Protein: 31 g.

986. Chicken Pita Sandwich

Preparation Time: 10 minutes
Cooking Time: 9 to 11 minutes
Servings: 4
Ingredients:

- 2 boneless, skinless chicken breasts, cut into 1-inch cubes
- 1 small red onion, sliced
- 1 red bell pepper, sliced
- 1/3 cup Italian salad dressing, divided
- ½ tsp. dried thyme
- 4 pita pockets, split
- 2 cups torn butter lettuce
- 1 cup chopped cherry tomatoes

Directions:

1. Select the Bake function and preheat Maxx to 380°F (193°C).
2. Place the chicken, onion, and bell pepper in the Air Fryer basket. Drizzle with 1 tablespoon of the Italian salad dressing, add the thyme, and toss.
3. Bake for 9 to 11 minutes, or until the chicken is 165°F (74°C) on a food thermometer, stirring once during cooking time.
4. Transfer the chicken and vegetables to a bowl and toss with the remaining salad dressing.
5. Assemble sandwiches with pita pockets, butter lettuce, and cherry tomatoes. Serve immediately.

Nutrition:
Calories: 311, Fat: 11 g, Carbohydrate: 22 g, Protein: 31 g.

987. Veggie Salsa Wraps

Preparation Time: 5 minutes
Cooking Time: 7 minutes
Servings: 4
Ingredients:

- 1 cup red onion, sliced
- 1 zucchini, chopped
- 1 poblano pepper, deseeded and finely chopped
- ½ cup salsa
- 8 ounces (227 g) Mozzarella cheese

Directions:

1. Place the red onion, zucchini, and poblano pepper in the Air Fryer basket. Select the Air Fry function and cook at 390°F (199°C) for 7 minutes, or until they are tender and fragrant.
2. Divide the veggie mixture among the lettuce leaves and spoon the salsa over the top. Finish off with Mozzarella cheese. Wrap the lettuce leaves around the filling.
3. Serve immediately.

Nutrition:
Calories: 140, Fat: 4 g, Fiber: 3 g, Carbohydrates: 5 g, Protein: 7 g.

988. Cheesy Shrimp Sandwich

Preparation Time: 10 minutes
Cooking Time: 5 to 7 minutes
Servings: 4
Ingredients:

- 1¼ cups shredded Colby, Cheddar, or Havarti cheese
- 1 (6-ounce / 170-g) can tiny shrimp, drained
- 3 tbsp. mayonnaise
- 2 tbsp. minced green onion
- 4 slices whole-grain or whole-wheat bread
- 2 tbsp. softened butter

Directions:

1. In a medium bowl, combine the cheese, shrimp, mayonnaise, and green onion; mix well.
2. Spread this mixture on two of the slices of bread. Top with the other slices of bread to make two sandwiches. Spread the sandwiches lightly with butter.
3. Select the Air Fry function and cook at 400°F (204°C) for 5 to 7 minutes, or until the bread is browned and crisp and the cheese is melted.
4. Cut in half and serve warm.

Nutrition:
Calories: 602, Fat: 23.9 g, Carbohydrates: 46.5 g, Sugar: 2.9 g, Protein: 11.3 g, Sodium: 886 mg.

989. Smoky Chicken Sandwich

Preparation Time: 10 minutes
Cooking Time: 11 minutes
Servings: 2
Ingredients:

- 2 boneless, skinless chicken breasts (8 ounces / 227 g each), sliced horizontally in half and separated into 4 thinner cutlets
- Kosher salt and freshly ground black pepper, to taste
- ½ cup all-purpose flour
- 3 large eggs, lightly beaten
- ½ cup dried bread crumbs
- 6 ounces (170 g) smoked Mozzarella cheese, grated
- 2 store-bought soft, sesame-seed hamburger or Italian buns, split

Directions:

1. Season the chicken cutlets all over with salt and pepper.
2. Set up three shallow bowls: Place the flour in the first bowl, the eggs in the second, and stir together the bread crumbs and smoked paprika in the third. Coat the chicken pieces in the flour, then dip fully in the egg.
3. Dredge in the paprika bread crumbs, then transfer to a wire rack set over a baking sheet and spray both sides liberally with cooking spray.
4. Transfer 2 of the chicken cutlets to the Air Fryer oven.
5. Select the Air Fry function and cook at 350°F (177°C) for 6 minutes, or until they begin to brown.
6. Spread each cutlet with 2 tablespoons of the marinara sauce and sprinkle with one-quarter of the smoked Mozzarella.

7. Increase the temperature to 400°F (204°C) and air fry for 5 minutes more, or until the chicken is cooked through and crisp and the cheese is melted and golden brown.
8. Transfer the cutlets to a plate, stack them on top of each other, and place them inside a bun. Repeat with the remaining chicken cutlets, marinara, smoked Mozzarella, and bun.
9. Serve the sandwiches warm.

Nutrition:
Calories: 311, Fat: 11 g, Carbohydrate: 22 g, Protein: 31 g.

990. Nugget and Veggie Taco Wraps

Preparation Time: 5 minutes
Cooking Time: 15 minutes
Servings: 4
Ingredients:

- 1 tbsp. water
- 4 pieces commercial vegan nuggets, chopped
- 1 small yellow onion, diced
- 1 small red bell pepper, chopped
- 2 cobs, grilled corn kernels
- Mixed greens, for garnish

Directions:

1. Over medium heat, sauté the nuggets in the water with the onion, corn kernels, and bell pepper in a skillet, then remove from the heat.
2. Fill the tortillas with the nuggets and vegetables and fold them up. Transfer to the Air Fryer basket. Select the Air Fry function and cook at 400°F (204°C) for 15 minutes.
3. Once crispy, serve immediately, garnished with the mixed greens.

Nutrition:
Calories: 140, Fat: 4 g, Fiber: 3 g, Carbohydrates: 5 g, Protein: 7 g.

991. Cheesy Greens Sandwich

Preparation Time: 15 minutes
Cooking Time: 10 to 13 minutes
Servings: 4
Ingredients:

- 1½ cups chopped mixed greens
- 2 garlic cloves, thinly sliced
- 2 tsp. olive oil
- 2 slices low-sodium low-fat Swiss cheese
- 4 slices low-sodium whole-wheat bread
- Cooking spray

Directions:

1. Select the Bake function and preheat Maxx to 400°F (204°C).
2. In a baking pan, mix the greens, garlic, and olive oil. Bake for 4 to 5 minutes, stirring once until the vegetables are tender. Drain, if necessary.
3. Make 2 sandwiches, dividing half of the greens and 1 slice of Swiss cheese between 2 slices of bread. Lightly spray the outsides of the sandwiches with cooking spray.
4. Bake the sandwiches in the Air Fryer oven for 6 to 8 minutes, turning with tongs halfway through, until the bread is toasted and the cheese melts.
5. Cut each sandwich in half and serve.

Nutrition:
Calories: 140, Fat: 4 g, Fiber: 3 g, Carbohydrates: 5 g, Protein: 7 g.

992. Cheesy Chicken Sandwich

Preparation Time: 10 minutes
Cooking Time: 5 to 7 minutes
Servings: 1
Ingredients:

- ⅓ cup chicken, cooked and shredded
- 2 Mozzarella slices
- 1 hamburger bun
- ¼ cup shredded cabbage
- 1 tsp. mayonnaise
- ¼ tsp. smoked paprika
- ¼ tsp. black pepper
- ¼ tsp. garlic powder
- Pinch of salt

Directions:

1. Select the Bake function and preheat Maxx to 370°F (188°C).
2. Brush some butter onto the outside of the hamburger bun.
3. In a bowl, coat the chicken with garlic powder, salt, pepper, and paprika.
4. In a separate bowl, stir together the mayonnaise, olive oil, cabbage, and balsamic vinegar to make coleslaw.
5. Slice the bun in two. Start building the sandwich, starting with the chicken, followed by the Mozzarella, the coleslaw, and finally the top bun.
6. Transfer the sandwich to the Air Fryer oven and bake for 5 to 7 minutes.
7. Serve immediately.

Nutrition:
Calories: 311, Fat: 11 g, Carbohydrate: 22 g, Protein: 31 g.

993. Lettuce Fajita Meatball Wraps

Preparation Time: 10 minutes
Cooking Time: 10 minutes
Servings: 4
Ingredients:

- 1 pound (454 g) 85% lean ground beef
- ½ cup salsa, plus more for serving
- ¼ cup chopped onions
- ¼ cup diced green or red bell peppers
- 1 large egg, beaten
- 1 tsp. fine sea salt
- ½ tsp. chili powder
- ½ tsp. ground cumin
- 1 clove garlic, minced
- Cooking spray

For Servings:

- 8 leaves Boston lettuce
- Pico de gallo or salsa - Lime slices

Directions:

1. Coat the Air Fryer basket with cooking spray.

2. In a large bowl, mix all the ingredients until well combined.
3. Shape the meat mixture into eight 1-inch balls. Place the meatballs in the Air Fryer basket, leaving a little space between them.
4. Select the Air Fry function and cook at 350°F (177°C) for 10 minutes, or until cooked through and no longer pink inside and the internal temperature reaches 145°F (63°C).
5. Serve each meatball on a lettuce leaf, topped with pico de gallo or salsa. Serve with lime slices.

Nutrition:
Calories: 576, Fat: 49 g, Total Carbohydrates: 8 g, Fiber: 2 g, Protein: 25 g.

994. Easy Homemade Hamburgers
Preparation Time: 5 minutes
Cooking Time: 15 minutes
Servings: 2
Ingredients:
- ¾ pound lean ground chuck
- Kosher salt and ground black pepper, to taste
- 3 tbsp. onion, minced
- 1 tsp. garlic, minced
- 1 tsp. soy sauce
- ½ tsp. cayenne pepper
- ½ tsp. mustard seeds
- 2 burger buns

Directions:
1. Thoroughly combine the ground chuck, salt, black pepper, onion, garlic, and soy sauce in a mixing dish.
2. Season with smoked paprika, ground cumin, cayenne pepper, and mustard seeds. Mix to combine well.
3. Shape the mixture into 2 equal patties.
4. Spritz your patties with a nonstick cooking spray. Air fry your burgers at 380°F for about 11 minutes or to your desired degree of doneness.
5. Place your burgers on burger buns and serve with favorite toppings. Devour!

Nutrition:
Calories: 433, Fat: 17.4 g, Carbohydrates: 40 g, Protein: 39.2 g, Sugars: 6.4 g.

995. Easy Beef Burritos
Preparation Time: 5 minutes
Cooking Time: 25 minutes
Servings: 3
Ingredients:
- 1 pound rump steak
- Sea salt and crushed red pepper, to taste
- ½ tsp. shallot powder
- ½ tsp. porcini powder
- ½ tsp. celery seeds
- 1 tsp. lard, melted
- 3 (approx. 7-8") whole-wheat tortillas

Directions:
1. Toss the rump steak with the spices and melted lard.
2. Cook in your Air Fryer at 390°F for 20 minutes, turning it halfway through the cooking time. Place it on a cutting board to cool slightly.
3. Slice against the grain into thin strips.
4. Spoon the beef strips onto wheat tortillas; top with your favorite ingredients, roll them up and serve. Enjoy!

Nutrition:
Calories: 368, Fat: 13 g, Carbohydrates: 20.2 g, Protein: 35.1 g, Sugars: 2.7 g.

996. Beef Parmigiana Sliders
Preparation Time: 5 minutes
Cooking Time: 15 minutes
Servings: 2
Ingredients:
- ½ pound lean ground chuck
- 1-ounce bacon bits
- 2 tbsp. tomato paste
- 3 tbsp. shallots, chopped
- 1 garlic clove, minced
- ¼ cup parmesan cheese, grated
- 1 tsp. cayenne pepper
- Salt and black pepper, to taste
- 4 pretzel rolls

Directions:
1. Thoroughly combine the ground chuck, bacon bits, tomato paste, shallots, garlic, parmesan cheese, cayenne pepper, salt, black pepper.
2. Shape the mixture into 4 equal patties.
3. Spritz your patties with a nonstick cooking spray. Air fry your burgers at 380°F for about 11 minutes or to your desired degree of doneness.
4. Place your burgers on pretzel rolls and serve with favorite toppings. Enjoy!

Nutrition:
Calories: 516, Fat: 20.7 g, Carbohydrates: 42 g, Protein: 34.3 g, Sugars: 5.1 g.

997. Chicago-Style Beef Sandwich
Preparation Time: 5 minutes
Cooking Time: 25 minutes
Servings: 2
Ingredients:
- ½ pound chuck, boneless
- 1 tbsp. olive oil - 1 tbsp. soy sauce
- ¼ tsp. ground bay laurel
- ½ tsp. shallot powder
- ¼ tsp. porcini powder
- ½ tsp. garlic powder
- ½ tsp. cayenne pepper
- Kosher salt and ground black pepper, to taste
- 1 cup pickled vegetables, chopped
- 2 ciabatta rolls, sliced in half

Directions:
1. Toss the chuck roast with olive oil, soy sauce, and spices until well coated.

2. Cook in the preheated Air Fryer at 400°F for 20 minutes, turning over halfway through the cooking time.
3. Shred the meat with two forks and adjust seasonings.
4. Top the bottom halves of the ciabatta rolls with a generous portion of the meat and pickled vegetables. Place the tops of the ciabatta rolls on the sandwiches. Serve immediately and enjoy!

Nutrition:
Calories: 385, Fat: 17.4 g, Carbohydrates: 28.1 g, Protein: 29.8 g, Sugars: 6.2 g.

998. Mediterranean Burgers with Onion Jam

Preparation Time: 5 minutes
Cooking Time: 25 minutes
Servings: 2
Ingredients:
- ½ pound ground chuck
- 2 tbsp. scallions, chopped
- ½ tsp. garlic, minced
- 1 tsp. brown mustard
- 2 Kosher salt and ground black pepper, to taste
- 2 burger buns
- 2 ounces Haloumi cheese
- 1 medium tomato, sliced
- Romaine lettuce leaves

Onion jam:
- 2 tbsp. butter, at room temperature
- red onions, sliced
- Sea salt and ground black pepper, to taste
- 2 cups red wine
- 1 tbsp. honey
- 2 tbsp. fresh lemon juice

Directions:
1. Mix the ground chuck, scallions, garlic, mustard, salt, and black pepper until well combined; shape the mixture into two equal patties.
2. Spritz a cooking basket with a nonstick cooking spray. Air fry your burgers at 370°F for about 11 minutes or to your desired degree of doneness.
3. Meanwhile, make the onion jam. In a small saucepan, melt the butter; once hot, cook the onions for about 4 minutes. Turn the heat to simmer, add salt, black pepper, and wine, and cook until liquid evaporates.
4. Stir in the honey and continue to simmer until the onions are a jam-like consistency; afterward, drizzle with freshly squeezed lemon juice.
5. Top the bottom halves of the burger buns with the warm beef patty. Top with halloumi cheese, tomato, lettuce, and onion jam.
6. Set the bun tops in place and serve right now. Enjoy!

Nutrition:
Calories: 474, Fat: 26.5 g, Carbohydrates: 32.9 g, Protein: 29 g, Sugars: 26.1 g

999. Italian Piadina Sandwich

Preparation Time: 5 minutes
Cooking Time: 20 minutes
Servings: 2
Ingredients:
- ½ pound ribeye steak
- 1 tsp. sesame oil
- Sea salt and red pepper, to taste
- 2 medium-sized piadinas
- 2 ounces Fontina cheese, grated
- 4 tbsp. Giardiniera

Directions:
1. Brush the ribeye steak with sesame oil and season with salt and red pepper.
2. Cook at 400°F for 6 minutes. Then, turn the steak halfway through the cooking time and continue to cook for a further 6 minutes.
3. Slice the ribeye steak into bite-sized strips. Top the piadinas with steak strips and cheese. Heat the sandwich in your Air Fryer at 380°F for about 3 minutes until the cheese melts. Top with Giardiniera and serve. Bon appétit!

Nutrition:
Calories: 384, Fat: 24.8 g, Carbohydrates: 11.1 g, Protein: 31.1 g, Sugars: 4.9 g

1000. Taco Stuffed Avocados

Preparation Time: 5 minutes
Cooking Time: 15 minutes
Servings: 2
Ingredients:
- 1/3 pound ground beef
- 2 tbsp. shallots, minced
- ½ tsp. garlic, minced
- 1 tomato, chopped
- 1/3 tsp. Mexican oregano
- Salt and black pepper, to taste
- 1 chipotle pepper in adobo sauce, minced
- ¼ cup cilantro
- 2 avocados, cut into halves and pitted
- ½ cup Cotija cheese, grated

Directions:
1. Preheat a nonstick skillet over medium-high heat. Cook the ground beef and shallot for about 4 minutes.
2. Stir in the garlic and tomato and continue to sauté for a minute or so. Add in the Mexican oregano, salt, black pepper, chipotle pepper, and cilantro.
3. Then, remove a bit of the pulp from each avocado half and fill them with the taco mixture.
4. Cook in the preheated Air Fryer at 400°F for 5 minutes. Top with Cotija cheese and continue to cook for 4 minutes more or until cheese is bubbly. Enjoy!

Nutrition:
Calories: 521, Fat: 42.1 g, Carbohydrates: 23.1 g, Protein: 20.2 g, Sugars: 4.8 g.

1001. Beef Taco Roll-Ups with Cotija Cheese

Preparation Time: 5 minutes
Cooking Time: 25 minutes
Servings: 4

Ingredients:
- 1 tbsp. sesame oil
- 2 tbsp. scallions, chopped
- 1 garlic clove, minced
- 1 bell pepper, chopped
- ½ pound ground beef
- Sea salt and ground black pepper, to taste
- ½ cup Cotija cheese, shredded
- 8 roll wrappers

Directions:
1. Start by preheating your Air Fryer to 395°F.
2. Heat the sesame oil in a nonstick skillet over medium-high heat. Cook the scallions, garlic, and peppers until tender and fragrant.
3. Add the ground beef, oregano, marjoram, and chili powder. Continue cooking for 3 minutes longer or until it is browned. Stir in the beans, salt, and pepper. Divide the meat/bean mixture between wrappers previously softened with a little bit of water. Top with cheese.
4. Roll the wrappers and spritz them with cooking oil on all sides.
5. Cook in the preheated Air Fryer for 11 to 12 minutes, flipping them halfway through the cooking time. Enjoy!

Nutrition:
Calories: 417, Fat: 15.9 g, Carbohydrates: 41 g, Protein: 26.2 g, Sugars: 1.5 g.

1002. Quick Sausage and Veggie Sandwiches

Preparation Time: 5 minutes
Cooking Time: 35 minutes
Servings: 4
Ingredients:
- 4 bell peppers - 2 tbsp. canola oil
- 4 medium-sized tomatoes, halved
- 4 spring onions - 4 beef sausages
- 4 hot dog buns - 1 tbsp. mustard

Directions:
1. Start by preheating your Air Fryer to 400°F.
2. Add the bell peppers to the cooking basket. Drizzle 1 tablespoon of canola oil all over the bell peppers.
3. Cook for 5 minutes. Turn the temperature down to 350°F. Add the tomatoes and spring onions to the cooking basket and cook for an additional 10 minutes.
4. Reserve your vegetables.
5. Then, add the sausages to the cooking basket. Drizzle with the remaining tablespoon of canola oil.
6. Cook in the preheated Air Fryer at 380°F for 15 minutes, flipping them halfway through the cooking time.
7. Add the sausage to a hot dog bun; top with the air-fried vegetables and mustard; serve.

Nutrition:
Calories: 627, Fat: 41.9 g, Carbohydrates: 41.3 g, Protein: 23.2 g, Sugars: 9.3 g.

1003. Cheesy Beef Burrito

Preparation Time: 5 minutes
Cooking Time: 20 minutes
Servings: 4
Ingredients:
- 1 pound rump steak
- 1 tsp. garlic powder
- Salt and ground black pepper, to taste
- 1 cup Mexican cheese blend
- 4 large whole wheat tortillas
- 1 cup iceberg lettuce, shredded

Directions:
1. Toss the rump steak with garlic powder, onion powder, cayenne pepper, Piri pudinas powder, Mexican oregano, salt, and black pepper.
2. Cook in the preheated Air Fryer at 390°F for 10 minutes. Slice against the grain into thin strips. Add the cheese blend and cook for 2 minutes more.
3. Spoon the beef mixture onto the wheat tortillas; top with lettuce; roll up burrito-style and serve.

Nutrition:
Calories: 468, Fat: 23.5 g, Carbohydrates: 22.1 g, Protein: 42.7 g, Sugars: 2.3 g.

1004. Burgers with Caramelized Onions

Preparation Time: 5 minutes
Cooking Time: 30 minutes
Servings: 4
Ingredients:
- 1 pound ground beef
- Salt and ground black pepper, to taste
- 1 tsp. garlic powder
- ½ tsp. cumin powder
- 1 tbsp. butter - 1 red onion, sliced
- 1 tsp. brown sugar
- 1 tbsp. balsamic vinegar
- 1 tbsp. vegetable stock
- 4 hamburger buns
- 8 tomato slices - 4 tsp. mustard

Directions:
1. Start by preheating your Air Fryer to 370°F. Spritz the cooking basket with nonstick cooking oil.
2. Mix the ground beef with salt, pepper, garlic powder, and cumin powder. Shape the meat mixture into four patties and transfer them to the preheated Air Fryer.
3. Cook for 10 minutes; turn them over and cook on the other side for 8 to 10 minutes more.
4. While the burgers are frying, melt the butter in a pan over medium-high heat. Then, add the red onion and sauté for 4 minutes or until soft.
5. Add the brown sugar, vinegar, and stock and cook for 2 to 3 minutes more.
6. To assemble your burgers, add the beef patties to the hamburger buns. Top with the caramelized onion, tomato, and mustard. Serve immediately and enjoy!

Nutrition:
Calories: 475, Fat: 21.1g, Carbohydrates: 33.3g, Protein: 36.2g, Sugars: 6.1g

30 Day Meal Plan

30 DAYS	BREAKFAST	LUNCH	DINNER
DAY 1	Coconut-Blueberry Cereal	Roasted Hamburgers	Saucy Chicken with Leeks
DAY 2	Air Toasted Cheese Sandwich	Pan-Seared Roasted Strip Steak	Chili Chicken Slider
DAY 3	Citrus Blueberry Breakfast Muffins	London Broil Steak	Spicy Chicken Ginger Soup
DAY 4	Peanut Butter and Jelly Breakfast Donuts	Summer Sausage	Chicken with Artichoke Hearts
DAY 5	Raspberry Oatmeal	Meatball Venison	Chicken Shawarma
DAY 6	Bacon, Egg and Cheese Breakfast Hash	Smoked Ham Sausage	Tender & Juicy Chicken
DAY 7	Air Toasted French Toast	Venison Loaf	Greek Chicken
DAY 8	Breakfast Radish Hash Browns	Bologna	Roasted Pepper Chicken
DAY 9	Breakfast Egg and Tomatoes	Squirrel Dish	Chicken Paillard
DAY 10	Maple Glazed Sausages and Figs	Swedish Meatballs	Crispy Breaded Pork
DAY 11	Breakfast Strata	Spaghetti and Meatballs	Lemongrass Pork Chops
DAY 12	Scrambled Eggs Wonton Cups	Cheese Garlicky Pork Chops	BBQ Pork Ribs
DAY 13	Sheet Pan Shakshuka	Garlic Lemon Pork Chops	Spicy Pork Chops
DAY 14	Breakfast Casserole	Herb Cheese Pork Chops	Easy Pork Patties
DAY 15	Air-Fried Omelet	Tender Pork Chops	Lemon Pepper Seasoned Pork Chops
DAY 16	Sunny Side up Egg Tarts	Asian Pork Chops	Flavorful Pork Chops
DAY 17	Crunchy Zucchini Hash Browns	Easy & Delicious Pork Chops	Pesto Pork Chops
DAY 18	French Toast	Dash Seasoned Pork Chops	Coconut Butter Pork Chops
DAY 19	Sausage Omelet	Easy Pork Butt	Crispy Pork Chops
DAY 20	Zucchini Fritters	Sweet and Sour Pork	BBQ Lamb
DAY 21	Scrambled Egg	Pork Ratatouille	Lamb Meatballs
DAY 22	Sausage Wraps	Moist Lamb Roast	Glazed Lamb Chops
DAY 23	Bacon Brussels Sprouts	Thyme Lamb Chops	Garlic Lamb Shank
DAY 24	Sausage Swiss Cheese Egg Bite	Baked Lamb Chops	Indian Meatball with Lamb
DAY 25	Spicy Chicken Wings	Meatballs	Roasted Lamb
DAY 26	Fajita Chicken	Rosemary Roasted Leg of Lamb	Lamb Gyro
DAY 27	Lemon Chicken Breasts	Air Fried Whole Chicken	Garlic and Bell Pepper Beef
DAY 28	Salmon Dill Patties	Air Roasted Turkey	Beef and Green Onion Marinade
DAY 29	Chicken Fritters	Spanish Chicken Bake	Short Ribs and Beer Sauce
DAY 30	Delicious Chicken Burger Patties	Barbeque Air Fried Chicken	Beef and Cabbage Mix

Air Fryer Cooking Chart

Air Fryer Cooking Temps and Times (approximate)

VEGETABLES	Temp (C)	Time (min.)	CHICKEN	Temp (C)	Time (min.)
Asparagus (sliced 2.5 cm)	200	5	Breast, bone in (566 g)	185	25
Beets (whole)	200	40	Breasts, boneless (110 g)	190	12
Broccoli (florets)	200	6	Drumsticks (1.13 kg)	185	20
Brussel Sprouts (halved)	190	15	Thighs, bone in (1 kg)	190	22
Carrots (slice 1 cm)	190	15	Thighs, boneless (680 g)	190	18-20
Cauliflower (florets)	200	12	Legs Turkey, bone in (800 g)	190	30
Corn on the Cob	195	6	Wings (1 kg)	200	12
Eggplant (3.5 cm cubes)	200	15	Game Hen (halved - 1 kg)	195	20
Fennel (quartered)	185	15	Whole Chicken (3 kg)	180	75
Green Beans	200	5	Tenders	180	8-10
Kale Leaves	125	12	**BEEF**		
Mushrooms (sliced 1/2 cm)	200	5	Beef Eye Round Roast (1.8 kg)	195	45-55
Onions (pearl)	200	10	Burger (110 g)	185	16-20
Parsnips (1 cm chunks)	190	15	Filet Mignon (225 g)	200	18
Peppers (2.5 cm chunks)	200	15	Flank Steak (680 g)	200	12
Potatoes (small baby, 680 g)	200	15	Meatballs (2.5 cm)	190	7
Potatoes (2.5 cm chucks)	200	12	Meatballs (8 cm)	190	10
Potatoes (baked whole)	200	40	Ribeye, bone in (2.5 cm 225 g)	200	10-15
Squash (1 cm chunks)	200	12	Rotisserie Beef (1.1 kg)	190	40
Sweet Potato (baked)	190	30-35	Sirloin Steak (2.5 cm 340 g)	200	9-14
Tomatoes (cherry)	200	4	Standing Rib (1.7 kg)	195	60
Tomatoes (halves)	175	10			
Zucchini (1 cm sticks)	200	12			

PORK AND LAMB	Temp (C)	Time (min.)	FROZEN FOODS	Temp (C)	Time (min.)
Bacon (regular)	200	5-7	Cheese Sticks (310 g)	200	8
Bacon (thick cut)	200	6-10	Chicken Nuggets (340 g)	200	10
Lamb Loin Chops (2.5 cm thick)	200	8-12	Crumbed Prawns	200	9
Lamb Roast bone in (2.2 KG)	190	50	Fish Fillets (1 cm, 280 g)	200	14
Lamb Roast boneless (600 g)	180	40	Fish Fingers (285 g)	200	10
Loin (1 kg)	180	55	French Fries Thick (180 g)	200	18
Pork Chops, bone in (2.5 cm 185 g)	200	12	French Fries Thin (560 g)	200	14
Rack of Lamb (680 g - 900 g)	190	22	Onion Rings (340 g)	200	8
Sausages	190	15	Pot Sticker Dumplings (280 g)	200	8
Tenderloin (500 g)	185	15	Spring Rolls (280 g)	195	12-14

FISH AND SEAFOOD	Temp (C)	Time (min.)	SNACKS AND BAKING	Temp (C)	Time (min.)
Calamari (225 g)	200	4	Cake (280 g)	160	20-25
Fish Fillet (2.5 cm, 225 g)	200	10	Quiche (400 g)	180	20-22
Prawns/Shrimp	200	5	Muffins (280 g)	190	15-18
Salmon, Fillet (170 g)	190	12			
Scallops	200	5-7			
Swordfish steak	200	10			
Tuna Steak	200	7-10			

Measurement Conversion

COOKING CONVERSION CHART

Measurement

CUP	ONCES	MILLILITERS	TABLESPOONS
8 cup	64 oz	1895 ml	128
6 cup	48 oz	1420 ml	96
5 cup	40 oz	1180 ml	80
4 cup	32 oz	960 ml	64
2 cup	16 oz	480 ml	32
1 cup	8 oz	240 ml	16
3/4 cup	6 oz	177 ml	12
2/3 cup	5 oz	158 ml	11
1/2 cup	4 oz	118 ml	8
3/8 cup	3 oz	90 ml	6
1/3 cup	2.5 oz	79 ml	5.5
1/4 cup	2 oz	59 ml	4
1/8 cup	1 oz	30 ml	3
1/16 cup	1/2 oz	15 ml	1

Temperature

FAHRENHEIT	CELSIUS
100 °F	37 °C
150 °F	65 °C
200 °F	93 °C
250 °F	121 °C
300 °F	150 °C
325 °F	160 °C
350 °F	180 °C
375 °F	190 °C
400 °F	200 °C
425 °F	220 °C
450 °F	230 °C
500 °F	260 °C
525 °F	274 °C
550 °F	288 °C

Weight

IMPERIAL	METRIC
1/2 oz	15 g
1 oz	29 g
2 oz	57 g
3 oz	85 g
4 oz	113 g
5 oz	141 g
6 oz	170 g
8 oz	227 g
10 oz	283 g
12 oz	340 g
13 oz	369 g
14 oz	397 g
15 oz	425 g
1 lb	453 g

Bonus 1—How to Reheat Food

A lot of people often have the problem of not knowing how to reheat the food they bought. Here's a guide on how you can do this activity!

Let's say you bought spaghetti sauce and it came in a jar with a lid. If that jar is emptied out, then the spaghetti sauce will be able to cool for 40 minutes before it starts cooking again. So, after 40 minutes have passed, put the spaghetti sauce back into its jar and put it in your oven at 350°F for 30–40 minutes or until it starts cooking again.

If the spaghetti sauce is jarred with a lid, it will cook just like a casserole.

Recipe for Reheating Food

1. Put the food you want to reheat into a bowl and use your food thermometer to see how hot it needs to be cooked. If you want the food to reheat well without getting too dry, cook it at 392°F for 10 minutes (the time used for steaks). If you don't have a thermometer, then use an oven thermometer or candy thermometer and make sure that the food gets heated up for about 30–40 minutes before cooling off again.
2. If you have a microwave, then put the food into a microwave-safe bowl and make sure that the edges of the bowl don't stick out, or else it will heat unevenly. Use your thermometer to see if the food is hot enough to go back in the refrigerator so that it cools off before reheating again at 392°F during step 3. If you have an oven, then put your food into a covered dish and place it in the oven for at least 30 minutes at 392°F.
3. After your food is cooled down (different foods cook differently: see step 2), then reheat it back up to 392°F or until it's hot again as per instruction in step 1.

Bonus 2—Cooking Frozen Foods

A lot of people are looking for ways to cook frozen food. That's because frozen food can be a convenient and low-calorie option when you're in a hurry or just don't have the time to cook. In most cases, there's nothing wrong with that. But having just the right technique to cook frozen food is important.

Here's how to do it:
1. Use a Level Plate. You'll need a clean, level, well-oiled frying pan—one that doesn't absorb any moisture and one with a lip that will allow you to slide the frozen food around in it without burning it.

Once your pan is ready, have ready the following ingredients:
- 3 tbsp. of butter (a small amount)
- 2 tsp. each: ground black pepper and allspice
- 1 tsp. dry mustard

Directions:
1. Place the frozen food in your pan.
2. As it begins to thaw, it will release water. Use a spoon to baste the food with this water so that the bottom doesn't get too dry.
3. Add the butter, spices, and mustard.
4. Cook at a slow flame for 10 minutes or until the food is completely thawed and heated through.
5. Slide-out onto a plate to serve.

You can also add some finely chopped onions or bell peppers if you like your meat well-seasoned, but remember that frozen vegetables do not contain any salt. Season carefully if you add any vegetables in addition to the product you're cooking!

Conclusion

An Air Fryer is a kitchen gadget that may be preferable to the oven for preparing crispy French fries, chicken wings, and other fast-cooking foods. Air Fryers use an air circulation system with hot air at 300°F that does not require oil. It will be less messy than frying on the stovetop and probably take less time. Many of them are on the market today to choose from, and most are not too expensive.

To conclude, some tips about Air Fryers:

1. A study in 2013 compared the nutritional value of fried chicken cooked in an Air Fryer with that of fried chicken cooked in a deep fryer using the same amount of fat. Nutrient levels varied from being lower to higher depending upon the food item. The study included chicken wings, French fries, and fish sticks. The flavor changed between foods but overall was rated as good or better than routinely cooked items.
2. When you buy an Air Fryer, notice how often it needs to be cleaned. Some models are not dishwasher safe and need to be washed by hand.
3. Sometimes, the temperature remains very high in the Air Fryer, and you may encounter overheating.
4. A small amount of food is enough to generate a large amount of heat in an Air Fryer.
5. The main advantage of an Air Fryer is that it can also cook food without oil.
6. It is essential to read the instruction manual that comes with the Air Fryer and follow the instructions.
7. Cleaning up after cooking in an Air Fryer is similar to cooking on the stovetop with a large saucepan.
8. The Air Fryer also has other uses aside from just preparing food for consumption. One advantage is that foods can be cooked in them even when they are not in season (such as when you want to cook chicken or fish in winter).
9. There are many different types of Air Fryers on the market today, and some of these are more suited for particular uses than others.
10. Air Fryers are not to be confused with convection Air Fryers because these do not require the use of hot air but use a fan instead.
11. An Air Fryer is considered a safer alternative than a Deep Fat Fryer because there is less risk of burns while preparing food. It will be less messy than frying on the stovetop and probably take less time.
12. There may be some disagreement over whether food cooked in an Air Fryer tastes better or worse than it would if you were to prepare it using other methods, but most people agree that it lacks flavor and may have a cardboard taste to it sometimes.
13. There are several different Air Fryers on the market today, and most are not too expensive.
14. It would help if you kept the lid closed while cooking at all times when using an Air Fryer. This helps maintain the temperature in your kitchen and prevents overheating if this should occur.
15. These devices are not intended to be used in a microwave and should not be used for storing food.
16. Air Fryers aren't meant to be put in the dishwasher. You'll need some elbow grease to clean it well after use.
17. Air Fryers are not designed for freezing because they are too small, and the food would be a soggy mess after freezing.
18. You can wash the Air Fryer by hand, but you should use a paper towel or a Plamadry pad to dry it.
19. You may find some of the foods being cooked in an Air Fryer stick to each other inside the appliance because there is no oil involved, so use a paper towel to clean it well when done!
20. Air Fryers are compact appliances with multiple settings and can cook almost anything!
21. Air Fryers can cook the food quickly using heated air instead of oil. Consequently, it is much healthier and lower in fat than many other cooking methods.
22. As the cost of these devices has come down, they have become more prevalent in recent years for home use.
23. Air Fryers do not require a lot of oil to cook food because hot air dries out the food as it boils, stopping some of the absorptions of fats and oils into the food being cooked.
24. One of the most extraordinary things an Air Fryer can do is reduce the amount of, Fat: and calories in your food.

A cooking appliance with the same versatility as a fryer, a grill, and an oven, the Air Fryer is an excellent addition to your kitchen with all those features, and more than just that makes it worth it. Another good thing about this appliance is that you get all these features for less than $200. And it doesn't need oil to cook food; instead, it uses air!

An inward sandwich grill with ten settings? Yes, please! This innovative grill cooks everything from sandwiches to chicken wings in minutes with no mess. The best part is that it doesn't use oil or grease. I toast my bread and make honey mustard chicken on it, which I couldn't do with other grills because it would soak up all the oils. Not anymore, thanks to this great invention! It's also perfect for making healthy alternatives to those greasy potato chips like kale chips or sweet potato fries. Who says you can't indulge on your cheat day anymore?

Made in the USA
Monee, IL
17 September 2022

14114515R00142